GOOD HOUSEKEEPING
NEW COLOUR COOKERY

GOOD HOUSEKEEPING
NEW COLOUR COOKERY

by Good Housekeeping Institute

EBURY PRESS London

izza napoletana
ee page 100).

Published by Ebury Press
National Magazine House
72 Broadwick Street
London W1V 2BP

First published in Great Britain October 1967
Second impression January 1970
Revised edition 1971
Reprinted 1972
Reprinted 1973
Reprinted 1975
Reprinted 1976
Completely revised and reset edition 1979

ISBN 0 85223 111 3

Line drawings by Hilary Evans
Designer Derek Morrison

Filmset by BAS Printers Limited, Over Wallop, Hampshire
Printed and bound by New Interlitho s.p.a., Milan

CONTENTS

Colour photography by Melvin Grey, Stephen Baker, Frank Apthorp, Bryce Attwell, Anthony Bake, Barry Bullough, John Cook, Frank Coppins, Philip Dowell, Gina Harris, Michael Leale, Ian Reid, Kenneth Swain, Roger Tuff

The following firms kindly loaned china and accessories for use in colour photographs:

Bush and Hall, London
Casa Pupo
Elizabeth David
Grayshot Potteries, Surrey
The Hop Kiln Potteries, Farnham, Surrey
Lintern and Peters, Farnham, Surrey
Peter Jones, London
Sallamanger, Farnham, Surrey

Jacket photograph shows Lamb kebabs (see page 43); Glazed orange cheesecake (see page 148); Scampi provençale (see page 36); Light fruit cake (see page 179); French-style pâté maison (see page 55); Raspberry and banana creams (see page 152) and Dinner rolls (see page 168).

FOREWORD

With this book on your shelf, you need never be left wondering what to give the family to eat, or what delicious menu to prepare for your guests. This collection of over a thousand Good House-keeping tried and tested recipes has the answer for every occasion.

Start with soups, for example, and then enjoy the more sophisticated art of soufflé making, try our sandwich and snack ideas and finish with a bout of home baking or preserving. Main courses with meat, chicken, eggs and fish also feature largely in this book and are made all the more useful by their accompanying notes on how to buy the best fresh foods and how to prepare them.

Who could resist trying such recipes as Pork and prune hot pot, Egg flip and potato pie, Rainbow salads or Orange ambrosia? The 64 pages of colour pictures add to the fun of using this completely updated Good Housekeeping favourite. The recipes are given in metric and imperial measures and have all been double tested in the Good Housekeeping Institute kitchens.

GOOD HOUSEKEEPING INSTITUTE

HANDY COOKERY CHARTS

CONVERSION TO METRIC MEASUREMENTS

The metric measures in this book are based on a 25 g unit instead of the ounce (28·35 g). Slight adjustments to this basic conversion standard were necessary in some recipes to achieve satisfactory cooking results.

If you want to convert your own recipes from imperial to metric, we suggest you use the same 25 g unit, and use 600 ml in place of 1 pint, with the British Standard 5-ml and 15-ml spoons replacing the old variable teaspoons and tablespoons; these adaptations will sometimes give a slightly smaller recipe quantity and may require a shorter cooking time.

Note Sets of British Standard metric measuring spoons are available in the following sizes – 2·5 ml, 5 ml, 10 ml and 15 ml.

When measuring milk it is more convenient to use the exact conversion of 568 ml (1 pint).

For more general reference, the following tables will be helpful.

METRIC CONVERSION SCALE

Liquid				Solid		
Imperial	Exact conversion	Recommended ml		Imperial	Exact conversion	Recommended g
¼ pint	142 ml	150 ml		1 oz	28·35 g	25 g
½ pint	284 ml	300 ml		2 oz	56·7 g	50 g
1 pint	568 ml	600 ml		4 oz	113·4 g	100 g
1½ pints	851 ml	900 ml		8 oz	226·8 g	225 g
1¾ pints	992 ml	1 litre		12 oz	340·2 g	325 g
				14 oz	397·0 g	400 g
				16 oz (1 lb)	453·6 g	450 g

For quantities of 1¾ pints and over, litres and fractions of a litre have been used.

1 kilogram (kg) equals 2·2 lb

Note Follow either the metric or the imperial measures in the recipes as they are not interchangeable.

OVEN TEMPERATURE CHART

°C	°F	Gas mark
110	225	¼
130	250	½
140	275	1
150	300	2
170	325	3
180	350	4
190	375	5
200	400	6
220	425	7
230	450	8
240	475	9

SERVINGS
All recipes give 4 servings unless otherwise stated.

SOUPS

Well-flavoured stock is the best possible basis for soups, and with a little forethought you can have a supply of it always at hand. Good stock can be made from bones, meat or poultry and from vegetables; gristle, trimmings and bacon rinds may be included, but fat must not be added. This type of stock is suitable for all types of soup, except consommé, for which a clear bone stock clarified with egg shells is essential. Stock made from raw meat or poultry, not from already cooked pieces, is known as 'first' stock.

To make the stock a stock pot is ideal, but by no means essential. Use any saucepan with a well-fitting lid, or a pressure cooker – which saves time and fuel.

Stock will keep for a week in a refrigerator or 2–3 months in a freezer. When no refrigerator is available it should be boiled up daily and not kept for more than 2–3 days.

If more convenient, use self-raising flour instead of plain for thickening soup.

Some soup-making do's and don'ts

Do chop or divide ingredients finely to extract the flavour.

Do sauté the ingredients carefully, to absorb the fat.

Do give long, gentle cooking (with a lid on the pan), to extract the flavours and soften the fibres.

Do stir cream in slowly; single cream is best.

Do skim the stock when it comes to the boil, removing all the scum.

Do sieve soup carefully and thoroughly – unless all the vegetables, etc., are put through the sieve, the soup will be flavourless and thin. If you have a blender, it's ideal for this job.

Do add the thickening agent carefully, with the pan off the heat; stir continuously to prevent lumps forming.

Do serve soup hot; heat the individual dishes or tureen.

Don't over-garnish soup.

Accompaniments and garnishes

Certain soups have a recognised accompaniment or garnish, but with others you can ring the changes on a variety of simple and more elaborate finishing touches. Here are notes on some of the most useful additions:

Mushrooms Slice thinly and sauté in a little butter, bacon fat or dripping before adding to thick soups.

Onion If a soup lacks flavour, add a little chopped onion and cook for a further few minutes before serving. Onion rings, cut thinly, dipped in egg white and flour and fried until golden brown and crisp in a little dripping, bacon fat or butter, give a good flavour; they can be added to the soup just before serving.

Leek Fried, chopped leek is a particularly good addition to potato soup.

Radishes Slice thinly and add to the soup immediately before serving.

Cucumber Slice very finely and serve with soup of any flavour, but especially with chicken.

Celery Pick the tender sprigs from the ends of the stems, wash well and serve one or two in each bowl.

Lemon Neatly cut wedges are delicious with many of the clear soups and with tomato soups.

Cheese Freshly grated hard cheese is a pleasant accompaniment to almost any vegetable soup. To add interesting colour, flavour and vitamins, mix freshly chopped parsley or watercress with the grated cheese just before serving. Grated cheese is usually handed separately, but may also be sprinkled on the soup just before serving.

Bacon Rind some lean rashers, cut into small strips or dice and fry lightly. Suitable for thick soups.

Sausages and sausagemeat Left-over cooked sausages go well with vegetable soups such as spinach. They should be cut into rounds or small strips and heated through in the soup just before serving. Raw sausagemeat may also be used. Roll it into pieces about the size of a marble, dust with flour and grill, fry or bake; alternatively, poach them in the soup for 10–15 minutes.

Melba toast Cut stale bread into very thin slices, lay them on baking sheets and dry off in the bottom of a very slow oven. Before serving brown them lightly in a warm oven 170°C (325°F) mark 3 or under a very slow grill.

Fried croûtons Cut bread about 1 cm (½ inch) thick and fry until golden brown in a little dripping, bacon fat or lard. Cut into cubes and serve immediately. (If preferred, the bread can be cubed before frying.)

Toast croûtons Make toast just before serving the soup and cut into small dice.

Savoury fritters Make a fritter batter with 100 g (4 oz) plain flour, 1 egg and about 150 ml (¼ pint) milk, season well and add some mixed herbs and, if liked, a little chopped fried bacon or onion. Fry in a little hot fat until golden brown on both sides. Cut into neat strips and add to the soup just before serving.

Rice Left-over dry boiled rice may be added to soup shortly before it is served, together with some freshly chopped parsley or chives. Rice may also be cooked in the actual soup or broth; in this case, it is added about 30 minutes before the end of the cooking time.

Macaroni and spaghetti These are good with minestrone and any thin soup. They should be broken into short lengths and added to the soup about 30 minutes before it is to be served. Other types of Italian pasta, such as alfabeto, small conchiglia, cappellini and tagliatelle (broken in small pieces), look more unusual for special occasions; use in small quantities only.

Quick soups and broths

Canned and packet soups are an excellent standby and particularly good results can be obtained by adding individual flavourings and garnishes or by combining two different-flavoured soups. Bouillon cubes also make it possible to produce stock quickly and easily, since all you have to do is to dissolve them in boiling water; the usual proportion is one cube to 400 ml (¾ pint) water, but this may vary with different brands.

Minestrone

450 g (1 lb) mixed vegetables, finely diced
50 g (2 oz) butter or margarine
1·1 litres (2 pints) stock
½ bayleaf
a sprig of thyme
25 g (1 oz) macaroni
seasoning to taste
grated cheese to garnish

Sauté the vegetables in the butter or

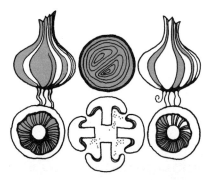

margarine until they are soft – about 15 minutes. Add the stock, herbs and macaroni and boil for 15 minutes to reduce the soup, then simmer for 30 minutes. Check the seasoning and garnish with cheese.

Cream of spinach soup

700 g (1½ lb) spinach, cooked
40 g (1½ oz) butter or margarine
25 g (1 oz) plain flour
600 ml (1 pint) chicken stock
300 ml (½ pint) milk
salt and pepper
142-ml (5-fl oz) carton single cream
butter to garnish

Sieve the spinach. Make a sauce with the fat, flour, stock and milk; add the spinach and season to taste. Stir in the cream and re-heat (but do not boil). Before serving, put a knob of butter on each bowl of soup.

Celery soup

1 head of celery
900 ml (1½ pints) stock or water
300 ml (½ pint) milk
1 onion, skinned and sliced
50 g (2 oz) butter or margarine
50 g (2 oz) plain flour
142-ml (5-fl oz) carton cream (optional)

Cut up the celery and cook in the stock or water. Sieve or liquidise. Place the milk and onion in a small pan and bring to the boil. Remove the onion and add the flavoured milk to the celery purée. Melt the fat in a pan, add the flour and blend together. Gradually add the purée, with the cream if used, re-heat and season to taste. Garnish if liked with celery leaves.

Mixed vegetable soup

450 g (1 lb) prepared mixed vegetables
600 ml (1 pint) stock
568 ml (1 pint) milk
1 slice of onion
5 ml (1 level tsp) mixed herbs
50 g (2 oz) butter or margarine
50 g (2 oz) plain flour
salt and pepper
parsley sprigs to garnish

Cook the vegetables in the liquids with the onion and herbs for 20 minutes. Sieve or liquidise. Melt the fat, make a roux with the flour and gradually add the vegetables, stirring well. Season, re-heat and garnish.

Sweetcorn soup

100 g (4 oz) frozen whole sweetcorn kernels
1 onion, skinned and chopped
1 small red pepper, seeded
1 bayleaf
600 ml (1 pint) stock
10 ml (2 level tsp) cornflour
300 ml (½ pint) milk
salt, pepper and cayenne pepper
chopped chives and cayenne to garnish

Put the sweetcorn, onion, red pepper, bayleaf and stock into a pan, bring to the boil and simmer gently for 15–20 minutes, then sieve. Return the soup to the pan, add the cornflour blended with a little milk and cook for 2–3 minutes. Add the remaining milk and bring to the boil. Season, then garnish with the chopped chives and a little cayenne pepper.

Fresh tomato soup

900 g (2 lb) fresh tomatoes
15 ml (1 level tbsp) cornflour
568 ml (1 pint) milk
1 bayleaf
1 clove
6 peppercorns
2 slices of onion
15 ml (1 tbsp) tomato purée
salt and pepper

Cut the tomatoes into quarters. Blend the cornflour with a little milk and add the rest of the milk. Pour into a saucepan, add the tomatoes, bayleaf, clove, peppercorns and finely chopped onion. Slowly bring to simmering point (this helps to prevent curdling) and simmer until the tomatoes are soft, then sieve. Add the tomato purée, re-heat and season to taste.

Cream of mushroom soup

225 g (8 oz) mushrooms
300 ml (½ pint) stock
1 small onion, skinned and sliced
25 g (1 oz) butter or margarine
25 g (1 oz) plain flour
400 ml (¾ pint) milk
salt and pepper
1 egg yolk

Wipe the mushrooms, chop finely and cook for 30 minutes in the stock with the onion; sieve or liquidise. Melt the fat in a saucepan, stir in the flour and add the milk gradually. Bring to the boil, stirring, then add the mushroom purée and seasoning and simmer for 15 minutes. Remove from the heat, allow to cool slightly, then stir in the beaten egg yolk. Cook for a few minutes, but do not boil, or the egg is likely to curdle. If liked, add a garnish of cooked, sliced mushrooms.

Onion soup

8 small onions, skinned
50 g (2 oz) butter or margarine
50 g (2 oz) plain flour
1·1 litres (2 pints) chicken stock
1 bayleaf
6 peppercorns

Slice the onions very thinly into rings. Melt the fat and sauté the onion until quite soft. Add the flour and gently re-cook to absorb the excess fat. Add the stock to the onion, with the bayleaf and peppercorns, and simmer for 30 minutes; check the seasoning.

Carrot soup

1 small potato, peeled and sliced
6–8 carrots, pared and sliced
1 onion, skinned and sliced
900 ml (1½ pints) chicken stock
300 ml (½ pint) milk
25 g (1 oz) butter or margarine
50 g (2 oz) plain flour
salt and pepper
chopped parsley to garnish

Simmer the potato, carrots and onion in the stock; sieve or liquidise and add the milk. Melt the fat in a saucepan, blend in the flour, gradually add the sieved soup and re-heat, stirring all the time. Season to taste and garnish with parsley.

Potato soup

4 medium potatoes, peeled and sliced
1 small onion, skinned and sliced
1 bayleaf
salt and pepper
celery salt
grated nutmeg
milk
chopped parsley and grated cheese to garnish

Cover the potatoes and onion with water, add the bayleaf and some salt, bring to the boil and simmer until the onion is soft. Sieve, then season well, adding a pinch of celery salt and a pinch of grated nutmeg. Thin the soup to the required consistency with milk and re-heat at once. Serve garnished with chopped parsley and grated cheese.

PRESSURE-COOKED SOUPS

Using a pressure cooker is an obvious way to produce soups and broths quickly. Always follow manufacturers' instructions for using a pressure cooker. Remember that the pan should be no more than two-thirds full and the rack should not be used. It is usual to cook at 'high' pressure. After cook-

Kidney soup with herb dumplings (see page 18).

ing, the pressure is reduced under the cold tap – except in the case of dried vegetables, which tend to block the air vent if the pressure is reduced too quickly.

Ordinary soup recipes can be used by reducing the liquid to three-quarters the normal quantity and the cooking time to one-third.

Oxtail soup

1 oxtail
2 onions, skinned
1 carrot, pared
2 stalks of celery, trimmed
25 g (1 oz) dripping
1·1 litres (2 pints) stock
25 g (1 oz) bacon
a bunch of herbs
salt and pepper
25 g (1 oz) plain flour
a little port wine (optional)
a squeeze of lemon juice

Wash and dry the oxtail; cut up the vegetables. Melt the fat in the pressure cooker and sauté the oxtail and vegetables. Cover with stock, bring to the boil, add the bacon, herbs and seasonings, put on the lid and bring to pressure. Lower the heat and pressure cook for 45 minutes, then reduce the pressure. Strain the stock, cut all the

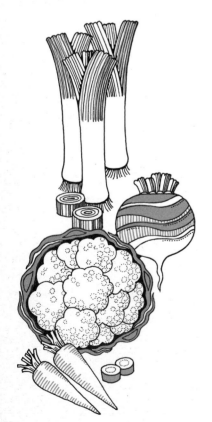

meat off the bones and return the stock and meat to the pan, with extra seasoning if required. Bring to the boil, thicken with the flour blended with the wine or water and boil for 5 minutes, adding the lemon juice.

Scotch broth

450–700 g (1–1½ lb) scrag end of lamb
1·1 litres (2 pints) water
salt and pepper
25 g (1 oz) pearl barley
1 small carrot, pared and diced
1 onion, skinned and diced
1 turnip, pared and diced
chopped parsley to garnish

Cut the meat into small pieces, removing the fat. Place in the pressure cooker and add the water, seasonings and barley. Fix the lid and bring steadily to pressure, lower the heat and cook for 20 minutes. Reduce the pressure, open the lid and skim any fat off the surface of the soup. Add the diced vegetables and pressure-cook for 5 minutes, then reduce the pressure. Serve in a tureen, sprinkled with the parsley.

Lentil soup

15 g (½ oz) dripping or butter
1 onion, skinned
1 carrot, pared
2 medium potatoes, peeled
175 g (6 oz) lentils
900 ml (1½ pints) stock or water
salt and pepper
a bunch of herbs
150 ml (¼ pint) milk

Melt the fat in the pressure cooker, cut up the vegetables and sauté in the fat with the lentils. Add the liquid, seasonings and herbs. Put on the lid, bring steadily to pressure, lower the heat and cook for 15 minutes. Let the pressure drop slowly to zero. Sieve the soup, or remove herbs and liquidise, add the milk, re-heat and serve.

CANNED SOUP VARIATIONS

Note The number of servings obviously depends on the size of can you use.

Combine 1 can of oxtail and 1 can of tomato soup, add lemon juice or sherry to taste and heat thoroughly; serve with grated cheese or croûtons.

Combine 1 can of pea soup and 1 can of tomato soup; heat thoroughly. Meanwhile grill 4 bacon rashers until crisp, then chop; alternatively, mince 50 g (2 oz) cooked ham. Sprinkle over the soup before serving.

Drain and roughly chop 1 small can of crabmeat, mix with 1 can of asparagus soup and heat thoroughly. Serve sprinkled with chopped parsley.

Mix 1 can of chicken noodle soup with 1 can of cream of mushroom and heat. Garnish with watercress.

Combine 1 can of pea soup with 1 can of asparagus soup, heat thoroughly and serve garnished with 25 g (1 oz) chopped shrimps.

Combine 1 can of vegetable broth with 1 can of tomato soup, then add 25 g (1 oz) broken noodles and simmer for 15 minutes. Serve with grated Parmesan cheese.

Combine 1 can of celery and 1 can of mushroom soup, heat thoroughly; serve garnished with sour cream and sprinkled with chopped chives or about 50 g (2 oz) sliced and lightly fried mushrooms.

Fry 15 ml (1 tbsp) mixed red and green peppers in a small knob of butter. Combine with 1 can of cream of chicken soup and simmer for 10 minutes before serving.

Fry 15 ml (1 tbsp) each of finely chopped onion, parsley and almonds in 15 ml (1 tbsp) oil for 5 minutes. Add 1 can cream of chicken soup and simmer for 10 minutes.

Make up 1 packet of French onion soup and simmer for 5 minutes; add 1 can of oxtail soup with 1 bayleaf and 10 ml (2 level tsp) curry powder; simmer for a further 10 minutes.

Fry 5 ml (1 tsp) finely chopped onion with 50 g (2 oz) chopped mushrooms in a small knob of butter for 5 minutes. Pour in 1 can of kidney soup and ⅓ can of milk or water and simmer for 10 minutes. Just before serving, add 15 ml (1 tbsp) instant rice (cooked separately).

EMERGENCY SOUPS

Quick satisfying soups can be made by adding a variety of ingredients to stock made from bouillon cubes. Here are some of the innumerable variations.

Almond soup

Heat 30 ml (2 tbsp) olive oil and fry 100 g (4 oz) finely chopped almonds, 15 ml (1 tbsp) chopped onion, 2·5 ml (½ tsp) chopped garlic and 5 ml (1 tsp) chopped parsley, stirring all the time with a spoon. The mixture should be well cooked but not browned. Add 25 g (1 oz) breadcrumbs and cook very slowly for a further 3 minutes. Pour on 1·1 litres (2 pints) stock made from chicken bouillon cubes, season well and simmer for 15 minutes.

Spanish tomato soup

Make a roux from 25 g (1 oz) butter or margarine and 25 g (1 oz) flour, add hot stock made from chicken cubes and 600 ml (1 pint) water. Blend carefully, then add 600 ml (1 pint) tomato pulp and season well with salt and pepper. Bring to the boil and simmer for 3 minutes. Cook 225 g (8 oz) vermicelli in boiling salted water, drain and add to the soup. Garnish with chives or parsley and serve with grated Cheddar or Parmesan cheese handed separately.

Chicken and rice soup

Cook 50 g (2 oz) instant rice in 1·1 litres (2 pints) stock made from chicken cubes and water for 10 minutes. Remove from the heat and cool slightly. Pour on to 2 egg yolks, gently whisking all the time. Finally, add the juice of 1 lemon and serve at once, garnished with parsley.

Cheese soup

Make a roux with 50 g (2 oz) butter or margarine and 25 g (1 oz) plain flour. Add 1·7 litres (3 pints) stock made from chicken bouillon cubes and water and cook for 10 minutes. Add 50 g (2 oz) cooked noodles and 50 g (2 oz) grated cheese and heat for a few minutes longer. Serve sprinkled with 15 ml (1 tbsp) chopped chives or some chopped parsley.

French onion soup

Classic soups

Crème Dubarry

1 firm white cauliflower
40 g (1 ½ oz) butter or margarine
25 g (1 oz) plain flour
900 ml (1 ½ pints) white stock
salt, pepper and nutmeg
142-ml (5-fl oz) carton double cream
2 egg yolks

Divide up the cauliflower, discarding the green leaves, and wash well in salted water. Melt the fat in a strong pan, remove from the heat and mix in the flour carefully; return the pan to the heat, then cook for a few minutes. Stir in the stock gradually, add the cauliflower (reserving a few well-shaped pieces), bring to the boil and simmer for 30 minutes. Meanwhile, cook the remaining florets in salted water until tender but not broken. Sieve or liquidise the soup, season well and add a pinch of grated nutmeg. Whisk the cream and egg yolks together and add, stirring carefully; re-heat the soup gently (but do not boil) until it thickens. Serve garnished with the cauliflower florets.

Watercress soup

2 bunches of watercress – about 225 g (8 oz)
a small knob of butter or margarine
600 ml (1 pint) stock
salt and pepper
15 ml (1 level tbsp) cornflour
150 ml (¼ pint) milk
30–45 ml (2–3 tbsp) single cream

Wash the watercress well and remove the coarse stalks. Melt the fat in a saucepan, add the watercress (reserving a few sprigs) and toss over a very gentle heat for 2–3 minutes. Add the stock, salt and pepper, then cover and simmer gently for 20–30 minutes. Sieve or liquidise, return to the pan, add the cornflour, blended with the milk, bring to the boil, stirring, and cook for 5–8 minutes. Add more seasoning if necessary and just before serving stir in the cream. Garnish with watercress.

French onion soup

225 g (8 oz) onions, skinned
40 g (1 ½ oz) butter or margarine
15 g (½ oz) plain flour
900 ml (1 ½ pints) boiling stock
salt and pepper
1 bayleaf
slices of French bread
grated cheese

Slice the onions or chop finely, then fry in the melted fat until well and evenly browned – take care not to let the pieces become too dark. Add the flour, mixing well. Pour in the boiling stock, season, add the bayleaf and simmer for 30 minutes. Put the slices of bread into a soup tureen, pour on the soup and top with cheese.

Alternatively, put the soup in a fireproof casserole, float the slices of bread on it and cover with grated cheese; the soup is then heated in a hot oven for a few minutes.

Consommé

100 g (4 oz) lean beef
1·1 litres (2 pints) cold brown stock
2 carrots, pared
2 sticks of celery, trimmed
1 small onion, skinned and scalded
1 white eggshell
1 blade of mace
6 peppercorns
salt to taste

Trim any fat from the meat, then cut it up finely and soak it in 150 ml (¼ pint) cold water for 15 minutes. If necessary, skim any fat from the stock. Chop the vegetables. Place all the ingredients in a pan and bring slowly to the boil, whisking constantly. When boiling point is reached stop whisking and boil fiercely for 1 minute. Let the soup stand for 15 minutes, then strain it through a cloth. Re-heat and add any desired garnish.

Prawn bisque

Illustrated in colour on page 19

1 large carrot, diced
100 g (4 oz) onion, skinned and chopped
100 g (4 oz) butter or margarine
600 ml (1 pint) fresh prawns in their shells

Bouquet garni
1 bayleaf
3 parsley stalks
5 ml (1 level tsp) dried thyme

30 ml (2 tbsp) brandy
45 ml (3 tbsp) dry white wine
900 ml (1 ½ pints) water
40 g (1 ½ oz) flour
1 lemon
salt and pepper
1 egg yolk
75 ml (5 tbsp) double cream
snipped chives to garnish

Sauté the vegetables, covered, in half the butter or margarine for 10 minutes. Peel the prawns. Tie the shells in muslin with the bouquet garni. Flambé the brandy and pour on to the vegetables. When the flames have died, add the shells. Pour the wine and water over and simmer gently, covered, for

30 minutes. Chop the shelled prawns finely.

Melt the remaining fat in a pan. Off the heat, stir in the flour and cook for 2 minutes. Discard the muslin bag. Gradually add the stock to the roux, stirring. Bring to the boil, stirring, and simmer for 5 minutes. Stir in the juice from ½ lemon and all but a few chopped prawns. Adjust the seasoning. Blend the egg yolk and cream. Add a little soup, return to the saucepan, stirring. Reheat, but do not boil. Before serving, transfer to a tureen, float thin slices of the remaining lemon on top and sprinkle with chives and chopped prawns. *Serves 4–6.*

Asparagus soup

1 bundle of asparagus
1·1 litres (2 pints) white stock
salt and pepper
25 g (1 oz) butter or margarine
25 g (1 oz) plain flour
150 ml (¼ pint) milk
a little cream

Prepare the asparagus in the usual way, discarding the woody part, and cut it into short lengths. Cut off a few of the tips and tie in muslin: these are removed from the soup when tender and used as a garnish. Put the asparagus into a pan with the stock, add the seasonings, cover and boil gently until tender. Sieve or liquidise (reserving tips). Melt the fat and stir in the flour to form a roux. Add the asparagus purée and bring to the boil, stirring, then cook gently for 2–3 minutes. Add the milk, re-season if necessary and stir in the cream and asparagus tips to garnish.

Celeriac soup

450 g (1 lb) celeriac, peeled
1 large potato, peeled
1 small onion, skinned
25 g (1 oz) butter or margarine
900 ml (1 ½ pints) stock, or milk and stock mixed
salt and pepper
15 g (½ oz) plain flour
30–45 ml (2–3 tbsp) milk or cream
thin slices of toast
grated cheese (optional)

Slice the vegetables. Melt the fat, add the vegetables and cook for 5 minutes. Add the stock and seasoning, cover and simmer gently until all the vegetables are tender. Blend the flour smoothly with the milk or cream. Sieve or liquidise, return to the pan with the blended flour and stir until boiling and creamy in consistency. Re-season and serve with the toast. A little grated cheese stirred into the soup just before serving gives a delicious flavour.

Asparagus soup

Tomato soup

100 g (4 oz) onion, skinned
3 cloves
907-g (2-lb) can tomatoes
sprig of parsley
1 bayleaf
5 ml (1 level tsp) salt
pepper
1.25 ml (¼ level tsp) grated nutmeg
50 g (2 oz) butter or margarine
45 ml (3 level tbsp) flour
400 ml (¾ pint) milk
150 ml (¼ pint) light stock
30–45 ml (2–3 tbsp) single cream
chopped parsley or croûtons to garnish

Cut the onion into small chunks. Stud one piece with the cloves. Place the onion, tomatoes with juice, sprig of parsley, bayleaf, seasoning and nutmeg in the saucepan. Bring to the boil, reduce the heat, cover and simmer for 1 hour. Melt the butter or margarine in another pan, blend in the flour. Cook the roux for 2–3 minutes before gradually stirring in the milk, giving a smooth paste. Bring to the boil, stirring, then reduce the heat and simmer for about 5 minutes.

Remove the bayleaf, cloves and parsley from the tomato mixture. Purée in an electric liquidiser. Pass through a fine sieve to remove the pips. Add to the white sauce. Blend well together, or combine both and liquidise together. Stir in the stock and cream, adjust the seasoning and re-heat to serving temperature. Do not boil.

Just before serving, whirl some cream over the surface. *Serves 4–6*

Split pea soup

175 g (6 oz) yellow split peas
2 potatoes
2 carrots
900 ml (1 ½ pints) stock (made from pork bones)
2·5 ml (½ level tsp) dried thyme (tied in muslin)
225 g (8 oz) button onions, skinned

Soak the peas for 24 hours; boil until soft and sieve. Peel and dice the potatoes and carrots. Combine the pea purée and stock and add the potatoes, carrots and thyme. Boil the soup until the vegetables are tender. Boil the prepared onions separately in 300 ml (½ pint) water and when tender add them, with their cooking liquor, to the soup.

Hearty soups

Kidney soup with herb dumplings

Illustrated in colour on page 15

25 g (1 oz) butter or margarine
1 onion, skinned
2 sticks of celery, trimmed
1 carrot, pared
225 g (8 oz) kidney, skinned and cored
1 litre (1¾ pints) stock
salt, pepper and thyme to taste
herb dumplings (see page 71)
25 g (1 oz) cornflour
75 ml (5 tbsp) milk

Heat the fat and sauté the chopped vegetables; add the chopped kidney, the stock and seasonings. Bring to the boil and simmer for 2–2 ½ hours. Meanwhile, make the dumplings. Sieve or liquidise the soup, add the blended cornflour, milk and dumplings. Simmer for a further 30 minutes, until dumplings are cooked.

Onion soup with cheese

6–8 onions, skinned
50 g (2 oz) butter or margarine
1·1–1·7 litres (2–3 pints) water
salt
75–100 g (3–4 oz) cheese, grated
paprika
chopped parsley or croûtons to garnish

Mince the onions and brown them lightly in the hot fat in the saucepan; add the water

Prawn bisque (see page 17).

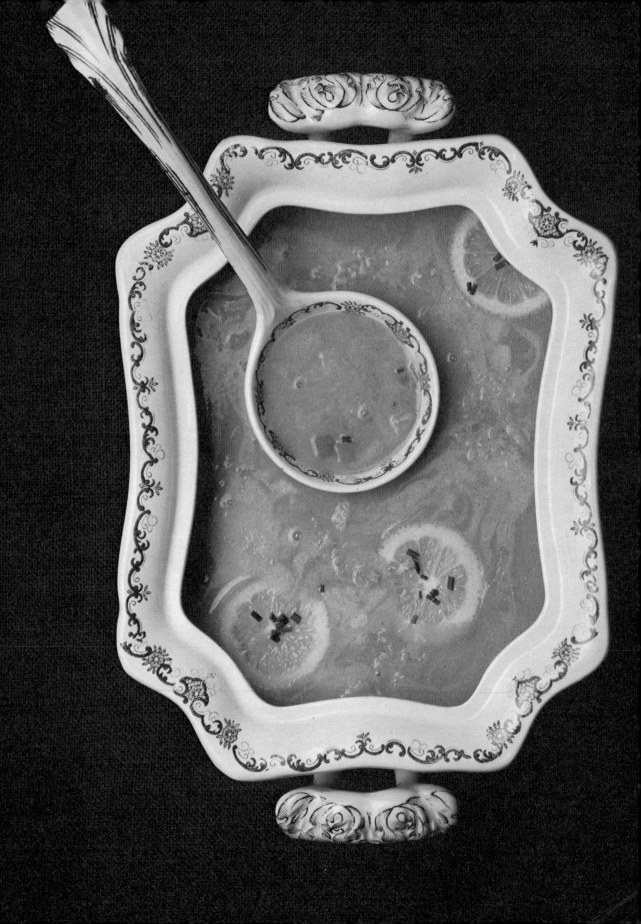

and some salt and allow to simmer until the onions are quite clear. Put the grated cheese in a warmed soup tureen and just before serving, pour the boiling soup over it, stirring constantly. Add some paprika to taste and serve the soup at once, garnished with parsley or croûtons.

Leek and potato soup with meat balls

325 g (12 oz) leeks, trimmed
325 g (12 oz) potatoes, peeled
25 g (1 oz) butter or margarine
1 litre (1¾ pints) white stock (eg, chicken)
salt and pepper
5 ml (1 tsp) mixed herbs
25 g (1 oz) plain flour
150 ml (¼ pint) milk

For the meat balls
100 g (4 oz) minced beef
½ onion, skinned and grated
10 ml (2 tsp) tomato ketchup
salt and pepper
1·25 ml (¼ tsp) mixed herbs
½ egg
25 g (1 oz) plain flour

Wash and slice the leeks and dice the potatoes, then sauté both in the fat for 5 minutes. Add the stock, seasoning and herbs; bring to the boil and simmer for 1 hour. Sieve or liquidise, add the blended flour and milk and re-boil, stirring until thick.

To make the meat balls, mix the meat with the onion, tomato ketchup, salt, pepper and herbs, then bind with the egg. Form into small balls and toss in the flour, add to the thickened soup and simmer for 30 minutes.

Country chicken soup

1 onion, skinned
½ green pepper
50 g (2 oz) butter or margarine
50 g (2 oz) plain flour
600 ml (1 pint) chicken stock
300 ml (½ pint) milk
50 g (2 oz) mushrooms
100 g (4 oz) peas
chunks of chicken
1 bayleaf
salt and pepper
toast croûtons (see page 13)

Chop the onion and pepper finely and sauté for 5 minutes in the butter. Add the flour and stir until cooked but not brown, then mix in the stock and milk gradually. Add the sliced mushrooms, peas, chicken and seasonings and bring to the boil, stirring all the time. Simmer gently for 1 hour. Serve with croûtons of toast.

Mulligatawny soup

1 onion, skinned and chopped
1 carrot, pared and grated
225 g (8 oz) tomatoes, chopped
½ green pepper, seeded and chopped
2 sticks of celery, trimmed and chopped
1 apple, grated
25 g (1 oz) butter or margarine
1 litre (1¾ pints) chicken stock
5 ml (1 level tsp) curry powder
2 cloves
15 ml (1 tbsp) chopped parsley
sugar, salt and pepper to taste
25 g (1 oz) cornflour
150 ml (¼ pint) milk
leftovers of cold cooked chicken, cut in neat pieces
25 g (1 oz) rice, cooked

Sauté the vegetables and apple in the fat for 5 minutes. Add the stock, flavourings and seasonings and simmer for 2–2½ hours, then sieve. Blend the cornflour with the milk and stir it into the soup. Add the chicken and the rice and re-boil the soup until it is thick.

Thick tomato soup

1 small onion, skinned
1 carrot, pared
2 sticks of celery, trimmed
25 g (1 oz) butter or margarine
450 g (1 lb) tomatoes
1 clove
1 bayleaf
5 ml (1 level tsp) sugar
salt, pepper and paprika to taste
1 litre (1¾ pints) stock
25 g (1 oz) cornflour or plain flour
150 ml (¼ pint) milk
25 g (1 oz) pasta or rice
Parmesan cheese

Chop the onion, carrot and celery and sauté in the fat for 5 minutes. Add the quartered tomatoes, flavourings, seasonings and stock, bring to the boil and simmer for 1½ hours. Sieve the soup. Blend the cornflour with the milk, add to the soup and re-boil, stirring until thick. Add the pasta or rice and simmer gently for 30 minutes. Serve with grated Cheddar or Parmesan cheese.

Potato and leek soup

325 g (12 oz) leeks
25 g (1 oz) butter or margarine
700 g (1½ lb) potatoes
1·7 litres (3 pints) light stock
bouquet garni
salt and pepper
French bread and grated cheese to serve

Discard a third of the green top from the leeks. Slice the remainder finely and wash thoroughly. Drain and place with the fat in a large saucepan, cover and sauté for 5 minutes.

Meanwhile, peel and roughly dice the potatoes and add to the pan with the stock, bouquet garni and seasoning. Bring to the boil, reduce the heat, cover and simmer for about 1 hour until the potatoes are soft. Discard the bouquet garni. Purée in an electric liquidiser or pass through a sieve. Return to the pan, thin down with a little extra stock, if liked; adjust the seasoning. Serve with slices of French bread, topped with grated cheese and grilled. *Serves 6*

Cabbage soup with meat balls

700 g (1½ lb) white cabbage
50 g (2 oz) butter or margarine
1·7 litres (3 pints) hot beef stock
2·5 ml (½ level tsp) mixed spice
6 peppercorns
10 ml (2 level tsp) salt

For the meat balls
100 g (4 oz) minced veal
100 g (4 oz) minced pork
30 ml (2 tbsp) dry breadcrumbs
15 ml (1 tbsp) chopped onion
5 ml (1 level tsp) salt
pepper
60 ml (4 tbsp) double cream

First make the meat balls. Combine the dry ingredients and gradually mix in the cream. Shape into small balls, using about a teaspoonful for each.

Trim the cabbage and cut into cubes, discarding the core and tough portions. Melt the fat in a thick-based pan, add the cabbage and brown it. Add the stock, flavourings and salt, cover and simmer until the cabbage is tender – up to about 30 minutes. Add the meat balls for the last 5 minutes of the cooking time.

Chicken soup with eggs

900 ml (1½ pints) chicken broth
300 ml (½ pint) undiluted canned consommé
8 2·5-cm (1-inch) slices of French bread
butter or margarine
4 eggs
grated Parmesan or Cheddar cheese

Heat the broth and consommé in a saucepan and bring to the boil; meanwhile sauté the bread in hot fat in a large frying pan until browned on both sides. Poach the eggs in the hot (not boiling) soup in the usual way, then place one egg in each soup plate. Pour some broth over the eggs (strain it if liked). Sprinkle the sautéed bread with cheese, place 2 slices beside each egg and serve with additional cheese.

Lentil and bacon soup

450 g (1 lb) lentils
1·1 litres (2 pints) water
1 clove garlic to taste
a small bunch of parsley
salt
225 g (8 oz) bacon, rinded and diced
450 g (1 lb) potatoes, peeled

Wash the lentils and soak overnight. Boil them in the same water, adding the garlic clove, coarsely chopped parsley and some salt. Add the bacon and allow to simmer until both lentils and bacon are cooked. Then add the potatoes, cut into very small dice, and cook for a further 20 minutes. If a thicker soup is required, brown some butter or margarine with a little flour and add just before serving.

Creamy vegetable soup

900 g (2 lb) prepared mixed vegetables
    (eg, carrots, onions, celery, turnips,
    tomatoes)
50 g (2 oz) dripping
1·1 litres (2 pints) stock
salt and pepper
50 g (2 oz) pearl barley
20 g (¾ oz) cornflour
milk
carrot, turnip and peas for garnish

Cut the vegetables into neat pieces and sauté in the hot dripping until all the fat is absorbed. Add the stock, bring to the boil and season well. Cover and simmer gently for 1 hour, or until tender. Sieve or liquidise, return to the pan with the barley and continue to cook. Blend the cornflour with a little milk and add a few minutes before the soup is ready. Meanwhile, cut strips and balls of carrot and turnip, using a Parisian potato-cutter, and cook in boiling salted water; add the peas just before the end of the time. Garnish the soup with these extra vegetables.

Fish chowder

450 g (1 lb) fresh haddock
300 ml (½ pint) fish stock
1 onion, skinned and sliced
a few bacon rinds
a small knob of butter or margarine
2–3 potatoes, peeled and sliced
425-g (15-oz) can tomatoes
salt and pepper
1 bayleaf
2 cloves
chopped parsley to garnish

Skin the fish and simmer the skins in 300 ml (½ pint) water to make the stock. Fry the onion and bacon rinds in the fat for 5 minutes. Add the sliced potatoes and the

fish, cut into cubes. Beat the tomatoes to a thick purée, combine with the fish mixture and add the seasoning and flavourings. Simmer for 30–45 minutes. Remove the bayleaf and cloves and garnish with parsley before serving.

Cold soups

Watercress and orange soup

Illustrated in colour on page 22

25 g (1 oz) butter or margarine
1 medium onion, skinned and chopped
2 bunches of watercress
900 ml (1½ pints) chicken stock
grated rind and juice of 1 orange
30 ml (2 tbsp) chopped fresh parsley
15 ml (1 tbsp) chopped fresh thyme
salt and pepper
15 ml (1 level tbsp) cornflour
60 ml (4 tbsp) single cream

Melt the fat in a large pan, add the onion and cook for 5 minutes, until soft. Trim the stalks of the watercress, wash thoroughly and drain well. Chop coarsely, add to the pan and cook for 2–3 minutes. Stir in the stock, orange rind and juice, parsley, thyme and seasoning. Bring to the boil, cover and simmer gently for 25–30 minutes. Cool and purée the soup in an electric liquidiser or rub through a sieve. Return the soup to a clean pan. Blend the cornflour to a smooth paste with a little cold water and stir into the soup. Bring the soup to the boil, stirring, and

cook for 1–2 minutes until thick. Serve hot or cold, garnished with a swirl of cream.

Iced cucumber soup

1 small onion, skinned
900 ml (1½ pints) stock
1 large cucumber
1 sprig of mint
5 ml (1 level tsp) arrowroot
60 ml (4 tbsp) cream or top of the milk
salt and pepper
green food colouring

Chop the onion and simmer for 15 minutes in a pan with the stock. Peel the cucumber thinly, cut into small pieces (reserving a little for garnish) and add to the stock, with the mint sprig; simmer until the cucumber is tender. Blend the arrowroot and cream together. Sieve or liquidise, return to the pan and season. Add the cream and arrowroot mixture and slowly re-heat until boiling point is reached; pour into a large bowl to cool. Tint the soup delicately with green colouring and chill it. Serve sprinkled with small cucumber dice or shredded mint.

Crème vichyssoise

4 leeks
50 g (2 oz) butter or margarine
1 onion, skinned and chopped
salt and pepper
1·1 litres (2 pints) chicken stock
2 potatoes, peeled
142-ml (5-fl oz) carton single cream
chives to garnish

Prepare the leeks, cut up finely and cook gently for 10 minutes in the fat, together with the onion and seasoning: do not allow to brown. Add the stock and the thinly cut potatoes. Cook until tender, then sieve or liquidise. Adjust the seasoning, stir in the cream and chill. Sprinkle with chopped chives before serving.

Iced curry soup

100 g (4 oz) onion, skinned and finely
    chopped
25 g (1 oz) butter or margarine
15 ml (1 tbsp) curry paste
25 g (1 oz) plain flour
1·1 litres (2 pints) chicken stock
1 strip of lemon rind
1 bayleaf
10 ml (2 level tsp) arrowroot

Fry the onion in 20 g (¾ oz) fat until it is soft but not brown; add the curry paste and cook for 5 minutes. Add the rest of the fat, stir in the flour and pour on the stock. Bring to the boil, add the lemon rind and bayleaf and simmer for 20 minutes. Strain the soup and return it to a clean pan. Mix the

arrowroot with 15 ml (1 tbsp) water and add to the soup; bring back to the boil, strain and allow to cool. Chill in the refrigerator before serving.

Iced tomato soup

30 ml (2 tbsp) water
425-g (15-oz) can tomato juice
142-ml (5-fl oz) carton single cream
15 ml (1 tbsp) sherry
salt and pepper
10 ml (2 level tsp) sugar
chopped parsley to garnish

Mix all the ingredients together in a basin and chill in the refrigerator. Immediately before serving add the chopped parsley.

Cold cream of mushroom soup

40 g (1½ oz) butter or margarine
25 g (1 oz) flour
900 ml (1½ pints) chicken stock
210-g (7½-oz) can mushrooms
284-ml (10-fl oz) carton single cream
mushroom slices or tarragon leaves to garnish

Melt the fat, add the flour and cook for 1 minute. Add the stock and blend well, then bring to the boil. Drain and purée the mushrooms; add to the soup with the cream. Simmer for about 3 minutes and

pour into a bowl; cover and allow to cool, whisking occasionally. When the soup is very cold, whisk again and pour into cups. Sprinkle with the mushroom slices or 2–3 tarragon leaves before serving.

Chilled bortsch

1·1 litres (2 pints) good beef stock or 2 cans consommé
142-ml (5-fl oz) carton soured cream or yoghurt
450 g (1 lb) cooked beetroot
30 ml (2 tbsp) lemon juice
a good bunch of chives, finely chopped
double cream or soured cream
chives to garnish

Beat the stock with the cream or yoghurt until smooth. Add the beetroot, skinned and cut into small, neat dice. Add the lemon juice and chives and chill for several hours. Serve in cups with a spoonful of whipped cream or soured cream on each cup and garnish with chopped chives. (If preferred, this soup may be puréed.)

Consommé

Jellied consommé is a traditional summer delight. Follow the recipe on page 17 and allow to cool.

Here are some variations of cold consommé:

1 Add 30–45 ml (2–3 tbsp) chopped herbs

(chives, parsley and tarragon) to 1·1 litres (2 pints) consommé. Dissolve 10 g (¼ oz) of gelatine in a little sherry or Madeira, add to the mixture and chill until jellied. Serve roughly broken up in soup cups and garnish with whipped cream which has been flavoured with curry powder or sprinkled with toasted almonds.

2 Add 300 ml (½ pint) tomato juice to 1·1 litres (2 pints) consommé. Stir in 1 envelope of gelatine dissolved in a little lemon juice. Chill until jellied and serve broken up and garnished with sliced lemon and parsley.

3 To 1·1 litres (2 pints) of consommé add some chopped mint leaves. Dissolve 10 g (¼ oz) of gelatine in about 60 ml (4 tbsp) of sherry and add. Chill until jellied, then break up and serve in cups; garnish with whipped cream mixed with chopped mint.

4 Dissolve 10 g (¼ oz) of gelatine in 30 ml (2 tbsp) water and add 1·1 litres (2 pints) consommé with ½ a cucumber, peeled and finely diced. Chill until jellied. Serve broken up, in soup cups, and garnish each cup with a spoonful of soured cream and a twist of cucumber.

5 Blanch a red and a green pepper in boiling water for 5 minutes, then dice them, removing the seeds. Dissolve 10 g (¼ oz) gelatine in 30 ml (2 tbsp) white wine and add to 1·1 litres (2 pints) consommé, with the peppers. Chill until jellied and serve broken up, in soup cups.

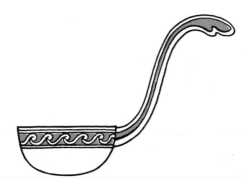

Watercress and orange soup (see page 21).

FISH COOKERY

Buying fish

Whatever fish you buy, the first essential is that it should be absolutely fresh; the fish should smell pleasant, with no trace of ammonia; it should be firm, not flabby, and scales should be lustrous and easy to rub off. Any spots and markings should be bright, the gills should be red and the eyes bright, clear and not sunken. The largest fish are not always the best – usually medium-sized ones have a better flavour and finer texture.

Bream White-fleshed fish of delicate flavour. Sea bream is available all the year; best from June to December; fresh-water bream in season July to February. Bream can be baked, grilled, poached or fried.

Brill A good-flavoured fish, not unlike turbot and cooked in the same ways. In season practically all the year, but only in small quantities.

Cod Available all the year; best from October to May. The close, white flesh is somewhat lacking in flavour, but is improved if cooked with herbs, stuffing or vegetables. Can be grilled, baked, fried in batter or used in made-up dishes.

Smoked cod fillet is used like smoked haddock.

Coley A meaty fish, part of the cod family. Takes particularly well to ingredients with robust flavours. Its greyish flesh turns whiter during cooking. Available all year round.

Dabs Small flat fish of the plaice family. Available all the year – best from June to February. Suitable for frying, baking, steaming and poaching.

Eel Best during autumn and winter. Suitable for baking, frying, stewing or serving jellied.

Flake (Sometimes called Dogfish) Available all the year; best from October to June. Suitable for frying, poaching, steaming and for made-up dishes.

Flounder Resembles plaice, but less good flavour and texture. Available in small quantities most of the year. Suitable for frying, steaming and poaching.

Gurnet and Gurnard Available all the year but not so good April to June. Suitable for baking, frying and poaching. Excellent cold with salad.

Haddock Available all the year; best from September to February. Suitable for cooking by all methods.

Smoked haddock, golden cutlets and smoked haddock fillet can be poached, grilled or used in made-up dishes such as kedgeree.

Hake Good flavour and texture. Available all the year; best from June to January. Cooked like cod. The dark-coloured Scotch hake is cheaper than Devonshire hake.

Halibut A large fish with delicate flavour, cheaper than turbot and not quite so good. Available all the year; best from August to April. Suitable for cooking by all methods; excellent cold with salad.

Herring These fish are good value as they're nutritious, rich in oils and vitamins. Two main home seasons – May to August and October to December. Suitable for cooking by most methods, including sousing and serving cold. Also prepared in various ways, as under:

Kippers Herrings that have been split open, soaked in brine, then smoked over wood chips and sawdust to give them their unique smoky flavour. Some of them are now dyed. They are usually poached or grilled.

Bloaters Herrings that have been soaked in brine, smoked and cured; unlike kippers, they are cured whole and for a shorter period.

Salt herrings The fish are gutted and preserved between layers of salt in barrels.

Rollmops The herrings are filleted, packed in barrels with brine and vinegar, then later rolled up and packed in jars with spices, onions or other flavourings, according to the manufacturer's particular recipe.

Bismark herrings are pickled and spiced like rollmops, but left whole.

Buckling herrings Smoked whole, at a higher temperature and for a longer time than kippers, so that they are lightly cooked during the curing. Very delicate in flavour.

John Dory An ugly fish with delicious flavour. In season October to December. Can be poached or baked whole, or filleted and then cooked as for sole; it may also be served cold, with salad.

Lemon sole Available all the year; best from July to February. Cook by any method.

Mackerel In season October to July; at its best April to June. Cook as for herring. Mackerel must be perfectly fresh.

Plaice Flat fish distinguished by red spots on dark side. Available all the year; best from May to January. Suitable for all methods of cooking, including serving cold.

Red mullet Firm, white flesh with delicious flavour. Best in summer months. Suitable for baking, poaching and grilling; good cold with salad.

Salmon Small and medium sizes are best. Seasons: English and Scottish, February to August; Irish, January to September. Suitable for poaching, grilling, baking and also for serving cold.

Salmon trout In season March to August. Serve poached, grilled, baked or cold with salad.

Skate A coarse white fish with a large percentage of bone. Suitable for poaching or frying, or to serve cold with salad.

Sole A flat fish, with firm, deliciously flavoured white flesh. Seasonable all the year. Suitable for any method of cooking.

Sprats Best from November to March, but supplies affected by weather. Best deep-fried or grilled.

Trout (River) Much prized for its delicate flavour. In season February to early September, but best from April to August. Serve grilled, baked or fried. Delicious served cold.

Turbot Considered the finest of the flat fish. Seasonable most of the year; best from March to August. Grill, bake or cook by any method. Excellent cold with salad.

Whitebait Tiny silver fish, the young of the herring and sprat. Most seasonable May to July. Best deep-fried.

Whiting Available all the year, best in winter months. The traditional fish for invalids. Serve poached, steamed, baked or fried.

Cooking fish

Grilling Ideal for thick steaks, cutlets and for herring, trout, etc. See recipes for grilled sole and grilled herrings, etc, and remember these points: season the fish well and brush liberally with fat; score whole fish on each side. Pre-heat the grill, put the fish on to the hot greased grid and turn the heat to moderate; grill gently until tender – 5–10 minutes, according to size – turning it once or twice.

Baking Small cod, hake or haddock (stuffed or plain), and good-sized cutlets are excellent this way. The recipes for Baked Stuffed Mackerel and Cod Véronique show the main methods, in which fish is cooked in fat or liquid. To enjoy baked fish at its best, season it well, cook in a covered dish and bake gently – usually in a moderate oven 180°C (350°F) mark 4; allow 10–15 minutes for small pieces, 25 minutes per 450 g (lb) for stuffed fish.

Poaching One of the simplest methods, suitable for thin cuts, fillets and smoked fish. Put the fish in a shallow pan, half-cover with milk or milk and water, add salt and pepper and cook very gently over a low heat, allowing 5–10 minutes according to thickness. Make a sauce with the liquor.

Boiling This method is suitable for large whole fish. Put enough water in a fish kettle to cover the fish, bring to the boil and lower the fish in. (Failing a fish kettle, put the fish on a plate and lower it with the aid of a muslin sling.) To improve the flavour, add 1–2 skinned onions, a bayleaf, a blade of mace and some thyme. Simmer slowly, over a low heat, allowing 8–10 minutes per 450 g (lb) – don't let the water boil again.

Steaming Steamed fish need not be insipid if you pay attention to seasoning and accompaniments. Small pieces, which take about 10–15 minutes, can be steamed between two plates placed over a pan of boiling water.

Cook larger pieces or whole fish in a steamer, allowing 30 minutes for cutlets, 15 minutes per 450 g (lb) for whole fish; adjust the heat so that water in steamer boils steadily. Season the fish and dab with butter before cooking.

Shallow frying Excellent for such whole fish as sole, and for fillets, etc – see Fried Plaice. First coat the fish; the simplest way is to use seasoned flour; other methods are to dip it in seasoned flour, into milk, then into flour again, or to coat with flour, then with beaten egg and finally with breadcrumbs. Use just enough really hot fat to prevent sticking; brown on either side, then fry gently.

Deep frying Used for small fish or pieces, which must be coated with egg and breadcrumbs or batter. The fat is all-important – oil, clarified beef fat or lard is suitable; it must be pure, free from moisture, and heated in a deep pan to 180°–190°C (350°–375°F). Put the fish in a frying basket, remove the pan from the heat, lower in the basket, quickly replace over the heat and cook until the fish is golden. Drain well and serve at once.

CHEF'S TIPS

Fish is sufficiently cooked when it will readily separate from the bone (test with the back of a knife), or when the flesh is opaque, white and firm.

When filleting and skinning fish, use a really sharp, pliable knife, and dip your fingers in coarse salt to get a good grip.

To minimise the smell of such fish as herrings cook them in a covered container or wrap in greaseproof paper or aluminium foil.

Wipe fish pans, dishes and cutlery with kitchen paper towel immediately after use and rinse in cold water. A little mustard in the washing-up water will kill the smell.

Whenever 'olive oil' or 'oil' is mentioned, you can use any form of cooking oil.

Frozen fish can be substituted in many of these recipes; canned fish is good in made-up dishes.

Fish recipes

Cod véronique

4 cod cutlets
1 shallot, skinned and sliced
50 g (2 oz) button mushrooms
fish stock
a little white wine (optional)
salt and pepper
25 g (1 oz) butter or margarine
25 g (1 oz) flour
150 ml (¼ pint) milk
a few white grapes, peeled, halved and pipped

Wash the fish and put into a baking dish. Add the shallot and mushrooms and cover with stock and the wine, if used. Season and bake in the oven at 190°C (375°F) mark 5 for 20 minutes. Drain off 150 ml (¼ pint) of the liquid, and arrange the fish on a dish. To

make a sauce, melt the fat, add the flour and gradually stir in 150 ml (¼ pint) stock and the milk. Season and boil the sauce until it thickens; add most of the grapes. Pour this sauce over the fish and garnish with remaining grapes and mushrooms.

Tipsy cod

2 onions, skinned and finely chopped
25 g (1 oz) butter or margarine
700 g (1½ lb) cod fillet
1 bayleaf
a little chopped thyme
chopped parsley
peppercorns
salt and pepper
brown ale
15 g (½ oz) cornflour

Fry the onions in the fat until faintly coloured, then spread in the bottom of an ovenproof dish. Put the pieces of cod fillet on this mixture, add the herbs and seasoning and cover with ale. Cook in the oven at 180°C (350°F) mark 4 for about 25 minutes. Strain the liquid from the fillets and thicken it with the cornflour, blended with a little water. Bring to the boil, stirring all the time, and pour over the fish.

Savoury fish stew

700 g (1½ lb) cod or haddock fillet
25 g (1 oz) seasoned flour
50 g (2 oz) lard or dripping
2 onions, skinned and sliced
1 clove of garlic, skinned and crushed
10 ml (2 tsp) chopped parsley
150 ml (¼ pint) vinegar
15 ml (1 tbsp) tomato paste
150 ml (¼ pint) water
100 g (4 oz) prawns, shelled

Wash the fish, cut into 5-cm (2-inch) squares and coat with seasoned flour. Melt the fat, fry the fish and place in a casserole. Fry the onions until golden and add to the fish,

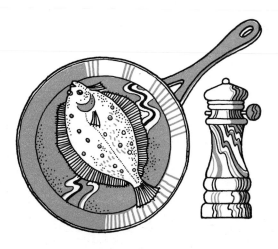

with the crushed garlic and parsley. Pour in the mixed vinegar, tomato paste and water. Cook in the oven at 180°C (350°F) mark 4 for 40 minutes, adding the prawns 10 minutes before cooking is complete. Serve with spaghetti or rice.

Fish pie

700 g (1½ lb) cod fillet
50 g (2 oz) shelled prawns
2 hard-boiled eggs
300 ml (½ pint) white sauce
225 g (8 oz) mashed potato
beaten egg to glaze

Cook the cod, then remove all the bones and skin and flake the fish. Put it in a casserole, together with the prawns and sliced eggs, and cover with the sauce. Cream the potato, adding a little milk if necessary, and fork or pipe over the pie. Brush with the egg and cook in the oven at 200°C (400°F) mark 6 for 35 minutes.

Haddock hotpot

450 g (1 lb) haddock
1 onion, skinned and chopped
100 g (4 oz) French beans
100 g (4 oz) cheese, grated
salt and pepper
a small can of tomatoes
2–3 large potatoes, peeled and sliced

Skin the fish and cut into cubes. Cover with

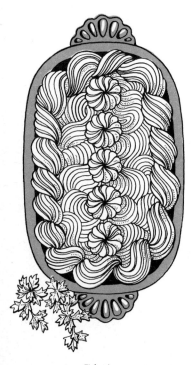

Fish pie

the chopped onion, the beans, half the grated cheese and the seasoning. Add the tomatoes, cover with the sliced potatoes and season again. Bake in the oven 180°C (350°F) mark 4 for 1 hour. Take from the oven, cover with the remaining cheese and brown under the grill.

Italian fish

Illustrated in colour opposite

4 cod cutlets or fillets of hake
25 g (1 oz) butter or margarine
1 clove of garlic, skinned and finely chopped
5 ml (1 tsp) chopped chives
100 g (4 oz) button mushrooms, sliced
15 ml (1 tbsp) chopped parsley
5 ml (1 level tsp) flour
30–45 ml (2–3 tbsp) stock
150 ml (¼ pint) white wine
salt and pepper
olive oil
chopped parsley to garnish

Prepare the fish. Melt the fat in a saucepan, add the garlic, chives, mushrooms and parsley, and cook for a few minutes. Stir in the flour, and cook for a further 3 minutes. Add very slowly the stock and wine, season, and bring to the boil. Cover, and simmer gently for 10 minutes. Meanwhile, fry the fish in oil. Drain, put into a hot dish, and cover with the sauce. Garnish with parsley.

Baked fish, Spanish style

4 cod steaks
5 ml (1 level tsp) salt
2·5 ml (½ level tsp) pepper
1·25 ml (¼ level tsp) cayenne pepper
1·25 ml (¼ level tsp) grated nutmeg
15 ml (1 tbsp) olive oil
1 large onion, skinned and thinly sliced
22·5 ml (1½ tbsp) chopped pimiento
4 anchovy fillets
4 tomatoes, peeled and cut in thick slices
45 ml (3 tbsp) chopped chives
100 g (4 oz) mushrooms, thinly sliced
30–45 ml (2–3 tbsp) white wine
50 g (2 oz) butter or margarine, melted
100 g (4 oz) white breadcrumbs

Wash the fish and dry it. Sprinkle with a mixture of salt, pepper, cayenne and nutmeg. Put the oil into a large ovenproof dish and add the onion and chopped pimiento. Arrange the seasoned fish slices side by side on top of the onion, then place one anchovy fillet on each. Cover the fish with tomato and sprinkle with chives. Scatter the mushrooms over all, then pour on the wine. Cover and bake for 30 minutes in the oven at 200°C (400°F) mark 6. Meanwhile, mix the melted fat and breadcrumbs.

Sprinkle this mixture on top of the fish and continue baking, uncovered, until well browned – about 5–10 minutes.

Coley with oriental sauce

25 g (1 oz) butter or margarine
175 g (6 oz) onion, skinned and chopped
1 clove garlic, skinned and chopped
3 sticks celery, thinly sliced
63-g (2¼-oz) can tomato paste
45 ml (3 tbsp) concentrated curry sauce
400 ml (¾ pint) light stock
50 g (2 oz) sultanas
25 g (1 oz) desiccated coconut
1 large piece stem ginger, chopped
30 ml (2 tbsp) redcurrant jelly
15 ml (1 level tbsp) cornflour
30 ml (2 tbsp) lemon juice
900 g (2 lb) coley fillet, skinned
1 onion, skinned and sliced
chopped parsley to garnish

Melt the fat in a large shallow pan. Add the onion, garlic and celery, cook until soft and transparent. Stir in the tomato paste, curry sauce and stock, bring to the boil, then reduce to a simmer. Add the sultanas, coconut, ginger and redcurrant jelly. Cook, covered, for 30 minutes. Blend the cornflour with the lemon juice. Stir it into the sauce, bring to the boil then simmer for 10 minutes. Wipe the fish and cut into large pieces. Stir the fish into the curry sauce and simmer for 20 minutes, stirring occasionally until fish is cooked. Carefully pour into serving dish and garnish with onion rings and parsley.

Halibut and cucumber in cheese sauce

4 steaks of halibut
salt and pepper
6 peppercorns
a few parsley stalks
150 ml (¼ pint) dry cider
50 g (2 oz) butter or margarine
½ cucumber, peeled and diced
25 g (1 oz) flour
milk
50 g (2 oz) cheese, grated

Wash and trim the halibut steaks, place in an ovenproof dish or casserole with the seasoning and flavourings and pour the cider over them. Cover with foil and bake in the oven at 180°C (350°F) mark 4 for about 20 minutes, until tender. Using 25 g (1 oz) fat, simmer the cucumber with seasoning for about 10 minutes in a covered pan, until tender. When the fish is cooked, remove the peppercorns and parsley and drain off the cooking liquid. Make a sauce from the remaining fat, the flour and the cooking liquid from the fish, made up to 300 ml

Italian fish (see above).

(½ pint) with milk. When it has thickened, remove from the heat, stir in half the cheese and season to taste. Pour over the fish, sprinkle with the remaining cheese and brown under a hot grill. Serve garnished with the cucumber.

Scalloped smoked haddock with cheese

Illustrated in colour on page 31

148-g (5 ¼-oz) pkt instant potato
75 g (3 oz) butter
1 egg, beaten
450 g (1 lb) smoked haddock
1 bayleaf
50 g (2 oz) plain flour
150 ml (¼ pint) milk
300 ml (½ pint) fish stock
100 g (4 oz) mature Cheddar cheese, grated
juice of ½ lemon
salt and pepper
parsley sprigs and lemon wedges to garnish

Make up the potato following the packet instructions. Add 25 g (1 oz) butter and the egg. Poach the fish in sufficient water to cover, adding the bayleaf. When it is tender, strain off and reserve the fish liquor. Discard any bones and skin from the fish. Melt the remaining butter in a saucepan and stir in the flour; cook for 1 minute. Add the milk all at once, with the fish stock, off the heat. Whisk or beat well, return the pan to the heat and bring to the boil, stirring. Add the cheese to the sauce, with the lemon juice and seasoning to taste.

Spoon the potato into a piping bag fitted with a large vegetable nozzle. Butter 4–6 large natural scallop shells or individual ovenproof dishes and pipe potato round each outside edge. Divide the roughly flaked fish between the shells. Spoon the sauce over and bake in the oven at 200°C (400°F) mark 6 for about 30 minutes or reheat under a moderate grill until the sauce is bubbling and the potato golden. Garnish with parsley and lemon. *Serves 4–6*

Haddock and cider casserole

450 g (1 lb) haddock or cod fillet, skinned
225 g (8 oz) tomatoes, sliced
50 g (2 oz) button mushrooms, sliced
15 ml (1 tbsp) chopped parsley
salt and pepper
150 ml (¼ pint) cider
30 ml (2 tbsp) fresh breadcrumbs
30 ml (2 tbsp) grated cheese

Wash the fish, cut it into cubes and place in an ovenproof dish. Cover with the tomatoes and mushrooms, parsley and season-ing and pour the cider over. Cover with foil and bake in the oven at 180°C (350°F) mark 4 for about 20–25 minutes. Sprinkle with the breadcrumbs and cheese and brown under a hot grill.

Devilled herrings

2 herrings
50 g (2 oz) butter or margarine
2·5 ml (½ level tsp) curry powder
10 ml (2 tsp) curry paste
30 ml (2 tbsp) lemon juice
lemon slices to garnish

Clean and fillet the herrings. Cream the fat and work in the curry powder, paste and lemon juice. Spread over the fish and grill. Serve at once on a hot dish, garnished with lemon.

Grilled herrings

To clean the fish, cut off the heads with a sharp knife or scissors, removing the inside at the same time. Remove any black skin from inside and wash clean. Scrape off the scales with the back of a knife and cut off the fins and tails with scissors. Rinse the fish thoroughly and dry well. Score the fish on both sides. Brush the herrings over with melted butter or dripping and put on a hot grid. Cook under a hot grill, browning first one side, then the other, then lower the heat to finish cooking – they should take about 3 or 4 minutes on each side. Serve at once on a hot dish, garnished with lemon slices and sprigs of parsley.

Fish and potato casserole

2 large salt herrings
450 g (1 lb) boiled potatoes, sliced
15 ml (1 tbsp) chopped onion or spring onion
30 ml (2 tbsp) melted butter or margarine
3 eggs
568 ml (1 pint) milk
2·5 ml (½ level tsp) pepper
25 g (1 oz) dried breadcrumbs

Soak the fish for 6 hours, skin and bone them and cut in long strips. Grease a baking dish and put in a layer of potato, then one of herring, with a little onion; repeat, finishing with a potato layer, and pour the melted fat over the top. Beat the eggs, add the milk

Grilled herrings

and pepper, pour into the baking dish and sprinkle with breadcrumbs. Bake in the oven at 180°C (350°F) mark 4 for 30–40 minutes or until browned.

Canned salmon may be used instead of salt herring.

Apple-stuffed mackerel fillets

Illustrated in colour on page 33

1 large cooking apple, peeled and cored
75 g (3 oz) celery
50 g (2 oz) butter or margarine
2·5 ml (½ level tsp) dried parsley
5 ml (1 tsp) lemon juice
45 ml (3 level tbsp) fresh breadcrumbs
salt and pepper
2 large mackerel, filleted
1 green eating apple, cored and sliced, to garnish
150 ml (¼ pint) pure apple juice
5 ml (1 level tsp) arrowroot
5–10 ml (1–2 level tsp) sugar
lemon slices to garnish

Chop the apple and celery. Melt 25 g (1 oz) fat in a saucepan and cook the apple and celery together until the apple is pulpy. Add the parsley, lemon juice, breadcrumbs and seasoning to taste. Mix well to combine. Spread the stuffing over the fish fillets; fold each in half. Place in an ovenproof dish and bake, uncovered, in the oven at 180°C (350°F) mark 4 for 25–30 minutes.

Melt the remaining fat in a pan and gently fry the apple slices for 1–2 minutes on each side. Blend a little apple juice with the arrowroot and sugar. Warm the remaining juice and add the arrowroot mixture. Bring to the boil to thicken. Glaze the mackerel with some of the sauce. Garnish with the fried apple and lemon slices. Serve the remaining sauce separately. *Serves 2–4*

Baked stuffed mackerel

4 mackerel
butter or margarine to baste

For the stuffing
25 g (1 oz) shredded suet
25 g (1 oz) ham or bacon, chopped
50 g (2 oz) fresh white breadcrumbs
5 ml (1 tsp) chopped parsley
a pinch of mixed herbs
grated rind of ½ lemon
salt and pepper
beaten egg

Cut off the heads and tails of the fish, clean them, remove the roe and take out the backbone. Mix all the stuffing ingredients together, binding them with the beaten egg. Stuff the fish, lay them in a greased baking dish, and cook for 40 minutes in the

oven at 170°C (325°F) mark 3, basting well with fat during the cooking.

Baked red mullet

Clean one mullet for each person and put into a well-buttered ovenproof dish. Add salt and pepper, put a little butter on each fish, cover with greased greaseproof paper and cook for about 20 minutes in the oven at 180°C (350°F) mark 4.

Fried plaice

8 fillets of plaice
beaten egg
breadcrumbs for coating
fat or oil for frying
parsley and lemon to garnish

First skin the fillets, using a sharp knife; put the fish, skin side down, on a board; hold the tail with your left hand and slide the fish off the skin with the knife held in the right hand. Brush the fillets with egg and dip in crumbs. Fry in shallow fat for about 2 minutes on each side. Garnish and serve.

Baked stuffed plaice

2 plaice, whole but cleaned
50 g (2 oz) fresh breadcrumbs
25 g (1 oz) suet
15 ml (1 tbsp) chopped parsley
2·5 ml (½ level tsp) dried thyme
grated rind of ½ lemon
salt and pepper
milk or egg to bind
25 g (1 oz) butter or margarine
150 ml (¼ pint) dry white wine
chopped parsley and lemon wedges to garnish

Get the fishmonger to make a slit down the backbone of the fish and lift the top fillets slightly to form two pockets. Mix together the crumbs, suet, herbs, lemon rind and seasoning and bind with milk or egg. Divide this mixture between the two fish, stuffing into the pockets. Place the fish in a large, shallow ovenproof dish and dot with the fat. Pour in the wine, cover the dish with foil and bake in the oven at 180°C (350°F) mark 4 for about 20 minutes, or until tender. Spoon the cooking liquid over the fish and serve garnished with parsley and lemon wedges.

Portuguese plaice

8 fillets of plaice
15 ml (1 tbsp) chives
3 tomatoes, skinned and sliced
25 g (1 oz) butter or margarine
a little white wine
salt and pepper

Prepare the fish. Chop the chives and fry

with the tomatoes in the fat for a few minutes, then pour into an ovenproof dish. Fold each fillet in three and put on top of the tomatoes; cover with wine, season and bake in the oven at 180°C (350°F) mark 4 for 25 minutes.

Plaice and cheese casserole

8 fillets of plaice
salt and pepper
75 g (3 oz) cheese, grated
25 g (1 oz) butter or margarine
25 g (1 oz) flour
300 ml (½ pint) milk
225 g (8 oz) tomatoes
tomato slices to garnish

Fold the fillets of plaice in half, sprinkle with salt and pepper and put in a casserole. Cover with half the grated cheese and bake for 10–15 minutes in the oven at 190°C (375°F) mark 5 until the fish is cooked. Meanwhile, melt the fat, add the flour, cook for a minute, then gradually add the milk. Bring to the boil, stirring all the time, and add nearly all the remaining cheese. Cut up the tomatoes and add to the sauce, season well, and allow to cook slowly for about 5 minutes; then pour over the fish. Cover with the remaining grated cheese and sliced tomatoes and grill until golden brown.

Grilled salmon cutlets

The cutlets should be about 2·5 cm (1 inch) thick. Wipe them dry and brush with oil or melted butter. Grease the grill pan and cook the fish under a fairly hot grill, allowing about 10 minutes for each side, as necessary, and adding a little more fat as it cooks. Serve garnished with lemon and watercress, accompanied by melted butter, maître d'hôtel butter or Belgian Cucumber (see page 107).

Grilled salmon cutlets

29

Baked salmon cutlets

4 salmon cutlets, about 1 cm (½ inch) thick
100 g (4 oz) butter or margarine
lemon
150 ml (¼ pint) dry white wine
cucumber
salt and pepper
chopped parsley
watercress to garnish

Wipe the cutlets. Melt half the fat and pour into a casserole; then add the salmon, with the juice of half a lemon and the white wine. Cover and bake in the oven at 180°C (350°F) mark 4 for 25–30 minutes, until the flesh is opaque and will leave the bone readily. Meanwhile peel and dice the cucumber, simmer in salted water until tender, then drain it and add the rest of the fat, salt, pepper and some chopped parsley. Serve the fish and garnish with the cucumber mixture and watercress, or with asparagus, when available.

Salmon patties

Illustrated in colour on page 37

25 g (1 oz) butter
300 g (11 oz) plain flour
150 ml (¼ pint) milk
198-g (7-oz) can red or pink salmon, drained
salt and pepper
15 ml (1 tbsp) lemon juice
pinch of cayenne pepper
65 g (2½ oz) butter or margarine
65 g (2½ oz) lard
50 g (2 oz) Cheddar cheese, grated
1 egg yolk
beaten egg to glaze

Melt the butter in a saucepan. Stir in 25 g (1 oz) flour. Cook for 1 minute. Gradually add the milk and bring to the boil, stirring. Remove any black skin and large bones from the salmon. Flake the flesh and add to the sauce. Season to taste with salt, pepper and lemon juice. Set aside to cool.

Sift 275 g (10 oz) plain flour with the cayenne pepper and a pinch of salt. Rub in the fats until the mixture resembles fine crumbs. Stir in the cheese. Mix to a dough with the egg yolk, blended with a little water. Roll the pastry out and cut 16 ovals, eight 11·5 cm (4½ inches) in length and eight 12·5 cm (5 inches) in length, using cutters or an oval template. Place the small ovals on a baking sheet and divide the filling between them leaving a rim. Damp the edges. Place the lids in position and crimp the edges together. Brush with beaten egg. Cut fluted rounds from thinly rolled pastry scraps and place on the patties. Glaze with beaten egg and bake at 220°C (425°F) mark

7 for 30–35 minutes until golden brown. Serve with a cucumber salad tossed in French dressing. *Makes 8*

Grilled sole

Wash the sole and remove the black skin. Sprinkle with salt, brush with melted butter or margarine and grill under a hot grill for 2–3 minutes on each side. Serve with maître d'hôtel butter (see page 71).

Sole meunière

1 small sole, whole or filleted, per person
salt and pepper
flour
butter or margarine
lemon juice
chopped parsley

Season the sole with salt and pepper, flour it lightly on both sides and fry it in the fat until the fish is cooked and golden brown on both sides. Serve on a hot dish, sprinkle with lemon juice and parsley, then pour on some lightly browned melted butter.

Sole au vin blanc

1 small sole per person
2 shallots, skinned and finely chopped
a small knob of butter or margarine
150 ml (¼ pint) white wine
15 g (½ oz) flour
a few button mushrooms
salt and pepper

Put the soles into an ovenproof dish. Fry the shallots in the fat for 3–4 minutes, add the wine and pour over the soles. Cover and bake in the oven at 190°C (375°F) mark 5 for 7 minutes. Drain off the liquid and add the flour, blended with a little water. Bring to the boil, add the mushrooms and boil gently for 2–3 minutes. Season well and pour over the sole.

Sole colbert

1 small sole per person
10 ml (2 level tsp) seasoned flour
beaten egg
browned crumbs
fat or oil for deep frying
25 g (1 oz) maître d'hôtel butter (see page 71)
fried parsley

Ask the fishmonger to clean and skin the soles, leaving the fish whole. With a sharp knife, cut down the centre of the fish on one side, loosening both fillets a little from the bone, so that they can be rolled back, leaving a long depression in the centre of

the fish. Dust the fish with seasoned flour, then brush with egg and coat with browned crumbs, shaking off any surplus. Fry the sole in deep fat until golden brown. Serve them garnished with maître d'hôtel butter (placing this in the hollow in the centre of the fish) and with fried parsley.

Paupiettes of sole with mushroom sauce

8 fillets of sole
50-g (2-oz) pkt frozen shrimps
40 g (1½ oz) butter or margarine
50 g (2 oz) button mushrooms
300 ml (½ pint) milk
salt and pepper
25 g (1 oz) flour

Roll up the fillets with 2 or 3 shrimps inside each one and stand them upright in an ovenproof dish. Put a very small knob of fat on each and cover with greaseproof paper. Bake in the oven at 180°C (350°F) mark 4 for 20 minutes. Meanwhile, wipe the mushrooms and stew them gently in the milk with salt and pepper for 10–15 minutes. Drain off the liquid. Melt 25 g (1 oz) of the fat and add the flour, then gradually add the milk and fish liquor. Bring to the boil, add the mushrooms and pour over the fish.

Sole with orange

4 sole, skinned
seasoned flour
175 g (6 oz) butter or margarine
4 small oranges
60 ml (4 tbsp) sherry
30 ml (2 tbsp) tarragon vinegar
chopped parsley to garnish

Coat the fish with seasoned flour. Melt 100 g (4 oz) of the fat and fry the fish on both sides. Meanwhile peel the oranges and cut into slices, retaining any juice. Gently heat the orange slices, juice, sherry and vinegar in a small pan. Clean out the frying pan and lightly brown the remaining fat. Put the fish in a serving dish and arrange the orange slices in a line down them. Add the liquid in which the sole were cooked to the browned fat and pour over the fish. Garnish with the parsley and serve at once.

Scalloped smoked haddock with cheese (see page 28).

Sole véronique

2 sole, filleted
2 shallots, skinned and chopped
2–3 button mushrooms, sliced
a few sprigs of parsley
½ bayleaf
salt and pepper
150 ml (¼ pint) dry white wine
150 ml (¼ pint) water
100 g (4 oz) green grapes
20 g (¾ oz) butter or margarine
20 g (¾ oz) flour
30–45 ml (2–3 tbsp) single cream

Wash the fillets, fold in three and lay in a greased ovenproof dish, with the shallots, mushrooms, herbs, seasonings, wine and water. Cover with foil and bake in the oven at 180°C (350°F) mark 4 for 20 minutes. Meanwhile poach the grapes for about 5 minutes in a little water (or extra wine), then peel them and remove the pips. Strain the liquid from the cooked fish and keep the fish warm while making a roux sauce from the fat, flour and cooking liquid (made up to 300 ml (½ pint) if necessary). When it thickens, remove from heat and stir in the cream and the grapes (retaining a few). Pour over the fish and serve garnished with the remaining grapes.

Sole with mushrooms

2 sole, filleted
2 shallots, skinned and chopped
100 g (4 oz) button mushrooms
45 ml (3 tbsp) dry white wine
15 ml (1 tbsp) water
1 bayleaf
salt and pepper
40 g (1½ oz) butter or margarine
juice of ½ lemon
20 g (¾ oz) flour
about 150 ml (¼ pint) milk
30–45 ml (2–3 tbsp) single cream
mushroom caps to garnish

Wash the fillets of sole, fold each of them in three and place in a greased ovenproof dish with the shallots, the chopped mushroom stalks, wine, water, bayleaf and seasoning. Cover and bake for 15–20 minutes in the oven at 180°C (350°F) mark 4 until tender. Drain off the cooking liquid; remove the flavouring vegetables and keep the fish warm. Meanwhile simmer the mushroom caps gently in half the fat, with a squeeze of lemon juice and some salt and pepper. Make a roux sauce from the remaining fat, the flour and the cooking liquid, made up to 300 ml (½ pint) with milk. When the sauce has thickened, remove from the heat, stir in the cream, add a squeeze of lemon juice and adjust the seasoning if necessary. Pour over the fish and serve garnished with mushroom caps.

Grilled trout

4 small trout
olive oil
salt and pepper
lemon slices and watercress to garnish

Prepare the trout, then brush them with olive oil and sprinkle with salt and pepper. Put them on a hot grill and cook for 5–10 minutes on each side. Serve at once, garnished with lemon and watercress.

Trout vin rouge

4 small trout, cleaned
100 g (4 oz) button mushrooms, sliced
1 bayleaf
1 clove
salt and pepper
150 ml (¼ pint) dry red wine
20 g (¾ oz) butter or margarine
20 g (¾ oz) flour
30–45 ml (2–3 tbsp) single cream or
   top of milk

Wash the fish and cut off the fins. (Leave the head on, or remove if preferred.) Place in a shallow ovenproof dish and add the mushrooms, herbs, seasoning and wine. Cover with foil and bake in the oven at 180°C (350°F) mark 4 for about 20 minutes, until tender. Strain off the cooking liquid, retaining the mushrooms, and keep the fish warm. Make a roux sauce from the fat, flour and cooking liquid, made up to 300 ml (½ pint) if necessary with water or stock. When the sauce has thickened, remove it from the heat and stir in the mushrooms and the cream. Adjust the seasoning if necessary and pour over the fish.

American tuna casserole

2 × 198-g (7-oz) cans tuna
30 ml (2 level tbsp) plain flour
2·5 ml (½ level tsp) salt
a little pepper
300 ml (½ pint) milk
30 ml (2 tbsp) sherry or brown table
   sauce
1 cup crumbled potato crisps

Put into a double saucepan 30 ml (2 tbsp) of

the oil from the tuna; gradually stir in the flour, salt, pepper and milk and cook, stirring, until smooth and thickened, then add the sherry or brown sauce. Cover the bottom of a greased 1·7-litre (3-pint) casserole with a quarter of the potato crisps. Add a third of the tuna, in chunks, then one-third of the sauce. Repeat, making 3 layers; top with the rest of the crisps. Put a lid on the casserole or cover with foil and bake in the oven at 190°C (375°F) mark 5 for 20 minutes, then take off the lid and bake for a further 10 minutes, or until brown.

Turbot with shrimp sauce

4 pieces of turbot
½ bayleaf
1 clove
salt and pepper
150 ml (¼ pint) dry red wine
milk
25 g (1 oz) butter or margarine
25 g (1 oz) flour
50–100 g (2–4 oz) shrimps
30–45 ml (2–3 tbsp) single cream

Wash the turbot and place in an ovenproof dish or casserole, add the bayleaf, clove and seasoning and pour the wine over. Cover with foil and bake in the oven at 180°C (350°F) mark 4 for about 20 minutes, or until tender. Remove the bayleaf and clove, strain off the cooking liquid and make up to 300 ml (½ pint) with milk. Make a sauce from the fat, flour and liquid and when it thickens, stir in the shrimps and cream; re-heat for 2–3 minutes. Adjust the seasoning if necessary, then pour over the fish and serve.

Fried whitebait

Wipe the fish well with a clean cloth and dust them with flour. Put the whitebait into a frying basket and shake off any excess flour. Heat some lard or oil in a deep frying pan and when the fat is hot enough to brown a cube of bread in 1 minute, plunge the fish into it. Fry it for about 2 minutes, shaking the basket once or twice during the frying. Drain the whitebait on kitchen paper in the oven, and serve piled on a napkin and garnished with lemon slices. Serve brown bread and butter with the fish.

Fish mornay

450 g (1 lb) cooked white fish
25 g (1 oz) butter or margarine
25 g (1 oz) flour
300 ml (½ pint) milk
salt and pepper
25–50 g (1–2 oz) cheese, grated
2 or 3 tomatoes, chopped

Remove the skin and bones from the fish

Apple-stuffed mackerel fillets
(see page 29).

and flake it roughly with a fork. Melt the fat and add the flour; cook for a minute, and then gradually add the milk. Bring to the boil, season and add most of the cheese. Mix with the fish and pour into a shallow ovenproof dish, together with the tomatoes. Sprinkle with grated cheese and bake for 30 minutes in the oven at 200°C (400°F) mark 6.

Fish mousse

225 g (8 oz) cooked fish
pepper
45 ml (3 tbsp) lemon juice
150 ml (¼ pint) salad cream
2·5 ml (½ level tsp) celery salt
20 g (½ oz) gelatine
300 ml (½ pint) fish stock
150 ml (¼ pint) unsweetened evaporated milk

Mix the fish, pepper, lemon juice, salad cream and celery salt together. Dissolve the gelatine in the stock and allow to cool before adding it to the fish; whisk the evaporated milk. When the fish and gelatine mixture is almost setting, fold the milk into it. Turn out when set.

To make the dish more decorative, line the serving dish with lettuce leaves and garnish with crimped cucumber and tomato twists – see page 115 for directions.

Savoury fish croquettes

225 g (8 oz) mashed potatoes
225 g (8 oz) cooked white fish
10 ml (2 tsp) chopped parsley
25 g (1 oz) butter or margarine
salt and pepper
egg to bind
egg and breadcrumbs
fat or oil for deep frying
lemon and watercress to garnish

Mix the potatoes, flaked fish and parsley together. Melt the fat in a saucepan, add the fish and potatoes, seasoning and enough egg to bind. Divide the mixture into 8 portions and form into cork-shaped pieces; coat with egg and crumbs and fry in the fat. Garnish and serve.

Shellfish recipes

Dressed crab

Pull the top shell from the body of the crab by putting your thumb at the head and pulling the shell gently away. Break off all the claws. Remove the flesh from the shell, keeping the brown meat separate from the white. Discard all the greyish-white 'dead man's fingers' and remove the stomach – a

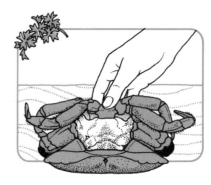

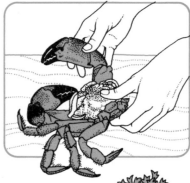

Dressing a crab

small sac near the head. Crack the claws with a hammer or a weight and remove all the flesh. If liked, season the flesh with mayonnaise or lemon juice and oil. Wash the shells and replace the meat, putting the brown in the centre and the white on either side. Garnish with paprika, chopped parsley and lemon wedges.

Lobster mayonnaise

1 lobster, cooked
1–2 lettuces
150 ml (¼ pint) mayonnaise
cucumber

Remove the flesh from the lobster, retaining the coral for garnishing. (The claws and head may be also used for this purpose. Flake the flesh, or cut it into small pieces. Wash the lettuce and tear into pieces, keeping the heart and some of the leaves whole; arrange these on a dish. Mix the lobster flesh with the mayonnaise and pile on to the salad. Decorate with lobster coral in hollowed out cucumber 'boats', and place the remaining lettuce leaves round the edges of the serving dish.

Lobster cocktail

225 g (8 oz) cooked lobster flesh, or a 220-g (7¼-oz) can lobster
2 tomatoes, peeled and sliced
lettuce
mayonnaise
cress to garnish

Dice the lobster flesh and mix with the tomatoes. Line some glasses with lettuce leaves, pile the lobster and tomato in each and coat with mayonnaise. Garnish with cress and serve chilled.

Crabmeat or Dublin Bay prawns, similarly prepared, also provide excellent fish cocktails.

Lobster thermidor

900-g (2-lb) lobster, cooked
50 g (2 oz) butter or margarine
1 small onion, skinned and finely chopped
25 g (1 oz) flour
150 ml (¼ pint) milk
25 g (1 oz) Cheddar cheese, grated
15 ml (1 tbsp) white wine
pinch of paprika pepper
salt and pepper
grated Parmesan cheese
lettuce, watercress and lemon slices to garnish

Using a large, sharp-pointed knife cut the lobster carefully down the centre back, open out the two halves and take out all the flesh. Discard the intestine, which looks like a small vein running through the centre of the tail, the stomach, which lies near the head, and the spongy gills, which are not edible. Clean the shells and rub them with oil. Twist the large and small claws from the shells and, using a rolling pin, crack the large claws and carefully remove all the flesh using a small, pointed knife and a skewer.

Cut all the flesh into pieces about 1 cm

(½ inch) long. Heat half the fat in a small frying pan and add the lobster meat. Sauté gently, turning occasionally.

Meanwhile, in a small pan, heat the remaining fat. Add the onion and sauté until soft. Add the flour and blend thoroughly. Add the milk, stirring, and bring to the boil. Simmer for a few minutes and add the cheese. Mix thoroughly over a low heat, add the wine and paprika; season. Pour the sauce over the lobster in the frying pan and mix well. Cook over a low heat for a few minutes. Place the cleaned lobster shells on a grill rack, then spoon the lobster mixture into them. Sprinkle thickly with grated Parmesan cheese and place under a preheated grill until the sauce is bubbling and golden brown. Place on a bed of lettuce. Garnish with watercress and lemon slices. *Serves 2*

Lobster Newburg

2 small cooked lobsters
25 g (1 oz) butter or margarine
60 ml (4 tbsp) Madeira or sherry
2 egg yolks
142-ml (5-fl oz) carton single cream
salt and cayenne pepper
boiled rice
chopped parsley

Halve the lobsters, carefully remove all the meat and slice it thinly. Melt the fat, arrange the lobster meat in the pan and heat gently for about 5 minutes. Add the Madeira and continue as for Prawns Newburg (right).

Oysters

These are at their best when eaten *au naturel* as an hors d'oeuvre. The renowned Colchester and Whitstable oysters are among the best for serving in this way, but oysters from the Helford river beds in Cornwall, though small, have an excellent flavour and are less expensive.

Oysters should ideally be eaten as soon as they are opened – and not longer than an hour afterwards. They may be opened by the fishmonger if bought near enough to the serving time, but after a little practice you could open them yourself.

Allow 4–6 per person and serve in the deeper shell, with lemon wedges, cayenne and brown bread and butter.

Prawns Newburg

225 (8 oz) prawns, peeled
25 g (1 oz) butter or margarine
60 ml (4 tbsp) Madeira or sherry
2 egg yolks
142-ml (5-fl oz) carton single cream
salt and cayenne pepper
boiled rice or toast
chopped chives or parsley

Sauté the prawns very gently in the fat for about 5 minutes. Stir in the Madeira or sherry and cook for a further 2–3 minutes. Mix the egg yolks and cream and pour into the prawn mixture, add seasoning to taste and heat very gently, until a thickened creamy consistency is obtained. Pour at once over boiled rice or toast. Serve sprinkled with chives or parsley and garnished with whole prawns.

Shrimps can of course be used in the same way.

Prawn risotto

2 chicken bouillon cubes
25 g (1 oz) butter or margarine
1 onion, skinned and chopped
1 clove of garlic, skinned and chopped
225 g (8 oz) long grain rice
150 ml (¼ pint) dry white wine
salt and pepper
50 g (2 oz) button mushrooms, sliced
225 g (8 oz) prawns, peeled
grated Parmesan cheese for serving

Make up 1·1 litres (2 pints) chicken stock with the cubes. Melt the fat and fry the onion and garlic for 5 minutes, or until soft but not coloured. Add the rice and continue cooking gently until the grains are golden and transparent. Stir in the wine and allow to bubble briskly until well reduced. Stir in 300 ml (½ pint) stock and the mushrooms. Season and cook in an open pan until all the stock has been absorbed. Continue adding the stock in 300-ml (½-pint) amounts until it has all been used; with the final addition stir in the prawns and cook for a further 5–10 minutes, or until they are heated through and all the liquid is

absorbed. Serve at once, sprinkled with Parmesan cheese.

Grilled scallops

8 scallops
olive oil
salt and pepper
50 g (2 oz) butter
1 clove of garlic, skinned and finely chopped
chopped parsley and lemon wedges to garnish

Brush the scallops with oil and sprinkle with salt and pepper. Place under a medium grill and grill for 3–4 minutes on each side; put on to a very hot dish. Heat 45 ml (3 tbsp) olive oil with the butter and garlic and pour over the scallops. Garnish with parsley and lemon wedges.

Scallops in cream

6–8 scallops
30 ml (2 tbsp) olive oil
lemon juice
seasoned flour
50 g (2 oz) butter or margarine
50 g (2 oz) button mushrooms, sliced
1 shallot, skinned and finely chopped
30–45 ml (2–3 tbsp) white wine
142-ml (5-fl oz) carton single cream
salt and cayenne pepper
50 g (2 oz) Parmesan cheese, grated

Clean and cut up the scallops. Mix the oil and 5 ml (1 tsp) lemon juice and marinade the scallops for 1 hour. Drain well, then toss in the seasoned flour and cook in the fat. Place the scallops in 4 shells, then fry the mushrooms and shallot lightly in the fat. Add the wine and reduce well, then stir in the cream. Heat gently, season and add a few drops of lemon juice. Pour over the scallops, sprinkle with the cheese and brown under a hot grill. Serve as an hors d'œuvre.

Fried scampi

225 g (8 oz) scampi or Dublin Bay prawns
seasoned flour
100 g (4 oz) plain flour
a pinch of salt
15 ml (1 tbsp) oil
1 egg, separated
30–45 ml (2–3 tbsp) water or milk and water
fat or oil for deep frying

If fresh scampi or prawns are used, discard their heads, remove the flesh from the shells and remove the dark veins; if frozen, allow to defrost, then drain well. Dip the scampi in the seasoned flour. Mix the plain flour, salt, oil and egg yolk with sufficient

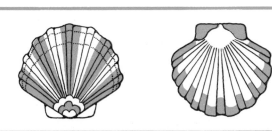

liquid to give a stiff batter which will coat the back of the spoon; beat until smooth. Just before cooking, whisk the egg white stiffly and fold it into the batter. Dip the scampi in the batter. Heat the fat until a cube of bread dropped into it takes 20–30 seconds to brown. Fry the scampi, a few at a time, until they are golden brown. Drain and serve with tartare or tomato sauce.

Alternatively, the scampi can simply be coated with beaten egg and fresh bread-crumbs and fried until golden brown.

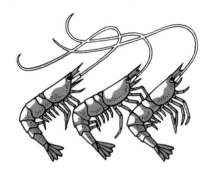

Scampi provençale

Illustrated in colour on the jacket

2 small onions, skinned and chopped
30 ml (2 tbsp) oil
1 rasher of bacon, rinded and chopped
225 g (8 oz) tomatoes, skinned
15 g (½ oz) flour
150 ml (¼ pint) stock or water
salt and pepper
100 g (4 oz) shelled scampi
sliced lemon and cucumber to garnish

Fry the onions in the oil until they are just starting to turn a light brown, then add the bacon and chopped tomatoes and continue frying for about 1 minute. Then add the flour and the stock or water, boil over a low heat for 5–10 minutes, then sieve. Season well and add the scampi. Re-heat and serve in scallop shells as an hors d'œuvre, accompanied by slices of brown bread and butter.

Snails à la bourguignonne

1 can snails
300 ml (½ pint) dry white wine
salt and pepper
a bouquet garni
1 small onion, skinned
6 cloves
150 ml (¼ pint) brandy (optional)

For the snail butter
100 g (4 oz) butter
1 shallot, skinned and chopped
1 garlic clove, skinned and crushed
5–10 ml (1–2 tsp) chopped parsley
a pinch of mixed spice
salt and pepper

Prepare the snails according to the directions on the can. For extra flavour add the remaining ingredients and re-heat slowly. Allow to cool, drain and push the snails into the shells.

To make the snail butter, cream the butter with the other ingredients. Fill up the stuffed snail shells with this butter, place the snails in a shallow ovenproof dish and bake in the oven at 220°C (425°F) mark 7 for about 10 minutes, or until really hot. Serve with rolls or garlic bread as an hors d'œuvre.

36

Shrimp Créole

25 g (1 oz) butter or margarine
1 onion, skinned and chopped
1 small green pepper, seeded and chopped
25 g (1 oz) flour
396-g (14-oz) can tomatoes
5 ml (1 level tsp) dried orégano or mixed herbs
salt and pepper
5 ml (1 level tsp) sugar
150 ml (¼ pint) dry white wine
225 g (8 oz) shrimps (or prawns)

Melt the fat and fry the onion and pepper until soft – 5–10 minutes. Stir in the flour, then add the tomatoes, herbs, seasoning and sugar and simmer for 15 minutes. Stir in the wine and shrimps and cook for a further 5–10 minutes, until the flavours are well blended. Serve in a border of boiled rice.

Shrimps in wine sauce

325 g (12 oz) shelled shrimps
25 g (1 oz) flour
30 ml (2 tbsp) olive oil
45 ml (3 tbsp) white wine
10 ml (2 tsp) tomato paste
30 ml (2 tbsp) warm water
salt, pepper and cayenne pepper
sliced lemon and chopped parsley to garnish

Coat the shrimps with flour and fry them in the oil until golden brown. Add the wine to the shrimps and cook for about 3 minutes. Add the tomato paste, water, and season-ing and cook gently for about 2 minutes. Garnish and serve as a hot hors d'œuvre.

Seafood cocktail

100 g (4 oz) prawns or shrimps, peeled
15–30 ml (1–2 tbsp) dry white wine
30 ml (2 tbsp) tomato ketchup
30 ml (2 tbsp) salad cream
15 ml (1 tbsp) single cream
15 ml (1 tbsp) white wine or medium sherry
salt, pepper and cayenne pepper
1 lettuce

Sprinkle the prawns with wine and leave for

30 minutes, turning them from time to time. Make a sauce by combining the ketchup, salad cream, cream and wine, with season-ing. Wash and shred the lettuce and divide between 4 small dishes. Place the drained prawns on the lettuce. Spoon the sauce over just before serving. Serve with lemon wedges and brown bread and butter.

Sauces and accompaniments

Egg sauce

25 g (1 oz) butter or margarine
25 g (1 oz) flour
300 ml (½ pint) milk
salt and pepper
2 hard-boiled eggs, shelled and chopped

Melt the fat and add the flour. Cook over a low heat for a minute, then add the milk. Bring to the boil, season, add the chopped egg and re-heat.

Serve with any plainly cooked fish.

Fresh tomato sauce

225 g (8 oz) tomatoes
25 g (1 oz) butter or margarine
25 g (1 oz) flour
300 ml (½ pint) milk
salt and pepper

Using a fork or skewer, hold the tomatoes over a flame until the skin splits, or place in boiling water for a few moments, then peel them and cut into small pieces. Melt the fat, add the flour, then gradually stir in the milk and bring to the boil. Season, add the tomatoes and allow to simmer gently for about 5 minutes.

White sauce

25 g (1 oz) butter or margarine
25 g (1 oz) flour
300 ml (½ pint) milk
salt and cayenne pepper

Melt the fat and add the flour, then grad-ually add the milk. Bring to the boil and add the seasonings.

Caper sauce Stir in 15–30 ml (1–2 tbsp) chopped capers.

Cheese sauce Stir in 75 g (3 oz) grated cheese

Mushroom sauce Add 50–100 g (2–4 oz) sautéed sliced mushrooms

Parsley sauce

Stir 15–30 ml (1–2 tbsp) freshly chopped parsley into a white sauce. Serve with any plainly cooked fish.

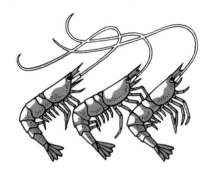

Salmon patties (see page 30).

Shrimp or prawn sauce

50 g (2 oz) frozen shrimps or prawns
25 g (1 oz) butter or margarine
25 g (1 oz) flour
300 ml (½ pint) milk
salt and pepper

Open the packet of shrimps and let them thaw. Melt the fat and add the flour, then cook over a low flame for a minute. Gradually add the milk, stirring well, and bring to the boil. Season well and add the shrimps. Serve with baked or steamed fish.

Wine sauce

1 shallot, skinned
50 g (2 oz) butter or margarine
5 ml (1 tsp) anchovy essence
150 ml (¼ pint) red wine
2·5 ml (½ level tsp) caster sugar
5 ml (1 tsp) chopped parsley

Chop the shallot very finely and fry it in the fat until golden brown, then add the anchovy essence, red wine and sugar. Boil together until the mixture is reduced by half, then add the parsley.

Piquant sauce

a blade of mace
a few peppercorns
300 ml (½ pint) milk, or milk and stock
25 g (1 oz) butter or margarine
25 g (1 oz) flour
5 ml (1 tsp) vinegar
5 ml (1 tsp) chopped parsley

Infuse the mace and peppercorns in the milk for 10 minutes over a low heat. Melt the fat and add the flour to make a roux; strain the milk and gradually add to the roux. Bring to the boil and add the vinegar and parsley.

Serve with steamed fish.

Quick tomato sauce

25 g (1 oz) mushrooms, finely chopped
1 small onion, skinned and finely
  chopped
20 g (¾ oz) butter or margarine
300 ml (½ pint) tomato juice
5 ml (1 level tsp) sugar
salt and pepper
10 ml (2 level tsp) cornflour

Fry the mushrooms and onion in the fat for about 2 minutes. Add the tomato juice, sugar and seasoning and cook for 5–10 minutes. Blend the cornflour with a little water, add to the tomato mixture and boil for about 1 minute.

Serve this sauce with steamed or fried fish.

Beurre rouge

1 shallot, skinned and finely chopped
salt and pepper
a pinch of sugar
150 ml (¼ pint) red wine
150 g (5 oz) butter

Cook the shallot, salt, pepper and sugar in the wine until the wine is reduced. Gradually add the butter, beating all the time. Keep the sauce warm and serve with plain baked or steamed fish.

Black butter sauce

50 g (2 oz) butter
15 ml (1 tbsp) chopped parsley
15 ml (1 tbsp) vinegar

Melt the butter in a pan and allow it to become golden brown, then add the parsley and fry until it is crisp. Pour into a sauce-boat. Boil the vinegar in the pan and add to the butter in the sauce-boat.

Melted butter sauce

With a fine-flavoured fish such as salmon and sole, plain melted butter is delicious.

Roe stuffing

50 g (2 oz) soft herring roes
90 ml (6 tbsp) milk
salt and pepper
a small knob of butter or margarine
15 g (½ oz) flour
cayenne pepper
lemon juice
25 g (1 oz) fresh white breadcrumbs

Wash the roes and cook in a little milk seasoned with salt and pepper. When they are cooked, drain off the milk. Melt the fat, add the flour, then stir in the milk; bring to the boil and add the cayenne pepper and a squeeze of lemon juice. Mash the roes and add them to the sauce together with the breadcrumbs.

Rice stuffing

50 g (2 oz) rice, cooked
1 small onion, skinned and chopped
50 g (2 oz) almonds, blanched and
  chopped
50 g (2 oz) raisins
30 ml (2 tbsp) chopped parsley
25 g (1 oz) butter or margarine, melted
salt and pepper
1 egg, beaten (optional)

Combine all the ingredients, season and bind them well together. This can also be used for chicken, meat or vegetables.

MEAT COOKERY

Choosing meat

Many people find the task of selecting meat quite a problem, especially when they first start cooking. They often hesitate to purchase an unfamiliar cut because they don't know how to cook it to the best advantage, so they miss many a good and inexpensive buy. We hope that the wide range of recipes in this chapter will help you to choose wisely, cook successfully and provide varied and economical meals.

Try to find a good butcher who sells meat only in prime condition for cooking; even the highest quality meat, if offered for sale without the proper hanging, will lack flavour and be tough. Don't be afraid to ask for the butcher's advice, remembering that he is an expert and will gladly help you to select the meat which is best suited to your particular purpose.

Most butchers nowadays sell both fresh home-killed meat and chilled or frozen imported meats. Imported meat is often less expensive than meat from our own farms and this difference may make a considerable saving if you are catering for a family on a limited allowance.

Most frozen meat is thawed out by the butcher and sold ready to cook. If, however, it is still icy when you buy it, allow it to thaw out at ordinary room temperature before cooking it: never put it in a hot place or pour hot water over it to speed the process. When it is thawed, treat as for fresh meat.

Generally speaking, select meat which has not got an undue amount of fat, as this is wasteful. What fat there is should be firm and free from dark marks or discoloration. Lean meat should be finely grained, firm and slightly elastic. The following points are characteristic of the different types of meat:

Beef The lean of good beef should be bright red in colour and it should be finely marbled with creamy streaks of fat. The solid portions of fat should be smooth, firm and creamy. Avoid joints which show more than the thinnest line of gristle between fat and lean meat.

Mutton The flesh is darker and more purple in colour than that of beef. Lean meat should be firm and close in texture: the fat should be white and very firm.

Lamb The flesh is lighter in colour than in mutton and the joints considerably smaller. The fat should be very white and waxy.

Veal The meat should be pale in colour (not red, which indicates age), smooth and very finely grained, with a small amount of fat, which should be white.

Pork Avoid very fat pork. The lean should be pale in colour, firm and finely grained and the fat should be firm and white.

Salted or pickled meats Most butchers sell beef, pork and tongues which they have salted ready for cooking. This saves the housewife time and trouble; although the process is not a difficult one and can be carried out at home if necessary (see page 70), it does take several days before the meat is ready to cook, so often it is more convenient to buy ready-to-cook pickled meat. It is always advisable to consult your butcher in good time if you want to buy salted meat, so that he knows your requirements.

Offal All internal meats, as well as heads, feet and trotters, are included in this category and a variety of both special-occasion and economical dishes can be prepared from them. Internal organs should be cooked soon after they are purchased and kept in the refrigerator until needed.

Storing meat

Remove the wrapping papers from meat when you reach home and either put it on to a plate, or wrap it with freezer wrap or clingfilm, leaving the ends open for ventilation. Store it in the coolest place available – the coldest part of a refrigerator, below the freezing unit, is ideal. In some of the larger refrigerators a special meat drawer or container is available and meat need not be wrapped or covered, but placed straight into this. Although the controlled temperature allows uncooked meat to be safely left for several days, the refrigerator must not be regarded as a storage place for a long period; the low temperature only slows down the process of deterioration and does not completely prevent it. Minced raw meat, sausages and offal are particularly perishable and should be used if possible within 24 hours of purchase.

When no refrigerator is available, keep meat in a cool, well-ventilated place, lightly wrapped and protected from flies.

Cooked meats which are put into a refrigerator should be wrapped to prevent drying. Leftover stews or casseroles should be allowed to become quite cold and then left in a covered dish: re-heat thoroughly before using them the next day.

Beef

Here is a list of some cuts of beef, with the best ways of cooking them:

Topside
    Roast, pot-roast, braise
Sirloin
    Roast (on the bone, or boned and rolled)
Ribs
    Roast (on the bone, or boned and rolled)
Buttock steak
    Braise, stew, pot-roast or use in pies
Rump steak
    Grill or fry
Fillet steak
    Grill or fry
Chuck steak
    Stew
Silverside (pickled)
    Boil
Wing rib
    Roast
Shin (gravy beef)
    Stew, or use for pies, puddings, beef tea
Flank (thick and thin)
    Use for pies, stews; boil it if pickled
Aitch bone
    Roast; boil it if pickled
Brisket
    Braise, stew; boil if pickled

Roast beef

Choose a choice cut – sirloin, ribs or topside. Weigh, then calculate cooking times as follows:

High-temperature method Roast in the oven at 220°C (425°F) mark 7. Allow 15 minutes per 450 g (lb) plus 15 minutes, if required rare; 20 minutes per 450 g (lb) plus 20 minutes for medium-done. Sirloin and ribs may be cooked in this way.

Moderate-temperature method Roast in the oven at 190°C (375°F) mark 5. With sirloin and ribs, unboned, allow 25 minutes per 450 g (lb) for medium to well-done; if joint is boned and rolled, 30 minutes per 450 g (lb).

Slow roasting Roast in the oven at 180°C (350°F) mark 4. For cheaper roasting cuts on the bone (eg, brisket) allow 40 minutes per 450 g (lb) to give a medium to well-done result; if boned and rolled, allow 45 minutes per 450 g (lb).

Cooking and serving Place the weighed joint on a rack or straight in the roasting tin.

Sprinkle with flour and add some dripping or lard if the meat is lean. When it is cooked, remove it from the tin and keep it hot while making the gravy. Basting is necessary only when the meat is very lean. For 'self-basting', use aluminium foil and cook at high temperature; either brown the joint first and then place it in the foil, or open the foil for the last 20 minutes.

Potatoes, parsnips, carrots, onions and marrow are all good when roasted with the joint; par-boiling (except in the case of marrow) shortens the cooking time and gives an excellent result.

Serve beef with gravy, horseradish cream or sauce and Yorkshire pudding or popovers. The horseradish cream may be put in apricot halves for a special occasion.

Spiced silverside

1·8 kg (4 lb) pickled silverside
flavouring vegetables
8 cloves
100 g (4 oz) brown sugar
5 ml (1 level tsp) cinnamon
2·5 ml (½ level tsp) dry mustard
75 g (3 oz) breadcrumbs
1 orange
1 lemon
1 wineglass sherry

Simmer the meat with a few chopped vegetables for 2–2½ hours and allow to cool in the liquor. Put into a greased tin or casserole and stick the cloves in the meat. Mix the sugar with the cinnamon, mustard, crumbs and a little grated orange and lemon rind and spread over the top of the beef. Bake in the oven at 180°C (350°F) mark 4 for about 40 minutes, basting with the orange and lemon juice and the sherry – pour these over the meat about half-way through the time.

Boiled beef

1·8 kg (4 lb) salted silverside or brisket
6–8 carrots, pared
6 onions, skinned
2–3 turnips, peeled
8 peppercorns
a bouquet garni
dumplings (optional)

Skewer or neatly tie the meat, cover with cold water, bring slowly to the boil and remove all scum. Add the carrots, cut lengthways, the onions and the thickly sliced turnips, the peppercorns and bouquet garni. Cover and cook very gently, allowing 25 minutes per 450 g (lb) of meat, plus 25 minutes. Remove the string and serve the meat surrounded by the vegetables (and the dumplings, if included).

Grilled steak with onion rings

Choose fillet or rump steak about 2·5–4 cm (1–1½ inches) thick. If rump steak is used, beat it on a board with a rolling-pin; fillet steak, being very tender, should not require this treatment. Season with salt and pepper (and a little garlic juice, if this flavour is enjoyed). Brush the meat over with oil or melted fat, place under a hot grill and cook for 2–3 minutes on each side first, turning the meat carefully to avoid losing the juices (use tongs if possible). Continue cooking, turning the meat frequently, for about 12–15 minutes, until done; the centre of the steak should be slightly underdone. Serve with fried onion rings, chipped potatoes and a pat of maître d'hôtel butter. Grilled mushrooms or tomatoes are also favourite accompaniments.

Steak Diane

Illustrated in colour opposite

4 fillet steaks (about 100 g (4 oz) each
  1 cm (½ inch) thick)
25 g (1 oz) butter
30 ml (2 tbsp) oil
30 ml (2 tbsp) Worcestershire sauce
15 ml (1 tbsp) lemon juice
15 ml (1 tbsp) grated onion
10 ml (2 tsp) chopped parsley
parsley sprigs and lemon slices to
  garnish

Fry the steaks in the butter and oil for about 2 minutes on each side. Remove and keep hot. Add the Worcestershire sauce and lemon juice to the pan juices. Stir well and warm through. Add the onion and parsley and cook gently for 1 minute. Serve the sauce spooned over the steaks. Garnish with parsley sprigs and lemon slices.

Minute steaks

Cut some fillet of beef into 0·5-cm (¼-inch) slices, trim neatly and flatten slightly with a wide-bladed heavy knife. Brush over with oil or melted fat and grill quickly for only 1–2 minutes on each side, or fry in a little butter or margarine for the same length of time. Serve with grilled mushrooms and maître d'hôtel butter.

American pot-roast

1·8 kg (4 lb) topside
salt and pepper
15 ml (1 tbsp) lard or bacon fat
300 ml (½ pint) stock
sliced cooked carrots
boiled potatoes
chopped parsley

Prepare and season the meat. Heat the fat

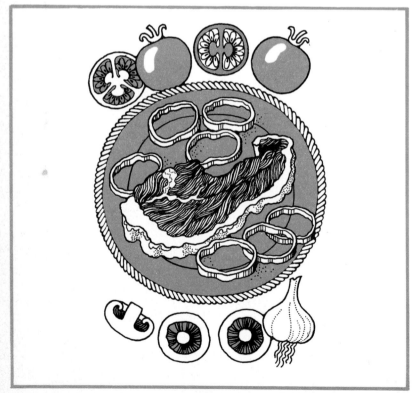

Steak Diane
(see above).

in a strong pan or casserole, add the meat and turn it several times, in order to brown it on all sides. Add the stock, cover closely and cook over a gentle heat or in the oven at 150°C (300°F) mark 2 for 3½–4 hours, adding a little more hot water if required. Serve surrounded by the vegetables, sprinkled with chopped parsley.

Collared beef

1·8 kg (4 lb) salted flank of beef
1 bayleaf
2 cloves
2 blades of mace
10 peppercorns
10 allspice berries
5 ml (1 level tsp) celery seeds
1 onion, skinned and sliced

Choose beef that is not too fat for this dish, which must be cooked the day before it is needed. Remove any gristle or bone from the beef, roll into a neat shape and secure it with fine string, then tie it in a pudding cloth. Put it in a pan with water to cover and add the spices, herbs and onion; cover and cook gently for about 4 hours. When it is cooked, lift it out of the pan and press it by placing it on a board, covering it with another board or plate and adding a heavy weight.

Leave until the next day. Remove the cloth and string and serve the beef sliced.

Steak and mushroom pie

700 g (1½ lb) braising steak
seasoned flour
50 g (2 oz) dripping
100 g (4 oz) mushrooms, sliced
1 onion, skinned and sliced
600 ml (1 pint) stock
salt and pepper
212-g (7½-oz) pkt frozen puff pastry
beaten egg to glaze

Cut the steak into neat pieces, discarding any excess fat. Dip the meat into seasoned flour and fry in the hot dripping until lightly browned. Add the mushrooms and onion and when these are fried, add the stock and seasonings. Cover and cook gently for about 2 hours, or until the meat is tender. Put into a pie dish and if possible leave until cold. Remove any fat from the surface and cover the pie with the thawed pastry. Decorate, glaze with egg and bake in the oven at 220°C (425°F) mark 7 for about 30 minutes.

Stuffed beef rolls

325 g (12 oz) lean beef, cut into thin slices
1 onion, skinned and sliced
1 carrot, pared and sliced
2 rashers of bacon, rinded and chopped
salt and pepper
1 wineglass red or white wine
150 ml (¼ pint) stock
a bouquet garni
15 ml (1 tbsp) tomato paste

For the stuffing
1 rasher of bacon, chopped
1 clove of garlic, skinned and crushed
15 ml (1 tbsp) chopped parsley
30–45 ml (2–3 tbsp) breadcrumbs
grated rind of ½ lemon
salt and pepper
grated nutmeg

First make the stuffing by frying the bacon until brown, adding the remaining ingredients and mixing well. Divide the stuffing between the slices of beef, roll up and tie with string or thread. Put the onion, carrot and bacon into a pan, lay the meat rolls on top. Season, cover and cook gently until the meat has lightly browned. Pour in the wine and stock and add the bouquet garni and tomato paste. Put into a casserole and cook in the oven at 170°C (325°F) mark 3 for 2½ hours, until the meat is tender. Untie the rolls, strain the sauce and pour over the meat.

Large Cornish pasty

175–225 g (6–8 oz) chuck steak
1 large onion, skinned and chopped
225 g (8 oz) raw potatoes, peeled and diced
salt and pepper
200 g (7 oz) shortcrust pastry
beaten egg to glaze

Remove any excess fat or gristle from the steak and cut the meat into small, neat pieces. Mix with the onion, potatoes and seasoning. Roll out the pastry into a round the size of a dinner plate and put the filling in the centre. Damp the edges, draw the

pastry together with the join on top. Press the edges firmly and knock together with a knife; crimp to a wavy line. Brush with beaten egg to glaze. Bake in the oven at 220°C (425°F) mark 7 for 15 minutes, then reduce to 170°C (325°F) mark 3 and bake for a further 1¼ hours until the filling is cooked. *Serves 2–3*

Old English steak pudding

Illustrated in colour on page 45

350 g (12 oz) self-raising flour
175 g (6 oz) shredded suet
salt and pepper
200 ml (about 12 tbsp) water
50 g (2 oz) flour
a pinch of nutmeg
700 g (1½ lb) chuck steak, cubed
225 g (8 oz) kidney, cored and chopped
100 g (4 oz) small mushrooms, wiped and quartered
99-g (3½-oz) can smoked oysters, drained (optional)
150 ml (¼ pint) boiling stock
150 ml (¼ pint) red wine

Sift the self-raising flour into a basin, add the suet, season well and stir in the water. Mix to a soft but manageable dough. Knead lightly on a floured surface, roll out two-thirds and use it to line a 2-litre (3½-pint) basin. Mix the 50 g (2 oz) flour with the nutmeg and season well. Toss the steak and kidney in the flour. Add the mushrooms and oysters. Mix well. Place the meat mixture in the basin. Pour over the boiling stock and wine. Place a pastry lid on top. Cover with greased greaseproof paper and foil, pleated across the centre, and secure with string.

Place the pudding in a large saucepan. Pour in enough boiling water to come two-thirds of the way up the basin, cover with a lid and boil gently for 4½–5 hours. From time to time replenish with boiling water. After the cooking time, remove from the water. Lift the paper off the pudding and, if you wish, place in a preheated oven at 200°C (400°F) mark 6 for about 20 minutes to dry the pastry lid to a pale golden brown. Serve with vegetables in season and creamed potatoes. *Serves 6–8*

Lamb

These are the best-known cuts of lamb, and the best ways of cooking them:
Leg (whole, or cut into shank and fillet)
    Roast
Loin (on the bone or boned, stuffed and rolled)
    Roast

Loin chops
    Fry or grill
Best end of neck
    Roast or braise; as cutlets, fry or grill
Middle neck
    Stew, casserole, use in broths and hot-
        pots
Scrag end of neck
    Stews, pies, broths
Breast
    Stew, braise or roast if boned and rolled
Shoulder (whole or half)
    Roast

Roast lamb

Leg, shoulder, loin and best end of neck are
the favourite roasting joints. Calculate the
roasting time, allowing 27 minutes per 450 g
(lb) plus 27 minutes, according to thickness.
Cook in the oven at 180°C (350°F) mark 4,
basting occasionally with the hot dripping.
Do not serve lamb underdone, but avoid
overcooking, which tends to dry up the
flesh. Serve with mint sauce and gravy.

Rolled stuffed breast of lamb

2 breasts of lamb
100 g (4 oz) breadcrumbs
15 ml (1 tbsp) chopped parsley
a pinch of mixed dried herbs
salt and pepper
a little grated lemon rind
beaten egg
dripping
stock
flavouring vegetables (optional)

Ask the butcher to bone the breast, or do it
yourself, using a small sharp knife. (Use the
bones for stock or soup.) Make the stuffing
by mixing the dry ingredients with egg to
bind, then spread over the meat. Roll up
neatly and secure with string. Melt a little
dripping in a heavy flameproof casserole
and brown the roll in this. Remove any
excess dripping, add enough stock to cover
the bottom of the pan well, put on the lid
and cook the meat slowly for 2 hours. Add
vegetables and extra stock if required.

Lamb kebabs

Illustrated in colour on the jacket

325 g (12 oz) lean lamb, cut from the leg
4 lamb's kidneys
8 mushrooms
4 tomatoes
4 rashers of bacon
1 corn on the cob
olive oil

Cut the lamb into small, neat pieces about

2·5 cm (1 inch) across. Skin and halve
the kidneys, removing the core. Blanch the
mushrooms; halve the tomatoes; cut each
rasher in half and roll up; cut the corn on the
cob into 4 pieces. Thread the ingredients on
to 4 skewers and brush over with oil. Cook
under a hot grill, turning frequently, for
about 8 minutes. Serve (still on skewers) on a
bed of yellow rice (see page 88) with peas
and a mixed salad.

Boiled leg of lamb with caper sauce

1 small leg of lamb or half a larger leg
salt and pepper
4 onions, skinned
2 turnips, peeled
450 g (1 lb) carrots, pared
caper sauce (see page 71)

Wipe and weigh the meat, put in a pan
and cover with fast-boiling water. Boil for a
few minutes, skimming frequently, then
reduce heat to a gentle simmer. Add salt
and pepper and the thickly sliced or quar-

tered vegetables, cover and cook gently,
allowing 20 minutes to each 450 g (lb) of
meat, plus 20 minutes. Serve with caper
sauce poured over and surrounded by
vegetables.

Neck of lamb may be cooked similarly.
Onion sauce (see page 71) may be served
instead of caper sauce.

Barbecued lamb slices

325–450-g (³⁄₄–1-lb) piece cold cooked lamb
40 g (1½ oz) butter or margarine
15 ml (1 tbsp) vinegar
60 ml (4 tbsp) redcurrant jelly
150 ml (¼ pint) stock
a little dry mustard
salt and pepper
pickled walnuts (optional)

Cut the lamb into neat slices. Melt the
fat in a frying pan, add the vinegar,
redcurrant jelly, stock and seasonings. Add
the slices of meat and turn them in the
sauce until they are well covered and
heated through. Place on a heated serving

dish, pour the remaining hot sauce over the meat and serve at once.

A few pickled walnuts may be chopped up and added to the sauce if liked.

Fried lamb cutlets

Buy some best end of neck and ask the butcher to saw the rib bones to about 7·5 cm (3 inches) in length and to remove the chine bone, before cutting it into cutlets. Trim the cutlets and scrape the end of the bone clean. Coat with beaten egg and breadcrumbs and leave for a little while to dry before cooking. Fry in shallow hot fat for about 8 minutes, turning them occasionally, and drain well. Serve with onion or tomato sauce (pages 36, 71) and accompanied by potatoes or noodles, fried onions and a green vegetable.

Grilled lamb chop platter

Choose good chops about 2·5 cm (1 inch) thick. Take out the bone, curl the 'tail' of the chop round the 'eye' and put a narrow streaky rasher round the edge of each chop, securing it with wooden cocktail sticks. Brush the chops with oil and grill on both sides, turning them often, for about 10 minutes. Serve with creamed potatoes, peas and small whole carrots.

For a simpler dish, omit the bacon and serve the chops with grilled tomatoes.

Paprika lamb chops

Illustrated in colour on page 49

700 g (1½ lb) middle or best end of neck
40 g (1½ oz) butter or margarine
175 g (6 oz) onion, finely chopped
450 g (1 lb) tomatoes, skinned and sliced
15 ml (1 tbsp) chopped parsley
5–10 ml (1–2 level tsp) paprika pepper
salt
142-ml (5-fl oz) carton soured cream or yoghurt

Chine the meat and trim away any excess fat, then cut it into chops. Heat the fat and brown the chops on both sides; remove from the pan. Fry the onion in the fat until

beginning to brown. Add the tomatoes, parsley, paprika and salt to taste. Replace the chops, cover and simmer gently for 1½–2 hours or bake in a covered casserole in the oven at 170°C (325°F) mark 3 for about 1–1½ hours.

Stir in the soured cream or beaten yoghurt, re-season and bring back to simmering point. Serve with noodles and buttered courgettes.

Lamb and potato pasties

Illustrated in colour on page 53

15 ml (1 tbsp) oil
225 g (8 oz) potatoes, peeled and diced
1 small onion, skinned and diced
350 g (12 oz) boned lean shoulder of lamb, coarsely minced
1 beef bouillon cube
salt and pepper
368-g (13-oz) pkt frozen puff pastry, thawed
milk to glaze

Heat the oil in a frying pan and gently fry the potato and onion for 3–4 minutes. Lift out using a draining spoon. Fry the meat quickly to seal, then mix with the potato, onion, crumbled bouillon cube, salt and pepper. Cool.

Roll out the pastry thinly and cut out four 18-cm (7-inch) rounds, using a saucepan lid as a guide. Divide the filling between the rounds, brush the edges with milk, then bring the pastry up and seal on top by pressing together with the fingertips. Place the pasties on a baking sheet, brush with milk and bake at 220°C (425°F) mark 7 for 15 minutes then reduce the heat to 180°C (350°F) mark 4 for a further 20–25 minutes until pasties are golden brown.

Mixed grill

The ingredients can be varied to suit individual circumstances, but a typical mixed grill includes a chop or a piece of steak, a piece of kidney or liver, bacon, a sausage, tomato and mushroom. Prepare the various ingredients according to type and brush them all over with melted fat or oil. Heat the grill thoroughly and begin by cooking the ingredients requiring the longest time. Keep everything very hot and serve attractively garnished with watercress, putting a pat of maître d'hôtel butter on each chop or piece of steak. Potato chips or crisps are a popular accompaniment; pineapple rings may be served instead of a vegetable, particularly when a gammon steak is included.

The following are the approximate grilling times:

Pork chops	15–20 minutes
Sausages: thick	15 minutes
thin	10 minutes
Steak	10–15 minutes
Lamb chops	10–15 minutes
Kidneys	10 minutes
Liver	5–10 minutes
Tomatoes	5 minutes
Mushrooms	5 minutes

Pork

Below is a list of the most usual cuts of pork, and the best ways of cooking them:
Leg (whole or divided)
　Roast; if pickled, boil it
Shoulder (blade-bone)
　Bone and stuff, then roast, pot-roast or braise
Loin
　Roast; grill or fry when divided into chops
Belly or streaky
　Roast, boil, braise; if pickled, boil or stew
Hand
　Roast, boil or stew
Spare rib
　Roast; grill or fry when cut into chops
Fillet
　Slit and stuff; then roast
Pork pieces
　Stew or use in pies
Pork must always be well cooked and should never be served even slightly underdone. To counteract its richness, it is usually served with a sharp accompaniment such as apple sauce.

Roast pork

Illustrated in colour on pages 56–57

Ask the butcher to score the rind closely and deeply, to make carving easier. Rub the outside with salt and oil before cooking – this gives a good crackling. Put the joint on a rack and roast in one of the following ways:
High-temperature method Roast in the oven at 220°C (425°F) mark 7 allowing 25 minutes per 450 g (lb), plus 25 minutes for joints with bone; this method ensures a crisp crackling.
Moderate-temperature method Roast in the oven at 190°C (375°F) mark 5, allowing 30–35 minutes per 450 g (lb) for boned and rolled joints; this gives a fairly crisp crackling. Serve with boiled, mashed or roast potatoes and a green vegetable, celery or onions; brown gravy and apple sauce are the accepted accompaniments and cranberry or redcurrant jelly may also be served.

Old English steak pudding (see page 42).

Barbecued spare ribs

30 ml (2 tbsp) oil
175 g (6 oz) onion, skinned and chopped
1 clove garlic, skinned and crushed
30 ml (2 tbsp) tomato paste
60 ml (4 tbsp) malt vinegar
1·25 ml (¼ level tsp) dried thyme
1·25 ml (¼ level tsp) chilli powder
45 ml (3 level tbsp) honey
1 beef bouillon cube
900 g (2 lb) pork spare ribs

Heat the oil in a saucepan, add the onion and sauté until transparent. Add the flavourings, honey and beef cube, dissolved in 150 ml (¼ pint) hot water. Bubble the mixture gently for 10 minutes. Place the spare ribs in a roasting tin in a single layer. Brush with a little of the sauce; roast in the oven at 190°C (375°F) mark 5, for 30 minutes. Pour off the fat and spoon the remaining sauce over the meat; cook for a further 1–1¼ hours.

Pork chops with glazed apples

4 loin pork chops
fat or oil for frying
30 ml (2 tbsp) finely chopped onion
150 ml (¼ pint) tomato juice
salt and pepper
10 ml (2 tsp) grated orange rind
120 ml (8 tbsp) orange juice
100 g (4 oz) granulated sugar
4 firm red apples

Choose lean chops (or trim off the surplus fat). Heat a little fat in a thick pan, add the meat and brown on both sides until it is a rich gold. Add the onion, tomato juice and seasoning, cover and simmer gently until the meat is tender – about 30 minutes. Meanwhile, heat the orange rind, juice and sugar until the sugar dissolves. Wipe and quarter the apples, without peeling, remove the core and cook carefully in the orange syrup until soft but unbroken. Put the chops on a dish with the glazed apples and pour any remaining liquid over them.

Veal

These are the usual cuts, with cooking methods:
Shoulder (whole or divided into two)
    Roast, stew
Loin
    If whole, bone, stuff, roll and roast; if cut into chops, grill or fry
Best end of neck
    Roast or cut into cutlets and fry or grill
Scrag-end of neck
    Stew

Fillet leg
    Roast, cut into slices for frying as es-calopes, or fricassee
    Sometimes boned and stuffed before roasting
Knuckle
    Boil, braise, stew
Breast
    Stew, braise, boil

Roast veal

Veal for roasting is often boned and stuffed with forcemeat, while forcemeat balls may be served with an unstuffed joint. Veal should be served well cooked and as the flesh lacks fat, it must either be well basted during the roasting, or protected with pieces of fat bacon.

Roast in the oven at 190°C (375°F) mark 5, allowing 20 minutes per 450 g (lb) for a joint with bone, or 30 minutes per 450 g (lb) for a boned and rolled joint.

Serve with bacon rolls, gravy, roast potatoes and young carrots, peas or other green vegetables.

Veal rolls with rice

450–700 g (1–1½ lb) thinly cut fillet of veal
herb stuffing (see page 71)
50 g (2 oz) dripping
stock
boiled rice
sieved spinach

Beat the veal, cut it into even-sized oblongs and spread with the stuffing. Roll up each oblong tightly and secure with thread. Brown in the hot dripping and then pour off any excess fat and add stock, almost covering the meat. Cover the pan and cook very gently for about 1 hour. Remove the threads, serve the rolls on a ring of hot rice, the centre filled with spinach. Serve with a gravy made from the veal stock.

Wiener schnitzel

veal escalopes (thinly cut slices taken from the fillet)
seasoned flour
beaten egg
fine browned breadcrumbs
butter or margarine for frying

Beat the escalopes to make them of an even thickness, and if necessary trim them to a good shape. Dip into the seasoned flour, then coat them with egg and bread-crumbs. Melt plenty of fat in a frying pan and when it is hot, add the meat; turn occasionally to brown both sides evenly. Serve on a hot dish, with any remaining fat strained round.

There are many versions of this popular dish. One is to serve each escalope on a croûte of fried bread spread with anchovy butter.

Veal flambé

4 veal cutlets
salt and pepper
½ onion, skinned and finely chopped
50 g (2 oz) butter or margarine
30–45 ml (2–3 tbsp) brandy
100 g (4 oz) mushrooms, sliced
30 ml (2 tbsp) stock or water
a dash of sherry and Worcestershire sauce
142-ml (5-fl oz) carton double cream

Season the cutlets with salt and pepper, then fry with the onion in half the fat until golden. Add the brandy and set it alight. When the flames die down, add the mush-rooms, remaining fat, stock, sherry and sauce. Simmer gently for 10 minutes. Lift out the cutlets and put on a warm serving dish. Add the cream to the sauce, stir well, then pour over the meat.

Veal suprême

25 g (1 oz) butter or margarine
25 g (1 oz) flour
300 ml (½ pint) milk
225 g (8 oz) cooked lean veal
salt and pepper
2 hard-boiled eggs
a squeeze of lemon juice
1 wineglass sherry
hard-boiled egg to garnish

Melt the fat and stir in the flour. Add the milk gradually and stir until the mixture thickens and becomes smooth. Cut the veal into small cubes and add to the pan, with some salt and pepper. Simmer gently in a covered pan for a few minutes, then add the chopped eggs, lemon juice and sherry. Serve garnished with sliced hard-boiled egg.

Escalopes fines herbes

50 g (2 oz) butter or margarine
40 g (1½ oz) flour
salt and pepper
4 escalopes of veal
10 ml (2 tsp) tomato paste
1 wineglass sherry
1 wineglass red wine
50 g (2 oz) mushrooms, sliced
2·5 ml (½ level tsp) mixed herbs
60 ml (4 tbsp) single cream
226-g (8-oz) can tomatoes
5 ml (1 level tsp) sugar
50 g (2 oz) cheese, grated

Heat 25 g (1 oz) of the fat in a frying pan. Mix

25 g (1 oz) of the flour with seasoning and toss the meat in this. Cook the escalopes gently for 2–3 minutes on each side in the hot fat; remove and keep hot. Add the remaining flour to the pan, stir in the tomato paste, sherry and wine and bring slowly to the boil; add the mushrooms, herbs and lastly the cream. Season as required. Cook very gently for 5 minutes.

Heat the remaining fat in a pan, add the canned tomatoes and sugar and heat through. Pour into a dish, put the meat on top, pour the sauce over, sprinkle with the cheese and brown under the grill.

Fresh tomatoes may be used instead of canned; peel and chop them and omit the sugar.

Raised veal and ham pie

325 g (12 oz) plain flour
2·5 ml (½ level tsp) salt
75 g (3 oz) lard
150 ml (¼ pint) water
450 g (1 lb) fillet of veal
225 g (8 oz) ham
1–2 hard-boiled eggs
salt and pepper
meat stock
beaten egg to glaze

Sift the flour and salt together and make a well in the centre. Heat the fat and water to boiling point, then pour into the dry ingredients. Mix with a wooden spoon, then knead the dough well until smooth. Keep a quarter of the pastry warm to make the lid and mould the rest into a pie shape, then fasten 3–4 folds of greased greaseproof paper round it to hold its shape; alternatively, line a 12·5- or 15-cm (5- or 6-inch) cake tin or a raised pie mould with the pastry. Cut the veal and ham into small dice and mix with the finely chopped eggs. Fill the pastry case with this mixture, adding seasonings as required and a little meat stock. Put on a pastry lid and decorate the pie as desired, making a hole in the top for steam to escape. Glaze with beaten egg

and decorate. Bake in the oven at 200°C (400°F) mark 6 for about 30 minutes, then reduce the heat to 180°C (350°F) mark 4 and cook for about 1 ½ hours longer: cover the pastry with a double sheet of greaseproof paper when it is sufficiently brown. Fill up the pie, through the hole in the top, with some aspic jelly (made with powdered aspic) and leave until cold: *Serves 6–8*

Bacon and ham

BACON

Bacon is made by curing fresh pork. Pigs for bacon are specially bred to have small bones, a long back, small shoulders and large plump gammons. Most bacon today is cured traditionally by a combination of brine injection and dry salting followed by immersion in brine and a period of maturation. When mature the sides have a pale cream rind with pink meat and the characteristic bacon flavour.

Some bacon goes through the additional process of smoking. This browns the rind and gives the meat a firmer texture and a smoked flavour. In the old days smoked bacon was prized for its good keeping qualities but this is not so important today when bacon can be put in a freezer.

One of the best things about bacon joints from the cook's point of view is that they are mostly boned and prepared before being sold so there is very little waste. Bacon joints are equally good hot or cold and any left over makes excellent savouries or supper dishes, so once you have cooked the joint it will give several good meals with little extra trouble. Rashers are an excellent standby for meals throughout the day.

Good bacon has a pleasant fresh aroma. The fat should be white and firm with the lean areas pinky in colour, firm with a good bloom without being soft: rind a good pale

cream colour if unsmoked. The rind of smoked bacon is light or dark golden brown depending on regional preference. Unsmoked bacon is sometimes called 'green' or 'pale' bacon.

Cuts of bacon
These vary from one part of the country to another. Many localities have their own method of cutting and selling so that it is difficult to generalise or to describe all available cuts. In some areas gammon is referred to as 'ham', see page 48.
Back bacon A prime rasher with a good eye of lean and a distinct layer of fat. Used for frying and grilling and can also be bought in the piece for boiling.
Streaky Narrow rashers in which lean and fat are mixed. It is good for grilling and frying and provides plenty of fat for frying bread, eggs, etc. It can also be boiled in the piece.
Middle cut or through cut Long rashers in which back and streaky are joined. Sold flat or rolled. Good value for family meals and usually priced between back and streaky. Makes a handsome roast or boiling joint with stuffing.
Bacon chops Boneless rib back chops cut between 0·5–1 cm (¼–½ inch) or thicker. Quick to fry or grill.
Gammon steaks and rashers Gammon steaks about 1 cm (½ inch) thick, usually 100–225 g (4–8 oz), almost circular in shape, are the leanest and most expensive cut for grilling and frying. Thinner gammon rashers are just as lean, more economical.
Collar Prime collar is one of the best boiling and baking joints and is good for braising. Whole joints weigh 3·6 kg (8 lb) but are usually sold in small pieces; end of collar which weighs about 900 g (2 lb) is an inexpensive cut. Collar rashers are substantial and meaty.
Forehock Whole hocks can be very inexpensive bought bone in, and weigh about 3·2–3·6 kg (7–8 lb) including knuckle. Can be boiled or roasted, knuckle used for

Raised veal and ham pie

soup, bacon pieces. Small boneless fore-hock joints 700–900 g (1½–2 lb) are popular boiling pieces, especially prime forehock.

Gammon The most prized part of the bacon side for leanness, flavour and fine texture of the meat, little fat. Often sold as a cooked meat. Whole or half gammons popular for weddings, special occasions. Smaller joints, usually boneless, are middle gammon, corner gammon, slipper gammon. Gammon knuckle is considerably meatier than forehock knuckle.

Storage of bacon

Store bacon at a cool temperature in the refrigerator or larder. Wrap closely in foil or cling film. This applies to joints not in a bag or vacuum packet and rashers bought loose. Do not use greaseproof paper which is porous and allows the bacon to dry out, causing surface saltiness. Refrigerate for up to 1 week.

Preparing rashers

Rind rashers thinly with kitchen scissors or a sharp knife unless, of course, the bacon is bought already rinded. Remove any bone. Thick rashers or chops should be snipped at intervals along the fat edge to help them remain flat and attractive looking during the cooking process. If you suspect that chops or other thick bacon or gammon slices are salty, soak them or poach them in water for a few minutes, throw away the water and cook as desired. Very salt bacon should also be blanched before it is used in large amounts in made up dishes or the flavour may be too strong.

For bacon rolls, use thin cut rashers and remove the rind. Stretch the rashers by stroking along the length with a heavy knife. Either roll up the whole rasher or cut each in half crosswise before rolling.

Cooking rashers

Streaky or back For frying, lay the bacon rashers in a cold pan, with the lean parts over the fat; for grilling arrange them in the reverse way. Lean rashers are better brushed with fat or oil for grilling. Cook quickly to obtain a crisp effect, slowly if you prefer the rashers softer. Thread bacon rolls on a skewer the same way as for kebabs and grill until crisp for 3–5 minutes, turning once.

Gammon Choose rashers that are not less than 0·5 cm (¼ inch) thick. Cut off the rind with scissors and clip the fat at intervals. Grilling is the ideal way of cooking. Pre-heat the grill at medium. Put the rashers on to a lightly greased grill grid, brush with melted fat or a little oil and cook under a medium

heat for about 5 minutes. Turn them, brush the second side with butter or oil and continue for a further 5–10 minutes until tender. For a special finish after cooking the first side, spread the second side with any of the following before grilling: melted butter and a sprinkling of brown sugar – preferably soft brown – marmalade sharpened with a little vinegar or lemon juice, brown sugar mixed with a pinch of dry mustard or ground ginger and moistened with orange or pineapple juice. Serve with apple or pineapple rings, basted with the juices from the meat and added to the grill towards the end of the cooking.

To boil bacon joints

The need to soak bacon joints is con-siderably reduced by milder cures. Today more and more housewives find soaking unnecessary. If soaking is preferred, do not allow more than 2–3 hours. Overnight soaking, if done at all should be reserved for larger joints – 8 hours is sufficient. A more practical method with an average size joint if you are worried about saltiness is to place the piece of bacon in cold water to cover, bring to the boil, throw away the water and start again with fresh cold water. Cooking – weigh the bacon joint, then calculate the cooking time, allowing 20–25 minutes per 450 g (lb) plus 20 minutes over. If you are cooking a joint 4·5 kg (10 lb) or over, allow 15–20 minutes per 450 g (lb) plus 15 minutes. Place the bacon in a large pan, skin side down, cover with cold water and bring slowly to the boil, skimming off any scum that forms. Time the cooking from this point. Cover and simmer until cooked. For extra flavour add 2 onions, skinned and quartered, 2 carrots, pared and quartered, 1 bayleaf and 4 peppercorns. When the bacon is cooked, ease away the rind and serve the joint hot with a sauce such as parsley. Or after removing from the liquid remove rind and press browned bread-crumbs into the fat and serve cold with salad, in sandwiches or to partner chicken or turkey.

To bake and glaze a bacon joint – weigh the joint, calculate the cooking time and boil as above for half the cooking time, then drain and wrap in foil. Place on a baking sheet and now bake in the centre of the oven at 180°C (350°F) mark 4 until 30 min-utes before cooking time is complete.

Raise the oven temperature to 220°C (425°F) mark 7. Open the foil, remove the rind from the bacon, score the fat in diamonds, stud with cloves and sprinkle the surface with demerara sugar; pat in. Return the joint to the oven and cook until crisp and golden.

HAM

Ham, strictly speaking, is the leg of a pig cut from the whole carcass and then cured and matured individually. When selecting a ham choose a short, thick leg without too much fat, and a thin rind. More often than not hams are cooked prior to purchase but if not, soak for about 12 hours or more depending on the type of ham (one that has been hung for a long time and is very dry may need 24 hours). Scrape and brush the ham and trim off any coloured parts – bloom is the sign of a good ham. To cook a York ham follow directions supplied or cook as for gammon. A popular finish after cooking is to score the rinded fat in tri-angles, baste with a few tablespoonfuls of sherry, port or Madeira then thickly coat with soft brown sugar. Put in the oven at 230°C (450°F) mark 8 until a golden crust forms – about 15 minutes.

Braised bacon

a piece of gammon, collar or forehock bacon
1 onion, skinned and sliced
4 carrots, pared and sliced
½ turnip, pared and sliced
2 sticks of celery, trimmed and sliced
45 ml (3 tbsp) oil
stock
a bouquet garni
salt and pepper

Soak the bacon or gammon for 1 hour (or overnight if you think it is likely to be very salty). Boil it for half the cooking time, allowing 20–25 minutes per 450 g (lb) 20 minutes over. Lightly fry the vegetables in hot fat or oil for 3–4 minutes. Put them in a casserole, put the bacon on top and add enough stock to cover the vegetables. Add the bouquet garni and the seasoning, cover and cook in the oven at 180°C (350°F) mark 4 for the remainder of the cooking time. Half an hour before the bacon is done, remove the rind and continue cooking, uncovered, for the final 30 minutes. Re-move the bouquet garni.

Bacon and bean casserole

175 g (6 oz) haricot beans, soaked overnight
325–450 g (¾–1 lb) piece of bacon
2 sticks of celery, sliced
1 large onion, skinned and sliced
15 ml (1 level tbsp) sugar
15 ml (1 tbsp) treacle
2·5 ml (½ level tsp) dry mustard
salt and pepper
cold water

Drain the beans. Cut the bacon in large pieces, put it in a casserole, surround it with

Paprika lamb chops (see page 44).

beans, then add the other ingredients, with enough water just to cover. Put on the lid and bake in the oven at 150°C (300°F) mark 2 for about 4 hours, adding water from time to time if necessary. About 1 hour before the casserole is ready, remove the lid and raise the bacon above the other ingredients. Return the casserole to the oven and continue cooking until the bacon is crisp.

Bacon pancakes

100 g (4 oz) plain flour
a pinch of salt
1 egg
300 ml (½ pint) milk
100 g (4 oz) lean bacon, rinded and minced
fat or oil for frying

Sieve the flour and salt and mix with the egg and sufficient milk to make a creamy batter. Beat thoroughly until the mixture is covered with bubbles, then stir in the rest of the milk and the minced bacon; put the batter into a jug. Melt a little fat in a frying pan, pour off any excess and then pour in just enough of the savoury batter to cover the bottom of the pan when this is tilted. Cook until golden, toss or turn and cook the other side. Roll up, keep hot while the other pancakes are cooked and serve with spinach, purple sprouting broccoli or another green vegetable. *Serves 2*

Bacon chops with mushrooms and brown lentils

175 g (6 oz) large brown lentils
30 ml (2 tbsp) corn oil
4 lean bacon chops, about 1 cm (½ inch) thick
about 600 ml (1 pint) chicken stock
100 g (4 oz) onion, skinned and finely sliced
3 sticks celery, washed and sliced
100 g (4 oz) button mushrooms, wiped and sliced
salt and pepper
chopped parsley to garnish

Soak the lentils overnight in cold water. Drain. Heat 15 ml (1 tbsp) oil and fry the bacon chops until golden on both sides. Drain off all the fat and add enough stock to just cover the chops. Cover and simmer for 15 minutes.

In another pan, heat the remaining oil and sauté the onion, celery and mushrooms for about 2 minutes. Drain the stock from the chops and pour it over the vegetables. Add the lentils and seasoning to taste. Cover and simmer for 15 minutes

until the lentils are tender. Meanwhile keep the chops hot. Serve the chops on the bed of lentils, garnished with parsley.

Bacon and liver pie

225 g (8 oz) streaky bacon, rinded
225 g (8 oz) calf or pig liver
225 g (8 oz) onions, skinned
700 g (1½ lb) potatoes, peeled
5 ml (1 level tsp) dried sage
salt and pepper
stock
butter or margarine

Cut the bacon and the washed and dried liver into small pieces. Slice the onions and potatoes. Grease a pie dish and put a layer of potatoes at the bottom, then a layer of onion and a layer of bacon and liver sprinkled with the herbs and seasonings. Continue with the layers finishing with potatoes. Pour in a little stock and put shavings of fat over the top. Cover and cook in the oven at 180°C (350°F) mark 4 for 1 hour, then remove the cover and bake for 20–30 minutes longer, until the potatoes are browned.

Bacon baked in cider

1·4–1·8 kg (3–4 lb) gammon hock or corner gammon, in a piece
2 onions, skinned and quartered
2 carrots, pared and quartered
1 bayleaf
4 peppercorns
100 g (4 oz) brown sugar
5 ml (1 level tsp) dry mustard
whole cloves
150 ml (¼ pint) cider

Soak the joint for 3–4 hours, then calculate the cooking time, allowing 20 minutes per 450 g (lb) and 20 minutes over. Put the joint with the onions, carrots, bayleaf and peppercorns into a large pan, cover with fresh water and bring slowly to the boil. Simmer gently for *half* the calculated cooking time. Remove the joint, wipe it dry and wrap in foil. Bake in the oven at 190°C (375°F) mark 5 for the remaining time.

About 20 minutes before the end of the cooking time, remove the joint from the foil and take off the skin, using a sharp knife. Score the fat in diamonds. Mix the sugar and mustard and spread this over the joint. Stud with cloves, pour the cider round the joint and return it to the oven for the last 20 minutes until golden brown.

Garnish the joint with tomato wedges and cress or apricot halves, peach slices or pineapple rings. For another variation try a Raisin Sauce: to make this, blend 25 ml (1½ level tbsp) cornflour with 300 ml (½ pint) cider in a pan, add 50 g (2 oz) brown sugar, a

pinch of salt, 50 g (2 oz) seedless raisins, 4 cloves and a pinch of cinnamon. Simmer together for 10 minutes, stirring, then stir in a small knob of butter before serving.

Bacon Montmorency

50 g (2 oz) lard
1 onion, skinned and chopped
1 carrot, pared and sliced
2 rashers of bacon, chopped
50 g (2 oz) flour
600 ml (1 pint) stock (made from bouillon cubes)
15 ml (1 tbsp) tomato paste
a bouquet garni
15 ml (1 tbsp) sherry or cider
24 black sweet cherries
4 thick gammon rashers
a little oil
15 ml (1 tbsp) redcurrant jelly
15 ml (1 tbsp) horseradish cream

Melt the fat in a pan, add the onion, carrot and bacon and fry gently until lightly browned. Remove these, draining the fat back into the pan, then stir in the flour and fry until well browned, to give the sauce a good colour. Gradually stir in the stock, return the vegetables, add the tomato paste, bouquet garni and sherry or cider. Bring to the boil and simmer, stirring the sauce occasionally, for 30 minutes. Alternatively, pour the sauce into a casserole and put in the oven at 150°C (300°F) mark 2 for 4 hours, where it will cook slowly with little attention.

Stone the cherries. Trim the gammon rashers and snip the edges to prevent their curling. Fifteen minutes before serving the meal, brush the rashers with oil and grill for 7 minutes. Meanwhile strain the sauce and return it to the pan. Turn the rashers over, brush with some more oil and grill for a further 7 minutes. Stir the redcurrant jelly and horseradish cream into the sauce, bring to the boil and simmer for 4 minutes. Add the cherries and allow them to heat through. Serve the gammon rashers with the sauce poured over them.

Bacon roly-poly

225–325 g (8–12 oz) lean bacon
1 small onion, skinned and finely chopped
chopped parsley
225 g (8 oz) self-raising flour
2·5 ml (½ level tsp) salt
100 g (4 oz) chopped suet
cold water to mix
tomato sauce or gravy

Mince the bacon and mix it with the finely chopped onion. Fry very lightly and add the parsley. Meanwhile sieve the flour and salt and mix with the suet and enough cold water to give a soft dough. Roll out into an oblong, spread with the bacon mixture to within 1 cm (½ inch) of the sides and damp these with water. Roll up tightly and either tie in a pudding cloth and steam for 2–2½ hours, or put on to a baking tin and bake in the oven at 190°C (375°F) mark 5 for about 1 hour. Serve with tomato sauce or a good brown gravy (see pages 36/71).

Savoury ham spaghetti

100 g (4 oz) spaghetti
4 hard-boiled eggs, shelled
2 tomatoes, skinned
100 g (4 oz) ham or cooked bacon
25 g (1 oz) butter or margarine
25 g (1 oz) plain flour
400 ml (¾ pint) milk
100 g (4 oz) cheese, grated
salt and pepper

Cook the spaghetti in boiling salted water and drain well. Slice the eggs and tomatoes and chop the ham. Melt the fat and add the flour, then gradually add the milk. Bring to the boil. Remove from the heat and stir in half the cheese and the seasoning. Put alternate layers of spaghetti, tomato, egg and ham in the casserole (reserving some egg and tomato to garnish). Pour the sauce over and sprinkle the other half of the cheese on top. Cook in the oven at 180°C (350°F) mark 4 for 30 minutes, until the top is browned. Garnish with slices of hard-boiled egg and tomato.

Layer potatoes with ham

60 ml (4 tbsp) soured cream
30 ml (2 tbsp) double cream
5 ml (1 level tsp) salt
100 g (4 oz) butter or margarine
450 g (1 lb) cold cooked potatoes, thinly sliced
3 hard-boiled eggs, shelled
100 g (4 oz) ham or cooked bacon, finely diced
75 g (3 oz) fresh breadcrumbs
1.25 ml (¼ level tsp) celery salt

Mix together in a bowl the soured cream, double cream and salt. Using half the fat, generously grease a 1-litre (1¾-pint) oven-proof dish and put a third of the potatoes in a layer on the bottom. Cover with a layer of sliced egg and pour over one-third of the cream mixture. Add another third of the potatoes in a layer, sprinkle with two-thirds of the diced ham, then pour over the remaining cream mixture. Top with the remaining sliced potatoes. Melt the remaining 50 g (2 oz) of the fat and toss the rest of the ham, the breadcrumbs and the celery salt in this and sprinkle evenly over the potatoes. Bake in the oven at 180°C (350°F) mark 4 for 30 minutes until the topping bubbles.

Ham and egg supper dish

4 hard-boiled eggs, shelled
225 g (8 oz) ham or cooked bacon
salt and pepper
100 g (4 oz) butter or margarine
90 ml (6 tbsp) fresh breadcrumbs, browned
300 ml (½ pint) white sauce (see page 36)
chopped parsley

Roughly chop the eggs and the ham and season lightly. Melt the fat and mix with the crumbs. Put a layer of this into a pie dish, then a layer of egg mixed with ham, followed by some sauce. Continue with these layers, finishing with the crumb mixture. Bake in the oven at 190°C (375°F) mark 5 for about 30 minutes and garnish with parsley.

Noodles milanaise

225 g (8 oz) broken noodles
salt and pepper
3 eggs
60 ml (4 tbsp) single cream
2.5 ml (½ level tsp) grated nutmeg
175 g (6 oz) minced ham
chopped parsley or watercress to garnish

Cook the noodles in plenty of boiling salted water until tender (about 10–15 minutes), then drain them. Season well with salt and pepper and mix with the beaten eggs, cream, nutmeg and ham. Turn into a buttered ring mould and stand this in a baking tin half-filled with water. Bake in the oven at 180°C (350°F) mark 4 for about 30 minutes, or until set. Turn out, garnish and serve hot with vegetables or a green salad.

Ham réchauffé

325 g (12 oz) cooked ham
100 g (4 oz) peas
2 onions, skinned and sliced
225 g (8 oz) potatoes, peeled and sliced
3–4 peppercorns
a pinch of mixed herbs
150 ml (¼ pint) water or chicken stock

Cut the ham into 2.5-cm (1-inch) squares. Arrange ham and vegetables in layers in a casserole, with a final layer of potato. Add the peppercorns and herbs, then half-cover with water. Cover and cook in the oven at 180°C (350°F) mark 4 for 1 hour. Remove the lid for the last 20 minutes to brown the potatoes.

Offal

Internal meats, such as liver, kidneys, hearts and brains, and the heads and tails of certain animals, are nearly all very nutritious and valuable foods; some of them are also quite inexpensive.

All offal needs careful washing and preparation before cooking. Kidneys, liver and hearts are often available in a frozen condition and should be allowed to thaw slowly at ordinary room temperature.

Some of the cheapest meats are particularly good for making nutritious soups, broths and stews and recipes are given under the appropriate headings.

As mentioned on page 39, all offal is very perishable and must be used within 24 hours of purchase.

Boiled ox tongue

Tongues are frequently purchased already pickled by the butcher and then only need to be cooked. If, however, a fresh tongue is bought, it must be thoroughly scraped and washed, rubbed over with coarse salt (see page 70) and left overnight to drain. The next day it is immersed in a pickling solution and left steeping in this for a week.

Before cooking the pickled tongue, soak it in cold water for several hours (overnight if the tongue has been smoked). Skewer it into a convenient shape if very large and put it into a pan with water to cover. Bring gradually to the boil and drain. Add flavouring ingredients such as sliced carrot, onion, turnip, peppercorns and a bouquet garni, cover with fresh cold water, bring to the boil and simmer for 3–4 hours, until tender. Skin the tongue, taking out any small bones or pieces of gristle.

To serve cold Put the tongue into a convenient sized cake tin (an 18-cm (7-inch) tin is required for a 2.7-kg (6-lb) tongue). Fill up with a little of the stock, put a plate on top, weigh down with a heavy object and leave to set. Turn out and garnish.

To serve hot Sprinkle the skinned tongue with browned crumbs and garnish with sliced lemon and parsley. Serve with parsley or tomato sauce.

Grilled kidneys

Cut the washed kidneys in half and cut out the core. Thread them on to a skewer, cut side uppermost, brush over with oil and sprinkle with salt and pepper. Cook under a hot grill, uncut side first and then cut side, so that the juices gather in the cut side. Serve on fried bread, with grilled or fried bacon, or with fried or diced potatoes and maître d'hôtel butter.

Either sheep's or pig's kidneys may be cooked in the same way; the former make delicious savouries when placed on fried croûtes and sprinkled with chopped parsley or served with a small pat of devilled butter (see page 71).

Stewed ox kidney

Wash 450 g (1 lb) ox kidney thoroughly in cold water. Cut it into pieces, removing the white core with kitchen scissors. Season 15 ml (1 level tbsp) flour with salt and pepper and roll the pieces of kidney in it. Melt 40 g (1½ oz) dripping in a stewpan or casserole and when hot, fry the kidney and a sliced onion until brown. Add 600 ml (1 pint) stock or water, cover and cook very gently for about 1½ hours. If necessary, thicken the gravy with a little flour, blended smoothly with cold water or stock. Serve the kidney in a border of piped or forked creamed potatoes or dry boiled rice.

Casseroled kidneys

450 g (1 lb) kidneys
3 small onions, skinned and chopped
25 g (1 oz) dripping or lard
3 rashers of bacon
salt and pepper
plain flour
150 ml (¼ pint) stock
mashed potatoes
egg or melted butter to glaze
chopped parsley or red pepper to
garnish

Halve and skin the kidneys, removing the cores, then soak them in cold salted water for 5 minutes. Fry the onions in the hot dripping or lard until light golden brown. Place in a casserole and arrange the drained kidneys on top. Cut the bacon into pieces and add to the kidneys; season and dredge lightly with flour. Pour the stock over, cover and cook in the oven at 180°C (350°F) mark 4 for about 30 minutes, or until tender.

Meanwhile line an ovenproof dish with mashed potato and glaze the edges with egg or melted butter; brown slightly in the oven. To serve, place the kidneys in the dish and sprinkle with finely chopped parsley or red pepper.

Boiled rice or buttered noodles make equally good accompaniments to serve instead of the mashed potatoes.

Kidneys in red wine

50 g (2 oz) butter or margarine
1 onion, skinned and chopped
4–6 sheep's kidneys
25 g (1 oz) flour
150 ml (¼ pint) red wine
150 ml (¼ pint) stock
a bouquet garni
15 ml (1 tbsp) tomato paste
salt and pepper
100 g (4 oz) mushrooms, sliced

Melt the fat and fry the onion until golden. Skin and core the kidneys and cut them into small pieces; add to the pan and cook for 5 minutes, stirring occasionally. Stir in the flour, pour in the wine and stock and bring slowly to the boil. Then add the bouquet garni, tomato paste and some salt and pepper. Simmer for 5 minutes. Add the mushrooms and simmer for a further few minutes. Remove the bouquet garni before serving and check the seasoning.

Brawn

1 pickled pig's head
a bouquet garni
salt
1 large onion, skinned
pieces of carrot and turnip
1 hard-boiled egg

Cut off the ears and remove the brains and all gristle from the head. Scald the ears, scrape them free of hair and wash well. Place the head in a pan with the bouquet garni, salt, vegetables and pig's ears and cover with water, then bring to the boil. Skim carefully and allow it to cook slowly

until the meat is quite tender – about 3 hours is usually sufficient. Strain off the liquid, remove the meat from the bones and cut into small pieces, removing any fat or gristle. Cut the ears into strips. Skim off the fat from the remaining liquid, then boil it until reduced to half. Garnish the bottom of a mould or cake tin with chopped egg white, pack the meat in tightly and pour some of the liquid over. Put a saucer and weight on it and leave until cold and set. When the brawn is required for use, dip the mould into hot water and turn the brawn on to a dish.

Brains in black butter sauce

4 pairs of lamb brains
15 ml (1 tbsp) vinegar
2·5 ml (½ level tsp) salt
100 g (4 oz) butter
15 ml (1 tbsp) wine vinegar
salt and pepper
chopped parsley

Wash the brains and soak for an hour in cold water. Remove as much of the skin and membrane as possible and put the brains into a pan with the vinegar, salt and enough water to cover well. Bring to simmering point and cook gently for 15 minutes. Put into cold water, then dry on a towel. Heat half of the butter in a frying pan, add the brains, brown on all sides and put on to a very hot dish. Add the rest of the butter and heat it until dark brown, without allowing it to burn. Add the wine vinegar and pour over the brains; sprinkle with salt, pepper and parsley.

Braised sweetbreads

450 g (1 lb) sweetbreads
1 rasher of bacon, chopped
25 g (1 oz) butter or margarine
1 carrot, pared and sliced
1 onion, skinned and sliced
a bouquet garni
1 wineglass white wine (optional)
salt and pepper
stock
juice of 1 lemon

Wash and soak the sweetbreads in cold water for several hours, changing the water as it becomes discoloured. Blanch by covering with cold water, with a few drops of lemon juice added, bringing slowly to boiling point. Boil for 5 minutes. Drain, put into cold water, pull off any fat and skin that will come away easily and cut the sweetbreads into even-sized pieces. Fry the bacon in the fat with the carrot and onion. Put in a casserole with the drained sweetbreads, bouquet garni, wine and seasoning. Almost cover with stock and cook for 2–3

Spiced lamb with aubergines (see page 63) and Lamb and potato pasties (see page 44).

hours in the oven at 150°C (300°F) mark 2. To serve, remove the sweetbreads, vegetables and bacon from the casserole, strain the cooking liquid and boil to reduce it; add the lemon juice and pour this sauce over the sweetbreads. Serve with boiled rice.

Sweetbread hotpot

450 g (1 lb) sweetbreads
1 onion, skinned and chopped
225 g (8 oz) shelled peas
100 g (4 oz) mushrooms, sliced
25 g (1 oz) butter or margarine
50 g (2 oz) plain flour
600 ml (1 pint) stock
salt and pepper
5 ml (1 level tsp) mixed herbs
toast triangles to garnish

Soak the sweetbreads in salted water until free from blood. Cover with water, bring slowly to the boil, then pour off the liquid. Sauté the onion, peas and mushrooms slowly for 5 minutes in the fat. Add the flour and stir until cooked. Add the liquid slowly, season, add the herbs and bring to the boil. Chop the sweetbreads and add. Cook in the oven at 170°C (325°F) mark 3 for about 2 hours. Serve with triangles of toast.

Casserole of lambs' tongues

4 lambs' tongues
25 g (1 oz) dripping or lard
1 onion, skinned and sliced
1 carrot, pared and grated
4 large tomatoes, skinned and sliced
15 ml (1 tbsp) chopped parsley
salt and pepper
stock
bacon rolls (optional)

Wash the tongues and trim if necessary. Heat the fat, fry the onion until it's golden brown and place in a casserole. Add the tongues, carrot, tomatoes, parsley and seasoning, and just enough stock to cover. Put in the oven at 190°C (375°F) mark 5 and cook for 1½ hours. If preferred the tongues may be skinned and then re-heated in the liquor before serving. Grilled or baked bacon rolls make a good garnish.

Rich casseroled heart

1 ox heart, weighing 1·1–1·4 kg
(2½–3 lb)
50–75 g (2–3 oz) butter or margarine
2 onions, skinned and sliced
25 g (1 oz) flour
300 ml (½ pint) stock
225 g (8 oz) carrots, pared and grated
½ small swede, peeled and grated
rind of 1 orange, finely shredded
6 walnuts, chopped

Cut the heart into 1-cm (½-inch) slices, remove the tubes, and wash it well. Melt the fat in a frying pan and sauté the slices of meat until slightly browned. Remove the meat, sauté the onions, then put both in a casserole. Add the flour to the remaining fat and brown slightly. Pour in the stock, bring to the boil and simmer for 2–3 minutes, then strain over the slices of heart in the casserole. Cover and cook for 3½–4 hours in the oven at 150°C (300°F) mark 2. Add the carrots and swede after 2½–3 hours. Cook the orange rind in boiling water for 10–15 minutes, then strain. Add the orange rind and walnuts 15 minutes before the cooking is completed. *Serves 5–6*

Lamb's heart casserole

4 small lambs' hearts
100 g (4 oz) fresh breadcrumbs
1 medium onion, skinned and finely chopped
45 ml (3 tbsp) melted butter or margarine
2·5 ml (½ level tsp) ground ginger
salt and pepper
30 ml (2 level tbsp) seasoned flour
25 g (1 oz) dripping
600 ml (1 pint) stock
12 small white onions, skinned
8 carrots, pared and quartered

Wash the hearts, slit open, remove any tubes or gristle and wash again. Fill with a stuffing made from mixing the breadcrumbs, onion, melted fat, ground ginger and seasoning. Tie the hearts firmly into their original shape with string, dredge with seasoned flour and brown quickly in the hot dripping. Place in a casserole with the stock, cover and cook in the oven at 180°C (350°F) mark 4 for 2½ hours, basting and turning them frequently. Add the whole onions and the carrots for the last 45 minutes of the cooking time.

Oxtail casserole

1 oxtail, jointed
25 g (1 oz) dripping or lard
2 onions, skinned and sliced
25 g (1 oz) plain flour
400 ml (¾ pint) stock
a pinch of mixed herbs
1 bayleaf
2 carrots, pared and sliced
10 ml (2 tsp) lemon juice
salt and pepper

Fry the oxtail until golden brown, then place it in a casserole. Fry the onions and add to the meat. Sprinkle the flour into the fat and brown it, add the stock gradually and bring to the boil, then pour over the meat. Add the herbs, carrots and lemon juice. Season, cover and cook in the oven at

190°C (375°F) mark 5 for 30 minutes then reduce to 150°C (300°F) mark 2 and simmer very gently for a further 2½–3 hours.

Oxtail hotpot

1 oxtail, jointed
seasoned flour
50 g (2 oz) fat
2 onions, skinned and sliced
225 g (8 oz) carrots, pared and diced
4 tomatoes, diced
2 potatoes, peeled and diced
salt and pepper
dried herbs
stock

Wash the oxtail, dip in flour and fry until golden brown; place in a casserole. Sauté the onions until golden brown, then add to the meat, with the other vegetables. Season well, adding some herbs. Half-cover the meat and vegetables with stock, put the lid on the dish and cook in the oven at 150°C (300°F) mark 2 for 4 hours.

Liver and vegetable casserole

450 g (1 lb) liver
seasoned flour
2 carrots, pared and chopped
2 small onions, skinned and chopped
4 potatoes, peeled and thinly sliced
300 ml (½ pint) stock
5–10 ml (1–2 level tsp) dried mixed herbs
salt and pepper
75 g (3 oz) cheese, grated

Wash the liver and remove any skin or tubes. Toss it in the seasoned flour. Place half the carrot and onion in the bottom of the casserole. Sprinkle with half the herbs and some seasoning, then cover with the liver. Add the remaining carrot and onion and finish with the sliced potatoes; pour in the stock. Sprinkle with seasoning and the remaining herbs, cover and cook in the oven at 180°C (350°F) mark 4 for 1½ hours. Uncover, sprinkle with cheese and bake for a further 15 minutes, or until the cheese topping looks golden and bubbly.

Baked stuffed liver

450 g (1 lb) liver
seasoned flour
forcemeat stuffing
4 rashers of back bacon
300 ml (½ pint) stock or gravy
chopped parsley to garnish

Wash and dry the liver, cut it into 4 pieces, dip in seasoned flour and place in a greased baking tin. Put a little stuffing on each piece of liver and a rasher of bacon on top. Add the stock, cover the baking tin with a lid or with greased paper and cook in the oven at 190°C (375°F) mark 5 until the liver is tender – about 40 minutes. Serve the liver on a hot dish and pour the stock or gravy over. Garnish with parsley.

Liver hotpot

325 g (12 oz) liver
seasoned flour
1 onion, skinned and diced
50 g (2 oz) mushrooms, sliced
3 tomatoes, skinned and sliced
5 ml (1 level tsp) mixed herbs
salt and pepper
450 g (1 lb) potatoes, peeled and thinly
    sliced
stock

Wash and trim the liver, toss in the seasoned flour and place in an ovenproof dish. Cover the meat with the vegetables and add the herbs and seasoning; then add the potatoes. Half cover the hotpot with stock and cook in the oven at 180°C (350°F) mark 4 for 1–1½ hours.

Liver Marsala

Illustrated in colour on page 64

450 g (1 lb) calf's or lamb's liver
lemon juice
seasoned flour
50 g (2 oz) butter
45 ml (3 tbsp) Marsala or sherry
150 ml (¼ pint) stock
60 ml (4 tbsp) single cream
whole grilled tomatoes, matchstick
    potatoes and chopped parsley
    to garnish

Wash and slice the liver. Sprinkle it with the lemon juice and coat with seasoned flour. Melt the butter in a frying pan and fry the liver quickly on both sides until lightly browned. Stir in the Marsala and stock. Simmer until the liver is just cooked and the sauce syrupy. Stir in the cream and reheat

without boiling. Arrange the liver on a serving dish and garnish with the tomatoes, potatoes and parsley.

French-style pâté maison

Illustrated in colour on the jacket

100 g (4 oz) bacon rashers, rinded
700 g (1½ lb) calf's or lamb's liver
225 g (8 oz) chicken livers
1 clove of garlic, skinned and crushed
1 egg, beaten
30 ml (2 tbsp) double cream
10 ml (2 tsp) brandy
salt and pepper

Line a 900-g (2-lb) loaf or pâté tin with the strips of bacon. Mince the two kinds of liver and add the garlic, egg, cream, brandy and seasoning to taste. Mix well, place in the tin and cover with foil. Stand the tin in a shallow dish of water and cook in the oven at 170°C (325°F) mark 3 for about 2 hours. Allow to cool, cover with a plate, put a weight on top to press the pâté and chill overnight. Turn it out of the mould just before serving and slice thinly.

Mexican liver with rice

325 g (12 oz) liver
25 g (1 oz) seasoned flour
50 g (2 oz) dripping
2 onions, skinned and sliced
225 g (8 oz) tomatoes, skinned and sliced
1 red pepper, seeded and sliced
25 g (1 oz) plain flour
300 ml (½ pint) stock
salt and pepper
100 g (4 oz) rice

Wash the liver and remove any skin or tubes. Slice it, toss in seasoned flour, fry lightly in the hot fat, then put in a casserole. Fry the onions, tomatoes and pepper (reserving a few slices of the pepper). When these vegetables are quite soft, add to the liver. Make a sauce with the fat left in the pan, the flour and the stock; season well, pour over the liver and cook in the oven at 180°C (350°F) mark 4 for 45 minutes.

Meanwhile cook the rice in boiling salted water (see page 128) and poach the remaining slices of pepper for a garnish. Serve the liver on a hot dish, with the rice and sliced pepper.

Tripe and onions

450 g (1 lb) prepared tripe
4 onions, skinned and sliced
568 ml (1 pint) milk
25 g (1 oz) butter or margarine
25 g (1 oz) plain flour
salt and pepper
a pinch of ground mace
chopped parsley

Wash the tripe and cut it into small pieces. Place in a casserole with the onions and milk and cook in the oven at 180°C (350°F) mark 4 for 2½ hours. When the tripe is tender, strain it, retaining the milk. Melt the fat in a pan, stir in the flour and cook for 1 minute. Add the milk gradually and bring to the boil, stirring all the time. Boil this sauce gently for 5 minutes, adding some seasonings and ground mace to taste, then add the tripe and re-heat. Serve sprinkled with a little chopped parsley.

Lyonnaise tripe

700 g (1½ lb) prepared tripe
50 g (2 oz) butter or margarine
40 g (1½ oz) flour
stock or water
5 ml (1 tsp) tomato paste
salt and pepper
2 large onions, skinned and chopped
wine vinegar
chopped parsley

Cut the tripe into neat pieces and cook in the hot fat until golden. Sprinkle in the flour to absorb the extra fat, and when it has cooked a little while, add just enough stock or water to cover the tripe. Add the tomato paste, salt and pepper, then the onions; cover, and cook gently until tender – about 1½–2 hours. Add the wine vinegar and parsley just before serving.

Ragoût of tripe

450 g (1 lb) prepared tripe
25 g (1 oz) dripping
1 onion, skinned and chopped
25 g (1 oz) flour
400 ml (¾ pint) stock
1 carrot, pared and sliced
2 tomatoes, chopped or 15 ml (1 tbsp)
    tomato paste
salt to taste
2 cloves
6 peppercorns
1 blade of mace
a pinch of mixed herbs
1 bayleaf
30–45 ml (2–3 tbsp) vinegar
gravy browning

Wash the tripe and cut into neat pieces. Melt the dripping, fry the onion lightly, mix in the flour and add the stock by degrees. Bring to the boil, stirring continuously, then add the carrot, tomatoes, salt, spices and herbs (tied in muslin). Lastly add the tripe and vinegar. Cover and simmer very gently for about 2 hours, until the tripe is really tender, taking care not to let the sauce stick or burn and removing the bag of herbs after about 1 hour. Re-season and if necessary add a little gravy browning to give a rich brown colour.

55

Overleaf:
Roast pork (see page 44).

Tripe Romana

700 g (1½ lb) prepared tripe
30 ml (2 tbsp) vinegar
30 ml (2 tbsp) oil
50 g (2 oz) butter or margarine
1 large or 2 small onions, skinned and
**   thinly sliced**
100 g (4 oz) mushrooms, thinly sliced
25 g (1 oz) flour
226-g (8-oz) can tomatoes made into a
**   purée**
salt and pepper
100 g (4 oz) fresh breadcrumbs
1 small pkt frozen peas

Cut the tripe into narrow strips, 5 cm (2 inches) long, and soak for 30 minutes in the mixed vinegar and oil. Melt 40 g (1½ oz) of the fat and fry the onions and mushrooms for 3–4 minutes. Remove vegetables and add the flour to the pan and brown slightly. Pour in the tomato purée and season to taste. Grease a casserole or ovenproof dish and line the base with half the tripe. Add the mushrooms and onions and sprinkle on half the breadcrumbs. Place another layer of tripe on this, pour the sauce over, sprinkle the top with the remaining crumbs and dot with the rest of the fat. Bake in an uncovered dish in the oven at 200°C (400°F) mark 6 for 25–30 minutes. Towards the end of the time, cook the peas and use to garnish the tripe.

Sausages

Both beef and pork sausages are made in several styles, so choose the size and type most suitable for your particular purpose. Sausagemeat is the most convenient purchase for made-up dishes, where separate sausages are not required. 450 g (1 lb) of sausages serves 4 people when used as a main dish. The smallest chipolata sausages are used mainly for buffet and cocktail party snacks – they are grilled or fried and served on sticks. Pork sausages require longer cooking than beef.
To fry Separate the links. Coat with flour and cook in a little hot fat until evenly browned, turning them over to cook on all sides. Serve as desired – on fried bread, with bacon or with mashed potatoes and gravy.
To grill Place under a hot grill and cook for 10–18 minutes according to type, turning frequently. Serve with grilled tomatoes, etc.
To bake Place on a greased tin and cook in the oven at 180°C (350°F) mark 4 for about 30 minutes.

Toad-in-the-hole

Skin 225 g (8 oz) sausages or not, as preferred. If they are skinned, roll them lightly in a little flour to form each into a roll. Heat 15 g (½ oz) dripping in a Yorkshire pudding tin until smoking and pour in 300 ml (½ pint) Yorkshire pudding batter (see page 71). Arrange the sausages in rows and bake in the oven at 220°C (425°F) mark 7 for about 45 minutes.

Sausagemeat balls with Spanish rice

450 g (1 lb) sausagemeat
seasoned flour
fat or oil for frying
175 g (6 oz) long-grain rice
50 g (2 oz) butter or margarine
1 onion, skinned and finely chopped
1 small green pepper, seeded and
**   chopped**
2 sticks of celery, trimmed and chopped
226-g (8-oz) can tomatoes
salt and pepper
chopped parsley to garnish

Form the sausagemeat into about 6 balls or cakes and roll them in a little seasoned flour. Fry on all sides until well cooked, turning carefully to prevent them from breaking.

Boil the rice in plenty of salted water until tender and drain. Melt the fat, stir in the onion, pepper and celery and cook gently for about 15 minutes. Add the tomatoes and the seasoning and when hot, stir in the rice. Heat all together, stirring, then put on to a hot dish. Arrange the sausagemeat balls over the top and garnish with parsley.

Herby sausage flan

100 g (4 oz) shortcrust pastry, using
**   100 g (4 oz) flour etc.**
1 onion, skinned and chopped
4 rashers of streaky bacon
a small knob of lard
325 g (12 oz) sausagemeat
5 ml (1 level tsp) mixed herbs
salt and pepper
1 egg, whisked
tomato slices to garnish

Line a 15-cm (7-inch) pie plate with the pastry, trim and crimp the edges. Rind the bacon and cut into 1-cm (½-inch) strips. Melt the lard in a frying pan and fry the onion and bacon until golden; drain well. Mix the sausagemeat, onion, bacon, herbs, salt and pepper, add the egg and beat well. Spread over the pastry case and bake in the oven at 200°C (400°F) mark 6 for 15 minutes, or until the pastry is set; reduce the oven temperature to 180°C (350°F) mark 4

and cook for a further 25 minutes, until the sausagemeat is cooked. Garnish with sliced tomato.

Sausage and potato pie

450 g (1 lb) sausages
1 onion, skinned and sliced
325 g (12 oz) tomatoes, skinned and
**   quartered**
450 g (1 lb) cooked potatoes
a little milk
butter or margarine
salt and pepper
chopped parsley

Fry the sausages and then let them cool slightly. Skin most of them, cut in half lengthways and put into a pie dish. Fry the onion and tomatoes in the same pan. Meanwhile cream the potatoes with milk and butter and season well. Put the vegetables over the sausages, cover with the potatoes and fork the top. Slice the remaining sausages and place round the edge of the dish, dot with small shavings of fat and bake in the oven at 220°C (425°F) mark 7 for 15 minutes to brown the potatoes. Sprinkle with parsley.

Sausage and bacon casserole

100 g (4 oz) bacon
225 g (8 oz) pork sausages
225 g (8 oz) apples, peeled, cored and
**   sliced**
100–225 g (4–8 oz) tomatoes, skinned
**   and sliced**
1 green pepper, seeded and sliced
30–45 ml (2–3 tbsp) stock
salt and pepper

Wrap each slice of bacon around 2 sausages, fry (or brown lightly under the grill) and place in a casserole. Arrange the apples, tomatoes and pepper in layers on top of the sausages and bacon. Add the stock and seasoning and cook in the oven at 200°C (400°F) mark 6 for about 40 minutes. *Serves 2*

Bouquet garni

Hotpots, casseroles and stews

BEEF

Beefsteak hotpot

700 g (1 ½ lb) stewing steak
flour
salt and pepper
2 onions, skinned
100 g (4 oz) mushrooms
3 carrots, pared
2–3 potatoes, peeled
ground nutmeg
stock

Cut the steak into 2·5-cm (1-inch) cubes and coat with seasoned flour. Put into a casserole with layers of sliced onions, mushrooms, carrots and potatoes, sprinkling each layer with a pinch of nutmeg and some seasoning. Cover with stock and cook in the oven at 180°C (350°F) mark 4 for 2 ½ hours.

Burgundy beef

25 g (1 oz) lard or dripping
1 large onion, skinned and cut into rings
2 green peppers, seeded
700 g (1 ½ lb) chuck steak
300 ml (½ pint) Burgundy
30 ml (2 tbsp) concentrated tomato
    purée
salt and pepper
150 g (5 oz) sweetcorn kernels

Melt the fat and fry the onion until golden brown; remove and place in a casserole. Cut the flesh of the peppers into thin strips, fry lightly and add these to the onions in the casserole. Cut the meat into 2·5-cm (1-inch) cubes, removing any gristle, and fry until brown. Stir in the Burgundy and tomato purée and season to taste. When well blended, add to the vegetables in the casserole. Cook in the oven at 180°C (350°F) mark 4 for 1 ½–2 hours, then add the sweetcorn kernels and continue cooking for a further 10–15 minutes.

Beef and kidney casserole

450 g (1 lb) rump steak
225 g (8 oz) kidney
plain flour
salt and pepper
50 g (2 oz) lard or dripping
2 medium onions, skinned and sliced
100 g (4 oz) mushrooms, sliced
225 g (8 oz) potatoes, peeled and diced
400 ml (¾ pint) stock
150 g (5 oz) frozen peas (optional)

Trim the steak and kidney, cut into even-sized cubes and coat with seasoned flour. Melt the fat, fry the onions until tender, remove and place in a casserole. Fry the meat until brown and put this also into the casserole. Add the mushrooms and potatoes and pour the stock over. Cook in the oven at 180°C (350°F) mark 4 for about 2 hours, then add the peas (if used), and cook for a further 15–20 minutes.

Beef and olive casserole

450 g (1 lb) rump steak
45 ml (3 tbsp) olive oil
1 carrot, pared and sliced
1 onion, skinned and sliced
2–3 sticks of celery, cut in 2·5-cm
    (1-inch) pieces
300 ml (½ pint) red wine
150 ml (¼ pint) wine vinegar
a bunch of fresh herbs
1 clove of garlic, skinned and crushed
a few peppercorns
salt and pepper
325 g (12 oz) fat bacon
100 g (4 oz) black and green olives
3–4 tomatoes, skinned and sliced

Wipe and trim the meat, then make a marinade. Heat the oil and add the vegetables. Cook until brown, add 150 ml (¼ pint) wine, the vinegar, herbs, garlic, peppercorns, salt and pepper. Bring to boil and simmer for 15 minutes, then leave until quite cold. Cut the meat into thick chunks and cover with the strained marinade.

Fry half the bacon and remove from the pan, then fry the meat on both sides and put into an ovenproof casserole. Add the marinade to the meat with the remaining bacon (diced), wine and olives. Cover and cook in the oven at 170°C (325°F) mark 3 for 2 ½ hours. Shortly before serving, remove any excess fat and add tomatoes. Serve with noodles and grated cheese.

Beef and celery casserole

½ head of celery
1 onion, skinned
50 g (2 oz) butter or dripping
salt and pepper
25 g (1 oz) flour
450 g (1 lb) minced beef
4 tomatoes, skinned and sliced
300 ml (½ pint) stock
scone topping (see below)
egg or milk to glaze

Dice the celery, chop the onion and sauté them together in the hot fat; put into a casserole. Season and flour the meat and brown it in the fat, then add to the casserole, with the tomatoes and stock. Cover and cook in the oven at 180°C (350°F) mark 4 for about 45 minutes, then remove the lid, raise the oven temperature to 220°C (425°F)

mark 7 and put on the scone rounds, overlapping them over the top. Glaze and continue to cook for about 15 minutes.

Scone topping Makes a good finish for a family-style casserole or ragoût. Make a scone dough, using 225 g (8 oz) self-raising flour, 50 g (2 oz) margarine, seasoning and sufficient milk to give a soft, pliable dough. Roll out about 0·5–1 cm (¼–½ inch) thick and cut into rounds. Put these on top of the cooked casserole, brush over with beaten egg yolk and milk and cook in the oven at 220°C (425°F) mark 7 for about 15 minutes.

Beef and macaroni hotpot

175 g (6 oz) macaroni
2 onions, skinned
3–4 sticks of celery
1 red pepper, seeded
50 g (2 oz) butter or margarine
450 g (1 lb) minced beef
290-g (10 ½-oz) can condensed
    mushroom soup plus 1 can water
salt and pepper
2·5 ml (½ level tsp) dried marjoram
30 ml (2 tbsp) chopped parsley

Cook the macaroni in boiling salted water. Drain. Dice the vegetables and sauté in the fat for 5 minutes. Add the meat and cook for a further 5 minutes. Pour in the soup plus the water, season with salt and pepper and add the marjoram. Place a layer of macaroni in an ovenproof dish (retaining enough to garnish the dish when cooked) and cover with the meat mixture. Cook for 1 hour in the oven at 180°C (350°F) mark 4, adding extra stock if necessary. Serve in a border of macaroni, sprinkled with chopped parsley.

Beef goulash

2 onions, skinned
700 g (1 ½ lb) lean stewing beef
50 g (2 oz) dripping
40 g (1 ½ oz) flour
600 ml (1 pint) stock
2 tomatoes, skinned and chopped
a bouquet garni
paprika pepper
salt
150 ml (¼ pint) red wine
lemon juice
creamed potato
cooked peas

Slice the onions and cut the meat into cubes. Melt the fat and fry the onion and meat. Transfer them to a casserole, add the flour to the dripping and cook until it browns. Then add the stock, tomatoes, bouquet garni, paprika pepper and salt. Pour over the meat and onions and cook gently in the oven at 180°C (350°F) mark 4 for about 2 hours, with the lid on; after an hour, stir in the wine and a good squeeze of lemon juice. About 15 minutes before the dish is to be served, remove the lid and pipe rings of creamed potato over the top; allow to brown, then fill with peas.

Russian casseroled beefsteak

700 g (1½ lb) braising steak
25 g (1 oz) plain flour
fat or oil for frying
2 potatoes, peeled and sliced
6 small cabbage leaves
2 carrots, pared
6 peppercorns
3 tomatoes, skinned

Wipe the steak and beat well, then cut up into 10-cm (4-inch) squares, coat with flour and fry until lightly browned. Put into a deep casserole layers of steak, potato, whole cabbage leaves and sliced carrot, with the peppercorns and sliced tomatoes. Add 15 ml (1 tbsp) stock or water and a little melted fat if necessary, but the juice from the meat and vegetables may give enough liquid – the casserole should be kept fairly dry. Cover and cook in the oven at 180°C (350°F) mark 4 for about 2 hours.

Greek aubergine moussaka

2 aubergines
45–60 ml (3–4 tbsp) olive oil
4–5 medium onions, skinned
450 g (1 lb) minced beef or lamb
4 tomatoes, skinned
150 ml (¼ pint) stock
150 ml (¼ pint) tomato pulp
2 eggs
142-ml (5-fl oz) carton single cream
salt and pepper

Slice the aubergines and fry them in some of the oil in a frying pan, then arrange them in the bottom of an ovenproof dish. Slice the onions and fry until they are lightly browned. Place layers of onion and minced meat on top of the aubergines and lastly add some fried slices of tomato. Pour in the stock and tomato pulp and bake in the

oven at 180°C (350°F) mark 4 for about 30 minutes. Beat together the eggs and cream, add salt and pepper and pour this mixture into the casserole. Put it back into the oven for 15–20 minutes, until the sauce is set, firm and golden brown.

Hotpot of beef olives with orange

325 g (12 oz) rump steak
fat or oil for frying
2 carrots, pared
2 sticks of celery
100 g (4 oz) shelled peas
stock
cornflour or plain flour to thicken

For the filling
50 g (2 oz) mushrooms, chopped
grated rind of ½ orange
2–3 tomatoes, chopped
30 ml (2 tbsp) fresh breadcrumbs
salt and pepper

Trim the meat and beat until thin, then cut into strips. Prepare the filling by mixing all the ingredients together, adding seasoning to taste. Spread the filling on the strips of meat, roll each up and tie with cotton. Fry lightly in the hot fat and place in an ovenproof dish. Add the diced carrots and celery and the peas, half-cover with stock and bake in the oven at 180°C (350°F) mark 4 for about 1½ hours. Remove the cottons, thicken the gravy with cornflour or flour and serve with the beef olives.

Rich beef and tomato casserole

Illustrated in colour opposite

700 g (1½ lb) chuck steak
15 ml (1 level tbsp) dry mustard
30 ml (2 level tbsp) flour
oil for frying
5 ml (1 level tsp) dried garlic chips
1 small onion, skinned and finely chopped
2 caps canned pimiento
30 ml (2 tbsp) chopped celery leaves
15 ml (1 tbsp) chopped parsley
300 ml (½ pint) tomato chutney
400 ml (¾ pint) water
30 ml (2 level tbsp) demerara sugar
a pinch of cayenne pepper
225 g (8 oz) button mushrooms
creamy mashed potato
celery leaves to garnish

Cut the steak into largish pieces, having trimmed off excess fat. Toss in a mixture of mustard and flour. In a frying pan, put just enough oil to cover the base of the pan. Fry the meat until well coloured.

Meanwhile, in a saucepan mix together the remaining ingredients, except the mushrooms and potato, and boil for 10 minutes. Put the meat in a casserole dish, pour the boiled ingredients over. Cover tightly and cook in the oven at 150°C (300°F) mark 1–2 for about 2½ hours until the meat is tender. Stir in the whole sautéed mushrooms. Pipe creamed potato to form a collar round the edge. Brown quickly under a hot grill. Garnish with celery leaves.

Summer casserole

900 g (2 lb) shin beef
25 g (1 oz) dripping
15 g (½ oz) flour
2·5 ml (½ level tsp) dry mustard
2 chopped chillies
5 ml (1 level tsp) celery salt
15 ml (1 tbsp) soft brown sugar
600 ml (1 pint) tomato juice
salt and pepper
fresh vegetables as available (see below)

Wipe the beef and remove any sinews and skin. Cut in cubes, fry in hot fat until golden brown, drain and place in a casserole. Add the flour, mustard, chillies, celery salt, sugar and tomato juice to the fat in the pan. Bring to the boil, season to taste and pour over the meat. Simmer in the oven at 170°C (325°F) mark 3 for 2 hours. Prepare all the vegetables and add to the casserole, then cook for a further 45 minutes–1 hour, until they are tender. *Serves 6*

Suggested vegetables
1 small cauliflower, in florets
1 carrot, pared and diced
1 onion, skinned and sliced
100 g (4 oz) tomatoes, quartered
100 g (4 oz) frozen sweetcorn
100 g (4 oz) frozen French beans

Australian hotpot

450–550 g (1–1¼ lb) braising steak
15 ml (1 tbsp) dripping
2 onions, skinned and sliced
2 cooking apples, cored and sliced
2 tomatoes, sliced
10 ml (2 level tsp) curry powder
50 g (2 oz) sultanas
25 g (1 oz) seeded raisins
300 ml (½ pint) stock
15 ml (1 level tbsp) plain flour
salt
brown sugar
parsley, 3 hard-boiled eggs, 1 pkt potato crisps to garnish

Cut up the meat. Heat the dripping in a pan, add the meat, onion and apple and fry until golden brown. Add the tomatoes and curry powder and cook for a few minutes longer.

Rich beef and tomato casserole (see above).

Place the mixture in a casserole, add the dried fruit and barely cover with stock. Put a lid on the casserole and cook in the oven at 180°C (350°F) mark 4 for 1½ hours. Blend the flour with a little extra water, stir into the casserole and cook for a further 5 minutes. Season to taste with a little salt and brown sugar. Garnish with parsley and sliced egg, surround the casserole with potato crisps and serve at once.

Carbonade of beef

Illustrated in colour on page 65

900 g (2 lb) stewing steak, cut into cubes
salt and pepper
50 g (2 oz) fat or oil
75 g (3 oz) lean bacon, rinded and chopped
60 ml (4 level tbsp) plain flour
300 ml (½ pint) beer
300 ml (½ pint) stock or water
30–45 ml (2–3 tbsp) vinegar
a pinch of nutmeg
a pinch of sugar
15 ml (1 level tbsp) tomato paste
450 g (1 lb) onions, skinned and chopped
1 clove garlic, skinned and chopped
a bouquet garni

Season the meat and fry in the fat or oil until brown – about 5 minutes. Add the bacon and continue cooking for a few minutes. Remove the meat and bacon from the pan, stir in the flour and brown lightly. Gradually add the beer, stock, vinegar, nutmeg, sugar and tomato paste, stirring continuously until the mixture thickens. Fill a casserole with layers of meat, bacon, onion and garlic. Pour the sauce over and add the bouquet garni. Cover and cook for about 3 hours in the oven at 150°C (300°F) mark 2. Add a little more beer while cooking, if necessary. Just before serving, remove the bouquet garni. Serve with plain boiled potatoes.

Yugoslavian beef casserole

450 g (1 lb) stewing steak
¼ white cabbage, shredded
1 small carrot, pared and sliced
2 tomatoes, skinned and sliced
2 large potatoes, peeled and sliced
1 green pepper, seeded and sliced
1 small parsnip, peeled and sliced
a few haricot beans
¼ red cabbage, shredded
2 small onions, skinned and sliced
salt
a few peppercorns
½ bottle of white wine

Slice the meat and put into a casserole in

alternate layers with the vegetables, lightly salting each layer and adding the peppercorns. Pour the white wine over, cover the casserole closely and simmer for at least 2½ hours. Do not stir or the vegetables will break up and become mushy, spoiling the consistency of the sauce.

Boeuf bourguignon

700 g (1½ lb) braising beef, cut into
2·5-cm (1-inch) cubes
50 g (2 oz) lard
225 g (8 oz) onions, skinned and sliced
2 rashers of bacon, rinded and chopped
100 g (4 oz) mushrooms, sliced
15 g (½ oz) flour
150 ml (¼ pint) Burgundy
300 ml (½ pint) stock
a bouquet garni
salt and pepper

Brown the meat quickly in the hot fat, then remove it from the pan and add the onions, bacon and mushrooms. Fry slowly, then stir in the flour. Put the meat in a 2·3-litre (4-pint) casserole and add the wine, stock, bouquet garni and seasoning. Cook in the oven at 170°C (325°F) mark 3 for 1½ hours. Add the onions, bacon and mushrooms and cook for 1 hour longer. Remove the bouquet garni before serving.

Goulash with beer

450 g (1 lb) stewing steak
seasoned flour
2 medium onions, skinned and chopped
1 green pepper, seeded and chopped
a little dripping
45 ml (3 tbsp) tomato paste
salt and pepper
grated nutmeg
50 g (2 oz) flour
300 ml (½ pint) stock
2 large tomatoes, chopped
a bunch of mixed herbs
150 ml (¼ pint) beer
10 ml (2 level tsp) paprika pepper

Cut the steak up small and dip in seasoned flour. Fry the onions and pepper lightly in a little dripping. Add the meat and fry lightly on all sides. Stir in the tomato paste, seasonings and flour and add the stock, tomatoes and herbs. Put into a casserole and cook in the oven at 170°C (325°F) mark 3 for 1 hour. Add the beer and paprika and cook for another 30 minutes–1 hour, or until the meat is tender; remove the herbs. Serve with sauerkraut and caraway-flavoured dumplings which can be added to the casserole 30 minutes before the end of cooking time. The goulash may also be served with a green salad.

LAMB

Lamb hotpot

700 g (1½ lb) scrag end of neck of lamb
seasoned flour
25 g (1 oz) dripping
2 large carrots, pared and sliced
2 medium onions, skinned and sliced
salt and pepper
15 ml (1 tbsp) pearl barley
10 ml (2 level tsp) dried lovage
300 ml (½ pint) stock and water
2 large potatoes, peeled and thinly sliced
chopped parsley to garnish

Trim the meat, removing the excess fat, and chop it into 4 pieces. Dip in the seasoned flour. Melt the fat and brown the meat, then remove it and brown the carrots and onions lightly. Season and place in a casserole, arrange the meat on top and sprinkle with pearl barley and lovage. Pour the liquid over and cover with a layer of potatoes. Put on a tightly fitting lid and bake in the oven at 170°C (325°F) mark 3 for 2¼ hours. Raise the heat to 220°C (425°F) mark 7, remove the lid and brown the potatoes. Serve the hotpot dusted with freshly ground pepper and some chopped parsley.

Lancashire hotpot

700–900 g (1½–2 lb) best end of neck of lamb
100 g (4 oz) mushrooms, sliced
225 g (8 oz) onions, skinned and sliced
450 g (1 lb) potatoes, peeled and sliced
salt and pepper
stock
dripping

Divide the meat into chops, removing any excess fat. Put the meat into the bottom of a casserole and cover with a layer of sliced mushrooms, then add the onions and lastly the potatoes, seasoning each layer. Pour in enough stock to half-fill the casserole and dot the potatoes with shavings of dripping. Cover and cook in the oven at 170°C (325°F) mark 3 for about 2½–3 hours, removing the lid towards the end of the time to brown the potatoes – allow 15–20 minutes.

Irish stew

450 g (1 lb) middle neck of lamb
900 g (2 lb) potatoes, peeled and sliced
2 large onions, skinned and sliced
salt and pepper
chopped parsley

Prepare the meat by wiping thoroughly, removing the marrow and cutting into neat joints. Place alternate layers of vegetables and meat in a pan, finishing with a layer of potatoes. Add salt and pepper and sufficient water to half-cover. Bring to the boil and simmer gently for about 2 hours, or until the meat and potatoes are tender.

Pile the meat, gravy and some of the potatoes in the centre of a hot dish. Place the rest of the potatoes at either end of the dish and sprinkle a little chopped parsley over them.

Lamb and oyster hotpot

700 g (1 ½ lb) lamb chops
8 oysters
a knob of butter or margarine
900 g (2 lb) potatoes, peeled and sliced
100 g (4 oz) mushrooms, quartered
2 onions, skinned and sliced
salt and pepper
300 ml (½ pint) rich brown sauce (see page 71)

Trim the chops and remove most of the fat. Beard the oysters and retain the liquid. Brush the inside of an ovenproof dish with melted fat. Put a thick layer of the potatoes over the bottom, arrange the chops on this, with a piece or two of mushroom and an oyster on each. Put the remaining oysters and mushrooms in the centre of the dish, scatter the onion over and season well. Layer the rest of the potatoes on top. Mix about 150 ml (¼ pint) of the sauce with the oyster liquor and pour in at the side of the dish. Brush the potatoes well with melted fat and cover with a piece of greased greaseproof paper. Cook in the oven at 180°C (350°F) mark 4 for 2–2 ½ hours. About 30 minutes before the end of the cooking time, add the rest of the sauce and remove the greaseproof paper to brown the potatoes.

Country casserole

4 shoulder of lamb chops
25 g (1 oz) lard
1 clove of garlic, skinned and finely chopped
4 medium potatoes, peeled
4 small onions, skinned
125-g (4 ½-oz) pkt frozen green beans
1·25 ml (¼ level tsp) ground cloves
5 ml (1 level tsp) salt
pepper
298-g (10 ½-oz) can condensed mushroom soup
150 ml (¼ pint) stock or water
paprika pepper to garnish

Trim some of the fat from the chops. Heat the lard, add the garlic and fry the chops on both sides. Place the chops in a casserole and arrange the halved potatoes and onions round them. Add the beans, cloves,

salt, pepper, soup and stock, cover and cook in the oven at 180°C (350°F) mark 4 for about 1 hour. Sprinkle with paprika pepper before serving.

You can use veal chops in a similar way, and the flavouring can be varied by using other types of condensed soups.

Lamb with apples

50 g (2 oz) butter or margarine
4 loin chops or a piece of loin of lamb
8 small potatoes, peeled and sliced
4 onions, skinned and sliced
15 ml (1 level tbsp) plain flour
300 ml (½ pint) stock
salt and pepper
60 ml (4 tbsp) white wine or vinegar
4 apples, sliced
a little grated cheese

Melt the fat in a frying pan and fry the meat until browned. Arrange some sliced potato and onion at the bottom of a casserole, add the meat and cover with another layer of vegetables. Add the flour to the remaining fat in the frying pan and brown. Stir in the stock, seasoning and wine, mix and strain over the meat. Place the sliced apple over the top and sprinkle with grated cheese. Put on the lid and cook in the oven at 190°C (375°F) mark 5 for 1–1 ½ hours, until the meat and vegetables are tender.

American cabin casserole

4 lean lamb chops
25 g (1 oz) dripping
1 rasher of bacon, chopped
4–5 large onions, skinned and sliced
4–5 large tomatoes, skinned and sliced
salt to taste
a little curry powder

Fry the chops lightly in the dripping with the bacon. Place the onions and tomatoes in alternate layers in a greased casserole, sprinkling each layer with salt and curry powder. Place the browned chops on top, cover the dish tightly and bake in the oven at 190°C (375°F) mark 5 for 45 minutes. Remove the lid and cook for a further 30 minutes.

Pineapple lamb casserole

4 lamb chops
lard or oil
8 chipolata sausages
4 slices of pineapple
8 mushrooms
butter or margarine
salt and pepper
150 ml (¼ pint) pineapple juice

Trim the chops and fry in the hot fat until

golden brown. Cut the sausages into small pieces and fry until brown. Place the chops in a casserole, put a slice of pineapple on each chop and add the sausages. Prepare the mushrooms, leaving them whole, add to the casserole, place a knob of fat on each and sprinkle with seasoning. Pour in the pineapple juice, cover and bake in the oven at 180°C (350°F) mark 4 for about 1 hour, or until the chops are tender.

Swiss braised lamb with wine

700 g (1 ½ lb) thickly cut leg of lamb
salt and pepper
cooking fat
150 ml (¼ pint) white wine
450 g (1 lb) potatoes, peeled and chopped
225 g (8 oz) carrots, pared and chopped
1 small celeriac, peeled and chopped
1–2 medium onions, skinned and chopped
1 clove of garlic, skinned and crushed (optional)

Beat the meat, rub with salt and pepper and fry in the fat in a flameproof casserole until browned on all sides. Add the white wine. Place the vegetables round the meat, cover the casserole with a well-fitting lid and braise in the oven at 200°C (400°F) mark 6 for 1 ¼–1 ½ hours.

Pork can be cooked in the same way.

Spiced lamb with aubergines

Illustrated in colour on page 53

1 kg (2 ¼ lb) lean breast of lamb, boned
25 g (1 oz) lard
225 g (8 oz) onion, skinned and chopped
5 ml (1 level tsp) turmeric
5 ml (1 level tsp) chilli seasoning
5 ml (1 level tsp) ground cumin
5 ml (1 level tsp) salt
30 ml (2 level tbsp) curry paste
45 ml (3 level tbsp) mango chutney
75 g (3 oz) sultanas
30 ml (2 level tbsp) peanut butter
15 ml (1 tbsp) Worcestershire sauce
300 ml (½ pint) beef stock
450 g (1 lb) aubergines, sliced
chopped parsley to garnish

Mince the lamb coarsely and fry in the melted lard to seal. Add the next six ingredients and cook for 5 minutes, stirring. Stir in the chutney, sultanas, peanut butter, Worcestershire sauce and stock. Bring to the boil, reduce the heat and simmer for 1 hour. Sprinkle the sliced aubergines with salt and leave for 5 minutes. Rinse and dry thoroughly and add to the pan. Simmer gently for a further 30 minutes. Garnish and serve with plain boiled rice. *Serves 6*

Overleaf:
Liver Marsala (see page 55).
Carbonade of beef (see page 62).

63

PORK

Pork and apple hotpot

4 loin pork chops
225 g (8 oz) cooking apples, sliced
1 onion, skinned and sliced
50 g (2 oz) butter or margarine
3 tomatoes, skinned
450 g (1 lb) potatoes, peeled and diced
salt and pepper

Bone and roll the chops. Fry the apples and onion in the fat until golden brown. Place the chops in a dish, cover with the apple and vegetables, add seasoning and half-cover the meat and vegetables with water. Cover the dish and cook in the oven at 180°C (350°F) mark 4 for 1½ hours.

Pork and prune hotpot

100 g (4 oz) prunes
juice and rind of 1 lemon
450 g (1 lb) pork
25 g (1 oz) plain flour
salt and pepper
a small knob of dripping

Cover the prunes with cold water, leave to soak for a few hours, then stew them with the rind of the lemon until tender. Strain off the juice and keep it. Remove the stones from the prunes. Wipe the pork, cut it into neat pieces and dip in the seasoned flour. Melt the dripping in a frying pan and fry the pork until brown. Place the pork and prunes in alternate layers in a casserole. Make some brown gravy with the remaining fat, flour and about 300 ml (½ pint) of the prune juice and pour this over the pork. Add the lemon juice, cover the casserole and cook in the oven at 180°C (350°F) mark 4 for about 1 hour. Serve in the casserole.

Braised pork chops

50 g (2 oz) butter or margarine
4 loin pork chops, 2·5 cm (1 inch) thick
1 onion, skinned and thinly sliced
1 carrot, pared and thinly sliced
a bouquet garni
150 ml (¼ pint) Sauternes
150 ml (¼ pint) stock
salt and pepper
100 g (4 oz) mushrooms, sliced
75 ml (5 tbsp) milk and water
15 ml (1 level tbsp) plain flour

Melt the fat and brown the chops on both sides; remove them and sauté the onion and carrot for 5 minutes. Remove and place in a casserole, with the chops on top. Add the bouquet garni, wine and seasoned stock and cook in the oven at 180°C (350°F) mark 4 for 1 hour. Meanwhile put the mushrooms in a pan with the milk and water; season, cover and simmer for 5 minutes. Blend the flour with the fat left in the frying pan to make a roux. Drain off the liquid from the casserole and that from the mushrooms and add gradually to the roux, stirring until the sauce has boiled. Add the mushrooms and pour over the chops in the casserole.

Pork chops with prune stuffing

225 g (8 oz) prunes
4 lean pork chops, 2·5 cm (1 inch) thick
30 ml (2 tbsp) lemon juice
25 g (1 oz) brown sugar
25 g (1 oz) fat
salt and pepper
4 potatoes, peeled and sliced
45–60 ml (3–4 tbsp) hot water

Soak the prunes in boiling water for 5 minutes, drain and stone. Bone the chops and make a pocket in each; to do this slit each chop from the bone side almost to the fat. Cut up the prunes with scissors, add the lemon juice, sugar and 15 ml (1 tbsp) water and cook together for a few minutes. Stuff the chops with this mixture and brown them in the fat, then sprinkle with seasoning. Place in a shallow casserole, cover with the potato and add the hot water. Bake in the oven at 180°C (350°F) mark 4 for 1 hour with the lid on, until the chops are tender. If liked, take off the lid for the last 15 minutes to brown the top surface of the casserole.

VEAL

Veal casserole with wine

700 g (1½ lb) stewing veal
50 g (2 oz) lard or dripping
2 cloves of garlic, skinned
salt and pepper
300 ml (½ pint) tomato juice
150 ml (¼ pint) white wine
2·5 ml (½ level tsp) rosemary or sage
a strip of lemon rind
15 ml (1 level tbsp) plain flour

Slice the meat or cut it into small pieces. Heat the fat in a casserole and cook the chopped garlic until lightly browned. Add the meat and seasoning and continue cooking until the meat is golden brown. Stir in the tomato juice, wine, rosemary and lemon rind, cover tightly and cook in the oven at 180°C (350°F) mark 4 until the meat is tender – about 1–1½ hours. Before serving, thicken the liquid with the flour, blended with a little cold water.

Veal hotpot

450 g (1 lb) veal fillet
seasoned flour
grated rind of 1 lemon
2·5 ml (½ level tsp) mixed herbs
2 carrots, pared and chopped
1 onion, skinned and chopped
100 g (4 oz) peas, shelled
450 g (1 lb) potatoes, peeled and thinly
  sliced
salt and pepper
stock

Trim and cube the meat and toss in the seasoned flour. Place in a casserole and sprinkle with lemon rind and herbs. Add the carrots, onion and peas to the hotpot and cover with the potatoes. Season and half-cover with stock. Cook in the oven at 180°C (350°F) mark 4 for 1¼ hours.

Braised veal cutlets

4 veal cutlets
65 g (2½ oz) butter or margarine
100 g (4 oz) chopped ham
15 ml (1 tbsp) chopped onion
15 ml (1 tbsp) chopped parsley
salt and pepper
150 ml (¼ pint) red wine

Trim the cutlets into a neat shape and fry until golden brown in 50 g (2 oz) of the fat. Remove and put on one side. Fry the ham and onion, add the parsley and season with salt and pepper. Cover the cutlets with this stuffing, place in a casserole and add the wine and a little water to come half-way up the meat. Cook in the oven at 180°F mark 4 with a lid on for about 45 minutes. Take out the cutlets and keep them hot while reducing the liquid slightly; just before serving, add the remaining fat to the liquor and replace the cutlets in it.

Rich veal stew

700 g (1½ lb) fillet of veal
cold water
salt and pepper
1 large onion, skinned and sliced
a bouquet garni
mushrooms to garnish
40 g (1½ oz) butter or margarine
25 g (1 oz) flour
600 ml (1 pint) stock
15 ml (1 tbsp) single cream
1 egg yolk
a squeeze of lemon juice
chopped parsley
bacon rolls (optional)

Trim the veal and cut it up into neat pieces. Put it into a saucepan with sufficient cold water to cover and add the seasoning, onion and bouquet garni. Cover and cook slowly for about 1 hour, removing any

...cum from the surface occasionally. Wash ...nd trim the mushrooms and cook them in ...5 g (½ oz) fat for about 5 minutes, ...emove them and keep hot. When the veal ... tender, strain off and reserve the stock.

Make a white sauce, using 25 g (1 oz) of ...he fat, the flour and 600 ml (1 pint) of stock. ...Mix the cream with the egg yolk and stir ...nto the sauce, with a little lemon juice. ...leat, stirring, but do not boil, then add to ...he veal. Season to taste and serve gar-...ished with the mushrooms and chopped ...arsley and, if liked, grilled bacon rolls. ...erves 4–5

Alternatively, omit the mushroom gar-...ish and use small triangles of fried bread or ...oast.

Veal à la royale

...00 g (2 lb) veal, cut into 2·5-cm (1-inch)
  cubes
...0 g (2 oz) lard
  rashers of bacon, rinded and chopped
...½ onion, skinned and sliced
...5 ml (3 tbsp) brandy
...0 g (2 oz) flour
...alt and pepper
...50 ml (¼ pint) red wine
...00 ml (¾ pint) stock
  bouquet garni

...rown the cubes of veal in the hot lard with ...he chopped bacon rashers; drain them ...arefully and put into a 2·3-litre (4-pint) ...asserole. Fry the onion until golden and ...dd to the meat. Add the brandy to the pan, ...et it alight, then when the flames die down, ...tir in the flour, salt, pepper, wine and stock. ...our over the meat, add the bouquet garni, ...over with the lid and cook for 2 hours in ...he oven at 180°C (350°F) mark 4. Serves 5–6

Osso bucco

Illustrated in colour on page 69

...00 g (2 lb) shin of veal (4 pieces)
...alt and pepper
...0 g (2 oz) margarine
  medium onion, skinned and finely
    chopped
  carrots, pared and sliced
  sticks of celery, trimmed and sliced
  clove garlic, skinned and crushed
...5 ml (1 level tbsp) flour
...00 ml (½ pint) chicken stock
...50 g (12 oz) tomatoes, skinned and
    quartered
  pinch of dried rosemary
...0 ml (2 tbsp) chopped parsley
...rated rind of 1 lemon

...eason the veal with salt and pepper. Melt ...he margarine in a saucepan large enough ...o take the veal in one layer. Brown the veal,

then put aside. If necessary, add a little more margarine before gently frying the onion, carrots and celery until they are just beginning to brown. Add the crushed garlic. Return the meat to the pan, add the flour and cook for a few minutes, then add the stock. Cover and cook gently for 1 hour. Transfer to a large shallow casserole. Add the tomatoes and rosemary, cover and continue to cook gently in the oven at 180°C (350°F) mark 4, for 1 hour, until the meat is tender. Sprinkle with parsley and lemon rind before serving.

Rabbit hotpot

450 g (1 lb) rabbit
225 g (8 oz) carrots, pared and sliced
450 g (1 lb) potatoes, peeled and diced
1 pkt onion soup mix

Wash and joint the rabbit. Blanch by putting into a saucepan, covering with water and bringing to the boil. Remove the joints from the pan and place in a dish; over the top arrange the carrots and potatoes. Make up the soup with 600 ml (1 pint) water and pour over the top. Cook in the oven at 180°C (350°F) mark 4 for 2 hours.

Ideas for the cold table

Meat platter

A variety of sliced meats can be served on a platter garnished with radish roses, celery curls, tomato lilies, etc. Cold roast meats can be supplemented by the wide variety of Continental specialities, sausages and salamis available.

Alternatively, spread the meat slices with a savoury filling and serve rolled up and secured with cocktail sticks. Suggested combinations: ham with cream cheese and raisins or cranberry jelly; beef with horseradish sauce or potato salad; pork with sage and onion stuffing or apple sauce.

Rounds of salami or Continental sausage can be rolled into cones and filled in a similar way with mixed vegetables in salad cream, asparagus tips, cream cheese, pimiento or cocktail onions.

Ham potato salad

Make a potato salad, using new waxy potatoes and flavouring it well with onion and chopped parsley. Then mix in some strips of lean cooked ham before adding the mayonnaise. Garnish with watercress, hard-boiled egg and small tomatoes.

Alternatively, make a jellied tomato ring mould containing sliced eggs, peas, etc, and put the salad in it.

Veal, ham and tongue mould

600 ml (1 pint) aspic jelly
3 hard-boiled eggs
225 g (8 oz) cooked veal, diced
225 g (8 oz) cooked tongue, diced
225 g (8 oz) cooked ham, diced

Line a 1·1-litre (2-pint) mould or tin with almost-setting aspic jelly and decorate it with slices of hard-boiled egg. Chop up any remaining egg and mix it with the diced meats. Put the mixture into the tin and cover with aspic. When set, turn out and serve cut into 8 slices.

A colourful accompaniment is a salad of cooked asparagus and tiny red tomatoes stuffed with cubes of cucumber and green peas tossed in mayonnaise.

Beef mayonnaise

225–325 g (8–12 oz) cold cooked beef
2 lettuce hearts
225 g (8 oz) tomatoes, skinned and sliced
½ cucumber, sliced
radishes
2 egg yolks
salt and pepper
about 300 ml (½ pint) oil
juice of ½ lemon
1 hard-boiled egg

Cut the meat into small dice. Line a salad bowl or platter with some of the larger lettuce leaves; cut the firm hearts into quarters and place these at intervals round the sides. Put the meat, tomatoes, cucumber and radishes into a bowl and mix with the mayonnaise, made as follows: put the egg yolks into a bowl with the salt and pepper, mix with a wooden spoon and then gradually stir in the oil drop by drop, adding a squeeze of lemon juice at intervals. The mayonnaise should be thick and creamy when ready. Pile the meat and mayonnaise mixture on the lettuce and decorate the dish with sliced hard-boiled egg and a few tomato slices, etc.

Ready-made mayonnaise may be used instead.

Marbled veal

Chop up or mince equal quantities of cold cooked tongue and veal, keeping them separate. Line a mould or glass pie dish with jellied stock and decorate with a pattern of sliced hard-boiled egg and tomato. When this is set, fill up the mould with irregular layers of the two meats, adding jellied stock to cover. When set, turn out and serve sliced, with salad.

In the Salads chapter of this book are recipes for a wide range of both well-known and unusual salads: many of them would be excellent with these cold meat dishes.

Carving meat

Beef joints
This meat, particularly when cold, is best carved thinly.

Sirloin or ribs (unboned) (see line drawings) Remove the chine or end bone and cut the meat from the top of the joint in thin slices from the outer fat down to the rib bone.

Turn the sirloin over and cut rather thicker slices from the fillet or undercut, this time cutting again down to the bone in even slices. Serve a slice of undercut with a slice of top meat and a little fat.

Rolled ribs, sirloin or topside Carve boneless joints of meat horizontally, in thin slices.

Fillet Carve across the grain, but rather thickly, in 0·5-cm (¼-inch) slices; cut downwards towards the dish.

Lamb joints
This is carved in rather thicker slices than beef.

Best end of neck If chined, this is easy to carve, as it has only to be divided by cutting between the bones.

Loin Cut the joint right through downwards between the bones, to divide it into individual chops.

Shoulder (see line drawings) Place the joint so that the bladebone points away from the carver. Insert the fork securely in the meat and with the aid of the fork, raise the far side of the joint slightly, then make a vertical cut through the centre of the meat up to the bone; this will cause the joint to open out slightly, making it appear as if a slice had already been removed. Cut thick slices from each side of this gap, as far as the bladebone on the one side and the knuckle on the other. Slices of the knuckle also may be carved for those who appreciate it. Next turn the joint so that the bladebone faces the carver and carve the meat on top of the bladebone downwards in strips, parallel with the central 'fin' of the bone. Finally,

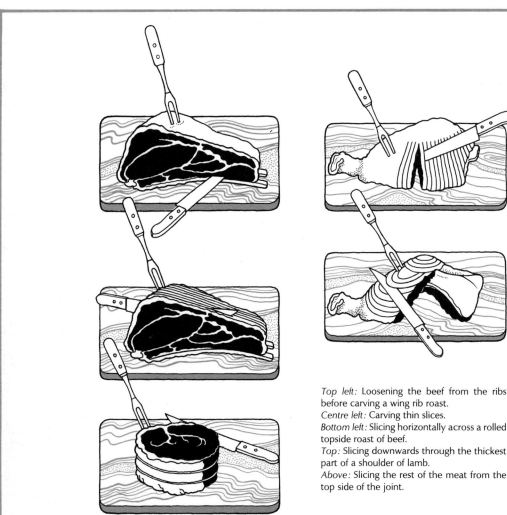

Top left: Loosening the beef from the ribs before carving a wing rib roast.
Centre left: Carving thin slices.
Bottom left: Slicing horizontally across a rolled topside roast of beef.
Top: Slicing downwards through the thickest part of a shoulder of lamb.
Above: Slicing the rest of the meat from the top side of the joint.

Osso bucco
(see page 67)

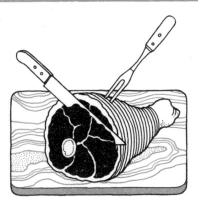

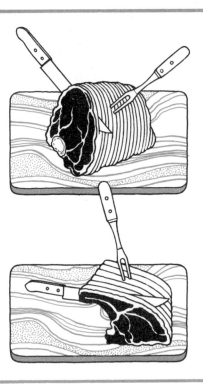

Above: Carving a leg of pork.
Above right: Carving a loin of veal.
Right: Slicing down between the bones of a best end neck of veal.

turn the joint upside down and slice meat horizontally from underside.

Leg Start cutting at the thick end and work towards the shank, cutting in slices down to the bone, then turn it over and cut rather more sloping slices, working from the shank to the fillet end.

Stuffed breast of lamb Cut downwards right through the joint in fairly thick slices.

Pork joints

This meat is cut moderately thick.

Leg (see line drawing) This is cut in the same way as a leg of lamb, but the cuts should be made between the cuts in the crackling and each person should be given a piece of crisp crackling with the meat.

Loin Divide between the bones to form chops, or cut into thinner slices for more economical carving.

Spare rib Cut between the score marks into moderately thick, even-sized slices.

Veal joints

Loin (see line drawing) Slice the meat downwards towards the serving dish, in medium-thick slices.

Fillet If the bone is left in, cut the meat down to the bone on one side, then turn the joint over and do the same on the underside. The joint is often boned and stuffed and when this is done it can be cut right

through into slices of medium thickness.

Best end of neck (see line drawing) Divide by cutting between the bones.

Shoulder Carve as for shoulder of lamb.

Pickling meat

Ox tongue, pig's head, leg or belly of pork and silverside or brisket of beef are particularly suited to pickling. Trim and wash the meat, then rub it over with salt to remove all traces of blood. Use a large earthenware crock, bowl or basin, or a polythene bowl and cover with a board to exclude the dust.

Wet pickle This is the easier method. Put 4·5 litres (8 pints) water, 700 g (1½ lb) sea or common salt, 25 g (1 oz) saltpetre and 175 g (6 oz) brown sugar in a large pan, bring to the boil and boil for 15–20 minutes, skimming carefully. Strain into a bowl, allow to cool, put in the meat and cover.

Dry pickle Pound 225 g (8 oz) sea salt, mix with 225 g (8 oz) common salt, 225 g (8 oz) brown sugar, 25 g (1 oz) saltpetre, 15 g (½ oz) black pepper and 5 ml (1 level tsp) allspice. Rub the meat daily with this mixture, working it well in. Leave the meat in the covered crock.

Times for pickling meat Home-pickled meat is best done in the cold weather and the meat may remain in the salt mixture for a variable length of time. A thick cut of beef needs about 10 days, whereas a thinner cut or a pig's head split in half, may be sufficiently salted in 4–5 days.

Cooking salted or pickled meat Remove the meat from the pickle and wash thoroughly in cold water. If liked, it may be soaked for 1 hour in cold water before cooking. Put the meat (neatly tied up if necessary) into a pan of cold water, bring slowly to the boil and skim. The first water may be thrown away and this process repeated if required. Add herbs and vegetables if desired, then allow the water to simmer very gently for the required time. (Retain the liquid for use in making soups etc.)

For salt beef and pork allow 50 minutes cooking time per 450 g (lb). Ox tongue requires 3–4 hours, according to size; it should be tested for tenderness with a small skewer.

If the meat is to be pressed or collared (see pages 42 and 52), it is best to remove the skin and any bones before the meat becomes cold; do this as soon as it is cool enough to handle. Tongue and ham skin comes away quite easily, but take care not to break up the meat.

Sauces and accompaniments

Apple sauce

450 g (1 lb) cooking apples, peeled, cored and sliced
25–50 g (1–2 oz) butter or margarine
sugar, if required
lemon juice

Cook the apples gently to a pulp in a covered pan. Beat with a wooden spoon until smooth and add the fat. Sugar may be added if desired, but a tart apple sauce is just the right accompaniment to pork. If the apples are sweet, add a little lemon juice.

Mint sauce

5 ml (1 level tsp) sugar
15 ml (1 tbsp) boiling water
30 ml (2 tbsp) chopped mint
22·5 ml (1½ tbsp) vinegar

Dissolve the sugar in the boiling water in a sauceboat, add the mint and stir in vinegar to taste. Cool.

Brown sauce

1 small onion, skinned and sliced
20 g (¾ oz) dripping
20 g (¾ oz) flour
300 ml (½ pint) stock
1 small carrot, pared and sliced
1 piece of turnip, peeled and sliced
salt and pepper

Fry the onion in the dripping, then stir in the flour and cook it, allowing it to become a golden brown colour before removing it from the heat. Stir in the stock gradually and add the other vegetables. Simmer for 20–30 minutes, season, strain and re-heat before serving.

For a richer sauce, add about 30 ml (2 tbsp) sherry.

Mushroom sauce

To 300 ml (½ pint) well-seasoned white sauce (see page 36) add 50–100 g (2–4 oz) sautéed mushrooms.

Onion sauce

Add 1–2 chopped boiled onions to 300 ml (½ pint) white sauce (see page 36).

Caper sauce

Make some white sauce in the usual way (see page 36), but use half meat liquor and half milk. Add about 25 ml (1½ tbsp) coarsely chopped capers to 300 ml (½ pint) sauce.

Devilled butter

Beat 50 g (2 oz) butter until soft, then mix in a little lemon juice, cayenne pepper, and 2·5 ml (½ level tsp) curry powder.

Maître d'hôtel butter

25 g (1 oz) butter
5 ml (1 tsp) chopped parsley
5 ml (1 tsp) lemon juice
salt and pepper

Mix all the ingredients thoroughly into a creamy paste, using a fork or wooden spoon. Shape into pats and chill before serving.

Horseradish cream

15–30 ml (1–2 tbsp) grated horseradish
15 ml (1 tbsp) vinegar
single cream or evaporated milk
salt and pepper
sugar

Soak the grated horseradish in the vinegar for 10–15 minutes. Stir in enough cream to give a soft consistency and season with salt, pepper and sugar.

Sage and onion stuffing

2 large onions, skinned
25 g (1 oz) butter
100 g (4 oz) fresh breadcrumbs
10 ml (2 level tsp) dried sage
salt and pepper

Blanch the onions, strain and cover with fresh boiling water, cook until tender. Drain well and chop finely. Add to the other ingredients and mix well.

Herb (parsley) stuffing

50 g (2 oz) suet
25–50 g (1–2 oz) cooked ham or bacon
100 g (4 oz) fresh breadcrumbs
10 ml (2 tsp) chopped parsley
2·5 ml (½ level tsp) mixed herbs
grated rind of ½ lemon
salt and pepper
1 egg yolk

Chop the suet and ham finely and mix with the crumbs; add the parsley, herbs and lemon rind, season and bind with the egg yolk. Use as required; for example to stuff bacon rolls or to make forcemeat balls. (This is sometimes called Veal Forcemeat.)

Dumplings

100 g (4 oz) self-raising flour
1·25 ml (¼ level tsp) salt
50 g (2 oz) chopped suet
a few fresh or dried herbs (optional)
cold water to mix

Mix the dry ingredients with water to a soft, elastic dough, roll into balls and add to soups or stews 30 minutes before serving.
Herb dumplings Include ½ onion, skinned and finely grated, and 2·5 ml (½ level tsp) mixed dried herbs.

Yorkshire pudding

Sift 100 g (4 oz) plain flour and 1·25 ml (¼ level tsp) salt and make a well in the centre. Add 1 egg and enough milk or milk and water (about 150 ml (¼ pint)) to give a creamy, smooth batter. Beat thoroughly with a wooden spoon until full of air bubbles, then stir in about another 150 ml (¼ pint) liquid. Heat a small knob of dripping in a Yorkshire pudding tin or in several deep patty tins and pour in the batter, only half-filling small tins. Bake in the oven at 220°C (425°F) mark 7 for about 45 minutes (15–20 minutes for small puddings).

Gravy

Either clear or thickened gravy is always served with roast joints and with many other meat dishes. Stock or vegetable water should be used for gravy, if possible, and it should be made in the baking tin, in order to make use of the juices which may have run into the fat.
Thin gravy Pour off all the fat from the tin and add a little boiling stock or water, stirring well in order to mix in any meat juices. Add as much extra liquid as required, season and add gravy browning, if necessary.
Thick gravy Pour off all but about 15 ml (1 tbsp) dripping from the tin and add to this 5–10 ml (1–2 level tsp) flour, according to the thickness of gravy required. Stir it over a low heat until smooth and lightly browned, then draw the tin off the heat and add about 300 ml (½ pint) stock or vegetable water. Return the tin to the heat and stir until the gravy boils and thickens. Season to taste and colour if necessary.

POULTRY AND GAME

Recipes give 4 servings, unless otherwise indicated

Poultry includes chickens, guinea fowls, ducks, geese and turkeys. Quite a lot of it nowadays is frozen, which means there is a good all-the-year-round supply (see notes below on frozen poultry). Most poultry is sold ready for cooking – that is, cleaned, plucked and trussed. Both fresh and frozen chickens and ducks, and often turkeys are available in separate joints as well as whole.

Hanging and storing Poultry should be hung for 2–3 days after killing before it is cooked. In cold weather it can if necessary be hung for about a week but, unlike game, it is not kept until it is 'high'. Poultry is usually plucked before hanging (see below), though this is not essential, but the inside should be left in.

Hang the bird by the feet in a cool, airy larder and protect it from flies, using muslin if the larder is not fly-proof. If poultry is to be put in a refrigerator, remove the inside and wrap the bird loosely or put it in a covered dish.

Frozen poultry Deep-frozen poultry must be allowed to thaw out at room temperature; the time required depends on the size of the joint or bird – single joints take from about 1 hour and large turkeys up to 24–48 hours. If you need to speed up the defrosting process, hold the bird under cold (not hot) running water.

The giblets are usually wrapped in polythene and placed inside the body cavity, so remove them before cooking the bird. Frozen birds are usually sold ready for stuffing. We include also a few recipes for game.

Stuffings and sauces

Recipes for Herb Stuffing and Sage and Onion Stuffing appear on page 71. Here are some others:

Sausage stuffing

1 large onion, skinned and chopped
450 g (1 lb) pork sausagemeat
25 g (1 oz) lard
salt and pepper
10 ml (2 level tsp) chopped parsley
5 ml (1 level tsp) mixed herbs
25 g (1 oz) fresh breadcrumbs (optional)

Mix the onion with the sausagemeat. Melt the lard and fry the sausagemeat and onion lightly for 2–3 minutes. Add the rest of the

ingredients and mix well. Use with chicken; for turkey, double the quantities.

Chestnut stuffing

50 g (2 oz) bacon, rinded and chopped
100 g (4 oz) fresh white breadcrumbs
5 ml (1 level tsp) chopped parsley
25 g (1 oz) butter or margarine, melted
grated rind of 1 lemon
225 g (8 oz) chestnut purée (see note)
salt and pepper
1 egg, beaten

Fry the bacon gently in its own fat for about 3–5 minutes, until crisp. Drain and add the rest of the ingredients, binding with the beaten egg.

This stuffing is suitable for a turkey.
Note Chestnut purée may be made from fresh chestnuts. Boil 450 g (1 lb) chestnuts for 2 minutes to soften the skins, remove from the heat and peel them while they are hot. Simmer the peeled chestnuts in milk for about 40 minutes, until soft. Sieve them or put them in an electric blender.

Apricot stuffing

75 g (3 oz) dried apricots
75 g (3 oz) fresh breadcrumbs
1·25 ml (¼ level tsp) mixed spice
1·25 ml (¼ level tsp) salt
1·25 ml (¼ level tsp) pepper
15 ml (1 tbsp) lemon juice
25 g (1 oz) butter or margarine, melted
1 small egg, beaten

Soak the apricots overnight in cold water. Drain off the liquid, chop the fruit, stir in the remaining ingredients and bind with the egg.

Use for stuffing a chicken, or make double the quantity for stuffing the neck end of the turkey.

Bread sauce

1 medium onion, skinned
2 cloves
400 ml (¾ pint) milk
salt
a few peppercorns
20 g (¾ oz) butter or margarine
75 g (3 oz) fresh white breadcrumbs
½ small bayleaf

Stud the onion with the cloves, place in a saucepan with the milk, salt and peppercorns; bring almost to boiling point and leave in a warm place for about 20 minutes, in order to extract the flavour from the onion. Remove the peppercorns and add the fat and crumbs, with the bayleaf. Mix and cook very slowly for about 15 minutes, then remove the onion.

If liked, remove the onion before adding the breadcrumbs, but a better flavour is obtained by cooking it with the crumbs, as this allows the taste of the onion to penetrate them.

Serve with roast chicken, turkey or pheasant.

Chicken recipes

When buying a fresh (non-frozen) bird, feel the tip of the breast-bone with the thumb and finger. In a young bird it is soft and flexible; if it is hard and rigid the bird is probably too old to roast satisfactorily and will have to be steamed or boiled. Look at the feet also – in a young bird they are smooth with small (not coarse) scales and with short spurs.

Many different terms have been used at times to classify chickens, but the main categories nowadays are:

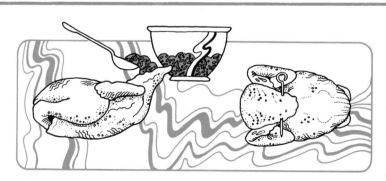

Spooning stuffing into the neck end of a chicken and securing the folded over neck skin with a skewer

Crunchy fried drumsticks with relish and Chicken sauté with pineapple (see page 76

Poussins Very small chickens, 450–900 g (1–2 lb); 6–8 weeks old; one serves 1–2 people.

Broilers Small birds 1·1–1·6 kg (2½–3½ lb); 12 weeks old; one serves 3–4 people. (Frozen chickens are usually broilers.)

Large roasters Generally young cockerels or hens, but may be capons. 'Young roasters' are 1·8–2·3 kg (4–5 lb) and one serves 5–6 people; capons weigh up to 3·6 kg (8 lb) and one serves 6–10 people.

Boiling fowls Older, tougher birds 1·8–3·2 kg (4–7 lb). They should be 18 months old, but may in some cases be older. Usually served in casseroles or made-up dishes; allow 100–175 g (4–6 oz) meat per person.

Roast chicken

When you buy a chicken it will usually be already prepared for cooking, so all you need do is stuff it if you wish. Different stuffings can be used, to give variety.

Make up the chosen stuffing. Loosen the chicken's wings, so that you can pull up the flap of skin over the breast, and fill the cavity with the forcemeat, making the breast a good shape. Remember that the stuffing, being made of bread or rice, will swell somewhat, so don't pack too tightly. Pull the flap down again and secure it with a skewer. (See page 72).

Put the chicken in a roasting tin, cover the breast with fat bacon and put some dripping over the rest of the bird. Roast in the oven at 200°C (400°F) mark 6 for 45–60 minutes, according to size; baste occasionally.

Serve the chicken with bread sauce and gravy and, if desired, garnish with bacon rolls and chipolata sausages. As very young chickens are delicately flavoured, you may not always want to stuff them, so try just rubbing the inside with a piece of garlic and adding a knob of butter; reduce the cooking time to about 45 minutes.

Gravy Remove the chicken to a hot dish, and pour away most of the dripping from the tin, leaving about 15 ml (1 tbsp): add 10 ml (2 level tsp) flour and stir in 300 ml (½ pint) giblet stock. Season well and bring to the boil, stirring well all the time. Add a little gravy browning if necessary.

Chicken roasted in foil

Wrap the chicken entirely in foil, making the join along the top, and roast in the oven at 200°C (400°F) mark 6 for 1 hour. Undo the join and loosen the foil for the last 10 minutes of the cooking time, so that the bird can brown, which makes it look more attractive. Serve with the usual accompaniments.

Chicken roasted on a spit

Some cookers are provided with a spit which can be attached to the roasting tin. This provides a very good way of roasting young chickens, as the birds can be evenly browned all over and the fat simply drips into the tin.

Put the chicken on to the spit and brush it with melted fat, place in position and roast for 50–60 minutes, according to size – see the book given with your cooker for details. Baste the chicken with the fat in the tin. Serve in the usual way, or with salad.

Baked chicken with cheese sauce

Divide a chicken into joints, put in a roasting tin with some fat and cook in the oven at 200°C (400°F) mark 6 for about 45 minutes, until tender. Place in an ovenproof dish, coat with 300 ml (½ pint) well-flavoured cheese sauce and put under the grill for a few minutes, until pale golden brown.

Fried chicken

Joint the chicken and cut the breast away from the bone, keeping the pieces as large as possible. Dip each piece in egg and fresh white breadcrumbs and fry in hot fat until golden brown and tender – 10–15 minutes. Serve at once with peas, sweetcorn fritters and mushroom sauce. Alternatively, garnish with grapes which have been peeled and tossed in melted butter.

French fried chicken

100 g (4 oz) flour
150 ml (¼ pint) milk
1 egg
15 g (½ oz) butter or margarine, melted
1 chicken, jointed
fat for frying

Make a batter with the flour, milk, egg and melted fat, beating it well. Dip each piece of chicken into the batter and then fry in hot fat until golden brown. Finish cooking in the oven at 180°C (350°F) mark 4 until the chicken is tender – about 30 minutes. Serve with a good tomato sauce (see page 36).

Southern-style fried chicken

Cut a broiler into 4 pieces, dip quickly in and out of cold water and drain. Dip each piece into seasoned flour until thoroughly coated. Fry the chicken in hot fat until each piece is tender and brown on both sides. Arrange on a hot dish, garnish with peas and keep hot while you make the gravy. Put 30 ml (2 tbsp) of the fat used for frying into a

saucepan, add 15 ml (1 level tbsp) flour, and stir in 150 ml (¼ pint) milk or cream and 15 ml (¼ pint) giblet stock; if desired, add few sliced mushrooms. Allow to cook for minute or two. Season well before serving

Deep-fried whole poussins

Small, tender birds are excellent fried whole – in fact, it is the quickest way of cooking them and gives a deliciously appetising crisp finish to the skin. Buy poussins weighing about 450 g (1 lb) each. Get ready a pa large enough to hold one, with enough o to cover the bird. Remove the giblets from inside the poussin and dry the bird. Hea the oil to 171°C (340°F) and carefully lowe the bird into it. Cook (uncovered) over moderate heat for 15 minutes, turning th bird several times during the cooking Repeat with the other poussins and serve hot or cold.

The above method of cooking can be used when you wish to make poussin flambé – an excitingly spectacular dish for special occasion.

Put the cooked poussin on a warmed serving dish. Warm 1 wineglass of brand and just before serving the poussin, se light to the spirit and pour it over the bird while it is still flaming.

Serve with a green salad and new pot atoes.

Chinese fried chicken

1 large chicken
90 ml (6 tbsp) soy sauce
90 ml (6 tbsp) sherry
5 ml (1 level tsp) sugar
2 spring onions, trimmed and chopped
flour
fat or oil for deep frying

Cut the chicken into about 12 pieces and soak them in the soy sauce, sherry, suga and onions for about 1 hour. Drain the chicken and dip each piece in flour. Fry in hot fat for about 5 minutes, until golden brown. Serve with plain boiled rice, adding a little soy sauce and sherry. (Any soy sauce and sherry that is left over can be used in sauces and soups.) *Serves 4–6*

Matabele fried chicken

1 chicken, jointed
olive oil
salt and pepper
4 rashers of bacon, rinded and sliced
1 red pepper, seeded and sliced
1 green pepper, seeded and sliced
1 large onion, skinned and sliced
325 g (12 oz) rice
2 rounds of pineapple
chopped chives

Marinade the chicken in seasoned olive oil for about 30 minutes. Boil the giblets to make stock for the rice. Heat 30 ml (2 tbsp) oil in a frying pan and fry the bacon, peppers and onion. Then add the rice and fry until it becomes opaque. Add enough chicken stock to cover the rice, then pour in one and a half times as much again. Season well and simmer gently until all the liquid is absorbed and the rice is tender. Add the diced pineapple 5 minutes before the rice finishes cooking. Meanwhile, fry the chicken in hot oil until tender and golden brown. Serve it on the rice, sprinkled with chopped chives.

This makes a good buffet party dish.

Grilled chicken

Young, small and tender broilers are very good when grilled. Split the chicken down the back, but without cutting through the skin of the breast, then flatten the bird out, removing the breastbone and breaking the joints where necessary. Skewer the legs and wings closely to the body. Alternatively, divide it into portions. Brush over with melted butter or oil, sprinkle with salt and pepper and put on the greased grid, skin side up. Cook under a moderate heat for 15 minutes, then turn the chicken and grill on the underside for a further 15 minutes or until tender. Serve garnished with watercress and accompanied by a clear giblet gravy.

Another method is to split the chicken then, after brushing it with oil, to sprinkle it with a mixture of very finely chopped onion, parsley and fresh white breadcrumbs and cook as above. Serve garnished with watercress and accompanied by brown or tomato sauce.

Devilled grilled chicken

1 chicken
22.5 ml (1½ level tbsp) curry powder
60 ml (4 tbsp) honey
60 ml (4 tbsp) French mustard

Cut the chicken into 4 pieces and rub all over with curry powder. Mix the honey, mustard and remaining curry powder and brush some of the mixture over the chicken. Grill the chicken for about 15 minutes, turning it every 5 minutes and basting with the sauce. Serve on rice, accompanied by a green salad.

Chicken poached in white wine

Cut the chicken into joints and put these into a flat saucepan. Add a bayleaf and a piece of parsley. Pour in enough white wine to cover the chicken almost entirely. Simmer very gently for 40 minutes, until the chicken is tender, then lift out the bird, drain it and place in a serving dish. Make a sauce as follows: melt 50 g (2 oz) butter or margarine, add 50 g (2 oz) flour and gradually stir in 600 ml (1 pint) of the strained wine; add some salt, bring to the boil and add 15 ml (1 tbsp) cream or top of the milk. Pour this over the bird and serve at once.

Sweet-sour chicken

1 small can pineapple pieces
175 g (6 oz) mushrooms, quartered
75 ml (5 tbsp) dry white wine
4 chicken joints
15 ml (1 tbsp) oil
25 g (1 oz) butter or margarine
142-ml (5-fl oz) carton soured cream
300 ml (½ pint) chicken stock
10 ml (2 tsp) lemon juice
15 ml (1 level tbsp) cornflour
25 g (1 oz) roasted almonds
salt and pepper

Drain the pineapple pieces and place them in a saucepan with the mushroom quarters and white wine; simmer gently for 5–7 minutes. Sauté the chicken joints in the oil and fat until they are a light golden brown. Transfer to a 1·7-litre (3-pint) casserole. Remove the mushrooms and pineapple from the heat and carefully blend a little of the liquor with the soured cream. Return this mixture to the pan and heat gently, but do not boil. Pour the pineapple and mushrooms over the chicken joints. Blend the stock, lemon juice and cornflour together and add to the fat remaining in the pan; bring to the boil and boil for 1 minute. Add the roasted almonds and seasoning and pour over the chicken joints. Cook in the oven at 150°C (300°F) mark 2 for 1½ hours.

Chicken Kiev

4 large chicken breasts, skinned (about 225 g (8 oz) each, with bone)
100 g (4 oz) butter
grated rind of ½ lemon
15 ml (1 tbsp) lemon juice
15 ml (1 tbsp) chopped parsley
1 clove garlic, skinned and crushed
25 g (1 oz) seasoned flour
1 egg, beaten
100 g (4 oz) fresh white breadcrumbs
fat or oil for deep frying

Using a small sharp knife, carefully work the flesh off the bone. Take care to keep the flesh in one piece. With a slightly dampened heavy knife beat out each piece. Work together the butter, lemon rind, juice, salt, pepper, parsley and garlic. Place it on a sheet of non-stick or waxed paper, form into a roll and chill until firm. Cut into 4 pieces and place one on each piece of chicken; roll up, folding the ends in to enclose the butter completely and secure with cocktail sticks. Coat with seasoned flour, then in the beaten egg and breadcrumbs, patting the crumbs well in. Chill until required. Heat the oil to 170°C (325°F).

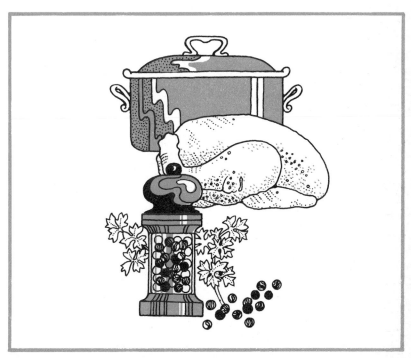

Place 2 chicken portions in a frying basket and carefully lower into the oil; fry for about 15 minutes and drain. Fry the remaining chicken. Serve at once, on a bed of savoury rice.

Chicken à la crème

1 roasting chicken
2 small onions, skinned and sliced
25 g (1 oz) butter or margarine
30 ml (2 tbsp) oil
salt
25 g (1 oz) flour
150 ml (¼ pint) dry white wine
a bouquet garni
142-ml (5-fl oz) carton single cream
black pepper (optional)

Joint the chicken. Sauté the chicken joints and onions in the fat and oil. Season with salt, reduce the heat, cover and cook for 20 minutes. When the joints are nearly done, remove the onions (which are used for flavouring only); stir in the flour. Cook for a minute or two, without browning. Add the wine and bouquet garni and continue to cook for a further 10–15 minutes. Add the cream very carefully to the wine in the pan, but do not allow to boil. Remove the joints and place on a serving dish. Discard the bouquet garni, pour the remaining sauce over the chicken and grind some black pepper over it before serving.

Crunchy fried drumsticks with relish

Illustrated in colour on page 73

6 chicken drumsticks
150 ml (¼ pint) evaporated milk
100 g (4 oz) cornflakes, crushed
salt and pepper
25 g (1 oz) butter or margarine

For the relish
2 sweet red peppers
4 large ripe tomatoes, skinned
5 ml (1 level tsp) sugar
60 ml (4 tbsp) oil
30 ml (2 tbsp) red wine vinegar
1 clove of garlic, skinned and crushed
5 ml (1 level tsp) tomato paste
5 ml (1 level tsp) paprika
5 ml (1 level tsp) salt
2·5 ml (½ level tsp) freshly ground
    pepper

Remove the skin from the drumsticks and dip each one first in evaporated milk and then in the crushed cornflakes. Season with the salt and pepper, then place on a baking sheet. Dot with the fat and bake in the oven at 190°C (375°F) mark 5 for 30–40 minutes.

76

To make the relish, discard the seeds from the peppers and cut into strips. Cut the tomatoes into 1.25-cm (½-inch) slices. Combine with the peppers and sprinkle with the sugar. In a pan, bring the oil to the boil with the vinegar, garlic, tomato paste, paprika, salt and pepper. Pour over the peppers and tomatoes, spoon through and cool. Serve with the chicken drumsticks.

Coq au vin

75 g (3 oz) bacon, rinded and chopped
175 g (6 oz) mushrooms, sliced
15 button onions (or 4 medium onions,
    skinned and sliced)
25 g (1 oz) butter or margarine
15 ml (1 tbsp) oil
4 chicken joints
¾ bottle of red wine
15 ml (1 level tbsp) cornflour
75 ml (5 tbsp) brandy
5 ml (1 level tsp) sugar
a pinch of grated nutmeg
salt and pepper
a bouquet garni

Sauté the bacon, mushrooms and onions in the fat and oil until they are golden brown. Remove from the pan and place half of the mixture in a 1·7-litre (3-pint) casserole. Sauté the chicken joints until golden brown; remove from the pan and place in the casserole. Add the remaining bacon, mushrooms and onions to the casserole. Gradually stir the blended wine and cornflour into the fat remaining in the pan; bring to the boil and allow to cook for 1–2 minutes. Add the brandy and pour over the joints in the casserole. Finally, add the sugar, nutmeg, salt, pepper and bouquet garni and cook in the oven at 180°C (350°F) mark 4 for 45 minutes, or until the chicken is tender. Before serving, remove the bouquet garni.

Chicken jambalaya

½ cooked chicken
2 onions, skinned and sliced
1 green pepper, seeded and chopped
2 sticks of celery, trimmed and sliced
30 ml (2 tbsp) oil
100 g (4 oz) mushrooms, sliced
325 g (12 oz) fresh tomatoes, skinned
    and quartered
150 ml (¼ pint) chicken stock
150 ml (¼ pint) dry white wine
175 g (6 oz) long-grain rice
100 g (4 oz) cooked ham, chopped
pepper

Cut the chicken flesh into cubes. Sauté the onions, pepper and celery in the oil until they are golden brown. Add the mush-

rooms, tomatoes, stock, wine and rice and cook gently on top of the stove until the rice is tender (15–20 minutes). Add the chicken and ham and heat through. Season to taste and turn into a serving dish.

French-style roast chicken

1·1–1·4 kg (2½–3 lb) roasting chicken
5–6 sprigs of tarragon or parsley
75 g (3 oz) unsalted butter
salt and pepper
50 g (2 oz) butter or margarine, melted
2 rashers of bacon, rinded
150 ml (¼ pint) chicken stock
150 ml (¼ pint) dry white wine
watercress to garnish
25 g (1 oz) flour

Wipe the inside of the chicken, then put the sprigs of tarragon or parsley inside it, with the unsalted butter and some pepper. Brush the breast of the bird with the melted fat. (Alternatively, cover with the rashers of bacon or, if preferred, use both fat and bacon.) Put the bird in a roasting tin, add the stock and wine and cook in the oven at 200°C (400°F) mark 6 for 45–50 minutes, basting every 15 minutes with the stock. Alternatively, roast it on a spit, if available. Remove the bacon during the last 15 minutes, to let the breast brown. Place the chicken on a serving dish and garnish with watercress. Thicken the liquor with 25 g (1 oz) flour and season to taste; serve separately.

Chicken sauté with pineapple

Illustrated in colour on page 73

700 g (1½ lb) poussin
25 g (1 oz) butter or margarine
15 ml (1 tbsp) oil
50 g (2 oz) onion, skinned and chopped
50 g (2 oz) button mushrooms, sliced
227-g (8-oz) can pineapple pieces,
    drained
150 ml (¼ pint) chicken stock
salt and pepper
30 ml (2 level tbsp) cornflour
25 g (1 oz) anchovies, drained
4 stuffed olives, sliced

Split the poussin in two and wipe the halves. Heat the fat and oil in a frying pan and sauté the poussin well on all sides until evenly browned. Transfer to a small casserole dish in which the halves fit side by side. Re-heat the juices in the frying pan and fry the onion and mushrooms together until the onion is transparent. Add the pineapple, stock and seasoning and pour over the poussin in the casserole. Cover the dish and cook in the oven at 200°C (400°F)

Hot chicken and pepper pie
(see page 80).

mark 6 for about 40 minutes until tender. Drain the poussin and keep warm. Blend the cornflour with a little water, combine with the sauce and heat gently to thicken. Adjust the seasoning to taste and pour over the poussin. Cut the anchovies into strips with scissors, arrange in a lattice over the poussin and place slices of olive in between. Serve immediately. *Serves 2*

Chicken Marengo

4 chicken joints (frying)
45–60 ml (3–4 tbsp) oil
100 g (4 oz) mushrooms, sliced
150 ml (¼ pint) rich brown sauce
150 ml (¼ pint) tomato sauce
300 ml (½ pint) chicken stock
5 ml (1 tsp) tomato paste
30 ml (2 tbsp) medium sherry
a bouquet garni
salt and pepper

Sauté the chicken joints in the oil until golden brown. Transfer them to a large casserole. Add the mushrooms to the fat remaining in the pan and sauté until tender; remove from the pan and add to the casserole. Mix together the brown sauce, the tomato sauce, chicken stock, tomato paste and sherry and heat: then pour over the chicken joints. Add the bouquet garni to the casserole, season, cover and cook for 45 minutes in the oven at 180°C (350°F) mark 4. Remove the bouquet garni before serving.

Chicken risotto with bananas

700 g (1½ lb) cooked chicken
a bouquet garni
salt and pepper
900 ml (1½ pints) chicken stock
2–3 onions, skinned
100 g (4 oz) mushrooms
40 g (1½ oz) dripping
325 g (12 oz) rice
4 bananas
grated cheese

Cut the chicken flesh into neat pieces and boil the bones with the bouquet garni and seasoning to make the stock. Chop the onions and half the mushrooms and fry in the dripping, then add the rice and fry this until opaque. Add the boiling stock and some salt and cook gently until the liquor is absorbed and the rice tender: do not stir while it is cooking, but if necessary fork it gently. Lay the chicken on top of the rice for about 10 minutes, to heat through. Fry the remaining mushrooms and the bananas for a garnish. Put the rice and chicken on an ovenproof dish, sprinkle with cheese and

brown under the grill. Serve with green salad. *Serves 6*

Chicken bourguignon

1 chicken
butter or margarine
3–4 button onions, skinned
3 rashers of bacon, rinded and diced
a bouquet garni
salt and pepper
1 wineglass of red Burgundy
50 g (2 oz) mushrooms, sliced
mashed potatoes

Joint the chicken, fry it in the fat with the onions and bacon until brown. Add the bouquet garni, salt, pepper and wine, cover with a lid and simmer gently until the chicken is tender – about 30 minutes. Meanwhile fry the mushrooms; 10 minutes before the end of the cooking time remove the bouquet garni and add the mushrooms. Serve in a border of mashed potato.

Chicken au gratin

1·8 kg (4 lb) chicken
seasoned flour
butter and oil for browning
heated chicken stock
50 g (2 oz) butter or margarine
40 g (1½ oz) flour
salt and pepper
60 ml (4 tbsp) fresh white breadcrumbs
60 ml (4 tbsp) grated cheese

Joint the chicken and dredge with seasoned flour. Brown in hot fat on all sides. Cover with the stock and simmer until the chicken legs are tender. Lift out the chicken and put into an ovenproof dish. Melt the fat and stir in the flour, cook without colouring and then add about 400 ml (¾ pint) of the chicken stock. Season well to taste and pour over the chicken. Sprinkle with the breadcrumbs and cheese mixed together and bake in the oven at 200°C (400°F) mark 6 or place under the grill until the surface is brown. *Serves 6*

Viennese chicken

1 chicken
juice of 2 lemons
olive oil
1 bayleaf
a little thyme and parsley
1 egg
breadcrumbs
fat or oil for frying
1 egg yolk
150 ml (¼ pint) milk
100 g (4 oz) small mushrooms
salt and pepper
chopped parsley to garnish

Joint the chicken and marinade for about 2 hours in the juice of 1 lemon and some olive oil, with the bayleaf, thyme and parsley. Drain the chicken, dip in beaten egg, coat with breadcrumbs and fry in hot fat until golden brown and tender. Beat the egg yolk with the milk, add mushrooms, salt and pepper and stir over a gentle heat until thick. At the last minute pour in the remaining lemon juice and pour the sauce around the fried chicken. Garnish with chopped parsley.

Chicken hotpot

4 pieces of chicken
seasoned flour
50 g (2 oz) fat
1 onion, skinned and sliced
2–3 rashers of bacon, rinded and diced
225 g (8 oz) shelled peas
225 g (8 oz) carrots, pared and sliced
4 tomatoes, skinned and sliced
50 g (2 oz) long-grain rice
salt and pepper
150 ml (¼ pint) chicken stock
50–75 g (2–3 oz) frozen prawns

Dip the chicken pieces in seasoned flour and fry until golden brown in the hot fat; put on to a plate. Sauté the onion until golden. In a basin mix together the onion, bacon, peas, carrots, tomatoes and rice; add the seasoning. Arrange this mixture and the chicken pieces in layers in a casserole, then pour the stock over. Cover and cook for 1 hour in the oven at 190°C (375°F) mark 5; 10 minutes before serving, add the prawns.

Chicken Louisette

4 chicken joints
15 ml (1 tbsp) oil
50 g (2 oz) butter or margarine
1 onion, skinned and sliced
1 clove of garlic, skinned and crushed
25 g (1 oz) flour
150 ml (¼ pint) stock
150 ml (¼ pint) medium white wine
a bouquet garni
½ cucumber, peeled and sliced
50 g (2 oz) cooked ham, chopped
salt and pepper
2 egg yolks
45 ml (3 tbsp) single cream

Sauté the chicken joints in the oil and 25 g (1 oz) of the fat until they are golden brown, then remove from the pan. Add the onion and garlic to the fat and continue to brown. Sprinkle on the flour and cook for 1 minute. Gradually add the stock and wine, bring to the boil and cook until thickened. Replace the chicken joints, add the bouquet garni and simmer on top of the stove for 20–30 minutes. Cook the cucumber in the remaining fat. Add the ham and seasoning and simmer for a further 4–5 minutes. When the chicken joints are tender, strain off the liquor. Mix the egg yolks and cream and add a little of the chicken liquor to blend. Add this mixture and the remaining chicken liquor to the pan containing the cucumber and ham and heat very gently until the sauce thickens. Place the chicken joints on a serving dish and pour the sauce over.

As a variation, mushrooms may replace cucumber.

Spanish chicken

1 chicken
seasoned flour
50 g (2 oz) bacon, rinded and diced
50 g (2 oz) butter or dripping
2 Spanish onions, skinned and sliced
2 green peppers, seeded and sliced
225 g (8 oz) tomatoes, skinned
150 ml (¼ pint) sherry or stock
salt and pepper
chopped parsley to garnish

Joint the chicken and dip the pieces in the seasoned flour. Fry the bacon until cooked, then take it out and add the butter or dripping. Fry the chicken several pieces at a time, until all are browned on the surface, then transfer the bacon and the chicken to a casserole and add the onions, peppers and tomatoes, the sherry or stock and a little seasoning. Cover and cook gently for 30 minutes and serve the chicken garnished with chopped parsley.

Chicken galantine

1 large chicken
325 g (12 oz) sausagemeat
175 g (6 oz) cooked ham, chopped
2 hard-boiled eggs
salt and pepper
a little powdered spice
1 onion, skinned and sliced
1 carrot, pared and sliced
1 stick of celery, trimmed and sliced
1 wineglass of sherry
stock or water to cook the galantine
aspic, sliced tomato and lettuce to
**   garnish**

First, bone the chicken. To do this, first cut off the end joints of the wing pinions and the feet, severing these at the first joint of the leg. Begin boning at the neck and down the backbone. Using a small, sharp knife, carefully turn the flesh back from the bone. To do the wings and legs, cut through from the inside out to withdraw the bone, then turn them back again.

Spread the chicken out, skin side downwards and spread the sausagemeat over it. Arrange the ham over the sausage. Put the hard-boiled eggs along the centre, sprinkle with salt and pepper and a little spice. Roll up, making into a neat shape and tie securely in muslin.

Put the galantine into a saucepan with the vegetables, salt, sherry and stock and simmer it gently for about 2 hours. Take it out, re-tie the cloth as tightly as possible, then put it on a dish and put a weight on top. When it is cold, remove the cloth, brush with liquid aspic and garnish with chopped aspic, tomato and lettuce. *Serves 8*

Chicken in aspic

1 cooked chicken
600 ml (1 pint) aspic
1 hard-boiled egg
asparagus tips
150 g (5 oz) frozen peas

Cut up the chicken into small pieces. Make up the aspic and when it is cold, pour a little into an oblong mould; when this sets, decorate with hard-boiled egg and asparagus. Pour a little more aspic over the decoration and allow to set in the refrigerator. Mix the chicken with most of the aspic, keeping back just enough to mix with the peas, and pour it in; put the mould in a cold place to set. Meanwhile cook the peas, and when they are cold, mix with the remaining aspic and pour into the mould. Leave to set and turn out when required. Serve with salad.

Chaudfroid of chicken

1 chicken
radish, cucumber, truffles, hard-boiled
**   egg, etc**
aspic jelly
salad

For the chaudfroid sauce
tomato purée
300 ml (½ pint) white sauce
300 ml (½ pint) liquid aspic jelly

Steam the chicken, skin it and allow to become cold. Next make the chaudfroid sauce. Add sufficient tomato purée to the white sauce to colour it well, then mix with the aspic; pour over the skinned chicken when cold but not set. Allow to set firmly,

Chaudfroid of chicken

then decorate with pieces of radish, cucumber skin, etc, dipping these in cold liquid aspic jelly. Finally pour a thin layer of cold aspic over the chicken to hold the decorations in place.

Barbecued chicken

Tender young chickens are one of the best things to roast at an open-air barbecue.

Make a good fire – a glowing red fire without smoke – and if possible erect a revolving spit over it. Put the chicken on the spit, brush it over with fat or oil and roast over the hot coals for about 40 minutes, turning it round at intervals to cook and brown evenly. When the bird is cooked, it should be so tender that you can pull it apart. Serve it plain, or with a bowl of barbecue sauce (see below), into which the joints may be dipped.

Barbecue sauce for chicken

25 g (1 oz) dripping
3 large onions, skinned and chopped
450 g (1 lb) tomatoes, skinned and chopped
30 ml (2 level tbsp) flour
150 ml (¼ pint) stock
salt and pepper
a pinch of sugar
a pinch of mixed herbs

Melt the dripping and fry the onions until almost tender, then add the tomatoes. Continue frying for a few minutes, then add the flour and mix it in well. Gradually add the stock, bring to the boil and add the seasonings, with a pinch of mixed herbs. Allow to simmer gently for about 10 minutes, then sieve and re-heat before serving.

Hot chicken and pepper pie

Illustrated in colour on page 77

2 kg (4 lb) oven-ready chicken
flavouring vegetables
50 g (2 oz) butter or margarine
175 g (6 oz) onion, skinned and chopped
225 g (8 oz) red peppers, seeded and finely sliced
50 g (2 oz) green chillies, halved and seeded
60 ml (4 level tbsp) flour
600 ml (1 pint) chicken stock (see method)
100 g (4 oz) mature Cheddar cheese, grated
salt and pepper
369-g (13-oz) pkt frozen puff pastry, thawed
1 egg, beaten

Simmer the chicken in water with flavour-ing vegetables for about 2 hours. Reduce the liquor to 600 ml (1 pint) by rapid boiling, then strain. Melt the fat in a saucepan and sauté the onion, peppers and chillies for 10 minutes. If preferred, remove the chillies at this stage. Carve the chicken and cut the flesh into smallish pieces, discarding the skin. Place in a 1·7-litre (3-pint) pie dish with a funnel.

Stir the flour into the sautéed vegetables and slowly add the strained stock, stirring. Bring to the boil. When the stock thickens, add the cheese, adjust the seasoning and spoon over the chicken. When the filling is cool, cover with a puff pastry lid, scoring the pastry into a diamond pattern with a knife. Glaze with egg, place on a baking sheet and cook in the oven at 230°C (450°F) mark 8 for 30 minutes. Reduce the heat to 170°C (325°F) mark 3 and cook for a further 30 minutes. *Serves 6–8*

Other poultry and game recipes

Roast goose

Pluck the bird and remove the stumps from the wings. Cut off the feet and the wing tips at the first joint. Cut off the head, then, forcing back the neck skin, cut off the neck where it joins the back. Draw the bird and clean the inside with a cloth wrung out in hot water. Put a thick fold of cloth over the breast-bone and flatten it with a mallet or rolling pin. Stuff with sage and onion stuffing or a fruit stuffing.

Working with the breast side uppermost and tail end away from you, pass a skewer through one wing, then through the body and out again through the other wing. Pass a second skewer through the end of the wing joint on one side, through the thick part of the leg, through the body and out the other side in the same way. Pass a third skewer through the loose skin near the end of the leg, through the body and out the other side in the same way. Enlarge the vent, pass the tail through it and fix with a small skewer. Wind string round the skewers, keeping the limbs firmly in position, but avoid passing the string over the breast of the goose. Tuck the neck skin in under the string.

Sprinkle the bird with salt, put in a baking tin on a rack or trivet (as goose tends to be fatty) and cover with the fat taken from inside, then with greased paper. A sour apple put in the tin during the cooking adds flavour to the gravy.

Roast in the oven at 200°C (400°F) mark 6 for 15 minutes per 450 g (lb) plus 15 minutes, basting frequently. To cook by the slow method, roast in the oven at 180°C (350°F) mark 4 for 25–30 minutes per 450 g (lb). Remove the paper for the last 30 minutes, to brown the bird.

Serve with giblet gravy (made in the roasting tin after the fat has been poured off) and apple or gooseberry sauce. Apple rings which have been dipped in lemon juice, brushed with oil and lightly grilled, also make an attractive garnish.

Roast duck

Pluck, draw and truss in the usual way, except that the wings are not drawn across the back; tie the legs with fine string.

A young duckling does not require stuffing, but it is usual to stuff an older bird with sage and onion stuffing at the tail end. Sprinkle the breast with salt and pepper. Cook in the oven at 200°C (400°F) mark 6; allow 20 minutes per 450 g (lb). Remove the trussing strings and skewers; serve the bird garnished with watercress and accompanied by apple sauce, potatoes, peas and thin brown gravy. Orange salad is also a favourite accompaniment for roast duck.

Rouen duck

1 large duck
50 g (2 oz) butter or margarine
25 g (1 oz) shallots, skinned and chopped
25 g (1 oz) flour
300 ml (½ pint) chicken stock
1 wineglass claret
a bouquet garni
lemon juice

For the stuffing
heart and liver of the duck, chopped
30 ml (2 tbsp) fresh breadcrumbs
1 small onion, skinned and chopped
5 ml (1 tsp) chopped parsley
25 g (1 oz) butter or margarine
salt and pepper

First, make the stuffing. Mix all the ingredients for the stuffing together and stuff the duck with it. Sauté the duck lightly in the fat until golden brown; remove and place in a 1·7-litre (3-pint) casserole. Add the shallots to the remaining fat and lightly sauté until golden brown; add to the casserole. Make a roux with the remaining fat and the flour and gradually add the stock; finally add the claret. Pour over the duck in the casserole, add the bouquet garni and a good squeeze of lemon juice and cook for 1½ hours in the oven at 180°C (350°F) mark 4. Remove the trussing

Rich pigeon casserole (see page 83).

strings and put the duck on a serving dish. Strain the sauce over it.

Duck in red wine

1 duck
½ clove of garlic, skinned
50 g (2 oz) flour
400 ml (¾ pint) red wine
50 g (2 oz) mushrooms, sliced
1 bayleaf
sprigs of parsley
2·5 ml (½ level tsp) dried thyme
5 ml (1 level tsp) salt
450 g (1 lb) small onions, skinned
450 g (1 lb) small carrots, pared

Remove the skin and fat from the duck and place the skin with the giblets into a pan. Cover with water and simmer for 1 hour. Skim off the fat and cool the stock.

Cut the duck into joints. Heat 30 ml (2 tbsp) of the duck fat in a pan, then brown the duck joints on all sides. Remove them from the fat and put in a casserole. Add the crushed garlic to the fat and fry for 1 minute. Stir in the flour. Add the wine, mushrooms, bayleaf, parsley, thyme and salt. Bring to the boil, stirring constantly, until the sauce thickens.

Put the onions, carrots and duck giblets in the casserole, pour the sauce over, cover

Duck à la portugaise

1 roasting duck
15 ml (1 tbsp) oil
25 g (1 oz) butter or margarine
1 small onion, skinned and chopped
1 green pepper, de-seeded and finely chopped
225 g (8 oz) tomatoes, skinned and quartered (or a 226-g (8-oz) can)
½ small can of pimientos, finely chopped
25 g (1 oz) flour
150 ml (¼ pint) chicken stock
150 ml (¼ pint) red wine
a bouquet garni
a dash of paprika
salt and pepper

Joint the duck and sauté in the oil and fat until the joints are golden brown; remove from the heat and place in a 1·1-litre (2-pint) casserole. Sauté the onion and green pepper in the remaining fat until lightly browned. Add the tomatoes and pimientos and sprinkle in the flour; cook for 1–2 minutes. Gradually add the stock and wine and bring to the boil. Add the bouquet garni, a dash of paprika and seasoning to

and cook in the oven at 180°C (350°F) mark 4 for about 1¼ hours.

taste. Pour over the duck joints and cook in the oven at 180°C (350°F) mark 4 for 1–1½ hours, or until the duck is tender. Remove the bouquet garni before serving.

Salmi of poultry

1 duck (or any poultry or game in season), roasted
1 orange
1 shallot, skinned and chopped
900 ml (1½ pints) chicken stock
300 ml (½ pint) rich brown sauce
150 ml (¼ pint) red wine
15 ml (1 tbsp) port
50 g (2 oz) white grapes, skinned

Cut the bird into joints, remove the skin and break up the carcass into small pieces; put into a saucepan. Peel the orange and divide into sections. Add the orange peel, shallots and stock to the duck; bring to the boil and simmer for 30 minutes. Mix together the rich brown sauce, red wine and 150 ml (¼ pint) of the strained stock. Place the duck joints in a pan, add the mixed stock and sauce and simmer until heated through. Arrange the joints on a serving dish. Add the port to the sauce and reduce until the mixture is of coating consistency. Pour over the duck and garnish with the orange segments and grapes.

Casseroled pheasant

1 pheasant
50 g (2 oz) butter or margarine
100 g (4 oz) cooked ham, diced
salt and pepper
400 ml (¾ pint) stock
100 g (4 oz) button mushrooms
60 ml (4 tbsp) redcurrant jelly

Prepare the bird and fry on all sides in the melted fat until browned. Put in a casserole, add the ham, salt, pepper and stock and cook in the oven at 180°C (350°F) mark 4 for 2 hours. Add the mushrooms after about 1½ hours and stir in the jelly just before serving.

Rich pigeon casserole

Illustrated in colour on page 81

45 ml (3 tbsp) vegetable oil
4 large pigeons
salt and pepper
175 g (6 oz) button onions, skinned
100 g (4 oz) streaky bacon, rinded and
   chopped
30 ml (2 level tbsp) flour
300 ml (½ pint) chicken stock
300 ml (½ pint) red wine
30 ml (2 level tbsp) tomato paste
1·25 ml (¼ level tsp) dried thyme
1 bayleaf
100 g (4 oz) button mushrooms

Heat the oil in a pan and gently fry the seasoned pigeons, flesh side down, until golden brown. Drain and place in a large casserole. Add the onions and bacon to the pan and fry for 5 minutes. Drain and place in the casserole. Add the flour to the pan and cook for 1 minute. Gradually stir in the stock, wine, tomato paste, thyme and bayleaf. Bring to the boil, stirring. Add the mushrooms and pour into the casserole. Cover and cook in the oven at 170°C (325°F) mark 3 for about 1½ hours until the pigeons are tender. Remove the bayleaf before serving.

Pigeons à la Catalan

2 pigeons
15 ml (1 tbsp) oil
25 g (1 oz) butter or margarine
25 g (1 oz) ham, roughly chopped
25 g (1 oz) flour
15 ml (1 tbsp) tomato paste
150 ml (¼ pint) chicken stock
150 ml (¼ pint) dry white wine
1 strip of orange peel
3 cloves of garlic, skinned and crushed
a bouquet garni
salt and pepper

For the stuffing
pigeon livers, chopped
100 g (4 oz) fresh breadcrumbs
50 g (2 oz) ham, chopped
1 clove of garlic, skinned and crushed
15 ml (1 tbsp) chopped parsley
1 egg, beaten

Prepare the pigeons. Make the stuffing by combining the livers, breadcrumbs, ham, garlic and parsley with the beaten egg. Stuff the pigeons and sauté them in the oil and fat until golden brown; then transfer them to a 1·7-litre (3-pint) casserole. Sprinkle the chopped ham over the pigeons. Blend the flour with the fat remaining in the pan and make a roux. Gradually add the tomato paste, stock and wine, bring to the boil and cook for 1 minute. Remove from the heat and pour over the pigeons. Add the orange peel, garlic, bouquet garni and seasoning, then cook in the oven at 180°C (350°F) mark 4 for 35–45 minutes. Remove the bouquet garni before serving.

Wild duck with raisin stuffing

2 wild ducks
slices of fat bacon
orange-flavoured gravy or orange salad
watercress to garnish

For the stuffing
175 g (6 oz) fresh white breadcrumbs
4 sticks of celery, chopped
1 onion, skinned and sliced
175 g (6 oz) seedless raisins
chopped nuts
salt and pepper
1 egg
200 ml (⅓ pint) hot milk

Dress the birds. Combine together the breadcrumbs, celery, onion and raisins. Some chopped nuts may also be added. Season and bind together with the beaten egg and the milk. Stuff the birds with this mixture and sew them up or secure with small skewers. Place pieces of fat bacon over the birds and roast in the oven at 200°C (400°F) mark 6 for 20–30 minutes, taking care not to over-cook. Serve with a good gravy, with some orange juice added, or with a simple salad made by tossing sliced peeled oranges in a French dressing. Garnish with watercress.

CURRIES

Whether you use ready-prepared curry powder and/or paste, or mix your own, do remember that thorough cooking, especially during the preliminary frying, is needed to remove the raw flavour of the spices.

Always cook curries slowly, to develop the characteristic richness. Indian curry is rarely thickened with flour – the long cooking should give the required consistency. Cut the meat, poultry or fish into bite-sized portions, so that the curry can be eaten with a fork.

When you are frying the onions (and perhaps garlic), cook them slowly, with a lid on, to prevent browning.

Although true Indian curries do not include apple, in this country it is often used as a substitute for mangoes; again, the sultanas which we also include, might be used in an accompanying pellao (pilaff), but not in curry.

The custom of garnishing a dish of curry with rice, which has become traditional in Europe is not seen in the East, where the rice is served separately.

The rice should be the Patna or long-grain type.

In the East, curries are usually accompanied by a variety of side dishes – see the notes on page 90.

CURRY POWDER AND PASTE

Providing you can buy a reliable brand and use it while fresh, you can obtain a very pleasing result with a ready-prepared mixture. (Paste, incidentally, usually contains certain ingredients that keep better in this form than in a dry, powdered state.) However, you can achieve even better results by making your own mixtures from fresh spices, bought in seed or 'whole' form or already ground. Buy only a little at a time and keep spices and curry powder in airtight containers.

Home-made curry powder

25 g (1 oz) turmeric
15 g (½ oz) coriander seed
15 g (½ oz) red chillies
15 g (½ oz) black pepper
50 g (2 oz) cumin seed
40 g (1½ oz) fenugreek
15 g (½ oz) powdered ginger
5 ml (1 level tsp) poppy seed

Any ingredients which are not already powdered must first be crushed using a pestle and mortar. Mix all well together, then sift to remove any imperfectly

crushed seeds and pound these again before re-mixing. Store in an airtight jar.

This gives a powder of medium strength; for a hotter flavour, increase the quantity of chillies.

COCONUT AND COCONUT MILK

Grated fresh coconut or desiccated coconut may be added to a curry to give a mellow flavour.

Coconut milk is also a very common ingredient. For best results it should be made from a fresh nut, but desiccated coconut can be used. Grate the coconut and pour over it enough boiling water to cover. Leave for 20–30 minutes, to obtain a well-flavoured infusion, then squeeze the liquid out through a fine strainer. A thinner milk is obtained by using the coconut a second time.

Curry recipes

Curried eggs

5 eggs, hard-boiled
50 g (2 oz) butter or margarine
2 small onions, skinned and finely chopped
a small piece of apple, finely chopped
5–10 ml (1–2 tsp) curry powder
25 g (1 oz) flour
300 ml (½ pint) stock
salt
10 ml (2 tsp) lemon juice
stuffed olives to garnish

Curried eggs

Slice 3 of the eggs. Melt the fat, fry the onion lightly, add the apple, curry powder and flour and cook for a few minutes. Gradually add the stock, salt and lemon juice, boil up and skim, then simmer for about 15 minutes. Heat the sliced eggs in this sauce, then turn the mixture into a hot dish and surround with boiled rice. Garnish with olives and the remaining eggs, cut in wedges. Serve this mild curry with lemon, preserved ginger and coconut.

Calcutta beef curry

450 g (1 lb) stewing steak
5 ml (1 level tsp) ground coriander
5 ml (1 level tsp) turmeric powder
5 ml (1 level tsp) chilli powder
a pinch of black pepper
a pinch of ground ginger
300 ml (½ pint) thick coconut milk
1 onion, skinned and sliced
1 clove of garlic, skinned and crushed
25 g (1 oz) butter or margarine
stock
salt
lemon juice

Cut the meat into pieces, removing any fat. Mix the powdered ingredients and make into a paste with a little of the coconut milk. Fry the onion and garlic in the fat until tender and add the paste, then fry for a further 3–4 minutes. Add the meat and a little stock, bring slowly to the boil and simmer for about 1 hour. Add the remaining coconut milk, some salt and lemon juice and serve at once, accompanied by boiled rice and a fruit or vegetable sambol (see page 90).

Chicken Dopyaza

700 g (1½ lb) chicken, skinned and jointed
2.5 ml (½ level tsp) ground ginger
2.5 ml (½ level tsp) salt
450 g (1 lb) onions, skinned
½ clove of garlic, skinned and crushed
25 g (1 oz) butter or margarine
seeds of 1 cardamom
10 ml (2 level tsp) turmeric
5 ml (1 level tsp) ground cumin
10 ml (2 level tsp) ground coriander
142-ml (5-fl oz) carton yoghurt
300 ml (½ pint) water
4 peppercorns

If possible, use an enamelled iron casserole for this curry. Wipe the chicken, prick with a skewer, rub in the ginger and salt and leave for 30 minutes. Chop half the onions, and fry these with the crushed garlic in the fat until brown, then remove from the pan,

Bengal chicken curry (see page 87).

draining well. Cook the cardamom seeds in the fat for 1 minute, then add the other spices, yoghurt and chicken; simmer gently until nearly all the yoghurt has been absorbed. Pound the cooked onions (or put them in a liquidizer) and add with the water to the chicken. Slice the rest of the onions thinly, put on top with the peppercorns, cover the pan tightly and cook in the oven at 170°C (325°F) mark 3 for 1 hour. 'Dopyaza' means 'twice onion' – strictly speaking, this curry should contain onions in two different forms, added at two different stages of the cooking, as in this recipe.

Ceylon prawn curry

600 ml (1 pint) prawns or 12 Dublin Bay prawns
50 g (2 oz) butter or margarine
1 onion, skinned and finely chopped
1 clove of garlic, skinned and finely chopped
15 ml (1 level tbsp) flour
10 ml (2 level tsp) turmeric
5 ml (1 level tsp) ground cloves
5 ml (1 level tsp) ground cinnamon
5 ml (1 level tsp) salt
5 ml (1 level tsp) sugar
150 ml (¼ pint) coconut milk (see page 84)
300 ml (½ pint) stock
5 ml (1 tsp) lemon juice

Shell the prawns. Melt the fat and fry the onion and garlic lightly, then add the flour, turmeric, cloves, cinnamon, salt and sugar. Cook gently for 10 minutes and add the coconut milk and stock. Simmer gently for 10 minutes, add the cooked prawns and lemon juice, re-season as necessary and cook for a further 10 minutes. Garnish with a few prawns heated separately; serve this mild curry with boiled rice and a hot chutney.

Shrimps may be used instead of the prawns.

Pork and pineapple curry

450 g (1 lb) pork fillet
50 g (2 oz) butter or margarine
1 clove of garlic, skinned and crushed
1 medium onion, skinned and chopped
1 red pepper, seeded and sliced
15 ml (1 tbsp) shrimp or anchovy essence
40 g (1½ oz) fresh (or green) ginger, finely chopped
15 ml (1 level tbsp) grated lemon rind
5 ml (1 level tsp) ground coriander
50 g (2 oz) blanched almonds, chopped
300 ml (½ pint) water
312-g (11-oz) can pineapple chunks
1·25 ml (¼ level tsp) powdered saffron

Cut the pork into small pieces and sauté in the hot fat with the garlic, onion and pepper. Combine the fish essence, ginger, lemon rind, coriander powder and almonds. Add this mixture to the pork and continue frying gently for a few minutes, then add the water and cook until the meat is tender – about 1½ hours. Finally, add the pineapple chunks and saffron and cook for a few minutes longer. Serve with boiled rice.

Fish curry

450 g (1 lb) filleted fish (eg, cod or halibut)
2 small onions, skinned and sliced
1 clove of garlic, skinned and crushed
50 g (2 oz) butter or margarine
1 tomato, quartered
10 ml (2 level tsp) curry powder
salt to taste

Prepare the fish. Fry the onions and garlic in the fat, then add the tomato and 15 ml (1 tbsp) water, to make a thick paste. Sprinkle the fish with curry powder and salt, add to the pan and cook until golden brown. Pour in 200 ml (⅓ pint) warm water and let the curry cook in the pan with the lid on until the fish is tender when tested; take care not to let it break up. Serve with rice or puris (see page 88).

Lemon juice may be included if desired, and the tomato may be replaced by tomato paste, a little extra stock or water being added.

Vegetable curry

1 large cauliflower, cut in large pieces
6 tomatoes
6–8 small potatoes, peeled and quartered
100 g (4 oz) peas
100 g (4 oz) French beans, sliced
5 ml (1 level tsp) turmeric
22·5 ml (1½ level tbsp) mild curry powder
2·5 ml (½ level tsp) salt
50 g (2 oz) butter or margarine
6 small onions, skinned and finely shredded
1 clove of garlic, skinned and crushed
300 ml (½ pint) stock

Place the raw vegetables on a large plate. mix the spices and salt and sprinkle over the vegetables. Melt the fat in a heavy pan and sauté the finely shredded onions and garlic. Add the vegetables, then a little stock, cover, bring to the boil and simmer until tender. Serve with plain boiled rice.

Lamb kofta (Meat ball curry)

450 g (1 lb) lean lamb
2 large onions, skinned and sliced
100 g (4 oz) butter or margarine
1 full garlic bulb, skinned and minced
10 ml (2 level tsp) chilli powder
10 ml (2 level tsp) ground coriander
2·5 ml (½ level tsp) turmeric
5 ml (1 level tsp) ground cumin
1·25 ml (¼ level tsp) ground ginger
5 ml (1 level tsp) allspice
450 g (1 lb) tomatoes, skinned
400 ml (¾ pint) water
10 ml (2 level tsp) salt
1 sprig of mint

Mince the lamb. Fry the onions in the fat until soft and browned. Mix the garlic and the powdered ingredients (except for 2·5 ml (½ tsp) of the allspice) and blend with 15 ml (1 tbsp) water. Add to the onions, with the tomatoes; mix well and fry until the tomatoes are soft. Remove 15 ml (1 tbsp) of this mixture, then add the water and salt to the remainder and simmer for 10 minutes.

Mix the remaining allspice, the 15 ml (1 tbsp) tomato mixture, the mint and the minced meat and knead well. Form into small balls and drop them into the sauce. Simmer gently for 30 minutes, shaking the pan so that the koftas are well coated with the sauce.

Koftas, which are very popular in the Deccan and Central India, may be made from a great variety of ingredients.

Bengal chicken curry

Illustrated in colour on page 85

15 ml (1 tbsp) oil
2 onions, skinned and chopped
1 clove of garlic, skinned and crushed
5 ml (1 level tsp) dry mustard
5 ml (1 level tsp) curry powder
4 chicken joints
300 ml (½ pint) chicken stock
30 ml (2 tbsp) tomato paste
salt and pepper
watercress to garnish

Heat the oil and sauté the onions and garlic. Mix together the mustard and curry powder and rub into the chicken joints. Add the joints to the pan and brown lightly. Mix together the stock and tomato paste, pour over the chicken and add a little salt and

pepper. Cover and bake in the oven at 180°C (350°F) mark 4 for 1 hour. Serve this curry with yellow rice and various sambols. Garnish with watercress.

Dry veal curry

450 g (1 lb) lean veal
2 medium onions, skinned and finely chopped
1 clove of garlic, skinned and crushed
25 g (1 oz) butter or margarine
10 ml (2 level tsp) curry powder
5 ml (1 tsp) curry paste
salt to taste
a few pickled gherkins
10 ml (2 tsp) chutney
juice of ½ lemon
150 ml (¼ pint) stock

Cut the meat into small pieces. Fry the onions and garlic lightly in the fat. Add the curry powder and paste and cook thoroughly for about 5 minutes, stirring all the time. Add the meat and salt and cook until well browned. Finally, add gherkins, chutney, lemon juice and stock and cook very slowly for 2–2½ hours, stirring occasionally. Serve with plain boiled or yellow rice and lemon.

Madras curry (hot)

50 g (2 oz) chopped almonds
50 g (2 oz) butter or fat
2 onions, skinned and chopped
1 clove of garlic, skinned and crushed
5 ml (1 level tsp) ground coriander
5 ml (1 level tsp) black pepper
2·5 ml (½ level tsp) chilli powder
2·5 ml (½ level tsp) ground cardamom
2·5 ml (½ level tsp) ground cumin
a small piece of cinnamon stick
2·5 ml (½ level tsp) ground cloves
10 ml (2 level tsp) flour
600 ml (1 pint) stock or water
450 g (1 lb) meat, chopped
10 ml (2 level tsp) turmeric
5 ml (1 level tsp) sugar
salt
juice of 1 lemon

Cover the almonds with 150 ml (¼ pint) boiling water and leave for 15 minutes, then strain the infusion. Melt the fat and lightly fry the onions. Add the garlic, spices and flavourings (except turmeric), with the flour, cook for 5 minutes, then add stock and meat. Simmer until tender – 1½–2 hours. Add the almond infusion, turmeric, sugar and salt and simmer for 15 minutes; finally, add lemon juice to taste.

Note Serve this hot curry with plain boiled rice and various sambols, e.g. banana, cucumber (see page 90).

Dry beef curry

450 g (1 lb) stewing steak
15 ml (1 level tbsp) ground coriander
5 ml (1 level tsp) turmeric
1 bayleaf
2 cloves
1·25 ml (¼ level tsp) chilli powder
2·5 ml (½ level tsp) ground cumin
a pinch of ground cinnamon
tamarind water or diluted vinegar
50 g (2 oz) butter or margarine
1 onion, skinned and finely chopped
1 clove of garlic, skinned and finely sliced
5 ml (1 tsp) curry paste
300 ml (½ pint) stock or water
salt to taste

Cut up the meat. Mix the spices and tamarind water to form a paste. Melt the fat and fry the onion and garlic, then fry the spices and curry paste thoroughly, stirring constantly. Add the meat and cook slowly for about 1 hour, stirring occasionally. Add the stock, cover, and cook gently for another hour, until the liquid is absorbed. Adjust the seasoning, if necessary. Serve with rice or dhal (see page 88) and chutney.

Accompaniments for curries

Besides rice, these can include poppadums, chapattis, puris, chutneys, pickles, Bombay duck and innumerable 'sambols'. Some are usually bought ready prepared, like Bombay duck and poppadums; others can be made at home and some recipes are given here.

Sambols (see page 90) are served with the curry in scallop shells, silver bowls or other little dishes, which are grouped either on a large tray or in the centre of the table. Each guest is given a large platter and takes a little of everything.

Some simple accompaniments which need little or no preparation are gherkins, water-melon, guava jelly, green olives, preserved ginger and pickled mangoes.

Boiled rice

Method I Allow 225 g (8 oz) long-grain rice, 1·7 litres (3 pints) water and 5 ml (1 level tsp) salt for 4–6 persons. Put the washed rice in fast-boiling salted water and boil for 10 minutes, then drain it in a sieve and pour cold water through to get rid of the loose starch. Put the rice back into fresh boiling water and cook for 2–3 minutes, keeping the pan uncovered throughout cooking.

Drain the rice and serve at once, or keep it warm in the oven at 150°C (300°F) mark 2, covered with foil or a cloth.

Method II Soak the rice for 15–30 minutes in cold water and drain. Put in a pan with fresh cold water, which should come about 2·5 cm (1 inch) above the rice; add salt. Put the pan over a high heat, stirring occasionally to prevent sticking. Reduce the heat and cook gently until all the water is absorbed – about 20 minutes – by which time the rice should be tender. Remove from the heat, pour cold water over it, then drain thoroughly. Cover with a cloth and warm through in the oven at 150°C (300°F) mark 2.

To re-heat rice Put it in a pan of boiling salted water, stir and bring to the boil; drain well.

Yellow rice

Illustrated in colour on the jacket

225 g (8 oz) long-grain rice
10 ml (2 level tsp) salt
6 cloves
1 stick of cinnamon
3 bayleaves
4 whole black peppercorns
2·5 ml (½ level tsp) turmeric
a little melted butter
50 g (2 oz) sultanas
50 g (2 oz) blanched almonds

Place all the ingredients except the almonds and butter in a pan of boiling water and simmer for 12–15 minutes. Drain, removing the spices. Melt the butter in a small saucepan and sauté the almonds until golden brown. Stir into the rice and serve with meat curries or lamb kebabs (see page 43).

Pellao

2 onions, skinned
50 g (2 oz) butter or margarine
450 g (1 lb) long-grain rice
chicken stock
salt to taste
a few cloves
a little ground cardamom
a few pieces of stick cinnamon
a few peppercorns
a few sultanas

Mince 1 onion, fry it in the hot fat until pale golden brown, then add the uncooked rice and fry for about 5–6 minutes. Now add some stock, salt and the spices, adding more stock as the rice swells. When the rice is well cooked, put the pellao in the oven at 180°C (350°F) mark 4 for 30 minutes to dry it off (or it may be dried by placing it in a saucepan over a very gentle heat – but Indian cooks generally find the oven more satisfactory). Slice the other onion, fry with a few sultanas until it is golden brown and crisp and sprinkle the mixture over the rice. *Serves 8–10*

Saffron pellao

225 g (8 oz) long-grain rice
175 g (6 oz) butter or margarine
2 small onions, skinned and sliced
30 ml (2 tbsp) raisins or sultanas, stoned
30 ml (2 tbsp) almonds, blanched and toasted
2·5-cm (1-inch) cinnamon stick
seeds from 3 cardamoms
2 bayleaves
8 peppercorns
salt
stock or water
a few cooked peas
15 ml (1 tbsp) saffron water

Wash and drain the rice. Heat 50 g (2 oz) of the fat in a saucepan and fry the onions until golden brown. Now add the rice with the remaining fat and cook, stirring frequently, until the rice has absorbed most of the fat. Add the raisins, almonds, cinnamon, cardamoms, bayleaves, peppercorns and salt. Just cover with hot stock or water, cover the pan and simmer until the rice is tender and all the liquid absorbed. Add the peas and saffron water, stir lightly, put in an ovenproof dish and dry off in the oven at 180°C (350°F) mark 4.

Puris (Fried bread)

100 g (4 oz) wholemeal flour
salt and pepper
water to mix
fat for frying

Mix the flour and a little salt and pepper with some water to form a stiff dough. If time permits, allow the dough to stand for 1 hour. Roll out thinly and cut into 10-cm (4-inch) rounds. Fry in the hot fat, one or two at a time, holding them down with a wide draining slice to distribute the air, which gives the characteristic puffy shape. When golden brown, remove carefully, drain on absorbent paper and serve at once.

The puris may be rolled out and shaped beforehand; cover them with a damp cloth and cook immediately before they are required for serving.

Chapattis

These large, thin unleavened girdle cakes may be bought from some shops specializing in Eastern foods and from Indian restaurants.

Poppadums

Poppadums are savoury wafer-like biscuits, which are usually purchased, as they are laborious to make at home; stored in an airtight tin, they will keep for several months. White ones are fairly mild, red ones very hot. To cook poppadums, choose a frying pan much larger than the size of the raw biscuit, as they expand considerably during cooking. Allow 1–2 per person. Place them one at a time in hot fat and fry for about 20–30 seconds, keeping them flat by holding under with a flat draining spoon. When crisp, drain and serve hot.

The poppadums may be heated through in the oven or under the grill.

Use them as an accompaniment to rice or curry, or crumble them over the surface.

Dhal (Lentil purée)

100 g (4 oz) red lentils
300 ml (½ pint) cold water
salt and pepper
1 medium onion, skinned and chopped
fat for frying
25 g (1 oz) butter or dripping

Wash the lentils – there is no need to soak them – put them in the water, add pepper and salt and cook steadily, adding more water if they get too dry. Meanwhile, fry the onion. When the lentils are tender, remove them from the heat and stir vigorously. Add the butter or dripping and onion and stir well over the heat.

Yoghurt and cucumber

½ cucumber, peeled and thinly sliced
5 ml (1 level tsp) sugar
15 ml (1 tbsp) vinegar
2 tomatoes, chopped
½ small onion, skinned and chopped
½ green pepper or 2 small green chillies
1·25 ml (¼ level tsp) pepper
2·5 ml (½ level tsp) salt
284-ml (10-fl oz) carton natural yoghurt
chopped parsley to garnish

Place the cucumber in a bowl, sprinkle with sugar and vinegar and marinade for 10 minutes. In another bowl mix lightly the tomatoes, onion and green pepper; add the drained and seasoned cucumber. Mix with the yoghurt and garnish with parsley.

Bombay duck

This is actually a fish (bummalo), which is sold salted and dried. It is a very popular accompaniment to many curries and is also often used as an ingredient. The smell when

Egg and prawn mayonnaise (see page 94).

it is being prepared is rather unpleasant, but the taste is appetising.

Bake in a hot oven or toast under the grill until crisp and brown; if necessary, flatten during the cooking. Alternatively, fry in hot fat and drain well.

Break the Bombay duck into small pieces or crumble up and sprinkle over the curry at table.

Sambols

Coconut Slice or grate some fresh coconut and serve with chopped green and red peppers. Desiccated coconut may be substituted for fresh, when necessary.

Peppers Red and green peppers can be parboiled, sliced, egg-and-crumbed and then fried, or they can be sliced and used raw.

Bananas Use firm bananas; slice and sprinkle with salt, lemon juice and a little chilli powder.

Aubergine (Eggplant) Boil until soft, then skin, mash the pulp and add a little finely chopped onion, 1–2 chopped chillies, a little coconut milk to moisten and salt to taste.

Cucumber Fry a chopped onion and a garlic clove in a little oil until soft but not coloured; add chopped cucumber, with a little crumbled Bombay duck and curry powder, a squeeze of lemon juice and a little coconut milk. Simmer until the cucumber is just soft. Serve hot or cold.

Tomato Skin and slice several tomatoes, mix with some fresh or pickled green chillies, cut lengthwise, a pinch of ground red chillies and a squeeze of lemon juice; add salt to taste. Sprinkle with freshly grated or desiccated coconut and a little chopped onion.

Onions Slice thinly and add lemon juice, seasonings and some chopped fresh (or pickled) chillies.

Potatoes Cut several cold cooked potatoes into cubes and blend lightly with a few chopped green chillies, a little finely chopped onion or spring onion and some olive oil; season them to taste and add a little lemon juice. Alternatively, mix some cold mashed potato with desiccated coconut, coconut milk, a little chopped onion and a few coarsely chopped red chillies; add a little olive oil and lemon juice and season to taste.

Dried peas Soak the peas overnight, then simmer them until tender, drain and serve sprinkled with lemon juice and paprika pepper.

Eggs Cut 2 hard-boiled eggs lengthwise into quarters and lightly blend with 1 finely chopped small onion, 2 fresh green (or pickled) green chillies, coarsely chopped, 15 ml (1 tbsp) lemon juice and salt to taste. Sprinkle with fine desiccated coconut or preferably with fresh scraped coconut if this is available.

Pickles, chutneys and relishes

Very hot, pungent chutneys and pickles are served in the East, but in this country somewhat milder types are probably more popular. Mango chutneys, prepared in different ways to give a very sweet, a hot or a mild effect, are among the best-known kinds.

Salted mangoes are served as an accompaniment to fish curries; chopped mangoes, both green and ripe, also mango sauce, are often included in the actual curries.

Other items sold by firms specializing in Eastern foods include lime, green chilli, lemon, aubergine (brinjal), bamboo, sweet turnip and mustard pickles, tamarind chutney and guava jelly. The taste for some of these is, however, only gradually acquired by most Europeans.

Hot Indian chutney

700 g (1½ lb) marrow
900 g (2 lb) tomatoes, skinned and chopped
450 g (1 lb) onions, skinned and chopped
100 g (4 oz) shallots, skinned and chopped
1 clove of garlic, skinned and chopped
450 g (1 lb) sugar
25 g (1 oz) salt
700 g (1½ lb) apples, peeled, cored and chopped
2-cm (¾-inch) piece of whole root ginger
20 ml (4 level tsp) chillies
20 ml (4 level tsp) cloves
20 ml (4 level tsp) white peppercorns
25 g (1 oz) mustard seed
900 ml (1½ pints) vinegar

Sprinkle the vegetables and garlic with the sugar and salt and leave overnight. Put the apples with the prepared vegetables into a pan. Add the spices, tied in a muslin bag, and the vinegar, and boil together slowly for at least 4 hours, until the mixture is thick. Pot and cover. Store for several months before use.

EGG AND CHEESE COOKERY

Eggs

Store eggs in a cool place; if they are put in the refrigerator, keep them well away from the freezer and take them out some time before using, to give them time to reach room temperature, otherwise they crack when being boiled and are also difficult to whisk. Use the refrigerator racks or boxes provided, as these are designed to protect the eggs. Don't store eggs next to cheese, fish or onions, as they will absorb strong flavours.

The more lightly egg dishes are cooked, the better (except in the case of hard-boiled eggs). This applies particularly to fried and baked egg dishes and to omelettes, where too long cooking makes the eggs tough.

Cook custards and similar dishes containing eggs very slowly over a low heat or stand them in a water bath or double saucepan.

Cheese

Though cheese often requires months – sometimes years – to bring it to full maturity, once ripe it deteriorates comparatively rapidly. So buy only enough to last a few days to a week and store it in a cool place, such as a cold larder; cover it loosely to protect it from the air, but do not make it air-tight. If entirely exposed to the air, cheese will become hard and dry and if tightly covered it is likely to mould.

A refrigerator is not ideal for storing cheese, but if it must be used, the cheese should first be wrapped in cling film or foil or tightly covered.

The less cooking cheese has, the better. Over-heating tends to make it tough, so when making a dish such as Welsh Rarebit or cheese sauce, heat the cheese very gently and don't cook the mixture more than necessary once the cheese is added.

Egg dishes

Baked eggs

Place the required number of individual ovenproof dishes or cocottes on a baking sheet, with a knob of butter in each dish. Put them in the oven for 1–2 minutes, until the butter has melted. Break an egg into each dish, sprinkle with a little salt and pepper, place in the centre of the oven at 180°C (350°F) mark 4 and leave until the eggs are just set – about 5–8 minutes. Serve at once, plain for breakfast or with vegetables as a snack. If you don't wish to use the oven, prepare the eggs as above, sprinkle them with white breadcrumbs or grated cheese, then cook them under the grill until the yolks are just setting.

Flamenco eggs

2–3 slices of cooked ham
15 ml (1 tbsp) chopped onion
olive oil or butter
225 g (8 oz) tomatoes, skinned and chopped
225 g (8 oz) cooked peas
225 g (8 oz) cooked potatoes
a little good stock
225 g (8 oz) continental-type sausage, sliced
6 asparagus tips, cooked, and strips of sweet pepper to garnish
4 eggs

Cut the ham in small pieces and fry with the onion in the oil or butter until they begin to colour. Add the tomatoes, peas and potatoes, with stock to moisten, then sauté gently for a few minutes, stirring carefully. Add the sausage and put into an ovenproof dish; garnish with asparagus tips and sweet pepper, break the eggs on top and put into the oven at 220°C (425°F) mark 7 for a few minutes, until the eggs are set.

Scrambled eggs

Break the eggs separately then beat them together lightly, season to taste and add 15 ml (1 tbsp) milk for each egg. Melt a little butter in a small pan, allowing about 25 g (1 oz) for 4 eggs, then add the egg-and-milk mixture, stirring. Stir and cook slowly until creamy, pile the mixture on to buttered toast and serve at once.

Variations
Try adding (to a 4-egg mixture) 50 g (2 oz) lightly cooked chopped mushrooms; 2 skinned tomatoes, chopped and cooked with a diced rasher of fried bacon; 45–60 ml (3–4 tbsp) well-drained canned sweetcorn; 50 g (2 oz) chopped ham, tongue or other meat; leftovers of cooked fish, eg, fresh haddock, smoked haddock, kipper, removing all bones and skin and flaking it carefully.

Asparagus with poached eggs

1 bundle of asparagus
4 rounds of buttered toast
4 eggs
salt and pepper
chopped parsley or paprika pepper

Cook and drain the asparagus and keep it hot. Make and butter the toast and poach the eggs. Arrange the asparagus on the toast and top with the eggs; season and sprinkle with parsley or paprika pepper.

Mushroom-stuffed crisp rolls

4 crisp dinner rolls
25 g (1 oz) butter or margarine
1 small onion, skinned and chopped
50 g (2 oz) mushrooms, chopped
3 tomatoes, skinned and chopped
3 eggs
salt and pepper

Remove a lid from each roll and scoop out some of the soft inside. Melt the fat, add the vegetables and sauté gently for 5–10 minutes, until soft. Beat the eggs with some seasoning, pour into the pan and stir with a wooden spoon over a low heat until the mixture thickens. Pile it into the bread shells, replace the lids, put on a baking sheet and cook in the oven at 180°C (350°F) mark 4 for about 15 minutes, until the rolls are crisp and the filling thoroughly heated. Serve at once.

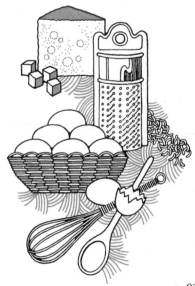

Potato nests

450 g (1 lb) creamed potatoes
4 eggs
salt and pepper
25 g (1 oz) cheese, grated

Pipe a border of creamed potato round 4 scallop shells or dishes (or put the potato into a greased ovenproof dish and make 4 wells in it). Break an egg into each dish (or well) and sprinkle with salt, pepper and grated cheese. Bake in the oven at 180°C (350°F) mark 4 until the eggs are set – about 10–15 minutes – and serve with green peas.

Eggs à la florentine

450 g (1 lb) spinach
salt and pepper
a small knob of butter or margarine
50 g (2 oz) Parmesan cheese, grated
4 eggs
30–45 ml (2–3 tbsp) single cream
a sprig of parsley to garnish

Wash the spinach well, put it into a pan with a little salt and just the water that clings to the leaves and cook for 10–15 minutes, until tender. Drain well, chop roughly and mix with the fat and seasoning. Put into an ovenproof dish and cover with most of the grated cheese. Break the eggs into a saucer and slide side by side into the cheese; bake in the oven at 180°C (350°F) mark 4 for 10 minutes. Remove from the

oven, spoon the cream over and sprinkle with the remaining cheese. Return the dish to the oven and bake for a further 10–15 minutes, until the eggs are firm. Serve garnished with parsley.

Alternatively, fill the bottoms of small individual casseroles with the spinach purée, add cheese and an egg to each and finish as above.

For a simpler dish, serve poached eggs on creamed spinach.

Savoury eggs

4 crumpets (pikelets)
butter or margarine
anchovy paste
4 poached eggs
chopped parsley

Toast and butter the crumpets, spread with paste, top with the eggs and sprinkle with parsley.

Scalloped eggs

Grease 4 scallop shells and put a sliced hard-boiled egg in each. Cut 4 anchovies in small pieces and mix with 15 ml (1 tbsp) capers and 300 ml (½ pint) white sauce. Pour this over the eggs, sprinkle with browned crumbs and re-heat for 10 minutes in the oven at 180°C (350°F) mark 4.

Egg ramekins

100 g (4 oz) cooked ham
50 g (2 oz) butter or margarine
25 g (1 oz) flour
300 ml (½ pint) milk
salt and pepper
4 eggs

Chop the ham finely. Make a white sauce with half the fat, the flour and the milk; season to taste and mix with the ham. Lightly butter 4 small individual dishes and spread the bottom and sides with the mixture. Break the eggs one by one into a cup, slide one into each dish, dot with the remaining fat and bake in the oven at 180°C (350°F) mark 4 until set – about 12 minutes.

Eggs in baked potatoes

4 large raw potatoes
25 g (1 oz) butter or margarine
salt and pepper
30 ml (2 tbsp) top of the milk
4 eggs

Scrub the potatoes then, using a sharp-pointed knife, mark around the tops in a circle. Bake the potatoes in the oven at 180°C (350°F) mark 4 for 1 hour, or until soft. Remove the insides of the potatoes and mash with butter or margarine, seasoning and milk. Return about half the mixture to each potato skin, break an egg in each, return them to the oven and cook until the egg has set. If liked, the rest of the creamed potato may then be piped round the top and the potatoes browned under the grill.

Egg fricassee

Illustrated in colour opposite

6 eggs
200 ml (⅓ pint) milk
slice onion, carrot, bay leaf, 6
**   peppercorns for flavouring**
25 g (1 oz) butter or margarine
30 ml (2 level tbsp) plain flour
142-ml (5-fl oz) carton soured cream
2·5 ml (½ level tsp) dried or 10 ml (2 tsp)
**   scissor-snipped fresh tarragon**
salt and pepper
sprig of fresh tarragon when available
212-g (7 ½-oz) packet frozen puff pastry

Place the eggs in boiling water to cover; boil very gently for 10 minutes. Remove, tap the shell and place in cold water. Bring the milk to the boil with the flavourings and leave to infuse for 10 minutes; strain. Melt the fat in a small heavy-based pan. Off the heat, stir in the flour, milk, soured cream, tarragon and seasoning. Return to the heat, bring to the boil, stirring all the time and simmer for

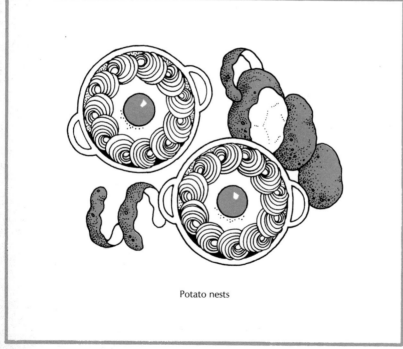

Potato nests

Egg fricassee
(see above).

about 5 minutes. Stir in the shelled and sliced eggs, reserving the yolk from one and simmer to warm the eggs; adjust the seasoning. Serve garnished with the reserved egg yolk (sieved), snipped tarragon, and accompanied by pastry triangles. For pastry triangles: roll out thawed pastry to an oblong 25·5 cm × 10 cm (10 × 4 inches). Divide into two lengthwise and cut each strip into ten triangles. Bake at 220°C (425°F) mark 7 for 12–15 minutes, or until golden brown and well risen.

Spicy ham and eggs

6 eggs
25 g (1 oz) butter or margarine
25 g (1 oz) flour
5 ml (1 level tsp) dry mustard
2·5 ml (½ level tsp) salt
a large pinch of pepper
300 ml (½ pint) milk
5 ml (1 tsp) grated horseradish
15 ml (1 tbsp) brown table sauce
15 ml (1 tbsp) chilli sauce
a dash of tabasco sauce
225 g (8 oz) cooked ham, diced
a few sliced stuffed olives
100 g (4 oz) sharp processed cheese, diced
grated cheese and breadcrumbs for topping

Hard-boil the eggs, peel and slice them. Make a spicy sauce as follows: melt the fat in a saucepan, stir in the flour, mustard, salt and pepper, then the milk. Cook, stirring until the mixture thickens. Stir in the horseradish and the brown, chilli and tabasco sauces. In a 900-ml (1½-pint) casserole, arrange layers of egg, ham, olives, cheese and sauce (reserving some egg and olives). Sprinkle with cheese and breadcrumbs and bake uncovered in the oven at 200°C (400°F) mark 6 for 25–30 minutes. Garnish with the remaining egg and olives. *Serves 6*

Oeufs soubise au gratin

450 g (1 lb) onions, skinned
salt and pepper
65 g (2½ oz) butter or margarine
75 g (3 oz) mature cheese, grated
50 g (2 oz) fresh breadcrumbs
4 eggs
15 ml (1 level tbsp) flour
300 ml (½ pint) milk
a pinch of marjoram

Roughly slice the onions and boil in salted water for 5 minutes; drain and chop finely. Melt 50 g (2 oz) of the fat, add the onion and cook with the lid on the pan until tender but not coloured; season. Meanwhile mix to-

gether the cheese and breadcrumbs and place half over the bottom of a greased ovenproof dish. Cover with half the onion. Soft-boil the eggs (ie, cook in boiling water for 4 minutes), then put immediately into cold water; carefully remove the shells. Place the eggs on the bed of onion, cover with a white sauce made from the remaining fat, the flour and the milk; season with pepper, salt and marjoram. Spoon the remainder of the onion on top of the sauce and finally add the rest of the cheese and the crumbs, dotting with pieces of butter. Place in the oven at 220°C (425°F) mark 7 and cook for 15 minutes.

Egg and prawn mayonnaise

Illustrated in colour on page 89

175 g (6 oz) long grain rice
1 large cucumber
30 ml (2 tbsp) single cream
300 ml (½ pint) mayonnaise
garlic salt
paprika pepper
4 hard-boiled eggs
175 g (6 oz) shelled prawns
watercress to garnish

Cook the rice in boiling salted water for 12 minutes. Drain, rinse in cold water and drain again. Peel the cucumber and cut into small chunks. Stir the cream into the mayonnaise, adding garlic salt to taste. Stir 45 ml (3 tbsp) mayonnaise into the rice and turn into a serving dish. Cut the eggs in half lengthways and place on top of the rice, cut side down. Coat the eggs in mayonnaise and dust with paprika. Arrange the cucumber and prawns down the sides of the dish. Garnish with watercress sprigs.

Egg flip and potato pie

2 eggs
150 ml (¼ pint) milk
salt and pepper
225 g (8 oz) cooked potatoes, sliced
100 g (4 oz) tomatoes, skinned and sliced
100 g (4 oz) Cheddar cheese, grated
chopped parsley to garnish

Beat the eggs thoroughly and add the milk, salt and pepper. Grease a pie dish and put in a layer of potatoes and tomatoes, adding a sprinkling of cheese, salt and pepper. Add 10–15 ml (2–3 tbsp) of the egg mixture and then another layer of potatoes, tomatoes and cheese. Add a similar quantity of egg, finish with a layer of grated cheese and pour in any remaining egg mixture. Bake in the oven at 180°C (350°F) mark 4 for about 40 minutes, until the egg flip has set and the cheese topping is golden brown. Garnish with parsley. *Serves 2–3*

Scotch eggs

4 hard-boiled eggs
a little flour
275 g (10 oz) sausagemeat
beaten egg
breadcrumbs
fat or oil for deep frying

Peel the eggs and dust with flour. Coat each with 50–75 g (2–3 oz) sausagemeat, keeping it a good shape. Brush with beaten egg, coat with breadcrumbs and fry in deep fat for about 7 minutes. Drain well and allow to cool. Serve cut in halves with salad.

Cheese and egg fricassee

4 hard-boiled eggs
300 ml (½ pint) white sauce (see page 36)
salt and pepper
5 ml (1 tsp) finely chopped parsley
50 g (2 oz) cheese, grated
browned breadcrumbs
watercress to garnish

Quarter the eggs, add to the white sauce and season well. Heat through without allowing to boil, then add the parsley and put into individual dishes. Cover the top thickly with the grated cheese and breadcrumbs and brown for a minute or two under a hot grill. Garnish with watercress and serve immediately with toast.

Pickled eggs

600 ml (1 pint) white wine or cider vinegar
6 cloves of garlic, skinned
25 g (1 oz) pickling spice
a small piece of orange peel
a piece of mace
6 hard-boiled eggs

Boil all the ingredients (except the eggs) for 10 minutes in a heavy pan with a well-fitting lid. When the mixture is cool, strain it into a wide-mouthed glass jar with a screw-lid or a tight cork. Put in the eggs (shelled but whole) and leave for at least 6 weeks before eating.

More hard-boiled eggs can be added as convenient, but they must always be covered by the liquid.

Serve as a buffet dish or snack, with salad.

SAVOURY AND SWEET OMELETTES

The first essential for omelette-making is a reliable pan, either a special omelette one

or a small-sized frying pan; whichever is used, it must be thick and smooth-surfaced. Before use, prepare it as follows: heat it gently, rub it over with salt and a small pad of kitchen paper and wipe it out with a dry cloth. Heat the pan thoroughly and evenly before putting in the egg mixture.

Plain omelette

3 eggs
salt and pepper
15 g (½ oz) butter or margarine

Whisk the eggs lightly; don't make them frothy as overbeating spoils the texture of the finished omelette. Season with salt and pepper. Heat the fat, tilting the pan so that the fat covers the base. Pour the beaten eggs into the hot fat. Stir gently with a fork or spatula until no more liquid egg can be seen. When the mixture is just set, tilt the pan and fold the omelette over, inserting any filling that is to be used. Turn the omelette out on to a warmed plate, garnish according to the type of filling and serve at once. *Serves 2*

Variations
Mushroom Fry 50 g (2 oz) sliced mushrooms in a little fat until tender and sprinkle over surface of cooked omelette before folding. Add a little sherry to egg mixture before cooking, if liked.
Herb Add chopped parsley, chives, thyme or other herbs to the eggs before cooking.
Kidney Cut up 1–2 sheep's kidneys, add 5 ml (1 tsp) finely chopped onion and fry lightly in fat until cooked. Bind with sauce or gravy and fold into the omelette.

Spanish omelette

1 small onion, skinned and chopped
olive oil
1 tomato, skinned and chopped
2 cooked potatoes, diced
2 canned pimientos, chopped
30 ml (2 tbsp) cooked peas
4 eggs
salt and pepper

Fry the onion lightly in a little oil; add the vegetables and cook for a few minutes, stirring. Beat the eggs, season well and pour them into the pan. Cook the omelette in a very little oil, shaking the pan occasionally. When one side is lightly and evenly browned, cover with a plate, turn the omelette and cook the other side. Do not fold; serve hot, with tomato sauce.

Spanish omelette, served cold, makes an excellent picnic dish.

Making and folding an omelette

Omelette cardinal

4 eggs
salt and pepper
25 g (1 oz) butter or margarine
1 orange
175 g (6 oz) prawns
15 ml (1 tbsp) single cream
150 ml (¼ pint) white sauce (see page 36)

Mix the eggs with a fork and season. Heat the fat, pour in the eggs and cook in the usual way. Peel the orange thinly and carefully, in order to obtain only the outer rind, then cut this into very thin Julienne strips. Finish peeling the orange, remove the pith and slice the flesh. Just before folding the omelette, fill it with half the Julienne strips and half the prawns, mixed with the cream. Fold the omelette and slide on to a hot serving dish, make a lengthwise incision and fill with remaining prawns. Pour the sauce over both ends. Arrange the orange slices around and sprinkle the rest of the Julienne strips on top.

Soufflé omelette

3 eggs, separated
45 ml (3 tbsp) milk or water
salt and pepper
15 g (½ oz) butter or margarine

Beat the egg yolks and add the liquid, with seasoning if required. Whisk the egg whites stiffly, then fold into the yolk mixture; work lightly and avoid overmixing. Melt the butter and tip the pan so that the sides are greased. Spread the egg mixture over the surface. Cook the omelette carefully over a moderate heat until it is an even golden brown on the underside. Lightly brown the top under a grill, add any required filling and fold the omelette in half. *Serves 2*

Variations
Cheese Sprinkle the surface liberally with grated cheese before browning the top.
Shrimp Heat 50 g (2 oz) shrimps in a little white sauce. Add a few drops anchovy essence to the yolks and insert the shrimps before folding omelette.
Ham or meat Add 50 g (2 oz) minced ham, cooked meat, liver, tongue or chicken to the yolk mixture.

Sausage and pepper omelette

Illustrated in colour opposite

3 eggs
30 ml (2 tbsp) creamy milk
salt and pepper
50 g (2 oz) butter or margarine
225 g (8 oz) pork chipolata sausages
1 small green pepper, seeded and finely sliced
1 small bunch of spring onions, trimmed and sliced
50 g (2 oz) cooked haricot beans

Lightly beat together the eggs, milk and seasoning. Melt a small knob of the fat in a 24-cm (9½-inch) frying pan and quickly cook the sausages until golden on all sides. Remove, cut each across in half and keep hot. Wipe the pan with absorbent kitchen paper and melt half the remaining fat. Sauté the pepper, spring onions and beans for about 2 minutes. Remove and keep hot.

Wipe out the pan and melt the remaining fat. Pour the egg mixture into the pan and cook quickly, stirring lightly with the back of a fork, until it begins to set. Add the sausages to the pan with the vegetables. Continue to heat until the egg is just set but still remains creamy. Serve at once. *Serves 2*

Asparagus omelette

a few cooked or canned asparagus spears
4 eggs, separated
15 ml (1 tbsp) water
salt and pepper
100 g (4 oz) Cheddar cheese, grated

Cut off the green tips of the asparagus, with about 2·5 cm (1 inch) of the stalk; chop the rest. Make a soufflé omelette in the usual way, adding the chopped asparagus and 75 g (3 oz) of the grated cheese to the egg yolks. Cook as usual, but do not fold; slide it on to a warm plate, make a slight incision in the middle of the omelette with the point of a knife, put in the asparagus tips in a bundle and sprinkle with the rest of the cheese.

Sweet soufflé omelettes

Make as above, but omit the seasoning.
Jam Spread the cooked omelette with hot jam, fold and sprinkle with sugar.
Rum Add 15 ml (1 tbsp) best quality rum to the egg yolks. Put the cooked omelette on a hot dish and pour 45–60 ml (3–4 tbsp) warmed rum round, ignite and serve.
Apricot Add the grated rind of an orange or tangerine to the egg yolks. Spread thick apricot pulp, fresh or canned, over the omelette before folding and serve liberally sprinkled with caster sugar.

Cheese dishes

Savoury cheese and onion pie

175 g (6 oz) shortcrust pastry
2 medium onions, par-boiled
15 ml (1 level tbsp) seasoned flour
75–100 g (3–4 oz) cheese, grated
30 ml (2 tbsp) milk

Divide the pastry in half and roll out one part to cover an 18-cm (7-inch) deep ovenproof pie plate. Slice the onions finely, dip into seasoned flour, place on the pastry and add the cheese and milk. Cover the pie with the rest of the pastry, cut into strips and worked lattice-fashion. Bake in the oven at 220°C (425°F) mark 7 for about 40 minutes, until the pastry is golden brown.

Alternatively, mix the onions with a little well-flavoured cheese sauce, sprinkle with grated cheese and finish as before.

Cheese and fish pie

900 g (2 lb) potatoes, peeled
65 g (2½ oz) butter or margarine
milk
salt and pepper
450 g (1 lb) white fish
40 g (1½ oz) flour
175 g (6 oz) cheese, grated
tomatoes, mushrooms, stuffed olives to garnish

Cook the potatoes and mash with 25 g (1 oz) of the fat, a little milk and seasoning to taste. Pipe a border of this creamed potato round an ovenproof dish and leave to brown under the grill. Meanwhile place the fish in a pan, cover with water, put on the lid and bring slowly to the boil, turn off the heat and leave the fish for 5 minutes. Drain the fish well (reserving 150 ml (¼ pint) of the liquor), skin and flake it. Make a white sauce with the remaining fat, flour, fish stock and 150 ml (¼ pint) milk. When it thickens, remove from the heat, stir in 150 ml (4 oz) of the cheese and season. Combine with the fish and pour into the piped potato border. Sprinkle with the remaining cheese and grill until the cheese bubbles. Garnish with tomatoes, mushrooms or stuffed olives.

Welsh rarebit

175 g (6 oz) Cheddar cheese, grated
1·25 ml (¼ level tsp) dry mustard
salt and pepper
beer or stout
Worcestershire sauce
hot buttered toast
chopped parsley to garnish

Put the cheese into a double saucepan and allow it to melt slowly over hot water. Add the seasonings, then stir in slowly as much beer or stout as the cheese will take up, and flavour to taste with Worcestershire sauce; the mixture should be smooth and creamy. Pour it over the hot toast and brown under the grill, if desired. Serve at once, garnished with parsley.

Sausage and pepper omelette (see above).

Buck rarebit Make as before and serve topped with a poached egg.
Yorkshire rarebit Top with a slice of boiled bacon and a poached egg.

Cheesy chicken

4 portions of chicken
100 g (4 oz) butter or margarine
2 slices of onion
thyme
150 ml (¼ pint) stock
40 g (1½ oz) flour
150 ml (¼ pint) dry cider
142-ml (5-fl oz) carton single cream
salt and pepper
10 ml (2 tsp) mild mustard
100 g (4 oz) strong Cheddar cheese, grated

Fry the chicken in the fat until tender (about 20 minutes). Put the pieces on to a heatproof dish and keep hot. Simmer the onion with a pinch of thyme in the stock. Strain and add the flour, stirring all the time. Stir in the cider, cream, seasonings and half the cheese; allow to simmer for 10 minutes. Pour this sauce over the chicken, sprinkle with the remaining cheese and brown under a very hot grill.

Cheese and ham croquettes

3 hard-boiled eggs
75 g (3 oz) cooked ham
25 g (1 oz) butter or margarine
25 g (1 oz) flour
150 ml (¼ pint) milk
salt and pepper
100 g (4 oz) cheese, grated
5 ml (1 tsp) chopped parsley
beaten egg and white breadcrumbs
fat for deep frying
watercress to garnish

Chop the eggs and ham very finely. Melt the fat in a small pan, stir in the flour, add the milk and bring to the boil. Season, add the cheese, parsley, eggs and ham and turn on to a plate to cool. When the mixture is cold, shape into croquettes, coat with egg and breadcrumbs and fry in deep fat until golden brown. Drain well and serve garnished with watercress.

Bacon and cheese peppers

4 green peppers
1 onion, skinned and chopped
100 g (4 oz) mushrooms, chopped
50 g (2 oz) butter or margarine
60 ml (4 tbsp) fresh breadcrumbs
salt and pepper
100 g (4 oz) Cheddar cheese, grated
4 rashers of streaky bacon, rinded
150 ml (¼ pint) stock

Halve the peppers lengthwise, remove the seeds and cook the cases in boiling salted water for 5 minutes, then drain and put into an ovenproof dish. Cook the onion and mushrooms in the fat until tender. Add the breadcrumbs, seasoning and most of the cheese. Put this mixture into the peppers, sprinkle with the rest of the cheese and put half a rasher of bacon on each. Put the stock in the dish, cover and bake in the oven at 200°C (400°F) mark 6 for about 20 minutes; remove the cover and cook for a further 10 minutes.

Ham and leeks au gratin

8 medium leeks, washed and trimmed
salt and pepper
butter or margarine
50 g (2 oz) flour
300 ml (½ pint) milk
nutmeg
100 g (4 oz) Gruyère cheese, grated
8 slices of cooked ham
toasted breadcrumbs
chopped parsley to garnish

Put the leeks into boiling salted water and cook gently until soft, about 15 minutes. Drain in a colander, keeping back about 300 ml (½ pint) of the liquid, and leave for about 5 minutes. Make a well-seasoned cheese sauce with 50 g (2 oz) fat, the flour, milk, leek liquor, a little grated nutmeg and 50 g (2 oz) of the cheese.

Wrap each leek in a slice of ham and put in an ovenproof dish, pour the sauce over, top with breadcrumbs and the remaining cheese. Dot with butter and put under the grill until golden brown. Garnish with parsley.

Tuna cheese casserole

50 g (2 oz) butter or margarine
25 g (1 oz) plain flour
400 ml (¾ pint) milk
salt and pepper
5 ml (1 tsp) salad cream
2 × 198-g (7-oz) cans tuna
175 g (6 oz) Cheddar cheese, grated
700 g (1½ lb) potatoes, cooked and mashed

Melt 25 g (1 oz) of the fat in a small saucepan, add the flour and cook, stirring, for 1 minute. Add the milk gradually, stirring constantly, and cook until smooth. Remove from the heat and stir in some seasoning, the salad cream, tuna fish and cheese. Grease a deep ovenproof dish and arrange in it a deep layer of potato; pour in the cheese mixture, top with remaining potato and brush well with melted butter. Bake in the oven at 180°C (350°F) mark 4 for 1 hour.

Ham and leeks au gratin

Cauliflower au gratin

1 cauliflower
40 g (1½ oz) butter or margarine
40 g (1½ oz) flour
400 ml (¾ pint) milk
salt and pepper
100 g (4 oz) cheese, grated
4 tomatoes, halved
4 hard-boiled eggs, shelled and quartered

Prepare the cauliflower, leaving it whole but cutting a cross in the base of the stem part to help it to cook. Quickly cook it in boiling salted water for 15–20 minutes. Make a roux with the fat and flour and then gradually add the milk; stir until the sauce boils, season to taste and add 75 g (3 oz) of the grated cheese. Grill the tomatoes lightly. Drain the cauliflower and place in an ovenproof dish. Arrange the eggs round the cauliflower, keeping back a few pieces for garnish. Quarter the tomatoes and arrange these also round the cauliflower, keeping a few pieces for garnish. Coat the cauliflower, tomatoes and eggs with the sauce, sprinkle with the remaining cheese, garnish with egg and tomato and place under the grill for 5 minutes. Serve hot.

Cheese pudding

6–8 thin slices of bread and butter
2 eggs
a little made mustard
salt and pepper
1 onion, skinned and chopped
10 ml (2 tsp) tomato sauce
100 g (4 oz) cheese, grated
568 ml (1 pint) milk
25 g (1 oz) breadcrumbs
toast triangles to garnish

Cut the buttered bread into neat pieces and put into a pie dish. Beat the eggs with the seasonings, onion and tomato sauce, add 75 g (3 oz) of the cheese and the milk. Pour this mixture over the bread and allow to stand for 10–15 minutes. Mix the remainder of the cheese with the breadcrumbs and sprinkle over the top. Bake in the oven at 180°C (350°F) mark 4 for about 45 minutes, until set and golden. Garnish with toast triangles and serve with baked tomatoes.

Devilled ham casserole

50 g (2 oz) cooked ham, finely chopped
30 ml (2 tbsp) chilli sauce
5 ml (1 tsp) made mustard
5 ml (1 tsp) finely chopped onion
5 ml (1 tsp) brown table sauce
5 ml (1 tsp) horseradish sauce
4 thin slices of bread
a little butter
3 eggs, beaten
2·5 ml (½ level tsp) salt
400 ml (¾ pint) milk
75 g (3 oz) cheese, grated

Combine the ham, chilli sauce, mustard, onion, brown sauce and horseradish and spread the bread with this mixture. Place overlapping layers in a baking dish and dot with knobs of butter. Mix together the eggs, salt and milk, pour over the bread and sprinkle with cheese. Place in a roasting tin of warm water and bake in the oven at 170°C (325°F) mark 3 for 1–1¼ hours.
Serves 2–3

Ham and cheese pancakes

50 g (2 oz) flour
salt
1 large egg
150 ml (¼ pint) milk and water
fat for frying
4 slices of ham
75 g (3 oz) cheese, grated
rings of green pepper to garnish

Put the flour into a bowl, add the salt and the egg, then gradually stir in the liquid, mixing to a smooth batter. Heat the fat in a frying pan and when it is really hot, pour in sufficient batter to form a thin layer over the base of the pan. Cook the pancake on one side, turn and cook the other side; keep it hot while making 3 more pancakes. Put a slice of ham on each pancake, sprinkle it with cheese and roll up. Arrange the pancakes in a serving dish, sprinkle the rest of the cheese over the top and brown lightly under the grill. Serve garnished with the green pepper rings.

Sweetcorn special

3 large eggs
425-g (15-oz) can sweetcorn
75 g (3 oz) butter or margarine
salt and pepper
3 large tomatoes
75 g (3 oz) Cheddar cheese, grated
chopped parsley to garnish

Hard-boil the eggs. Heat the corn in a saucepan with 50 g (2 oz) of the fat and some seasoning for 6 minutes. Halve the tomatoes, dot with the rest of the fat and grill for 5 minutes. Drain and shell the eggs. Drain the sweetcorn and pour into an ovenproof dish. Halve the eggs lengthwise and arrange down the centre of the dish, on top of the corn. Season, cover with cheese and brown for 4 minutes under the grill. Put the tomatoes round the edge of the dish, garnish with parsley and serve at once.
Serves 3

Creamy salmon dip

113-g (4-oz) can salmon
100 g (4 oz) cottage cheese
2 rashers streaky bacon, rinded
142-ml (5-fl oz) carton soured cream
2 gherkins, chopped
salt and pepper
15–30 ml (1–2 tbsp) mayonnaise
chopped parsley to garnish
potato crisps

Drain the excess liquid from the salmon and flake it into a basin; add the cottage cheese. Fry the bacon until crisp, crush and fold into the salmon mixture, then add the soured cream and gherkins. Check the seasoning and finally fold in the mayonnaise. Garnish with a sprig of parsley and serve with potato crisps for dipping.

CHEESE SAVOURIES AND PASTRIES

Cheese pastry

75 g (3 oz) butter or margarine
75 g (3 oz) cheese, grated
100 g (4 oz) plain flour

Blend together the fat and cheese until soft. Add the flour gradually and stir until the mixture begins to stick together. Collect it into a ball, knead until smooth and if possible refrigerate before using.

Cheese straws

Roll out some cheese pastry fairly thinly and cut into fingers about 7·5 cm (3 inches)

Cheese straws

long and 0·5 cm (¼ inch) wide. Stamp out some rings, using 2 greased cutters, put all on a baking sheet and bake in the oven at 200°C (400°F) mark 6 for about 10 minutes. When the biscuits are cold, dip the ends of the straws into paprika pepper or finely chopped parsley and insert into the rings.

Hot cream cheese tartlets

100 g (4 oz) cheese pastry (see above)
25 g (1 oz) cream cheese
salt and pepper
2·5 ml (½ tsp) Worcestershire sauce
150 ml (¼ pint) thick white sauce
  (see page 36)
1 egg, separated
finely grated Parmesan cheese

Roll out the pastry and use it to line 6–8 small tartlet tins. Beat the cream cheese until soft, then add the seasonings, the sauces and the egg yolk. Beat the egg white until stiff and fold it into the mixture. Three-quarters fill the pastry cases with this mixture and bake in the oven at 190°C (375°F) mark 5 for about 15 minutes. Before serving, sprinkle a little grated Parmesan cheese on top of each tartlet.

Quick pizza

100 g (4 oz) self-raising flour
a pinch of salt
cooking oil
45–60 ml (3–4 tbsp) water
226-g (8-oz) can tomatoes
2·5 ml (½ level tsp) dried sage, mixed
  herbs or oregano
75 g (3 oz) cheese, diced
a few anchovy fillets and stuffed olives
  to garnish

Mix the flour and salt with 15 ml (1 tbsp) oil and the water to a soft dough. Roll out into a 15-cm (6-inch) round and fry the pizza gently in a little oil in a shallow pan for about 5 minutes, or until it is browned on the underside. Turn it over and cover with the well-drained tomatoes, herbs and cheese; garnish with the anchovy fillets and sliced olives. Fry on the second side for a further 5 minutes, then place under a hot grill until the topping is golden brown. Serve with a green salad.

Although the dough is made by a quick method, the topping given above is a traditional one; however, you can vary it by using other mixtures:

1 Spread with canned tomatoes, sprinkle with chopped ham or crisply fried bacon, add diced cheese.

2 Use sliced mushrooms dotted with butter to replace the anchovies.

3 Spread with canned tomatoes, then

sprinkle with chopped sautéed green pepper and diced cheese.

4 Spread with sardines or pilchards in tomato sauce, then sprinkle with diced cheese.

Pizza napoletana

Illustrated in colour on page 6

about 150 ml (¼ pint) water
2·5 ml (½ level tsp) sugar
7·5 ml (1 ½ level tsp) dried yeast or
**   15 g (½ oz) fresh yeast**
225 g (8 oz) strong plain flour
5 ml (1 level tsp) salt
a small knob of lard
cooking oil

For the topping
450 g (1 lb) onions, skinned and chopped
2 × 425-g (15-oz) cans tomatoes, drained
10 ml (2 level tsp) dried marjoram
salt and pepper
100 g (4 oz) Bel Paese or Mozzarella
**   cheese, cut into small dice**
2 × 60-g (2-oz) cans anchovy fillets,
**   drained**
black olives

Warm the water to blood heat and dissolve the sugar in it. Sprinkle the dried yeast on and leave in a warm place until frothy. If you are using fresh yeast, blend it with the water and use at once; omit the sugar. Mix the flour and salt, rub in the lard and pour in the yeast mixture. Hand mix and beat until the dough leaves the bowl clean. Knead on a floured board until smooth and elastic. Put the dough in an oiled polythene bag; leave in a warm place until doubled in size. Turn the dough on to a floured surface and roll to a long strip. Brush with oil and roll it up like a Swiss roll.

Repeat 3 times. Grease a 30-cm (12-inch) plain flan ring on a baking sheet, and roll out the dough to fit this (if no flan ring is available, roll out the dough to a 30-cm (12-inch) round and place on a baking sheet). Brush with oil. Sauté the onions in a little oil until soft but not coloured. Spread to within 2 cm (¾ inch) of the edge of the dough. Arrange the tomatoes on top, sprinkle with marjoram and seasoning and bake in the oven at 230°C (450°F) mark 8 for 20 minutes. Scatter the cheese over, lattice with anchovies and arrange olives in the spaces between. Cover loosely with foil and cook for a further 20 minutes. Serve hot in wedges with a mixed salad. *Serves 6*

Cocktail titbits

Arrange a variety of appetising morsels on cocktail sticks and skewer these into a small cheese, a grapefruit or whole rosy apples. Choose from the following:

Cheddar cheese with celery, a cocktail onion or a chunk of pineapple and a cocktail cherry.

A tiny sausage, a piece of Cheddar cheese and a cocktail onion.

Stoned dates or prunes, or split and seeded grapes, filled with cream cheese.

Savoury bacon rolls Roll a strip of bacon round a piece of pineapple or apricot, a prune or date stuffed with cheese, a stuffed olive, pickled onion or cocktail sausage, then grill until crisp. Serve hot.

Cheese balls Form some cream cheese into balls and roll them in chopped parsley, walnuts or minced ham.

Cheese and bacon quiche

Illustrated in colour opposite

For the pastry
200 g (7 oz) plain flour
a pinch of salt
100 g (3 ½ oz) block margarine
cold water to mix

For the filling
100 g (4 oz) lean streaky bacon, rinded
**   and chopped**
1 small onion, skinned and chopped
75 g (3 oz) Cheddar cheese, grated
2 eggs
milk
salt and pepper
2 tomatoes, skinned and sliced
chopped parsley to garnish

Make up the pastry in the usual way and use to line a 21-cm (8½-inch) fluted flan ring. Bake 'blind' in the oven at 200°C (400°F) mark 6 for 20 minutes.

For the filling, sauté the bacon and onion together in the bacon fat until the onion is soft and the bacon crisp. Spoon into the flan case and top with half the cheese. Beat the eggs lightly and make up to 200 ml (⅓ pint) with milk. Season well and pour over the filling. Sprinkle the remaining cheese over the filling and arrange tomato slices around the edge. Return to the oven at 190°C (375°F) mark 5 for about 40 minutes, until the filling is set. Garnish with parsley and serve with an apple and celery salad.

Hot cheese puffs

2 egg whites
1·25 ml (¼ level tsp) baking powder
salt and pepper
100 g (4 oz) cheese, grated
small toast canapés
watercress to garnish

Whisk the egg whites stiffly and whisk in the baking powder and the seasonings. Fold in the cheese and pile the mixture on to the canapés. Cook under a moderately hot grill until golden and puffy and serve hot, garnished with watercress.

Bacon, date and cheese savouries

Rind some bacon rashers and cut each into two; stone some dates. Stuff each date with a strip of cheese and wrap a piece of bacon round. Grill for 8–10 minutes.

Camembert canapés

Butter some fingers of toast about 7·5 cm (3 inches) long by 1 cm (½ inch). Cut slices of Camembert cheese slightly smaller, place on the toast, then toast quickly under a hot grill. Sprinkle with paprika pepper and serve at once.

Cheese éclairs

50 g (2 oz) butter or margarine
150 ml (¼ pint) boiling water
100 g (4 oz) plain flour, sieved
3–4 eggs
filling (see method)

Put the fat and water into a small pan and when the fat has melted, add the flour and stir vigorously. Cook gently until a smooth ball of paste is formed, then remove from the heat; cool slightly and mix in the eggs, adding them one at a time and beating very thoroughly. The paste should finally be of such a stiffness that it can be piped easily, but will retain its shape. Using a forcing bag fitted with a 1-cm (½-inch) nozzle, pipe 5-cm (2-inch) lengths of the paste on to a baking tin and bake in the oven at 220°C (425°F) mark 7 for 20–30 minutes, or until the éclairs are well risen and light. When they are cooked, split them open, cool and fill with a rich, creamy cheese sauce or with softened cream cheese mixed with a little anchovy paste.

Cheese dartois

100 g (4 oz) flaky pastry
1 egg
50 g (2 oz) Parmesan cheese, finely
**   grated**
salt, pepper and cayenne pepper
25 g (1 oz) butter or margarine, melted

Roll the pastry out thinly and divide it into two portions. Beat the egg and add the cheese, seasonings and melted fat; spread the mixture over one half of the pastry

Cheese and bacon quiche (see above) served with a crunchy salad of apple and celery in a vinaigrette dressing

damp the edges and place the other piece of pastry on top. Press the edges well together and mark across in strips. Bake in the oven at 230°C (450°F) mark 8 for about 15 minutes, until the pastry is golden brown. Divide into fingers and serve either hot or cold.

Savoury cheese slice

75 g (3 oz) butter or margarine
225 g (8 oz) self-raising flour
150 g (5 oz) cheese, grated
1 egg, beaten
a little milk (if needed)
1 small onion, skinned and finely chopped
100 g (4 oz) streaky bacon, rinded and chopped
2·5–5 ml (½–1 level tsp) mixed herbs
salt and pepper

Rub 50 g (2 oz) of the fat into the flour until it resembles breadcrumbs. Stir in 75 g (3 oz) of the cheese, then mix to a fairly soft dough with egg and some milk if necessary. Fry the onion and bacon gently for about 5 minutes in the remaining 25 g (1 oz) fat. Divide

the dough into 2 pieces and roll out each piece into a 20·5-cm (8-inch) square. Place one piece on a greased baking sheet, cover with the onion and bacon and sprinkle with the herbs and seasoning, Wet the edges and cover with the second piece of dough, pressing the edges together. Brush with milk and sprinkle with the remaining cheese. Bake in the oven at 200°C (400°F) mark 6 for about 20 minutes, until crisp and golden. Serve hot or cold, cut in fingers or wedges.

Variation

Fry 2–3 skinned and chopped tomatoes with the onion and bacon.

York fingers

100 g (4 oz) flaky pastry
100 g (4 oz) Wensleydale or processed cheese
beaten egg
finely grated cheese
minced ham
horseradish sauce

Roll out the pastry thinly and cut the

cheese into very thin slices. Put the cheese on to one half of the pastry, fold the other half over and roll it out again. Cut the pastry into fingers about 7·5 cm (3 inches) long and 1 cm (½ inch) wide, brush with beaten egg and sprinkle with grated cheese. Bake in the oven at 230°C (450°F) mark 8 until golden, then spread with ham mixed with horse-radish sauce.

Croûtes of fried cheese

6 Petit Suisse cheeses (or 100 g (4 oz) Gruyère)
1 egg, beaten
50 g (2 oz) breadcrumbs
rounds of bread
25–50 g (1–2 oz) butter or margarine
watercress to garnish

Divide each small cheese in half (or cut rounds of the Gruyère cheese). Brush over with beaten egg, coat with breadcrumbs and repeat this process twice, to make a really firm covering. Fry the rounds of bread in the fat until golden brown, then fry the cheese. Place the cheese on the croûtes and garnish with watercress.

VEGETABLES

Keep vegetables in a cool, airy place – for example, in a vegetable rack placed in a cool larger or in the vegetable compartment of the refrigerator. Green ones should be used as soon as possible after gathering, while their vitamin C value is at its highest.

Prepare all vegetables as near the time of cooking as possible, to retain both flavour and vitamin C content.

Serve fried vegetables very hot and don't cover them with a lid or they will become soggy.

Add a knob of butter to boiled and steamed vegetables.

A sprinkling of chopped herbs added before serving also improves vegetables – try parsley on carrots, mint on peas, tarragon on courgettes. A little grated nutmeg gives an interesting flavour to cabbage.

A well-flavoured white or cheese sauce makes a change with such vegetables as cauliflower, marrow, leeks and onions, broad beans and carrots.

A platterful of assorted vegetables, arranged in rows or circles, looks attractive and is a good accompaniment to boiled meat.

A–Z of vegetables

Artichoke (Jerusalem) Scrub the artichokes; using a stainless steel knife or peeler, peel quickly and immediately plunge them into cold water, keeping them under water as much as possible to prevent discoloration. A squeeze of lemon juice (or a few drops of vinegar) in the water helps to keep them a good colour. Cook in boiling salted water to which a little lemon juice (or vinegar) has been added, until just tender, about 15–20 minutes. Drain, garnish with chopped parsley and serve with melted butter or a white, cheese or similar sauce.

Allow 175–225 g (6–8 oz) per portion.

Artichokes (Globe) The artichokes should be of a good green colour, with tightly clinging, fleshy leaves – leaves that are spreading, and fuzzy, purplish centres indicate over-maturity. Cut off the stem close to the base of the leaves and take off the outside dry or discoloured leaves. As globe artichokes have close-growing leaves, they need soaking in cold water for about 30 minutes, to ensure that they are thoroughly cleaned; drain well. Cook in boiling salted water until the leaves will pull out easily – 20–40 minutes, depending on size, Drain upside-down. Serve with melted butter.

Globe artichokes may also be served cold with a vinaigrette dressing (see page 126).

When eating them, pull off the leaves with the fingers; the soft end of each leaf is dipped in the sauce and sucked. When you reach the centre, remove the choke (or soft flowery part), if it has not already been taken out, and eat the bottom – the chief delicacy – with a knife and fork.

Allow 1 artichoke per person.

Asparagus Cut off the woody end of the stalks and scrape the white part lightly, removing the coarse spines. Tie in bundles with the heads together and place upright in a pan of boiling salted water – the water should be almost up to the tips. Bring to the boil and cook gently for 10 minutes, then lay them flat and cook for a further 10–15 minutes. Don't over-cook asparagus – the tips should not be mushy. Drain and untie before serving with melted butter.

Asparagus may also be served cold, with a vinaigrette dressing or mayonnaise (see page 126).

To eat, hold a stick by the stem end and dip the tip in the butter or sauce. It is not usual to eat the stem end.

Allow 8–12 stems per serving.

Aubergine or eggplant Aubergines should be of a uniform purple colour, firm, smooth and free from blemishes. Cut off the stem, wash the vegetables and if necessary peel them. Aubergines are usually fried or stuffed and baked.

Allow about 175 g (6 oz) per serving.

Beans (Broad) Shell beans and cook in boiling salted water until tender – 15–20 minutes. If liked, serve with parsley sauce. When the beans are very young and tender the whole pods may be washed, cooked and eaten.

Allow 225–325 g (8–12 oz) (weight as bought) per serving.

Beans (French and runner) Top, tail and string the beans. Slice runners thinly; French beans may be left whole. Cook in boiling salted water until soft – young beans 8–12 minutes, larger beans 15–20 minutes. Remove any scum that rises during cooking. Drain and toss with salt and pepper and a knob of butter.

Allow 100–225 g (4–8 oz) per serving.

Beetroot Cut off the stalks 2·5 cm (1 inch) or so above the root, then wash the beetroots, taking care not to damage the skin or they will 'bleed' when boiled. Boil in salted water until soft – the time depends on age and freshness: small, early beetroot will take about 30 minutes, larger, older ones about 1½ hours. Rub off the skin and slice or cube. Serve hot, coated with a white sauce, or cold, sliced and in a little vinegar.

The cooking time may be much reduced if the beets are peeled and sliced and then cooked until tender in a very little water in a covered pan, the liquid being used to make a sauce; the time varies, but is about 30 minutes.

Allow 100 g (4 oz) per serving when served as a vegetable.

Broccoli There are several varieties of this vegetable, the chief being:

White broccoli, with a fairly large flower head, which is cooked and served in the same way as cauliflower. Buy by the head, judging by size.

Purple broccoli and Calabrese (a green sprouting broccoli), with a more delicate flavour. Cook like cauliflower, allowing 10–15 minutes. Serve plain, or with melted butter sauce.

Allow 100–175 g (4–6 oz) per serving.

Brussels sprouts Wash the sprouts, removing discoloured leaves, and cut a cross in the stalks. Cook in boiling salted water until soft – 10–15 minutes – drain, return them to the pan and re-heat with a knob of butter and salt and pepper.

Allow 100–175 g (4–6 oz) per serving.

Cabbage – green, red, kale, greens Remove coarse outer leaves, cut the cabbage in half and take out the hard centre stalk. Wash thoroughly, shred finely and cook rapidly in about 2·5 cm (1 inch) of boiling salted water for about 10 minutes, or until cooked. For red cabbage add 15 ml (1 tbsp) vinegar to the water. Drain well and toss with a knob of butter, a sprinkling of pepper and a pinch of grated nutmeg (optional).

Allow 100–175 g (4–6 oz) per serving.

Carrots, new Trim off the leaves, then scrape lightly with a sharp knife. Small new carrots are usually cooked whole. Simmer in salted water for about 15 minutes, or until cooked. Serve tossed with a little butter, pepper and chopped parsley. **Old** Peel thinly, cut up, cook and serve as above.

Allow 100–175 g (4–6 oz) per serving.

Cauliflower Remove the coarse outer leaves, cut a cross in the stalk end and wash the cauliflower. Cook stem side down in fast-boiling salted water for 10–15 minutes, depending on size. Drain well and serve coated with white sauce or cheese sauce.

Cauliflower can also be divided into florets and cooked as above for about 8–10 minutes; drain and serve tossed with butter and a sprinkling of pepper, or with sauce.

A medium cauliflower serves 4 people.

Celeriac (The root of turnip-rooted celery.) Peel fairly thickly; small roots may be cooked whole, but larger ones are sliced thickly or diced. Cook in boiling salted water or stock until tender – 45 minutes–1 hour. Drain well and serve with melted butter or white sauce.

Allow 100–225 g (4–8 oz) per serving.

Celery Wash, scrub and cut into 5-cm (2-inch) lengths. Cook in boiling salted water until tender – 10–20 minutes, depending on its coarseness. Drain well and serve with a white, parsley or cheese sauce.

Allow 1 head of celery per serving if small, 2–3 sticks if really large.

Chicory To prepare, cut off a thin slice from the base; using a pointed knife, re-move the core. Pull away any damaged outer leaves and wash quickly under cold water – don't soak. To cook, put into boiling salted water with a little lemon juice added and cook gently for about 20 minutes. Serve plain or with a cheese or tomato sauce.

Allow 1–2 heads per serving.

Corn on the cob Choose cobs which are plump, well formed and of a pale golden

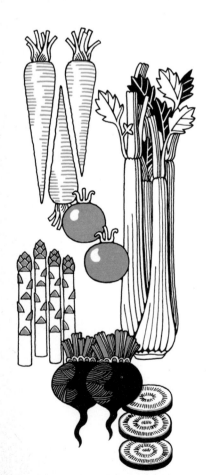

yellow colour and use them while still really fresh. Remove the outside leaves and silky threads. Put the cobs into boiling unsalted water (salt toughens them) and cook for 8–15 minutes, depending on size, but don't overcook them, which also makes them tough. Drain well and serve with melted butter, salt and freshly ground pepper.

Allow 1 cob per serving.

Courgettes These are a variety of small vegetable marrow, normally cooked un-peeled, either left whole or cut in rounds. They may be boiled in the minimum of water for 10–15 minutes, steamed or fried and are served with melted butter and chopped parsley or tarragon.

Allow 100 g (4 oz) per serving.

Leeks Remove the coarse outer leaves and cut off the roots and tops. Wash the leeks very well, splitting them down the centre to within 2·5 cm (1 inch) or so of the base, to ensure that all grit is removed; if necessary, cut them right through. Cook in boiling salted water until tender – 10–15 minutes. Drain very thoroughly. Serve coated with a white or cheese sauce.

Allow 1–2 leeks per serving.

Marrow Large ones must be peeled; the seeds are removed and the flesh cut in even-sized pieces. Cook in boiling salted water until tender – about 10–20 minutes – and drain well. Serve coated with a white or cheese sauce. Marrow can also be roasted in the dripping round the meat or stuffed and baked – either whole or in thick rings.

Allow 175 g (6 oz) per serving when cooked unstuffed.

Mushrooms Most of the mushrooms bought today are cultivated and require only wiping before being used. Cut off the earthy end of each stalk – the rest of the stalk can be included in the dish or as an ingredient in stuffing. Field mushrooms may need skinning.

Allow 25–75 g (1–3 oz) per serving, de-pending on whether the mushrooms are to be used as a garnish or vegetable.

Onions These vary considerably in both size and flavour. Shallots are smaller than the average true onion, but have a stronger flavour. Spanish onions are larger but milder than English ones. Skin and trim, cut up if desired and cook in boiling salted water for 25–35 minutes, according to size. Drain and use as required. Onions may also be fried, braised and stuffed and baked.

Allow one onion per serving for braising, stuffing or roasting.

Parsnips Wash, peel, quarter and remove the hard centre core. Cut in slices, strips or dice and leave in water until required for cooking. Cook in boiling salted water for 30 minutes, until soft. Drain and toss in

butter, salt and pepper, with a little grated nutmeg if liked. To roast parsnips, par-boil for 5 minutes in salted water, drain and put in the fat round the joint for about 1 hour.

Allow 175–225 g (6–8 oz) per serving.

Peas The season for fresh peas lasts for about 6 weeks only, but they are sold preserved in various ways – canned, bottled, dried, dehydrated and frozen. Dehydrated and frozen peas are very similar to fresh when properly cooked and presented – follow the directions on the packet.

Allow 225 g (8 oz) fresh peas (in pods), 50–75 g (2–3 oz) canned, frozen, etc. per serving.

To cook fresh peas, shell, wash, place in boiling salted water with about 5 ml (1 level tsp) sugar and a sprig of mint and cook until tender – 10–15 minutes. Drain, remove the mint and if liked toss the peas with a knob of butter. For Petit Pois (a particularly small sweet type of pea much used on the Continent), cook with the addition of a little chopped onion and some butter.

Potatoes Peel as thinly as possible, using either a special peeler or a sharp, short-bladed knife. New potatoes are scraped o brushed. Cook potatoes as soon as you can after peeling or scraping; if it is necessary to let them stand for a bit, keep them under water, to prevent discoloration. Cook in boiling salted water for 15–20 minutes, drain and finish as desired. (See potato recipes on page 107.)

Allow 175–225 g (6–8 oz) per serving.

Spinach Wash well in several waters to remove all grit, and strip off any coarse stalks. Pack into a saucepan with only the water that clings to the leaves. Heat gently, turning the spinach occasionally, then bring to the boil and cook gently until soft – 5–10 minutes. Drain well and re-heat with butter and seasoning.

Allow 225 g (8 oz) per serving.

Swedes, turnips Peel thickly and put under water to prevent discoloration. Swedes are cut up. Young turnips can be left whole but older ones are sliced or diced. Cook in boiling salted water, allowing 20–30 minutes for swedes, 15–20 minutes for turnips. Swedes and older turnips are usually mashed with butter and seasoning. Whole turnips may be tossed in butter or a little top of the milk, with seasoning, or served in a white sauce.

Allow 175 g (6 oz) per serving.

CANNED, FROZEN AND DEHYDRATED VEGETABLES

There is a wide and ever-increasing selection of these products, and most people find it convenient to keep some frozen

Cheesy stuffed leek (see page 107).

canned and dehydrated kinds in store for emergency use. They require practically no time for preparation, cook quickly (follow the directions on the package) and may be used in many ways to make either accompaniments or main dishes.

Here are a few quick ways of presenting some of the most popular of these prepared vegetables.

Peas Cook and serve with chopped skinned tomatoes and spring onions which have been lightly fried in butter. Alternatively, cook some chopped celery in 4 cm (1½ inches) of water until tender, add a packet of peas and cook for a further 5 minutes.

Peas and carrots Add to the cooked vegetables a chopped onion which has been fried in butter.

Cut green beans Slice 50 g (2 oz) mushrooms, fry in butter and add to the cooked beans.

Sliced green beans Add some crisply fried bacon and chopped cooked onion to the cooked beans.

Broad beans Add the cooked beans to a cheese sauce, sprinkle with grated cheese and brown under the grill.

Spinach Add horseradish sauce to the cooked spinach.

Broccoli Fry some chives or grated onion in a little butter, add a few drops of lemon juice and pour over the broccoli. Top with toasted shredded almonds.

Sweetcorn kernels Cook and add 30 ml (2 tbsp) double cream.

Vegetable dishes

Artichokes with vinaigrette sauce

Allow one globe artichoke per person. Trim the stalk and cut the ends of the coarse outside leaves with scissors and wash the vegetables. Boil in salted water for about 30 minutes (or until the outer leaves will tear off easily), remove from the water and turn upside-down to drain. Pull out the centre in one piece and remove the 'choke'. Replace the centre and garnish with parsley. Serve hot or cold, with vinaigrette sauce.

Asparagus with egg sauce

Cut off the woody ends of the asparagus, lightly scrape away any coarse spines, and tie in bundles. Place upright in a pan of boiling salted water and boil for 5 minutes. Then lay the bundles flat and cook until tender – a further 10 minutes. Drain and untie the bundles. Meanwhile pipe some

creamed potato in the base of an ovenproof dish and keep warm. Arrange the asparagus on top, pour over 300 ml (½ pint) egg sauce (see page 36) and re-heat in the oven. Sieve hard-boiled egg yolk over the sauce to garnish.

Aubergines à la provençale

2 aubergines
salt and pepper
25 g (1 oz) butter or margarine
4 small tomatoes, skinned and chopped
1 shallot, skinned and chopped
1 onion, skinned and chopped
50 g (2 oz) fresh white breadcrumbs
50 g (2 oz) cheese, grated
parsley sprigs and baked tomatoes to garnish

Do not peel the aubergines, but wipe them. Bring to the boil and cook gently for about 20 minutes. When they are tender, cut them in half lengthways, scoop out the flesh, chop and season. Heat the fat in a pan and sauté the tomatoes, shallot and onion. Lastly, add the aubergine flesh and a few breadcrumbs. Stuff the aubergine cases with this, sprinkle with breadcrumbs and then with grated cheese. Grill until golden brown on top and serve garnished with parsley and baked tomatoes.

Braised haricot beans

225 g (8 oz) haricot beans
½ clove of garlic, skinned and crushed
3 tomatoes, sliced
100 g (4 oz) mushrooms, sliced
seasoned stock
450 g (1 lb) sausages
chopped parsley to garnish
chutney and French mustard to serve

Wash the beans, drain, cover with water and leave to soak overnight. Mix the beans, garlic, tomatoes and mushrooms. Add enough stock to cover, and cook in the oven at 150°C (300°F) mark 2 for 3–4 hours, until the beans are tender. Stir occasionally and if necessary add a little more stock: when the dish is cooked, most of the liquid should be absorbed. Bake or fry the sausages and arrange on top of the savoury beans. Garnish with chopped parsley, and serve with chutney and French mustard.

Vichy carrots

50 g (2 oz) butter or margarine
30–45 ml (2–3 tbsp) water
450 g (1 lb) young carrots, pared and sliced
salt and pepper
a little single cream
chopped parsley to garnish

Melt the fat in a saucepan, add the water

and sliced carrots, cover and cook until the carrots are tender and the liquid absorbed, about 40 minutes. Toss in cream and parsley before serving.

Sautéed cauliflower

Cook a cauliflower in boiling salted water until almost tender. Break off the sprigs and sauté them in 50 g (2 oz) melted butter or margarine until golden brown (toss rather than stir, to prevent the sprigs from breaking). Arrange on a dish in the cauliflower shape. Sieve 2 hard-boiled eggs and chop 15 ml (1 tbsp) parsley and sprinkle these over the cauliflower. Sauté 30 ml (2 tbsp) fresh white breadcrumbs in 50 g (2 oz) butter or margarine and when hot pour over the cauliflower.

Celeriac with cheese sauce

Peel a celeriac and cut into slices about 0·3 cm (⅛ inch) thick. Boil in salted water until tender – about 15 minutes – then drain well. Make some cheese sauce (see page 36), put a little in the bottom of an ovenproof dish and arrange the slices of celeriac on top. Add the rest of the sauce, sprinkle with grated cheese and brown in the oven.

Braised celery

Trim 4 celery hearts and place in a greased ovenproof casserole with 50 g (2 oz) butter or margarine. Add a dash of lemon juice and 300 ml (½ pint) stock, cover and cook in the oven at 170°C (325°F) mark 3 until the celery is tender – about 1 hour. Place it on a hot serving dish. If necessary reduce the liquor by boiling, then pour over the celery.

Celery hotpot

1 head of celery
65 g (2½ oz) butter or margarine
4 tomatoes, skinned and quartered
2 onions, skinned and finely chopped
5 ml (1 level tsp) seasoned flour
150 ml (¼ pint) vegetable stock
175 g (6 oz) self-raising flour
a pinch of salt
cold water to mix
wedges of cheese

Prepare the celery, melt 15 g (½ oz) of the fat and fry the tomatoes and onions for about 10 minutes; then add the seasoned flour and stock. Place in an ovenproof casserole or other suitable dish, and continue to cook for a further 15 minutes. To make the biscuit crust for the top, rub the rest of the fat into the flour, add the salt and mix with cold water to a soft dough. Roll out lightly on a floured board to about 1 cm (½ inch) thick, cut into rounds and place on

Stuffed onions

top of the vegetables. Bake in the oven at 220°C (425°F) mark 7 until the crust is golden brown – 20–30 minutes. Just before the end of the baking, add the wedges of cheese.

Buttered courgettes

Leave the courgettes (small young marrows) whole, and parboil them in salted water for 5 minutes, then drain. Put them in a casserole with 50 g (2 oz) melted butter, cover and cook in the oven at 150°C (300°F) mark 1 until tender – about 10–15 minutes – turning them occasionally while cooking. Serve sprinkled with salt, pepper and chopped parsley.

Belgian cucumber

4 small cucumbers
2 egg yolks
284-ml (10-fl oz) carton natural yoghurt
150 ml (¼ pint) mayonnaise (see page 126)
chopped dill to garnish

Peel the cucumbers, cut into 5-cm (2-inch) lengths and cook in boiling salted water until tender (about 5 minutes). Drain, and arrange in a hot dish. Beat the egg yolks, mix with the yoghurt and the mayonnaise and warm gently without boiling. Pour over the cucumber and sprinkle with chopped dill.

Cheesy stuffed leeks

Illustrated in colour on page 105

450 g (1 lb) leeks
4 rashers streaky bacon, rinded and finely chopped
50 g (2 oz) mushrooms, chopped
50 g (2 oz) fresh white breadcrumbs
75 g (3 oz) Cheddar cheese, grated
salt and pepper

Trim the leeks and remove the outer leaves. Split each leek lengthways, without cutting completely in half, and wash thoroughly under cold running water. Place in a pan with cold water, bring to the boil and cook for 1 minute. Drain thoroughly.

Meanwhile, fry the bacon in a pan until crisp. Add the mushrooms and cook for 2–3 minutes, stirring occasionally. Remove the pan from the heat, stir in half the breadcrumbs and half the cheese, season well. Arrange the leeks in a shallow ovenproof dish and spoon the stuffing equally into each. Stir the remaining breadcrumbs and cheese together and sprinkle over the leeks. Cook in the oven at 200°C (400°F) mark 6 for 15 minutes, until the topping is golden brown.

Stuffed marrow

1·4 kg (3 lb) marrow
175 g (6 oz) long grain rice
2 onions, skinned and sliced
50 g (2 oz) butter or margarine
½ red pepper, seeded and sliced
100 g (4 oz) mushrooms, sliced
5 ml (1 tsp) chopped parsley
salt and pepper
a pinch of dried thyme
4 hard-boiled eggs, chopped

Wash the marrow, then put it into a greased baking tin with a little water. Cover and bake in the oven at 180°C (350°F) mark 4 until tender (45 minutes). Meanwhile boil the rice for 15 minutes and drain it. Fry the onions in the fat until golden brown, then add the red pepper and mushrooms and cook for several minutes. Add the onions, pepper, mushrooms and parsley to the rice, with the seasoning and herbs, and mix lightly together. Lastly, add the hard-boiled eggs. When the marrow is tender, cut in half and scoop out the seeds and fill up the centre with the rice mixture. Serve with baked tomatoes or a tomato sauce. *Serves 4–6*

Mushroom casserole

325 g (12 oz) mushrooms, sliced
3 tomatoes, skinned and sliced
1 onion, skinned and sliced
25 g (1 oz) butter or dripping
1 sheep's kidney, skinned and cored
salt and pepper
15 ml (1 tbsp) chopped parsley
60 ml (4 tbsp) stock or water

Grease an ovenproof casserole. Fry the mushrooms, tomatoes and onion in the fat until golden brown. Cut up the kidney. Fill the dish with alternate layers of kidney and vegetables, seasoning well. Sprinkle with the parsley and finish with a layer of mushrooms. Add the liquid and cook gently in the oven at 180°C (350°F) mark 4 until tender – about 30 minutes. Pack the ingredients closely to allow for shrinkage during cooking.

Marrow with cheese sauce

Peel a marrow, cut in half lengthways, scoop out the seeds and cut the flesh into cubes. Put into a greased casserole, season, but do not add any liquid; cover and cook in the oven at 150°C (300°F) mark 1 for about 1 hour. When the marrow cubes are tender, toss them lightly in a cheese sauce (see page 36).

Stuffed onions

4 large onions, skinned
100 g (4 oz) carrot, grated
75 g (3 oz) cheese, grated
50 g (2 oz) walnuts, chopped
60 ml (4 tbsp) double cream
salt and pepper

Cook the onions in boiling salted water for 20–30 minutes, scoop out the centres and chop them. Mix the carrot, 50 g (2 oz) of the cheese and the walnuts with the chopped onion and the double cream. Season to taste. Fill the onion shells with this mixture, sprinkle the remaining grated cheese on top, and bake in the oven at 180°C (350°F) mark 4 for about 30 minutes. Serve with French beans and parsley sauce.

Layer potato casserole

700 g (1½ lb) potatoes, peeled and sliced
2 onions, skinned and sliced
salt and pepper
100 g (4 oz) butter or margarine
paprika pepper and chopped parsley to garnish

Grease an ovenproof casserole dish and place a layer of potatoes in the bottom, cover with a little onion, season well and dot with fat. Continue adding layers in this way until the dish is filled, finishing with potatoes. Cover and bake in the oven at 200°C (400°F) mark 6 for about 45 minutes, or until the potatoes are tender. Sprinkle with paprika and parsley.

Potatoes with onions

900 g (2 lb) potatoes, peeled
2 large onions, skinned
salt and pepper
600 ml (1 pint) stock
a little butter

Cut the potatoes in half lengthways, then cut across into slices about 1 cm (½ inch) thick. Slice the onions. Grease an ovenproof casserole and put in alternate layers of potato and onion, finishing with potato. Sprinkle with salt and pepper, add the stock and put knobs of butter on top. Cover and cook in the oven at 180°C (350°F) mark 4 for 1–1½ hours.

Potato matches

Peel some potatoes, slice and cut in thin fingers. Dry them in a tea towel. Heat some deep fat or oil in a pan to 190°C (375°F), place a few 'matches' in the frying basket, gently lower this into the fat and cook until the potatoes are golden brown. Lift out the basket, tap it lightly on the edge of the pan to shake off the surplus fat, and turn the potato matches on to crumpled absorbent paper to drain. Repeat until all the potato matches are cooked.

Creamy jacket potatoes

4 potatoes
butter
2 egg yolks
45–60 ml (3–4 tbsp) cream
salt, pepper and nutmeg
chopped parsley to garnish

Scrub the potatoes well, prick them and bake in the oven at 180°C (350°F) mark 4 until soft – about 1¼ hours. Cut each in half and remove the inside. Sieve the potato, and mix with a generous amount of butter, the egg yolks and the cream. Season, add grated nutmeg to taste and return the mixture to the potato cases. Dot with shavings of butter and bake until golden on top, about 10–15 minutes. Garnish with parsley.

Alternatively, the potatoes may be stuffed with tomatoes or chopped fried mushrooms.

Baked cheese potatoes

4 large potatoes
60 ml (4 tbsp) hot milk
100 g (4 oz) cheese, grated
salt and pepper
a little butter
paprika and parsley to garnish

Wash and scrub the potatoes, prick several times and bake in the oven at 180°C (350°F) mark 4 until well cooked – 1½–2 hours. Cut in half lengthways and scoop out the centre, leaving the skins intact. Put the potato in a basin and work with a fork until free from lumps. Add the milk, most of the cheese, and seasoning to taste. Mix until blended, then fill the potato shells with the mixture. Sprinkle the rest of the cheese on top, brush over lightly with a little melted butter and brown in the oven. Sprinkle with

108

paprika before serving, and garnish with parsley.

Alternatively, cut a cross in each potato after baking and add seasoning and a piece of cream cheese.

Potatoes Dauphine

325 g (12 oz) cooked potatoes
40 g (1½ oz) butter or margarine
150 ml (¼ pint) water
65 g (2½ oz) flour
1–2 eggs
salt and pepper
fat or oil for frying
parsley to garnish

Sieve the potatoes. Melt the fat, add the water and bring to the boil, then toss in the flour and mix well, until the mixture forms a ball. Beat in the eggs to give a soft mixture and finally beat in the sieved potato and season to taste. Heat some fat until it is smoking hot, drop in spoonfuls of the mixture and fry until golden. Serve very hot, with parsley. *Serves 3–4*

Lyonnaise potatoes

700 g (1½ lb) potatoes
butter or margarine
salt and pepper
225 g (8 oz) onions, skinned and chopped

Boil the potatoes in their skins, peel and leave to become almost cool. Slice them thinly and toss them in a pan with some very hot fat, adding the salt and pepper. When the potatoes are beginning to colour, add the onions. Continue cooking until the potatoes are all golden brown.

Anna potatoes

Wash and peel 4 large potatoes, slice them thinly and dry well. Grease a round cake tin or a small baking tin and arrange the potatoes in it in layers, with 25 g (1 oz) butter or margarine and seasonings between the layers; fill the tin two-thirds full. Put 25 g (1 oz) butter or margarine on top and bake in the oven at 190°C (375°F) mark 5 for about 1 hour. Test by inserting a skewer; when the potatoes are soft and brown; turn them out onto the serving dish and garnish with sprigs of parsley.

Duchesse potatoes

450 g (1 lb) cooked potatoes
25 g (1 oz) butter or margarine
1 egg
15 ml (1 tbsp) cream or milk
salt and pepper

Sieve the potatoes. Melt the butter in a

saucepan, add the potatoes, and when warm add the beaten egg yolk and cream; season well and mix thoroughly. Put the mixture into a forcing bag with a large star nozzle and pipe on to a greased tin in rosettes or other shapes, as desired. Glaze with beaten egg, and cook in the oven at 200°C (400°F) mark 6 until golden brown.

Sweet-sour red cabbage

Illustrated in colour opposite

900 g (2 lb) red cabbage
2 medium onions, skinned and sliced
2 cooking apples, peeled, cored and chopped
10 ml (2 level tsp) sugar
salt and pepper
bouquet garni
30 ml (2 tbsp) water
30 ml (2 tbsp) red wine vinegar
25 g (1 oz) margarine or butter

Shred the cabbage finely, discarding any discoloured outside leaves or coarse stems. Layer the cabbage in a casserole with the onions, apples, sugar and seasoning. Put the bouquet garni in the centre and pour the water and vinegar over. Cover tightly and cook in the oven at 150°C (300°F) mark 1–2 for 1 hour. Put the cabbage in the coolest part of the oven and continue cooking at 180°C (350°F) mark 4 for a further 1½ hours. Add the butter or margarine and mix into the cabbage at the end of the cooking time. This is excellent with pork. *Serves 4–6 as an accompaniment*

Vegetable macaroni casserole

225 g (8 oz) carrots, pared
1 small turnip, peeled
2 stalks of celery, washed and trimmed
2 leeks, trimmed
2 tomatoes
1 rasher of bacon, rinded
25 g (1 oz) dripping
1 clove of garlic, skinned and crushed
salt and pepper
150 ml (¼ pint) tomato juice
50 g (2 oz) macaroni
60 ml (4 tbsp) chopped parsley
fried onion rings to garnish
grated cheese to serve

Cut up the vegetables and dice the bacon. Heat the fat and sauté first the bacon then the vegetables for 10 minutes. Transfer to an ovenproof casserole, add the crushed garlic, seasoning and tomato juice and cook in the oven at 180°C (350°F) mark 4 for 1 hour. Meanwhile cook the macaroni; add to the casserole and top with parsley and onion. Serve with cheese.

Sweet-sour red cabbage
(see above).

Ratatouille

4 tomatoes, skinned
2 aubergines
1 small red pepper, seeded
1 small green pepper, seeded
2 onions, skinned
1 small marrow or 3 courgettes
30 ml (2 tbsp) oil
25 g (1 oz) butter or margarine
salt and pepper
1 clove of garlic, skinned and crushed
chopped parsley to garnish

Quarter the tomatoes, wipe and slice the aubergines. Chop the peppers and onions. Peel the marrow (but not courgettes, if used) and slice. Heat the oil and fat in an ovenproof casserole and add the vegetables, seasoning and garlic. Stir well, cover tightly and cook in the oven at 180°C (350°F) mark 4 for 1–1½ hours, or until tender. Garnish with parsley.

Pressure-cooking vegetables

Vegetables cooked in a pressure cooker retain flavour and colour and keep their valuable vitamin and mineral content. Pressure cooking is particularly suitable for root vegetables. Watch these points to obtain good results:

1 Choose vegetables of about the same size, or cut large ones into small, even-sized pieces.
2 Cook at 'high' pressure.
3 Time accurately – an extra minute may cause vegetables to be over-cooked: as they vary in size, age and toughness, the times quoted can only be a general guide.
4 Use the rack or separators, unless the vegetables are included as part of a meat dish.
5 Pour 150–300 ml (¼–½ pint) water into the pan – sufficient to reach the level of the rack – before putting vegetables in; do not add green vegetables until the water is boiling.
6 Season lightly, sprinkling with salt.
7 Bring quickly to pressure, and reduce pressure quickly.
8 Use the vegetable stock left in the cooker for making soups, sauces or gravies.

Vegetables with the same cooking times may be cooked together; stand them on the rack in separate piles, or wrap each kind in aluminium foil. If your pan is fitted with separators, use these to keep the vegetables apart. When the cooking times differ, put the vegetables needing the longest time in the pan first, and reduce the pressure

part way through the cooking to insert those taking a shorter time; eg, potatoes take 10 minutes and leeks 3 minutes, so reduce the pressure after 7 minutes to put in the leeks. Sometimes the cooking times can be made the same by leaving some vegetables whole and cutting those that take longer into smaller pieces.

Prepare and serve vegetables as described on pages 103–104.

Artichokes (Globe) Place on rack with water and a little salt and pressure-cook for 10 minutes. Reduce pressure immediately.
Artichokes (Jerusalem) Put on rack, with water, season and pressure-cook for 8 minutes.
Asparagus When water is boiling stand vegetable on rack and add a little salt. Pressure-cook for 2–3 minutes.
Beans (Broad) Place on rack with boiling water and a little salt and pressure-cook for 4–5 minutes.
Beans (French) Place on rack with boiling water and a little salt and pressure-cook for 3 minutes.
Beans (Runner) Place on rack with boiling water and add salt, then pressure-cook for 2–3 minutes, according to maturity of beans.
Beetroot Place on rack with a little salt and 600 ml (1 pint) water and pressure-cook for 10–35 minutes, according to age and size.
Brussels sprouts When water is boiling, put them on rack, season and pressure-cook for 3–4 minutes.
Carrots Pressure-cook for 2–10 minutes, according to size and age. Young whole carrots take 5–6 minutes; old ones, if diced about 2 minutes, if sliced 4–5 minutes, if halved or quartered 5 minutes, if whole 6–8 minutes.
Cauliflower When water is boiling, put vegetable on rack and season. Whole cauliflowers take 5–6 minutes, depending on size and maturity; sprigs 3–4 minutes.

Celery When water is boiling, put celery on rack and season. Pressure-cook for 3–4 minutes.
Corn on the cob Add water and a little salt and pressure-cook for 4 minutes.
Green vegetables (Cabbage, Greens, etc.) When water is boiling, add salt and pressure-cook for 2–4 minutes.
Leeks Put on rack with boiling water and a little salt and pressure-cook for 3–5 minutes.
Marrow Put on the rack, add water and some salt, and pressure-cook for 3–4 minutes.
Mushrooms Put on rack, add water and pressure-cook for 2–4 minutes.
Onions Place on rack with some salt and water and pressure-cook for 3–4 minutes in the case of sliced or quartered onions, 8–10 minutes for whole ones.
Parsnips If halved lengthways, they take 7–8 minutes' pressure-cooking; if sliced, 3–4 minutes.
Peas (green) When the water boils, place the peas on the rack with a sprig of mint. Pressure-cook for 3–4 minutes.
Potatoes Place on the rack or in a separator and add water and seasoning. Pressure-cook as follows:

In jackets: 8–10 minutes
Peeled, medium-sized: 4–5 minutes
Peeled and quartered: 3–4 minutes
New (add mint): 6–8 minutes.

Mashed potatoes Melt a little butter in the pan, add 150 ml (¼ pint) milk for every 700 g (1½ lb) potatoes, with seasoning to taste, and put in the potatoes, cut in small pieces. Pressure-cook for 3–6 minutes, according to size, then mash them in the pan.
Spinach Place on rack when water boils, season and pressure-cook for 1 minute.
Swedes and turnips Place on rack, add water and a little salt and pressure-cook for 4–5 minutes.
Tomatoes Stand them on the rack, with water, and pressure-cook for 1–2 minutes.
Braised vegetables The most suitable kinds are carrots, turnips, parsnips, celery and onions. For every 450 g (1 lb) of vegetables, place 25 g (1 oz) dripping in the pressure pan and sauté the vegetables over a low heat until the fat has been absorbed. Add 300 ml (½ pint) brown stock and pressure-cook for the time required by the various vegetables. Before serving, thicken the stock with 15 g (½ oz) cornflour to 300 ml (½ pint) liquid, or reduce it by boiling in an open pan.
Dried vegetables Before cooking, soak dried and split peas, butter beans and haricot beans (but not lentils) for 1–2 hours, or overnight, in boiling water; discard this water. Put the vegetables straight into the pan, without using the rack, and add 1·1

litres (2 pints) cold water and 10 ml (2 level tsp) salt for every 450 g (1 lb). Never fill the pan more than half-full, as dried vegetables swell during cooking. Bring slowly to 'high' pressure and cook butter and haricot beans and peas for 15–20 minutes, split peas and lentils for 15 minutes. Reduce the pressure gradually.

Vegetarian dishes

Chicory and rice

4 heads of chicory
50 g (2 oz) butter or margarine
stock
salt and pepper
30 ml (2 tbsp) long-grain rice (uncooked)
chopped parsley or grated cheese
**   to garnish**

Wash the chicory and cut in half lengthways, or leave whole if small. Melt the fat, add the chicory and cook for a few minutes, then half-cover with stock, season, put on a tightly-fitting lid and simmer for 10 minutes. Add the rice and cook until this is soft and almost all the liquor absorbed. Sprinkle with parsley or cheese.

Savoury pancakes

50 g (2 oz) flour
a pinch of salt
½ egg
150 ml (¼ pint) milk
4 hard-boiled eggs
100 g (4 oz) mushrooms, sliced
60 ml (4 tbsp) cooked peas
30 ml (2 tbsp) white sauce (see page 36)
fat or oil for frying

Make the batter by mixing the flour, salt, egg and milk together. Make the filling by mixing the chopped eggs and mushrooms, peas and sauce. Put some fat in a frying pan, pour in a little batter, and cook on both sides: keep hot on a plate over boiling water. Continue adding fat and batter to the pan until all the batter is used and 6 pancakes have been made. Put a little filling in the centre of each pancake and fold over in three. Serve hot, with baked potatoes or a mixed salad and a sauce. *Serves 3*

Cheese and leek pie

175 g (6 oz) shortcrust pastry
2–3 leeks, parboiled and cut into rounds
seasoned flour
100 g (4 oz) cheese, grated
30 ml (2 tbsp) top of the milk
beaten egg to glaze

Line an 18-cm (7-inch) pie plate with half the pastry. Put the leeks on the pastry and sprinkle with a little seasoned flour. Cover with the grated cheese and add the milk. Roll out the rest of the pastry and cut into strips, plait these lattice-fashion over the top. Brush with beaten egg and bake in the oven at 220°C (425°F) mark 7 for about 30 minutes.

Nutty-stuffed tomatoes

4 large tomatoes
50 g (2 oz) fresh white breadcrumbs
50 g (2 oz) walnuts, chopped
10 ml (2 tsp) grated raw onion
10 ml (2 tsp) chopped parsley
5 ml (1 tsp) chopped fresh mint
1 egg
salt and pepper
butter

Cut off a small round from the top of each tomato and reserve it for a lid. Scoop out the inside of the tomatoes and mix with the breadcrumbs, walnuts, onion and herbs. Bind with the egg, season, fill the tomatoes and dot each with a little butter. Put on the lid of each, put them on a greased baking tray. Cover and bake in the oven at 180°C (350°F) mark 4 for 15–20 minutes.

Vegetable pie

450 g (1 lb) cooked mixed vegetables
600 ml (1 pint) cheese sauce (see page 36)
900 g (2 lb) sieved cooked potato
50 g (2 oz) butter or margarine
beaten egg or milk
salt and pepper
grated cheese
mushrooms or tomatoes to garnish

Put the vegetables and sauce in layers in an ovenproof casserole. Mix the potato with the fat, egg and seasoning, and spread on top of the vegetables. Sprinkle with a little grated cheese and brown in the oven at 180°C (350°F) mark 4 for about 15 minutes. Garnish with mushrooms or tomatoes. *Serves 6*

Mushroom ring

50 g (2 oz) butter or margarine
1 small onion, skinned and chopped
225 g (8 oz) mushrooms, sliced
salt and pepper
grated nutmeg
50 g (2 oz) flour
150 ml (¼ pint) milk
2 eggs
50 g (2 oz) cheese, grated
30 ml (2 tbsp) cream or top of the milk
finely chopped parsley to garnish
tomato sauce to serve

Melt the fat and fry the onion and the mushrooms (reserving 1–2 whole ones for garnishing) for 5 minutes. Add salt, pepper and nutmeg. Gently stir in the flour, add the milk and continue stirring until the mixture comes to the boil. Remove from the heat, add the beaten eggs, cheese and cream. Turn the mixture into a greased 900-ml (1½-pint) ring mould and bake in the oven at 180°C (350°F) mark 4 for 30 minutes, or until firm. Gently turn out on to a warm dish, garnish with parsley and the reserved fried mushrooms and serve with tomato sauce. (Incidentally, if you do not require it as a strictly vegetarian dish, you can garnish the ring with fried or grilled bacon rolls.) Mushroom ring is also delicious served cold, with salad.

Cheese and egg pie

225 g (8 oz) shortcrust pastry
600 ml (1 pint) cheese sauce (see page 36)
4 hard-boiled eggs
100 g (4 oz) mushrooms or tomatoes
50 g (2 oz) cheese, grated

Make a 20·5-cm (8-inch) flan case with the shortcrust pastry and bake 'blind' in the oven at 200°C (400°F) mark 6. Make the cheese sauce and add the quartered hard-boiled eggs. Lightly fry the mushrooms (or skin and chop the tomatoes) and add to the sauce. Put the mixture into the pastry case, sprinkle the grated cheese on top and brown in a hot oven or under the grill.

Vegetable dumpling

Make 225 g (8 oz) cheese suetcrust pastry (see below) and use two-thirds of it to line a greased 900-ml (1½-pint) basin. Chop up a variety of cooked vegetables (eg, carrots, turnips, parsnips, onions, mushrooms, cauliflower and French beans) and moisten with 300 ml (½ pint) cheese sauce (see page 36). Put this mixture inside the pastry case and cover with the remaining pastry. Cover with greaseproof paper and then with aluminium foil and steam for 2½–3 hours in a pan, with boiling water coming half-way up the basin. Turn out and serve with tomato sauce.

Cheese suetcrust pastry

225 g (8 oz) flour
a pinch of salt
5 ml (1 level tsp) baking powder
100 g (4 oz) cheese, grated
50 g (2 oz) shredded suet
cold water to mix

Make the pastry by combining the dry ingredients and adding enough water to give a soft, elastic dough. Use as desired, eg, for Vegetable dumpling above.

SALADS

There are thousands of variations on the salad theme, and plenty of scope for people who enjoy creating recipes or who have artistic flair.

From the health point of view, salads have much to offer. Since the ingredients are mostly used uncooked and very fresh, their vitamin C value is retained; when the salad is coupled with a protein food such as eggs, cheese, fish or meat, it makes a very nutritious meal. Salads appeal particularly to those on a slimming diet, as the number of calories in the various ingredients is usually low.

Even the best of salads is improved by a good dressing, so we devote a section to salad dressings, with many variations. Remember not to use too much dressing; no surplus should be seen at the bottom of the bowl – there should be just sufficient clinging to the salad ingredients to flavour them appetisingly. A salad intended to accompany a main dish is usually tossed in a simple French dressing. Heartier salads, with mayonnaise or another rich dressing, may be served at a less formal lunch, dinner or supper, where the chief course is not very substantial, or they may indeed form the main course.

Salad ingredients

Avocados Just before serving slice in half, remove stone and peel and slice. Toss in lemon juice to prevent discoloration and use in mixed salads.

Beetroot Thinly peel or rub off the skin from the cooked beetroot. Cut into thin slices, if the beetroots are small; grate or dice them if large. The prepared beetroot can be sprinkled with salt, pepper and 5–10 ml (1–2 level tsp) sugar and covered with vinegar or vinegar and water – this helps it to keep and also gives it a better flavour.

Cabbage Wash the leaves in salted water, drain and cut into shreds with a sharp knife.

Celeriac Wash, slice and then peel. Dice or cut into matchstick shaped pieces. Blanch in boiling, salted water for 2–3 minutes. Drain and cool. Use tossed in mayonnaise or French dressing.

Celery Separate the sticks and wash them well in cold water, scrubbing to remove any dirt from the grooves. Slice, chop or make curls (see Salad garnishes).

Chicory Trim off the root end and any damaged leaves, wash the chicory in cold water and drain.

Chinese cabbage Trim the root ends and any damaged leaves, wash well. Use in salads finely shredded.

Cucumber Wipe the skin and either leave it on if liked or peel it off thinly. Slice the cucumber finely, sprinkle with salt and

112

Italian mixed meat salad (see page 118).

leave it for about 1 hour; pour off the liquid and rinse. Alternatively, you can soak the cucumber in a little vinegar, with salt and a pinch of sugar. If you like the cucumber crisp, use it when freshly sliced.

Endive Trim off the root end, remove the coarse outer leaves, separate remaining leaves, wash and drain well.

Fennel Trim off top stems and slice off base. Wash well in cold water and thinly slice. Fennel has a distinct aniseed flavour which is refreshing when used in salads.

Garlic Many of those who say they dislike garlic don't really know how to use it. True, it is pungent and needs using with discretion – you will find one clove ample for the average bowl of salad.

First remove the papery outside skin of the garlic clove, then crush the clove with a broad-bladed knife (do this on a plate, unless you have a board that you keep specially for onion chopping). Scrape the crushed garlic into the salad bowl or add it to the dressing. Alternatively, use a garlic press, if you have one.

Herbs in salads Parsley is an addition to any salad. Don't chop it very finely but snip it with scissors straight on to the salad, just before serving. A few leaves of fresh mint, sage, thyme, dill or tarragon (one at a time, not all together) can be chopped and sprinkled over a salad. Some people like verbena or rosemary, but don't be too liberal with these slightly scented flavours unless you know the tastes of the people you are serving.

Lettuce Remove the outer coarse leaves. Separate the inner leaves and wash them under a running cold tap or in a bowl of cold water. Drain them in a sieve or colander or shake them in a clean towel or a salad basket.

To 'revive' a withered lettuce, wash it in cold water, shake slightly to remove the excess moisture, place in a polythene bag or a bowl covered with a plate and put in the bottom of the refrigerator or in any cool place. In an hour or so the leaves will have crisped up.

Mushrooms Trim the base of the stalks. Skin or wipe and thoroughly dry, if necessary. Halve or slice thinly and use in salads.

Mustard and cress Trim off the roots and lower parts of the stems with scissors and place the leaves in a colander or sieve. Wash them under running cold water, turning the cress over and removing the seeds.

Peppers Wash, cut off the top to remove stalks, seeds and membrane from inside. Slice thinly and use in salads.

Radishes Trim off the root end and leaves and wash the radishes in cold water. Slice

thinly or cut into 'lilies' or 'roses' (see Salad garnishes).

Spinach Raw spinach leaves can replace lettuce and their dark green colour is a good contrast to other ingredients.

Spring onions Trim off the root end, remove the papery outer skin, trim the green leaves down to about 5 cm (2 inches) of green above the white and wash.

Tomatoes Remove the stem and wash or wipe the tomatoes. To remove the skins, plunge them for a minute into boiling water, then lift them out and put immediately into cold water; when they are cool, the skins will peel off easily with a knife. Alternatively, spear a tomato on the prongs of a fork and turn it gently over a gas jet until the skin bursts, then peel it off with a knife.

Watercress Trim the coarse ends from the stalks, wash the watercress and drain well before using.

Salad garnishes

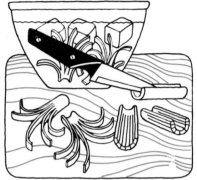

The classic green salad needs no garnish and only the simplest of touches is required to set off many other types – a dusting of chopped herbs on potato salad, a sprinkling of chopped onion or some thinly cut onion rings on a tomato salad, a few leaves of watercress on an orange salad. However, for those occasions when you want something a little more ambitious to set off a mixed salad or to garnish, say, a cold veal and ham pie, here are some attractive salad decorations that can quite easily be produced.

Radish roses Choose round radishes and wash them well, removing the root but leaving 2·5 cm (1 inch) or so of the stalk. Using a small, sharp knife or potato parer, peel the skin down in sections to look like petals, starting at the root end and continuing nearly as far as the stalk. Repeat all round, leaving the middle of the radish as the flower centre. Soak in cold water for a short time to make the petals open out; shake well before using.

Radish lilies Wash and trim the radishes, then cut each into sections down from the root end towards the stalk. Leave in cold water until they open like flowers.

Curled celery Cut into very thin shreds lengthwise and soak in cold or iced water until curled – about 1 hour. Drain well before using.

Curled spring onions Prepare as for celery.

Cucumber cones Cut thin slices. Take one slice, cut from centre to rim, then wrap one cut edge over the other to form a cone.

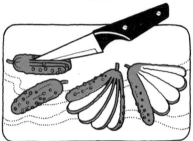

Top: Curled celery
Centre: Gherkin fans
Bottom: Lemon twists and butterflies

Crimped cucumber Working lengthways on a whole or half cucumber, remove strips of the cucumber skin about 0·3 cm (⅛ inch) wide at intervals of about 0·3 cm (⅛ inch). Now cut the cucumber crossways into thin slices.

Gherkin fans Choose long, thin gherkins. Cut each lengthways into thin slices, but leave these joined at one end. Fan out the slices.

Lemon twists and butterflies For a twist, cut to the centre of a slice from one side and twist the halves in opposite directions. For butterflies, cut out two triangular pieces from each slice.

Onion rings Cut the onion crossways. Use the rings in graduated sizes or singly to enclose another garnish such as chopped egg or beetroot.

Tomato twists Slice a firm tomato crossways. Slit each piece up to the core, leaving a piece at the top holding the halves together; turn halves in opposite directions to make the twist.

Use beetroot, lemon or cucumber similarly.

Tomato lilies Choose firm, even-sized tomatoes. Using a small sharp-pointed knife, make a series of V-shaped cuts round the middle of each, cutting right through to the centre. Carefully pull the halves apart.

Red pepper julienne Cut a red (or green) pepper into very thin strips, cutting across the vegetable and removing any pith or seeds.

Quick garnish Sprinkle finely chopped parsley on potato salad; finely chopped onion on beetroot; chopped spring onion on tomato; chopped mint, chives, tarragon or parsley on green salad.

Salads

Chicken and almond salad

175 g (6 oz) seedless raisins
100 g (4 oz) almonds
325 g (12 oz) cold cooked chicken
142-ml (5-fl oz) carton single cream
30 ml (2 tbsp) mayonnaise
salt and pepper
5 ml (1 tsp) lemon juice
15 ml (1 tbsp) grated onion
15 ml (1 tbsp) chopped parsley
lettuce

Cover the raisins with cold water and bring to the boil, leave to stand for 5 minutes, then drain. Blanch and toast the almonds. Cut the chicken into long shreds. Mix the cream with the mayonnaise and season with the salt, pepper and lemon juice. Put all the ingredients except the lettuce in a bowl and combine well with the mayonnaise mixture. Serve the salad on a dish lined with lettuce leaves.

Egg and yoghurt salad

4 hard-boiled eggs
1 head of celery, washed and trimmed
4 carrots, pared and grated
radishes, trimmed
½ cucumber, sliced
284-ml (10-fl oz) carton natural yoghurt
5 ml (1 level tsp) paprika pepper
5 ml (1 level tsp) sugar
15 ml (1 tbsp) lemon juice
15 ml (1 tbsp) orange juice
pepper
15 ml (1 tbsp) finely chopped parsley

Slice the eggs, lay them on a bed of shredded celery, cover with the raw grated carrot and surround with sliced radishes and cucumber. Cover with a dressing made by mixing the yoghurt with the paprika, sugar, strained fruit juices, a little pepper and the parsley. Chill and serve.

Duck and tangerine salad

2 lettuce hearts, washed
325–450 g (¾–1 lb) cooked duck
6 tangerines
a bunch of watercress
225 g (8 oz) cooked green peas
30 ml (2 tbsp) French dressing
chopped parsley to garnish

Arrange the lettuce heart leaves on a flat dish. Slice the duck and arrange neatly on the lettuce. Peel the tangerines, removing as much of the pith as possible, and divide 2 of them into segments. Push a small bunch of watercress into the top of each whole tangerine and put these on the dish. Toss the peas in French dressing and arrange round the duck. Garnish with parsley and tangerine segments.

Salmon and rice salad

175 g (6 oz) long grain rice
226-g (8 oz) can salmon
225 g (8 oz) tomatoes, skinned and chopped
60 ml (4 tbsp) chopped chives
90 ml (6 tbsp) whipped cream
90 ml (6 tbsp) mayonnaise
5 ml (1 level tsp) celery seeds
grated lemon rind
salt and pepper
lettuce
radishes to garnish

Cook the rice in boiling salted water and drain well. Drain and flake the salmon, add with the tomato and chives to the rice and mix lightly. Fold the whipped cream into the mayonnaise and add the celery seeds, with lemon rind, salt and pepper to taste. Fold in the rice mixture and press into a 1·1-litre (2-pint) ring mould. When the salad is set, turn it out on to a serving dish lined with lettuce leaves and garnish the ring with sliced radishes.

Ham and celery salad

4 sticks of celery, washed and trimmed
175 g (6 oz) lean ham
¼ cucumber
225 g (8 oz) cooked new potatoes
mayonnaise
1 red or green pepper (or a small pepper of each colour)
1–2 hard-boiled eggs
lettuce or endive

Cut the celery, ham, cucumber and potatoes into small, neat pieces. Combine with enough mayonnaise to bind and add any trimmings from the peppers and the eggs that are not required for garnishing the dish. Put some lettuce or endive leaves on a flat plate, pile the salad ingredients in the centre and put slices of hard-boiled egg and pepper rings round the outside.

Christmas salad

225 g (8 oz) cooked turkey
6 sticks of celery, washed and trimmed
150 ml (¼ pint) mayonnaise (see page 126)
salt and pepper
5 ml (1 tsp) lemon juice
lettuce

Dice the turkey and celery and combine with the mayonnaise. Season with the salt, pepper and lemon juice, chill and serve on lettuce leaves.

Ham and salami antipasto

Antipasto This Italian word means either hors d'œuvre or a salad. Most basic antipasto recipes contain tuna fish, anchovies, tomatoes and peppers. The flavours should contrast – spicy, sharp and bland – and the colours should be as varied and attractive as possible.

4 slices of Parma ham
4 slices of tomato
4 slices of Italian salami
4 sticks of celery, each cut in 4 5-cm (2-inch) strips
99-g (3½-oz) can tuna
4 anchovy fillets, divided in halves
141-g (5-oz) can red pimientos, cut in strips
4 black olives
4 green olives
20 ml (4 tsp) capers

Lay the slices of ham on a plate, lengthways and overlapping each other. Between them arrange the slices of tomato and salami alternately. Pile the celery at either end of the dish. Place the tuna fish across the centre and cover with anchovy fillets. Pile

the pimiento at one side of the dish. Stone the olives and slice into strips, then pile the black ones in two opposite corners and the green ones in the remaining corners. Place the capers down both sides of the fish.

Meat salad mould

25 g (1 oz) gelatine
150 ml (¼ pint) water
600 ml (1 pint) meat stock
2·5 ml (½ tsp) meat extract
salt and pepper
100 g (4 oz) cooked peas
15 ml (1 tbsp) chutney
100 g (4 oz) corned beef, diced
100 g (4 oz) breakfast sausage
radishes, sliced
1 tomato, sliced
cucumber, sliced
1 hard-boiled egg, sliced
lettuce, sliced tomato and mustard and
    cress to garnish

Dissolve the gelatine in the water and add it to the stock, meat extract and seasoning. Place a little of this jelly at the bottom of a 900 ml–1·1 litre (1½–2 pint) mould or cake tin and put this in a cold place to set. Meanwhile, add the peas, chutney, corned beef and breakfast sausage (reserving some for garnish) to the rest of the stock. Arrange the radishes, tomato, cucumber and hard-boiled egg attractively in the set jelly in the mould, together with the rest of the breakfast sausage. Pour on the rest of the jelly and allow to set in a cold place. Turn on to a dish and garnish.

Virginia chicken apple salad

½ small cooked chicken
225 g (8 oz) unpeeled apples
90 ml (6 tbsp) lemon juice
½ head of celery, washed and trimmed
6 stuffed olives
50 g (2 oz) slivered almonds
45 ml (3 tbsp) mayonnaise (see page 126)
113-ml (4-fl oz) carton double cream,
    whipped
5 ml (1 level tsp) salt
1 lettuce, washed
2 heads of chicory, trimmed
apple rings, cored but unpeeled, to
    garnish

Cut the chicken into chunks. Chop the apples and dip into 45 ml (3 tbsp) of the lemon juice to prevent their discolouring. Slice the celery and olives. Combine the above ingredients with the almonds. Blend the mayonnaise with the cream, 30 ml (2 tbsp) lemon juice and the salt; toss this with the chicken mixture, then leave to chill. Heap the salad on a layer of lettuce and chicory. Dip the apple rings in the rest of the
116

lemon juice, tuck some chicory leaves in each ring and use to garnish.

Carrot and raisin salad

75 g (3 oz) seedless raisins
1 orange
450 g (1 lb) carrots, grated
60 ml (4 tbsp) mayonnaise (see page 126)
15 ml (1 tbsp) lemon juice
5 ml (1 level tsp) sugar
1·25 ml (¼ level tsp) salt

Put the raisins in a bowl, pour boiling water over them and leave to stand for 5 minutes to plump them; drain well. Peel the orange and divide into sections, then chop. Add the orange and carrots to the raisins. Combine the mayonnaise, lemon juice, sugar and salt and toss the carrot mixture well into this dressing.

Waldorf salad

900 g (2 lb) red eating apples
lemon juice
5 ml (1 level tsp) sugar
150 ml (¼ pint) mayonnaise (see page
    126)
1 head of celery, washed and trimmed
50 g (2 oz) shelled walnuts
1 lettuce, washed

Core the apples; dice all but one, then slice this apple, dip in lemon juice to prevent it discolouring and reserve it for garnish. Toss the diced apples with 30 ml (2 tbsp) lemon juice, the sugar and 15 ml (1 tbsp) mayonnaise. Just before serving, slice the celery, chop the walnuts (keeping a few whole for garnish) and add both to the apple mixture. Add the rest of the mayonnaise and toss together very well. Serve in a bowl lined with lettuce leaves and garnish with the apple slices and the whole walnuts.

Cold curried chicken salad

175 g (6 oz) long grain rice
1 small chicken, cooked
1 small cauliflower
45 ml (3 tbsp) French dressing (see page
    126)
150 ml (¼ pint) mayonnaise (see page
    126)
15 ml (1 level tbsp) curry powder
2·5 ml (½ level tsp) salt
1·25 ml (¼ level tsp) pepper
30 ml (2 tbsp) milk
1 small green pepper, seeded
2 sticks of celery, washed, trimmed and
    sliced
2 onions, skinned and finely sliced
1 cos or round lettuce, washed

Cook the rice in boiling salted water until tender; drain very well and allow to dry. Cut the chicken into chunks. Remove the

green .outer leaves of the cauliflower and cut the 'flower' into 0·5-cm (¼-inch) strips, then toss with the rice in the French dressing. Combine the mayonnaise, curry powder, salt and pepper in a large bowl, slowly stir in the milk, add the chicken and toss together. Add the rice mixture, the green pepper, cut in strips, the celery and the onion rings. Line a plate with lettuce leaves and turn the mixture on to this. Serve with separate dishes of curry accompaniments – for instance, flaked coconut, salted peanuts, pineapple cubes, tomato wedges and redcurrant jelly.

Piquant potato salad

2 small onions, skinned
200 ml (⅓ pint) stock
50 g (2 oz) butter or margarine
150 ml (¼ pint) vinegar
salt and pepper
a little sugar
900 g (2 lb) cooked potatoes, sliced
    0·5 cm (¼ inch) thick
15 ml (1 tbsp) chopped chives or parsley

Slice the onions and boil until tender in the stock and fat. Add the vinegar, seasonings and sugar, then the potatoes, bring to the boil and cook for a few minutes. Allow to cool before serving, sprinkled with chopped chives or parsley.

Caesar salad

1 cos lettuce, washed
French dressing
1 egg, beaten
50 g (2 oz) Parmesan cheese, grated
60-g (2-oz) can anchovy fillets, finely
    chopped
garlic croûtons (see below)

Toss the lettuce in the dressing. Mix the egg, cheese and anchovy and add to the lettuce, mixing well.

Make some garlic croûtons by cutting 3 slices of French bread into cubes and frying them in oil with 2 cut cloves of garlic. When they are golden brown, remove the garlic and drain the croûtons on absorbent paper.

Immediately before serving the salad, add the croûtons.

Leek and tomato salad

1 clove of garlic, skinned
1 cos lettuce, washed
4 small leeks, washed and sliced
4 tomatoes, skinned and sliced
5 ml (1 tsp) chopped basil
5 ml (1 tsp) chopped chervil
45 ml (3 tbsp) French dressing (see page
    126)

Rub round the inside of a salad bowl with

Mexican bean salad
(see page 118).

the crushed clove of garlic and arrange the lettuce in it. Place the leeks and tomatoes on the lettuce and sprinkle with the basil and chervil. Pour the French dressing over.

Italian mixed meat salad

Illustrated in colour on page 113

2 green peppers
2 red peppers
3 courgettes, trimmed and sliced

For the dressing
30 ml (2 tbsp) red wine vinegar
30 ml (2 tbsp) olive oil
5 ml (1 tsp) Worcestershire sauce
5 ml (1 level tsp) tomato paste
2.5 ml (½ level tsp) paprika pepper
salt
a pinch of sugar

75 g (3 oz) pasta spirals, cooked
175 g (6 oz) cooked ham, diced
100 g (4 oz) garlic sausage, thickly sliced
50 g (2 oz) sliced salami, cut into quarters
black olives, stoned, to garnish

Slice the peppers and remove the core and seeds. Put the pepper and courgette slices in a pan of cold water, bring to the boil then drain and cool. Meanwhile, make the dressing. Put the dressing ingredients into a bowl and whisk well together. Place the vegetables, pasta and meats in a serving dish. Pour the dressing over and toss gently. Quarter the olives and use to garnish.

Salad of mushroom and shellfish

1 clove of garlic, skinned and crushed
225 g (8 oz) mushrooms
225 g (8 oz) frozen scampi, thawed
lemon and oil dressing

Rub 2 bowls with the crushed garlic. Slice the raw mushrooms thinly, then put them in one bowl and the shellfish in the other. pour half of the dressing over the mushrooms and the rest over the fish. Just before serving mix the two and sprinkle with parsley.

Golden slaw

1 medium Savoy cabbage
450 g (1 lb) red eating apples
225 g (8 oz) Gruyère cheese
salt and pepper
150 ml (¼ pint) mayonnaise (see page 126)
15 ml (1 tbsp) prepared mustard
a little sugar

Wash the cabbage well. Spread out the outer leaves, then cut round the base of the heart and scoop it out, leaving a 'bowl'.

Ingredients for Golden slaw

Finely shred the cabbage heart. Core and dice the apples. Cut the cheese into fine slivers, put in a basin with the cabbage and apples, sprinkle with salt and pepper and toss gently. Combine with mayonnaise with the prepared mustard and toss the salad mixture in this dressing until the ingredients are well coated. Serve in the scooped-out cabbage 'bowl', sprinkled with sugar.

Russian salad

225 g (8 oz) cold cooked meat
2 cooked beetroots, diced
4 cooked potatoes, diced
4 gherkins, chopped
½ cucumber, diced
2 hard-boiled eggs, chopped
French dressing (see page 126)
2.5 ml (½ tsp) made mustard

Dice the meat and mix with the beetroots, potatoes, gherkins and cucumber and the chopped eggs. Mix the French dressing with mustard and combine with salad.

Fruit, nut and cheese salad

225 g (8 oz) curd cheese
15 ml (1 tbsp) seedless raisins
lettuce, washed
4 canned peach halves
4 walnut halves
cucumber and watercress to garnish

Beat the cheese until smooth. Put the raisins into boiling water for 1–2 minutes to soften them, drain well and cool, then mix with the cheese. Put the lettuce on a dish in about 4 individual portions and place on each a peach half. Top each with a spoonful of the cheese and raisin mixture and a walnut half. Garnish the dish with cucumber and watercress.

'Swiss crest' salad

900 g (2 lb) asparagus
salted water
175 g (6 oz) ham, preferably smoked
225 g (8 oz) Gruyère cheese
225 g (8 oz) tomatoes
45 ml (3 tbsp) mayonnaise (see page 126)

Wash and prepare the asparagus and cook in salted water; strain and cool. Divide into 4 equal portions and place on a large round plate, forming a cross. Fill the gaps between the arms of the cross alternately with rolled slices of ham and slices of cheese. Surround with sliced tomatoes and fill the centre of the cross with mayonnaise. Serve cold.

Asparagus and corn salad

2 corn cobs
1 bundle of asparagus, cooked
15 ml (1 tbsp) chopped capers
150 ml (¼ pint) mayonnaise (see page 126)
2 lettuces, washed
1 hard-boiled egg and 2 tomatoes to garnish

Cook and drain the corn and allow to get cold. Cut the asparagus heads off to the depth of 5 cm (2 inches); keep a few for garnishing and put the remainder in a basin with the corn and capers. Add the mayonnaise and blend well. Pile into individual salad dishes and garnish with lettuce, sliced egg and tomato.

Mexican bean salad

Illustrated in colour on page 117

425-g (15-oz) can red kidney beans
4 sticks of celery, washed and chopped
25 g (1 oz) gherkins, sliced
30 ml (2 level tbsp) finely chopped onion
60 ml (4 tbsp) oil
30 ml (2 tbsp) malt vinegar
2.5 ml (½ level tsp) French mustard
1.25 ml (¼ level tsp) caster sugar
salt and pepper
2 eggs, hard-boiled
1 cos lettuce heart
a few celery leaves to garnish (optional)

Drain the kidney beans well and combine in a bowl with the chopped celery, gherkins and onion. Place the oil, vinegar, mustard, sugar, salt and pepper in a tightly lidded container. Shake well, pour over the bean mixture and mix well. Slice the eggs length-ways. Arrange 2 lettuce leaves on each plate, pile the bean mixture on to the base of these, spooning over any remaining dressing. Place 3 slices of hard-boiled egg on each and add a few celery leaves to garnish. Or arrange on one large serving plate. *Serves 6*

Rainbow salad

1 clove of garlic, skinned
1 small, close cabbage heart, chopped
1 beetroot, peeled and sliced
2 carrots, pared and sliced
2 tomatoes, skinned and sliced
½ cucumber, sliced
100–175 g (4–6 oz) cheese, grated
50 g (2 oz) green peas
French dressing (see page 126)
2 or 3 hard-boiled eggs to garnish

Rub a flat platter or dish with the cut garlic. Place the different ingredients in sections radiating from the centre of the dish. Sprinkle with French dressing (or serve this separately) and garnish with quartered eggs.

Potato and egg salad

30 ml (2 tbsp) vinegar
5 ml (1 level tsp) sugar
salt and pepper
900 g (2 lb) cooked potatoes, sliced
3 hard-boiled eggs, sliced
1 onion, skinned and grated
a few anchovy fillets, chopped
15 ml (1 tbsp) chopped parsley to
   garnish

Combine the vinegar, sugar and seasonings in the bottom of a dish. Put the potato and egg slices in layers in the dish, sprinkling each layer with onion and anchovy. Finish with a layer of egg and garnish with chopped parsley and a line of grated onion.

Mussel salad

4 small potatoes, skinned
8 mussels
5 ml (1 tsp) each chopped parsley, dill
   and chives
white wine dressing (see page 127)
lettuce leaves, washed
1 hard-boiled egg and 1 canned truffle,
   if available, to garnish

Cook the potatoes, drain, cool and dice them. Thoroughly clean the mussels and cook in boiling salted water until their shells open; remove from the shells, discard the beards and dice the mussels. Chop all the

herbs and mix them with the dressing. Toss the potatoes and mussels in the dressing and arrange on lettuce leaves. Garnish with chopped egg and truffle strips.

Crab salad

50 g (2 oz) black olives
8 sticks of celery, washed and trimmed
2 × 92-g (3¼-oz) cans crabmeat
90 ml (6 tbsp) mayonnaise (see page 126)
30 ml (2 tbsp) tomato ketchup
10 ml (2 tsp) lemon juice
lettuce

Cut the olives into wedges, slice the celery thinly and flake the crabmeat. Blend the mayonnaise, tomato ketchup and lemon juice and toss the other ingredients lightly in this mixture. Serve in lettuce 'cups'.

Sardine and beetroot salad

2 × 198-g (7-oz) cans sardines
2 eating apples
1 medium beetroot, peeled
60–90 ml (4–6 tbsp) seasoned
   mayonnaise
lettuce to garnish
lemon juice

Mash the sardines in a bowl. Grate 1 apple and the beetroot and mix with the sardines. Add mayonnaise to moisten and garnish with lettuce and sliced apple, dipped in lemon juice.

Sauerkraut salad

1 small can sauerkraut
142-ml (5-fl oz) carton natural yoghurt
sugar to taste

Rinse the sauerkraut in cold water, drain and mix with the yoghurt, adding sugar to taste.

Tomatoes stuffed with apple and celery

4 large tomatoes
salt and pepper
4 sticks of celery, washed
2 apples
60 ml (4 tbsp) lemon juice
5 ml (1 level tsp) sugar
60 ml (4 tbsp) soured cream
45 ml (3 tbsp) olive oil
15 ml (1 tbsp) grated horseradish
chives, watercress and radishes to
   garnish

Cut a 0·5-cm (¼-inch) slice from the stem end of each of the tomatoes; using a spoon, scoop out and reserve the pulp. Sprinkle the tomato cups with 5 ml (1 level tsp) salt and 1·25 ml (¼ level tsp) pepper, then place

them upside-down on a plate. Finely slice the celery, grate the unpeeled apples coarsely and put in a bowl; add the lemon juice, sugar and 2·5 ml (½ level tsp) salt. Combine the sour cream, olive oil, horse-radish, 2·5 ml (½ level tsp) salt and 1·25 ml (¼ level tsp) pepper. Drain the tomato pulp and chop it coarsely. Chill all these in-gredients. Combine the apple and sour cream mixtures, then add the tomato pulp. Use to fill the tomato cups, arrange these on a large dish and sprinkle with chopped chives. Garnish with watercress and radish roses or as desired.

Red cabbage salad

450 g (1 lb) red cabbage
2 sharp dessert apples
French dressing
1 hard-boiled egg to garnish

Quarter the cabbage and take out the root. Shred the cabbage finely. Grate the apples and put them straight into the dressing. Add the cabbage, toss lightly before serving and garnish with the sliced egg.

Curried mushroom salad

Illustrated in colour on page 121

225 g (8 oz) button mushrooms, trimmed
100 g (4 oz) cooked ham, diced
½ cucumber, diced
141-g (5-fl oz) carton natural yoghurt
15 ml (1 level tbsp) concentrated curry
   sauce or 5 ml (1 level tsp) curry
   powder
salt and pepper
10 ml (2 tsp) lemon juice
30 ml (2 level tbsp) mango chutney

Cut the larger mushrooms into quarters and leave the small ones whole. Stir the mushrooms, ham and cucumber together in a bowl. Mix the yoghurt, curry sauce or powder, seasoning and lemon juice to-gether in a separate bowl. Chop any large pieces of mango in the chutney and add to the yoghurt mixture. Pour the yoghurt mixture over the mushrooms, ham and cucumber and stir until well combined. Chill for 1–2 hours before serving.

Beetroot salad

450 g (1 lb) cooked beetroot
1 horseradish root
5 ml (1 level tsp) sugar
5 ml (1 level tsp) salt
2·5 ml (½ level tsp) caraway seeds
juice of 3 lemons

Peel and slice the beetroot and grate the horseradish. Mix the horseradish with the sugar, salt, caraway seeds and lemon juice and pour over the beetroot.

Raw celeriac salad

2 young celeriac roots
2 apples
French dressing

Peel and shred the roots carefully. Peel, core and shred the apples. Toss both thoroughly in the French dressing and chill for 3–4 hours before serving.

Avocado, grape and prawn salad

Illustrated in colour opposite

2 large avocados
lemon juice
175 g (6 oz) white grapes
4 sticks of celery, washed
175 g (6 oz) shelled prawns

For the dressing
30 ml (2 tbsp) lime cordial
5 ml (1 tsp) white wine vinegar
2·5 ml (½ level tsp) Dijon mustard
salt and pepper

50 g (2 oz) unshelled prawns to garnish

Cut the avocados in half and remove the stones. Peel thinly and cut each half into slices. Brush with lemon juice. Peel the grapes, remove the pips and place in a bowl. Finely slice the celery and add to the grapes with the shelled prawns. Place the dressing ingredients in a lidded container and shake well to combine the ingredients. Pour the dressing over the grapes, celery and prawns and stir gently until well mixed. Arrange the avocado slices around the edge of four serving dishes or one large dish, spoon the grape and prawn mixture in the centre and garnish with unshelled prawns.

Marguerite salad

4 heads of chicory
1 large apple, peeled
lemon juice
2 sticks of celery, washed
4 mushrooms
454-g (16-oz) can grapefruit segments
4 tomatoes, skinned and sliced
watercress, washed
mayonnaise to serve

Cut off the root end of the chicory, remove the outer leaves and wash in cold water. Core and slice the apple, toss in lemon juice; cut the celery and mushrooms into Julienne strips; drain the grapefruit segments. Arrange the chicory leaves round the edge of a dish, next add the grapefruit segments; then the tomatoes, with mushroom and celery piled between them. Lastly, add a circle of apple slices with a bunch of watercress in the middle. Serve with mayonnaise.

120

Ensalada Isabella

2 celery hearts
450 g (1 lb) cooked potatoes
4 apples
lemon juice
1 clove of garlic, skinned and crushed
1 egg yolk
salt and pepper
oil

Remove the outer stalks of the celery, leaving the crisp hearts; wash and leave in cold water until required. Slice the potatoes; peel and slice the apples, toss in lemon juice. Combine the garlic, egg yolk and seasoning and stir in the oil, a few drops at a time, until the mixture is thick, then stir in a little lemon juice to taste. Cut up the celery and toss this with the apples and potatoes in the mayonnaise.

Side salads

For the dressings used in these salads see pages 126–127.

Green salad

This is the traditional French accompaniment to steak. Use two or more green salad ingredients such as lettuce, cress, watercress, endive etc. See that the lettuce is fresh and crisp and take care to use the right proportions of oil and vinegar in the French dressing. Toss the leaves lightly in dressing until thinly coated.

Chicory and orange salad

Illustrated in colour on page 125

15 ml (1 tbsp) lemon juice
1·25 ml (¼ level tsp) salt
freshly milled pepper
1·25 ml (¼ tsp) French mustard
5 ml (1 tsp) clear honey
45 ml (3 tbsp) vegetable oil
3 oranges
4 heads of chicory, trimmed and washed

Blend the lemon juice, salt, pepper, mustard and honey together in small bowl. Gradually whisk in the oil until the dressing is smooth and creamy.

Grate the rind from 2 oranges and add to the dressing. Remove the skin and pith from the oranges, divide into segments and place in a serving bowl together with any juice. Thinly slice the chicory and add to the bowl. Pour over the dressing and toss gently.

Leave to stand for 1–2 hours.

Broccoli salad

325 g (12 oz) broccoli heads
45 ml (3 tbsp) French dressing
30 ml (2 tbsp) chopped chervil
10 ml (2 tsp) chopped capers
45 ml (3 tbsp) cream dressing
sprigs of watercress to garnish

To prepare the broccoli, plunge it into rapidly boiling water, bring back to the boil and boil fast for 10 minutes. Immediately it is tender, drain it in a colander and when cool, pile in a bowl and chill. Sprinkle with some of the French dressing and leave for

Curried mushroom salad (see page 119), Raisin and nut salad (see page 122), Avocado, grape and prawn salad (see above).

about 1 hour. Add the chopped chervil and capers to the cream dressing and pile this on the broccoli. Dip the watercress in the French dressing and arrange round the broccoli.

Tomato ice

450 g (1 lb) tomatoes
½ clove of garlic, skinned
1 bayleaf
5 ml (1 tsp) chopped basil
300 ml (½ pint) thick mayonnaise (see page 126)
5 ml (1 tsp) tomato purée
juice of 1 lemon
grated rind of 1 orange
113-ml (4-fl oz) carton double cream
a pinch of sugar
salt and pepper

Make a tomato pulp by stewing the tomatoes with the garlic, bayleaf and chopped basil; sieve or purée this mixture. Mix the pulp with the mayonnaise and add the tomato purée, lemon juice and orange rind. Partially whip the cream and add the tomato mixture, with the sugar, salt and pepper to taste. Pour into an ice tray and freeze in the refrigerator, stirring every 30 minutes until the mixture is half frozen, then leave it to freeze completely.

This is often used to accompany grilled sole.

Dressed fennel

Slice the fennel finely, sprinkle with salt and cover with lemon and oil dressing.

Tomatoes and black olives

4 tomatoes, skinned
½ clove of garlic
45 ml (3 tbsp) mayonnaise (see page 126)
black pepper
8 olives, stoned and coarsely chopped

Halve the tomatoes and scoop out the seeds and pulp. Put pulp in a bowl, mix well with the crushed garlic and add the mayonnaise. Pour this dressing over the tomatoes, filling each, and sprinkle lightly with pepper. Scatter the olives over the tomatoes.

Mint and onion salad

1 bunch of spring onions
1 dozen mint leaves
15 ml (1 level tbsp) caster sugar
vinegar

Slice the onions thinly and chop the mint finely. Arrange in layers in a small glass dish, sprinkling sugar between the layers. Cover with vinegar and let stand for 30 minutes before serving. This is good with cold lamb.

Salad niçoise

450 g (1 lb) tomatoes, skinned and sliced
1 small cucumber, sliced
salt and freshly ground black pepper
5 ml (1 tsp) chopped basil
5 ml (1 tsp) chopped parsley
grated rind of 1 lemon
100 g (4 oz) French beans, cooked
50 g (2 oz) black olives
½ clove of garlic
French dressing
8 anchovy fillets

Place layers of tomato and cucumber in a small dish and season well with salt and pepper. Sprinkle the herbs over the cucumber and tomato. Grate the lemon rind over the whole, then scatter the beans over. Halve and stone the olives, scatter these over the salad and season. Chop the garlic, add to the dressing and pour over the salad. Halve each anchovy fillet and make a lattice pattern on top of the salad. Serve with bread and butter and lemon.

Leek salad

Clean 4 young leeks and blanch them in boiling salted water for 8 minutes; lift out and drain carefully, then chill well. Sprinkle them with freshly ground black pepper and toss in French dressing.

Tomato herb salad

50 g (2 oz) seedless raisins, chopped
4 tomatoes, peeled and quartered
15 ml (1 tbsp) finely chopped lemon thyme
15 ml (1 tbsp) finely chopped tarragon
15 ml (1 tbsp) finely chopped marjoram
15 ml (1 tbsp) finely chopped chives
15 ml (1 tbsp) finely chopped basil
French dressing (see page 126)

Add the raisins to the tomatoes and sprinkle with the herbs. Pour the French dressing over and chill well.

Radishes with horseradish dressing

2 bunches of radishes, washed
30 ml (2 level tbsp) freshly grated horseradish
10 ml (2 tsp) lemon juice
10 ml (2 level tsp) caster sugar
1·25 ml (¼ level tsp) salt
cayenne pepper
142-ml (5-fl oz) carton double cream

Trim the radishes, reserve a few for garnish, cut the larger ones in half and leave the remainder whole. Stir the horseradish, lemon, sugar and seasoning together.

Whip the cream until it just holds its shape then fold in the horseradish mixture. Add the radishes, stir until well coated and turn into a serving dish. Slice the reserved radishes and use to garnish the dish.

Carrot hors d'œuvre

450 g (1 lb) carrots, pared
1 small onion or shallot, skinned
30 ml (2 tbsp) olive oil
5 ml (1 tsp) lemon juice
a pinch of salt
a pinch of sugar

Grate the carrots coarsely; grate the onion and mix well together. Mix oil, lemon juice, salt and sugar, pour on to the mixture and toss well before serving.

Mushroom salad

100 g (4 oz) well-opened cultivated mushrooms
15 ml (1 tbsp) lemon juice
45 ml (3 tbsp) olive oil
15 ml (1 tbsp) finely chopped parsley
salt and freshly ground black pepper

Wipe the mushrooms, if necessary; do not peel, but remove the stalks. Slice very thinly into a serving dish, add the lemon juice, oil, parsley and pepper and leave to soak in this dressing for 30 minutes. Salt lightly just before serving. This is a good accompaniment for fish.

Raisin and nut salad

Illustrated in colour on page 121

2 sharp dessert apples
100 g (4 oz) seeded raisins, chopped
50 g (2 oz) walnuts, broken
French dressing (see page 126)
lemon juice
1 bunch of watercress, washed and trimmed

Wipe the apples; do not peel them. Grate one into a basin. Add the chopped raisins and nuts and a little French dressing; mix lightly. Slice the remaining apple and dip in lemon juice. Pile the fruit and nut mixture in the centre of a serving dish. Garnish with the apple slices and sprigs of watercress.

Lettuce and bacon salad

1 lettuce
50 g (2 oz) bacon, diced
90 ml (6 tbsp) vegetable oil
15 ml (1 level tbsp) brown sugar
45 ml (3 tbsp) vinegar

Wash the lettuce and arrange in a salad bowl. Fry the bacon in the oil until crisp; add the sugar and vinegar and pour this hot dressing over the lettuce. Serve at once, while the lettuce is still warm from the dressing.

Spring salad

1 bunch of radishes
1 bunch of spring onions (optional)
1 lettuce, washed
1 bunch of watercress, washed
mustard and cress, washed
4 tomatoes, sliced
1 beetroot, sliced
½ cucumber, sliced
4 hard-boiled eggs, sliced

Wash the radishes and cut them into 'lilies'; wash the spring onions (if used) and cut the stalks into curls; soak both in a bowl of iced water to make them open. Arrange the lettuce, watercress and mustard and cress on a serving dish. Arrange the tomatoes, beetroot, cucumber and eggs attractively on the dish and serve with mayonnaise.

Celeriac salad

900 g (2 lb) celeriac, washed and peeled
45 ml (3 tbsp) mayonnaise
5 ml (1 tsp) prepared mustard
4 small pickled beetroots to garnish

Cut the celeriac into Julienne strips. Put into boiling salted water and cook for about 5 minutes, until tender; drain and allow to cool. Mix the mayonnaise with the mustard and combine with the celeriac. Garnish with a ring of the sliced pickled beetroots.

Rice salad ring

Illustrated in colour on page 129

225 g (8 oz) long-grain rice, cooked and
    drained
100 g (4 oz) French beans, cooked and
    chopped
100 g (4 oz) frozen peas, cooked
1 stick of celery, washed and chopped
1 small dessert apple, cored and
    chopped
10 ml (2 tsp) chopped chives or 5 ml
    (1 tsp) chopped onion
French dressing (well flavoured with
    mustard)
4 tomatoes, quartered
1 bunch of watercress, trimmed and
    washed, to garnish

Put the rice (which should be quite dry) into a bowl and add the beans, peas, celery and apple. Stir with a fork, adding the chives and enough dressing to moisten.

Pack the rice into a lightly oiled ring mould and chill in the refrigerator. Turn out, when required, and garnish with tomato quarters and watercress.

Italian cauliflower salad

1 medium cauliflower
7 anchovy fillets, cut into small pieces
10 ripe olives, stoned and sliced
15 ml (1 tbsp) bottled capers
15 ml (1 tbsp) minced shallot or onion
freshly ground pepper
45 ml (3 tbsp) vegetable oil
15 ml (1 tbsp) wine vinegar

Wash and trim the cauliflower and break into small florets. Cook in 2·5 cm (1 inch) of boiling salted water for about 10 minutes, or until tender-crisp. Drain, cool, then put in the refrigerator. Place the chilled cauliflower, anchovy fillets, olives, capers and shallot in a bowl, sprinkle generously with pepper and pour the oil and vinegar over all; toss well and refrigerate for 30 minutes before serving.

Fennel and cucumber salad

1 orange
½ cucumber
1 fennel root, trimmed
8 radishes, washed
chopped mint
lemon and oil dressing
1 clove of garlic, skinned and crushed
2 hard-boiled eggs

Peel the orange and divide into segments. Cut the unpeeled cucumber into 0·5-cm (¼-inch) slices, then cut each slice across into 4 pieces. Cut the fennel into short, thin strips; slice the radishes. Mix all these together and add a little chopped mint. Make the lemon and oil dressing, add the chopped garlic and pour over the salad. Quarter the eggs and arrange on the salad.

Fennel and Gruyère cheese

Shred 1 fennel root and add 100 g (4 oz) Gruyère cheese, cut into slivers. Season well with freshly ground black pepper and pour lemon and oil dressing over.

French beans with tuna fish

Cook 450 g (1 lb) French beans until just tender. Dice the contents of a 99-g (3½-oz) can of tuna fish. Make a French dressing, pour over the warm beans and top with the fish.

Courgette and rice salad

2 courgettes, sliced
100 g (4 oz) rice
2 tomatoes, sliced
8 black olives, stoned and chopped
French dressing
4 sprigs of mint and 10 ml (2 tsp)
    chopped basil to garnish

Cook the courgettes in boiling salted water

until just tender – about 5 minutes; drain and cool. Boil the rice, drain and allow to dry a little. Toss the tomatoes and olives in the dressing and garnish with the herbs.

Cabbage salad

1 small white cabbage
1 onion, skinned and chopped
45 ml (3 tbsp) French dressing
5 ml (1 level tsp) caraway seeds
2·5 ml (½ level tsp) dried marjoram
15 ml (1 tbsp) chopped parsley to
    garnish

Trim the cabbage, removing the outer leaves, then wash and shred it. Place in a bowl and pour some boiling water over it; after 10 minutes drain, then add the chopped onion. Make a French dressing, adding the caraway seeds and marjoram. Pour this mixture over the cabbage and sprinkle the salad with the chopped parsley.

Dandelion leaves salad

450 g (1 lb) dandelion leaves
142-ml (5-fl oz) carton soured cream
salt and pepper
2·5 ml (½ level tsp) paprika pepper

Wash the dandelion leaves very well indeed and put them in a bowl, pour boiling water over them and drain well. Put 45 ml (3 tbsp) boiling salted water into a saucepan and put in the leaves, cover the pan and cook for 10 minutes, shaking about 3 times during the cooking. Drain the leaves and chop coarsely. Heat the sour cream in a thick-based pan and add the salt and pepper. Stir the chopped dandelion leaves into the mixture, reduce the heat and slowly bring the cream just up to boiling point, but do not allow to boil. When cool, sprinkle with paprika pepper.

Scandinavian salads

In Scandinavia, salads as we know them are not very often eaten, but their place is taken to some extent by the almost universal Smørrebrød, which often consist of salad ingredients. Smørrebrød are often eaten as hors d'œuvre and in Norway they may form the midday meal, while together with a variety of fish, meat and other dishes, they play an important part in the Scandinavian cold table.

Roughly translated, Smørrebrød means 'buttered bread', but it has come to mean bread and butter with a topping of some kind – in other words, an open sandwich. Some Danish and Swedish restaurants serve certain tranditional Smørrebrød, always made up in the same way, but since such an enormous range of different ingredients can be used, it is simpler to leave yourself a free hand, using your imagination and your artistic ability to create your own tempting open sandwiches. Smørrebrød are becoming more and more popular in this country as a 'party piece' which can easily be prepared well in advance.

The base is usually Scandinavian rye-bread, which, like many varieties of crisp-bread, can now be bought in this country. Failing either of these, firm white or brown bread is quite satisfactory. The secret is to butter the bread or crispbread very well, so that the ingredients will stay firmly in place. Arrange the topping and garnish carefully, remembering that both in colour and in taste the garnish should suit the topping.

Assorted Smørrebrød

Lettuce, smoked salmon, sliced cucumber, lemon twists.
Liver sausage, slices of tomato, chopped chives.
Lettuce, sardine, caviare, lemon twist.
Liver pâté, ring of pimiento, cucumber cones, radish rose.
Salami slices, onion rings, chopped chives, black olives, mayonnaise.
Lettuce, smoked salmon, horseradish cream, lemon slice, parsley.
Salami, mayonnaise, half-slices of cucumber, parsley.
Sliced tomato, sliced hard-boiled egg and chives.
Caviare, chopped raw onion, raw egg yolk.

Other easy Smørrebrød

Lettuce, ham, scrambled eggs, cress.

Pork luncheon meat, sweet pickle, cucumber.
Tongue, Russian salad and a tomato twist.
Crisply grilled bacon, scrambled eggs.
Chopped pork, potato salad, watercress, sliced tomato.
Chopped hard-boiled eggs and chopped chives.

Garnishes for Smørrebrød

These can include anything from a simple sprig of parsley to radish roses, curled celery, cucumber cones, gherkin fans, onion rings, tomato twists and red pepper Julienne (see page 115 for instructions) or one of the following:

Egg strips Allow 4 eggs to 300 ml (½ pint) milk, beat well, strain and season; cook slowly over warm water until set, then leave until cold and cut in strips. As a quick alternative, scramble the eggs in the usual way and press lightly while cooling.

Horseradish salad Grate fresh horseradish into whipped cream; flavour with lemon juice and a little caster sugar.

Herbs Fresh dill is one of the most traditional garnishes, but when it is not in season, parsley sprigs are equally suitable.

The cold table

This usually includes a very large serving dish of cold meats such as pork, ham, tongue, liver pâté, beef, salami, chicken, etc. In addition there would be a large cheeseboard containing traditional Scandinavian and other cheeses such as goat's milk, Samsoe, Danish Blue, Gorgonzola, Danish Port Salut and so on. Assorted crispbreads are also offered, plus a liberal amount of butter. Herrings, Frikadeller and Fågelbo are almost indispensable. Here are some typical recipes:

Soused salt herrings

1 large salt herring
75 ml (5 tbsp) vinegar
30 ml (2 tbsp) water
10 whole allspice, crushed
2 sprigs of fresh dill
30 ml (2 tbsp) chopped onions
5 peppercorns, crushed
fresh dill sprigs and onion rings to garnish

Clean the herring, removing the head, rinse under cold running water, then soak it in cold water for 10–12 hours; change the water a few times. Cut the herring along the back, remove the big backbone and as many small ones as possible and pull off the skin. (The bones come out easily after the soaking.) Drain on absorbent paper, then place the fillets together one on another, so that they look like a whole fish. Slice thinly with a sharp knife, and remove to a long narrow dish, using a spatula. Mix the remaining ingredients in a saucepan, bring to the boil and simmer for a few minutes, cool, strain and pour over the herring. Garnish, chill and serve with small boiled potatoes.

Prawn salad

15 ml (1 tbsp) mayonnaise
25 g (1 oz) cream cheese
30 ml (2 tbsp) whipped cream
1 green pepper, finely chopped
15 ml (1 tbsp) chopped parsley
2 sticks of celery, washed
225 g (8 oz) frozen prawns, thawed
lettuce, washed
1 lemon, sliced, to garnish

Mix the mayonnaise and cream cheese and add the cream, green pepper and parsley; place in a small bowl in the centre of a serving dish. Cut the celery into fine strips and mix with the prawns. Place the lettuce on the dish, cover with the prawn-and-celery mixture and garnish with lemon.

Cucumber salad

2 cucumbers
15 ml (1 level tbsp) salt
150 ml (¼ pint) vinegar
150 ml (¼ pint) water
juice of ½ lemon
30–45 ml (2–3 level tbsp) sugar
a dash of black pepper

Do not peel the cucumbers unless the skin is tough. Wash them well, slice very finely, sprinkle with salt, put in a bowl with a weighted plate on top and leave for some hours or overnight. Discard the juice, rinse the slices and dry in a cloth.

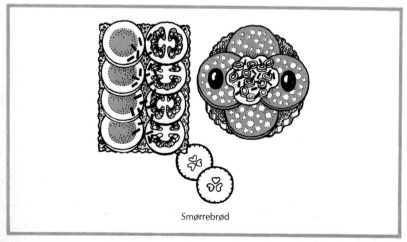

Smørrebrød

Chicory and orange salad (see page 120).

Make a dressing of the remaining ingredients, then pour it over the cucumber and leave for about 30 minutes. Serve as a side dish with fried meats, roasts and chicken, or use to garnish Smørrebrød.

Pickled beetroots

Wash 900 g (2 lb) small beets but do not peel; cook in plenty of water until tender for 1½–2 hours. Allow to cool, then peel, slice and put into a jar. Bring 600 ml (1 pint) vinegar, 300 ml (½ pint) water and 50–100 g (2–4 oz) sugar to the boil and pour over to cover the beets completely.

These will keep for 2–3 weeks – longer if strips of raw horseradish are boiled with the vinegar. Serve with any kind of roast, liver pâté or salads.

Fairy-tale salad

700 g (1½ lb) boiled potatoes, sliced
30 ml (2 tbsp) gherkin, chopped
30 ml (2 tbsp) cocktail onions
30 ml (2 tbsp) olive oil
15 ml (1 tbsp) vinegar
10 ml (2 tsp) French mustard
salt and pepper
a little sugar
chopped parsley and dill to garnish

Mix the sliced potatoes and the gherkins with the onions. Blend the oil, vinegar and mustard, then season with salt, pepper and sugar. Toss the salad in this dressing and marinade for 2 hours. Sprinkle with the herbs before serving.

Salad dressings

French dressing

1·25 ml (¼ level tsp) salt
a large pinch of pepper
1·25 ml (¼ level tsp) dry mustard
a pinch of sugar
15 ml (1 tbsp) vinegar
30 ml (2 tbsp) olive or vegetable oil

Put the salt, pepper, mustard and sugar in a bowl, add the vinegar and mix well. Beat in the oil with a fork and when the mixture thickens, use it at once. The oil separates out on standing, so if necessary whisk immediately before use. A good plan is to mix the dressing in a screw-topped jar, then shake up vigorously just before serving.

A little tarragon vinegar is sometimes added. The proportion of oil to vinegar varies with individual taste, but use vinegar sparingly.

French dressing variations

With chives Mix 30 ml (2 tbsp) French dressing with 15 ml (1 tbsp) chopped chives. Good with vegetable salads.

With herbs Mix 30 ml (2 tbsp) French dressing with 15 ml (1 tbsp) chopped parsley, 2·5 ml (½ level tsp) powdered marjoram and a pinch of powdered thyme. Good with vegetable or meat salads.

With pickles Mix 30 ml (2 tbsp) French dressing with 30 ml (2 tbsp) pickle relish or 30 ml (2 tbsp) chopped dill pickle. Good with vegetable, meat or fish salads.

With olives Mix 30 ml (2 tbsp) French dressing with a few sliced stuffed olives or a few chopped ripe olives. Good with vegetables, fruit or fish salads.

Vinaigrette dressing Add a little chopped parsley, chopped gherkin or capers and chives to 30 ml (2 tbsp) dressing.

Lemon and oil dressing

30–45 ml (2–3 tbsp) olive or vegetable oil
salt and pepper
15 ml (1 tbsp) lemon juice

Add the oil gradually to the condiments and when the salt is dissolved, pour in the lemon juice.

Mayonnaise

2 egg yolks
2·5 ml (½ tsp) made mustard
salt and pepper
about 150 ml (¼ pint) olive or vegetable oil
10 ml (2 tsp) white vinegar or strained lemon juice
5 ml (1 tsp) tarragon vinegar
5 ml (1 tsp) chilli vinegar

Put the egg yolks into a basin with the mustard, pepper and salt to taste. Mix thoroughly, then add the oil drop by drop, stirring hard with a wooden spoon or a whisk the whole time, until the sauce is thick and smooth. Add the vinegars gradually and mix thoroughly. If liked, lemon juice may be used instead of the vinegars or it may replace white vinegar only.

Note To keep the basin firmly in position, twist a damp cloth tightly round the base – this prevents it from slipping. In order that the oil may be added 1 drop at a time, put into the bottle-neck a cork from which a small wedge has been cut. Should the sauce curdle during the process of making, put another egg yolk into a basin and add the curdled sauce very gradually in the same way as the oil is added to the original egg yolks.

Mayonnaise variations

Caper Mix 30 ml (2 tbsp) mayonnaise with 5 ml (1 tsp) capers, 5 ml (1 tsp) chopped pimiento and 2·5 ml (½ tsp) tarragon vinegar. Good with fish and vegetable salads.

Cream Mix 30 ml (2 tbsp) mayonnaise and 142-ml (5-fl oz) carton of double cream, whipped. Particularly good with salads containing fruit.

Cucumber Mix 30 ml (2 tbsp) mayonnaise with ½ a small cucumber (pared, chopped and drained). Good with fish salads, particularly those made with crab, lobster and salmon.

Herb Mix 10 ml (2 tsp) mayonnaise with 10 ml (2 tsp) chopped chives and 15 ml (1 tbsp) chopped parsley. Good with meat or fish salads.

Spicy mixer mayonnaise sauce

2 egg yolks
5 ml (1 tsp) French mustard
5 ml (1 level tsp) sugar
5 ml (1 level tsp) salt
a very small pinch of cayenne pepper
a pinch of pepper
5 ml (1 tsp) lemon juice
300 ml (½ pint) olive or vegetable oil
30 ml (2 tbsp) white wine vinegar

Place the egg yolks, mustard, sugar, salt, peppers and lemon juice in the mixer bowl and blend, using speed 3–5. Place the oil in the juice extractor bowl, regulate the dripper and add the oil very gradually at first.

When the egg and oil emulsify, the oil may be allowed to run through the dripper more rapidly. When all the oil has been incorporated, add the vinegar gradually until the sauce is of the right consistency, ie, until it is stiff enough to hold its shape. Use as required; this mayonnaise is particularly good with grilled fish.

Foamy mayonnaise

2 egg yolks
salt and pepper
about 150 ml (¼ pint) olive or vegetable oil
about 30 ml (2 tbsp) lemon juice
1 egg white

Cream the yolks and seasonings and add the oil drop by drop, stirring hard all the time until the mayonnaise is thick and smooth. Stir in the lemon juice. Put in a cool place until required; just before serving, fold in the stiffly whisked egg white.

White salad cream

142-ml (5-fl oz) carton double cream
10 ml (2 tsp) tarragon vinegar
salt and pepper
10 ml (2 tsp) lemon juice
2 egg whites, whisked

Beat the cream until fairly stiff, then stir in the vinegar gradually. Season to taste, add the lemon juice and fold in the stiffly beaten egg whites.

Sour milk dressing

A simple dressing, practical in the summer time, is made from sour milk. Allow the milk to become solid, then beat up with salt, pepper and sugar to taste. It is particularly good with green salads.

French mustard dressing

10 ml (2 tsp) French mustard
30 ml (2 tbsp) olive oil
juice of ½ lemon
15 ml (1 level tbsp) sugar
salt and freshly ground black pepper

Blend the mustard and oil and slowly mix in the lemon juice; add the sugar and seasoning and use as required.

Boiled salad dressing

25 g (1 oz) flour
15 ml (1 level tbsp) sugar
10 ml (2 level tsp) dry mustard
15 ml (1 level tbsp) salt
150 ml (¼ pint) milk
2 eggs, beaten
50 g (2 oz) butter
150 ml (¼ pint) vinegar
142-ml (5-fl oz) carton soured cream or oil

Mix the dry ingredients, blend with the milk and bring to the boil, stirring continuously; boil for 5 minutes. Cool a little, add the eggs and butter, beat well and cook until thick, but do not boil. Add the vinegar gradually and beat well, then stir in the cream or oil and pour into a screw-topped jar. Shake well before using.

Cream dressing

salt and cayenne pepper
142-ml (5-fl oz) carton double cream
30 ml (2 tbsp) vinegar

Add the seasoning to the cream and whip until thick, then very gradually add the vinegar (French wine, for preference). Chill and use as required.

Horseradish dressing

fresh horseradish
142-ml (5-fl oz) carton soured cream
a pinch of sugar
5 ml (1 tsp) lemon juice
5 ml (1 tsp) vinegar
salt
cayenne pepper

Clean and grate the horseradish to give 45 ml (3 tbsp). Whip the cream until thick and add the horseradish, sugar, lemon juice and vinegar; season to taste.

Sour cream salad dressing

142-ml (5-fl oz) carton soured cream
30 ml (2 tbsp) white vinegar
30 ml (2 tbsp) chopped onion
2·5 ml (½ level tsp) sugar
5 ml (1 level tsp) salt
a little pepper

Mix all the ingredients thoroughly.

Spanish salad dressing

10 ml (2 level tsp) caster sugar
5 ml (1 level tsp) salt
5 ml (1 tsp) made mustard
a pinch of paprika
15 ml (1 tbsp) lemon juice
15 ml (1 tbsp) cold water
5 ml (1 tsp) piquant sauce
15 ml (1 tbsp) tomato ketchup
75 ml (5 tbsp) oil

Mix together in a basin the sugar, salt, mustard and paprika. Moisten these with the other ingredients, beat thoroughly and serve on any plain salad.

White wine dressing

75 ml (5 tbsp) olive or vegetable oil
75 ml (5 tbsp) white wine
5 ml (1 tsp) lemon juice
salt and pepper

Blend oil and wine as for a French dressing, stir in lemon juice and season to taste.

Gold dressing

300 ml (½ pint) mayonnaise (see page 126)
2·5 ml (½ level tsp) salt
a large pinch of pepper
a large pinch of paprika
10 ml (2 level tsp) sugar
30 ml (2 tbsp) vinegar
30 ml (2 tbsp) milk
10 ml (2 tsp) prepared mustard
2 egg yolks

Combine the ingredients and beat together until well blended.

Note In all salad recipes where mayonnaise is suggested, this can be replaced by commercial mayonnaise or salad cream when speed is important.

PASTA AND RICE

Though so different in origin and character, these can be used in similar ways.

Pasta

Pasta, which is Italian in origin, is made from special 'hard' wheats. Some continental shops sell freshly-made pasta, which should be used straight away, though the packeted kinds sold throughout the country will keep indefinitely. The main practical difference between fresh and packeted pasta is that the former takes about 5 minutes to cook, the packet pastas up to 20 minutes.

COOKING AND SERVING PASTA

Italians would reckon about 75–100 g (3–4 oz) per person, but in this country 50 g (2 oz) is enough for most people. Pasta should be cooked in a large quantity of fast-boiling salted water (see the chart below for times) until al dente, or just resistant to the teeth – it should never be mushy or slimy. Drain it as soon as it is cooked and serve on a heated dish.

These are the average times; if the pasta has been stored for some time, slightly longer may be needed.

Vermicelli, Spaghettini	5 minutes
Spaghetti	12–15 minutes
Macaroni	15–20 minutes
Fancy-shaped, eg, Farfalette, Tagliatelle, Noodles	10 minutes
Lasagne	10–15 minutes
Cannelloni, Large shells	20 minutes
Stuffed, eg, Ravioli	15–20 minutes

Rice

There are three main kinds of rice grain – long, medium and short. Long grains are best for made-up savoury rice dishes and for rice used as a savoury accompaniment. Medium grains are very suitable for rice rings, stuffings and croquettes. The short grain type is usually used for rice puddings and other sweet dishes.

PREPARING AND COOKING RICE

Rice sold in unbranded packs or loose should be washed in a strainer under the cold tap.

128

Boiled rice

Place 225 g (8 oz) long grain rice in a saucepan with 600 ml (1 pint) water and 5 ml (1 level tsp) salt. Bring quickly to the boil, stir well and cover with a tightly fitting lid. Reduce the heat and simmer gently for 14–15 minutes. Remove from the heat and before serving separate out the grains gently, using a fork – the rice will not need draining. For a drier effect, leave covered for 5–10 minutes.

This amount serves 3–4 people.

Oven-cooked rice

Place 225 g (8 oz) rice in an ovenproof dish. Bring 600 ml (1 pint) water and 5 ml (1 level tsp) salt to the boil, pour over the rice and stir well. Cover tightly with a lid or foil and bake in the oven at 180°C (350°F) mark 4 for 35–40 minutes, or until the grains are just soft and the cooking liquid has all been absorbed by the rice.

Pasta recipes

Spaghetti napolitana

225 g (8 oz) spaghetti
25 g (1 oz) butter or margarine
150–300 ml (¼–½ pint) tomato sauce (see page 36)
salt and pepper
25 g (1 oz) Parmesan cheese, grated

Cook the spaghetti in fast-boiling salted

Lowering spaghetti into boiling water, curling it into the pan as the ends soften

water in the usual way for 12–15 minutes. Drain and return it to the pan, with the fat, and shake it over a gentle heat for a minute or two. Serve on a heated dish, with the tomato sauce poured over it and the cheese sprinkled on top; if you prefer, the sauce and cheese may be served separately.

Buttered spaghetti

Have ready a large pan of boiling water. Allow 50 g (2 oz) spaghetti per person; hold the end of the bunch of spaghetti in the water and as it softens, coil it round in the pan. Boil rapidly for 12–15 minutes, moving the spaghetti occasionally to prevent sticking, until it is just cooked. Drain well and return it to the pan with 25–50 g (1–2 oz) butter and a good sprinkling of grated Parmesan cheese. Stir and leave for a few minutes for the butter and cheese to melt. Serve with more grated cheese in a separate dish. Any form of tubular or ribbon pasta can be cooked and served in this way.

Spaghetti alla bolognese

225 g (8 oz) spaghetti
grated Parmesan cheese

For the traditional Italian meat sauce
50 g (2 oz) bacon, chopped
a small knob of butter or margarine
1 small onion, skinned and chopped
1 carrot, pared and chopped
1 stick of celery, trimmed and chopped
225 g (8 oz) minced beef, raw
100 g (4 oz) chicken livers, chopped (optional)
15 ml (1 level tbsp) tomato paste
150 ml (¼ pint) dry white wine
300 ml (½ pint) beef stock
salt, pepper, nutmeg

Make the sauce first. Fry the bacon lightly in the fat for 2–3 minutes, add the onion, carrot and celery and fry for a further 5 minutes until lightly browned. Add the beef and brown lightly. Stir in the chicken livers, if used. Cook for about 3 minutes, then add the tomato paste and wine, allow to bubble for a few minutes and add the stock, seasoning and nutmeg. Cover and simmer for 30–40 minutes, until the meat is tender and the liquid in the sauce is well reduced. Re-season if necessary.

Meanwhile cook the spaghetti in the usual way in fast-boiling salted water for about 12–15 minutes. Drain and serve on a heated dish with the sauce poured over. Serve the cheese sprinkled over the sauce or in a separate dish.

Rice salad ring
(see page 123).

A more simple meat sauce may be made by omitting the chicken livers, wine, carrots and celery.

Macaroni cheese

175 g (6 oz) macaroni
40 g (1½ oz) butter or margarine
40 g (1½ oz) flour
568 ml (1 pint) milk
salt and pepper
a pinch of grated nutmeg or 2·5 ml (½ tsp) made mustard
175 g (6 oz) cheese, grated
30 ml (2 tbsp) fresh white breadcrumbs (optional)

Cook the macaroni in fast-boiling salted water for 15 minutes only and drain it well. Meanwhile melt the fat, stir in the flour and cook for 2–3 minutes. Remove the pan from the heat and gradually stir in the milk. Bring to the boil and continue to stir until the sauce thickens; remove from the heat and stir in the seasonings, 100 g (4 oz) of the cheese and the macaroni. Pour into an ovenproof dish and sprinkle with the breadcrumbs (if used) and the remaining cheese. Bake in the oven at 200°C (400°F) mark 6 for about 20 minutes, or until golden. Quick macaroni can also be used – cook it as directed.

Variations

Add to the sauce any of the following:
1 small onion, skinned, chopped and boiled
100 g (4 oz) bacon or ham, chopped and lightly fried
½–1 green pepper, seeded, chopped and blanched
½–1 canned pimiento, chopped
50 g (2 oz) mushrooms, sliced and lightly fried

Mediterranean pasta

175–225 g (6–8 oz) pasta
2 medium onions, skinned and chopped
40 g (1½ oz) butter or 30–45 ml (2–3 tbsp) oil
1 clove of garlic, skinned and crushed
425-g (15-oz) can Italian tomatoes
141-g (5-oz) can tomato paste
5 ml (1 level tsp) dried marjoram or rosemary
5 ml (1 level tsp) sugar
salt and pepper
100 g (4 oz) mushrooms, sliced

Cook the pasta in the usual way. Fry the onions gently in 25 g (1 oz) of the butter for 5 minutes, until soft but not coloured. Stir in the garlic, tomatoes, tomato paste, herbs, sugar and seasoning, cover and sim-

mer for 30 minutes, until the sauce is thick. Fry the mushrooms gently for about 3 minutes in the remaining butter and add. Adjust the seasoning and serve over the pasta.

Macheroni alla carbonara

175 g (6 oz) macaroni, in short lengths
100 g (4 oz) cooked ham
25 g (1 oz) butter or margarine
2–3 eggs, beaten
salt and pepper
30 ml (2 tbsp) grated Parmesan cheese

Cook the macaroni in the usual way in fast-boiling water for 15–20 minutes, until soft, and drain it well. Fry the ham lightly for 2–3 minutes in the fat, until heated through, and stir in the drained macaroni, beaten eggs and seasoning. Stir over a gentle heat until the mixture is well blended and the eggs are just beginning to thicken. Add the cheese, mix well and serve straight away.

Quick macaroni can also be used – cook as directed on the packet.

Lasagne al forno

2 × 226-g (8-oz) cans Italian tomatoes
92-g (3¼-oz) can tomato paste
2·5–5 ml (½–1 level tsp) dried marjoram
salt and pepper
5 ml (1 level tsp) sugar
225 g (8 oz) cooked veal or ham, diced
100 g (4 oz) lasagne
175 g (6 oz) Ricotta or cream cheese
50 g (2 oz) Parmesan cheese
225 g (8 oz) Mozarella cheese

Mediterranean pasta

Combine the canned tomatoes, tomato paste, marjoram, seasonings and sugar simmer gently for about 30 minutes and add the veal or ham. Cook the lasagne in boiling salted water in the usual way for about 10–15 minutes (or as stated on the packet) and drain well.

Cover the base of a fairly deep ovenproof dish with a layer of the tomato and meat sauce. Add half the lasagne, put in another layer of the sauce, then cover with the cheeses, using half of each kind. Repeat these layers with the remaining ingredients finishing with a layer of cheese. Bake in the oven at 190°C (375°F) mark 5 for 30 minutes, until golden and bubbling on top. Serve at once. This sauce can be replaced by a Bolognese sauce (see page 128).

Spinach and liver-stuffed cannelloni

Illustrated in colour on page 132

100 g (4 oz) onion
225 g (8 oz) pig's liver
25 g (1 oz) butter or margarine
226-g (8-oz) pkt frozen chopped spinach, thawed
40 g (1½ oz) fresh white breadcrumbs
salt and pepper
a pinch of nutmeg
12 cannelloni
400-g (14-oz) can tomatoes
300 ml (½ pint) chicken stock
50 g (2 oz) Cheddar cheese, grated

Skin and very finely chop the onion and liver, or place together in an electric liquidiser for a few seconds. Melt the margarine and sauté the onion and liver gently for 8–10 minutes. Stir frequently. Stir in the well drained spinach, breadcrumbs and season to taste with salt, pepper and nutmeg. Use to stuff the uncooked cannelloni. Pack tightly in a shallow, greased ovenproof dish in a single layer. Break up the tomatoes roughly and spoon over with juice then the stock. Cover with foil and bake in the oven at 190°C (375°F) mark 5 for 30 minutes. Uncover, sprinkle with the cheese and return to oven until the cheese has melted.

Ravioli

In Italy, supplies of ravioli and its variants are made and cooked fresh daily. In this country, freshly made ravioli can be bought in some Italian shops and restaurants. Failing this, you can find ready-cooked ravioli in some delicatessen shops and it can also be bought in cans.

To cook fresh ravioli Put the ravioli into boiling salted water, adding about 10–15

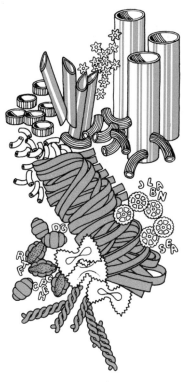

Pasta shapes and varieties

pieces at a time, and cook for 15–20 minutes (don't cook more than this at any one time, as the pieces tend to break up if the pan is crowded). Remove them with a slotted spoon and keep warm until all are cooked. Toss them with a little butter and then serve sprinkled with finely grated Parmesan cheese.

As a variation, the cooked ravioli can be layered with tomato sauce in a greased ovenproof dish, sprinkled with grated Parmesan cheese and baked in the oven at 200°C (400°F) mark 6 for about 15 minutes, until golden.

Rice recipes

Flavoured rice

1 Rice may be cooked in various liquids to give extra flavour and variety. Replace water by any of these:

Chicken or beef stock (fresh or made from a cube).

Canned tomato juice, undiluted or used half-and-half with water.

Orange juice – used half-and-half with water.

2 Alternatively, rice can be flavoured as follows:

Savoury rice Fry chopped onion, pepper, celery or bacon in a little butter in the pan before adding the rice.

Herby rice Add a pinch of dried herbs with the cooking liquid (eg, sage, marjoram, thyme, mixed herbs).

Raisin rice Add stoned raisins (or currants or sultanas) and if liked a pinch of curry powder.

Variety rice When the rice is cooked stir in: diced pineapple, chopped canned pimiento, slivered browned almonds, grated cheese, or chopped fresh herbs.

Fried rice with egg

100 g (4 oz) long grain rice
2 eggs, beaten
60 ml (4 tbsp) oil
2·5 ml (½ level tsp) salt
½ onion, skinned and finely chopped
50 g (2 oz) mushrooms, thinly sliced
30 ml (2 tbsp) frozen peas
50 g (2 oz) cooked ham, diced
10 ml (2 tsp) soy sauce

Boil the rice. Make a plain omelette from the eggs, cut it into thin strips and set aside. Fry the drained rice for about 5 minutes in 30 ml (2 tbsp) of very hot oil with the salt, stirring all the time; remove from the pan and set aside. Clean the pan and add the remaining oil. Fry the onion for about 3 minutes, until lightly browned, add the remaining vegetables and the ham and fry lightly for a further 3 minutes, stirring well. Slowly add the rice and when well mixed, stir in the soy sauce and shredded omelette; serve hot, to accompany chicken.

Paella

6–8 mussels, fresh or bottled
50–100 g (2–4 oz) Dublin Bay prawns (or frozen scampi)
1 small cooked lobster
1 small chicken
60 ml (4 tbsp) oil
1 clove of garlic, skinned and crushed
1 onion, skinned and chopped
1 green pepper, seeded and chopped
4 tomatoes, skinned and chopped
225–325 g (8–12 oz) long grain rice
1·1–1·7 litres (2–3 pints) chicken stock (made from a cube)
salt and pepper
a little powdered saffron
a small pkt of frozen peas
garnish

This famous Spanish dish takes its name from the pan in which it is cooked – a shallow oval metal dish with handles at each side. There are few hard-and-fast rules about making a paella, although the following ingredients are traditionally included – chicken, lobster, shellfish of various kinds, onion, green or red peppers and rice. Paella is rather elaborate and somewhat expensive to prepare in this country, but it makes an attractive party dish. The quantities given should serve at least 8 people.

Shell or drain the mussels and peel the prawns, if fresh. Remove the lobster meat from the shell and dice it, retaining the claws for decorating. Cut the meat from the chicken into small pieces. Put the oil into a large *paella* or frying pan and fry the garlic, onion and green pepper for 5 minutes, until soft but not browned. Add the tomatoes and chicken pieces and fry until the chicken is lightly browned. Stir in the rice and add half the stock, the seasoning and saffron (blended with a little of the stock). Bring to the boil, then reduce the heat and simmer for about 20–25 minutes, until the chicken is tender and the rice just cooked.

Stir in the mussels, prawns, lobster meat and peas and simmer for a final 5–10 minutes, until heated through. Serve garnished with a few extra strips of green pepper or pimiento and the lobster claws. Mussels in their shells can also be used as a garnish.

Risotto

Risotto is the main rice dish in the north of Italy, where rice takes the place of pasta. Risotto is usually a dish complete in itself (with the exception of Milanese Risotto, which is served as an accompaniment to such well-known Italian dishes as Osso bucco).

The difference between a risotto and a pilau is that the former is moister, being made from a special type of rice with short, fat grains. In this country a long grain rice may have to be substituted, but the risotto should still be more moist than a pilau.

Chicken risotto

½ boiling chicken or 2–3 good-sized chicken portions (uncooked)
75 g (3 oz) butter or margarine
2 small onions, skinned and finely chopped
1 stick of celery, trimmed and finely chopped
1 clove of garlic, skinned and crushed
1 green pepper, seeded and finely chopped
50 g (2 oz) mushrooms, sliced
50 g (2 oz) bacon or ham, chopped
150 ml (¼ pint) dry white wine
chicken stock
salt and pepper
chopped fresh herbs as available (eg marjoram, thyme or basil)
225 g (8 oz) long grain rice
grated Parmesan cheese

131

Skin the chicken, bone it and cut the flesh in strips. Melt 25 g (1 oz) of the fat and fry one of the onions gently for 5 minutes, until soft. Add the chicken, the remaining vegetables and the bacon or ham and fry for a further few minutes, stirring all the time. Add the wine and let it bubble until well reduced; just cover with chicken stock and add the seasoning and herbs. Put on the lid and leave to simmer for about 1 hour, until the chicken is really tender.

Fry the remaining onion in 25 g (1 oz) of the remaining fat for about 5 minutes, until soft. Add the rice and stir until transparent. Add about 300 ml (½ pint) of chicken stock and cook over a moderate heat, un-covered, until the stock has been absorb-ed; continue to cook, adding more stock as required, until the rice is just soft (15–20 minutes). Pour in the chicken mixture, stir well and continue cooking until the two mixtures are well blended and the liquid all absorbed. Stir in the remaining butter and some Parmesan cheese and serve.

Shellfish risotto

Shellfish risotto

1 onion, skinned and finely chopped
75 g (3 oz) butter or margarine
225 g (8 oz) long grain rice
150 ml (¼ pint) dry white wine
900 ml (1½ pints) boiling chicken stock
salt and pepper
1 clove of garlic, skinned (optional)
225 g (8 oz) frozen scampi or prawns, thawed
grated Parmesan cheese

Prepare the risotto as above, using 50 g (2 oz) of the fat. Just before the rice becomes tender, gently fry the garlic (if used) and the shellfish in the remaining 25 g (1 oz) butter for 5 minutes. Stir into the risotto and serve with the cheese.

A few sliced button mushrooms can be fried with the shellfish or a few frozen peas or strips of canned pimiento can be added to the risotto just before the rice is cooked. Other shellfish, such as crab or lobster meat (fresh or canned) may also be used; a mixture of shellfish, with possibly a few mussels (canned or fresh) will give a more unusual touch.

Basic pilau

225 g (8 oz) long grain rice
50 g (2 oz) butter or margarine
1·7 litres (3 pints) boiling chicken stock
salt and pepper

Fry the rice gently in the melted fat for about 5 minutes, stirring all the time, until it looks transparent. Add the stock pouring it in slowly, as it will tend to bubble rather a lot at first. Add the seasoning, stir well, cover with a tightly fitting lid and leave over a very low heat for about 15 minutes, until the water is absorbed and the rice grains are just soft. (The idea is that the rice should cook in its own steam, so don't stir mean-while.) Remove the lid, cover the rice with a cloth, replace the lid and leave in a warm place to dry out for at least 15 minutes before serving. (This is a traditional part of making a pilau).

To serve, stir lightly with a fork to separate the grains, add a knob of butter and serve at once.

Liver pilau

225 g (8 oz) calf's liver, cut in strips
50 g (2 oz) butter or margarine
2 onions, skinned and finely chopped
25 g (1 oz) shelled peanuts or almonds
175–225 g (6–8 oz) long grain rice
salt and pepper
a pinch of mixed spice
50 g (2 oz) currants
2 tomatoes, skinned and chopped
1·1–1·7 litres (1½–2 pints) chicken or meat stock (boiling)
a little chopped parsley

Fry the liver lightly in the fat for 2–3 minutes and remove it from the fat with a slotted spoon. Fry the onions for 5 minutes in the same fat until soft but not brown. Add the nuts and rice and fry for a further 5 minutes, stirring all the time. Add the seasoning, spice, currants, tomatoes and stock, stir well, cover with a tightly fitting lid and simmer for about 15 minutes, until all the liquid has been absorbed. Stir in the liver and parsley, cover again and before serving leave for 15 minutes in a warm place (but without further cooking). The liver if pre-ferred may be replaced by cooked chicken or lamb.

Spinach and liver-stuffed cannelloni (see page 130).

HOT PUDDINGS

Although the modern trend is towards serving a light sweet or fresh fruit at the end of a meal, there are still times when a good, substantial hot pudding is just what the family needs. Here is a wide selection for all occasions, including hearty steamed, suet and baked puddings, lighter milk puddings and batters and delicious soufflés, not forgetting the ever-popular fruit pie in many guises.

Steamed puddings

General rules for steaming

1 Put on the steamer with the base half filled with water so that this is boiling by the time the pudding is made. If you have no steamer, half fill a large saucepan with water, bring this to the boil and stand the pudding basin in it.
2 Grease the pudding basin well.
3 Cut double greaseproof paper or a piece of foil to cover the pudding basin and grease well.
4 Fill the basin not more than two-thirds full with mixture.
5 Cover the basin tightly with the paper or foil to prevent steam or water entering.
6 Keep the water in the steamer boiling rapidly all the time and have a kettle of boiling water ready to top it up regularly, or the steamer will tend to boil dry.

Saxon pudding

100 g (4 oz) sponge cake crumbs
50 g (2 oz) ground almonds
30 ml (2 tbsp) cream or top of milk
30 ml (2 tbsp) milk
50 g (2 oz) caster sugar
50 g (2 oz) butter or margarine
2 eggs
50 g (2 oz) pineapple, shredded or diced
grated rind of 1 lemon

Grease a 900-ml (1½-pint) pudding basin thoroughly. Put the crumbs and ground almonds into a basin, pour on the cream and milk and leave to soak for about 30 minutes. Cream together the sugar and fat and beat in the egg yolks alternately with the soaked mixture and the drained pineapple. Beat in the lemon rind and lastly fold in the stiffly beaten egg whites. Pour into the basin, cover with greased greaseproof paper or foil. Steam carefully for 1½–2 hours, turn out, decorate with pieces of pineapple and serve with pineapple sauce – see next recipe.

Pineapple sauce

100 g (4 oz) caster sugar
150 ml (¼ pint) water
30 ml (2 level tbsp) apricot jam, sieved
10–15 ml (2–3 tsp) lemon juice
30 ml (2 level tbsp) shredded pineapple
10 ml (2 level tsp) cornflour
a little red food colouring if liked

Dissolve the sugar in the water and add the apricot jam, lemon juice and pineapple. Blend the cornflour with a little cold water and add to the hot syrup, bring to the boil and add colouring.

Rich chocolate pudding

50 g (2 oz) plain chocolate
150 ml (¼ pint) milk
100 g (4 oz) fresh white breadcrumbs
40 g (1½ oz) butter or margarine
40 g (1½ oz) caster sugar
1 egg
vanilla essence
1·25 ml (¼ level tsp) baking powder
almonds to decorate

Break the chocolate into small pieces, melt it in the milk, pour on to the crumbs and leave to soak for 15–20 minutes. Cream together the fat and sugar until soft and light, beat in the egg yolk, then beat in the soaked crumbs. Add a few drops of vanilla essence and the stiffly beaten egg white. Lastly, fold in the baking powder, put the mixture into a greased 900-ml (1½-pint) pudding basin. Cover with greased greaseproof paper or foil and steam gently for 1–1½ hours, until well risen and firm. Turn it out on to a hot dish, decorate with a few blanched almonds and serve with chocolate sauce – see next recipe.

Chocolate sauce

40 g (1½ oz) plain chocolate
200 ml (⅓ pint) water
5 ml (1 level tsp) cornflour
a pinch of salt
50 g (2 oz) caster sugar
a few drops of vanilla essence
a small knob of butter or margarine

Break up the chocolate, add half of the water and dissolve over a gentle heat. Mix the cornflour and salt to a smooth cream with a little of the remaining cold water, heat the remainder, and when boiling pour on to the blended cornflour, stirring. Return it to the saucepan and bring to the boil, still stirring. Add the dissolved chocolate and sugar and cook for 4–5 minutes, stirring and beating. Lastly, stir in the vanilla essence and butter or margarine.

Canary pudding

100 g (4 oz) plain flour
a pinch of salt
2·5 ml (½ level tsp) baking powder
100 g (4 oz) butter or margarine
100 g (4 oz) caster sugar
2 eggs
30 ml (2 tbsp) milk
a few drops of vanilla essence

Sift together the flour, salt and baking powder. Cream the fat and sugar until soft and white, then beat in the eggs separately with a sprinkling of flour. Stir in the remaining flour lightly and add the milk and essence. Put into a greased 1·1-litre (2-pint) pudding basin, two-thirds filling it, cover with greased greaseproof paper or foil and steam for 1½ hours. Turn out and serve with jam sauce (see page 135).

Some variations of Canary pudding are given below.

Jam canary pudding

Put 30 ml (2 tbsp) jam (or marmalade or golden syrup) in the basin before adding the pudding mixture.

Orange or lemon sponge

Add the grated rind of 1 lemon or orange and serve with a sauce made with the fruit juice.

Cherry sponge

Add 50 g (2 oz) chopped glacé cherries to the Canary pudding mixture, combining them with the dry ingredients. Serve with a custard sauce flavoured with Maraschino or sherry.

Chocolate sponge

Add 40 g (1½ oz) cocoa and a pinch of baking powder to the flour and mix to a soft dropping consistency, adding a little more milk if necessary. Serve with chocolate or custard sauce.

Sponge ring

100 g (4 oz) butter or margarine
100 g (4 oz) caster sugar
2 eggs
175 g (6 oz) plain flour
2·5 ml (½ level tsp) baking powder
grated rind of 1 lemon
mixed stewed fruits, eg, cherries,
**   apricots, currants, gooseberries**
a little cornflour

Grease a 900-ml–1·1-litre (1½–2-pint) ring

mould. Cream together the fat and sugar until fluffy and light, beat in the eggs one at a time, then lastly fold in the flour, baking powder and grated lemon rind. Put the mixture into the mould, cover with greased greaseproof paper or foil, and steam for 1½ hours. Turn it out, then pile the hot mixed fruit into the centre and round the dish. Serve the pudding with some of the fruit juice, thickened with a little cornflour.

Marmalade pudding

Illustrated in colour on pages 136–137

100 g (4 oz) plain flour
1·25 ml (¼ level tsp) salt
5 ml (1 level tsp) baking powder
100 g (4 oz) fresh white breadcrumbs
75–100 g (3–4 oz) shredded suet
1 egg, beaten
60 ml (4 tbsp) marmalade
milk to mix
marmalade sauce

Sift the flour, salt and baking powder together. Add the crumbs and suet and mix well, then add the egg, marmalade and sufficient milk to give a soft dropping consistency. Put the mixture into a greased 900-ml (1½-pint) pudding basin, cover with greased greaseproof paper or foil and steam for 1½–2 hours. Turn out and serve with marmalade sauce – see recipe below.

Marmalade (or jam) sauce

15 ml (1 tbsp) marmalade (or jam)
5 ml (1 level tsp) caster sugar
150 ml (¼ pint) water
2·5 ml (½ level tsp) cornflour
a little lemon juice
food colouring (optional)

Put the marmalade (or jam), sugar and water in a saucepan and bring to the boil.

Add the cornflour, mixed with a little cold water, and boil up until the sauce is clear and the cornflour cooked – about 5 minutes. Add the lemon juice and colouring (if used). Strain if necessary.

Suet syrup pudding

225 g (8 oz) plain flour
a pinch of salt
100 g (4 oz) shredded suet
5 ml (1 level tsp) ground ginger
30 ml (2 tbsp) golden syrup
5 ml (1 level tsp) bicarbonate of soda
milk to mix

Put the flour, salt, suet and ginger into a basin, make a well in the centre and add the syrup. Dissolve the bicarbonate of soda in 15 ml (1 tbsp) of the milk. Mix the pudding to a very soft dough with milk and add the bicarbonate of soda. Put the mixture into a greased 900-ml-1·1-litre (1½–2-pint) pudding basin, cover with greased greaseproof paper or foil and steam for 2½ hours. Turn out and serve with syrup or custard sauce. Decorate if desired with chopped crystallised ginger.

Spotted dick or plum duff

100 g (4 oz) plain flour
a pinch of salt
5 ml (1 level tsp) baking powder
100 g (4 oz) fresh white breadcrumbs
100 g (4 oz) shredded suet
100 g (4 oz) currants
water to mix

Sift the flour, salt and baking powder together. Add the breadcrumbs, suet and currants and mix to a soft dough with water. Turn out on to a floured board and shape into a roll, put this into a piece of greased greaseproof paper then roll it in foil. Steam over rapidly boiling water

Suet syrup pudding

for 1½–2 hours. Unwrap and serve with butter and brown sugar, or with custard sauce.

Steamed fruit pudding

900 g (2 lb) fruit
225 g (8 oz) suet crust pastry (see page 144)
50–100 g (2–4 oz) caster sugar
a little water, as required

Thoroughly grease a 1·7-litre (3-pint) basin and prepare the fruit. (Apples, rhubarb, apricots, gooseberries, plums and so on are all suitable.) Cut off a quarter of the pastry, roll the rest out into a round and line the basin with it. Fill the basin well with fruit until it is piled high, putting a good sprinkling of sugar between the layers, and add a very little water – the amount varies according to the fruit, juicy ones needing least water. Roll out the rest of the pastry into a round for the top, damp the edges and fix firmly. Cover with greaseproof paper, then with foil, and tie down lightly. Steam for 2½–3 hours. Turn out and serve with custard or a sauce.

Christmas pudding

175 g (6 oz) plain flour
5 ml (1 level tsp) mixed spice
2·5 ml (½ level tsp) grated nutmeg
75 g (3 oz) fresh white breadcrumbs
100 g (4 oz) shredded suet
100 g (4 oz) raisins, stoned and chopped
225 g (8 oz) currants, cleaned
225 g (8 oz) sultanas, cleaned
100 g (4 oz) apple, peeled, cored and chopped
75 g (3 oz) Demerara sugar
grated rind of 1 lemon
2 eggs, beaten
200 ml (⅓ pint) strong ale

Grease a 1·1-litre (2-pint) basin. Sift together the flour and spices. Add the breadcrumbs, suet, dried fruit, apple, sugar and lemon rind. Mix well and gradually stir in the eggs and ale. Stir again thoroughly.

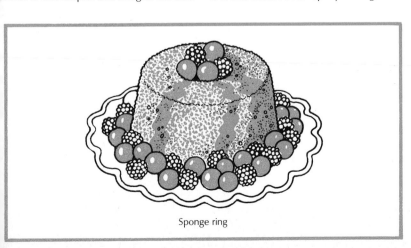

Sponge ring

135

Marmalade pudding (see page 135),
Pineapple and cherry pancakes (see page 142),
Chocolate pear upside-down pudding (see page 138).

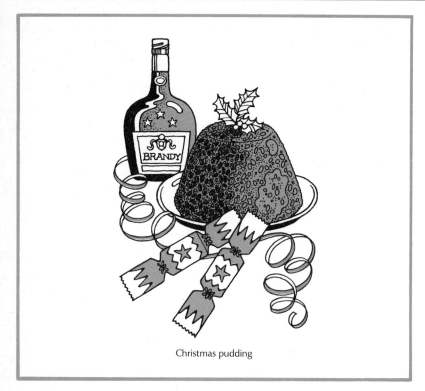

Christmas pudding

Turn the mixture into the basin, cover with greased greaseproof paper and then with foil or a pudding cloth. Either place the pudding in a pan with water half-way up the sides of the basin and, after bringing it to the boil, reduce the heat and simmer for 6 hours, or alternatively cook it in a steamer for 8 hours. Leave the greaseproof paper in position, but when the pudding is cold, cover with a fresh piece of foil or cloth before storing.

Re-boil for 3–4 hours before serving with Fluffy sauce – see recipe below – or Brandy butter – (see page 162). *Serves 5–6*

Fluffy sauce for Christmas pudding

50 g (2 oz) butter
100 g (4 oz) icing sugar, sifted
2 eggs, separated
30 ml (2 tbsp) brandy
142-ml (5-fl oz) carton double cream

Cream the butter and sugar. Beat in the beaten egg yolks. Gradually beat in the brandy and add the cream. Place in a double saucepan and cook over a gentle heat until of the consistency of thick custard. Pour slowly on to the beaten egg whites, whisking all the time. Keep warm in the double pan, but don't continue to cook. Stir before serving.

138

Baked puddings

Apple and rhubarb cobbler

Illustrated in colour on page 237

538-g (1 lb 3 oz) can rhubarb
700 g (1 ½ lb) cooking apples, peeled and cored
100 g (4 oz) caster sugar
25 g (1 oz) stem ginger, chopped
100 g (4 oz) butter
vanilla essence
150 g (5 oz) self raising flour
crushed cornflakes

Drain the rhubarb and measure off 150 ml (¼ pint) of the syrup. Thickly slice the apples into a saucepan, sprinkle over the 25 g (1 oz) caster sugar and add the measured syrup. Bring to the boil, then simmer gently for about 20 minutes until tender. Combine the fruit and ginger. Pour into a 1·1-litre (2-pint) ovenproof dish. Cream the butter and remaining sugar together until soft and fluffy. Beat in a few drops of vanilla essence and the egg yolk. Gradually stir in the flour and mix to a smooth dough. With wet hands divide the mixture into 24 small balls. Roll these in cornflakes. Arrange over the fruit. Bake at 190°C (375°F) mark 5 for about 30 minutes until golden brown. Serve with pouring custard. *Serves 6*

Baked jam roll

Roll 225 g (8 oz) shortcrust pastry into an oblong, damp the edges with a little water and spread to within 2·5 cm (1 inch) of the sides with jam. Roll up and put into a greased ovenproof dish. Pour a little milk into the dish and bake in the oven at 180°C (350°F) mark 4 for 30–40 minutes, until brown and crisp. Serve with more jam, if required.

Pineapple upside-down pudding

226-g (8-oz) can pineapple rings, drained
25 g (1 oz) glacé cherries
45–60 ml (3–4 tbsp) melted golden syrup
175 g (6 oz) self-raising flour
100 g (4 oz) butter or margarine
100 g (4 oz) caster sugar
2 eggs
30–45 ml (2–3 tbsp) milk

Grease the base of an 18-cm (7-inch) square cake tin well and line with greased greaseproof paper, arrange the pineapple and cherries decoratively in it and cover them with the syrup. Using the same method as for Canary pudding (see page 134), make a cake mixture from the remaining ingredients and spread it carefully and evenly over the fruit. Bake in the oven at 180°C (350°F) mark 4 for about 45 minutes. Turn out on to a plate and serve hot or cold, accompanied by whipped cream or by the pineapple juice thickened with arrowroot. (Allow 10 ml (2 level tsp) arrowroot to 150 ml (¼ pint) juice.)

Chocolate pear upside-down pudding

Illustrated in colour on pages 136–137

For the topping
45 ml (3 level tbsp) brown sugar
15 g (½ oz) butter, melted
439-g (15 ½-oz) can pear halves, drained
25 g (1 oz) walnuts, chopped

For the chocolate sponge
100 g (4 oz) butter or margarine
100 g (4 oz) caster sugar
2 eggs, beaten
75 g (3 oz) self-raising flour
25 g (1 oz) cocoa powder

Grease and line a 20-cm (8-inch) round cake tin. For the topping, sprinkle the base of the tin with brown sugar and spoon over the melted butter. Fill the centre of each pear half with walnuts and place cut side down in the tin.

Cream the butter and sugar together until pale and fluffy. Gradually beat in the eggs and fold in the flour and cocoa powder. Spoon the sponge mixture over the pears and smooth the top. Bake in the oven at 190°C (375°F) mark 5 for 35–40 minutes. Turn out the pudding and serve hot or cold with whipped cream.

Adam and Eve pudding

75 g (3 oz) Demerara sugar
grated rind of 1 lemon
450 g (1 lb) cooking apples, peeled, cored and sliced
50 g (2 oz) butter or margarine
50 g (2 oz) sugar
1 egg
50 g (2 oz) flour
1·25 ml (¼ level tsp) baking powder

Add the Demerara sugar and lemon rind to the apples and put them into a 900-ml (1½-pint) ovenproof dish or pie dish with 15 ml (1 tbsp) water. Cream the fat and sugar thoroughly, add the egg and beat well, then stir in the flour and baking powder and spread on top of the apples. Bake in the oven at 200°C (400°F) mark 6 for about 30 minutes, or until the apples are tender and the cake mixture well risen and firm.

Apple-Anna

Peel and slice an apple, put in a casserole and sprinkle with 30 ml (2 level tbsp) brown sugar. Slice a banana and arrange on top, then slice another 2 apples and put over the banana. Sprinkle with 45 ml (3 level tbsp) sugar and dot with a little butter. Cover the casserole and bake for 20 minutes in the oven at 190°C (375°F) mark 5, then take off the lid and bake for about 15 minutes longer, or until the fruit is tender. Serve with cream.

Danish apple cake

1 kg (2¼ lb) cooking apples, peeled and sliced
100 g (4 oz) caster sugar
100 g (4 oz) butter or margarine
100 g (4 oz) coarse breadcrumbs (preferably half white, half brown)
jam or marmalade
ground cinnamon
142-ml (5-fl oz) carton double cream (whipped) to decorate

Stew the apples with or without a little water, according to type. Add half the sugar. Melt the fat and mix in the breadcrumbs, then add the remaining sugar, stirring this into the fat until light brown in colour. Grease a cake tin and in it place alternate layers of crumbs, apples, jam or marmalade and a light sprinkling of cinnamon, finishing with crumbs. Press down

firmly, then cook for 30 minutes in the oven at 180°C (350°F) mark 4. Turn it out and decorate the top with whipped cream and jam or marmalade.

Orange pudding

100 g (4 oz) butter or margarine
100 g (4 oz) caster sugar
3 eggs
grated rind and juice of 1 orange
150 ml (5 oz) plain flour
1·25 ml (¼ level tsp) baking powder
orange curd
100 g (4 oz) caster sugar for meringue topping

Cream the fat and sugar until light and creamy. Beat in 2 of the egg yolks and one whole egg, the orange rind and the juice, then fold in the flour and baking powder. Put into a greased 1·1-litre (2-pint) ovenproof dish and bake in the oven at 180°C (350°F) mark 4 until well risen and firm – 30–40 minutes – and then spread the top with a little orange curd. Whisk the remaining egg white until stiff, fold in the caster sugar and whisk well. Pile on top of the

pudding and bake in the oven at 150°C (300°F) mark 1 until golden brown – 15–20 minutes.

Bakewell tart

100 g (4 oz) shortcrust pastry (see page 143)
30 ml (2 tbsp) red jam
40 g (1½ oz) butter or margarine
50 g (2 oz) caster sugar
1 egg
50 g (2 oz) ground almonds
50 g (2 oz) cake crumbs
5 ml (1 tsp) almond essence

Line a 15-cm (6-inch) pie plate with the pastry and spread the jam over the bottom. Cream the fat with the sugar until soft and white, then add the beaten egg a little at a time. Stir in the ground almonds and cake crumbs and add the almond essence. Spread the mixture on the top of the jam and add strips of pastry cut from the trimmings. Bake in the oven at 180°C (350°F) mark 4 until the mixture is firm and the pastry lightly browned – 30–40 minutes. Serve hot or cold, with or without custard.

Pineapple upside-down pudding

Milk and custard puddings

Rice pudding

Illustrated in colour opposite

40 g (1 ½ oz) short grain rice
568 ml (1 pint) milk
15–25 g (½–1 oz) caster sugar
a little butter
grated nutmeg

Wash the rice and put it into a greased pie dish with the milk and sugar. Put a few shavings of butter over the top, with a little grated nutmeg. Bake in the oven at 150°C (300°F) mark 1 for 2–3 hours, stirring once or twice during the first hour, then leave undisturbed for the remaining time.

Semolina pudding

568 ml (1 pint) milk
40 g (1 ½ oz) semolina
15 g (½ oz) caster sugar
1 egg, separated

Heat the milk and when almost boiling sprinkle in the semolina, stirring. Stir until boiling, then simmer for 10–15 minutes, until the grain is soft, stirring frequently. Remove from the heat, add the sugar and cool slightly. Beat the egg yolk into the semolina and mix well. Whisk the white stiffly and fold in. Pour into a greased pie dish and bake in the oven at 180°C (350°F) mark 4 for about 30 minutes, until the pudding is lightly browned.

Apricot semolina meringue

Illustrated in colour opposite

568 ml (1 pint) milk
a knob of butter
60 ml (4 level tbsp) semolina
50 g (2 oz) granulated sugar
2 eggs, separated
425-g (15-oz) can apricot halves
50 g (2 oz) sultanas
50 g (2 oz) caster sugar
toasted flaked almonds

Heat the milk with the butter and sprinkle on the semolina. Continue to heat, stirring, until the milk boils and the mixture thickens. Cook for 2–3 minutes, stirring. Off the heat, stir in the 50 g (2 oz) granulated sugar and the beaten egg yolks. Pour into a greased 1·1-litre (2-pint) ovenproof dish. Place on a baking sheet and bake in the oven at 170°C (325°F) mark 3 until set – about 40 minutes.

Drain the apricots and measure 150 ml

(¼ pint) juice into a saucepan. Add the sultanas and boil in the open pan until the sultanas are plumped up and most of the liquid has evaporated. Purée the apricots, stir in the sultanas and spread over the semolina. Beat the egg whites and whisk in 25 g (1 oz) caster sugar. When stiff, fold in a further 25 g (1 oz) caster sugar. Pile over the apricot layer to mask and return to the oven at 200°C (400°F) mark 6 for 5–10 minutes. Sprinkle with toasted flaked almonds and serve hot. *Serves 4–6*

Queen of puddings

400 ml (¾ pint) milk
40 g (1 ½ oz) butter or margarine
75 g (3 oz) breadcrumbs
40 g (1 ½ oz) caster sugar
grated rind of 1 lemon
2 eggs, separated
50 g (2 oz) caster sugar
jam

Bring the milk to the boil with the fat and pour over the crumbs, sugar and rind; stir and leave to cool. Add egg yolks and mix well, then pour into a 1·1-litre (2-pint) pie dish and bake in the oven at 180°C (350°F) mark 4 until set, about 25–30 minutes. Meanwhile whisk the egg whites stiffly and fold in the sugar. Spread the pudding with melted jam and pile or pipe the meringue on top. Bake in the oven at 150°C (300°F) mark 1 until the meringue is crisp – about 30 minutes.

If preferred, this pudding may be made and served in individual dishes.

Baked custards

300 ml (½ pint) milk
1 egg
15 g (½ oz) sugar
nutmeg

Heat the milk without boiling it. Beat the egg with the sugar and pour the milk on to it, stirring well. Strain the mixture into individual dishes, sprinkle with a little grated nutmeg and bake in the oven at 150°C (300°F) mark 1 for about 20 minutes, until set.

The dish containing the custard can be stood in a shallow tin containing water – this helps to ensure that the custard does not separate through overheating.

Caramel custard

125 g (4 ½ oz) caster sugar
150 ml (¼ pint) water
568 ml (1 pint) milk
4 eggs

Put 100 g (4 oz) sugar and the water into a small pan, dissolve, then heat without

stirring until the mixture becomes a rich brown colour, but don't make the caramel too dark, or it will taste bitter. Pour it quickly into a hot 15-cm (6-inch) cake tin, then, holding the tin with a cloth, coat the inside well all over. Leave to set. Heat the milk; beat the eggs and remaining sugar and pour the hot milk on to the eggs. Strain the mixture over the cooled caramel. Place the tin into a shallow tin of water and bake in the oven at 170°C (325°F) mark 3 for about 1 hour until set. Leave in the tin until quite cold before turning out.

Caramel crisp pudding

100 g (4 oz) caster sugar
60 ml (4 tbsp) water
75 g (3 oz) white bread, diced
2 eggs
400 ml (¾ pint) milk

Dissolve the sugar in the water and boil rapidly until it caramelises. Leave to cool slightly, then carefully add another 60 ml (4 tbsp) water and re-boil. Grease an ovenproof dish and put the diced bread into it, then pour the caramel over and leave to soak. Meanwhile, beat the eggs, heat the milk to boiling point and pour on to the eggs. Strain this mixture over the soaked bread and leave to stand for 15 minutes, then bake in the oven at 150°C (300°F) mark 1 for 20–30 minutes, until the custard has set and the bread (which rises to the top) is crisp and brown.

Bread and butter pudding

5–6 slices of white bread and butter
50 g (2 oz) dried fruit
25 g (1 oz) caster sugar
15 ml (1 tbsp) marmalade (optional)
2 eggs
568 ml (1 pint) milk

Rice pudding and
Apricot semolina pudding (see above).

Grease an ovenproof dish. Cut the bread and butter into triangles; clean the fruit and mix it with the sugar. Arrange the bread and butter, fruit and sugar in layers in the dish, and spread the top layer with marmalade (if used).

Beat the eggs and pour on the cold milk, then pour this mixture over the bread and butter and soak for 1 hour. Bake in the oven at 150°C (300°F) mark 1 for 45 minutes–1 hour, until the custard is set and the top lightly browned.

Chocolate marshmallow pudding

400 ml (¾ pint) milk
1 egg, beaten
50 g (2 oz) sponge cake crumbs
75 g (3 oz) ground almonds
25 g (1 oz) cocoa
25 g (1 oz) caster sugar
5 ml (1 tsp) vanilla essence
100 g (4 oz) marshmallows

Heat the milk and pour it on to the egg. Put the dry ingredients into a bowl and pour on the egg and milk, add the sugar and vanilla essence, then pour into a greased dish and bake in the oven at 180°C (350°F) mark 4 until set – about 1 hour. Remove from the oven, arrange the marshmallows on top and brown them under a hot grill. Serve with marshmallow sauce – see recipe below.

Marshmallow sauce

100 g (4 oz) granulated sugar
45 ml (3 tbsp) water
8 marshmallows
1 egg white
vanilla essence
a little food colouring

Dissolve the sugar in the water, then boil together for about 15 minutes. Add the marshmallows, cut into small pieces with scissors. Beat the egg white very stiffly, then gradually fold in the marshmallow mixture. Add essence and colouring.

Batter mixtures

Pancakes

100 g (4 oz) plain flour
a pinch of salt
1 egg
300 ml (½ pint) milk or milk and water
lard for frying

Mix the flour and salt, make a well in the centre and break in the egg. Add half the liquid and beat the mixture until it is smooth. Add the remaining liquid gradually and beat until well mixed.

Heat a little lard in a frying pan until really hot, running it round to coat the sides of the pan; pour off any surplus. Pour in a little batter, running it round to cover the base of the pan thinly and cook quickly until golden brown underneath. Turn with a palette knife or by tossing and cook the second side until golden. Slide out on to sugared paper, sprinkle with sugar and a squeeze of lemon, roll up and serve at once, with sugar and lemon wedges.

If you are cooking a large number of pancakes, keep them warm by putting them as they are made between 2 plates in a warm oven. Finally, roll up all the pancakes and serve at once.

Pancakes with a difference

Pineapple and cherry pancakes
Illustrated in colour on pages 136–137
Combine drained canned pineapple (cut into pieces) and cherries. Blend a little cornflour with the reserved pineapple juice, bring to the boil and cook until thickened. Add the fruit and heat through. Spoon some filling on to each pancake, fold into quarters, arrange on a serving dish and pour over the remaining sauce.

Layered pancakes Instead of rolling the pancakes, use a filling (for instance whipped cream and jam) to layer the pancakes one on top of the other. Cut in wedges.

A mixture of drained canned fruit (such as peaches, apricots, strawberries and raspberries) and whipped cream, makes another delicious filling.

Surprise pancakes Make the pancakes in the usual way, spoon some ice cream into the centre of each pancake and fold in half, like an omelette. Serve with jam sauce or a sauce made from sieved raspberries.

French pancakes

50 g (2 oz) butter or margarine
50 g (2 oz) caster sugar
2 eggs
50 g (2 oz) plain flour
300 ml (½ pint) milk
jam

Cream the fat and sugar, add the eggs one at a time, with some of the flour, then fold in the rest of the flour and lastly stir in the very slightly warmed milk. (At this stage the mixture will probably curdle, but this does not matter.) Half-fill 4–6 greased patty tins or saucers with the mixture and bake in the oven at 200°C (400°F) mark 6 for 10–15 minutes. Turn the pancakes out on to sugared paper, place a spoonful of hot jam

in each and fold over like an omelette, or sandwich together with jam.

Fritters

100 g (4 oz) plain flour
a pinch of salt
15 ml (1 tbsp) oil
150 ml (¼ pint) tepid water
2 egg whites
fat for deep frying
4 bananas, 16 apple slices, or 10 pineapple rings
caster sugar

Sift together the flour and salt, make a well in the centre and add the oil and half the water. Draw in the flour from the sides and mix and beat well. Add sufficient water to bring to a coating consistency. Just before using the batter, whisk the egg whites until stiff and fold them into the mixture. Heat the fat until a 2·5 cm (1 inch) cube of bread will brown in 60 seconds. Dip the pieces of fruit into the batter, drain well and lower carefully into the hot fat. Allow to brown on one side, then turn the fritters and cook on the other side until they are golden brown. Remove, draining well, then put on to crumpled kitchen paper to finish draining. Serve sprinkled with caster sugar.

American waffles

175 g (6 oz) plain flour
a pinch of salt
7·5 ml (1½ level tsp) baking powder
15 ml (1 level tbsp) caster sugar
2 eggs
300 ml (½ pint) milk
50 g (2 oz) butter, melted
a few drops of vanilla essence

Sift the flour, salt and baking powder into a basin, and stir in the sugar. Make a well in the centre of the dry ingredients and add the egg yolks. Mix these in, adding the milk and melted fat alternately, then stir in the vanilla essence. Whip up the whites of egg very stiffly and fold in lightly. Pour the batter into the heated waffle iron and cook according to the maker's directions. Serve the waffles immediately, with butter and maple syrup or golden syrup.

Hot soufflés

Vanilla soufflé

50 g (2 oz) caster sugar
4 large eggs
60 ml (4 level tbsp) plain flour
300 ml (½ pint) milk
2·5 ml (½ tsp) vanilla essence
icing sugar (optional)

Butter an 18-cm, 1·7-litre (7-inch, 3-pint) soufflé dish. Cream the sugar with one whole egg and one yolk until pale cream in colour. Stir in the flour. Pour on the milk and mix until smooth. Bring to boiling point, stirring, and simmer for 2 minutes. Cool slightly, then beat in the remaining yolks and vanilla essence. Fold in the stiffly beaten egg whites. Pour into the soufflé dish and bake for about 45 minutes at 180°C (350°F) mark 4, until well risen, firm to the touch and pale golden. If you wish, after 30 minutes cooking, quickly dust the soufflé with icing sugar and continue to bake.

Variations

Line the base of the buttered soufflé dish with sliced banana, previously sautéed in butter and dredged with sugar. Top with the vanilla soufflé mixture. Or omit vanilla essence and stir in the finely grated rind and juice of 1 lemon before adding the egg white. Serve with a thin orange sauce (see page 162). Or marinade sliced fresh strawberries in a little sugar, orange juice and orange curaçao. Drain and retain the juice. Line the base of the soufflé dish with strawberries. Top with vanilla soufflé mixture. Serve baked soufflé with whipped cream flavoured with marinade.

Baked orange soufflé

Illustrated in colour on page 149

2 medium oranges
60 ml (4 tbsp) Grand Marnier
75 g (3 oz) sponge cake crumbs
300 ml (½ pint) milk
25 g (1 oz) butter
75 g (3 oz) caster sugar
65 g (2½ oz) plain flour
4 egg yolks
5 egg whites
icing sugar to dust

Cut the thinly pared rind from one orange into thin strips. Cook in boiling water until soft. Drain. Marinate in 15 ml (1 tbsp) Grand Marnier. Peel the oranges and remove the segments by cutting between each one, close to the dividing membrane. Soak the crumbs in 45 ml (3 tbsp) Grand Marnier, then add the orange segments. Butter a 1·7-litre (3-pint) soufflé dish.

In a saucepan, bring the milk, less 100 ml (6 tbsp), to the boil with the butter and sugar. Blend the flour and the 100 ml (6 tbsp) milk to a smooth paste. Whisk into the boiling milk, bring back quickly to the boil. Heat until the mixture leaves the side of the pan. Beat 4 yolks one by one into 'panada'. Stir in the liquor drained from the marinated orange and peel. Fold the stiffly whisked whites into the mixture. Pour half

into the soufflé dish. Sprinkle in the orange segments and crumbs. Pour over the remaining mixture. Bake at 200°C (400°F) mark 6 for about 45 minutes. Dust with icing sugar and marinated orange julienne strips. *Serves 6*

Lemon soufflé

50 g (2 oz) butter or margarine
50 g (2 oz) caster sugar
juice of ½ lemon
2 eggs, separated
15 g (½ oz) plain flour
grated lemon rind

Cream together the fat and sugar, then beat in the lemon juice and egg yolks. Stand the basin over boiling water and whisk until the mixture is thick and creamy. Fold in the flour and grated lemon rind and add the stiffly beaten egg whites. Grease a 15-cm (6-inch) soufflé dish and pour in the mixture, stand the tin in another tin half-filled with water and bake in the oven at 180°C (350°F) mark 4 for 30 minutes. Dust the top with icing sugar and serve immediately with cream.

Chocolate soufflé

Use the same recipe and method as for Vanilla Soufflé, but dissolve 40 g (1½ oz) plain chocolate in the milk before using it for making the panada mixture.

Liqueur soufflé

2 sponge cakes
75 ml (5 tbsp) Kirsch
40 g (2½ oz) mixed glacé fruits
50 g (2 oz) butter or margarine
25 g (1 oz) plain flour
150 ml (¼ pint) milk
50 g (2 oz) caster sugar
3 eggs, separated

Cut the sponge cakes into fingers and soak in 15 ml (1 tbsp) kirsch. Rinse the glacé fruits in very hot water to remove the excess sugar, cut into small pieces and allow to soak in 15 ml (1 tbsp) Kirsch.

Melt the fat, add the flour and beat well. Remove from the heat and gradually add the milk, stirring all the time. Return it to the heat and cook for 5 minutes. Cool slightly and beat in the sugar, egg yolks and 45 ml (3 tbsp) Kirsch, then fold in the stiffly beaten egg whites. Pour half this mixture into a greased 1·7-litre (3-pint) soufflé dish, place over it a layer of sponge cakes and glacé fruit, cover with the remaining soufflé mixture and bake in the oven at 220°C (425°F) mark 7 for 15 minutes; lower the heat to 180°C (350°F) mark 4 and continue to bake for 30 minutes. Serve at once.

Pastries and pies

Shortcrust pastry

225 g (8 oz) plain flour
a pinch of salt
100 g (4 oz) fat – half butter or block margarine and half lard
cold water to mix

Sift the flour and salt into a bowl, put in the fat, cover with flour and break into pieces. Using the finger-tips, rub the fat into the flour until the mixture is as fine as breadcrumbs; raise the hands high in the basin to incorporate as much cold air as possible. Add the water slowly, using just enough to make the mixture bind when stirred. Use a round-ended knife to mix. Finally, knead gently into a smooth ball, leaving the bowl clean. The pastry is now ready to roll out and use.

Allow 5 ml (1 tsp) cold water to each 25 g (1 oz) flour to bind. The usual oven temperature is 200°–220°C (400°–425°F) mark 6–7.

Rich shortcrust or flan pastry

225 g (8 oz) plain flour
a pinch of salt
150 g (5 oz) butter (or block margarine and butter)
5 ml (1 level tsp) caster sugar
1 egg yolk
cold water

Sift the flour and salt into a basin. Rub in the fat with the tips of the fingers until the mixture resembles fine breadcrumbs: do this very lightly or the mixture will become greasy and heavy. Add the sugar. Beat the egg yolk and add 15–30 ml (1–2 tbsp) cold water, then add just sufficient of this liquid to mix to a firm dough. Turn on to a floured board, knead or pat lightly into a round, roll out and use as required.

This pastry should be cooked at 200°C (400°F) mark 6.

Flaky pastry

225 g (8 oz) plain flour
a pinch of salt
175 g (6 oz) block margarine and lard, mixed
a squeeze of lemon juice
cold water to mix

Sift the flour and salt into a basin. Soften the fat and divide it into 4 portions. Rub one quarter well into the flour and mix to a stiff paste with lemon juice and water. Knead the paste on a lightly floured board, then roll it into an oblong and flake another quarter of the fat over two-thirds of the pastry: to prevent the fat working through at the edges when the pastry is rolled out, keep it about 1 cm (½ inch) in from the edges. Fold the pastry into three, first bringing the bottom third up, then the top third down to cover it. Seal the edges lightly with the rolling pin and turn the pastry towards the left. Repeat the processes of flaking, folding and turning with the two remaining portions of the fat. Fold and roll once more, then leave the pastry in a cool place for 30 minutes before using it as required.

The usual oven setting for flaky pastry is 220°C (425°F) mark 7.

Note Bought ready made puff pastry is frequently used to replace home-made flaky rough puff and puff pastry. Buy a 212-g (7 ½-oz) packet to replace homemade pastry made with 225 g (8 oz) flour.

Suet crust pastry

225 g (8 oz) plain flour (or 175 g (6 oz) flour and 50 g (2 oz) fine breadcrumbs)
5 ml (1 level tsp) baking powder
2·5 ml (½ level tsp) salt
75–100 g (3–4 oz) suet, shredded or chopped
cold water to mix

Sift the flour, baking powder and salt, mix in the suet and add the breadcrumbs, if used. Make a well in the centre and pour in enough cold water to give a soft but not sticky dough. Place this on a lightly floured board and gently knead it. Use as required.

PIE EDGINGS

The appearance of a tart or pie can be greatly improved by means of a decorative edge. After putting on the top crust of the pie a better finish is obtained if the edges are 'knocked up' with a sharp knife – see

Fruit pie

picture **1**. This apples particularly to the richer pastries, such as flaky or rough puff. For a decorative finish suitable for a plate pie, a scalloped edge can be made, as shown in picture **2**; the width of the scallops can be varied as required, but is usually fairly small for sweet pies. Picture **3** shows a fluted edge, made by pressing the forefinger on one side of the pastry, against the finger and thumb held on the other side. A further decoration for a plate pie is shown in picture **4**; this is made by cutting strips of pastry and twisting them on to the damped edge of the top crust. Several other pastry decorations can be devised which will use the left-over pastry trimmings.

Fruit pie

Illustrated in colour opposite

225 g (8 oz) shortcrust pastry
about 900 g (2 lb) fruit (see note)
sugar to sweeten
cold water
milk or egg white to glaze

Make the pastry (see page 143), and prepare the fruit according to kind. Half-fill a 1·1-litre (2-pint) pie dish with fruit, sprinkle well with sugar, and well fill the dish with the rest of the fruit. Add sufficient water to cover the bottom of the dish. Roll the pastry out to 0·5 cm (¼ inch) thickness, making it the shape of the pie dish but about 2·5 cm (1 inch) larger all round. Cut off a strip of pastry wide enough to cover the rim of the dish. Damp the dish rim, press on the strip and damp the pastry edge. lift the rest of the pastry on a rolling pin, lay it over the fruit and press lightly on to the rim, then trim off the rough edges. 'Knock up' the edges and mark with a fork. Glaze with milk or egg white and make a hole at each end to allow the steam to escape. Bake in the oven at 220°C (425°F) mark 7 for 15–20 minutes, until the pastry has set and lightly browned, then reduce the heat and cook until the fruit is quite tender. Serve hot dusted with caster sugar.

Note Use plums, rhubarb or apple and cherry combined to make a refreshing change.

Spiced apple and cheese pie

175 g (6 oz) shortcrust pastry
450 g (1 lb) cooking apples
100 g (4 oz) caster sugar
30 ml (2 level tbsp) flour
5 ml (1 level tsp) powdered cinnamon
milk to glaze
2 slices of cheese

Divide the pastry into 2 even-sized pieces, roll out and use one piece to line a shallow

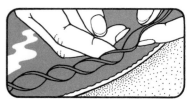

Pie edgings

15-cm (6-inch) pie dish. Peel, core and slice the apples; add the sugar, flour and cinnamon and mix well. Put this mixture into the dish, wet the edges of the pastry and cover with the second piece; flake and scallop the edges and brush the top with milk. Bake in the oven at 220°C (425°F) mark 7 for 10 minutes, then lower to 180°C (350°F) mark 4 and bake for a further 20–30 minutes to cook the fruit. Just before serving, decorate the top of the pie with triangles of cheese and return it to the oven until they just begin to melt. Serve hot, with cream or custard.

Summer berry pie

900 g (2 lb) mixed berry fruits
100 g (4 oz) caster sugar
225 g (8 oz) shortcrust pastry
egg white
caster sugar

Strawberries, raspberries, loganberries, gooseberries, red and blackcurrants, etc, can all be used in this pie. Pick the fruit over and wash it, half-fill a 1·1–1·7-litre (2–3-pint) pie dish with the mixed berries and sprinkle well with sugar, then pile the rest of the fruit high in the dish. Roll out the pastry and

Fruit pies (see above).

Blackcurrant galette

cover the dish as for fruit pie. Glaze with beaten egg white and caster sugar, and bake in the oven at 190°C (375°F) mark 5 for about 30 minutes, until the pastry is brown and the fruit tender. Serve hot or cold, with whipped cream.

Gooseberry plate pie

225 g (8 oz) flaky pastry (see page 143)
450 g (1 lb) gooseberries
150 ml (¼ pint) water
50–100 g (2–4 oz) sugar, as required
5 ml (1 level tsp) cornflour or arrowroot
egg white to glaze
caster sugar

Line a 20·5-cm (8-inch) pie plate with half the pastry. Prepare the gooseberries, rinse, then place in a saucepan with about 150 ml (¼ pint) water. Cover and cook very gently until tender, taking care to keep the berries whole. Drain in a colander. Measure 150 ml (¼ pint) of the juice, put this back in the saucepan with the sugar and add the

cornflour or arrowroot blended with a spoonful of cold water. Cook, stirring, until the mixture boils and thickens. Add the gooseberries and set aside to cool, then pour into the lined pie plate. Cover with the pastry, glaze with beaten white of egg and dust with caster sugar. Bake in the oven at 220°C (425°F) mark 7 for about 10 minutes, then reduce the heat to 180°C (350°F) mark 4 and cook for about 30 minutes, until the pie is well risen and nicely browned. Serve hot with cream.

Blackcurrant galette

Illustrated in colour on page 153

225 g (8 oz) plain flour
100 g (4 oz) butter or block margarine
50 g (2 oz) lard
30 ml (2 level tbsp) caster sugar
cold water
1 small egg, beaten
50 g (2 oz) semolina
50 g (2 oz) caster sugar
700 g (1 ¼ lb) blackcurrants, destalked

Sift the flour into a bowl, grate the fat straight from the refrigerator into the flour and rub in lightly. Add the 30 ml (2 tbsp) caster sugar and mix to a firm dough with cold water. Roll out and line a greased 23-cm (9-inch) fluted ovenproof flan dish. Trim off excess pastry, prick the base with a fork and brush with a little beaten egg. Chill. Mix together the semolina and caster sugar, layer up with the blackcurrants in the pastry-lined dish. Roll out the pastry trimmings, cut into strips with a pastry wheel. Use these to lattice the flan dish. Brush with beaten egg and bake in the oven at 220°C (425°F) mark 7 for 30–40 minutes. *Serves 8*

Swiss plum tart

175 g (6 oz) shortcrust pastry
225 g (8 oz) plums
a little sugar
a small knob of butter

Line an 18-cm (7-inch) pie plate with the pastry and decorate the edges. Cut the plums in half, remove the stones and then cut them in quarters. Arrange these quarters in overlapping circles on the pastry. Sprinkle with sugar and some fine shavings of butter and bake in the oven at 220°C (425°F) mark 7 until the pastry is lightly browned – 10 minutes – then reduce the heat to 180°C (350°F) mark 4 until the fruit is tender – about 30 minutes in all.

Sliced apples or black cherries (stoned) may also be used for making this type of tart.

Blackberry trellis pie

175 g (6 oz) flaky pastry
milk or egg for glazing
450 g (1 lb) blackberries
25–50 g (1–2 oz) caster sugar
30 ml (2 tbsp) condensed milk
grated rind of 1 lemon

Line an 18-cm (7-inch) plate with the pastry, flute the edges with a sharp knife, prick the bottom of the pie and bake blind in the oven at 220°C (425°F) mark 7 until cooked – about 15 minutes. Roll out the pastry trimmings and make into a trellis, glaze and bake separately for 5–10 minutes, then allow to cool. Mix the blackberries, sugar, condensed milk and lemon rind, put into the pie case and place the trellis on top. Serve immediately.

COLD PUDDINGS

Cold sweets and desserts can range from hearty fruit tarts and flans to feathery confections of cream and meringue, but they all share the advantage of being easy to prepare in advance. Although for the really elaborate ice-cream creations a refrigerator is essential, there are dozens of delicious and simply made sweets which will become sufficiently chilled in a cool larder.

Desserts

Raspberry and pineapple rings

Cream 2 squares of demi-sel cheese or a mild cream cheese spread with the grated rind of 1 lemon, 10 ml (2 level tsp) sugar and enough lemon juice to give a soft consistency. Sandwich some pineapple rings together in pairs with this mixture; decorate with toasted flaked almonds and serve with raspberry sauce. Chill both the pineapple rings and the sauce thoroughly before serving.

To make the sauce, blend 10 ml (2 level tsp) arrowroot with 150 ml (¼ pint) of juice taken from a can of raspberries, boil until the sauce thickens and then fold in the drained raspberries. Alternatively, use fresh raspberries crushed with sugar or puréed in a blender.

Savarin aux fruits

45 ml (3 tbsp) warm milk
15 g (½ oz) fresh yeast or 7·5 ml (1½ level tsp) dry yeast and 5 ml (1 level tsp) caster sugar
100 g (4 oz) plain strong flour
1·25 ml (¼ level tsp) salt
15 ml (1 level tbsp) caster sugar
2 eggs, beaten
50 g (2 oz) butter, softened
syrup (see method)
60–90 ml (4–6 tbsp) warm apricot glaze
fruit salad (see method)

Blend together the milk and yeast, then stir in 25 g (1 oz) flour. Stand the bowl in a warm place for about 20 minutes. Add the remaining flour, salt, sugar, eggs and butter and beat for 3–4 minutes. Well grease a 900-ml (1½-pint) metal ring mould with lard and dust with flour. Fill with the mixture. Cover, allow to rise until two-thirds full. Bake in the oven at 200°C (400°F) mark 6 for about 20 minutes. Cool for a few minutes, ease out on to a wire rack, and while still warm, prick finely. Spoon enough

syrup over to saturate the savarin, reserving the remainder. Brush with the apricot glaze and cool. Place carefully on a serving dish, fill and decorate with fruit salad. Serve with cream.

For the syrup: Dissolve 175 g (6 oz) sugar in 225 ml (8 fl oz) water. Add 4 strips of lemon rind. Boil for 5 minutes. Cool, add 45 ml (3 tbsp) kirsch.

For the fruit salad: Peel 1 orange and segment without the membrane. Peel and slice 1 pear and 1 banana. Leave the skin on 1 red apple, core and dice. Stone 100 g (4 oz) mixed grapes. Toss all the fruits in 30 ml (2 tbsp) lemon juice and the remaining sugar syrup.

Summer pudding.

450 g (1 lb) soft fruits (raspberries, currants, blackberries, etc)
sugar
thin slices of bread
custard or whipped cream

Stew the fruit with sugar and water, keeping it as whole as possible. Arrange the fruit and bread in alternate layers in a 600–900-ml (1–1½-pint) basin, retaining some of the juice; pour this over the mixture, then place a piece of bread on the top, cover with a plate and press down with a heavy weight. Leave overnight in a cool place. If possible chill before serving with custard or cream.

Melon and fruit salad deluxe

Choose a medium-sized ripe honeydew or cantaloup melon. Cut a slice off the top and scoop out the seeds and then the flesh, leaving a rim of flesh round the top edge. Cut the melon pulp into cubes, retaining the juice, and mix with a selection of fresh or canned fruits, the juice of a lemon and a little Kirsch and leave to stand. Just before serving, fill the melon with the fruit salad, top with scoops of ice cream and sprinkle with some chopped nuts. Place on a dish, decorate with extra fruits and serve at once.

Brandied melon and ginger

1 canteloup melon
5–10 ml (1–2 level tsp) powdered ginger
about 100 g (4 oz) caster sugar
75 ml (5 tbsp) brandy

Halve the melon, scoop out the flesh and dice it; place in a bowl with the ginger and sufficient sugar to sweeten (the amount depends on your own tastes). Chill until the sugar has dissolved and the juice flows, then stir in the brandy. Serve in the half

melon shell or in individual dishes, accompanied by cream.

Cherries in red wine

450 g (1 lb) red cherries
red wine
30 ml (2 tbsp) redcurrant jelly
arrowroot

Stew the cherries in just enough red wine to cover, with the recurrant jelly. Strain off the juice and thicken with arrowroot – 15 g to 600 ml (½ oz to 1 pint) juice. Put the fruit in individual glasses and pour the juice over. Chill.

Orange ambrosia

4 sweet oranges
caster sugar to taste
50 g (2 oz) desiccated coconut
15–30 ml (1–2 tbsp) Curaçao or Grand Marnier

Peel the oranges, removing as much of the pith as possible; slice across very thinly. Place the oranges in individual glasses, layered with the sugar, coconut and liqueur, and chill before serving.

Peaches in white wine

Allow one or more yellow peaches per person. Peel and slice each into a wine glass, pour on some white wine and leave for a few minutes. The peach is eaten first, then the wine is drunk. (The most suitable wine is a sweet white Italian one, such as Orvieto).

Pears in port wine

4 large ripe pears
150 ml (¼ pint) port
150 ml (¼ pint) water
75 g (3 oz) caster sugar
rind of 1 lemon
30 ml (2 tbsp) redcurrant jelly (or to taste)
cream

Peel the pears, cut in quarters lengthways and remove the cores. Make a syrup from

the port, water, sugar and lemon rind. Add the pears and simmer gently until tender. Remove the fruit, add the redcurrant jelly, then boil the syrup rapidly until it is well reduced. Place 4 pear slices in each glass and pour the syrup over. Allow to cool and serve with cream.

Gala pineapple

Select a fairly large pineapple with a good crown of green leaves. Following the markings in the pineapple skin, stick in slanting rows of cocktail sticks; on these fix rows of fresh fruits, eg, grapes, cherries, strawberries, slices of banana, chunks of redskinned apple, pieces of pineapple and also chunks of cheese. (Dip the apple and banana slices in lemon juice to prevent their discolouring.) This makes a good item at a buffet or cocktail party.

Grilled grapefruit

Cut 2 grapefruit in half and loosen the segments in the usual way. Brush each half well with melted butter, sprinkle with 15 ml (1 level tbsp) brown sugar, 10 ml (2 tsp) rum or sherry and a little powdered cinnamon, then grill gently for 10 minutes, until tender and bubbling. Serve alone or with whipped cream.

Blackberry fool

450 g (1 lb) blackberries (or a 425-g (15-oz) can)
sugar to taste
300 ml (½ pint) custard and/or cream

Stew the blackberries in a little water with sugar as required (unless canned fruit is used); sieve the fruit. Mix the purée with the custard or cream (or a half-and-half mixture) and sweeten to taste. Pour into glasses, decorate with chopped nuts or as desired. Serve with shortbread or Savoy biscuits.

This sweet is equally good made with other fruits, especially gooseberries, rhubarb and berry fruits.

Apricot dessert

850-g (1 lb 14-oz) can apricots
40 g (1 ½ oz) cornflour
50 g (2 oz) ground almonds
50 g (2 oz) caster sugar
2 eggs, separated
5 ml (1 tsp) almond essence
10 ml (2 tsp) lemon juice
142-ml (5-fl oz) carton double cream
blanched angelica

Sieve the apricots with their juice (keeping 8 for decoration) and make up to 1·1 litres (2 pints) with water. Mix the cornflour, almonds, sugar and egg yolks to a smooth paste with a little of the cold fruit mixture. Bring the rest of the fruit to the boil, add to the cornflour, return the mixture to the pan and cook for 3 minutes. Remove from the heat and add the essence and lemon juice. Whisk the egg whites stiffly and fold in. Spoon the mixture into individual glasses. When cold, cover with half-whisked cream and put an apricot half and angelica 'leaves' on each. Whisk the remaining cream and pipe some into each apricot. *Serves 8*

Strawberry orange sponge flan

Illustrated in colour on page 157

2 large eggs
50 g (2 oz) caster sugar
50 g (2 oz) plain flour
4 medium juicy oranges
60 ml (4 level tbsp) apricot jam
5 ml (1 level tsp) arrowroot
142-ml (5-fl oz) carton double cream
15 ml (1 tbsp) milk
100 g (4 oz) strawberries

Prepare a fatless sponge mixture using the eggs, sugar and plain flour. Bake in a prepared 21·5-cm (8 ½-inch) sponge flan tin in the oven at 220°C (425°F) mark 7 for about 15 minutes until well risen and golden brown. Turn out carefully and cool on a wire rack. Squeeze the juice from one orange. Peel remaining oranges free of all pith. Using a knife over the bowl of juice, cut along both sides of each, dividing membrane and lift out the sections. Squeeze the membrane into the bowl.

In a saucepan, bring to the boil 150 ml (¼ pint) orange juice, the apricot jam and arrowroot blended together. Cook for a few minutes then sieve. Whip the cream and milk together until it holds its shape, hull and chop all but 3 strawberries. Put the chopped berries in the base of the flan and spread the cream over. Cover with orange segments and remaining hulled, sliced strawberries. Glaze with warm, but not hot, orange juice and apricot jam mixture. *Serves 6*

Glazed orange cheesecake

Illustrated in colour on the jacket

225 g (8 oz) digestive biscuits
100 g (4 oz) butter or block margarine, melted
15 g (½ oz) powdered gelatine
225 g (8 oz) cream cheese
2 large thin skinned oranges
50 g (2 oz) caster sugar
2 eggs, separated
75 g (3 oz) granulated sugar

Crush the biscuits finely and combine with the melted butter or margarine. Press into a 23-cm (9-inch) loose-bottomed flan tin to line the base and sides. Place in the refrigerator to set. Dissolve the gelatine in 45 ml (3 tbsp) boiling water and cool. Beat the cream cheese until soft and add the finely grated rind and strained juice of one orange with the caster sugar and egg yolks. Stir in the cooled gelatine. Whisk the egg whites until stiff and fold into the cream cheese mixture. Pour into the biscuit case and leave to set.

Meanwhile, wipe and very thinly slice the remaining orange. Place the granulated sugar in a large shallow pan with 150 ml (¼ pint) water. Add the sliced orange, cover and poach gently for about 50 minutes until the peel is tender. Drain the orange slices and arrange around the top edge of the cheesecake. Boil the remaining syrup to a glaze and brush over the oranges. Chill again before serving. *Serves 6–8*

Fruit salad Pavlova

225 g (8 oz) caster sugar
25 g (1 oz) cornflour
3 egg whites
225 g (8 oz) fresh or canned fruit (oranges, grapes, cherries, banana, etc)

Draw a circle 15 cm (6 inches) in diameter on a piece of waxed or greaseproof paper, then place this on a greased tray. Sieve the sugar and cornflour together very thoroughly. Beat the egg whites until foamy, add half the sugar-and-cornflour mixture and beat until stiff. now add the rest of the sugar-and-cornflour and fold in until it is well blended. Place a forcing bag fitted with a vegetable star pipe and pipe round the pencil line on the paper and over the entire centre. Pipe round the edge to build up a 'basket' shape. Bake in the oven at 130°C (250°F) mark ½ for 2–3 hours, until quite dry and crisp. While the meringue case is cooking, peel and slice oranges and apples, halve and seed grapes, stone cherries, slice banana and cut pineapple into chunks.

Take the meringue case off the paper while it is still warm and lift it on to a cooling

Baked orange soufflé
(see page 143).

rack. When it is cool, arrange the fruit attractively in the meringue basket.

Basic fruit salad

Make a syrup by boiling together 100 g (4 oz) sugar and 300 ml (½ pint) water and when cool add the juice of 1 lemon. Prepare according to type 2 oranges, 2 bananas, 2 red-skinned apples, 100 g (4 oz) black or green grapes, 1 small can of cherries and 1 can of peaches or pineapples. Add all to the syrup. Supplement with other fruits in season, eg, strawberries, raspberries, apricots, melon, plums or pears, 30–45 ml (2–3 tbsp) fruit liqueur or spirit can be added to the syrup. Chill before serving.

Serve in a glass dish or, for a change, in hollowed oranges or melons (serrate the edges with a knife) or in a brandy balloon or punch bowl. The rim may be frosted by painting it with egg white and coating with sugar crystals.

Hedgerow delight

225 g (8 oz) blackberries
225 g (8 oz) damsons
sugar to sweeten
1 sponge sandwich
whipped cream and chopped almonds to decorate

Stew the two fruits, separately with sugar to sweeten, adding no water to the blackberries and very little to the damsons. Remove the stones from the latter then cook the damsons with the blackberries for a few minutes. Lay the first sponge layer in a dish, pour over it half of the fruit and put the other cake layer on top, then add the rest of the fruit. Leave for 4–6 hours in a cool place, then transfer to a glass dish. Put some cream on top and sprinkle with chopped almonds.

Loganberry whirls

Illustrated in colour on page 161

225 g (8 oz) loganberries or raspberries
75 g (3 oz) granulated sugar
1 pkt raspberry jelly
150 ml (¼ pint) crushed ice or iced water
15–30 ml (1–2 tbsp) lemon juice
113-ml (4-fl oz) carton double cream
grated chocolate or chocolate leaves to decorate (see method)

Poach the fruit gently in a syrup made of the sugar and 300 ml (½ pint) water. Pull the jelly into cubes and dissolve in the hot fruit mixture. While still warm, purée in an electric liquidiser with the crushed ice or iced water and strain through a nylon sieve,

adding lemon juice to taste. Cool the mixture until almost set, whisk well to make it light and airy, and spoon into four tall glasses. Swirl a little unwhipped cream through each; refrigerate until set. Decorate with the remaining cream, whipped, and coarsely grated chocolate or chocolate leaves.

To make chocolate leaves, use melted plain chocolate cake covering to pipe a leaf outline on non-stick paper (from a small paper forcing bag minus nozzle). Fill in with chocolate; when firm, pipe 'veins' on each leaf. Peel off the paper for serving.

Peach and strawberry Romanoff

4 peaches
450 g (1 lb) strawberries
caster sugar
1 glass of Curaçao
vanilla ice cream
15 ml (1 tbsp) cream

Skin and slice the peaches, place with three-quarters of the strawberries in a dish and sprinkle with caster sugar. Crush the remaining strawberries to a pulp, add the

Curaçao, ice cream and cream, then mix well together. Pour over the fruit and chill before serving.

Cherry trifle

175 g (6 oz) caster sugar
450 g (1 lb) cherries, stoned
sponge cakes or cake crumbs
cherry jam or redcurrant jelly
300 ml (½ pint) custard
50 g (2 oz) almonds
142-ml (5-fl oz) carton double cream
chopped pistachio nuts to decorate

Make a syrup with the sugar and sufficient water to cover the fruit; wash the cherries and stew them in the syrup. Split the sponge cakes and spread them with the cherry jam or redcurrant jelly; if cake crumbs are used, a thin layer of jam may be spread on top of them. Pour the stewed cherries over and leave for about 30 minutes for the sponge cakes to soak, then cover with the custard. Blanch the almonds and shred each into about three; sprinkle these on top of the custard, reserving a few for decoration. Whip the cream stiffly with a little caster sugar and pile in rocky heaps on top of the nuts. Decorate with pistachios.

Fruit salad

Strawberry mousse

200 ml (⅓ pint) strawberry purée
50 g (2 oz) caster sugar
juice of 1 lemon
15 g (½ oz) gelatine
75 ml (5 tbsp) water
284-ml (10-fl oz) carton double cream,
    lightly whipped
2 egg whites, stiffly whisked
strawberries and cream to decorate

Combine the strawberry purée, sugar and lemon juice. Dissolve the gelatine in the water over gentle heat and add. When the mixture is about to set, fold in the cream and lastly the egg whites. Put into a wetted 900-ml (1½-pint) mould and leave to set. Turn out and decorate with whole strawberries and a little whipped cream.

Alternatively, omit the gelatine and 75 ml (5 tbsp) water and put the mixture into the freezer of the refrigerator to make a frozen mousse.

Damson whip

450 g (1 lb) damsons
75 g (3 oz) caster sugar
15 g (½ oz) gelatine
1 small can evaporated milk
1 egg white
double cream and nuts to decorate

Stew the damsons with the sugar and 150 ml (¼ pint) water until tender, then sieve them. Dissolve the gelatine in 150 ml (¼ pint) hot water and stir it into the fruit purée; add the milk and leave to cool. When the mixture is almost set, add the egg white and whisk until light and frothy. Pile into glasses and decorate with whipped cream and some chopped nuts.

Redcurrant floats

Illustrated in colour on page 165

75 ml (5 tbsp) water
10 ml (2 level tsp) powdered gelatine
45 ml (3 level tbsp) redcurrant jelly
225 g (8 oz) redcurrants
142-ml (5-fl oz) carton double cream
45 ml (3 tbsp) milk

For the float
10 ml (2 level tsp) arrowroot
90 ml (6 tbsp) water
90 ml (6 level tbsp) redcurrant jelly
a few drops of red food colouring
    (optional)
redcurrants on the stem to decorate

Place the water in a cup, sprinkle the gelatine over and leave for a few minutes to swell. Gently heat the redcurrant jelly with the redcurrants, bring just to the boil then reduce the heat. Add the gelatine and leave to dissolve. Press the redcurrant mixture

Strawberry mousse

through a nylon sieve. Whip the cream with the milk until it holds its shape. Using a metal spoon, fold the purée mixture into the cream, until evenly combined. Divide the mixture between six glasses.

In a saucepan, blend the arrowroot with the water and add the redcurrant jelly; bring to the boil, stirring. Boil for a few minutes until clear, adding a few drops of red food colouring if liked. Cool. Pour over the creams and decorate with sprays of redcurrants. *Serves 6*

Orange and raspberry bavarois

1 pkt raspberry jelly
1 pkt orange jelly
100 g (4 oz) fresh raspberries
30 ml (2 level tbsp) custard powder
15 ml (1 level tbsp) sugar
300 ml (½ pint) milk
142-ml (5-fl oz) carton single cream
142-ml (5-fl oz) carton double cream
whipped cream and orange slices to
    decorate

Place the jelly cubes in a measure, make up to 400 ml (¾ pint) with boiling water and stir to dissolve. Make up 150 ml (¼ pint) of the liquid jelly to 300 ml (½ pint) with cold water, then pour into the base of a 1·4-litre (2½-pint) fancy mould. Drop in the prepared fruit and leave to set.

Make up a custard, using the custard powder, sugar and milk, and leave to cool. Stiffly whisk the single and double creams.

Whisk the cooled custard into the remaining jelly when this is on the point of setting. Fold the cream through the mixture and pour into the mould; chill. Turn out, and decorate with orange slices and whipped cream.

Orange baskets

4 large oranges
100 g (4 oz) grapes
2 bananas
1 dessert pear
a few canned apricots
a few canned or glacé cherries
angelica

Wipe the oranges and cut the top off each. Remove the pulp carefully without piercing the skin and squeeze it in muslin to obtain the juice. Stone the grapes, slice the bananas and cut up the other fruit. Pour the orange juice over the mixed fruit. Notch the edges of the orange baskets with scissors and fill with the fruit mixture. Soak the angelica in a little water and cut it in strips to form basket handles.

Frosted fruit pyramid

This makes an excellent centrepiece for a formal dinner table or buffet. For it you need a selection of fruits; for example, green and black grapes, clementines, dessert dates, green and red-skinned apples. Leave the apples whole; leave some clementines whole but divide 2–3 of them into segments; separate grapes into small bunches. Dip the fruits into lightly beaten egg white, then into caster sugar, making sure that the whole surface of each is thoroughly coated; leave overnight for the frosting to become firm. The next day, build the fruit up into a pyramid, using a silver cakeboard as a base and securing the layers of fruit with cocktail sticks. Decorate the base of the pyramid with sections of clementine and sprays of frosted fern.

Meringue pyramid

4 egg whites
225 g (8 oz) caster sugar
284-ml (10-fl oz) carton double cream
sugar to sweeten cream
225 g (8 oz) green and black grapes
50 g (2 oz) shelled walnuts
chocolate curls or flakes to decorate

Whisk the egg whites very stiffly. Add the sugar a little at a time, beating well after each addition. Put the mixture into a forcing bag fitted with a plain nozzle and pipe on to lightly oiled greaseproof paper in a small round meringues. Bake in the oven at 130°C (250°F) mark ½ for 3–4 hours, until crisp and dry but not coloured.

Whip and sweeten the cream. Remove the seeds from the grapes and chop the nuts roughly. Place a layer of meringue on a plate and cover with some of the cream and grapes. Continue piling up layers of meringue, fruit and cream in this way (retaining a little cream for decoration); form into a pyramid and finish with meringues. Pipe stars of cream between the meringues and decorate with grapes and walnuts, then sprinkle with chocolate flakes.

Raspberry and banana creams

Illustrated in colour on the jacket

2 eggs, separated
75 g (3 oz) caster sugar
150 ml (¼ pint) raspberry purée
15 g (½ oz) powdered gelatine
30 ml (2 tbsp) raspberry juice
3 bananas
150 ml (¼ pint) double cream
whipped cream and crystallised mint leaves to decorate

Whisk the egg yolks, sugar and raspberry purée over boiling water until the mixture is thick and creamy. Dissolve the gelatine in the raspberry juice and add to the mixture; sieve and add two of the bananas. Whip the cream and whisk the egg whites until stiff. When the fruit mixture is cool, add the whipped cream and lastly the egg

whites. Pour into individual glass dishes and when set decorate with whipped cream, sliced banana and crystallised mint leaves.

Stuffed pears

50 g (2 oz) seedless raisins
30 ml (2 tbsp) rum
30 ml (2 tbsp) water
25 g (1 oz) crystallized ginger, chopped
142-ml (5-fl oz) carton double cream, whipped
30 ml (2 level tbsp) caster sugar
850-g (1 lb 14-oz) can pear halves
maraschino cherries to decorate
shortbread fingers

Simmer the raisins gently in the rum and water for about 10 minutes, until the fruit is soft and has absorbed the spirit. Allow to cool, drain the fruit and mix with the ginger, cream and sugar. Pile this mixture on the well-drained pear halves, decorate each with a cherry and chill well. Serve with shortbread fingers.

Tahitian Pavlova

Illustrated in colour on page 165

4 egg whites
225 g (8 oz) caster sugar
10 ml (2 level tsp) cornflour
5 ml (1 tsp) vanilla essence
5 ml (1 tsp) vinegar
284-ml (10-fl oz) carton double cream
142-ml (5-fl oz) carton single cream
439-g (15½-oz) can guavas, drained
566-g (1 lb 4-oz) can lychees, drained

Draw a 20·5-cm (8-inch) circle on a piece of non-stick paper and place it on a baking

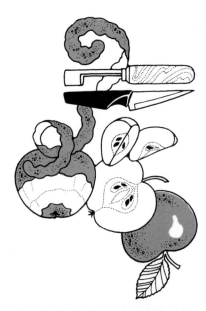

sheet. Whisk the egg whites until very stiff then gradually beat in the sugar until the mixture is shiny and thick. Beat in the cornflour, vanilla and vinegar and spread the mixture over the circle of paper. Bake in the oven at 150°C (300°F) mark 2 for 1 hour. Leave to cool, then carefully remove the paper.

Place the Pavlova on a serving plate. Whip the creams together in a basin until they hold their shape but are not stiff. Discard the seeds from the guavas. Cut each in half and reserve for decoration. Roughly chop the lychees and combine with half the cream. Pipe the remaining cream in a circle about 3 cm (1½ inches) from the edge of the Pavlova. Arrange guava 'petals' over the cream. Pile the cream and lychees over the top. Chill for 30 minutes before serving. *Serves 8*

Lemon snow

15 g (½ oz) gelatine
300 ml (½ pint) boiling water
175 g (6 oz) caster sugar
150 ml (¼ pint) lemon juice
3 egg whites
preserved lemon and glacé cherries to decorate

Dissolve the gelatine in the boiling water and add the sugar and lemon juice; leave to cool but do not allow it to set. Add the egg whites and whisk until light and fluffy. Put into individual glasses and decorate.

Bulgarian brandied fruit salad

2 apples
2 pears
1 orange
226-g (8-oz) can cherries
½ small melon
75 g (3 oz) sugar
400 ml (¾ pint) white wine
150 ml (¼ pint) brandy

Peel and thinly slice the apples, pears and orange. Stone the cherries. Scoop out balls from the melon with a Parisian cutter and mix the fruit thoroughly. Combine the sugar, wine and brandy, pour over the fruit and mix well, taking care not to break up the fruit pieces. Serve very cold.

Apple salad (Germany)

6 large eating apples
75 g (3 oz) hazelnuts, chopped
75 g (3 oz) walnuts, chopped
75 g (3 oz) seedless raisins
juice and grated rind of 1 lemon
75 g (3 oz) icing sugar, sifted
284-ml (10-fl oz) double cream

Strawberry shortcake (see page 160), Gooseberry ice cream flan (see page 159), Blackcurrant galette (see page 146).

Peel and slice the apples, mix with the nuts and raisins and sprinkle with lemon juice. Mix with the sugar and lemon rind, toss in the cream and serve chilled.

Delicious salad (South Africa)

2 oranges
1 pineapple
2 bananas
lemon juice
4 guavas
100 g (4 oz) sugar

Peel and thinly slice the oranges. Peel the pineapple, remove the core and cut the remaining flesh into slices. Peel and slice the bananas, toss in lemon juice to prevent discoloration. Do not peel the guavas, as their skins are attractive in colour – just slice them. Arrange the fruits in layers, generously sprinkle each layer with sugar and finish with a layer of orange slices. Leave the salad for several hours, so that the sugar can dissolve and form a syrup with the fruit juice.

Drunken prunes

325 g (12 oz) prunes
600 ml (1 pint) water
75–100 g (3–4 oz) sugar
grated rind and juice of 1 lemon
15 g (½ oz) gelatine
75 ml (5 tbsp) port
a few canned pears or apricots

Simmer the prunes in the water with the sugar, lemon rind and juice until tender. Sieve the fruit and juice to make a purée. Dissolve the gelatine in a little hot water, add to the fruit, then add the port. Pour the mixture into a refrigerator tray and leave to set. Chop it into large cubes and serve with the pears or apricots. *Serves 6*

Pineapple and peach salad (Germany)

150 ml (¼ pint) water
100 g (4 oz) granulated sugar
4 fresh peaches, halved
4 slices fresh pineapple
1 glass Rhine wine
50 g (2 oz) black grapes and icing sugar
to decorate

Make a syrup with the water and granulated sugar, cool and pour over the peaches; leave for 1 hour. Cut the pineapple slices into halves and arrange these in a circle on a flat dish, then fill the centre with the peach slices. Add the wine to the sugar syrup and pour over the fruit. Halve and seed the grapes, roll in icing sugar and use as decoration. Chill before serving.

Fruit salad in glasses

225 g (8 oz) strawberries, hulled
2 bananas, sliced
100 g (4 oz) cherries, stoned
juice of 1 lemon
150 ml (¼ pint) sweet clear jelly (liquid)
1 liqueur glass of maraschino
1 liqueur glass of brandy
75 ml (5 tbsp) sugar syrup

Put the 3 fruits in layers into individual goblet glasses. Strain the lemon juice and mix with the other liquids. Pour a little of this syrup over the fruit in each glass; chill well before serving.

Syrian chilled fruit salad

100 g (4 oz) dried apricots
100 g (4 oz) prunes
100 g (4 oz) dried figs
other dried fruit as available
50 g (2 oz) seedless raisins
50 g (2 oz) almonds
50 g (2 oz) pine kernels
50 g (2 oz) pistachio nuts
30 ml (2 tbsp) rose-water
sugar syrup or fruit syrup to taste

Wash the dried fruit, cover with cold water and leave to soak in a cool place for 24 hours. Blanch the nuts and add to the fruit, with the rose-water and enough syrup to sweeten. Keep in a cold place (preferably in a refrigerator) until needed; if possible, serve with ice cubes floating in the juice.

Scandinavian fruit salad

100 g (4 oz) redcurrants
100 g (4 oz) blackcurrants
100 g (4 oz) loganberries
100 g (4 oz) raspberries
150 ml (5 oz) caster sugar
300 ml (½ pint) red wine

Prepare the fruits and put them in a bowl. Sprinkle with the sugar, pour the wine over and leave to stand in a cool place for 1 hour before serving.

Orange salad (Switzerland)

4 oranges
10 ml (2 tsp) Kirsch
5 ml (1 tsp) Curaçao

Peel and quarter the oranges, place them in a salad bowl, sprinkle with the mixed liqueurs and chill

Fruit salad plus

Combine a can of peaches with 2 sliced red-skinned apples (unpeeled) and 225 g (8 oz) seeded black grapes. Mix 2 pkts cream

cheese with 25 g (1 oz) sugar, the grated rind of 1 orange, 25 g (1 oz) chopped walnuts and enough orange juice to give the consistency of thick cream. Serve the fruit salad topped with the cheese mixture and sprinkled with more walnuts.

Filled melon (West Africa)

1 melon
300 ml (½ pint) sugar syrup (made using 100 g (4 oz) sugar and 300 ml (½ pint) water)
1 orange, peeled and segmented
1 grapefruit, peeled and segmented
30–45 ml (2–3 tbsp) whisky
ice cream

Cut the top off the melon, then remove and dice the flesh. Mix the syrup with the melon, diced orange and grapefruit segments and add the whisky. Put all this in the melon shell and top with ice cream.

Vanilla ice cream

300 ml (½ pint) milk
75 g (3 oz) sugar
2·5 ml (½ level tsp) salt
3 egg yolks
142-ml (5-fl oz) carton double cream
vanilla essence

Boil the milk. Mix the sugar, salt and egg yolks in a basin, pour the milk over and cook in a double saucepan until the mixture thickens, stirring all the time. Let it cool; when cold pour into a freezing tray and freeze for 20–30 minutes. Turn out and whip until creamy. Add cream and essence, return mixture to tray and freeze. Stir at 30 minute intervals until half frozen and then leave until hard. *Serves 8*

Pineapple ice cream

Drain contents of a 425-g (15-oz) can of crushed pineapple. Whip 284-ml (½-pint) carton double cream, then add the juice of ½ a lemon, 25 g (1 oz) caster sugar and the pineapple pulp. Put into the ice tray and freeze; stir at intervals of 30 minutes until half-frozen, then leave until hard.

Strawberry liqueur ice cream

142-ml (¼-pint) carton double cream
225 g (8 oz) strawberries, puréed to give 150 ml (¼ pint)
2·5 ml (½ tsp) vanilla essence
15 ml (1 tbsp) rum or maraschino
50 g (2 oz) sugar (if fresh strawberries are used)

Whip the cream, then mix with all the other ingredients. Pour into a freezing tray of the refrigerator and freeze for 45 minutes–1 hour. Turn out and whisk until smooth, then return the mixture to the tray and freeze until firm.

Variations

Use raspberries instead of strawberries; in this case the purée may need sieving to remove the pips. Use a can of pineapple; drain off the juice from the can and crush the pineapple pieces well before adding to the cream.

Sundaes

Sundaes can be quickly and simply made, using the following basic ideas with your own individual variations:

Ice cream in various flavours with layers of fresh fruit that has been lightly crushed, mixed with sugar and a little liqueur (optional), then left to stand; top with cream.

Alternate layers of two ice creams, say, coffee and orange or vanilla and chocolate, topped with a chocolate, butterscotch or rum sauce and chopped nuts or flaked chocolate.

Alternate layers of chopped or whipped jelly, fruit and ice cream.

Zabaglione

4 egg yolks
30 ml (2 level tbsp) sugar
90 ml (6 tbsp) Marsala or Madeira wine

Whisk the egg yolks and sugar together until light and creamy. Add the wine and blend well. Heat the mixture over boiling water, whisking all the time and taking care not to let it curdle. As soon as it thickens, pour into individual glasses and serve hot; it may also be served over fruit.

Apple mousse

4 large apples, peeled and cut up
juice and grated rind of 1 lemon
15 g (½ oz) gelatine
2 eggs
284-ml (10-fl oz) carton double cream
50–75 g (2–3 oz) sugar (according to tartness of apples)
red eating apple to decorate

Cook the apples with the lemon rind and a little water, then sieve into a basin. Melt the gelatine with 75 ml (5 tbsp) lemon juice (add some water if necessary), leave to cool and then it starts to thicken add to the apple.

Whisk the eggs in a bowl over boiling water until thick and creamy; cool, stirring from time to time, add to the apple mixture, sweeten to taste, then fold in the cream. Pour into a 20·5-cm (8-inch) loose bottomed cake tin and leave to set, then turn out.

Cut wafer-thin slices of the eating apple, leaving the peel on to give extra colour, and use as decoration. (To prevent the slices going brown, dip them in a sugar syrup made by boiling 30 ml (2 level tbsp) sugar and 300 ml (½ pint) water together with 30 ml (2 tbsp) lemon juice.)

Syllabub

This old English sweet was traditionally made with milk straight from the cow poured from a height into wine, cider or ale: this gave a frothy mixture, which was sweetened to taste and flavoured with spices and spirit. here are two recipes – the first separates out and when eating it you dip a spoon through the frothy honeycomb layer into the wine-lemon whey; the second, which is more solid, may be made beforehand and kept for up to 2 days in a cool place (but not the refrigerator). Serve boudoir biscuits or macaroons separately.

Recipe I
2 egg whites
100 g (4 oz) caster sugar
juice of ½ lemon
150 ml (¼ pint) sweet white wine
284-ml (10-fl oz) carton double cream, lightly whipped

Whisk the egg whites until they form stiff peaks. Fold in the sugar, lemon juice and wine. Finally fold in the cream. Spoon into glasses and leave to separate. Decorate with a twist of lemon peel.

Recipe II
thinly pared rind of 1 lemon and 60 ml (4 tbsp) juice
90 ml (6 tbsp) white wine or sherry
30 ml (2 tbsp) brandy
50–75 g (2–3 oz) caster sugar
284-ml (10-fl oz) carton double cream
grated nutmeg

Place the lemon rind, juice, wine and brandy in a bowl; leave for several hours or overnight. Strain into a large bowl, add the sugar and stir until dissolved. Add the cream slowly, stirring all the time. Whisk until the mixture forms soft peaks, spoon into glasses and sprinkle with nutmeg.

Sherry prune mould

450 g (1 lb) prunes
300 ml (½ pint) water
rind of 1 lemon
50 g (2 oz) caster sugar
15 g (½ oz) gelatine
15 ml (1 tbsp) sherry
50 g (2 oz) split almonds
whipped double cream and browned almonds to decorate

Soak the prunes for several hours, then

cook them with the water, lemon rind and sugar until they are tender. Strain off 300 ml (½ pint) of the juice, dissolve the gelatine in it and add the sherry. Pour a little of the jelly into the bottom of a mould and when firm decorate with a few of the split almonds, then put another layer of jelly over these. Meanwhile sieve the prunes, add remaining nuts (chopped into rough pieces) and mix in the rest of the jelly. Pour into the decorated mould and leave to set. When the mixture is firm, turn it out of the mould on to a glass plate and decorate with whipped cream and a few lightly browned almonds.

Vanilla cheesecake

325 g (12 oz) curd or cottage cheese
175 g (6 oz) digestive biscuits
75 g (3 oz) caster sugar
75 g (3 oz) butter, melted
2 eggs, beaten
284-ml (10-fl oz) carton soured cream
vanilla essence
lemon peel to decorate

Sieve the cheese. Crush the biscuits and mix them with 25 g (1 oz) of the sugar and the butter. Butter a shallow ovenproof dish about 23 cm (9 inches) in diameter and press the crumb mixture against the sides and base. Bake in the oven at 180°C (350°F) mark 4 for 10 minutes.

Meanwhile beat the cheese until it is softened. Mix in the eggs, the rest of the sugar and the cream. Flavour with a little vanilla. Pour into the biscuit case, return it to the oven and cook for 30–35 minutes, until set. Decorate with a long twist of thinly pared lemon peel which should be removed just before slicing.

Charlotte russe

600 ml (1 pint) lemon jelly
few diamonds of angelica
300 ml (½ pint) milk
1 vanilla pod
45 ml (3 tbsp) water
30 ml (2 level tbsp) powdered gelatine
3 egg yolks
30 ml (2 level tbsp) caster sugar
10–12 soft sponge fingers
142-ml (5-fl oz) carton double cream

Pour a little jelly into a 900-ml (1½-pint) sloping-sided Russe tin. Allow to set. Arrange a pattern of angelica over and set carefully with a little more jelly. Place the remaining jelly in a basin and leave to set.

Heat the milk in a saucepan with the vanilla, do not boil; leave to infuse for 10 minutes. Put the water in a small bowl, sprinkle the gelatine over and leave to swell. Beat the yolks and sugar, pour the strained milk over and return to the pan. Cook gently to a coating consistency. Add the gelatine and stir until dissolved. Cool until beginning to set. Arrange sponge fingers (trimmed down each side) side by side round the tin. Lightly whip the cream and fold into the custard. Turn at once into the tin. Trim the sponge fingers level with the mixture. Place the trimmings over the top. Chill until set. Turn out as for a jelly and decorate with any remaining jelly, chopped. *Serves 6*

Note If packet jelly is used, add lemon juice as part of the measured water to sharpen.

Lemon soufflé

3 lemons
4 eggs, separated
175 g (6 oz) caster sugar
15 g (½ oz) gelatine
30 ml (2 tbsp) water
142-ml (5-fl oz) carton double cream
crystallised lemon slices, finely chopped nuts and whipped cream to decorate

Prepare a 15-cm (6-inch) soufflé dish: cut a band of firm paper 7·5 cm (3 inches) deeper than the sides of the dish and fix it round the outside, making sure that it is a good shape.

Combine the finely grated rind and the juice of the lemons with the egg yolks and sugar and whisk over hot water until thick and fluffy. Remove from the water and add the gelatine (dissolved in the water over very gentle heat). Leave in a cool place until the mixture begins to thicken, then fold in the whipped cream and stiffly whisked egg whites; pour into a prepared soufflé dish and leave to set. Remove the paper and decorate.

Chocolate soufflé

3 eggs
75 g (3 oz) caster sugar
150 ml (¼ pint) milk
15 g (½ oz) gelatine
45 ml (3 tbsp) water
50 g (2 oz) melted chocolate
284-ml (10-fl oz) carton double cream
whipped cream and flakes of chocolate to decorate

Prepare a soufflé dish as described for Lemon soufflé above. Put the egg yolks, sugar and 150 ml (¼ pint) milk in a basin over boiling water and whisk until thick and light.

Meanwhile dissolve the gelatine in the water and add to the mixture with the melted chocolate, and allow to cool. Whisk the cream and also the egg whites. Fold the cream into the egg yolk mixture, and lastly fold in the whisked egg whites. Pour into the prepared soufflé dish and leave to set firmly. Carefully remove the paper and decorate the soufflé with whipped cream and flaked chocolate.

Coffee soufflé

Make as for Chocolate Soufflé, but use 150 ml (¼ pint) strong black coffee to flavour.

Decorate with halved walnuts and angelica.

Apricot soufflé

425-g (15-oz) can apricots
3 eggs, separated
75 g (3 oz) caster sugar
15 ml (1 tbsp) lemon juice
15 g (½ oz) gelatine
15–30 ml (1–2 tbsp) orange liqueur or rum
142-ml (5-fl oz) carton double cream
50 g (2 oz) walnuts, chopped and cream to decorate

Prepare an 18-cm (7-inch) soufflé dish by cutting a band of firm paper about 7·5 cm (3 inches) deeper than its sides and fixing round the outside – make sure it is a good shape. Drain and reserve the syrup from the apricots. Sieve the fruit to make 150 ml (¼ pint) purée. Put the egg yolks, sugar, lemon juice and 30 ml (2 tbsp) fruit syrup in a basin over hot water and whisk until thick and creamy.

Dissolve the gelatine in 30 ml (2 tbsp) fruit syrup over gentle heat and add the liqueur. Fold into the whisked mixture, then fold in the fruit purée. Whisk the cream and egg whites separately. Fold the cream, then the egg whites into the fruit mixture. Pour into the prepared soufflé case and leave to set. Carefully remove the paper. Decorate the sides with nuts and the top with cream.

Strawberry soufflés

Illustrated in colour on page 165

4 eggs, separated
100 g (4 oz) caster sugar
300 ml (½ pint) strawberry purée, sieved
30 ml (2 tbsp) lemon juice
20 ml (4 level tsp) powdered gelatine
45 ml (3 tbsp) water
142-ml (5-fl oz) carton double cream
12 whole strawberries to decorate

In a basin over hot water, whisk the egg yolks and sugar until really thick and creamy. Remove from the heat and continue whisking occasionally until cold. Whisk in the purée and lemon juice. Dissolve the gelatine in the water over gentle heat. Cool slightly and stir into the fruit mixture. Allow to set to the consistency of unbeaten egg whites. Whip the cream to the same consistency as the strawberry mixture and fold into the strawberry base. Whisk the egg whites until firm but not dry, and fold in. Turn the mixture into six individual soufflé dishes with 6·5-cm (2½-inch) greaseproof paper collars. Chill until set. Remove the collars and place a whole strawberry in the centre of each

Strawberry orange sponge flan (see page 148).

souffle. Slice the remaining strawberries and place around the edges.

Note If the strawberries are pale in colour, add a little red edible food colouring or cochineal when incorporating the purée.

Serves 6

Honeycomb mould

2 large eggs
568 ml (1 pint) milk
40 g (1 ½ oz) caster sugar
vanilla essence
15 g (½ oz) gelatine
30 ml (2 tbsp) water

Separate the eggs. Make a custard with the egg yolks, milk and sugar and flavour it with vanilla. Dissolve the gelatine in the water and add it to the custard. Whisk the egg whites very stiffly and fold lightly into the cool custard mixture. Pour into a glass dish or mould and turn out when set. Serve with chocolate sauce or with stewed fruit (or jam) and whipped cream.

This is the traditional Honeycomb Mould, but if you wish you can replace the vanilla by grated orange or lemon rind or coffee essence. Chopped glacé fruit and nuts may be added.

Lemon chiffon cream

3 eggs, separated
75 g (3 oz) caster sugar
juice of 1 lemon
30 ml (2 tbsp) dry white wine
grated rind of ½ lemon
225 g (8 oz) fresh strawberries (optional)

Beat the egg yolks and sugar together until creamy, then gradually add the lemon juice, wine and lemon rind. Put into the top of a double boiler and heat gently, stirring all the time, until it thickens – do not overheat or it will curdle. Allow to cool. Whisk the egg whites stiffly and fold into the lemon cream mixture. Pile into individual glasses and chill before serving, with the strawberries, if used.

Choco-rum

175 g (6 oz) plain chocolate
4 eggs, separated
30 ml (2 tbsp) rum
142-ml (5-fl oz) carton double cream, whipped and 25 g (1 oz) nuts, chopped, to decorate

Melt the chocolate in a bowl over a pan of hot water and cool slightly. Beat the egg yolks into the chocolate, then add the rum. Whisk the egg whites until stiff and carefully fold into the chocolate mixture. Put into individual glasses and chill. Decorate with whipped cream and nuts.

Slimmers' melon fruit salad

Choose a ripe canteloup melon; cut a slice off the top and scoop out the seeds, with some of the pulp, then turn the melon upside-down to drain whilst preparing the filling. Cut the melon pulp up into small pieces and mix with some fresh fruit. (Raspberries, strawberries or redcurrants are probably the best fruits to choose.) Pile the fruit and melon mixture into the melon, pour on some lemon juice sweetened with artificial sweetener, and replace the lid.

Slimmers' citrus salad

1 grapefruit
2 oranges
1 mandarin or clementine
artificial sweetener

Remove the skin from the fruit, and remove the sections from the central pith with a sharp knife. The mandarin need not be cut, but should be sectioned and the outer pith removed with warm water. Sweeten with artificial sweetener.

Fresh fruit salad for slimmers

2 dessert pears
1 dessert apple
lemon juice
1 orange or tangerine
3 dessert plums
1 peach
100 g (4 oz) white and black grapes mixed
1 banana
a few cherries
artificial sweetener
juice of 1 lemon

Prepare the pears and remove the centres with the aid of a teaspoon; peel and core the apple, toss in lemon juice to prevent discoloration, and cut up into sections. Peel the orange or tangerine and divide into segments. Cut the plums and the peach in half and remove the stones, then slice into convenient-sized pieces. Place all these fruits in a chilled bowl, together with the grapes, sliced banana and cherries. Sweeten 150 ml (¼ pint) water with artificial sweetener to taste, add the lemon juice, and pour over the fruit.

Slimming summer cocktail

1 small honeydew melon
juice of 1 large grapefruit
artificial sweetener
mint and glacé cherries to decorate

Use a Parisian cutter to scoop out balls from

the melon flesh. Fill sundae glasses two-thirds full with melon. Sweeten the grape-fruit juice if necessary with artificial sweet-ener, pour over the fruit and chill. Garnish each cocktail with mint (if available) and half a cherry.

Raspberry delight

Arrange 325 g (12 oz) fresh raspberries in 4 sundae glasses. Pour 15 ml (1 tbsp) strained fresh orange juice into each, decorate with sprigs of mint and chill before serving. Sweeten, if liked.

Flans, tarts and pies

To make a flan case

Make flan pastry as directed on page 143. Place the flan ring on a baking tray. Roll the pastry out into a round 0·5 cm (¼ inch) thick and about 2·5 cm (1 inch) larger than the ring. With a rolling pin lift the pastry and lower into the flan ring. Press into position, making it quite flat at the base; trim the edges and prick the bottom lightly. If the flan is to be filled after cooking it is necessary to bake it 'blind'. For this place a piece of paper inside the pastry and half-fill with baking rice or beans; bake in the oven at 220°C (425°F) mark 7 until the pastry is set – about 15 minutes, then take out the beans and paper and carefully remove the ring. Put the pastry case back into the oven to finish cooking; when it is golden brown, remove it from the oven and cool on a rack.

Flan cases are usually made with flan (rich shortcrust) pastry, but plain shortcrust may be used if desired.

Fruit flans

Most fruits, when attractively arranged in a flan case, make good summer or party sweets. Hard or soft fruits, fresh or canned can be used equally well, and a mixture may also be used. Such soft fruits as loganberries, raspberries and strawberries are generally used raw, but other fruits are better if cooked beforehand in a syrup made with fruit juice or water, sweetened with sugar. Stone fruits should be halved if large, the stones being removed. When cooking the fruit take care to stew it very gently so that it will remain a good shape. Having arranged the fruit neatly in the flan case, cover it with one of the following: fruit jelly (which should be quite cold and just on the point of setting); sugar syrup (boiled until it is thick enough to coat a spoon); fruit purée. When the coating has set, the flan can be decorated with cream.

cream. Ar

Harlequin fruit tart

225 g (8 oz) shortcrust pastry
a variety of cooked fruits
300 ml (½ pint) lemon jelly
whipped cream (optional)

Roll the pastry out thinly and use to line a Swiss roll tin, flute the edges and bake 'blind' in the oven at 200°C (400°F) mark 6 until brown and cooked – about 15 minutes. Cool on a rack. Prepare the fruit (eg, cherries, raspberries, blackberries, apricots, sliced peaches, sliced pears and damsons), and arrange in separate rows across the pastry case. Make up the jelly and leave it in a cool place until nearly set, then quickly pour it over the fruit and leave to set. Serve piped with cream, if liked.

Chocolate coffee pie

175 g (6 oz) shortcrust pastry
568 ml (1 pint) milk
25 g (1 oz) cornflour
30 ml (2 level tbsp) cocoa
5 ml (1 level tsp) coffee extract
25 g (1 oz) butter or margarine
60 ml (4 level tbsp) caster sugar
whipped cream and grated chocolate to decorate

Line an 18-cm (7-inch) pie plate with pastry, brush over with milk, prick the bottom and bake in the oven at 220°C (425°F) mark 7 until cooked through. Meanwhile bring 400 ml (¾ pint) milk to the boil; blend the cornflour, cocoa and coffee extract with 30 ml (2 tbsp) cold milk to a smooth paste and pour on the hot milk. Return to the pan and bring to the boil, stirring; boil for a minute or two, then add the fat and sugar and beat for 1 minute. Pour this mixture into the pie shell and allow to become quite cold before decorating with cream and chocolate.

Gooseberry ice cream flan

Illustrated in colour on page 153

For the filling
50 g (2 oz) caster sugar
300 ml (½ pint) water
225 g (8 oz) gooseberries, topped and tailed
juice of 1 orange
15 ml (1 level tbsp) cornflour
483 ml (17 fl oz) Cornish ice cream

For the crust
100 g (4 oz) cornflakes
50 g (2 oz) butter or margarine
50 g (2 oz) Demerara or light soft brown sugar

First make the crust. Roughly crush the cornflakes. Melt the fat, stir in the sugar and heat, without boiling, until the sugar has

dissolved. Stir in the cornflakes and heat gently for about 3 minutes. Spoon the cornflake mixture into a 23-cm (9-inch) fluted porcelain flan dish. Press into the sides and base to form a shell. Chill.

To make the filling, dissolve the sugar in the water in a saucepan over a low heat. Add the gooseberries, halved if large, and simmer until just tender. Blend the orange juice with the cornflour. Stir in a little gooseberry juice and return to the pan, bring to the boil and simmer for 1 or 2 minutes. To serve, scoop the ice cream with a tablespoon and pack into the chilled crust. If a home freezer or a freezing compartment of a refrigerator is available, the pie can be kept here until required. Spoon the warm gooseberry sauce over just before serving. *Serves 6*

Custard pie

100 g (4 oz) shortcrust pastry
300 ml (½ pint) milk
2 eggs, beaten
30 ml (2 tbsp) caster sugar
nutmeg

Line a 15-cm (6-inch) pie dish with the pastry. Warm the milk to tepid heat and pour it on to the eggs and sugar. Strain the mixture into the pie dish, sprinkle well with grated nutmeg and bake in the oven at 220°C (425°F) mark 7 for 10 minutes, until the pastry is set, then reduce to 180°C (350°F) mark 4 and continue cooking for a total of 40 minutes, until the custard is set.

Cream cheese and apricot flan

175 g (6 oz) shortcrust pastry
225 g (8 oz) cream cheese
100 g (4 oz) caster sugar
226-g (8-oz) can apricots, halved
30 ml (2 tbsp) redcurrant jelly
30 ml (2 tbsp) water
15 ml (1 tbsp) lemon juice
angelica to decorate

Roll out the pastry and line a 20·5-cm (8-

Cream cheese and apricot flan

inch) flan case; bake the case blind in the oven at 220°C (425°F) mark 7 until crisp and golden brown. Cream the cheese and sugar together, then spread evenly over the bottom of the flan case. Arrange the halved apricots on top, cut side down. Make a glaze as follows: put the redcurrant jelly, water and lemon juice into a small, thick saucepan and stir over a gentle heat until dissolved; boil briskly until slightly tacky, then spoon carefully over the fruit. Decorate the flan with cut angelica.

Gooseberry marshmallow tart

450 g (1 lb) gooseberries
150 ml (¼ pint) water
175 g (6 oz) caster sugar
25 g (1 oz) cornflour
a pinch of salt
5 ml (1 level tsp) ground cinnamon
5 ml (1 level tsp) ground cloves
a little grated nutmeg
175 g (6 oz) shortcrust pastry
25 g (1 oz) butter or margarine
225 g (8 oz) marshmallows

Top and tail the fruit and cook with the water and 100 g (4 oz) sugar. Mix the rest of the sugar, the cornflour, salt and spices. When the fruit is tender, add this mixture and cook, stirring, until thick. Line a deep 20·5-cm (8-inch) pie plate with pastry and decorate the edges. Fill with fruit mixture and dot with fat. Cover with strips of the remaining pastry, arranged in a lattice pattern, and bake in the oven at 190°C (375°F) mark 5 for about 25–30 minutes. Place a marshmallow in each lattice 'hole' and return the pie to the oven to finish browning; alternatively, serve with whipped cream or custard.

Orange cream tart

15 g (½ oz) gelatine
15 g (½ oz) cornflour
300 ml (½ pint) milk
2 eggs, separated
150 g (5 oz) caster sugar
grated rind of 1 lemon
142-ml (5-fl oz) carton double cream, whipped
312-g (11-oz) can mandarin oranges
23-cm (9-inch) pastry case, cooked

Dissolve the gelatine in a little water. Blend the cornflour with a little of the milk and heat the remainder. Pour the boiling milk on to the cornflour, return the mixture to the pan and cook for 2–5 minutes. Remove from the heat and add the egg yolks, 25 g (1 oz) sugar, the gelatine and lemon rind. Cool, then fold in the cream. Arrange most of the mandarin oranges in the pastry case, spoon on the cream mixture and leave to cool. Beat the egg whites until stiff, whisk in half the remaining sugar and fold in the rest. Pile this mixture on to the cream filling, carefully covering right to the edge. Bake in the oven at 220°C (425°F) mark 7 for about 2–3 minutes until light brown. Decorate with the remaining orange.

Chocolate pear flan

Place scoops of plain ice cream in a flan case made from chocolate and ginger crust (see below). Top with drained pear halves and flaked almonds.

Chocolate and ginger crust Melt 100 g (4 oz) plain chocolate and 50–75 g (2–3 oz) butter in a bowl over hot water. Combine with 225 g (8 oz) crushed gingernuts, line a pie dish with the mixture and chill until set.

Apricot amber

900 g (2 lb) apricots (or 325 g (12 oz) purée)
50–75 g (2–3 oz) caster sugar
2 eggs, separated
50 g (2 oz) butter or margarine, melted
20·5-cm (8-inch) flan case
50 g (2 oz) caster sugar
angelica and glacé cherries to decorate

Sieve the apricots, mix with the sugar, egg yolks and melted fat, then pour the mixture into the prepared flan case. Bake in the oven at 200°C (400°F) mark 6 for 20–25 minutes, until firm. Whisk the egg whites until stiff and then whisk in half the caster sugar; fold in the rest of the sugar and pile this meringue in a ring on the filling. Sprinkle well with sugar and put into the oven at 150°C (300°F) mark 1 until it is light brown and crisp – about 25 minutes. Decorate with angelica and glacé cherries.

Lemon meringue pie

100 g (4 oz) shortcrust pastry
45 ml (3 level tbsp) cornflour
150 ml (¼ pint) water
juice and grated rind of 2 lemons
100 g (4 oz) caster sugar
2 eggs, separated
75 g (3 oz) caster sugar
glacé cherries and angelica to decorate

Roll out the pastry and line an 18-cm (7-inch) flan case or deep pie plate. Trim the edges and bake blind in the oven at 220°C (425°F) mark 7 for 15 minutes. Remove the paper and baking beans and return the case to the oven for a further 5 minutes; reduce the oven temperature to 180°C (350°F) mark 4. Mix the cornflour with the water in a saucepan, add the lemon juice and grated rind and bring slowly to the boil, stirring until the mixture thickens, then add the sugar. Remove from the heat, cool the mixture slightly and add the egg yolks. Pour into the pastry case. Whisk the egg whites stiffly, whisk in half the caster sugar and fold in the rest. Pile the meringue on top of the lemon filling and bake in the centre of the oven for about 10 minutes, or until the meringue is crisp and lightly browned. Decorate before serving with the glacé cherries and angelica.

Strawberry shortcake

Illustrated in colour on page 153

225 g (8 oz) plain flour
5 ml (1 level tsp) cream of tartar
2·5 ml (½ level tsp) bicarbonate of soda
a pinch of salt
50 g (2 oz) butter or block margarine
40 g (1½ oz) caster sugar
1 egg, beaten
45–60 ml (3–4 tbsp) milk
225 g (8 oz) strawberries, hulled
142-ml (5-fl oz) carton cream
15 ml (1 tbsp) milk
butter

Sift together the flour, cream of tartar, bicarbonate of soda and salt into a bowl. Rub in the fat and stir in the sugar. Make a well in the centre, add the beaten egg and milk to give a soft but manageable dough. Knead lightly on a floured surface, shape into an 18-cm (7-inch) round. Place on a baking sheet, dust lightly with flour and bake in the oven at 220°C (425°F) mark 7 for about 20 minutes. Cool a little on a wire rack, covered with a clean tea towel.

Slice the strawberries thickly. Whisk together the cream and milk until it holds its shape. Split the warm shortcake and lightly butter. Spread half the cream over the base, then add the fruit and the rest of the cream. Replace the top and serve at once. *Serves 6–8*

Crisp peach tart

100 g (4 oz) shortcrust pastry
425-g (15-oz) can peaches
grated rind of 1 lemon
50 g (2 oz) butter or block margarine
50 g (2 oz) brown sugar
50 g (2 oz) plain flour
5 ml (1 level tsp) mixed spice
50 g (2 oz) nuts or coconut, chopped

Line an 18-cm (7-inch) pie dish with the pastry. Drain the peaches, place most of them in the tart and cover with the lemon rind and a little peach juice. Rub together the fat, sugar, flour and spice until the mixture resembles fine breadcrumbs. Mix in the nuts and spread this crumbly topping over the fruit. Bake in the oven at 220°C (425°F) mark 7 for about 20 minutes, until crisp and golden. Decorate with the remaining peaches and serve with custard or cream. This unusual tart can be varied by using other fruit such as apricots, pears, stewed apples, gooseberries or rhubarb.

Milles-feuilles

225 g (8 oz) puff pastry or a 212-g (7½-oz) pkt frozen puff pastry, thawed
raspberry jam
142-ml (5-fl oz) carton double cream
312-g (11 oz) can pineapple, drained
green glacé icing
chopped nuts to decorate

Roll the pastry out 0·3–0·5 cm (⅛–¼ inch) thick and cut into 18-cm (7-inch) rounds – it should make 5–6. Put on a baking tray and prick them, then bake in the oven at 230°C (450°F) mark 8 for 8–10 minutes, until brown and crisp. Cool on a rack. Spread one layer of pastry with jam, place another round on this and cover with whipped cream and chopped pineapple (reserving a few pieces). Repeat to the last layer. Ice and decorate with pineapple and chopped nuts.

Speedy sweets

Poires Hélène

Put some lemon or vanilla ice cream into sundae glasses, place one canned pear in each, pour chocolate sauce over the top and decorate with almonds or crystallised violets.

Pêches aurore

284-ml (10-fl oz) carton single cream
vanilla ice cream
1 glass of Kirsch
red food colouring
4 large peaches, skinned
15 ml (1 tbsp) whipped cream to decorate

Make a sauce by mixing thoroughly the single cream, a little ice cream, Kirsch and a few drops of red colouring. Halve the peaches. Serve each peach with a little ice cream and pour the sauce over. Decorate with cream.

Speedy ice cream sweets

1 Place some ice cream in individual dishes, add 2 meringue halves to each and

Loganberry whirl (see page 150).

top with fruit, chocolate or butterscotch sauce and cream.

2 Fill éclairs or choux pastry balls with ice cream and sprinkle with chopped nuts.

Meringue balls

Cut 4 rounds of Swiss roll, place on a baking sheet, top with fresh or canned fruit and sprinkle with sherry. Whip 2 egg whites until stiff and beat in 30 ml (2 level tbsp) caster sugar. Pile this meringue over the cake and fruit, taking it right down to the baking tray. Bake in the oven at 220°C (425°F) mark 7 for a few minutes, until the meringue is just coloured. Serve at once.

Fruit cream flan

Instant whip puddings and flavoured custard and blancmange powders make a creamy filling for a flan. They can be alternated with layers of fruit, or the fruit can be folded into the mixture.

Suggested fillings and toppings Raspberry cream, whole raspberries decorated with crushed ratafias.

Chocolate cream, mandarins or oranges, decorated with cream.

Butterscotch cream, sliced bananas, decorated with crushed praline or cream.

Lemon cream, crushed pineapple, decorated with walnuts or crystallised ginger.

Quick apple flan

Spread a prepared flan case with raspberry jam and cover this with a layer of sweetened stewed apples. Make up some thick custard, using 30 ml (2 level tbsp) custard powder, 30 ml (2 level tbsp) sugar and 300 ml (½ pint) milk, and pour it carefully over the fruit. Sprinkle with flaked chocolate and serve chilled, with cream if desired.

Vary by leaving out the jam, by using other types of fruit (fresh, canned, or stewed), by flavouring the custard, or by sprinkling with chopped nuts or coconut.

Cream cheese and pineapple flan

2 × 85-g (3-oz) pkts cream or lactic cheese
45–60 ml (3–4 tbsp) chopped pineapple
50 g (2 oz) walnuts, chopped
sugar to taste
grated rind of 1 lemon
1 17·5-cm (7-inch) baked pastry flan case

Mix together the cream cheese, pineapple, 25 g (1 oz) of the walnuts, 25–50 g (1–2 oz) sugar and lemon rind. Stir until well mixed, adding a little pineapple juice if necessary to give the consistency of whipped cream.

Pile into the flan case and decorate with the remaining nuts.

Fruit creams

Put alternate layers of instant pudding mixture or flavoured custard and soft fruit in sundae glasses and decorate with cream, nuts, chocolate, praline, angelica, crystallised fruit or fresh fruits. Use similar combinations to those for Fruit Cream Flan.

Rice condé

Add 15 ml (1 level tbsp) sugar, the grated rind of 1 lemon and a pinch of salt to a 425-g (15-oz) can of rice pudding. Pour into individual dishes, top with half a peach, flat side downwards, and top with jam sauce.

Baked fruit Alaska

1 sponge round
1 block of ice cream
canned or stewed fruit
2 egg whites
100 g (4 oz) caster sugar

Place the cake on a baking sheet and put the ice cream on top. Pile on some fruit, taking care it does not slip off. Whisk the egg whites until stiff and fold in almost all the sugar. Coat the Alaska well with this meringue. Sprinkle with the remaining sugar and bake at 220°C (425°F) mark 7 for 4–5 minutes, until lightly coloured.

Swiss apple Charlotte

900 g (2 lb) cooking apples
50 g (2 oz) sugar
40 g (1½ oz) butter or margarine
30 ml (2 tbsp) golden syrup
15 g (½ oz) cornflakes
cream or evaporated milk

Peel, quarter and core the apples; cook in a little water until soft, then sieve. Add just a little sugar. Spoon into a bowl or individual glasses. Melt the fat and syrup in a saucepan and add the cornflakes, carefully turning them until evenly covered with syrup. Pour the cream or milk over the apple, then pile the cornflakes on top.

Sweet sauces

White sauce

25 g (1 oz) butter or margarine
25 g (1 oz) flour
400 ml (¾ pint) milk
sugar to sweeten
15 ml (1 tbsp) cream (optional)

Melt the fat, stir in the flour and blend thoroughly then add the cold milk gradually and bring to the boil. Add the sugar and boil for 5 minutes, stirring all the time. Lastly, stir in the cream.

Egg custard sauce

300 ml (½ pint) milk
a strip of lemon rind
1 egg or 2 yolks
25 g (1 oz) sugar

Heat the milk and lemon rind together, but do not boil, then pour on to the well-beaten egg, stirring. Return the mixture to the pan and cook over hot water until the sauce coats the back of the spoon thinly. Add the sugar, strain and cool, stirring occasionally, or serve hot if liked.

Lemon or orange sauce

1 large lemon or orange
15–30 ml (1–2 level tbsp) sugar
25 g (1 oz) butter or margarine
15 g (½ oz) flour or cornflour
300 ml (½ pint) water
1–2 egg yolks

Wipe the lemon or orange, grate the rind and add it to the sugar. Melt the fat in a saucepan and stir in the flour or cornflour then add the water gradually and stir until boiling. Simmer slowly for 2–3 minutes, and add the sugar and strained lemon or orange juice. Then remove the saucepan from the heat, and quickly stir in the egg yolks. Pour at once into a sauce-boat.

Syrup sauce

60 ml (4 tbsp) water
30 ml (2 tbsp) golden syrup
juice of ½ lemon

Mix all together and boil rapidly for a few minutes.

Brandy butter

Cream together 50 g (2 oz) butter and 100 (4 oz) icing sugar until light and creamy then beat in 30–45 ml (2–3 tbsp) brandy. Pil into a small dish, and put in a cool place t harden; sprinkle with a little more icin sugar just before serving.

To whip fresh cream

Use double cream: it should be as cool a possible, and the whipping should be don in a cool place. Put the cream in a bowl an sweeten with a little caster sugar if desire Use a fork or a rotary whisk. Continu beating until the cream is thick enough t stand up in points, but on no account ove beat, or it will separate.

YEAST COOKERY

Yeast cookery still has a slight aura of mystery, but there is nothing intrinsically difficult about it. The main thing is to realise that yeast, unlike other raising agents, is a living plant, requiring gentle warmth in order to grow. Like any other plant, yeast also requires food and water, and these it obtains from the carbohydrates in the flour and from the moisture used in making the dough. Under these conditions, yeast grows rapidly and as it grows a harmless and tasteless gas – carbon dioxide – is formed. The bubbles of this gas are responsible for the sponginess of the mixture; the growing yeast also produces alcohol, which gives the characteristic yeasty smell and taste to freshly baked bread.

YEAST

Fresh yeast This is rather like putty in colour and texture and should have a faint 'winey' smell. There should be no discoloration and it should crumble easily when broken. Although it will store for up to a month in a screw-topped jar or wrapped in cling film or foil in the refrigerator, the best results are obtained when it is absolutely fresh, so buy it in small quantities when required.

Fresh yeast is usually blended with a liquid, it is then ready to be added to the flour all at once. It can also be rubbed directly into the flour or else added as a batter. This batter is known as the sponge dough process where only some of the ingredients are mixed, forming a sponge that is allowed to ferment and is then mixed with the remaining ingredients to form a dough.

Using sugar to cream the yeast before adding the liquid is not advised as sugar kills some of the yeast cells and delays fermentation. The resulting bread has a strong yeasty taste. Fresh yeast is easiest measured by weight. According to the richness of the mixture, 25 g (1 oz) fresh yeast should be sufficient to raise 1·4 kg (3 lb) white flour.

Dried yeast This is sold in granulated form and is very convenient as it can be stored in an airtight container in a cool place for up to six months. Take care when buying it that it is bakers' yeast and not tonic or brewers' yeast as these have no rising powers. Dried yeast requires sugar and liquid to activate it. The sugar, in the proportion of 5 ml (1 level tsp) to 300 ml (½ pint) of tepid liquid, is dissolved in the liquid. The yeast granules are then sprinkled over the surface of the liquid and the mixture left

to froth for about 15 minutes before being ready for use. Dried yeast is easiest measured in 5 ml (1 tsp) or 15 ml (1 tbsp) spoonfuls. As it is more concentrated than fresh yeast, generally half the amount of dried yeast is required to fresh yeast. 15 ml (1 level tbsp) dried yeast is equivalent to 25 g (1 oz) fresh yeast.

FLOUR

The type to use depends of course on the bread being made, but it must always be a plain flour – self-raising flour should not be used, as it gives a close, cake-like texture. The best results are obtained by using a 'strong' plain flour. If a 'strong' plain flour is not available, a plain flour is suitable but will not give nearly such a good result.

These are other speciality flours:
Wholemeal 100 per cent wheat.
Wheatmeal 81–95 per cent wheat (ie some of the bran is removed).
Stone-ground More expensive, but of very good flavour, since the heat arising during the grinding 'toasts' the flour slightly. Available as wholemeal and wheatmeal.
Rye flour Gives the typical continental rye bread.

SALT

Salt improves the flavour. It should be measured accurately, as too little causes the dough to rise too quickly and too much kills the yeast and gives the bread an uneven texture. Salt is used in the proportions of 5–10 ml (1–2 level tsp) to 450 g (1 lb) flour.

FAT

The addition of fat to the dough enriches it and gives a moist, close-textured loaf with a soft crust. It also helps keep the bread fresh and soft for a longer time.

LIQUID

Water is most suitable for plain bread, producing a loaf with an even texture and a crisp crust. Milk and water, or milk alone, will give a softer golden crust and the loaf will stay soft and fresh for longer.

The amount of liquid used will vary according to the absorbency of the flour, as too much will give the bread a spongy and open texture. Brown flours are usually more absorbent than white.

The liquid is generally added to the yeast at a tepid temperature, ie 43°C (110°F).

GLAZES AND FINISHES

If a crusty finish is desired for bread or rolls, they can be brushed before baking with a glaze made by dissolving 10 ml (2 level tsp) salt in 30 ml (2 tbsp) water.

For a soft finish the surface should be brushed with oil and dusted with flour, or alternatively brushed with beaten egg or beaten egg and milk.

Some breads and yeast buns are glazed after baking to give them a sticky finish. To achieve this brush with warmed honey or a syrup made by dissolving 30 ml (2 level tbsp) sugar in 30 ml (2 tbsp) water; bring to the boil.

There are many ways of adding interest and variety to bread and rolls. After glazing and before baking, lightly sprinkle the surface with one of the following:
1 Poppy, caraway, celery or fennel seeds.
2 Sesame seeds. Particularly good sprinkled on to the soft baps used with hamburgers.
3 Cracked wheat or crushed cornflakes. Sprinkle them on top of wholemeal bread or baps.
4 A mixture of crushed rock salt and caraway. This is particularly good on rolls to be eaten with cheese or smoked sausage.

Step by step processes in breadmaking

The processes used in making yeast mixtures form the basis of the method followed for nearly all yeast cooking.
Mixing the dough Measure all the ingredients carefully and sift the dry ingredients (flour, salt, etc) into a large bowl.

Add the yeast dissolved in the liquid all at once and mix with the dry ingredients, using a wooden spoon or fork, until blended. Extra flour can be added at this stage if the dough is too slack. Beat the dough by hand until the mixture is completely smooth and leaves the sides of the bowl cleanly.
Kneading the dough Kneading is essential to strengthen the gluten in the flour, thus making the dough elastic in texture and enabling it to rise more easily. This is how to do it:

Turn the dough on to a floured working surface, knead the dough by folding it towards you and pushing down and away from you with the palm of the hand. Give the dough a quarter turn and continue kneading for about 10 minutes until it is firm, elastic and no longer sticky.

Using a dough hook If you have a mixer with a dough hook attachment it can take the hard work out of kneading. Follow the manufacturer's instructions; working with small amounts of dough is more successful than attempting a large batch all at once. Place the yeast dissolved in the liquid in the bowl, add the dry ingredients and begin at lowest speed and mix to form dough. Increase the speed for the recommended time.

Rising The kneaded dough is now ready for rising. Unless otherwise stated, place in a greased bowl and cover with a large sheet of polythene brushed with oil, to prevent a skin forming during rising.

Rising times vary with temperature. As only extreme heat kills the yeast and extreme cold retards the growth of yeast,

the method of rising can be arranged to suit yourself.

The best results are obtained by allowing the covered dough to rise overnight or up to twenty-four hours in the refrigerator. The dough must be allowed to return to room temperature before it is shaped.

Allow about 2 hours for the dough to rise at room temperature, 18°C (65°F). The dough can be made to rise in about 45 minutes–1 hour if placed in a warm place such as an airing cupboard or above a warm cooker. The risen dough should spring back when gently pressed with a floured finger.

Preparing tins While the dough is rising, prepare the tins or baking sheets by greasing and lightly flouring them. Whenever reference is made to a 450 g (1 lb) loaf tin, the approximate size to use is 20·5 × 10 × 6·5 cm (8 × 4 × 2 ½ inches), top

measurements. When reference is made to a 900 g (2 lb) loaf tin, use one with 23 × 13 × 7 cm (9 × 5 × 3 inches), top measurements.

Knocking back The best texture is obtained by kneading the dough for a second time after rising. Turn the risen dough on to a lightly floured working surface and knead for 2–3 minutes to 'knock' out any large bubbles and ensure an even texture. The dough is shaped as required and placed in tins or on baking sheets then covered with polythene. Tins should only be half filled to allow for proving.

Proving or second rise This is the last process before baking. The shaped dough should be allowed to 'prove', that is, left until it is doubled in size and will spring back when lightly pressed with a floured finger. This is done at room temperature. The dough is now ready for glazing and baking.

Baking Basic breads are baked in the oven at 230°C (450°F) mark 8.

When cooked the bread should be well risen and golden brown and when tapped underneath with the knuckles, it should sound hollow. Allow the bread to cool on wire racks before storing.

Storing Store in an airtight tin.

Refreshing bread Wrap the bread in aluminium foil and place in the oven at 230°C (450°F) mark 8, for 5–10 minutes. Allow the bread to cool in the foil before unwrapping. For a more crusty loaf omit the foil and bake as above.

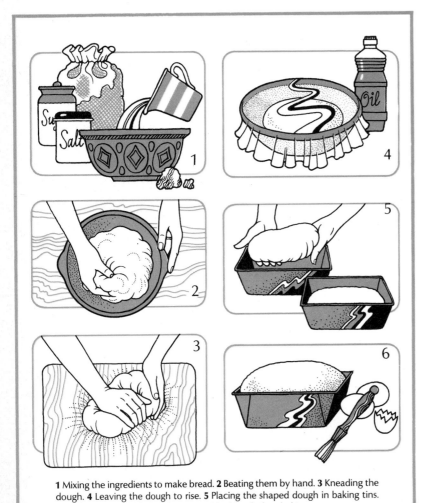

1 Mixing the ingredients to make bread. 2 Beating them by hand. 3 Kneading the dough. 4 Leaving the dough to rise. 5 Placing the shaped dough in baking tins. 6 Glazing the 'proven' loaf just before baking.

Breads, loaves and rolls

White bread

700 g (1 ½ lb) strong plain flour
10 ml (2 level tsp) salt
a knob of lard
15 g (½ oz) fresh yeast or 7·5 ml (1 ½ level tsp) dried yeast and 5 ml (1 level tsp) caster sugar
400 ml (¾ pint) tepid water (43°C (110°F))

Grease a 900-g (2-lb) loaf tin or 2 × 450-g (1 lb) loaf tins, or 2 baking sheets if making rolls.

Sift the flour and salt into a large bowl and rub in the lard. Blend the fresh yeast with the water. If using dried yeast, dissolve the sugar in the water, sprinkle the yeast over and leave until frothy. Mix the dry ingredients with the yeast liquid, adding the liquid all at once. Stir in with a wooden fork

Redcurrant floats (see page 151), Strawberry soufflé (see page 156), Tahitian Pavlova (see page 152).

or spoon. Work it to a firm dough, adding extra flour if needed, until it will leave the sides of the bowl clean. Do not let the dough become too stiff as it produces heavy 'close' bread.

Turn the dough on to a floured surface and knead thoroughly, to stretch and 'develop' it. To do this, hold the dough towards you, then push down and away with the palm of your hand. Continue kneading until the dough feels firm and elastic and no longer sticky – about 10 minutes. Shape it into a ball and place in a large bowl.

Cover the dough with lightly oiled polythene to prevent a skin forming and allow to rise until it is doubled in size and will spring back when pressed with a floured finger.

Allow time for the rising of the dough to fit with your day's arrangements, but the best results are achieved with a slow rise. Allow 45 minutes–1 hour in a warm place, ie above the cooker or in the airing cupboard at about 23°C (75°F), 2 hours at average room temperature, up to 12 hours in a cold larder or up to 24 hours in the refrigerator.

Refrigerated risen dough must be allowed to return to room temperature for about 1 hour before it is shaped.

Turn the risen dough on to a lightly floured surface, flatten it firmly with the knuckles to knock out the air bubbles, then knead to make it firm and ready for shaping (do not use too much flour or the colour of the crust be spoilt). Stretch the dough into an oblong the same width as the tin, fold it into 3 and turn it over so that the 'seam' is underneath. Smooth over the top, tuck in the ends and place in the greased 900-g (2-lb) loaf tin. For 2 small loaves, divide the dough into 2 and continue as above; for rolls, divide the dough into 50-g (2-oz) pieces and roll each into a ball, place on the baking sheets about 2·5 cm (1 inch) apart. *Makes about 18*

Cover the tin with lightly oiled polythene and leave to rise again until the dough comes to the top of the tin and springs back when pressed with a floured finger. Leave for 1–1½ hours at room temperature, or longer in a refrigerator. Leave rolls until doubled in size.

Remove the polythene, place the tin on a baking sheet and put in the centre of the oven. Put a pan of boiling water on the oven bottom. Bake at 230°C (450°F) mark 8 for 30–40 minutes, 15–20 minutes for rolls, until well risen and golden brown. Rolls will double in size. When the loaf is cooked it will shrink slightly from the sides of the tin, and will sound hollow if you tap the bottom of the tin. Turn out and cool on a wire rack.

Farmhouse loaf

To make a farmhouse loaf, shape 700 g (1½ lb) white bread dough and put it into a greased shallow loaf tin, taking care that the ends of the loaf do not touch the tin. Make a lengthways cut in the loaf and put to prove (see page 164). Bake in the oven at 230°C (450°F) mark 8 for 40–50 minutes, reducing the heat to 190°C (375°F) mark 5 after 20 minutes. If a floury appearance is liked, brush it with milk and water and sprinkle with flour before baking.

Cottage loaf

Illustrated in colour on page 169

Divide 450 g (1 lb) white bread dough into two portions, one larger than the other. Shape into rounds, place the smaller on top and push a floured finger down centre of both to fix firmly together. Prove as usual and bake in the oven at 230°C (450°F) mark 8 for about 45 minutes.

Coburg loaf

Illustrated in colour on page 169

Make a white bread dough. Mould each quarter of dough into a ball; place it on a baking sheet. Brush with milk and with a knife mark a cross on the top of each dough ball. Return to the polythene bag and leave the dough to double in size. Remove the polythene, brush again with milk and bake in the oven at 230°C (450°F) mark 8 for 30–40 minutes.

Enriched white bread

Illustrated in colour on page 169

450 g (1 lb) strong plain flour
15 g (½ oz) fresh yeast or 7·5 ml (1½ level tsp) dried yeast and 5 ml (1 level tsp) caster sugar
225 ml (8 fl oz) tepid milk
5 ml (1 level tsp) salt
50 g (2 oz) butter or block margarine
1 egg, beaten

Grease and flour two baking sheets. Sift 150 g (5 oz) of the flour into a large bowl. Crumble the yeast, add the milk and stir until dissolved. Add to the flour and set aside to froth – about 20 minutes.

Mix the remaining flour with the salt and rub in the fat. Add the egg and the flour mixture to the batter and mix well to give a fairly soft dough that will leave the sides of the bowl clean. Turn the dough on to a lightly floured surface and knead until it is smooth and no longer sticky – about 10 minutes. Place in a bowl. Cover the dough with lightly oiled polythene and leave to

rise until doubled in size. When risen, turn the dough on to a lightly floured surface, knead well and shape as required into plaited loaves, baps or fancy rolls. Place on the greased and floured baking sheets. Cover with lightly oiled polythene and put to prove until doubled in size. Glaze with beaten egg. Bake in the oven at 190°C (375°F) mark 5, 45–50 minutes for loaves and 10–15 minutes for rolls. Turn out and cool on a wire rack.

Poppy seed plait

Illustrated in colour on page 169

Using risen Enriched white bread dough, knead the dough lightly on a floured working surface. Divide in half and roll each half into an oblong. Cut each half into three strips lengthways, pinching the dough together at the top. Plait the strips, damp the ends and seal together. Place on a lightly greased baking sheet. Brush with beaten egg and sprinkle with poppy seeds. Prove again until doubled in size. Bake in the oven at 190°C (375°F) mark 5 for 45–50 minutes. Cool on a wire rack.

Crown loaf

Illustrated in colour on page 169

Using half quantity risen Enriched white bread dough, divide into six pieces. Roll each piece to a smooth ball, place five in a ring in a greased sandwich cake tin, then put the sixth in the centre. Prove, glaze and finish as above, and bake in the oven at 190°C (375°F) mark 5 for 30–35 minutes.

The crown looks particularly attractive for a dinner or lunch party, and it breaks easily into separate rolls.

Milk loaf

Illustrated in colour on page 169

550 g (1¼ lb) strong plain flour
10 ml (2 level tsp) salt
25 g (1 oz) lard
15 g (½ oz) fresh yeast or 7·5 ml (1½ level tsp) dried yeast and 5 ml (1 level tsp) caster sugar
300 ml (½ pint) tepid milk

Sift the flour and salt and rub in the fat. Dissolve the yeast in the milk. Make a well in the flour, add the liquid and sprinkle with a little flour. Cover and set aside in a warm place until frothy – 10–15 minutes for fresh yeast, 20 minutes for dried yeast. Mix to a soft dough, knead well on a floured board and leave to rise to double its size. Knead lightly, then divide into two. Press lightly into 2 greased and floured 450-g (1-lb) tins and prove until the dough has risen to the top of the tins. Bake in the oven at 240°C (475°F) mark 9 for 15 minutes, then reduce the heat to 190°C (375°F) mark 5 and bake for 45 minutes–1 hour in all. Glaze with sugar syrup.

French bread

450 g (1 lb) strong plain flour
5 ml (1 level tsp) salt
15 g (½ oz) fresh yeast or 7·5 ml (1½
    level tsp) dried yeast and 5 ml (1 level
    tsp) caster sugar
300 ml (½ pint) tepid water
a small knob of butter
beaten egg to glaze

Sift the flour and salt into a mixing bowl. Dissolve the yeast in the water, add the butter and stir well until melted. Pour the liquid ingredients into the flour and beat well with the hand until the dough leaves the bowl. Knead for 5 minutes on a floured board and return it to the bowl. Cover with oiled polythene and set to rise until double its size. Turn the dough out on to a floured board and knead. Roll the dough out to an oblong 38 × 25·5 cm (15 by 10 inches), then cut in half lengthways. Roll up each loaf tightly from the long edge, sealing the ends thoroughly. Point the ends, and place on greased baking sheets. Prove, brush with beaten egg and bake in the oven at 230°C (450°F) mark 8 for 10 minutes, then reduce heat to 190°C (375°F) mark 5 for a further 10–15 minutes. Allow to cool, then brush with salt water, and replace in the oven for 10 minutes longer. This produces a crisp crust similar to that on continental breads.

Wholemeal bread

1·4 kg (3 lb) wholemeal flour or 450 g
    (1 lb) white and 900 g (2 lb)
    wholemeal
25 g (1 oz) salt
50 g (2 oz) lard
25 g (1 oz) fresh yeast or 15 ml (1 level
    tbsp) dried yeast and 5 ml (1 level tsp)
    caster sugar
900 ml (1½ pints) tepid water

Sift the flour and salt, rub in the lard. Dissolve the yeast in half the tepid liquid. Make a well in the flour and add the yeast mixture and enough water to give a rather soft dough. Knead well, then put to rise until it doubles its size (see page 164). Re-knead, shape and put into 2 greased 900-g (2-lb) loaf tins. Prove, and bake in the oven at 240°C (475°F) mark 9 for 15 minutes, then reduce to 200°C (400°F) mark 6 and bake until the loaves are brown and sound hollow when tapped. Wholemeal generally requires more moisture than white flour and takes somewhat longer to cook.

To make a twisted loaf, divide the dough into three and knead each portion until smooth, then place in the prepared tin diagonally, pushing into place with the knuckles. During the proving, the three pieces will rise together.

Wholemeal flowerpots

Illustrated in colour on page 169

Divide 450 g (1 lb) Wholemeal bread dough into two portions. Shape each piece to half fill 2 clean 10–12·5-cm (4–5-inch) flowerpots (see note). Brush the tops with salt and water and sprinkle with cracked wheat. Put into a large greased polythene bag, tie loosely and put to rise until the dough has doubled in size and springs back when lightly pressed with a floured finger; remove the bag. Bake in the oven at 230°C (450°F) mark 8 for 40 minutes.
Note When using flowerpots, grease them before using and bake empty in a hot oven several times – this prevents the bread sticking.

Quick wholemeal bread

900 g (2 lb) wholemeal flour
450 g (1 lb) white flour
30 ml (2 level tbsp) salt
30 ml (2 level tbsp) caster sugar
50 g (2 oz) fresh yeast or 30 ml (2 level
    tbsp) dried yeast and 5 ml (1 level tsp)
    caster sugar
1 litre (1¾ pints) tepid water
cracked wheat (optional)

Mix the flour, salt and sugar. Dissolve the yeast in a little of the tepid water. Make a well in the centre of the flour and pour in the yeast mixture and remaining tepid water. Mix to a soft dough, then knead well for about 5 minutes, until smooth. Shape and half-fill 3–4 greased 450-g (1-lb) loaf tins, and set to rise in a warm place until doubled in size (about 30 minutes). Bake in the oven at 230°C (450°F) mark 8 for 20–30 minutes. The tins may first be dusted with cracked wheat, and some of this may be sprinkled on top of the loaves before proving, if liked.
This dough may be used as basis for various sweet tea breads – for example, the Apricot and Currant Bread on page 175.

Quick white loaf

450 g (1 lb) strong plain flour
5 ml (1 level tsp) salt
15 g (½ oz) fresh yeast or 7·5 ml (1½
    level tsp) dried yeast and 5 ml (1 level
    tsp) caster sugar
300 ml (½ pint) tepid water
egg and milk to glaze

Sift the flour and salt into a bowl. Dissolve

the yeast in the tepid water. Make a well in the centre of the flour and pour in the yeast mixture. Mix to a dough and knead for 5 minutes on a floured board, to make the dough very smooth. Place it in a greased and floured bread tin, and allow to rise until double its size. Glaze with beaten egg and milk and bake for 45 minutes in the oven at 230°C (450°F) mark 8, reducing the heat to 180°C (350°F) mark 4 after 15 minutes.

Currant bread

550 g (1¼ lb) strong plain flour
10 ml (2 level tsp) salt
25 g (1 oz) lard
225 g (8 oz) currants
25 g (1 oz) fresh chopped candied peel
15 g (½ oz) fresh yeast or 7·5 ml (1½
    level tsp) dried yeast and 5 ml (1 level
    tsp) caster sugar
about 400 ml (¾ pint) tepid milk

Sift the flour and salt and rub in the fat. Add the currants and peel and mix well. Dissolve the yeast in the milk. Make a well in the flour, add the liquid, sprinkle a little flour over the top, cover and put in a warm place until frothy. Mix to a soft dough, knead well on a floured board and leave to rise until doubled in size. Divide into two pieces, and knead each into a ball. Press lightly into greased and floured 450-g (1-lb) tins, or shape into smooth cobs, and place on a baking sheet. Prove until the dough has filled the tins. Bake the loaves in the oven at 240°C (475°F) mark 9 for 10 minutes, then reduce to 190°C (375°F) mark 5 and bake until cooked – 45 minutes in all – then brush over if desired with sugar glaze.

Rye bread

700 g (1½ lb) rye flour
450 g (1 lb) strong plain flour
15 ml (1 level tbsp) salt
25 g (1 oz) butter or lard
10 ml (2 level tsp) caraway seed
5 ml (1 level tsp) sugar
20 g (¾ oz) fresh yeast or 10 ml (2 level
    tsp) dried yeast and 5 ml (1 level tsp)
    caster sugar
675 ml (1 pint plus 5 tbsp) tepid milk
    and water
beaten egg to glaze

Sift the flours and the salt. Rub in the fat and add the caraway seeds. Dissolve the sugar and yeast and add most of the tepid liquid. Make a well in the flour, pour in the yeast mixture, and mix to a firm dough, adding the remaining liquid as required. Knead until smooth on a floured board, then place in the bowl and cover with oiled polythene. Leave to rise until doubled in size. Turn out and knead again, divide into two and shape into either an oval or round loaf. Put on to greased and floured baking sheets, and set to prove. The loaves may then be glazed with beaten egg and sprinkled with caraway seeds or left as they are, before baking in the oven at 230°C (450°F) mark 8 for 40 minutes.

Vienna loaf

450 g (1 lb) strong plain flour
5 ml (1 level tsp) salt
40 g (1 ½ oz) butter or margarine
300 ml (½ pint) tepid milk
15 g (½ oz) fresh yeast or 7·5 ml (1 ½
level tsp) dried yeast and 5 ml (1 level
tsp) caster sugar
1 egg, beaten

Sift the flour and salt into a bowl. Melt the fat in the milk and pour on to the yeast and beaten egg, then pour all into a well in the flour. Mix to a soft dough and beat well, until the mixture leaves the hand clean. Turn on to a floured board and knead well for 5 minutes. Leave to rise until it has doubled in size. Knead on a board and shape into 3 loaves. Cut slits along the length of each loaf. Place on a greased baking sheet, and put to prove. Glaze with milk or beaten egg, and bake in the oven at 230°C (450°F) mark 8 for 20–30 minutes, reducing the heat to 190°C (375°F) mark 5, after 8 minutes.

Milk rolls

450 g (1 lb) strong plain flour
2·5 ml (½ level tsp) salt
50 g (2 oz) lard
15 g (½ oz) fresh yeast or 7·5 ml (1 ½
level tsp) dried yeast and 5 ml (1 level
tsp) caster sugar
about 300 ml (½ pint) tepid milk
milk or egg to glaze

Sift the flour and salt together and rub in the lard. Dissolve the yeast and add most of the tepid milk. Make a well in the flour and pour in the liquid. Mix to a soft elastic dough, adding the remaining milk as required. Knead well and put to rise until doubled in size. Turn out on to a floured board and knead. Divide the mixture into small pieces and shape as desired. Apart from round balls and long finger rolls, favourite shapes are:

Plaits (divide each peace into three and pull these out into long strips; stick the ends together and plait loosely).

Twists (divide each piece into two and pull into long strips; twist the pieces together, sealing the ends with a little water).

Crescents (bend long finger rolls round to form a half-moon shape).

Place the rolls on a greased baking sheet and put to prove. Glaze with milk or beaten egg, and bake in the oven at 230°C (450°F) mark 8 for 15–20 minutes, according to size, until well risen, golden brown and hollow-sounding when tapped underneath. *Makes about 16*

Floury baps

Illustrated in colour opposite

Knead 450 g (1 lb) Enriched white bread dough (see page 166) on a floured surface for about 5 minutes. Place in a large bowl and cover with lightly oiled polythene and allow to rise until doubled in size. Lightly knead the dough, then cut into eight to ten even-sized pieces. Shape each into a ball, place on a floured baking sheet and press down to flatten slightly. Cover with oiled polythene and allow to rise until doubled in size – about 45 minutes at room temperature. Dredge the tops lightly with flour and bake at 200°C (400°F) mark 6 for 15–20 minutes. Cool on a wire rack.

Bridge rolls

225 g (8 oz) strong plain flour
a pinch of salt
15 g (½ oz) fresh yeast or 7·5 ml (1 ½
level tsp) dried yeast and 5 ml (1 level
tsp) caster sugar
60 ml (4 tbsp) tepid milk
1 egg, beaten
50 g (2 oz) butter or margarine, melted
beaten egg to glaze

Sift the flour and salt into a basin and make a well in the centre. Dissolve the yeast with half the liquid and pour into the flour. Beat the egg with the remainder of the milk and stir it into the flour with the melted fat, mixing to a soft, smooth dough. Knead well on a floured board. Leave the dough to rise until it has doubled in size. Turn on to a board and cut into narrow strips the size of bridge rolls, about 7·5 cm (3 inches) long. Roll in the hands, place them on greased baking tins and put to prove. Brush with beaten egg, and bake in the oven at 230°C (450°F) mark 8 for about 15 minutes. *Makes 12–16*

Dinner rolls

Illustrated in colour opposite and on the jacket

450 g (1 lb) white bread dough (see page 164)
beaten egg to glaze
poppy seeds, cardamom, coriander

Knead the dough until smooth, divide it into pieces. and shape.

There are endless variations, as shown in the colour photograph, eg:

Small cottage loaves made as described on page 166.

Knots Make by pulling dough into a strip and knotting.

Trefoils Make by dividing each piece into three balls and arranging on a baking sheet so that they are just touching.

Snails Coil a strip of dough from the outside to the centre.

Glaze with beaten egg and sprinkle with poppy seeds, cardamom or coriander. Bake in the oven at 230°C (450°F) mark 8 for 10–15 minutes.

These rolls are crusty and have quite a different texture from the richer, soft milk roll. *Makes about 16*

Brown rolls

Illustrated in colour opposite

Using half quantity of Quick wholemeal bread dough (see page 167), flatten the dough to 1 cm (½ inch) in thickness on a floured surface. Cut into rounds with a 7·5-cm (2 ½-inch) cutter, or divide the dough into 24 pieces and roll into rounds, using the palm of one hand; press down hard at first, then ease up. Place on a floured baking sheet.

For soft-sided rolls, the kind which you pull apart, pack the pieces of dough 2 cm (¾ inch) apart and dust with flour.

For crusty rolls, leave a 2·5-cm (1-inch) space all round, brush the tops with salt and water and sprinkle with cracked wheat, if liked.

Cover the rolls with greased polythene, put to rise until doubled in size, and bake in the oven at 230°C (450°F) mark 8 for 20–25 minutes.

Brioche

15 g (½ oz) fresh yeast or 7·5 ml (1 ½
level tsp) dried yeast and 5 ml (1 level
tsp) caster sugar
22·5 ml (1 ½ tbsp) warm water
225 g (8 oz) strong plain flour
a pinch of salt
15 ml (1 level tbsp) caster sugar
2 standard eggs, beaten
50 g (2 oz) butter, melted
beaten egg to glaze

Blend the fresh yeast with the water. For dried yeast, dissolve the sugar in the water, sprinkle the yeast over and leave until frothy. Sift together the flour, salt and 15 ml (1 level tbsp) sugar. Stir the yeast liquid into the flour, with the eggs and butter. Work to a soft dough, turn out on to a floured board and knead for about 5 minutes. Put the

Coburg loaf, Milk loaf, Enriched white bread, Crown loaf, Poppy seed plait (see page 166), Wholemeal flowerpots (see page 167), Cottage loaf (see page 166), Floury baps, Brown rolls, Dinner rolls (see above).

dough into a bowl and cover with lightly oiled polythene and leave to rise at room temperature for 1–1½ hours, until it is doubled in size and springs back when gently pushed with a floured finger. Brush a 1·1-litre (2-pint) fluted mould with oil.

Knead the dough well on a lightly floured surface. Shape three-quarters of it into a ball and place in the bottom of the mould. Press a hole in the centre as far as the tin base, and put in the middle the remainder of the dough, shaped as a 'knob'; press down lightly.

Cover the mould with oiled polythene and leave at room temperature until the dough is light and puffy and nearly reaches the top of the mould – about 1 hour. Brush it lightly with egg glaze and bake in the oven at 230°C (450°F) mark 8 for 15–20 minutes, until golden. Turn out and cool.

Note For small brioches divide the dough into 12 pieces, put into deep 7·5-cm (3-inch) fluted patty tins (oiled), and bake as above for about 10 minutes.

Breadsticks

700 g (1½ lb) strong plain flour
10 ml (2 level tsp) salt
20 g (¾ oz) fresh yeast or 10 ml (2 level tsp) dried yeast and 5 ml (1 level tsp) caster sugar
400 ml (¾ pint) tepid milk
50 g (2 oz) butter or margarine, melted

Sift the flour and salt together. Dissolve the yeast in half of the tepid milk. Make a well in the centre of the flour and pour in the yeast

Crumpets

mixture. Sprinkle with flour and put in a warm place to froth. Add the remaining milk and melted fat, and mix to a dough. Knead well and put to rise. Turn out on to a floured board and knead. Divide the dough into small pieces, then roll and pull these into sticks 15–20·5 cm (6–8 inches) long and as thick as a finger. Place on a greased baking sheet, and prove. Bake in the oven at 200°C (400°F) mark 6 for about 30–35 minutes, reducing the heat to 180°C (350°F) mark 4 after 10 minutes.

For salted breadsticks, brush over with milk and water before baking, and sprinkle with crushed rock salt.

These breadsticks will keep for about two weeks in an airtight tin, and can be crisped in a slow oven before serving.

Teatime specials

Sally Lunn teacakes

325 g (12 oz) strong plain flour
1·25 ml (¼ level tsp) salt
15 g (½ oz) fresh yeast or 7·5 ml (1½ level tsp) dried yeast and 5 ml (1 level tsp) caster sugar
200 ml (⅓ pint) tepid milk and water
1 egg, beaten
25 g (1 oz) butter or margarine
egg or milk and sugar to glaze
glacé icing

Sift the flour and salt into a basin. Dissolve

the yeast in the tepid liquid and pour into the centre of the flour. Add the beaten egg and melted fat, and mix to a light, soft dough, then knead well. Divide into 2 or 3 pieces, shape into rounds and put into small greased and floured tins, half filling them. Set to rise until the dough rises to the top of the tins, then bake them in the oven at 230°C (450°F) mark 8 for 15–20 minutes. Glaze a few minutes before finally removing from the oven, using a sugar glaze. When cold, cover with glacé icing. (If preferred slice across before icing.)

Yorkshire teacakes

Follow the recipe for Sally Lunn Teacakes, adding 50 g (2 oz) currants or sultanas and omitting the egg, if preferred. Allow the dough to rise in the bowl, then knead again and shape into flat, round cakes. Place on greased baking sheets and put to prove. Bake in the oven at 230°C (450°F) mark 8 for about 15 minutes. Glaze and leave on a rack to cool.

Crumpets (Pikelets)

15 g (½ oz) fresh yeast or 7·5 ml (1½ level tsp) dried yeast and 5 ml (1 level tsp) caster sugar
600 ml (1 pint) tepid milk and water
450 g (1 lb) strong plain flour
a pinch of bicarbonate of soda
5 ml (1 level tsp) salt

Dissolve the yeast in a little of the tepid liquid, add the rest and pour into the flour. Beat very thoroughly with the hand for 5 minutes, then cover and leave it to stand to froth – about 20 minutes. Dissolve the bicarbonate of soda and salt in a little warm water and add to the frothing mixture. Beat until very smooth. Have ready a greased girdle (see page 199), moderately hot; grease some crumpet rings and let them heat on the girdle. Pour in enough batter to cover the bottom of each ring thoroughly; cook gently until the top is set, remove the rings, turn the crumpets over and allow to dry for a few minutes on the underside. Toast on both sides, butter and serve hot.

Devonshire splits

Illustrated in colour on page 173

450 g (1 lb) strong plain flour
5 ml (1 level tsp) salt
50 g (2 oz) butter or margarine
15 g (½ oz) fresh yeast or 7·5 ml (1½ level tsp) dried yeast and 5 ml (1 level tsp) caster sugar
about 300 ml (½ pint) tepid milk
egg or milk to glaze

Sift the flour and salt together and rub in the fat. Dissolve the yeast and add some milk. Make a well in the flour and pour over the liquid, leave until frothy. Mix with enough liquid to give a soft dough. Knead it well on a floured board and place in a bowl, cover with oiled polythene. Allow to rise until doubled in size. Turn it out and knead well. Divide into 12–14 pieces. Knead each lightly into a ball and put on a greased and lightly floured tin. Leave to prove until doubled in size. Glaze with milk, and bake in the oven at 230°C (450°F) mark 8 for 10–15 minutes.

When cool, split and fill with jam, then pipe with whipped cream.

Cinnamon pinwheel ring

Illustrated in colour on page 176

450 g (1 lb) strong plain flour
5 ml (1 level tsp) salt
50 g (2 oz) butter or margarine
15 g (½ oz) fresh yeast or 7·5 ml (1½ level tsp) dried yeast and 5 ml (1 level tsp) caster sugar
about 300 ml (½ pint) tepid milk
40–50 g (1½–2 oz) butter or margarine, melted
ground cinnamon
ground almonds
caster sugar
a little beaten egg to glaze

Sift the flour and salt together and rub in the fat. Dissolve the yeast in most of the warmed milk. Pour into the flour and mix to a soft, elastic dough, adding more milk if required. Knead well and put to rise until doubled in size.

Turn the dough on to a floured board and knead well, until smooth. Roll out to an oblong 0·3 cm (⅛ inch) thick, spread with melted fat and sprinkle with cinnamon, ground almonds and sugar. Roll the dough up to form a long roll and join the ends to make a ring. Place on a greased and floured baking sheet and with scissors snip almost through into slices about 1 cm (½ inch) thick; then open these out and arrange as shown in the picture. Put to prove. Brush with beaten egg and bake in the oven at 190°C (375°F) mark 5 for 25–30 minutes.

Pinwheel slices

Prepare a roll as for Cinnamon Pinwheel Ring (left), but do not join it into a ring. Cut into slices 4 cm (1½ inches) thick, make 2 or 3 cuts almost through each slice, and arrange, opened out, on a baking sheet. Leave to prove, then bake in the oven at 190°C (375°F) mark 5 for 10–15 minutes. While it is still hot, brush with glacé icing.

Danish pastries

For the basic dough
25 g (1 oz) fresh yeast or 15 ml (1 level tbsp) dried yeast and 5 ml (1 level tsp) caster sugar
about 150 ml (¼ pint) water
450 g (1 lb) plain flour – not strong
5 ml (1 level tsp) salt
50 g (2 oz) lard
30 ml (2 level tbsp) sugar
2 eggs, beaten
300 g (10 oz) butter
beaten egg to glaze

Blend the fresh yeast with the cold water. For dried yeast, dissolve the sugar in tepid water, sprinkle the yeast over and leave until frothy. Mix the flour and salt, rub in the lard and stir in the 30 ml (2 level tbsp) sugar. Add the yeast liquid and beaten eggs and mix to an elastic dough, adding a little more water if necessary. Knead lightly. Cover the bowl and leave the dough to 'rest' in the refrigerator for 10 minutes. Work the butter with a knife until soft and form it into an oblong. Roll out the dough on a floured board into an oblong about three times the size of the butter, put the butter in the centre of the dough and enclose it, over-lapping the unbuttered sides just across the middle and sealing the open sides with a rolling pin.

Turn the dough so that the folds are to the sides and roll into a strip three times as long as it is wide; fold the bottom third up, and the top third down, cover and leave to 'rest' for 10 minutes. Turn, repeat, rolling, folding and resting twice more and use as required.

Imperial stars Roll out half of the dough thinly, cut into 7·5-cm (3-inch) squares and make diagonal cuts from each corner to within 1 cm (½ inch) of the centre. Put a piece of almond paste in the centre of the square and fold one corner of each section down to the centre, securing the tips with a little beaten egg. *Makes about 16 pastries*

Cushions Using 7·5-cm (3-inch) squares, put a little almond paste in the centre and either fold over 2 alternate corners to the centre or fold over all 4 corners, securing the tips with beaten egg.

Twists Roll out half dough as before. Cut each oblong length to give 4 pieces. Spread with cinnamon butter and fold the bottom third up and the top third down. Cut each across into thin slices. Twist these slices and put on a baking sheet. *Makes about 16 pastries*

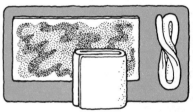
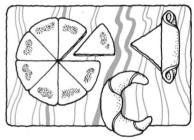

Shaping Danish pastries
Imperial stars, cushions, twists, crescents

Crescents Roll out half of the dough thinly and cut out two 23-cm (9-inch) rounds. Divide each into 8 segments and put a little almond paste or confectioners' custard mixture at the base of each. Roll up from the base and curl round to form a crescent. *Makes 16 pastries*

Pinwheels Roll out half of the dough into two oblongs 30 cm (12 inches) long and 20·5 cm (8 inches) wide. Spread with cinnamon butter and sultanas, roll up like Swiss rolls, cut into 2·5-cm (1-inch) slices and place cut side upwards on a baking sheet. *Makes about 16 pastries*

To finish Danish pastries After shaping them, prove for 20–30 minutes. Brush with beaten egg and bake in the oven at 220°C (425°F) mark 7 for about 15 minutes. While they are still hot, brush with thin white glacé icing (see page 206) and sprinkle them with flaked or chopped almonds which have been lightly browned under the grill. Finish the centres of imperial stars and cushions with a blob of confectioners' custard or redcurrant jelly.

Almond paste filling

15 g (½ oz) butter
75 g (3 oz) caster sugar
75 g (3 oz) ground almonds
1 egg, beaten
almond essence (optional)

Cream the butter and sugar, stir in the almonds and add enough egg to make a pliable consistency; add a few drops of almond essence if you wish.

Confectioners' custard or pastry cream

1 whole egg, separated
1 egg yolk
50 g (2 oz) caster sugar
30 ml (2 level tbsp) plain flour
30 ml (2 level tbsp) cornflour
300 ml (½ pint) milk
vanilla essence

Cream the egg yolks and sugar together until really thick and pale in colour. Beat in the flour and cornflour and a little cold milk to make a smooth paste. Heat the rest of the milk in a saucepan until almost boiling and pour on to the egg mixture, stirring well all the time. Return the mixture to the saucepan and stir over a low heat until the mixture boils. Beat the egg white until stiff. Remove the custard mixture from the heat and fold in the egg white. Return to the heat, add essence to taste and cook for a further 2–3 minutes. Cool before using.

Cinnamon butter filling

50 g (2 oz) butter
50 g (2 oz) caster sugar
10 ml (2 level tsp) ground cinnamon

Cream the butter and sugar and beat in the cinnamon.

Muffins

25 g (1 oz) fresh yeast or 15 ml (1 level tbsp) dried yeast and 5 ml (1 level tsp) caster sugar
600 ml (1 pint) tepid water
15 ml (1 level tbsp) salt
700 g (1½ lb) strong plain flour

Mix the yeast with the tepid water, add the salt to the sifted flour, and add the liquid and yeast by degrees. Beat well with the hand for 15 minutes; thorough beating at this stage is most essential. Cover with oiled polythene and allow to rise. Beat up again and leave for a further 30 minutes. Meanwhile, take a deep baking tin, dust very liberally with flour and put in a warm place. When the muffin mixture is ready, turn on to a floured board and cut into even-sized pieces. Although the mixture is very soft, only sufficient flour should be used to make handling easy. Roll the portions of dough into flat cakes, rather smaller than the muffin rings, and put them in the floured tin. Allow to prove. Have ready a moderately hot floured girdle or hot-plate, grease some muffin rings, and heat them. Drop the muffins in the rings and cook for 5 minutes; turn, and cook for another 5 minutes. Remove the rings and press the sides of the muffins to see if they are quite cooked. Butter generously.

Note These are one of the most delicious of the traditional teabreads and used to be sold in the streets by 'muffin men'.

Austrian toffee buns

450 g (1 lb) strong plain flour
100 g (4 oz) caster sugar
25 g (1 oz) fresh yeast or 15 ml (1 level tbsp) dried yeast and 5 ml (1 level tsp) caster sugar
245 ml (⅓ pint plus 3 tbsp) tepid milk
2·5 ml (½ level tsp) salt
2 eggs, beaten
275 g (10 oz) butter or margarine
stoned raisins
brown sugar
ground cinnamon

The dough is best made the day before. Into a large mixing bowl put 225 g (8 oz) flour and 5 ml (1 level tsp) sugar. Rub in the yeast, add the milk and mix well together to a batter. Leave in a warm place until frothy. Mix the remaining 225 g (8 oz) flour with the salt and add this to the yeast mixture, together with the beaten eggs, remaining sugar and 225 g (8 oz) softened fat. Beat the dough thoroughly for 5–10 minutes, then cover with aluminium foil, place in the refrigerator and leave overnight.

The next day, turn the dough out on to a floured board and leave for 1 hour to 'come to'. Then knead lightly, dealing with half at a time. Roll out into an oblong 0·3 cm (⅛ inch) thick. Brush with melted fat and sprinkle with raisins, brown sugar and cinnamon. Roll up tightly and cut into 2·5-cm (1-inch) slices. Prepare some patty tins

by brushing with fat and putting a small knob of butter and 15 ml (1 level tsp) brown sugar in each.

Place a slice in each tin and set to prove until well risen. Bake in the oven at 180°C (350°F) mark 4 for 10–15 minutes, until golden brown. Turn out immediately and leave upside-down. The butter and sugar will have formed a delicious toffee topping.

Lardy cake

800 g (1¾ lb) risen white bread dough (see page 164)
150 g (5 oz) lard
175 g (6 oz) caster sugar
75 g (3 oz) currants
sugar and water glaze

Make the white bread dough as described on page 164, then roll it into an oblong and spread on it half the lard, half the sugar and half the currants, covering only two-thirds of the dough. Fold the dough into three, bringing the uncovered portion up first, then fold over again; seal the ends by pressing them with a rolling-pin. Turn the dough half-way round, and again roll into an oblong. Spread the remaining lard, sugar and currants on to two-thirds of it, then fold and turn as before. Roll out to fit a tin about 18 cm (7 inches) square – the dough should be 2·5–4 cm (1–1½ inches) thick. Mark with a criss-cross pattern, using a sharp knife, and leave to rise. Bake in the oven at 200°C (400°F) mark 6 for 45 minutes–1 hour. When cooked, brush over with hot sugar and water glaze: to make this, dissolve 15 ml (1 level tbsp) sugar in 15 ml (1 tbsp) water and bring to the boil.

Honey and almond kuchen

a third of the Toffee Bun dough (see above)
melted butter or margarine
50 g (2 oz) blanched almonds
50 g (2 oz) currants
brown sugar

For the honey topping
25 g (1 oz) softened butter
25 g (1 oz) caster sugar
30 ml (2 tbsp) thick honey
15 g (½ oz) flour
25 g (1 oz) almonds, chopped

Divide the dough into three, then divide 2 pieces in halves again. Shape the 4 small pieces into rounds and roll out or flatten with the hand to fit a 15–18-cm (6- or 7-inch) cake tin. Place one round in the well-greased tin, brush with melted fat and sprinkle with the chopped almonds, currants and brown sugar. Place another

Devonshire splits (see page 170).

round on top, treat in the same way, and repeat yet a third time; place the last round on top, leaving it plain. Roll the large piece into a strip about 40·5 cm (16 inches) long and coil it loosely into the tin.

Put to prove until well risen. Meanwhile, blend all the ingredients for the topping, spoon this on to the Kuchen and bake in the oven at 200°C (400°F) mark 6 for 30–40 minutes, until well risen and golden brown. If it browns too quickly, turn the oven down to 180°C (350°F) mark 4 after 20 minutes.

This cake is delicious eaten either hot or cold.

Fruit braid

225 g (8 oz) strong plain flour
a pinch of salt
15 g (½ oz) fresh yeast or 7·5 ml (1½ level tsp) dried yeast and 5 ml (1 level tsp) caster sugar
150 ml (¼ pint) tepid milk
50 g (2 oz) butter or margarine, melted
50 g (2 oz) caster sugar
1 egg, beaten
beaten egg to glaze
glacé icing

For the filling
1 cooking apple, grated
75 g (3 oz) stoned raisins, halved
25 g (1 oz) finely chopped mixed candied peel
50 g (2 oz) Demerara sugar
grated rind of ½ lemon
a pinch of ground cinnamon

Sift the flour and salt into a bowl. Dissolve the yeast in the milk and add the melted fat, sugar and beaten egg. Make a well in the flour, pour in the liquid and beat thoroughly until the mixture leaves the hands clean. Cover, and set to prove. Knead on a floured board and roll out into a strip 35·5 × 15 cm (14 × 6 inches), then transfer to a baking sheet. Place the well mixed filling down the centre third of the strip. Slash the sides diagonally at 2-cm (¾-inch) intervals and fold the ends in alternately over the filling. Prove until doubled in size. Brush with beaten egg and bake in the oven at 200°C (400°F) mark 6 for 30–35 minutes. While still warm, brush with a little glacé icing.

Mincemeat ring

Make some dough as for Chelsea Buns (see page 175) and leave until doubled in size. Knead lightly and roll out into an oblong. Spread thinly with 25 g (1 oz) softened butter or margarine, then add a generous layer of mincemeat. Roll up tightly, join the ends and put into a ring tin. Using scissors, cut three-quarters of the way through the

ring at 1-cm (½-inch) intervals. Leave until doubled in size, then brush with sugar glaze (see page 163) and bake in the oven at 230°C (450°F) mark 8 for about 40 minutes. While it is still warm, decorate with a little thin glacé icing.

Yorkshire spice bread

450 g (1 lb) strong plain flour
1·25 ml (¼ level tsp) salt
100 g (4 oz) butter or margarine
100 g (4 oz) lard
15 g (½ oz) fresh yeast or 7·5 ml (1½ level tsp) dried yeast and 5 ml (1 level tsp) caster sugar
1 egg, beaten
about 150 ml (¼ pint) tepid milk and water
10 ml (2 tsp) golden syrup
50 g (2 oz) sultanas
100 g (4 oz) currants
25 g (1 oz) chopped candied peel
100 g (4 oz) caster sugar
5 ml (1 level tsp) grated nutmeg
5 ml (1 level tsp) ground cinnamon
sugar glaze

Sift the flour and salt together. Rub in the butter and lard and make a well in the centre of the flour. Dissolve the yeast and pour over the beaten egg. Warm the liquid and syrup gently, then add to the flour,

together with the yeast mixture. Mix to a soft dough with the hand, and knead well until smooth – about 5 minutes. Leave to rise until the dough has doubled in size. Turn the dough on to a floured board and knead until smooth, adding more flour if necessary. Work in the prepared fruit, sugar and spices. Divide the dough into two, shape it and place in 2 greased and floured 450-g (1-lb) bread tins. Put to prove until the dough reaches the top of the tins, then bake in the oven at 230°C (450°F) mark 8 for 1¼ hours, reducing heat to 180°C (350°F) mark 4 after 10 minutes. Brush with sugar glaze while still hot.

Rich dough cake

225 g (8 oz) strong plain flour
a pinch of salt
a pinch of grated nutmeg
40 g (1½ oz) butter or margarine
15 g (½ oz) fresh yeast or 7·5 ml (1½ level tsp) dried yeast and 5 ml (1 level tsp) caster sugar
150 ml (¼ pint) tepid milk and water
1 egg, beaten
15 g (½ oz) chopped peel
50 g (2 oz) currants
50 g (2 oz) chopped glacé cherries
25 g (1 oz) sugar
beaten egg to glaze
sugar glaze

Yorkshire spice bread

Sift the flour, salt and nutmeg, and rub in the fat. Dissolve the yeast with a little tepid milk and water. Make a well in the centre of the flour and pour in the yeast mixture, the remaining liquid and the beaten egg. Knead thoroughly on a floured board for 5 minutes, then knead in the peel, currants, cherries and sugar. When smooth, put into a greased and floured 15-cm (6-inch) cake tin; press lightly into the tin, and allow to rise until the dough reaches the top of the tin. Glaze with beaten egg, and bake in the oven at 220°C (425°F) mark 7 for about 30 minutes, turning the heat down to 190°C (375°F) mark 5 after 20 minutes. Brush with sugar glaze whilst still hot.

This cake may also be baked in a loaf tin and served cut into slices and buttered.

Apricot and currant bread

Into 325 g (12 oz) risen Quick Wholemeal dough (see page 167) work 100 g (4 oz) chopped dried apricots, 50 g (2 oz) currants and 25 g (1 oz) sugar. Knead well together, then place in a greased 450-g (1-lb) bread tin. Prove until it reaches the top of the tin, then bake in the oven at 230°C (450°F) mark 8 for 40–50 minutes. Brush with melted butter after baking.

Chelsea buns

225 g (8 oz) strong plain flour
15 g (½ oz) fresh yeast or 7·5 ml (1½ level tsp) dried yeast and 5 ml (1 level tsp) caster sugar
100 ml (4 fl oz) tepid milk
2·5 ml (½ level tsp) salt
a knob of butter or lard, about 15 g (½ oz)
1 egg, beaten
melted butter
75 g (3 oz) dried fruit
30 ml (2 tbsp) chopped mixed peel
50 g (2 oz) soft brown sugar
clear honey to glaze

Grease an 18-cm (7-inch) square cake tin. Put 50 g (2 oz) of the flour in a large bowl and blend together with the yeast and milk until smooth. Set aside in a warm place (about 23°C (75°F)) until the batter froths – 10–20 minutes. Mix the remaining flour and the salt; rub in the fat. Mix into the batter with the egg to give a fairly soft dough that will leave the side of the bowl clean after beating. Turn the dough out on to a lightly floured surface and knead until it is smooth – about 5 minutes. Leave to rise for 1–1½ hours. Knead the dough thoroughly and roll out to an oblong 30 × 23 cm (11¾ × 9 inches). Brush with melted butter and cover with a mixture of dried fruit, peel and brown sugar.

Chelsea buns

Roll up from the longest side like a Swiss roll, and seal the edge with water. Cut into 9 equal-sized slices and place these, cut side down, in the prepared cake tin. Prove until the dough feels springy – about 30 minutes. Bake the buns in the oven at 190°C (375°F) mark 5 for about 30 minutes.

While they are still warm, brush them with a wetted brush dipped in honey.

Nutty twists

Make up the mixture given for Chelsea Buns (above) and divide the risen dough into about 12 even-sized pieces. Cut each in half, form the halves into 2 rolls and twist them together. Put to rise on a greased tin and brush over with a sugar glaze. Bake in the oven at 230°C (450°F) mark 8 for 15–20 minutes, and just before baking is complete, brush over with more sugar glaze and sprinkle with chopped almonds or pine kernels.

Bath buns

450 g (1 lb) strong plain flour
25 g (1 oz) fresh yeast or 15 ml (1 level tbsp) dried yeast and 5 ml (1 level tsp) caster sugar
150 ml (¼ pint) milk
60 ml (4 tbsp) water
5 ml (1 level tsp) salt
50 g (2 oz) caster sugar
50 g (2 oz) butter, melted and cooled, but not firm
2 eggs, beaten
175 g (6 oz) sultanas
30–45 ml (2–3 tbsp) chopped mixed peel
beaten egg and crushed sugar lumps for topping

Put 100 g (4 oz) of the flour in a large mixing bowl. Add the yeast and 5 ml (1 level tsp) sugar. Warm the milk and water to about 43°C (110°F); add to the 100 g (4 oz) flour and mix well. Set aside in a warm place until frothy – about 20 minutes. Sift together the remaining flour and salt and add the 50 g (2 oz) sugar. Stir the butter and eggs into the frothy mixture, add the flour, sultanas and peel and mix well – the dough is fairly soft. Turn it out on to a floured surface and knead until smooth. Leave it to rise in a covered bowl until doubled in size. When it is ready, beat well. Place in about 18 spoonfuls on greased baking sheets, cover and leave to rise. Brush with egg and sprinkle with crushed sugar.

Bake in the oven at 190°C (375°F) mark 5 for about 15 minutes, until golden; cool on a rack. Serve buttered.

Lemon yeast buns

Follow the recipe for Bath Buns (above), replacing the fruit by 30 ml (2 tbsp) grated lemon and omitting the crushed sugar topping. Bake in the oven at 230°C (450°F) mark 8 for 15–20 minutes, then cool on a wire tray. Prepare a glacé icing from icing sugar, lemon juice and yellow colouring, and ice the buns when cold, decorating with lemon jelly slices.

Sugar currant buns

Use Currant Bread dough (see page 167), divide it into even-sized pieces and form into buns. Place on a greased baking tin and put to rise. Brush over with sugar glaze and bake in the oven at 230°C (450°F) mark 8 for 15–20 minutes; when nearly cooked, glaze again, and sprinkle with brown sugar.

Hot cross buns

450 g (1 lb) strong plain flour
25 g (1 oz) fresh yeast or 15 ml (1 level
  tbsp) dried yeast and 5 ml (1 level tsp)
  caster sugar
150 ml (¼ pint) milk
60 ml (4 tbsp) water
5 ml (1 level tsp) salt
2·5 ml (½ level tsp) mixed spice
2·5 ml (½ level tsp) powdered cinnamon
2·5 ml (½ level tsp) grated nutmeg
50 g (2 oz) caster sugar
50 g (2 oz) butter, melted and cooled,
  but not firm
1 egg, beaten
100 g (4 oz) currants
30–45 ml (2–3 tbsp) chopped mixed peel
50 g (2 oz) shortcrust pastry

For the glaze
60 ml (4 tbsp) milk and water
45 ml (3 level tbsp) caster sugar

Flour a baking sheet. Place 100 g (4 oz) of the flour in a large mixing bowl and add the yeast and 5 ml (1 level tsp) sugar. Warm the milk and water to about 43°C (110°F) add to the flour and mix well. Set aside in a warm place until frothy – 10–15 minutes for fresh yeast, 20 minutes for dried.

Sift together the remaining 350 g (12 oz) flour, salt, spices and 50 g (2 oz) sugar. Stir the butter and egg into the frothy yeast mixture, add the spiced flour and the fruit, and mix together. The dough should be fairly soft. Turn it out on to a lightly floured surface and knead until smooth. Leave to rise until doubled in size – about 1–1½ hours. Turn the risen dough out on to a floured surface and knock out the air bubbles, then knead.

Divide the dough into 12 pieces and shape into buns, using the palm of one hand. Press down hard at first on the table surface, then ease up as you turn and shape the buns. Arrange them well apart on the floured baking sheet, and put to rise for about 30 minutes. Roll out the pastry thinly on a floured board and cut into thin strips about 9 cm (3½ inches) long. Damp the pastry strips and lay two on each bun to make a cross. Bake in the oven at 190°C (375°F) mark 5 for 15–20 minutes, until golden brown and firm to the touch. Meanwhile, heat the milk and water and sugar gently together. Brush the hot buns twice with glaze, then leave to cool.

Note If time is short, omit the pastry crosses and mark on each bun with a sharp knife.

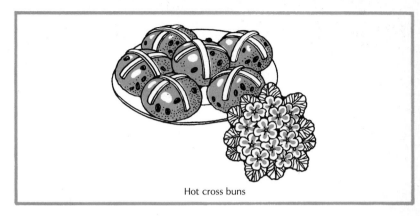
Hot cross buns

Swiss buns

Make dough as for Sally Lunn Teacakes (see page 170), but shape into finger-length rolls; glaze, and bake in the oven at 230°C (450°F) mark 8 for about 20 minutes. When the buns are cold, coat them with a little white glacé icing.

Cherry trefoil buns

Make the dough as for Chelsea Buns (see page 175), but replace the dried fruit by 50 g (2 oz) chopped glacé cherries. Cover the dough and put to rise. Turn on to a floured board, knead, and divide into small balls. Put 3 balls into each greased patty tin and put to rise. Brush lightly with beaten egg and milk, put a glacé cherry in the centre of each, and bake in the oven at 230°C (450°F) mark 8 for about 20 minutes.

Cinnamon pinwheel ring
see page 171).

CAKES, BUNS AND BISCUITS

We have tried to gather together some of the most popular recipes from the many Good Housekeeping books on this favourite subject.

At the end of the chapter you will find recipes for icings and frostings, with many variations, and some helpful notes on icing and simple decoration for formal cakes.

Family cakes

Gingerbread

450 g (1 lb) plain flour
5 ml (1 level tsp) salt
15 ml (1 level tbsp) ground ginger
15 ml (1 level tbsp) baking powder
5 ml (1 level tsp) bicarbonate of soda
225 g (8 oz) Demerara sugar
175 g (6 oz) butter or margarine
175 g (6 oz) treacle
175 g (6 oz) golden syrup
300 ml (½ pint) milk
1 egg

Sift together the flour, salt, ginger, baking powder and bicarbonate of soda. Warm the sugar, fat, treacle and syrup, but do not allow to get hot. Warm the milk and beat the egg. Combine all the ingredients, mixing very thoroughly until a smooth batter is obtained. Pour into a greased and lined 20·5-cm (8-inch) square tin and bake in the oven at 180°C (350°F) mark 4 for about 1¾–2 hours, or until firm to the touch. Allow to cool in the tin before turning out.

Madeira cake

225 g (8 oz) plain flour
a pinch of salt
10 ml (2 level tsp) baking powder
a little finely grated lemon rind
150 g (5 oz) butter or block margarine
150 g (5 oz) caster sugar
3 eggs
lemon essence
milk to mix
a slice of citron peel to decorate

Grease and line an 18-cm (7-inch) cake tin. Sift the flour, salt and baking powder together and add the grated lemon rind. Put the fat and sugar into a basin and cream together until they are light and fluffy. Beat in the eggs, adding a little at a time. Fold in the dry ingredients, a little lemon essence and some milk if required to give a soft dropping consistency. Put into the pre-

pared tin, place in the oven at 180°C (350°F) mark 4 and bake for 1–1¼ hours. Put the slice of citron peel on top of the cake as soon as it is set – if it is added before the cake is put in the oven, it is inclined to sink.

Date and nut family cake

325 g (12 oz) plain flour
175 g (6 oz) butter or block margarine
175 g (6 oz) caster sugar
325 g (12 oz) dates and nuts, chopped
5 ml (1 level tsp) ground cinnamon
300 ml (½ pint) apple purée
5 ml (1 level tsp) bicarbonate of soda
30–45 ml (2–3 tbsp) milk

For the cake topping
15 ml (1 tbsp) chopped nuts and dates, mixed together
10 ml (2 level tsp) sugar
2·5 ml (½ level tsp) ground cinnamon

Put the flour into a bowl and rub in the fat until the mixture resembles fine bread-crumbs. Add the sugar, dates and nuts and cinnamon. Make a well in the centre and add the apple purée. Lastly dissolve the bicarbonate of soda in the milk and add to the mixture; mix well and put into a greased and lined loaf tin measuring about 20·5 × 12·5 cm (8 × 5 inches). Mix the ingredients for the topping, sprinkle over the surface and bake the cake in the oven at 180°C (350°F) mark 4 for 1½ hours.

Date ripple loaf

Illustrated in colour on pages 200–201

225 g (8 oz) cooking apples, peeled and cored
150 g (5 oz) stoned cooking dates
grated rind and juice of 1 lemon
45 ml (3 tbsp) water
125 g (4 oz) butter or block margarine
125 g (4 oz) dark brown sugar
2 eggs, beaten
125 g (4 oz) self-raising flour

Chop the apple and 125 g (4 oz) dates and place in a saucepan with the lemon rind and juice and water. Cook over a gentle heat until a soft purée. Beat well and cool. Cream together the fat and sugar until light and fluffy. Gradually beat in the eggs then lightly beat in the flour. Spoon a third of the cake mixture into a non-stick rectangular cake tin that has a top measurement of 26 × 10 cm (10½ × 4 inches); spread the mixture over the base. On top of

this, spread half the apple and date mixture. Repeat the layering finishing with cake mixture. Cut the remaining 25 g (1 oz) dates into thin slivers and arrange in a line down the length of the cake. Bake at 170°C (325°F) mark 3 for about 1 hour 10 minutes. Cover with foil half way through cooking time. *Note* This mixture also fits a loaf tin with a top measurement of 21·5 × 11 × 6 cm (8¾ × 4⅜ × 2½ inches).

Spice cake

225 g (8 oz) butter or block margarine
225 g (8 oz) soft brown sugar
3 eggs
75 g (3 oz) almonds, chopped
a little grated orange peel
2·5 ml (½ level tsp) ground cloves
2·5 ml (½ level tsp) ground cinnamon
2·5 ml (½ level tsp) ground cardamoms
284-ml (10-fl oz) carton single cream
325 g (12 oz) plain flour
10 ml (2 level tsp) baking powder

Grease and flour a 20·5-cm (8-inch) square tin. Cream the fat and sugar until light and fluffy. Beat in the eggs a little at a time and mix in the nuts, flavourings and cream. Sift together the flour and baking powder and stir into the mixture. Put into the prepared tin and bake for 1 hour in the oven at 180°C (350°F) mark 4. Turn out and cool on a wire tray.

Roseylangen cake

450 g (1 lb) plain flour
225 g (8 oz) butter or block margarine
225 g (8 oz) currants
225 g (8 oz) raisins, stoned
100 g (4 oz) chopped mixed candied peel
325 g (12 oz) soft brown sugar
5 ml (1 level tsp) mixed spice
grated rind of 1 lemon
1 small bottle of brown ale
5 ml (1 level tsp) bicarbonate of soda
4 eggs

Sift the flour and rub in the fat, then add the fruit, sugar, spice and lemon rind. Warm the ale, pour over the bicarbonate of soda and quickly add to the other ingredients. Beat the eggs and mix in. Beat well until smooth, then put into a greased and lined loaf tin measuring 13·5 × 24 cm (5½ × 9½ inches) and bake in the oven at 170°C (325°F) mark 3 for about 3 hours.

This cake is best kept for a week before cutting.

Grasmere cake

Illustrated in colour on page 181

450 g (1 lb) plain flour
200 g (7 oz) butter or block margarine
225 g (8 oz) caster sugar
225 g (8 oz) currants
100 g (4 oz) sultanas
5 ml (1 level tsp) mixed spice
12·5 ml (2 ½ level tsp) bicarbonate of soda
400 ml (¾ pint) sour milk

Rub the fat into the flour and add the other dry ingredients. Mix with enough sour milk to form a soft dropping consistency and leave to stand overnight. Put in a greased and lined loaf tin, 13·5 × 24 cm (5 ½ × 9 ½ inches), and bake in the oven at 170°C (325°F) mark 3 for 2–2 ½ hours. Allow to cool in the tin before turning out.

Light fruit cake

Illustrated in colour on pages 200–201 and on the jacket

175 g (6 oz) butter or block margarine
175 g (6 oz) caster sugar
3 large eggs
125 g (4 oz) plain flour
150 g (5 oz) self-raising flour
50 g (2 oz) glacé cherries, halved
225 g (8 oz) mixed dried fruit
grated rind and juice of ½ lemon
walnut halves
15 ml (1 level tbsp) granulated sugar

Grease and line an 18-cm (7-inch) round cake tin. Cream the fat, add the sugar and continue creaming until light and fluffy. Beat in the eggs, one at a time. Combine the flours, cherries and mixed dried fruit. Fold into the creamed mixture alternately with the lemon rind and juice. Turn the mixture into the prepared cake tin; level the surface. Top with halved walnuts, sprinkle with granulated sugar and bake in the oven at 170°C (325°F) mark 3 for about 1 hour 40 minutes until firm to the touch. Turn out and cool on a wire rack.

Cherry cake

325 g (12 oz) glacé cherries
275 g (10 oz) plain flour
50 g (2 oz) self-raising flour
225 g (8 oz) butter or block margarine
225 g (8 oz) caster sugar
4 eggs
vanilla essence
milk to mix, if required

Wash the cherries, cut in half, dry on absorbent paper and dust with a little of the measured flour. Grease and line a 20·5-cm (8-inch) tin. Cream the fat with the sugar, then lightly whisk the eggs and beat into

the mixture. Lightly fold in the cherries and flour, with a few drops of vanilla essence. Add a little milk if necessary to make a soft dropping consistency. Put into the prepared tin and bake in the oven at 170°C (325°F) mark 3 for about 1 hour 50 minutes. Turn out and cool on a wire rack.

Seed cake

175 g (6 oz) plain flour
2·5 ml (½ level tsp) baking powder
a pinch of salt
10 ml (2 level tsp) caraway seeds
100 g (4 oz) butter or block margarine
100 g (4 oz) caster sugar
2 eggs
a little milk

Sift the flour, baking powder and salt together and add the caraway seeds. Put the fat and sugar into a basin, cream until pale in colour, then beat in each egg separately. Stir in the sifted flour, adding a little milk to make the mixture of a dropping consistency. Put into a greased and lined 18-cm (7-inch) tin and bake in the oven at 200°C (400°F) mark 6 for about 1 hour. Turn out and cool on a wire rack.

Malt loaf

45 ml (3 tbsp) malt extract
45 ml (3 tbsp) golden syrup
200 ml (⅓ pint) milk
225 g (8 oz) self-raising flour
75 g (3 oz) dates, chopped
1 egg
5 ml (1 level tsp) bicarbonate of soda

Put the malt, syrup and milk in a saucepan and heat until blended. Sift the flour and add the chopped dates. Beat the egg and add to the flour, together with the malt mixture, stirring all the time. Dissolve the bicarbonate of soda in a little water and add it to the mixture, then pour into a greased and bottom-lined loaf tin and bake at 190°C (375°F) mark 5 for about 1 hour, or until firm. Turn out and cool on a wire rack.

Moist almond butter tart

Illustrated in colour on pages 200–201

For the pastry
175 g (6 oz) butter
175 g (6 oz) plain flour
45 ml (3 tbsp) cold water
apricot jam or raspberry jelly

For the filling
125 g (4 oz) butter or block margarine
125 g (4 oz) caster sugar
2 eggs
125 g (4 oz) cake crumbs
100 g (4 oz) ground almonds
a few drops of almond essence

For the pastry, have butter at average room temperature, rub into the flour lightly with the tips of the fingers to mix to a soft but manageable dough with all the water. Knead the dough lightly on a well floured surface and roll out to fit a 24-cm (9 ½-inch) diameter fluted flan tin. Reserve the trimmings. Spread the base with the jam or jelly.

For the filling, cream together the butter and sugar. Beat in the eggs, cake crumbs, ground almonds and almond essence. Spread over the pastry. Decorate with shapes cut from the pastry trimmings. Bake in the oven at 200°C (400°F) mark 6 for 30 minutes. Reduce the heat to 170°C (325°F) mark 3 for a further 30 minutes. Cool in the tin.

Note Crumbled trifle sponges or plain sandwich or Madeira cake make the best crumbs.

Traditional cakes

Yorkshire parkin

225 g (8 oz) plain flour
2·5 ml (½ level tsp) salt
6·25 ml (1 ¼ level tsp) bicarbonate of soda
25 g (1 oz) mixed spice
100 g (4 oz) coarse oatmeal
175 g (6 oz) soft brown sugar
100 g (4 oz) butter or lard
75 g (3 oz) golden syrup or black treacle
150 ml (¼ pint) milk

Sift the flour, salt, soda and spice, then mix thoroughly with the oatmeal and sugar. Melt the fat with the syrup or treacle and add to the dry ingredients, with the milk. Spread into a 20·5-cm (8-inch) greased and lined square tin and bake in the oven at 180°C (350°F) mark 4 for about 50 minutes.

Pitcaithly bannock

150 g (5 oz) butter or block margarine
75 g (3 oz) caster sugar
200 g (7 oz) plain flour
25 g (1 oz) ground rice
1·25 ml (¼ level tsp) salt
25 g (1 oz) blanched almonds, finely chopped
25 g (1 oz) chopped peel

Work the butter and sugar together on a smooth surface until thoroughly blended, then draw in the sifted flour, ground rice and salt. Finally, mix in the almonds and peel. Form into a round cake about 2·5 cm (1 inch) thick, lay it on greaseproof paper on a baking tin, prick the top and pinch up the edge. Mark into triangles then pin a band of greaseproof paper round the edge of the bannock. Bake in the oven at 180°C (350°F) mark 4 for 30–40 minutes.

Simnel cake

450 g (1 lb) ready-made almond paste (see page 207)
225 g (8 oz) plain flour
a pinch of salt
2·5 ml (½ level tsp) grated nutmeg
2·5 ml (½ level tsp) powdered cinnamon
225 g (8 oz) currants, cleaned
100 g (4 oz) sultanas, cleaned
75 g (3 oz) chopped mixed peel
100 g (4 oz) glacé cherries, quartered
175 g (6 oz) butter or block margarine
175 g (6 oz) caster sugar
3 eggs
milk to mix, if required
egg white

Originally a Mothering Sunday cake, it is now more usual to bake this for Easter.

Grease and line an 18-cm (7-inch) round cake tin. Shape a third of the almond paste into a round slightly smaller than the cake tin.

Sift together the flour, salt and spices. Mix the currants, sultanas, peel and cherries. Cream the butter and sugar until pale and fluffy and beat in each egg separately. Fold the flour into the creamed mixture, adding a little milk, if required, to give a dropping consistency. Fold in the fruit. Put half the mixture into the prepared tin and place the round of almond paste on top. Cover with the rest of the mixture, spreading it evenly. Bake in the oven at 150°C (300°F) mark 2 for 2½–3 hours, until the cake is a rich brown and firm to the touch. Cool on a wire rack.

From the remaining almond paste, shape 11 small balls, then make the rest into a round to fit the top of the cake. Brush the top surface of the cake with egg white, place the almond paste round in position and smooth it slightly with a rolling pin. Pinch the edges into scallops with finger and thumb. Score the surface with a knife, arrange the almond paste balls in position and brush the whole with egg white. Grill until light golden brown and decorate with a ribbon and a bow when cold.

Pound cake (fruitless)

225 g (8 oz) butter or block margarine
225 g (8 oz) caster sugar
4 eggs
325 g (12 oz) self-raising flour
juice and grated rind of 1 lemon

Beat together the fat and sugar until light and fluffy. Beat the eggs and add to the mixture, alternately with the flour. Mix in the lemon juice and rind. Turn the mixture into a greased and lined loaf tin 12·5 × 16 × 9 cm (5 × 7 ½ × 3 ½ inches) and bake in the oven at 170°C (325°F) mark 3 for about 2 hours.

Norfolk cake

225 g (8 oz) plain flour
5 ml (1 level tsp) baking powder
2·5 ml (½ level tsp) mixed spice
100 g (4 oz) butter or block margarine
75 g (3 oz) caster sugar
2 eggs
100 g (4 oz) sultanas
50 g (2 oz) currants
grated rind of 1 lemon and 1 orange
15 ml (1 tbsp) melted chocolate
30 ml (2 tbsp) milk

Sift the flour, baking powder and spice and allow to stand in a warm place while you beat the fat and sugar to a light, fluffy cream. Beat the eggs and stir them into the butter mixture, alternately with the flour. Mix in the cleaned sultanas and currants, the orange and lemon rind and the chocolate, then the milk. Put into a greased and lined round 20·5-cm (8-inch) tin and bake in the oven at 170°C (325°F) mark 3 for about 2 hours.

Rich Christmas cake

Illustrated in colour on page 189

500 g (1 lb 2 oz) currants
225 g (8 oz) sultanas
225 g (8 oz) raisins, stoned
100 g (4 oz) mixed peel, chopped
175 g (6 oz) glacé cherries, halved
275 g (10 oz) plain flour
a pinch of salt
2·5 ml (½ level tsp) mixed spice
2·5 ml (½ level tsp) ground cinnamon
275 g (10 oz) butter or margarine
275 g (10 oz) soft brown sugar
grated rind of ½ lemon
6 eggs, beaten
45 ml (3 tbsp) brandy

Line a 23-cm (9-inch) cake tin, using 2 thicknesses of greaseproof paper. Tie a double band of brown paper round the outside.

Clean the fruit if necessary. Mix the prepared currants, sultanas, raisins, peel and cherries with the flour, salt and spices. Cream the fat, sugar and lemon rind until pale and fluffy. Add the eggs a little at a time, beating well after each addition. Fold in half the flour and fruit, using a table-spoon, then fold in the rest and add the brandy. Put into the tin, spread the mixture

Ingredients for Norfolk cake

Grasmere cake (see page 179)

evenly, making sure there are no air pockets, and make a dip in the centre. Stand the tin on a layer of newspaper or brown paper in the oven and bake at 150°C (300°F) mark 2 for about 4½ hours. To avoid over-browning the top, cover it with several thicknesses of greaseproof paper after 2½ hours.

When the cake is cooked, leave it to cool in the tin and then turn it out on to a wire rack. To store, wrap it in several layers of greaseproof paper and put it in an airtight tin. If a large enough tin is not available, cover the wrapped cake entirely with aluminium foil. If you like, you can prick the cake top all over with a fine skewer and slowly pour 30–45 ml (2–3 tbsp) brandy over it before storing. For icing and decoration see pages 206–208.

Apple cake

325 g (12 oz) self-raising flour
2·5 ml (½ level tsp) salt
5 ml (1 level tsp) ground cinnamon
2·5 ml (½ level tsp) grated nutmeg
2·5 ml (½ level tsp) ground cloves
5 ml (1 level tsp) bicarbonate of soda
400 ml (¾ pint) apple purée
100 g (4 oz) butter or block margarine
175 g (6 oz) moist brown sugar
1 egg, separated
100 g (4 oz) raisins

Sift together the flour, salt and spices. Add the bicarbonate of soda to the apple purée, stirring until dissolved. Cream the fat and sugar until light and fluffy, add the egg yolk and beat well. Now add the flour and apple purée alternately to the butter mixture, then add the raisins and lastly fold in the stiffly whipped egg white. Put the mixture into a greased and lined 20·5-cm (8-inch)

round cake tin and bake in the oven at 180°C (350°F) mark 4 for about 1–1½ hours.

Dundee cake

275 g (10 oz) plain flour
100 g (4 oz) currants
100 g (4 oz) raisins
100 g (4 oz) sultanas
100 g (4 oz) chopped orange and lemon peel
50 g (2 oz) whole almonds
1 orange
5 eggs
225 g (8 oz) butter or block margarine
225 g (8 oz) caster sugar
75 g (3 oz) ground almonds
a pinch of salt

Sift the flour. Prepare the fruit, blanch and split the almonds, grate the orange rind and beat the eggs. Cream the fat and sugar and add the eggs and flour alternately, beating well. Add the fruit, ground almonds, orange rind and salt. Turn the mixture into a greased and lined 20·5-cm (8-inch) cake tin, cover the surface with the split almonds and bake in the oven at 170°C (325°F) mark 3 for about 2½ hours. Cool on a wire rack.

Lincolnshire farmhouse dripping cake

450 g (1 lb) plain flour
2·5 ml (½ level tsp) salt
175 g (6 oz) dripping
50 g (2 oz) candied peel
225 g (8 oz) raisins
175 g (6 oz) granulated sugar
15 ml (1 tbsp) black treacle
about 300 ml (½ pint) milk
2 eggs, beaten
5 ml (1 level tsp) bicarbonate of soda

Sift the flour with the salt and rub in the dripping thoroughly. Chop the candied peel, stone the raisins and add both to the flour, with the sugar. Warm the treacle in half the milk, mix with the eggs and stir into the mixture, with just enough cold milk to make a dough which will just drop from the wooden spoon when shaken. Then add the bicarbonate of soda, dissolved in 15 ml (1 tbsp) milk; put at once into a prepared 20·5-cm (8-inch) square cake tin. Bake in the oven at 180°C (350°F) mark 4 for about 1½–2 hours, reducing the temperature to 170°C (325°F) mark 3 after the first hour.

This cake is very good if cut into squares or sliced thinly and buttered.

Maids of honour

568 ml (1 pint) milk
a pinch of salt
5 ml (1 level tsp) rennet
75 g (3 oz) butter or margarine
2 eggs
15 ml (1 tbsp) brandy
25 g (1 oz) blanched almonds, chopped
10 ml (2 level tsp) sugar
225 g (8 oz) puff pastry or a 212-g (7½-oz) pkt frozen puff pastry, thawed
a few currants (optional)

Warm the milk to blood heat, add the salt and rennet and leave to set; when firm, put into a piece of fine muslin and allow to drain overnight.

The next day, rub the curds and butter through a sieve. Whisk the eggs and brandy together and add to the curds, with the almonds and sugar. Line some deep patty tins with the pastry, half-fill with the curd mixture and if desired sprinkle currants over the top. Bake in the oven at 220°C (425°F) mark 7 for 15–20 minutes.

Ayrshire shortcake

100 g (4 oz) plain flour
100 g (4 oz) ground rice
a large pinch of salt
100 g (4 oz) butter
100 g (4 oz) caster sugar
1 egg yolk
15 ml (1 tbsp) cream

Sift the flour, ground rice and salt. Rub in the butter lightly, then add the sugar and mix well. Beat up the egg yolk and cream and add to the mixture; mix to a firm dough, then roll out thinly, cut into wedges, rounds or fingers and prick with a fork. Place on greased paper on a baking tin and bake in the oven at 170°C (325°F) mark 3 for about 25 minutes.

Ayrshire shortcake

Layer and sponge cakes

Victoria sandwich cake

100 g (4 oz) butter or margarine
100 g (4 oz) caster sugar
2 eggs
100 g (4 oz) plain flour
2·5 ml (½ level tsp) baking powder
a little milk, if necessary
jam
caster sugar to dredge

Cream the fat and sugar together until light and creamy, then beat in the eggs, adding a little at a time so that the mixture does not curdle. Sift the flour and baking powder together and fold very lightly into the mixture, together with a little milk if necessary to give a soft dropping consistency. Put into 2 greased 18-cm (7-inch) sandwich tins and bake in the oven at 190°C (375°F) mark 5 for 25–30 minutes. Cool on a cake rack and when cold sandwich together with jam or alternatively with jam and whipped cream. Dust lightly with caster sugar or decorate as desired.

Coffee almond layer

Illustrated in colour on pages 200–201

5 large eggs
30 ml (2 tbsp) coffee essence
150 g (5 oz) caster sugar
125 g (4 oz) plain flour
25 g (1 oz) cornflour
225 g (8 oz) unsalted butter
30 ml (2 tbsp) dark rum
275 g (10 oz) icing sugar
125 g (4 oz) flaked almonds, toasted
instant coffee powder

Grease and line two 21·5-cm (8½-inch) sandwich tins. In a deep bowl over a pan of hot, not boiling water, whisk the eggs, essence and caster sugar until pale and really thick. Remove from the heat. Sift the flours together and then re-sift over the egg mixture. Using a metal spoon, fold in the flour using a figure of eight movement. Divide between the two tins. Bake in the oven at 190°C (375°F) mark 5 for 25–30 minutes. Leave in the tins for 5 minutes. Turn out on to a wire rack to cool.

Cream the butter, gradually beat in the rum and sifted icing sugar. Sandwich the coffee sponges with some of the butter cream and use the rest to completely mask the cake. Press almonds into the butter cream. Dredge with icing sugar. Cover the top with a piece of paper with a 7·5-cm

(3-inch) circle cut from the centre. Sprinkle instant coffee over the hole and carefully remove the paper. *Makes 12 portions*

Orange sandwich cake

3 egg whites and 2 yolks
100 g (4 oz) butter or block margarine
100 g (4 oz) caster sugar
175 g (6 oz) plain flour
5 ml (1 level tsp) baking powder
grated rind of 1 orange
a little milk
orange butter cream (see page 206)

Beat the egg whites stiffly. Cream the fat and sugar until very light. Beat in the egg yolks. Sift the flour and baking powder and mix in the orange rind. Add to the creamed ingredients alternately with the milk; the mixture should be of a dropping consistency. Lastly, fold in the stiffly beaten egg whites. Put into 2 greased and bottom-lined 18-cm (7-inch) sandwich tins and bake in the oven at 180°C (350°F) mark 4 for about 25 minutes. When cool, sandwich together with orange butter cream.

Caramel nut gâteau

3 eggs
90 ml (6 level tbsp) caster sugar
10 ml (2 level tsp) instant coffee
60 ml (4 level tbsp) self-raising flour
65 g (2½ oz) ground almonds
75 g (3 oz) browned flaked almonds

For the filling
175 g (6 oz) icing sugar
75 g (3 oz) butter or margarine
10 ml (2 level tsp) instant coffee
15 ml (1 tbsp) water

For the caramel and topping
175 g (6 oz) granulated sugar
60 ml (4 tbsp) water
whole almonds to decorate

Beat the eggs and sugar, with the coffee, as for a whisked sponge (see Swiss Roll on page 184). Fold in the sifted flour and ground almonds, put into 2 greased and bottom-lined 18-cm (7-inch) sandwich tins and bake in the oven at 190°C (375°F) mark 5 for 20 minutes. Turn out and allow to cool. Make the filling: blend the icing sugar and margarine and flavour with the coffee dissolved in the water. Sandwich the cakes together with half this mixture and spread most of the remainder round the sides of the cake (reserving a little for decoration); press the flaked almonds into the butter cream.

Make the caramel by dissolving the sugar in the water in a pan (without stirring), then boiling until golden. Pour on to

the top of the cake and mark into portions with a knife before the caramel sets completely. Pipe with butter cream and decorate with almonds.

Tutti frutti layer cake

Illustrated in colour on page 185

175 g (6 oz) butter or margarine
175 g (6 oz) caster sugar
3 eggs, beaten
175 g (6 oz) self raising flour
grated rind of 1 lemon
15 g (1½ oz) angelica
25 g (1 oz) glacé cherries
15 g (1½ oz) flaked almonds

For the filling
40 g (1½ oz) butter
75 g (3 oz) icing sugar

Grease and base-line two 20·5-cm (8-inch) straight-sided sandwich tins. Cream the butter or margarine, add the sugar and beat until light and fluffy. Beat in the eggs, a little at a time. Lightly beat in the flour together with the lemon rind. Divide the mixture equally between the tins and level the surfaces. Scissor-snip the angelica and the cherries into small pieces and scatter with the almonds over the surface of one cake mixture. Bake at 180°C (350°F) mark 4 for about 25 minutes or until spongy to touch. Turn out and cool on a wire rack. For the filling, cream the butter and gradually beat in the icing sugar and lemon juice.

Lemon gâteau

175 g (6 oz) self-raising flour
50 g (2 oz) cornflour
a pinch of salt
225 g (8 oz) butter or block margarine
225 g (8 oz) caster sugar
juice and finely grated rind of 1 lemon
2 eggs, lightly beaten
90 ml (6 tbsp) apricot jam
angelica and mimosa balls to decorate

For the frosting
2 egg whites
350 g (12 oz) caster sugar
a pinch of salt
30 ml (2 tbsp) water
30 ml (2 tbsp) lemon juice
finely grated rind of 1 lemon
a pinch of cream of tartar
yellow food colouring

Grease and flour three 20·5-cm (8-inch) sandwich tins. Sift the flour, cornflour and salt on to a plate. Cream the fat, sugar and lemon rind until light and fluffy and gradually add the eggs, beating well. Fold in the flour and lightly stir in the lemon juice.

Divide the mixture evenly between the tins and bake in the oven at 180°C (350°F) mark 4 for 30 minutes until golden brown and springy to the touch. When the cakes are quite cold, spread jam evenly over 2 and sandwich all 3 layers together.

To make the frosting, whisk all the ingredients (except the colouring) lightly together; place the bowl over hot water and whisk until the mixture thickens sufficiently to hold peaks. Add a few drops of colouring, to tint it pale lemon-yellow. Using a palette knife, spread frosting over top and sides of cake. Rough up the surface and decorate with angelica and mimosa balls.

Chestnut gâteau

3 eggs
75 g (3 oz) caster sugar
75 g (3 oz) plain flour
15 ml (1 tbsp) warm water
apricot jam
100 g (4 oz) chopped browned almonds
142-ml (5-fl oz) carton double cream
   and a little chestnut purée to decorate

Whisk the eggs and sugar until thick and creamy. Fold in the sifted flour with a metal spoon, then fold in the warm water. Pour the mixture into a greased and lined Swiss roll tin 20·5 × 30·5 cm (8 × 12 inches) and bake in the oven at 230°C (450°F) mark 8 for 7–9 minutes, until golden brown and firm to the touch. Turn out on to a cooling rack.

When cool, cut across into 3 and sandwich together again with thin layers of apricot jam, sprinkled with almonds. Coat the sides with jam and press on chopped nuts. Decorate the top with whipped cream and chestnut purée piped in alternate lines.

Swiss roll

3 eggs
100 g (4 oz) caster sugar
100 g (4 oz) plain flour
15 ml (1 tbsp) hot water
caster sugar to dredge
warmed jam

Grease and bottom-line a Swiss roll tin 23 × 30·5 cm (9 × 12 inches). Put the eggs and sugar into a large basin and stand this over a saucepan of hot water, then whisk very briskly until the mixture is light, thick and firm enough to retain the impression of the whisk for a few seconds. Remove the basin from the heat. Sift about one-third of the flour over the surface of the mixture and fold in very slightly, using a large metal spoon. Add the remaining flour in the same way and lightly stir in the hot water.

Pour the mixture into the prepared tin, allowing it to run over the whole surface. Bake in the oven at 230°C (450°F) mark 8 for 7–9 minutes, until golden brown, well-risen and firm.

Meanwhile, have ready a sheet of greaseproof paper liberally sprinkled with caster sugar: if desired, place it over a tea

towel lightly wrung out of hot water, to help make the sponge pliable. Turn the cake quickly out on to the paper, trim off the crusty edges with a sharp knife and spread the surface with warmed jam. Roll up with the aid of the paper, making the first turn firmly, so that the whole cake will roll evenly and have a good shape when finished; roll more lightly after this first turn. Dredge the cake with sugar and cool on a cake rack.

Devil's food cake

225 g (8 oz) plain flour
1·25 ml (¼ level tsp) salt
2·5 ml (½ level tsp) bicarbonate of soda
10 ml (2 level tsp) baking powder
75 g (3 oz) chocolate, grated
300 ml (½ pint) less 15 ml (1 tbsp) milk
150 g (5 oz) butter or margarine
275 g (10 oz) caster or soft brown sugar
3 eggs, beaten
5 ml (1 tsp) vanilla essence
chocolate butter cream (see page 206)
quick frosting (see method)
chocolate flakes or vermicelli to
   decorate

Grease and bottom-line two 23-cm (9-inch) sandwich cake tins. Sift the flour with the salt and bicarbonate of soda on to kitchen paper. Warm the chocolate in the milk until it has dissolved. Cream the fat in a basin and beat in the sugar gradually until the mixture is soft and creamy. Add the eggs a little at a time and beat thoroughly. Stir in the sieved dry ingredients alternately with the chocolate milk. Add the vanilla essence and bake in the prepared tins in the oven at 180°C (350°F) mark 4 for 30–35 minutes.

When the cakes are cooked, cool on a wire tray, sandwich together with chocolate butter cream (or whipped cream) and coat with quick frosting. Decorate with flaked chocolate or chocolate vermicelli.

Quick frosting Put into a bowl 2 egg whites, 325 g (12 oz) caster sugar, a pinch of salt, a large pinch of cream of tartar and 60 ml (4 tbsp) water and whisk lightly. Place the bowl over hot water and whisk until the mixture thickens sufficiently to hold 'peaks'. Use at once.

Genoese sponge

75 g (3 oz) butter
65 g (2½ oz) plain flour
15 ml (1 level tbsp) cornflour
3 large eggs
100 g (4 oz) caster sugar
filling and/or icing

First clarify the butter. Heat it gently until melted, then continue heating slowly without browning until all bubbling has ceased

Swiss roll

Tutti frutti layer cake
(see page 183).

– this indicates that the water has been driven off. Now remove it from the heat and let it stand for a few minutes for the salt and any sediment to settle, then gently pour off the fat. If much sediment is present, strain the butter through muslin.

Grease and line a shallow 20·5-cm (8-inch) square tin. Sift the flour and cornflour. Put the eggs and sugar in a large basin, stand this over a saucepan of hot water and whisk briskly until the mixture is light, thick and stiff enough to retain the impression of the whisk for a few seconds. Remove the basin from the heat. Sift about half of the flour over the surface of the mixture and fold in very lightly. Add the remaining flour in the same way, alternately with the cooled clarified butter – Genoese sponge must be mixed very lightly or the fat will sink to the bottom and cause a heavy cake. Pour the mixture into the prepared tin and bake in the oven at 190°C (375°F) mark 5 until golden brown and firm to the touch, the time depending on the depth of the cake – about 45 minutes. Turn out and cool on a wire tray. Use as required for layer cakes, iced cakes, etc.

Party cakes

Orange liqueur gâteau

175 g (6 oz) butter or block margarine
175 g (6 oz) caster sugar
3 eggs, beaten
175 g (6 oz) self-raising flour, sifted
30–45 ml (2–3 tbsp) Grand Marnier
grated rind of 1 orange
284-ml (10-fl oz) carton double cream, whipped
chopped walnuts
15–30 ml (1–2 tbsp) fresh orange juice
150 g (5 oz) icing sugar, sifted
thin slices of orange to decorate

Grease and line two 18-cm (7-inch) sandwich tins. Cream the fat and the caster sugar until pale, soft and fluffy. Gradually beat in the eggs, beating well after each addition. Fold in the flour and then divide the mixture evenly between the tins, levelling the top with a knife. Bake in the oven at 190°C (375°F) mark 5 for about 35 minutes, until golden and beginning to shrink from the sides of the tin. Turn out and cool on wire trays. When cool, sprinkle some liqueur over each half.

Add the orange rind to the cream and use about half of the mixture to sandwich the two cakes together. Spread a little round the sides and then roll the cake in the chopped walnuts. Add sufficient orange

juice to the icing sugar to make an icing thick enough to coat the back of a spoon. Spread this over the top of the cake. When set, pipe with whirls of cream and decorate with thin slices of orange.

If preferred, spread the sides of the cake with apricot jam instead of cream; the amount of cream can then be cut down slightly.

Meringue torte

Prepare 3 rounds of greased greaseproof paper 20·5–23 cm (8–9 inches) in diameter, and place on baking trays. Whisk 5 egg whites until stiff, add 150 g (5 oz) caster sugar and whisk the mixture until it is again stiff. Gently fold in another 150 g (5 oz) sugar and place the mixture in a forcing bag fitted with a plain nozzle. Cover one round of paper with lines of piped meringue, pipe a lattice of meringue over another paper and a double ring round the edge of the last paper round. Dredge each lightly with caster sugar and place in the oven at 150°C (300°F) mark 2 until dry and firm. Remove from the paper. Drain a can of peaches and slice thinly. Lightly whip 300 ml (½ pint) cream and add a little vanilla essence and sugar. Spread cream over the first meringue, place the ring on top and fill with fruit and cream. Spread cream on the ring and cover with the lattice. Decorate with peaches and glacé cherries.

Orange and pineapple cake

Illustrated in colour on pages 200–201

125–175 g (4–6 oz) glacé pineapple cubes
50 g (2 oz) ground almonds
75 g (3 oz) self-raising flour
75 g (3 oz) plain flour
1 small orange
175 g (6 oz) butter or block margarine
175 g (6 oz) caster sugar
3 eggs
apricot jam
50 g (2 oz) icing sugar

With a wet sharp knife, cut each cube of the 125 g (4 oz) pineapple into four slices. When using 175 g (6 oz) pineapple, finely chop the extra 50 g (2 oz). In a bowl, combine the almonds, flours, grated rind of the orange and the chopped pineapple, if used. Squeeze the juice from the orange. Cream together the butter and sugar. When light and fluffy beat in the eggs, one at a time. Fold in the dry ingredients alternately with 30 ml (2 tbsp) of the orange juice. Turn into a base-lined 20·5-cm (8-inch) 1·1-litre (2-pint) moule à manqué tin. Level the surface and

bake in the oven at 180°C (350°F) mark 4 for 45–55 minutes until well risen and spongy to the touch. Turn out on to a wire rack to cool with base uppermost. Brush the base of cake with apricot jam. Arrange slices of pineapple over the jam. Blend the icing sugar with just enough orange juice or water to give a thin coating consistency. Spoon over the pineapple and leave to set.

Rich chocolate nut cake

175 g (6 oz) butter or block margarine
175 g (6 oz) caster sugar
75 g (3 oz) chocolate, melted
150 g (5 oz) ground almonds
30 ml (2 tbsp) fresh white breadcrumbs
15 ml (1 tbsp) rum
50 g (2 oz) plain flour
4 eggs, separated
butter cream (see page 206)
nut cream (see method)
chocolate vermicelli to decorate

Cream the fat and sugar and add the chocolate, almonds, the crumbs soaked in the rum, the flour and egg yolks. Beat the whites to a stiff froth and add them to the mixture, beating well. Put into two 20·5-cm (8 inch) sandwich tins: bake in the oven at 170°C (325°F) mark 3 for about 45 minutes–1 hour. Cool on a rack, then sandwich with butter cream and top with nut cream. Decorate with vermicelli.

To make nut cream, cream 50 g (2 oz) butter and 50 g (2 oz) sugar, then add 100 g (4 oz) ground almonds and 15 ml (1 tbsp) cream. Beat thoroughly and use as required.

Meringue nests

Make a meringue mixture as given on page 186, but use 3 eggs and 175 g (6 oz) caster sugar. Pipe it into rings on oiled paper, building the rings up to form 'nests'. Bake as directed. When cool, fill with cream and fresh strawberries (or any other fresh fruit). Alternatively, fill with coffee butter cream (see page 206) mixed with chopped walnuts and decorate each nest with a halved walnut.

Berry-whip squares

125 g (4 oz) butter or block margarine
125 g (4 oz) caster sugar
2 eggs
175 g (6 oz) self-raising flour
milk if required
topping (see below)
fruit or chopped nuts to decorate

Cream the fat and sugar, then beat in the eggs one at a time. Stir in the flour; if the mixture is too stiff, a little milk may be

...dded. Put into a greased and lined Swiss ...oll tin and bake in the oven at 180°C (350°F) ...ark 4 for 20–25 minutes. Turn out and ...ool, then cut into 5-cm (2-inch) squares. ...ust before serving, top with Berry-whip (see ...elow) and add a few pieces of canned fruit ...r chopped nuts to decorate.

...erry-whip topping

...egg white
...pinch of salt
...75 g (6 oz) caster sugar
...25 g (12 oz) strawberries or raspberries

...ut all the ingredients into a basin and ...hisk or beat with an electric beater until ...e mixture will stand up in stiff peaks when ...ted. (If frozen fruit is used, thaw it, then ...rain before adding.)

...offee-chocolate slice

...lustrated in colour on pages 200–201

...0 ml (2 level tbsp) granulated sugar
...0 ml (4 tbsp) water
...5 g (3 oz) butter
...25 g (4 oz) icing sugar
...25 g (8 oz) full fat soft cheese
...glacé cherries, chopped
...5 g (1 oz) walnut halves, chopped
...0 ml (2 level tbsp) nibbed almonds,
...toasted
...5 ml (1 tbsp) coffee essence
...× 184-g (6½-oz) pkt Nice biscuits
...(small size)

...or the icing
...00 g (4 oz) caster sugar
...5 ml (3 level tbsp) cocoa powder
...0 ml (2 tbsp) water
...ml (1 tsp) coffee essence
...5 g (3 oz) butter

...n a pan, dissolve the sugar in the water. ...ring to the boil then cool. Meanwhile, ...ream the butter with the sifted icing sugar, ...dd the cheese and beat well. Add the ...herries and nuts to a third; beat the coffee ...ssence into the remainder.

...Dip 15 biscuits, one at a time, in the sugar ...yrup; arrange in 3 rows of 5 on kitchen foil. ...pread each row with the coffee-cheese. ...dd a second and third layer of biscuits and ...lling. Pile the cherry and nut cheese along ...e centre row only. Put your hands under ...e foil and bring up the outer rows to meet ...n the centre, forming a triangle. Secure ...ith foil and chill.

For the icing, blend the sugar, cocoa ...owder, water and coffee essence together ...n a pan and bring to the boil. Off the heat, ...dd the butter, cut in pieces; beat well. ...ool to a coating consistency. Unwrap the ...ake, place on a rack, coat with the icing. ...hill overnight.

Chocolate peppermint ring

1 vanilla pod
60 ml (4 tbsp) milk
225 g (8 oz) plain chocolate
100 g (4 oz) plain flour
50 g (2 oz) ground rice
5 ml (1 level tsp) baking powder
225 g (8 oz) butter or margarine
175 g (6 oz) caster sugar
4 eggs, separated

For the butter cream and topping
150 g (5 oz) butter or margarine
225 g (8 oz) icing sugar, sifted
15 ml (1 tbsp) crème de menthe
a little green food colouring
chocolate vermicelli

Grease and flour a ring mould 23 cm (9 inches) in diameter by 6·5 cm (2½ inches) deep.

Infuse the vanilla pod in the milk for 30 minutes, then remove it. Melt the chocolate in the milk, taking care not to overheat. Sift together the flour, ground rice and baking powder. Cream the fat and sugar until light and fluffy. Beat in the egg yolks one at a time and then the cooled but still soft chocolate mixture. Whisk the egg whites and lightly fold into the cake mixture. Turn into the prepared tin and bake in the oven at 180°C (350°F) mark 4 for about 1¼ hours, until well risen.

Make the butter cream in the usual way. Coat the cooled cake with butter cream and sprinkle with chocolate vermicelli. *Note* As an alternative to the ring mould, use a 20·5-cm (8-inch) round cake tin.

Chocolate and coffee gâteau

Illustrated in colour on page 209

6 eggs
175 g (6 oz) caster sugar
15 ml (1 tbsp) coffee essence
25 g (1 oz) cocoa powder
100 g (4 oz) plain flour
25 g (1 oz) cornflour
25 g (1 oz) ground almonds
75 g (3 oz) butter (preferably unsalted)
coffee butter icing (see page 206)
50 g (2 oz) shelled walnuts, chopped
chocolate cobwebs (see method)
    and sugar coffee beans to decorate

Grease and line two 24-cm (9½-inch) straight-sided sandwich tins. Whisk the eggs and sugar in a large bowl over a pan of hot water until really thick and the mixture retains the impression of the whisk for a moment. Whisk in the coffee essence. Remove from heat. Whisk until cold.

Sift together the cocoa, flour, cornflour and almonds. Using a metal spoon, carefully fold in half the resifted flour then fold in the butter, melted but not oily, poured

round the side, alternately with the remaining flour. Divide between the prepared tins and bake at 190°C (375°F) mark 5 for about 30 minutes. Turn out and cool on a wire rack.

To finish, sandwich with coffee butter icing. Spread the sides as well; coat with walnuts. Top with more coffee butter icing and decorate with piping, chocolate cobweb leaves and sugar coffee beans. Keep in a cool place until firm. *Serves 8–10*
To make the Chocolate Cobwebs Put 50 g (2 oz) plain chocolate cake covering into a basin that's standing in a pan of hot water; allow to dissolve and fill a paper forcing bag fitted with a No. 2 icing nozzle. On non-stick paper, trace in pencil an outline around a medium – 9·5-cm (3¾-inch) – boat shape cutter. Pipe chocolate around the outline and fill in with a wriggly, continuous trelliswork to 'link' the holes. Chill until set, peel away the paper. The cobwebs can be made a few days ahead but keep them in a tin in a cool place.

Simple fruit gâteau

Make up a Victoria Sandwich mixture as on page 183, but use 175 g (6 oz) each of fat, sugar and flour and 3 eggs. Spread it evenly in a greased and lined 20·5-cm (8-inch) tin. Bake in the oven at 190°C (375°F) mark 5 for about 45 minutes. When the cake is cool, spread the sides with 100 g (4 oz) butter cream (see page 206) and roll the sides in finely chopped nuts. Put the cake on a plate and place well-drained canned fruit over the top. Thicken 150 ml (¼ pint) of the fruit juice with 5 ml (1 level tsp) cornflour and when the mixture clears, pour it over the fruit and allow to set.

Peach mallow cake

225 g (8 oz) marshmallows
566-g (1 lb 4-oz) can peaches
150 ml (¼ pint) peach juice
150 ml (¼ pint) Madeira or sherry
284-ml (10-fl oz) carton double cream
boudoir biscuits (about 2 pkts)

Grease and line the base of a loaf tin 23 × 12·5 cm (9 × 5 inches). Cut the marshmallows in quarters. Strain the juice from the peaches, mix with the Madeira or sherry and place with the marshmallows in a pan. Heat gently, stirring until the marshmallows dissolve, then refrigerate until the mixture cools and thickens slightly. Whip three-quarters of the cream and stir into the mixture. Arrange a layer of biscuits on the bottom of the tin, cover with half the peaches, roughly chopped, and half the marshmallow mixture. Repeat these layers, finishing with one of biscuits. Refrigerate overnight, unmould, decorate as desired and serve with the remaining cream.

Strawberry cake

225 g (8 oz) sweet biscuits
100 g (4 oz) butter or block margarine
100 g (4 oz) caster sugar
2 eggs, separated
grated rind of 1 lemon
225–325 g (8–12 oz) strawberries
284-ml (10-fl oz) carton double cream

Line an 18-cm (7-inch) square cake tin with waxed paper. Crush the biscuits and arrange half of them in the tin. Cream the fat and sugar until very soft and fluffy, beat in the egg yolks and lemon rind and gradually fold in the stiffly whipped egg whites. Spread this mixture over the crumbs. Hull, wash and slice the strawberries (reserving a few whole ones for decoration) and place on top of the lemon mixture. Whip the cream lightly, pour over the strawberries and cover with the remaining crumbs. Refrigerate overnight. Unmould and decorate, or serve cut in squares, surrounded with the remaining strawberries.

Chocolate velvet refrigerator cake

24–26 soft sponge fingers
175 g (6 oz) caster sugar
30 ml (2 level tbsp) cornflour
400 ml (¾ pint) milk
284-ml (10-fl oz) carton double cream (unwhipped)
50 g (2 oz) plain chocolate
2 egg yolks
25 g (1 oz) butter or margarine
5 ml (1 level tsp) gelatine
toasted almonds to decorate

Line a cake or loaf tin measuring 18 × 12·5 × 6·5 cm (7 × 5 × 2 ½ inches) with a strip of greaseproof paper. Arrange some sponge fingers to cover the base and sides. Blend the sugar and cornflour in a saucepan, then gradually add the milk and half the cream. Break the chocolate up roughly, add to the milk and bring slowly to the boil, stirring all the time. Boil for 3 minutes, by which time the chocolate will have melted. Cool a little.

Beat the egg yolks, pour on half the chocolate mixture and return this to the rest of the chocolate in the pan; boil for 1 minute. Beat in the fat. Dissolve the gelatine in 10 ml (2 tsp) hot water and stir into the chocolate mixture; cool, stirring

188

occasionally. When the mixture is beginning to thicken, pour half over the sponge fingers. Cover with a second layer of sponge fingers and pour on the remaining mixture. Leave overnight in the refrigerator. Turn out. Whip the rest of the cream lightly, cover the top of the cake and strew with the almonds.

Lemon coconut sponge

1 pkt lemon meringue pie filling
grated rind of 2 lemons
284-ml (10-fl oz) carton double cream
100 g (4 oz) desiccated coconut
2 × 18-cm (7-inch) sponge cakes
chocolate vermicelli to decorate

Make up the lemon meringue pie filling according to the directions on the packet and allow to cool, then fold in the lemon rind, the cream and 50 g (2 oz) of the coconut. Sandwich the cakes together with part of the lemon mixture and completely coat with the remainder. Refrigerate overnight and serve sprinkled with the remaining coconut and a little chocolate vermicelli.

Cakes from other countries

Sachertorte (Austria)

225 g (8 oz) plain chocolate
100 g (4 oz) unsalted butter
175 g (6 oz) caster sugar
5 eggs, separated
75 g (3 oz) ground almonds
40 g (1 ½ oz) self-raising flour
jam, blanched almonds and whipped cream to decorate

For the icing
150 g (5 oz) plain chocolate
150 g (5 oz) butter

Melt the chocolate and when soft, cream with the butter, sugar and egg yolks; beat all together thoroughly until thick and creamy. Fold in the almonds and sifted flour, then the stiffly beaten egg whites. Put into a greased and lined 23-cm (9-inch) cake tin and bake in the oven at 200°C (400°F) mark 6 for about 45 minutes. When the cake is quite cold, cut it in half and fill with a layer of jam.

To make the icing, melt the chocolate and butter, mix well together and allow to become fairly firm, then spread over the top and round the sides of the cake. Decorate with blanched almonds and piped whipped cream.

Sour cream devil's food cake (USA)

225 g (8 oz) self-raising flour
2·5 ml (½ level tsp) salt
75 g (3 oz) butter or margarine
225 g (8 oz) caster sugar
1 egg
5 ml (1 level tsp) bicarbonate of soda
142-ml (5-fl oz) carton soured cream
75 g (3 oz) chocolate, melted
90 ml (6 tbsp) hot water
5 ml (1 tsp) vanilla essence
grated chocolate to decorate

For the frosting
75 g (3 oz) butter or margarine
275 g (10 oz) icing sugar, sifted
30 ml (2 tbsp) cream
15–30 ml (1–2 tbsp) rum

Sift together the flour and salt. Cream the fat thoroughly, add the sugar gradually and beat until light and fluffy. Add the well beaten egg and beat well. Dissolve the soda in the soured cream. Add the flour to the creamed mixture alternately with the soured cream, a little at a time; beat well after each addition. Combine the chocolate and hot water and add to the above mixture, then beat until smooth and add the vanilla essence. Put into 2 greased and lined 23-cm (9-inch) cake tins and bake in the oven at 180°C (350°F) mark 4 for about 30 minutes.

To make the frosting, cream the fat until very soft, then gradually add the sifted icing sugar. Work in the cream and as much rum as desired. Beat the mixture well until light and fluffy. Using some of the frosting, sandwich the two cakes together, then spread the remainder evenly over the top and sides. Press grated chocolate on to the sides, using a palette knife.

This produces a cake much lighter in colour than the usual Devil's food cake.

Florentines

rice paper
100 g (3 ½ oz) butter or margarine
110 g (4 oz) caster sugar
110 g (4 oz) mixed broken walnuts and almonds
25 g (1 oz) sultanas
25 g (1 oz) chopped peel
25 g (1 oz) chopped crystallised cherries
15 ml (1 tbsp) whipped cream
100 g (4 oz) plain block chocolate

Place the rice paper on baking trays. Melt the fat, add the sugar and dissolve, then boil together for 1 minute. Add all the other ingredients (except the chocolate) and mix. Drop the mixture in small, well shaped heaps on to the lined trays and bake in the oven at 180°C (350°F

Rich Christmas cake (see page 180).

mark 4 for about 10 minutes, until golden brown. Remove from the oven and shape using a palette knife. Cool, remove the rice paper, then spread the backs with melted chocolate and draw a fork across to mark lines.

Retes-strudel (Hungary)

7·5 ml (1½ tsp) cooking oil
1 small egg
150 ml (¼ pint) water
275 g (10 oz) plain flour (unsifted)
225 g (8 oz) butter, melted and cooled
filling (see recipes following)
icing sugar

Combine the oil, egg and water; beat until smooth, using a fork. Measure the flour into a large bowl, make a well in the centre, pour in the oil mixture and stir well to form a soft dough. Turn the dough out on to a lightly floured surface and knead until elastic. Lightly brush the ball of dough with melted butter, cover with a large bowl and let stand in a warm place for 30 minutes.

Meanwhile, cover a small table with a clean cloth. Rub just enough flour into the cloth to cover it very well, so that it will prevent the dough from sticking; brush off any excess. Place the dough in the centre of the cloth; using a floured rolling pin, roll the dough out into a square of about 40·5 cm (16 inches). Using the fingers, spread the entire surface with melted butter.

Stretch the dough out so that it is thin enough to see through. Using scissors, snip off the thick edges all round and let the dough dry for 15 minutes, or until crisp. Start heating the oven to 190°C (375°F) mark 5 and measure out the ingredients for the desired filling.

When the dough is crisp, sprinkle it lightly with melted butter; then proceed as in the filling recipe (see below). Turn in the overhanging sides of the dough over the filling all the way round, to make a very neat square. Roll up the dough, then, using a sharp knife, cut the roll in half crossways so as to make 2 strudels. Using a broad spatula, lift them carefully on to a greased baking sheet or Swiss roll tin, side by side. Brush with melted butter and bake for about 55–60 minutes, brushing often with melted butter. Bake until crisp and golden brown. Serve warm, thickly sprinkled with sifted icing sugar. If desired, the strudel may be accompanied by 142-ml (5-fl oz) carton soured cream mixed with 5 ml (1 level tsp) grated nutmeg, well chilled.

190

Apple strudel filling

100 g (4 oz) dried white breadcrumbs
75 g (3 oz) walnuts, finely chopped
175 g (6 oz) granulated sugar
1·25 ml (¼ level tsp) grated nutmeg
1·25 ml (¼ level tsp) ground cinnamon
900 g (2 lb) apples, sliced, stewed and
    well drained
15 ml (1 level tbsp) grated lemon rind
50 g (2 oz) raisins

Combine the crumbs, walnuts, sugar, nutmeg and cinnamon and use to sprinkle over the half of the strudel dough nearest you. Toss the apples with the lemon rind and raisins and spoon over the crumb mixture.

Proceed as already described.

Cream cheese strudel filling

4 × 75-g (3-oz) packets cream cheese
3 egg yolks
75 g (3 oz) sugar
15 ml (1 level tbsp) grated lemon rind
50 g (2 oz) raisins, stoned
75 g (3 oz) dried white breadcrumbs

Combine the cheese, egg yolks and sugar and beat until smooth and blended. Stir in the lemon rind and the raisins. Now sprinkle the breadcrumbs evenly over the half of the strudel nearest you and spread the cheese filling over the crumbs. Proceed with the rolling of the strudel as already directed.

Mont Blanc aux marrons

3 eggs
100 g (4 oz) caster sugar
75 g (3 oz) butter or margarine
75 g (3 oz) plain flour
apricot purée
browned almonds
chestnut purée (see method)

Beat the eggs and sugar together over hot water until thick and frothy. Melt the fat and allow it to cool, then add the sifted flour and melted fat alternately to the whisked mixture and mix well. Pour into a greased and lined Swiss roll tin and bake in the oven at 200°C (400°F) mark 6 for 20–25 minutes; cool on a rack. Cut the cake into 5-cm (2-inch) rounds, using a scone cutter, and coat the sides and top of the pieces with apricot purée. Roll the sides of the cakes in chopped browned almonds and pipe the chestnut purée into whirls on top of each cake.

Chestnut purée Cook, peel and sieve 225 g (8 oz) chestnuts. Dissolve 75 g (3 oz) granulated sugar in 60 ml (4 tbsp) water and bring to the boil. Simmer gently until a hard ball forms when a drop of the syrup

is put into cold water. Mix with the chestnuts and flavour to taste with a little vanilla essence. Alternatively, use canned chestnut purée (sweetened as above with sugar syrup) or canned chestnut spread.

Polish cheesecake

For the pastry
100 g (4 oz) plain flour
50 g (2 oz) butter or block margarine
25 g (1 oz) caster sugar
1 egg yolk
a little water to mix

For the filling
225 g (8 oz) cream cheese
6 egg yolks
50 g (2 oz) butter, melted
225 g (8 oz) caster sugar
5 ml (1 tsp) vanilla essence
glacé icing (see page 206)

Make pastry as for shortcrust (see page 143) and line a 20·5-cm (8-inch) square baking tin. Now make the filling. Tie the cream cheese in muslin and squeeze out the moisture. When it is dry, crumble it into a mixing bowl. Add the egg yolks, melted butter, sugar and essence and beat thoroughly until quite smooth. Place in the pastry case and bake in the oven at 180°C (350°F) mark 4 for about 1 hour, until the cheese mixture is firmly set.

When the cake is cold, cut into squares and coat each with a little glacé icing.

Doboz torte (Austria)

4 eggs
175 g (6 oz) caster sugar
150 g (5 oz) plain flour
100–175 g (4–6 oz) caster sugar for
    caramel
3 egg whites
175 g (6 oz) icing sugar
225 g (8 oz) butter, softened
100 g (4 oz) chocolate, melted
crushed biscuits or chopped nuts to
    decorate

Grease and flour 6–7 baking sheets. Whisk the eggs, add the sugar gradually and whisk over hot water until very thick and fluffy. Fold in the sifted flour. Spread the mixture out on the baking sheets into large rounds – about 21·5 cm (8½ inches) across – and bake in the oven at 190°C (375°F) mark 5 for 7–10 minutes, until golden brown. Loosen from the tins and trim each cake to a neat shape with a sharp knife – a saucepan lid may be used as a guide. Lift on to wire cake racks to cool.

Take the round with the best surface

and lay it on an oiled rack or tray. Now prepare the caramel: put the sugar in a small, heavy saucepan, place over gentle heat and allow the sugar to dissolve without stirring; boil steadily to a rich brown, then pour it over the biscuit round, spreading it with an oiled knife. Mark into sections and trim around the edge.

Make a chocolate butter cream as follows: whip the egg whites and icing sugar over hot water until very thick. Cream the butter thoroughly and beat the meringue into it by degrees; add the melted chocolate. Sandwich the remaining biscuit rounds together in one stack with the butter cream and put the caramel-covered one on top. Spread the sides of the torte with butter cream and press either crushed biscuit crumbs or chopped nuts round the sides. Pipe the remaining butter cream round the top edge to make a decorative border.

Novelty cakes

Merry-go-round cake

Bake a Victoria sandwich cake mixture in a pair of 20·5-cm (8-inch) sandwich tins and when cool sandwich together with vanilla-flavoured butter cream (see page 206). Coat with white or pastel-coloured glacé-icing (see page 206).

Choose a striped or brightly-coloured drinking straw for the centre pole, and cut some narrow coloured ribbons into equal lengths; fix one end of each into one of the open ends of the drinking straw, holding them in place with a coloured hat pin. Fix the other ends of the ribbons to the outer edge of the cake with attractive candle-holders (we used tiny wooden dolls) and then carefully twist the centre straw to make the ribbons taut. Decorate the side of the cake with more ribbons.

Balloon cake

Coat a 20·5-cm (8-inch) cake with coloured glacé icing (see page 206). Before it has quite set, fix some flat round coloured sweets in bunches round the cake to represent bunches of balloons. Using a fine writing nozzle and a little chocolate butter cream (see page 206), pipe in the balloon strings. If the child's name is short, this can also be written in sweets on top of the cake. Place candles round the top edge.

Hedgehog cakes

Bake 18 small cakes in small patty tins, using the Victoria sandwich mixture (see page 183). When cool, coat with chocolate butter cream (see page 206), then rough it up slightly with the flat edge of a knife. Brown some slivered almonds under the grill and stick them into the cakes to represent the hedgehog's prickles. Use cloves for the eyes and almond halves for the feet.

Alphabet bricks

Make an oblong Victoria sandwich and when it is cool, cut it into 4-cm (1½-inch) cubes. Coat thoroughly with sieved apricot jam, then cover the bricks with a lemon butter cream of fairly soft consistency. Re-shape the bricks and smooth the edges with a knife, then draw a fork over the butter cream to mark all the sides. Make up a little chocolate butter cream and pipe large letters on each side of the bricks.

Sailing boats

Make an oblong Victoria sandwich. When it is cool use a boat-shaped cutter to cut out foundation shapes for the boats. Make up some vanilla butter cream (see page 206) and coat the boats with it, leaving a little on one side for decoration. Smooth the edges with a warm knife and reshape the sides. Add some chocolate colouring to the remaining butter cream and pipe port-holes on the sides of the boats. Cut sails from rice paper and fix into the butter cream.

Picture cake

Coat the top of a slab cake with glacé icing (either coloured or plain – see page 206). Using a plain writing pipe and stiff glacé icing of a contrasting colour, mark it into large squares. In each square outline some simple children's toys, eg, balloons, a beach ball, a bicycle, a train, a building brick, etc.

Jumbo cake

Fill a sandwich cake with a well-flavoured lemon filling and coat it with yellow glacé icing (see page 206). Trace a picture of an elephant on to a piece of cardboard and cut out the shape, leaving a stencil. Place this on the cake and fill the cut-out area with a chocolate butter cream (see page 206); smooth with a knife and leave to set before lifting off the stencil. Using

lemon icing, pipe the eyes, ears and other finishing touches. A saddle and decorative trappings may also be added in icing.

Mushroom cake

3 eggs
150 g (5 oz) caster sugar
75 g (3 oz) plain flour
1 egg white
225 g (8 oz) icing sugar
175 g (6 oz) butter or margarine
15–30 ml (1–2 level tbsp) cocoa
a little almond paste
desiccated coconut
green food colouring

Make a sponge (see Swiss roll, page 184) from the whole eggs, 75 g (3 oz) caster sugar and the flour and bake in 2 greased and lined 20·5-cm (8-inch) sandwich tins in the oven at 180°C (350°F) mark 4 for about 30 minutes. Make up a meringue mixture with the egg white and 50 g (2 oz) caster sugar (see page 186) and form into meringues of varying sizes. Make a butter cream with the icing sugar, fat and cocoa (see page 206).

When the cakes are cold, sandwich them together with some butter cream; spread most of the remainder over the sides and top, then furrow with a fork or icing card. Make stalks of almond paste and stick them to the base of the meringues with a little butter cream. Using a small writing nozzle, pipe underneath with butter cream to represent gills. Tint the coconut with a little green colouring dissolved in water. Place the cake on a board, surround with the coconut and decorate with the meringue mushrooms, placing some on the board and some on the cake itself.

'Number' birthday cake

175 g (6 oz) butter or margarine
175 g (6 oz) caster sugar
3 eggs
175 g (6 oz) self-raising flour
900 g (2 lb) icing sugar for glacé icing (see page 206)
yellow food colouring
100 g (4 oz) ground almonds
100 g (4 oz) icing sugar for almond paste
beaten egg
gravy browning
100 g (4 oz) icing sugar and 75 g (3 oz) butter for butter cream
cocoa powder

Obtain a cake tin representing the correct numeral and grease it very well; seal the bottom with foil. Make up a Victoria sandwich mixture from the 175 g (6 oz) fat, 175 g (6 oz) caster sugar, eggs and flour (see page 183), place in the tin and bake in the oven at 180°C (350°F) mark 4 for 1 hour. Cool on a rack. Place on a board and coat with 2 layers of pale yellow glacé icing.

Bind the ground almonds and 100 g (4 oz) icing sugar with beaten egg and knead in gravy browning until the paste is pale brown. Roll out on a board dusted with icing sugar, then cut out 4 mice of different sizes and a grandfather clock. (This will be easier to do if you first draw paper patterns.)

Make up a plain butter cream with the remaining sugar and butter (see page 206) and use a little to stick 3 mice in graded sizes round the sides of the cake and a mouse and the clock on top. Colour a little butter cream with cocoa and pipe a face and pendulum on the clock. With the remaining butter cream, tinted yellow, pipe a border round the base of the cake.

This design may need to be slightly adapted to suit the particular numeral.

Small cakes

Chocolate cakes

75 g (3 oz) butter or block margarine
75 g (3 oz) caster sugar
1 egg
150 g (5 oz) plain flour
25 g (1 oz) cocoa
5 ml (1 level tsp) baking powder
milk to mix
white glacé icing (see page 206)
chocolate shavings

Cream the fat and sugar and beat in the egg thoroughly. Sift the dry ingredients and add them, with milk to give a soft dropping consistency. Put into paper baking cases placed in patty tins and bake in the oven at 200°C (400°F) mark 6 for 20–25 minutes. When the cakes are cold, put a little icing on each and sprinkle with shavings of chocolate. *Makes about 10*

Rock buns

325 g (12 oz) self-raising flour
a pinch of salt
1·25 ml (¼ level tsp) grated nutmeg
1·25 ml (¼ level tsp) mixed spice
175 g (6 oz) butter or margarine
175 g (6 oz) caster sugar
75 g (3 oz) currants
40 g (1½ oz) chopped peel
1 egg
milk to mix
192

Sift the flour, salt and spices. Rub in the fat and add the sugar, fruit and peel. Mix with beaten egg and enough milk to bind. Using a teaspoon and a fork, place in rocky heaps on a greased baking sheet and bake in the oven at 200°C (400°F) mark 6 for 15–20 minutes. *Makes about 12*

Lemon or orange buns

225 g (8 oz) self-raising flour
a pinch of salt
100 g (4 oz) butter or margarine
100 g (4 oz) caster sugar
grated rind of 2 lemons
1 egg
milk to mix

Sift the flour and salt. Rub in the fat and add the sugar and lemon rind. Mix with lightly beaten egg and enough milk to give a soft dropping consistency. Put into greased patty tins or small paper cases, and bake for 15–20 minutes in the oven at 200°C (400°F) mark 6, until well-risen and firm to the touch.

To make orange buns, substitute the grated rind of 2 oranges for the lemon rind. *Makes about 10*

Queen cakes

100 g (4 oz) butter or block margarine
100 g (4 oz) caster sugar
2 eggs
100 g (4 oz) plain flour
2·5 (½ level tsp) baking powder
a little milk if necessary
50 g (2 oz) sultanas

Thoroughly cream the fat and sugar and add the eggs a little at a time, beating well. Fold the sifted flour and baking powder into the mixture, together with a little milk if necessary to give a soft dropping consistency. Add the fruit and place the mixture in spoonfuls in greased patty tins. Bake in the oven at 190°C (375°F) mark 5 for 15–20 minutes, until firm to the touch and golden brown in colour. *Makes about 10*

Frosted cup cakes

100 g (4 oz) butter or block margarine
75 g (3 oz) caster sugar
1 egg
175 g (6 oz) self-raising flour
milk to mix
vanilla essence or a little grated orange
or lemon rind
fluffy frosting (see page 206)
glacé cherries or nuts to decorate

Cream the fat and sugar and beat in the egg thoroughly. Add the sifted flour and

enough cold milk to give a soft dropping consistency; flavour with a few drops of essence or the rind. Put into paper cases standing in patty tins, three-quarters filling the cases, and bake in the oven at 190°C (375°F) mark 5 for about 15 minutes. When cool, remove from the paper cases, dip the top of each cake into the frosting and decorate with a glacé cherry or a piece of nut. *Makes 12–14*

Walnut and sultana rockies

Illustrated in colour opposite

225 g (8 oz) plain flour
a pinch of salt
2·5 ml (½ level tsp) mixed spice
50 g (2 oz) butter
50 g (2 oz) lard
100 g (4 oz) Demerara sugar
50 g (2 oz) walnuts, chopped
50 g (2 oz) sultanas
25 g (1 oz) chopped mixed peel
1 egg, beaten
a little milk if necessary

Sift the flour, salt and spice into a basin. Rub in the fats until the mixture resembles fine crumbs. Add the sugar, walnuts, sultanas and peel. Using a fork, bind them together with the egg and a little milk, if necessary, to give a very stiff dough that just holds together. Continue using a fork to make small rough heaps on greased baking sheets. Bake in the oven at 200°C (400°F) mark 6 for 15–20 minutes. Leave to cool for a short time before transferring to a rack to cool completely. *Makes about 12*

Fluted caraway buns

Illustrated in colour opposite

75 g (3 oz) butter or block margarine
50 g (2 oz) caster sugar
2 eggs
30 ml (2 level tbsp) lemon cheese or
curd
125 g (4 oz) self-raising flour
a pinch of salt
2·5 ml (½ level tsp) caraway seeds
glacé icing and glacé cherries to
decorate

Grease 9 fluted patty tins about 7 cm (2¾ inch) wide and 3 cm (1¼ inch) deep. Cream together the fat and caster sugar and beat in the eggs. Alternately fold in the lemon cheese and flour sifted with the salt. Lastly fold in the caraway seeds. Divide between the patty tins and bake in the oven at 170°C (325°F) mark 3 for about 25 minutes. Turn out and cool on a wire rack bottom sides up. Decorate each

Walnut and sultana rockies (see above), Mincemeat splits (see page 194), Ginger whirls (see page 195), Fluted caraway buns (see above).

with a little blob of stiff glacé icing and half a glacé cherry. Or serve the other way up, simply dusted with icing sugar. *Makes about 9*

Coconut tarts

100 g (4 oz) plain flour
a pinch of salt
50 g (2 oz) butter or block margarine
5 ml (1 level tsp) caster sugar
1 egg yolk
raspberry jam

For the filling
50 g (2 oz) butter or margarine
50 g (2 oz) caster sugar
1 egg, beaten
50 g (2 oz) desiccated coconut
25 g (1 oz) self-raising flour

Sift the flour and salt into a basin, rub in the fat lightly and stir in the sugar. Mix in the egg yolk and sufficient cold water to mix to a firm dough. Turn on to a floured board and knead lightly. Roll out this pastry and cut out rounds to fit small patty tins. Line the tins with the pastry and put a little jam into each.

For the filling, cream the fat and sugar together until light and fluffy. Beat in half the egg a little at a time. Fold in the coconut and flour, then add the remaining egg to give a soft dropping consistency. Place in spoonfuls in the lined patty tins and bake in the oven at 190°C (375°F) mark 5 for 20 minutes.

To make a Coconut Flan, use the same amounts of pastry and filling, place in an 18-cm (7-inch) flan ring and bake for about 30 minutes.

Macaroons

2 egg whites
100 g (4 oz) ground almonds
25 g (1 oz) ground rice (good measure)
225 g (8 oz) caster sugar
5 ml (1 tsp) orange-flower water
rice paper

To decorate
split almonds and glacé cherries
a little egg white

Beat the egg whites lightly with a fork. Stir in the almonds, ground rice, sugar and flavouring and mix thoroughly. Cover a greased baking sheet with rice paper and place the mixture on it in small heaps (or pipe with a forcing bag and large plain pipe), leaving room for spreading. Place an almond or piece of cherry on each biscuit, brush with egg white and bake in the oven at 170°C (325°F) mark 3 for about 20–25 minutes, until pale golden

brown. It is important to cook macaroons slowly, so that they colour evenly and acquire a good texture.

Sponge fingers

2 eggs
50 g (2 oz) caster sugar
50 g (2 oz) plain flour
caster sugar to dredge

Whisk the eggs and sugar together until thick and creamy, then fold in the flour. Grease and flour some sponge finger tins. Put the mixture into a forcing bag with a plain 1-cm (½-inch) nozzle and pipe it into the tins, sprinkle the top of each finger with a little sugar and bake in the oven at 200°C (400°F) mark 6 for 7–10 minutes.

When cold, the top of each finger may be iced with glacé icing (see page 206). Alternatively, sandwich them together in pairs with butter icing (see page 206), and dip the ends into melted chocolate.

Almond fingers

100 g (4 oz) plain flour
a pinch of salt
50 g (2 oz) butter or block margarine
5 ml (1 level tsp) caster sugar
1 egg yolk and cold water to mix

For the filling
1 egg white
100 g (4 oz) icing sugar
100 g (4 oz) almonds, blanched and chopped

Sift the flour and salt into a basin and

rub in the fat lightly. Mix in the sugar and add the egg yolk and sufficient cold water to mix to a firm dough. Turn on to a floured board and knead lightly. Use this pastry to line a tin measuring 25·5 × 12·5 cm (10 × 5 inches). Make the filling by whisking the egg white until stiff, then folding in the sifted icing sugar. Spread this mixture over the pastry base and sprinkle the chopped nuts evenly on top. Bake in the oven at 180°C (350°F) mark 4 for about 30 minutes. When cold, cut into fingers.

Mincemeat splits

Illustrated in colour on page 193

50 g (2 oz) butter
50 g (2 oz) white vegetable fat
75 g (3 oz) soft light brown sugar
1 large egg
45 ml (3 level tbsp) mincemeat
200 g (7 oz) plain flour
2·5 ml (½ level tsp) bicarbonate soda

For the mincemeat filling
50 g (2 oz) butter
75 g (3 oz) icing sugar
5 ml (1 tsp) lemon juice
45 ml (3 level tbsp) mincemeat

Grease 2–3 baking sheets. Cream the butter and the white fat until soft. Add the sugar and continue beating until light and fluffy. Beat in the egg and mincemeat. Sift the flour and bicarbonate of soda and gradually work into the creamed mixture. Leave in the refrigerator until firm. Using the hands, shape the dough into about

24 walnut-sized balls. Place well apart on baking sheets. Bake in the oven at 180°C (350°F) mark 4 for about 12 minutes until well risen and puffy. Lift on to a wire rack to cool. Sandwich in pairs with mincemeat filling.

For the filling, cream the butter with the sifted icing sugar, lemon juice and mincemeat until of a spreading consistency. *Makes 12–15*

Ginger and date cakes

175 g (6 oz) self-raising flour
a pinch of salt
75 g (3 oz) butter or block margarine
75 g (3 oz) caster sugar
50–75 g (2–3 oz) dates, chopped
25 g (1 oz) crystallised ginger
1 egg, beaten
milk to mix

Sift the flour and salt into a bowl and rub in the fat lightly. Stir in the sugar, dates and ginger, then mix in the egg and sufficient milk to form a stiff dropping consistency. Place in spoonfuls in greased patty tins and bake in the oven at 190°C (375°F) mark 5 for 15 minutes.

Ginger whirls

Illustrated in colour on page 193

225 g (8 oz) butter or block margarine
75 g (3 oz) icing sugar
200 g (7 oz) plain flour
25 g (1 oz) cornflour
10 ml (2 level tsp) ground ginger
ginger marmalade
stem ginger (optional)

Cream the fat, sift in the icing sugar and cream together until really light and fluffy. Sift in the flour, cornflour and ground ginger and beat into the mixture. Fill a fabric piping bag, fitted with a large star vegetable nozzle, with the ginger mixture and pipe a whirl into 12 paper cases. Place in a sheet of patty tins. Bake in the oven at 190°C (375°F) mark 5 for 15–20 minutes. Cool on a wire rack. Fill the centre of each with a little ginger marmalade and top each with a slice of stem ginger. *Makes 12*

Butterfly cakes

175 g (6 oz) self-raising flour
100 g (4 oz) butter or margarine
100 g (4 oz) caster sugar
2 eggs, beaten

For the filling
100 g (4 oz) butter or block margarine
175 g (6 oz) icing sugar
almond essence

Madeleines

Sift the flour. Cream the fat and sugar until light and fluffy, then beat in the eggs a little at a time. Fold in the flour to give a stiff dropping consistency. Place in spoonfuls in patty cases and bake in the oven at 190°C (375°F) mark 5 for 15–20 minutes.

For the filling, cream the fat until soft, beat in the sifted sugar gradually and add a few drops of essence. When the cakes are quite cold, cut a slice from the top of each and pipe or fork in a generous amount of filling. Cut each cake slice in half and replace at an angle in the cream, to represent butterflies' wings.

Madeleines

100 g (4 oz) butter or margarine
100 g (4 oz) caster sugar
2 eggs, beaten
100 g (4 oz) self-raising flour
red jam
desiccated coconut
glacé cherries and angelica to decorate

Beat the fat and sugar together until light and fluffy and gradually add the eggs, beating well. Fold in the flour. Grease 12 dariole moulds and three-parts fill with mixture. Bake in the oven at 180°C (350°F) mark 4 for about 20 minutes, or until firm and browned. Trim off the bottoms, so that the cakes stand firmly and are of even height. When the cakes are nearly cold, brush

with melted jam, holding them on a skewer, then roll them in coconut. On top of each madeleine place a cherry dipped in a little jam, then add 2 small leaves cut from angelica.

Doughnuts

225 g (8 oz) strong plain flour
a pinch of salt
50 g (2 oz) butter or margarine
15 g (½ oz) fresh yeast or 7·5 ml (1½ level tsp) dried yeast and 5 ml (1 level tsp) caster sugar
45–60 ml (3–4 tbsp) tepid milk
1 egg, beaten
jam
fat for deep frying
cinnamon (optional)
caster sugar

Warm the sifted flour and salt in a basin and rub in the fat. Dissolve the yeast in the milk and egg. Pour into the centre of the flour and mix to a soft dough. Beat well with a wooden spoon or the hand, knead on a floured board for 5 minutes. Leave to rise until the dough becomes twice the original size, then knead lightly. Divide into small pieces, shape each into a ball, flatten a little and place about 1·25 ml (¼ tsp) jam in the centre of each. Gather the edges together over the jam, forming balls. Place on a greased and floured tin and leave in a warm place for a few minutes to prove. Heat the fat

195

until smoking faintly but not too hot, then fry the doughnuts until golden brown and cooked through (about 5 minutes). Drain, turn out on to a paper and dredge with caster sugar – which can be mixed, if desired, with a little ground cinnamon. Serve fresh.

Quick cakes

If guests arrive at a time when you have no cakes to offer them, use a plain cake mix and add a variation of your own for quick results. A cake mix that's intended to give one large cake will equally well make 24 small cakes if the mixture is mixed to a slightly stiffer consistency, spooned into patty cases and baked in the oven at 190°C (375°F) mark 5 for 15–20 minutes.

Fruit buns Add 50 g (2 oz) mixed dried fruit.

Chocolate buns Add 50 g (2 oz) chopped up plain chocolate to the dry ingredients.

Coffee buns Add 15 ml (1 tbsp) instant coffee powder.

Cherry buns Add 100 g (4 oz) glacé cherries cut in half, washed and rolled in flour.

Orange buns Add the finely grated rind of 1 orange to the dry ingredients; use the juice to replace some of the water.

Cream horns

Illustrated in colour opposite

Roll out flaky or puff pastry to 0.3–0.5 cm (⅛–¼ inch) thick, into an oblong about 30.5 cm (12 inches) long and cut into 1-cm (½-inch) strips. Moisten one edge of each strip and roll round a cream horn tin, starting at the pointed end of the tin and overlapping the pastry very slightly. Bake in the oven at 230°C (450°F) mark 8 until crisp – 10–15 minutes. Slip off the tins and when cold, fill with a spoonful of jam or fruit, top with whipped cream and dredge with icing sugar.

Macaroon pastries

100 g (4 oz) rich shortcrust pastry
jam
100 g (4 oz) ground almonds
25 g (1 oz) plain flour
150 g (5 oz) caster sugar
2 egg whites

Line boat-shaped tins with the rich shortcrust pastry and add a little jam. Mix the almonds, flour and sugar; whisk the eggs very lightly and fold in the dry ingredients. Place a little mixture in each case and put strips of pastry across some. Bake in the oven at 190°C (375°F) mark 5 for 20

minutes, until the pastry and the macaroon mixture are golden.

Almond sandwich pastries

Roll out rich shortcrust pastry very thinly and cut into small rounds. Sandwich the biscuits in pairs with the above almond mixture and bake in the oven at 190°C (375°F) mark 5 for 15 minutes. When cold, coat the tops with white glacé icing (see page 206) and pipe stars in coffee butter cream (see page 206) round the sides. Decorate the edges with browned chopped almonds.

Meringues

2 egg whites
50 g (2 oz) granulated sugar
50 g (2 oz) caster sugar
142-ml (5-fl oz) carton double cream, whipped

Rub a trace of oil over the surface of a really clean baking sheet, or cover it with non-stick paper. Whisk the egg whites very stiffly, add granulated sugar and whisk again until the mixture retains its former stiffness. Lastly, fold in the caster sugar very lightly, using a metal spoon. Pipe through a forcing bag (or put in spoonfuls) on to the baking sheet and dry off in the oven at 130°C (250°F) mark ½ for several hours, until the meringues are firm and crisp but still white. When cool, sandwich together with cream.

Pink meringues can be made by adding 1–2 drops of red food colouring to the mixture with the sugar.

Coffee essence can be added when the sugar is folded in; allow 5 ml (1 tsp) to each egg white.

Chocolate meringues can be made by adding cocoa with the caster sugar – allow 5 ml (1 level tsp) per egg white.

The cream filling can be varied by adding finely chopped nuts, coffee essence, melted chocolate or liqueur.

Petits fours

Bake a shallow square or oblong of Victoria or Genoese sponge (see Layer and Sponge Cakes, pages 183 and 184). This can then be used as the base for many small fancy cakes – for example:
1 Cut it into fancy shapes, glaze completely with sieved apricot jam and allow to dry. Stand the cakes on a wire cooling tray and pour over them glacé icing (see page 206) which has been coloured or flavoured with a fruit essence, coffee, lemon or orange juice or melted choco-

late. When the icing is set, decorate with cut glacé cherry and angelica, chopped nuts, mimosa balls, crystallised flowers, etc or piped butter cream.
2 Cut cake into small squares and coat with sieved apricot jam. Roll the sides in chopped walnuts and pipe stars of coffee butter cream (see page 206) round the top edges. Heat 50 g (2 oz) sugar in a saucepan until melted and golden brown, allow to cool slightly, then pour a little in the centre of each cake.
3 Coat some small rounds of cake with butter cream (see page 206) and roll the sides in chopped walnuts, or coat with raspberry jam and roll the sides in desiccated coconut. Colour some almond paste pale green or pink, roll it out and cut into small petal shapes, allowing 5 for each cake. Arrange the petals on top of each cake and mark the centre of the flower with a mimosa ball.
4 Cut a long strip of cake, brush with apricot jam and place 3 small rolls of coloured almond paste along the top. Brush these with jam, then coat completely with glacé icing and decorate if desired with chopped nuts, angelica or glacé cherries. When set, cut up and serve in paper cases.

Chamonix

2-egg meringue mixture (see page 186)
226-g (8-oz) can chestnut purée
caster sugar
vanilla essence
142-ml (5-fl oz) carton cream, whipped
grated chocolate to decorate

Make a mixture as for meringues (see page 186); pipe in small rounds on to a baking sheet and dry out in the oven at 130°C (250°F) mark ½. Using a plain small pipe, pipe on to each meringue a swirl of chestnut purée (sweetened to taste and flavoured with vanilla essence). Fill the centres with a small blob of whipped cream and dust with grated chocolate.

Petites feuilletées

puff or flaky pastry
egg white
sieved apricot jam
chopped nuts and whipped cream to decorate

Roll the pastry thinly and cut into 7.5-cm (3-inch) squares. Fold the corners to the centre and join them with a tiny cut-out shape of pastry. Brush with white of egg and bake in the oven at 230°C (450°F) mark 8 for 10–15 minutes. When cool brush with jam, sprinkle with nuts and pipe with cream.

Palmiers (see page 198) and Cream horns (see above).

Chocolate cases

75 g (6 oz) plain block chocolate
100 g (4 oz) sponge cake
15 ml (1 tbsp) raspberry jam
sherry to taste
142-ml (5-fl oz) carton double cream
maraschino cherries

Line 8 small paper cases with melted chocolate and leave to set overnight. Peel off the paper carefully. Mix together the crumbled cake, jam and sherry and fill the cases with this mixture. Top each with whipped cream and a cherry.

Petits gâteaux millefeuilles

225 g (8 oz) puff pastry or 212-g (7½-oz)
**   pkt frozen puff pastry, thawed**
beaten egg
apricot or raspberry jam
142-ml (5-fl oz) carton double cream
chopped nuts to decorate

Prepare the pastry and roll it out to 0·3 cm (⅛ inch) thick. Prick and cut into small rounds, using a 5-cm (2-inch) plain cutter. Brush the top with beaten egg and bake in the oven at 230°C (450°F) mark 8 for about 8 minutes, until crisp and golden brown. Cool, then sandwich 3 layers of pastry together with sieved jam and whipped cream. Brush the top with jam, add a cream rosette and sprinkle with nuts.

Almond flower pastries

Roll some puff or flaky pastry out to about 0·5 cm (¼ inch) in thickness and cut out, using a small plain, round cutter. Put the rounds on to a baking tin, brush the tops over with a little beaten egg and bake in the oven at 230°C (450°F) mark 8 for 10–15 minutes. When the pastries are quite cold, put a little blackcurrant jelly on top of each and arrange some whole or halved blanched almonds round the top to resemble flower petals.

Palmiers

Illustrated in colour on page 197

Roll some puff pastry out evenly, until it is 0·5 cm (¼ inch) thick and about 51 cm (20 inches) long, then sprinkle it thoroughly with caster sugar. Fold the ends over to the centre until they meet and press with the rolling pin. Sprinkle thoroughly with sugar and fold the sides to the centre again. Press and sprinkle with sugar. Place the two folded portions together and press; then, with a sharp knife, cut into 0·5-cm (¼-inch) slices. Place the cut edge down on a baking sheet, allowing room

to spread, sprinkle with caster sugar and bake in the oven at 230°C (450°F) mark 8 until golden brown. Cool on a rack and just before serving spread sweetened whipped cream on half of the slices, sandwich with the remaining ones and dredge with icing sugar. (If liked, use jam with the cream.)

Coconut pyramids

Whisk 2 egg whites stiffly and fold in 150 g (5 oz) sugar and 150 g (5 oz) desiccated coconut. Pile in small pyramids on a greased tin covered with rice paper, press into shape and bake in the oven at 140°C (275°F) mark 1 until pale fawn – for about 45 minutes–1 hour. If desired, tint pink or green before baking.

Langues de chat

50 g (2 oz) butter or margarine
50 g (2 oz) sugar
1 egg
50 g (2 oz) self-raising flour
caster sugar to dredge
chocolate glacé icing to decorate (see
page 206)

Cream the fat and sugar and beat in the egg. Work in the flour to make a mixture of a consistency suitable for piping. Put in a forcing bag fitted with a plain 0·5-cm (¼-inch) piping nozzle and force on to a greased tin in fingers about 6·5–7·5 cm (2½–3 inches) long, spaced widely apart. Dredge with caster sugar and bake in the oven at 220°C (425°F) mark 7 for about

5 minutes. When the fingers are cold, sandwich them together in pairs with chocolate icing, and dip the ends of each in some more of the icing.

Eclairs

Illustrated in colour on page 209

40 g (1½ oz) butter or margarine
150 ml (¼ pint) water
65 g (2½ oz) plain flour
2 eggs
coffee glacé icing (see page 206)

Place the fat and water in a pan and bring to the boil. Remove the pan from the heat, stir in the flour, then beat until the paste forms a ball in the middle of the pan. Leave to cool very slightly whilst beating the eggs. Add these gradually to the mixture, beating lightly after each addition; use sufficient egg to give a mixture of piping consistency which will just hold its shape.

The paste is now ready for shaping. Put it into a forcing bag with a plain round pipe of 1-cm (½-inch) diameter and force in finger lengths 9–10 cm (3½–4 inches) long on to a greased baking sheet, keeping the lengths very even. Bake in the oven at 200°C (400°F) mark 6 for about 35 minutes, until well risen, crisp and of a golden brown colour. Remove from the tin, slit down the sides with a sharp-pointed knife to allow the steam to escape and leave on a cake rack to cool. When the éclairs are cold, fill with piped whipped cream and ice the tops with a little coffee glacé icing (see page 206).

Cream puffs Pipe the paste in small balls on to a baking sheet and bake as for éclairs until risen and golden. Split and cool on a rack. When cold, fill with whipped cream, glaze the tops with sieved apricot jam and sprinkle with chopped walnuts.

Chocolate truffles

100 g (4 oz) stale cake or cake trimmings
100 g (4 oz) caster sugar
100 g (4 oz) ground almonds
apricot jam
rum
chocolate glacé icing (see page 206) or covering chocolate
chocolate vermicelli to decorate

Crumble the cake finely and add the caster sugar, ground almonds and enough hot sieved apricot jam to bind. Add rum (or flavouring essence) to taste. Shape the mixture into 12–18 small balls and leave to become firm. Dip each ball into the glacé icing or covering chocolate and roll in chocolate vermicelli. When dry, put into small paper cases.

Nut fruit clusters

50 g (2 oz) chocolate, grated
a small knob of butter or margarine
25 g (1 oz) nuts, chopped
25 g (1 oz) seeded raisins, chopped
cornflakes

Melt the grated chocolate and then add the fat, nuts and dried fruit and sufficient cornflakes to make into a mixture which will bind together. Put in small rough clusters on to waxed paper and leave in a cool place to harden. Serve in little paper cases.

As a variation, replace the raisins by chopped glacé cherries or chopped crystallised ginger.

Scones and quick breads

A pre-heated baking sheet aids the rise of scones. Place the baking sheet in the oven when you start preparing the mixture. Lightly grease the sheet before placing the scones on it (this is not necessary if you are using a non-stick surface).

Plain oven scones

225 g (8 oz) self-raising flour
1·25 ml (¼ level tsp) salt
25–50 g (1–2 oz) butter or margarine
milk to mix – about 150 ml (¼ pint)

Sift the flour and salt into a basin and rub in the fat. Make a well in the centre and stir in enough milk to make a light, fairly soft dough – just firm enough to handle. Turn on to a floured board, knead very lightly if necessary to remove any cracks, then roll out to 2·5 cm (1 inch) thick. Cut in rounds with a sharp cutter dipped in flour, or shape into triangles with a sharp knife. Place on a floured pre-heated baking sheet, glaze if liked with beaten egg or milk, and bake in the oven at 230°C (450°F) mark 8 for 7–10 minutes, until well risen and nicely browned. Cool the scones on a wire cake rack.

Sour milk may be used in making these scones.

Fruit scones

Follow the above recipe but add 50 g (2 oz) currants, sultanas or raisins to the dry ingredients; chopped dates may be used if preferred.

Oatcakes

175 g (6 oz) medium oatmeal
50 g (2 oz) plain flour
1·25 ml (¼ level tsp) bicarbonate of soda
2·5 ml (½ level tsp) salt
40 g (1½ oz) butter or margarine, melted
boiling water to mix

Mix the oatmeal, flour, bicarbonate of soda and salt in a basin. Add the softened fat, with sufficient water to give a soft binding consistency. Knead lightly and roll out very thinly on a board sprinkled with a little oatmeal or flour. Cut into about a dozen rounds or triangles, place on a greased baking tray and bake in the oven at 200°C (400°F) mark 6 for about 15 minutes, or until the edges curl up and the oatcakes are crisp. Cool and serve with butter.

Griddle scones

If you do not possess a 'griddle' or 'girdle', use a thick-bottomed frying pan or the solid hot-plate of an electric cooker. To prepare a cast iron griddle, heat it well, rub with salt and kitchen paper, remove salt and reheat it slowly and thoroughly for 15 minutes. Before cooking the scones, lightly grease the griddle with a little lard or cooking oil. A griddle with a non-stick surface is ideal and requires no special treatment.

Make the mixture as for Plain Oven Scones, adding 50–75 g (2–3 oz) currants if desired. Roll the dough out to 0·5 cm (¼ inch) thick, cut out, and place on a moderately hot greased griddle or heavy-based frying pan. When the scones are brown, turn them and cook on the other side – about 5 minutes altogether.

Although these scones do not rise as much as ordinary scones, they taste just as good and are a useful alternative that save lighting the oven or to make when only a ring is available.

Drop scones

225 g (8 oz) plain flour
5 ml (1 level tsp) bicarbonate of soda
10 ml (2 level tsp) cream of tartar
60 ml (4 tbsp) caster sugar
2 eggs
300 ml (½ pint) milk

Sift the dry ingredients and add the sugar. Whisk the eggs and stir into the dry ingredients, with enough milk to make a batter the consistency of thick cream. Do this as quickly and lightly as possible. If a thin pancake is wanted, add rather more milk. Have ready a griddle, hot and lightly greased all over. Put the mixture in spoonfuls on the griddle; for round pancakes, drop from the point of the spoon, for oval, from the side. Keep the griddle at a steady heat, and when the bubbles rise to the surface of the pancakes and burst, turn the cakes over, using a knife, and cook until golden brown on the other side – 4–6 minutes in all. Put the pancakes on a cloth, cover with another and cool on a rack; this keeps in the steam and the pancakes do not become dry. Serve with butter or with whipped cream and jam.

These drop scones are also known as Scotch pancakes. Any that are left over are particularly good fried with bacon.

Baking powder bread

450 g (1 lb) plain flour
20 ml (4 level tsp) baking powder
5 ml (1 level tsp) salt
milk or water to mix (about 300 ml (½ pint))

Sift the flour, baking powder and salt into a basin, make a well in the centre and stir in enough liquid to make a soft, spongy dough. Turn on to a floured board, knead very lightly, and form into 2 flat loaves. Cut three marks on each with a knife. Put on a floured baking sheet and bake in the oven at 220°C (425°F) mark 7 for about 45 minutes, or until well risen, nicely browned on top and firm underneath.

This is a close textured 'sconey' bread which is useful if ordinary bread runs out.

Overleaf:
Light fruit cake (see page 179), Coffee-chocolate slice (see page 187), Coffee almond layer (see page 183), Moist almond butter tart (see page 179), Orange and pineapple cake (see page 186), Date ripple loaf (see page 178).

Plain and party biscuits

Vanilla biscuits

175 g (6 oz) plain flour
a pinch of salt
75 g (3 oz) butter or margarine
75 g (3 oz) caster sugar
1 egg
a few drops of vanilla essence
milk to mix

Sift the flour and salt. Cream the fat and sugar and when light and fluffy, beat in the egg. Add the essence, stir in the flour and mix to a stiff paste with milk. Roll the dough out to 0·3 cm (⅛ inch) thick on a lightly floured board, prick and then, using fancy cutters, shape into biscuits and put on a greased baking tin. Bake in the oven at 180°C (350°F) mark 4 for 10–15 minutes, until golden. *Makes about 24 biscuits*

Cherry rings

Add 40 g (1½ oz) chopped glacé cherries to the above mixture, and keep 15 g (½ oz) for decoration. Roll out the dough as above, then, using a round fluted cutter, cut it into rounds. Remove the centres with a small cutter, halve the cut-out pieces and decorate the rings with these; bake as above. *Makes about 30 biscuits*

Sultana pinwheels

Cut some Vanilla Biscuit dough into 5-cm (2-inch) diamonds. Fold over one point of each diamond, then put three diamonds together, damping the joins to make them hold, and press a few sultanas into the centre. Bake as for Vanilla Biscuits. *Makes 12 to 14 biscuits*

Chocolate cream sandwiches

Follow the Vanilla Biscuit recipe, but substitute 25 g (1 oz) cocoa for 25 g (1 oz) of the flour. Roll the dough out, prick, cut into fingers about 4 × 7·5 cm (1½ × 3 inches) and put on a greased baking sheet. Bake as above for 10–12 minutes. When cool, sandwich together with vanilla butter cream (see page 206). *Makes 12 biscuits*

Chocolate walnuts

Make some chocolate dough as directed in the above recipe and break off pieces the size of a walnut. Roll into balls, put on a greased baking tray, press half a walnut on each and bake as above for 15–20 minutes. *Makes about 30 biscuits*

Ginger biscuits

100 g (4 oz) butter or lard
60 ml (4 tbsp) golden syrup
100 g (4 oz) caster sugar
275 g (10 oz) plain flour
10–15 ml (2–3 level tsp) ground ginger
5 ml (1 level tsp) bicarbonate of soda
white glacé icing, preserved ginger and blanched almonds to decorate

Warm the fat, syrup and sugar slightly and beat to a cream. Add the flour, ginger and bicarbonate of soda and mix to a stiff dough. Roll out thinly and cut into rounds, place on a greased tray and bake in the oven at 190°C (375°F) mark 5 for 15–20 minutes. Allow the biscuits to cool slightly before lifting them off the tin. When they are cold, decorate some of the biscuits with glacé icing and triangles of preserved ginger and others with split almonds. *Makes 30 biscuits*

Shortbread

175 g (6 oz) plain flour
50 g (2 oz) caster sugar
100 g (4 oz) butter or margarine

Sift the flour and sugar, work in the fat and continue kneading until the mixture binds together. Divide into two, shape into rounds and smooth the top lightly with a rolling pin. Crimp the edges with the finger and thumb, mark each round into 8 sections with a knife and prick the surface, then place on a greased baking sheet. Bake in the oven at 150°C (300°F) mark 2 for 40–60 minutes.

If you have a shortbread mould, flour it well, press the dough in, invert on to the baking tin and bake.

Shortbread fingers

Roll the shortbread dough out on a board into an oblong about 7·5 cm (3 inches) wide and 1 cm (½ inch) thick. Score across with a knife or prick with a fork, then cut into about 30 fingers. Put on a greased tin and bake in the oven at 150°C (300°F) mark 2 for 20–30 minutes, until lightly browned.

Cinnamon bars

Illustrated in colour on page 205

100 g (4 oz) butter or margarine
75 g (3 oz) caster sugar
½ egg
150 g (5 oz) plain flour
a pinch of salt
10 ml (2 level tsp) ground cinnamon
chopped nuts to decorate

Cream the fat and sugar together until white and fluffy. Beat in the egg, reserving a little of the white for glazing the biscuits. Sift the dry ingredients and gradually add to the creamed mixture. Press the dough into an oblong tin about 20·5 × 15 cm (8 × 6 inches); brush the surface with egg white and sprinkle with chopped nuts. Bake in the oven at 170°C (325°F) mark 3 for 1 hour. Cut into slices and allow to cool in the tin, then place them on a wire tray and allow to become quite cold before storing. *Makes about 12 biscuits*

Cinnamon twists

Illustrated in colour on page 205

100 g (4 oz) butter or margarine
100 g (4 oz) caster sugar
2 egg whites
5 ml (1 level tsp) ground cinnamon
100 g (4 oz) plain flour

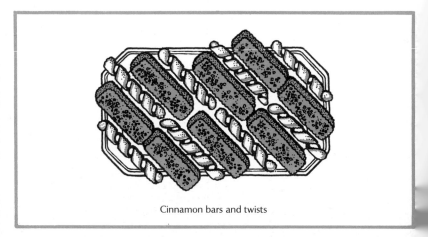

Cinnamon bars and twists

beat the fat and sugar together until light, then beat in the egg whites a little at a time, to form a smooth, light batter. Add the cinnamon and finally fold in the sifted flour. Using a 0·5-cm (¼-inch) piping tube, pipe the mixture into strips about 18 cm (7 inches) long on to a greased baking sheet, keeping them well apart, as they spread a good deal. Bake in the oven at 200°C (400°F) mark 6 for 7–10 minutes. (The edges of these biscuits are very thin and rapidly turn golden brown while the centre part still remains white.) As soon as the biscuits are removed from the oven, twist them into curly shapes and place on a rack. *Makes about 40 biscuits*

Gingernuts

Illustrated in colour on page 205

100 g (4 oz) self raising flour
2·5 ml (½ level tsp) bicarbonate of soda
5–10 ml (1–2 level tsp) ground ginger
5 ml (1 level tsp) ground cinnamon
  (optional)
10 ml (2 level tsp) caster sugar
50 g (2 oz) butter or block margarine
75 g (3 oz) golden syrup

Grease two baking sheets. Sift together the flour, bicarbonate of soda, ginger, cinnamon and sugar. Melt the fat, and stir in the syrup. Stir these into the dry ingredients and mix well. Roll the dough into small balls, place well apart on the greased baking sheets and flatten slightly. Bake in the oven at 190°C (375°F) mark 5, for about 15 minutes. The gingernuts will have the traditional cracked tops. Cool for a few minutes before lifting carefully from the baking sheet. Finish cooling on a wire rack and then store in an airtight tin.

If liked, these biscuits may be iced with lemon-flavoured glacé icing (see page 206). *Makes about 24 biscuits*

Brandy snaps

50 g (2 oz) butter or margarine
50 g (2 oz) caster sugar
30 ml (2 tbsp) golden syrup
50 g (2 oz) plain flour
1·25 ml (¼ level tsp) ground ginger
5 ml (1 tsp) brandy or rum essence
1·25 ml (¼ level tsp) grated lemon rind

Melt the fat, sugar and syrup in a pan. Remove from the heat, add the other ingredients and stir until well mixed. Drop the mixture in teaspoonfuls on to a baking sheet lined with non-stick paper, 5 cm (2 inches) apart, and bake in the oven at 180°C (350°F) mark 4 for 7–10 minutes, until just golden brown. While they are baking, grease 2–3 wooden spoon handles,

and get a wire cooling rack ready. Stand the tray on top of the cooker, so that biscuits cool without becoming too hard. Using a palette knife, remove the biscuits from the tray and roll them round the spoon handles. When they are quite cold, slip off carefully. If the last biscuits are too hard to get off the tray, place them over gentle heat for a minute. The secret of making good brandy snaps is to keep them warm enough to handle. When the rolled biscuits are cold, pipe or fill them with whipped cream. *Makes about 18 biscuits*

Brandy cornets

Illustrated in colour on page 209

Prepare and cook as for Brandy snaps. Meanwhile, grease some metal cream horn tins. Remove the biscuits from the oven and as they begin to firm, roll around the tins. When they are set, twist the tins gently to remove. (Brandy cornets will store for up to a week in an airtight tin.)

Chocolate logs

100 g (4 oz) plain flour
a pinch of salt
75 g (3 oz) butter or margarine
25 g (1 oz) caster sugar
50 g (2 oz) chocolate powder
2·5 ml (½ tsp) vanilla essence
milk to mix
50 g (2 oz) chocolate butter cream
  (see page 206)
icing sugar

Sift the flour and salt and rub in the fat with the finger-tips. Add the sugar, chocolate powder and essence, bind together with a little milk and put the dough on a lightly floured board. Shape into a long roll 2·5 cm (1 inch) in diameter, then cut into 5-cm (2-inch) lengths. Bake on a greased baking sheet in the oven at 190°C (375°F) mark 5 for 20–30 minutes. When cold, cover with the butter cream, mark with a fork to look like logs and finally dust with icing sugar. *Makes about 12 biscuits*

Lemon fingers

Illustrated in colour on page 205

100 g (4 oz) butter or margarine
100 g (4 oz) caster sugar
1 egg
grated rind of ½ lemon
225 g (8 oz) plain flour
lemon butter cream (see page 206)
caster or icing sugar to dredge

Cream the fat and sugar together and beat

in the egg and lemon rind; then gradually add the flour. Pipe the mixture in finger lengths on to greased baking sheets, using a large star nozzle. Bake in the oven at 190°C (375°F) mark 5 for 15–20 minutes, or until golden brown, and cool on a wire tray. Sandwich together in pairs with butter cream and dredge with either caster or icing sugar or dip the ends in melted chocolate. *Makes 12 biscuits*

Marshmallow creams

175 g (6 oz) plain flour
a pinch of salt
75 g (3 oz) butter or margarine
75 g (3 oz) caster sugar
1 egg, separated
milk to mix
15 ml (1 tbsp) golden syrup
colouring and flavouring
jam
walnut halves to decorate

Sift the flour and salt. Then cream the fat and sugar until light and fluffy, beat in the egg yolk, add the dry ingredients and stir in enough milk to give a soft dough. Turn out on to a floured board, roll out thinly and cut into 4-cm (1½-inch) rounds with a scone cutter. Place on a greased baking sheet, prick, and bake in the oven at 180°C (350°F) mark 4 for 10–15 minutes. Allow to cool and meanwhile make mock marshmallow as follows: whisk up the egg white and syrup over hot water until thick, fluffy and quite stiff; colour and flavour if desired (eg, with 1·25–2·5 ml (¼–½ tsp) coffee essence). Sandwich the biscuits together with jam and coat the tops with marshmallow, roughing it up if desired. Decorate, using halved walnuts on the biscuits topped with coffee-flavoured marshmallow. *Makes about 12 biscuits*

Meringue tops

50 g (2 oz) butter or margarine
100 g (4 oz) caster sugar
a few drops of vanilla essence
1 egg, separated
75 g (3 oz) plain flour
25 g (1 oz) chocolate powder
a pinch of salt
butter cream or apricot jam

Cream the fat and 50 g (2 oz) sugar with essence until quite soft. Whisk the egg yolk and lightly beat it into the creamed mixture. Sift the flour, chocolate powder and salt, add and stir in until mixture binds together; knead on a lightly floured board and roll out to 0·3 cm (⅛ inch) thick. Cut with a small fancy cutter, put on a greased baking sheet and bake in the oven at 200°C (400°F) mark 6 for 5–7 minutes. Whisk the egg white and 25 g (1 oz) sugar until very stiff, then fold in the remaining sugar. Put the meringue mixture into a forcing bag fitted with a star pipe and pipe in rosettes on to an oiled baking sheet. Bake in the oven at 150°C (300°F) mark 2 for 40–60 minutes, or until firm but not coloured. When both biscuits and meringues are cold, join a meringue to each biscuit with a little butter cream or apricot jam. *Makes about 24 biscuits*

Chocolate cookies

100 g (4 oz) self-raising flour
25 g (1 oz) sweetened chocolate powder
a pinch of salt
100 g (4 oz) butter or margarine
50 g (2 oz) caster sugar

For the filling
25 g (1 oz) sweetened chocolate powder
45 ml (3 tbsp) black coffee
50 g (2 oz) butter or margarine

Sift the flour, chocolate powder and salt on to a plate. Cream the fat and sugar and stir in the flour mixture. Form into balls the size of a walnut and place well apart on a greased baking sheet; flatten with a wet fork. Bake in the oven at 180°C (350°F) mark 4 for 15 minutes. Allow to cool before lifting on to a cooling rack.

Mix the chocolate powder and coffee for the filling in a small saucepan and heat gently until they form a thick cream. Cool slightly and beat in the fat. Sandwich the biscuits together with this cream and dust with icing sugar. *Makes about 9 cookies*

Chocolate whirls

Illustrated in colour opposite

100 g (4 oz) butter or margarine
100 g (4 oz) caster sugar
1 egg yolk
90 g (3 ½ oz) self-raising flour
100 g (4 oz) custard powder
15 g (½ oz) cocoa
milk to mix
melted chocolate or chocolate glacé icing (see page 206)
lemon glacé icing (see page 206) or desiccated coconut to decorate

Cream the fat and sugar and beat in the egg yolk. Mix the dry ingredients, with enough milk to give a fairly stiff dough, then knead lightly on a floured board and roll out. Cut out 20–24 rounds, removing the centres with a cutter if liked. Place the rings on a greased tin. Prick, then bake in the oven at 200°C (400°F) mark 6 for

about 15 minutes. When the biscuits are cold, coat with melted chocolate or chocolate icing, swirling it with a fork, and decorate as liked.

Melting moments

100 g (4 oz) butter or margarine
75 g (3 oz) caster sugar
½ egg
vanilla essence
150 g (5 oz) self-raising flour
crushed cornflakes

Cream the fat and sugar and beat in the egg and a few drops of essence. Work in the flour and mix to a stiff dough. Wet the hands, divide the mixture into small portions and roll into balls. Roll these in cornflakes, put on a greased baking sheet and bake in the oven at 190°C (375°F) mark 5 for 15–20 minutes. *Makes about 24 biscuits*

Mincemeat cookies

15 ml (1 heaped tbsp) mincemeat
30 ml (2 tbsp) water
325 g (12 oz) plain flour
salt
10 ml (2 level tsp) baking powder
200 g (7 oz) butter or margarine
200 g (7 oz) soft brown sugar
1 egg

Cook the mincemeat in the water until the latter has boiled away and the mincemeat is nearly dry. Sift the flour, salt and baking powder together. Cream the fat and sugar and beat in the egg, then add the dry ingredients and the cooled mincemeat. Form into sausage-shaped rolls, wrap in waxed paper and put in the refrigerator for 8 hours or overnight. When firm, roll out to 0·3 cm (⅛ inch) in thickness, cut into shapes and bake in the oven at 200°C (400°F) mark 6 for 8 minutes.

Chocolate pinwheels

Illustrated in colour opposite

175 g (6 oz) plain flour
5 ml (1 level tsp) baking powder
salt
90 g (3 ½ oz) butter or margarine
90 g (3 ½ oz) sugar
1 egg yolk
5 ml (1 tsp) vanilla essence
25 g (1 oz) chocolate

Sift the dry ingredients. Cream the fat and sugar together and beat in the egg yolk and essence, then stir in the flour. Melt the chocolate and add to one half of the dough, keeping the other half plain.

Put both into the refrigerator to chill and harden for about 3 hours; if it is too hard when you remove it, knead it a little with your hand. Roll each half into an oblong 0·3 cm (⅛ inch) thick and as nearly as possible the same size. Put one on top of the other and roll up like a Swiss roll. Wrap in waxed paper and put in the refrigerator to harden for about 12 hours; then, using a sharp knife, cut into 0·3-cm (⅛-inch) slices and bake in the oven at 200°C (400°F) mark 6 for 5–10 minutes; cool on a rack.

Marbled cookies

After making pinwheels, knead the left over pieces lightly together, roll into a sausage shape, wrap in waxed paper and put in the refrigerator to harden. Slice 0·3 cm (⅛ inch) thick and bake for 5–8 minutes in the oven at 200°C (400°F) mark 6. Sprinkle with caster sugar.

Orange cookies

275 g (10 oz) self-raising flour
salt
150 g (5 oz) butter or margarine
175 g (6 oz) caster sugar
1 egg
5 ml (1 tsp) grated orange rind

Sift the four and salt together. Cream the fat and sugar and beat in the egg and the orange rind; then fold in the flour. Either roll the dough into a sausage shape and wrap in waxed paper or put into a small loaf tin that has been lined with waxed paper and chill in the refrigerator for several hours, until firm; turn out and cut into wafer-thin slices with a sharp knife. Bake in the oven at 200°C (400°F) mark 6 for 8–10 minutes.

This recipe can be varied by the addition of grated lemon rind and chopped glacé cherries or desiccated coconut, or other flavourings.

Walnut cookies

125 g (4 ½ oz) plain flour
2·5 ml (½ level tsp) baking powder
a pinch of salt
25 g (1 oz) butter or margarine
25 g (1 oz) lard
90 g (3 ½ oz) brown sugar
½ egg
5 ml (1 tsp) vanilla essence
50–75 g (2–3 oz) walnuts, chopped

Sift the flour, baking powder and salt together. Cream the fats and sugar until fluffy and add the egg and essence, mixing well. Then stir in the dry ingredients

204

Gingernuts (see page 203), Cinnamon bars (see page 202), Chocolate pinwheels (see above),
Lemon fingers (see page 203), Chocolate whirls (see above), Cinnamon twists (see page 202)

and nuts. Shape into a roll, wrap and chill. The next day, slice thinly and bake in the oven at 200°C (400°F) mark 6 for 10–12 minutes.

Icings and frostings

Butter cream or icing

75 g (3 oz) butter or margarine
175 g (6 oz) icing sugar, sifted
vanilla essence
15–30 ml (1–2 tbsp) milk or warm water

Cream the fat until soft and gradually beat in the sugar, adding a few drops of essence and the milk or water.

This amount will coat the sides of an 18-cm (7-inch) cake, or give a topping and a filling. If you wish both to coat the sides and give a topping and filling, increase the amounts of butter and sugar to 100 g (4 oz) and 225 g (8 oz) respectively.

Orange or lemon butter cream Omit the vanilla essence and add a little finely grated orange or lemon rind and a little of the juice, beating well to avoid curdling.

Walnut butter cream Add 30 ml (2 tbsp) finely chopped walnuts; mix well.

Almond butter cream Add 30 ml (2 tbsp) very finely chopped toasted almonds; mix well.

Coffee butter cream Omit the vanilla essence and flavour with 10 ml (2 level tsp) instant coffee powder or 15 ml (1 tbsp) coffee essence.

Chocolate butter cream Flavour either by adding 25–40 g (1–1½ oz) melted chocolate or by adding 15 ml (1 level tbsp) cocoa dissolved in a little hot water (cool before adding).

Mocha butter cream Dissolve 5 ml (1 level tsp) cocoa and 10 ml (2 level tsp) instant coffee powder in a little warm water; cool before adding to the mixture.

Glacé icing

Put 100 g (4 oz) sifted icing sugar and (if liked) a few drops of any flavouring essence in a basin and gradually add 15–30 ml (1–2 tbsp) warm water. The icing should be thick enough to coat the back of a spoon. If necessary, add more water or sugar to adjust the consistency. Add a few drops of colouring if required and use at once.

For icing of a finer texture, put the sugar, water and flavouring into a small pan and heat, stirring, until the mixture is warm – don't make it too hot. The icing should

coat the back of a wooden spoon and look glossy.

This amount is sufficient to cover the top of an 18-cm (7-inch) cake.

Orange icing Substitute 15–30 ml (1–2 tbsp) strained orange juice for the water in the above recipe.

Lemon icing Substitute 15 ml (1 tbsp) strained lemon juice for the water.

Chocolate icing Dissolve 10 ml (2 level tsp) cocoa in a little hot water and replace same amount of plain water.

Coffee icing Flavour with either 5 ml (1 tsp) coffee essence or 10 ml (2 level tsp) instant coffee powder, dissolved in a little water.

Mocha icing Flavour with 5 ml (1 level tsp) cocoa and 10 ml (2 level tsp) instant coffee powder, dissolved in a little water.

Liqueur icing Replace 10–15 ml (2–3 tsp) of the water by liqueur.

American frosting

225 g (8 oz) caster sugar
60 ml (4 tbsp) water
1 egg white

Note To make this properly, it is necessary to use a sugar-boiling thermometer. If you do not possess one, you can make Seven-minute frosting (see below).

Gently heat the sugar in the water, stirring until dissolved. Then, without stirring, heat to 120°C (240°F). Beat the egg white stiffly. Remove the sugar syrup from the heat and when the bubbles subside, pour it on to the egg white; beat the mixture continuously. When it thickens and is almost cold, pour it quickly over the cake.

Makes sufficient frosting for an 18-cm (7-inch) cake.

Orange frosting Add a few drops of orange essence and a little orange colouring to the mixture while it is being beaten and before it thickens.

Lemon frosting Add a little lemon juice while beating.

Caramel frosting Substitute Demerara sugar for the white sugar; follow the same method as above.

Coffee frosting Add 5 ml (1 tsp) coffee essence while beating.

Chocolate frosting

150 g (5 oz) icing sugar, sifted
1 egg
2·5 ml (½ tsp) vanilla essence
25 g (1 oz) plain chocolate, melted
25 g (1 oz) butter or margarine

Beat all the ingredients together over ho water.

Fluffy frosting

200 g (7 oz) granulated sugar
60 ml (4 tbsp) water
a pinch of cream of tartar
2 egg whites, beaten
a few drops of vanilla essence
food colouring, if required

Put the sugar, water and cream of tarta into a pan and heat slowly until the suga dissolves, then cook without stirring unt the temperature reaches 120°C (240°F Pour this syrup on to the egg whites, beat ing all the time. Add the essence an colouring (if used) and beat until the icin is cool and thick enough to spread.

Seven-minute frosting

1 egg white
175 g (6 oz) caster sugar
a pinch of salt
30 ml (2 tbsp) water
a pinch of cream of tartar

Put all the ingredients into a bowl an whisk lightly. Place the bowl over ho water and continue whisking until the mix ture thickens sufficiently to hold 'peaks'.

The same variations can be made a for true American Frosting, except for the Chocolate and Fluffy versions.

Satin frosting

75 g (3 oz) soft butter or margarine
325 g (12 oz) icing sugar, sifted
45 ml (3 tbsp) cream
vanilla essence

Cream the fat and gradually beat in the sugar and cream; when smooth, flavou with vanilla essence.

Maple satin frosting Replace the crea by maple syrup.

Lemon satin frosting Omit the vanill essence and add the grated rind of ½ a lemon.

Fudge topping

225 g (8 oz) icing sugar
30 ml (2 level tbsp) cocoa powder
45 ml (3 tbsp) milk
75 g (3 oz) caster sugar
75 g (3 oz) vegetable fat, whipped

Sift the icing sugar and cocoa into a bow Heat the rest of the ingredients gently i a small pan until the sugar and fat ar dissolved. Bring to the boil, pour into th icing sugar, stir until mixed, then beat unt fluffy. Spread over the cake, using a knife rough up the surface and leave to set.

Sea foam frosting

90 ml (6 tbsp) golden syrup
3 egg whites
a pinch of salt
7·5 ml (1½ tsp) vanilla essence

Heat the syrup in a pan until it is boiling. Beat the egg whites until stiff, add the salt and slowly pour the syrup over the whites. Beat until the frosting is fluffy and stands up in peaks; add the vanilla essence and use at once.

Almond paste

450 g (1 lb) icing sugar
450 g (1 lb) ground almonds
2 eggs, lightly beaten
5 ml (1 tsp) vanilla essence
lemon juice

Sift the sugar into a bowl, then add the almonds, eggs, essence and enough lemon juice to mix to a stiff dough. Form into a ball and knead lightly. (For a slightly less smooth texture, substitute 225 g (8 oz) caster sugar for 225 g (8 oz) of the icing sugar, sifting the two together.) This makes 900 g (2 lb) almond paste – sufficient for a 23-cm (9-inch) cake.

To apply almond paste Trim the top of the cake if necessary. Measure round the cake with a piece of string. Brush the sides of the cake generously with sieved apricot jam. Take a quarter of the paste, form into a roll and roll out half as long as string and as wide as the cake is deep. Press the strip firmly half-way round the side of the cake, keeping the edges square. Roll out a second quarter of the paste in a similar way and press on to the other side, smoothing the join with a round-bladed knife. Brush the top of the cake with jam. Dredge the working surface generously with icing sugar, then roll out the remaining almond paste into a round to fit the top of the cake. Turn the cake upside-down, centring it exactly on the paste, and press it down firmly. Smooth the join, loosen the paste from the board and turn the cake the right way up. Check that the top edge is quite level. Leave for 2–3 days before coating with royal icing.

Almond paste decorations Simple but attractive decorations for an iced cake can be made from almond paste and they are particularly suitable for Christmas or birthday cakes. Draw the chosen shape on stiff paper and cut it out. (Stars, candles, holly leaves, Christmas trees, houses or engines make good designs as they have bold outlines.) Colour some almond paste by working edible colouring in evenly; roll out very thinly on a board sprinkled with icing sugar, lay the pattern on it and cut

round with a sharp-pointed knife. For holly berries, roll tiny balls of red-tinted paste. Leave the shapes on a plate till quite dry, then stick them on to the royal icing (which must be firm).

Royal icing

Allow 4 egg whites to every 900 g (2 lb) icing sugar, 15 ml (1 tbsp) glycerine may

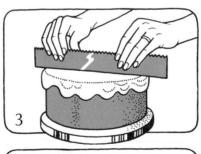

1 and **2** Applying almond paste. **3** and **4** Flat-icing a cake.

be added to give a softer texture. Sift the sugar twice. Separate the eggs, place the whites in a bowl and stir slightly – just sufficiently to break up the albumen, but without including too many air bubbles. Add half the icing sugar and stir until well mixed, using a wooden spoon; beat for about 5–10 minutes, or until the icing is smooth, glossy and white. Cover the bowl with a damp cloth or damped greaseproof paper and leave to stand for at least 30 minutes, to allow any air bubbles to rise to the surface.

Gradually add the remaining icing sugar until the required consistency is obtained. When the icing is intended for flat work, stand a wooden spoon upright in it – if the consistency is correct it will fall slowly to one side. For rough icing, the mixture should be stiff enough for peaks to be easily formed on the surface when you 'pull' it up with the spoon. Add any desired colouring. If possible, leave the icing overnight in an airtight container in a cool place before use. To obtain a really smooth result, just before using the icing, remove 15 ml (1 tbsp) of it and mix to a coating consistency with water; return it to the rest and mix until smooth.

Sufficient for a 23-cm (9-inch) cake.

Rough-icing a cake

Place 5 ml (1 tsp) of the icing on the cake-board and put on the cake firmly, centring it accurately. Spoon the icing on top of the cake. Working with a palette knife in a to-and-fro motion until the air bubbles are broken, cover the top and sides of the cake evenly. Now draw an icing ruler or palette knife across the top of the cake evenly and steadily, until the surface is smooth. Using a round-bladed knife, draw the icing up into peaks round the sides and in a border round the top of the cake – or as liked. Before the icing is set, you can put on some simple decorations.

If you want a very simply decorated cake, put almond paste on the top only of the cake and then royal icing on the top and down the sides for about 2·5 cm (1 inch) so that the almond paste is hidden. Rough-ice the sides and make a border round the cake as above. Decorate as desired and tie a ribbon round the cake below the icing. (For this sort of decoration use half the suggested amounts of almond paste and royal icing.)

Flat-icing a cake

Place the cake on the cake-board. Spoon most of the icing on top of it and cover the top of the cake as described above. Some of the icing will work down the sides

207

of the cake – return this to the bowl. Now draw an icing ruler or the palette knife across the top of the cake evenly and steadily. Draw it across again at right angles to the first stroke until the surface is smooth. If possible, leave the cake for 24 hours. (Put the icing from the bowl into a polythene bag and store in a refrigerator.)

Put the cake and board on an upturned plate or a turntable and work the remaining icing on to the sides of the cake. Draw a ruler, knife or baker's card round the sides until they are smooth. Smooth out the join between top and sides, then leave to set for at least 24 hours. Finally, remove any small uneven bumps with a sharp knife.

If liked, apply a second layer of icing to give a really smooth finish. Save 60 ml (4 tbsp) of the royal icing and mix it with a little water to give a coating consistency; pour on to the centre of the cake, then, using a knife, spread it over the top and down the sides. Knock the board gently up and down on the table to bring any air bubbles to the surface, so that they can be burst with a pin before the icing sets. Leave to harden for 2–3 days.

Decorating a formal cake

When you are decorating a royal-iced cake, let the flat coat of icing harden for several days before attempting the next stage. Plan out the scheme on a piece of greaseproof paper of the same size as the cake, lay this on the icing and with a pin prick out the design lightly, to act as a guide.

The icing used for piping must be free of all lumps, which might block the nozzles; it must also be of such a consistency that it can be forced easily through the pipe but will retain its shape.

Special icing pumps can be bought, but are more difficult to manage than paper forcing bags (made as follows) or small nylon forcing bags.

To make and use a paper forcing bag

1 Fold a 25·5-cm (10-inch) square of greaseproof or silicone paper into a triangle.
2 Holding the right angle of the triangle towards you, roll over one of the other corners to meet it. Roll the second corner over in the opposite direction to meet the first at the back of the bag. Adjust the two corners over one another until a point is formed at the tip.
3 Fold over the corners several times, to secure them in position.
4 Cut a small piece from the tip of the

bag and drop in the required metal nozzle or pipe.
5 To use the bag, place a little icing in it and fold the top over once or twice. When piping, hold the bag in one hand as though it were a pencil, with the thumb in the centre to give an even pressure. If you are inexperienced, first practice piping on an upturned plate. Remember that icing can easily be removed while it is still soft, so mistakes can be corrected.

The pipes or nozzles

For a simple design – which is often the most effective – these types of pipes or nozzles are usually needed:
1 Writing pipes in 3 sizes, to make lines, scallops, dots and words.
2 Star pipes for rosettes, zigzags and ropes.
3 Shell pipe.

For advanced work, use a petal pipe for flowers and bows and a leaf pipe for leaves.

What went wrong? Cake-making faults analysed

RUBBED-IN AND CREAMED MIXTURES

Close texture may be due to:
1 Insufficient creaming of the fat and sugar – air should be well incorporated at this stage.
2 Insufficient beating when the egg is added – air is incorporated at this stage also.
3 Curdling of the creamed mixture when eggs are added – a curdled mixture will not hold as much air.
4 Over-stirring or beating the flour into a creamed mixture.
5 Insufficient baking powder.
6 Too much liquid.
7(a) Too slow an oven – the air expands before the cake is set enough to hold its risen shape.
7(b) Too hot an oven – the crust sets before the air has time to expand and make the mixture rise.
Uneven and holey texture may be caused by:
1 Over-stirring when adding the flour.
2 Uneven or insufficient mixing in of the flour.
3 The mixture being put into the cake

tin small amounts at a time – this allows pockets of air to be trapped in the mixture.
Dry and crumbly texture may be due to:
1 Too much baking powder.
2 Too long a cooking time in too cool an oven.
Streakiness in the crust may be due to:
1 Flour being unevenly or insufficiently mixed into the creamed mixture.
2 Faulty mixing – if any of the mixture is left on the sides of the bowl without being combined with the flour and is then scraped into the cake tin, these scrapings will cause streakiness.
Unevenly risen cakes may be due to:
1 The mixture not being evenly spread in the tin.
2 The oven shelf being tilted.
3 The tin not being centrally placed on oven shelf.
'Peaking' and cracking may be caused by:
1 Too hot an oven.
2 The cake being placed too near top of oven.
3 Too stiff a mixture.
4 Too small a cake tin.
Fruit sinking in a cake may be due to:
1 Damp fruit. Though fruit needs cleaning, if it is washed, it must be dried by being spread out on trays and left in a warm place for 48 hours before use.
2 Sticky glacé cherries: if covered with thick syrup, they should first be washed, then lightly floured.
3 Too soft a mixture: a rich fruit cake mixture should be fairly stiff, to hold up the weight of the fruit.
4 Opening or banging the oven door while the cake is rising.
5 Using self-raising flour where the recipe requires plain, or using too much baking powder – the cake over rises, but cannot carry the fruit with it.
Dry fruit cakes may be due to:
1 Cooking at too high a temperature.
2 Too stiff a mixture.
3 Not lining the tin thoroughly – for a large cake the tin should be lined with double greaseproof paper.
Burnt fruit on the outside of a fruit cake may be caused by:
1 Too high a temperature.
2 Lack of protection: as soon as the cake begins to colour, a piece of brown paper or a double thickness of greaseproof paper can be placed over the top for the remainder of the cooking time, to prevent further browning.
A cake that sinks in the middle may be due to:
1 Too soft a mixture.
2 Too much raising agent.

Brandy cornets (see page 203), Eclairs (see page 198), Chocolate and coffee gateau (see page 187).

3 In the case of a gingerbread, too much syrup in the mixture.
4 Opening or banging the oven door while the cake is rising.
5(a) Too cool an oven, which means that the centre of the cake does not rise.
5(b) Too hot an oven, which makes the cake appear to be done before it is cooked through, so that it is taken from the oven too soon.
6 Too short a baking time.

WHISKED SPONGE MIXTURES

Close, heavy texture may be caused by:
1 The eggs and sugar being insufficiently beaten, so that not enough air is enclosed.
2 The egg and sugar mixture being over-heated, causing the egg to cook slightly and become rather tough and rubbery.
3 The flour being stirred in too heavily or for too long – very light folding movements are required and a metal spoon should be used.
4 The flour being added in a rush – it should be sieved in gently, so that it will not crush out too much of the air.
5 Too much flour being used in proportion to the eggs and sugar.

Lumps on the bottom of the cake may be caused by:
Careless or uneven mixing in of the flour – any unmixed lumps sink to the bottom of the cake.

Cracking of a Swiss roll may be due to:
1 An unlined tin – lining is necessary to prevent the edges overcooking.
2 Too big a tin – this makes the mixture too thin, giving a brittle instead of a spongy texture.
3 Too hot an oven or too long a cooking time – this makes the cake brittle and difficult to roll.
4 The edges not being cut off: since the edges are the crispest part, they should always be removed or the roll will split.
5 The cake not being rolled quickly enough: it must be rolled while it is still very soft and spongy – ie, immediately it is taken from the oven.

Heavy layer at base of a Genoese sponge may be due to:
1 The melted fat being too hot – it should be only lukewarm.
2 Uneven or insufficient folding in of fat and flour.
3 Adding all the fat at once – it should be added alternately with the flour.

BUFFET PARTY CATERING

As a general rule, 225 g (8 oz) pastry gives about 18–24 savouries, according to size.

Assorted savouries

Savoury bouchées

Roll out 225 g (8 oz) flaky pastry 0·5–1 cm (¼–½ inch) thick. Using a 5-cm (2-inch) cutter, cut into rounds and put on a baking tin. Cut half-way through the centre of each with a 1-cm (½-inch) round cutter, glaze the tops with egg and bake in the oven at 220°C (425°F) mark 7 for 10 minutes, then reduce the heat to 180°C (350°F) mark 4 for a further 5–10 minutes. Remove the soft centres and cool the cases on a rack. Fill the patties when cold.

The basis for most fillings is 300 ml (½ pint) white sauce (see page 36) combined with an ingredient such as the following:
175 g (6 oz) picked shrimps, prawns or other shellfish.
100 g (4 oz) chopped or minced chicken with 50 g (2 oz) minced or chopped ham or 50 g (2 oz) chopped fried mushrooms.
100–175 g (4–6 oz) flaked canned or fresh salmon.
100 g (4 oz) diced ham and 50 g (2 oz) tongue or cooked veal.
175 g (6 oz) chopped ham and 50 g (2 oz) cooked mushrooms.

Savoury horns

Illustrated in colour on page 217

212-g (7 ½-oz) packet frozen puff pastry, thawed
beaten egg
poppy seeds
100 g (4 oz) garlic sausage
75 g (3 oz) tomato, skinned and deseeded
30 ml (2 tbsp) thick mayonnaise
6 stuffed olives
parsley sprigs to garnish

Roll out the pastry to a strip approximately 66 × 10 cm (26 × 4 inches), brush with beaten egg. Trim the edges with a sharp knife. Cut 21·5-cm (8½-inch) ribbons from the pastry. Wind each round a cream horn tin, egg side uppermost. The pastry should not overlap the metal rim. Sprinkle with poppy seeds. Place the horns, join side underneath, on a damp baking sheet and bake in the oven at 220°C (425°F) mark 7

for 8–10 minutes. Cool for a few minutes. Hold in one hand and gently twist to remove case with the other hand.

Finely chop the garlic sausage. Dice the tomato into small pieces. Combine together with mayonnaise. Finely chop 4 olives and add to the mixture. Using a teaspoon, fill the cases. Decorate with the remaining olives cut into slices and parsley sprigs. Chill for 30 minutes before serving. *Makes 8 horns*

Note If preferred the pastry cases can be made a day ahead and refreshed in the oven for a few minutes on the day they are to be filled and served.

Crab tartlets

100 g (4 oz) flaky pastry
150 ml (¼ pint) white sauce (see page 36)
60-g (2-oz) can crab
40 g (1 ½ oz) cheese, grated
50 g (2 oz) almonds, blanched and chopped
salt and pepper

Roll the pastry out thinly and use to line tartlet tins. Mix all the other ingredients, reserving half the cheese and the nuts. Fill the cases with this and sprinkle the remaining cheese and nuts on top. Bake in the oven at 220°C (425°F) mark 7 for 15 minutes.

Cheese and bacon tartlets

Illustrated in colour on page 213

Roll out 100 g (4 oz) flaky pastry and use to line tartlet tins. Chop 50 g (2 oz) cooked bacon (or ham) and put a little in each tin. Beat up 1 egg, some seasoning and 150 ml (¼ pint) milk and divide between the tartlets. Sprinkle 100 g (4 oz) grated cheese over the custard filling. Bake in the oven at 200°C (400°F) mark 6 for about 15 minutes.

Cheese and smoked salmon tartlets

100 g (4 oz) shortcrust pastry
150 g (5 oz) cream cheese
salt and pepper
1 egg, beaten
40 g (1 ½ oz) ham
40 g (1 ½ oz) smoked salmon
25 g (1 oz) Gruyère or Cheddar cheese

Roll out the pastry and use to line tartlet tins. Beat the cream cheese, season and stir in the egg by degrees. Cut the ham and salmon into shreds and mix carefully. Fill the tartlet moulds with this mixture, cut the cheese in thin slices and lay these over the top of the tartlets. Bake in the oven at 220°C (425°F) mark 7 until golden brown and crisp – about 10 minutes.

Coleslaw clusters

Illustrated in colour on page 217

16 slices white bread
50 g (2 oz) butter, melted
50 g (2 oz) finely shredded white cabbage
1 stick celery, finely chopped
50 g (2 oz) carrot, grated
25 g (1 oz) onion, finely grated
15 ml (1 tbsp) chopped parsley
45 ml (3 level tbsp) thick mayonnaise
salt and pepper
canned or bottled mushrooms to garnish

Using a 7·5-cm (3-inch) diameter plain round cutter, stamp out 16 circles from the slices of bread. With a rolling pin press out each side to flatten the bread. With scissors, cut a slit from the outside edge to the centre of each slice so that it will fit patty tins snugly. Dip one side in melted butter, overlap cut edges slightly and fit butter-side down in tins. Press gently. Brush with more butter around the top edge. Bake at 200°C (400°F) mark 6 for about 10 minutes until golden brown. Invert casing to crisp the bottom and bake for a further 5 minutes. Allow to cool.

In a bowl combine the cabbage, celery, carrot, onion and parsley. Bind together with mayonnaise and adjust the seasoning. Fill the cases with slaw and garnish with 2–3 slices of drained button mushrooms. Chill before serving. *Makes 16*

Sausage rolls

175 g (6 oz) flaky pastry
225 g (8 oz) sausagemeat
beaten egg to glaze

Roll out the pastry thinly into an oblong 15 cm (6 inches) wide and cut it into 2 strips. Lay a roll of sausagemeat down the centre of each, brush the edges with egg and fold one side over the filling. Seal the two long edges together by flaking with a knife. Glaze the top of each roll with egg, cut into slices 2·5–4 cm (1–1½ inches) long and bake in the oven at 200°C (400°F) mark 6 for about 20 minutes.

Cheese aigrettes

50 g (2 oz) plain flour
15 g (½ oz) butter or margarine
150 ml (¼ pint) water
1 large egg
40 g (1½ oz) cheese, grated
salt and pepper
deep fat for frying

Make choux pastry with the flour, fat, water and egg (see recipe for éclairs). Add the cheese and seasoning. Heat a pan of deep fat until it will brown a cube of bread in a few seconds. Drop in the cheese mixture, teaspoonfuls at a time, and fry for about 5 minutes, until the aigrettes are a pale golden brown; drain well.

Cheese biscuits

50 g (2 oz) cheese pastry (see page 99)
cream cheese
a little milk
finely chopped parsley, paprika pepper, anchovies or sliced olives to garnish

Roll the pastry out thinly and cut into small rounds. Bake in the oven at 200°C (400°F) mark 6 for 10–15 minutes, then cool. Mix the cheese to a piping consistency with milk and pipe a large star or whirl on each round. Set 2 half-biscuits in the cheese to form wings and garnish.

Cheese pastry, cheese straws

See page 99.

Savoury whirls

Roll out 100 g (4 oz) cheese or shortcrust pastry (see pages 99 and 143) thinly into an oblong and spread with yeast or meat extract, leaving the edges free. Brush the edges with water, roll up like a Swiss roll, then slice thinly, put on a greased baking sheet and bake in the oven at 200°C (400°F) mark 6 for 10–15 minutes.

Cheese and tomato wedges

Illustrated in colour on page 217

100 g (4 oz) shortcrust pastry
15 g (½ oz) butter or margarine
50 g (2 oz) onion
100 g (4 oz) celery
salt and pepper
75 g (3 oz) mature Cheddar cheese, grated
175 g (6 oz) tomatoes, skinned
225 ml (8 fl oz) milk
2 eggs
chopped parsley to garnish

Use the pastry to line a 17·5-cm (7-inch) flan ring placed on a baking sheet. Fill with dried beans and bake blind at 190°C (375°F) mark 5 for about 15 minutes. Remove the beans and bake for a further 10 minutes. Take out of the oven but leave ring in position.

Melt the fat in a frying pan. Finely chop the onion and celery and sauté until transparent. Drain on kitchen paper towel. Place the fried vegetables over the pastry case. Season well. Sprinkle the cheese over, slice the tomatoes and arrange on top. In a bowl, whisk together the milk and eggs. Strain through a sieve. Pour over the tomatoes in the flan. Bake at 190°C (375°F) mark 5 for about 30 minutes until custard has set. Remove the flan ring. Garnish with chopped parsley. Serve in wedges, warm or cold. *Serves 8*

Anchovy twists

Illustrated in colour opposite

scraps of flaky or shortcrust pastry
anchovy fillets
lemon juice
beaten egg

Roll the pastry 0·3 cm (⅛ inch) thick and cut it into strips. Lay a strip of anchovy on top of each and sprinkle with lemon juice. Twist the two together, brush with beaten egg and bake in the oven at 220°C (425°F) mark 7 for about 10 minutes.

Cheese dartois

See page 100.

Glazed pâté slices

Illustrated in colour on page 217

325 g (12 oz) liver sausage
225 g (8 oz) garlic sausage
25 g (1 oz) onion, grated
pepper
1 egg, beaten
326-g (11½-oz) can lamb's tongue, diced
225 g (8 oz) plain flour
5 ml (1 level tsp) salt
50 g (2 oz) lard
90 ml (6 tbsp) milk or water

For the garnish
298-g (10½-oz) can whole carrots
stoned black olives
150–300 ml (¼–½ pint) aspic jelly

In a bowl, using an electric mixer, work the sausages until smooth. Add the onion, pepper, half the egg and the diced tongue. In another bowl sift the flour and salt. Melt the lard in the milk or water. Bring to the boil and pour into the dry ingredients, working quickly. Beat with a wooden spoon to a soft dough. Turn on to a floured board and knead until smooth. Roll out two-thirds of the pastry and use it to line a 1·3-litre (2¼-pint) greased loaf tin. Roll out the remaining pastry for the lid. Fill the lined tin with pâté mixture. Turn over the

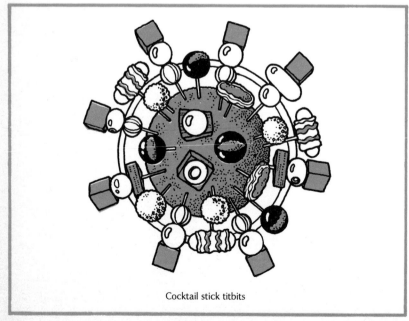

Cocktail stick titbits

Cheese and bacon tartlets (see page 211), Anchovy twists (see above), Sardine tricornes (see page 214),
Tuna cheese dunk (see page 214), Scandinavian-type open sandwiches (see page 215), Barrier reef (see page 218).

excess pastry edge, brush with egg and top with the lid, pricking the edges together with a fork. Glaze with some of the remaining beaten egg. Bake at 220°C (425°F) mark 7 for 20 minutes, reglazing the top pastry twice. Reduce heat to 190°C (375°F) mark 5 for 35 minutes or until the pastry is golden brown. Leave until cold. Ease round the edge, turn out and cut into slices. Garnish each slice with sliced carrot and stoned black olive halves. Glaze with nearly set aspic. Chill before serving. *Makes 12 slices*

Sardine tricornes

Illustrated in colour on page 213

175 g (6 oz) cheese or shortcrust pastry (see pages 99 and 143)
100 g (4 oz) sardines
150 ml (¼ pint) thick cheese sauce
egg or milk
stuffed olives or chopped parsley to garnish

Roll the pastry out thinly and cut into rounds 9–10 cm (3½–4 inches) in diameter. Mix the sardines with the sauce and place a spoonful of this filling in the centre of each round. Brush the outside edge with a little water, draw up over the filling and pinch to form a three-cornered shape. Brush with a little egg or milk and bake in the oven at 190°C (375°F) mark 5 for 15–20 minutes. Garnish with slices of olive or chopped parsley.

Small savouries

Thin wedges of melon wrapped round with a thinly cut slice of smoked or roast ham.
Asparagus tips or pineapple spears wrapped in slices of ham.
Asparagus tips wrapped in slices of smoked salmon.

Fish and chip balls

Illustrated in colour on page 217

225 g (8 oz) smoked haddock fillet
2 slices lemon
parsley stalks
175 g (6 oz) full-fat soft cheese
10 ml (2 tsp) lemon juice
15 ml (1 tbsp) chopped parsley
freshly ground black pepper
50 g (2 oz) plain crisps, crushed

Cook the fish with the slices of lemon and the parsley stalks in water to cover. Bring to the boil, reduce the heat and simmer until cooked. Drain well. Remove any skin, membrane and bones. Allow to cool, then flake finely. Cream the cheese with the lemon juice until fully blended. Add the

chopped parsley and freshly ground black pepper. Beat with the flaked fish until really smooth. With lightly floured hands, take small walnut-size portions of the mixture and roll into a ball shape. Roll the balls in crushed crisps, pressing them well into the mixture. Keep in a cool place. Serve on cocktail sticks. *Makes about 30*

Savoury bread

Slice a long French loaf diagonally into slices about 2·5 cm (1 inch) thick, but do not cut through the bottom crust. Spread the cut surfaces with one of these savoury fillings:
Cream cheese mixed with chopped chives
Cream cheese and chopped chutney
Cream cheese and caraway seeds
Cream cheese and tomato purée
Grated Cheddar cheese and chopped mango chutney
Wrap the loaf in foil and bake in the oven at 200°C (400°F) mark 6 for 10 minutes. Unwrap and serve immediately, with watercress.

Party skewers to serve with dips

1·1 kg (2½ lb) topside of beef
1·1 kg (2½ lb) middle leg of pork
300 ml (½ pint) dry red wine
90 ml (6 tbsp) corn oil
10 ml (2 level tsp) dried rosemary
5 ml (1 level tsp) dried sage
freshly ground black pepper

Cut the beef and pork into large pieces. Place in separate dishes each with 150 ml (¼ pint) wine, turn well and leave covered in a cool place for several hours or overnight. Drain the meats and add 45 ml (3 tbsp) oil and the rosemary to the beef and 45 ml (3 tbsp) oil and the sage to the pork. Turn each to distribute the oil and herb. Season with pepper. Place in separate baking tins or dishes and cook in the oven at 200°C (400°F) mark 6 for 1 hour, then reduce to 180°C (350°F) mark 4 for 30 minutes. Baste frequently with the pan juices, add a little of the wine marinade if wished and turn the meat 2 or 3 times during the cooking. When tender, place the meat on skewers and keep warm. Reduce the juices by rapid boiling, adjust the seasoning and spoon over respective meats. Serve with a selection of dips. *Serves 8*

Dips

Cream cheese can be combined with crushed avocado pears, pineapple, flaked salmon or tuna, minced ham, chopped shellfish, celery, onion, hard-boiled egg,

crisp bacon, nuts or chutney, or it may be mixed with cream, salad cream, white wine, beer or fruit juice and flavoured with herbs, curry powder or seasoned salt. Serve in a bowl, on a platter surrounded with assorted 'dunks' – pumpernickel strips, French bread, fingers of toast, crispbreads, pretzels, potato crisps, celery sticks, radishes, pineapple chunks, avocado chunks, prawns, grilled bacon rolls, chunks of chicken or ham, carrot sticks, cocktail onions, apple segments. Mount these on cocktail sticks if necessary.
Party Edam Cut the top from an Edam cheese and scoop out the centre. To decorate the outside, cut out shapes in the red skin with a cutter. The scooped-out cheese can then be finely chopped and mixed with extra cheese and any of the savoury ingredients suggested for dips (see above).

Cheesy egg dunk

175-g (6-oz) pkt soft cream cheese (preferably chive-flavoured)
30 ml (2 tbsp) mayonnaise
5 ml (1 tsp) prepared mustard
1·25 ml (¼ level tsp) salt
2·5 ml (½ tsp) Worcestershire sauce
a large pinch pepper
2 hard-boiled eggs, chopped
45 ml (3 tbsp) milk

Mix all the ingredients to a thick cream.

Tuna cheese dunk

Illustrated in colour on page 213

92-g (3¼-oz) can tuna
75-g (3-oz) pkt cream cheese
75 ml (5 tbsp) dry white wine
15 ml (1 tbsp) mayonnaise
30 ml (2 tbsp) chopped parsley
15 ml (1 tbsp) sweet pickle
15 ml (1 tbsp) grated onion
a dash of Tabasco
1·25 ml (¼ level tsp) salt
1·25 ml (¼ level tsp) garlic salt

Drain the tuna and blend with the cream cheese, then with the remaining ingredients.

Blue cheese dunk

Mix 65 g (2½ oz) blue cheese with 225 g (8 oz) cottage cheese, a little grated onion and 1 carton of plain yoghurt.

Cocktail stick titbits

See page 100 for directions for making.

Fancy sandwiches

HINTS ON SANDWICH-MAKING

1 Use a cut loaf (thinly sliced) and soften butter.

2 Prepare the fillings beforehand – they should be moist and well-seasoned. For layer sandwiches use well-contrasted fillings.

3 Pair the slices which lie next to each other in the loaf, so that the edges will match.

4 Use a sharp unserrated knife for cutting, as this is less likely to tear the bread. If fancy cutters are used, choose ones with sharp edges.

Sandwich fillings

Salmon, finely chopped onion and cucumber.

Liver pâté, crisp bacon bits and pickle.

Cream cheese, pimiento and celery or dates.

Scrambled egg and chopped ham or chopped chives.

Chopped turkey or chicken and cranberry jelly.

Chopped shrimps, celery, pineapple and salad cream.

Cream cheese sandwich loaf

210-g (7 ½-oz) can salmon
45 ml (3 tbsp) salad cream
15 ml (1 tbsp) lemon juice
2 eggs
50 g (2 oz) cheese, grated
5–10 ml (1–2 tsp) made mustard
50 g (2 oz) butter or margarine
30 ml (2 tbsp) chopped parsley
10 ml (2 tsp) chopped chives
5 ml (1 tsp) grated onion
salt and pepper
1 large tin loaf
325 g (12 oz) cream cheese
a little milk
sliced radishes and parsley to garnish

Flake the salmon and mix with the salad cream and lemon juice. Scramble the eggs, add the cheese and mustard and leave to cool. Cream the butter or margarine with the herbs and onion. Season all the fillings well. Cut the crusts from the top and short sides of the loaf, slice it into 6 lengthways and trim off the remaining crusts. Spread one slice with half the salmon mixture, cover with a second slice, then spread with half the egg mixture; add another slice, spread with savoury butter, put on a slice covered with the remaining egg mixture, a slice with the remaining salmon and finally a plain slice. Wrap the loaf in waxed paper, place between two boards and press well. Before serving, cover with cream cheese, softened with milk. Garnish with radishes and parsley.

Scandinavian-type open sandwiches

Illustrated in colour on page 213

Use small split bridge rolls, thin rounds from a French loaf, toast, crispbread, rye bread or savoury biscuits; spread with butter (possibly flavoured with minced onion, curry powder, mayonnaise or chopped herbs, such as parsley or chives); top with any decorative mixture of ingredients – for instance:
Shrimps, anchovies, crabmeat, tuna fish, salami, cold roast meats, liver pâté, smoked Continental sausage, cheese, cream cheese, eggs (scrambled or hard-boiled and sliced), salad ingredients, olives, gherkins, pickled walnuts.

Open sandwich toppings

Herring fillets, potato salad, chopped beetroot.

Cold cooked white fish coated with salad cream, topped with tomato or pimiento.

Scrambled egg topped with smoked salmon, on a base of a lettuce leaf on toast.

Shrimps surrounding hard-boiled egg halves, covered with salad cream and decorated with dill or lettuce.

Shrimps with cheese and cucumber cubes in curry-flavoured salad cream.

Liver pâté, an anchovy fillet, horseradish cream and parsley.

Salami, scrambled egg, slices of leek.

Egg and tomato slices with piped mayonnaise and chopped chives to garnish.

Pinwheel sandwiches

Cut off the end and top crusts from a new white loaf. Stand the loaf on end and cut off very thin slices down its whole length. Put these pieces flat on the table and pass the rolling pin lightly over them – this will make it easier to roll them up. Spread with a soft filling (either dark or brightly coloured, to provide a good contrast to the bread) and cut off the crusts. Roll up, starting at one narrow end, wrap each roll tightly in waxed or greaseproof paper, then put in the refrigerator for 30 minutes. When the rolls are firm, cut them in 0·5 cm (¼-inch) slices, as though cutting Swiss roll.

Rolled sandwiches

Illustrated in colour on page 217

Asparagus
454-g (1-lb) can green asparagus
1 Hovis-type loaf
175 g (6 oz) softened butter

Drain the asparagus. Cut the crusts from the loaf, then butter and slice thinly in the usual way. (Day-old bread is easier to handle with a sharp knife.) Place an asparagus tip on each slice. Roll up carefully like a Swiss roll. Secure the bread seam with butter if needed. Arrange rolls in groups of three. Wrap in cling film and keep in a cool place until required. *Makes 20 rolls*

Smoked salmon
1 large white uncut loaf
175 g (6 oz) softened butter
15 ml (1 tbsp) lemon juice
15 ml (1 tbsp) chopped parsley
325 g (12 oz) smoked salmon, cut very thinly
canned pimiento strips to garnish

Remove the crusts from the loaf and slice. In a bowl beat together the butter, lemon juice and parsley. Spread over the bread. If necessary, flatten the salmon with the back of a knife on a wooden board. Arrange on the buttered bread in a thin layer and roll up. Wrap in cling film and keep in a cool place until required. Serve garnished with pimiento. *Makes 30 rolls.*

Drinks

Elaborate drinks are out of place at a buffet party. Usually the host or hostess has to do the serving and this should not develop into a full-time job. Complicated cocktails, for example, which need mixing on the spot, are a nuisance and anyway rather old-fashioned. A wine or fruit cup, however, is a splendid standby. It can be prepared beforehand and only needs a punch bowl and ladle for quick, easy serving. A wide selection of drinks is also unnecessary. Asking the guests what they will have is easy if you offer a choice of only two or three drinks.

At a wine and cheese party, offer both red and white wine. At a beer party, offer bitter, lager and cider. If you rise to a champagne party – *not* so extravagant as it sounds – you only need to offer champagne. At the conventional 'come in for drinks', you can get by quite well with sherry and gin plus vermouth and tonic.

Do always offer a non-alcoholic drink as an alternative. You will most likely serve coffee at some stage, but you will also need fruit juice (canned or bottled), fruit squashes, mineral drinks of some kind or a cup (see pages 215–216) for non-drinkers.

Thirst-quenchers Alcohol adds to the gaiety of the occasion, but drinks are intended to quench the thirst and this alcohol does not do, so even wine-drinkers may like tonic or lemonade afterwards. Some people like to add water to their wine (a favourite hot-weather trick on the Continent).

Sale or return Your local wine merchant or off-licence will almost certainly let you buy drinks on a 'sale or return' basis. This means you can buy enough bottles to cope with your maximum expectations and any unopened bottles can be returned. Glasses can usually be hired.

Aperitifs

These should be served chilled and many of them are improved by ice and a twist of lemon peel.

Sherry	dry, medium or sweet
Port	coming back into fashion as an aperitif
Madeira	also becoming popular again
Vermouth	dry, sweet and *bianco* (white)
Dubonnet	excellent iced, with lemon peel
Campari	deliciously bitter-sweet when served with soda or tonic water and ice

Spirits

Whisky	traditionally served neat or with water, but many people like soda or ginger ale
Gin	serve with lime or other fruit squash; bitter lemon or tonic with a lemon peel twist; vermouth, Dubonnet or Angostura bitters (2 or 3 drops) and iced water
Rum	serve with lime, orange or cola drinks
Vodka	use like gin, or serve with tomato juice to make a 'Bloody Mary'

Wine

Broadly speaking, wine can be red, white or rosé and still or sparkling. It can cost anything you like to pay, but plenty of the cheaper kinds make excellent party drinking. There is no need to be snobbish about sticking to French wines – splendid wines are imported from other countries and in any case it is a complete waste of a true old vintage to serve it at a stand-up buffet party.

Many wines can be bought in 2·3-litre, 4·5 litre, 9-litre (½-gallon, 1-gallon and 2-gallon) jars and this generally works out cheaper.

216

What temperature? White wine is served chilled. Keep it in a cool place or put it in the refrigerator for an hour before serving. (Improvise an ice bucket if refrigerator space is limited.) Red wine is served at room temperature, rosé very slightly chilled.

Champagne is one of the easiest things to serve at a party and you need offer nothing else except a non-alcoholic drink. It can be drunk before, during and after eating and adds an air to any party without necessarily being ruinously expensive. There are plenty of good non-vintage champagnes and the champagne-style Spanish sparkling wines are very reasonable.

French wines The main divisions are into Bordeaux and Burgundy – which can be both red or white – and rosé, though there are countless other classifications.

Red Bordeaux (also known as Claret), such as St. Emilion or Médoc, is a light, dryish wine. White Bordeaux, such as Graves or Sauternes, is generally semi-sweet – Sauternes is indeed the sweetest of wines.

Red Burgundy, such as Beaune and Beaujolais, is fuller and richer than Bordeaux. White Burgundy, such as Chablis and Meursault, is dryish and fairly full.

Rosé, such as Anjou rosé or Tavel, is a light wine varying in colour from pale to dark; it can be sweet or dry.

Other wines Italian wines include Chianti (red or white) in wicker-basket bottles – probably the most popular, but not necessarily the best or cheapest Italian wine.

German wines include the deliciously light and fresh Hocks and Moselles.

Every wine merchant now has also a big selection of wines from Spain, Portugal, Algeria, Yugoslavia, Hungary, Cyprus, the Commonwealth countries (even perhaps one from Russia!) and many of these are cheap and very drinkable.

Yield per bottle

Wine	8 glasses
Sherry, Port	10–12 glasses
Champagne	6–8 glasses
Spirits	24 measures (varies a lot; some bars get 28 or even 30 tots from a bottle)
Squash	14–18 long drinks

Beer, Cider

Generally, light ale or lager is served at a party. You can order a small barrel (or pin) of bitter from your local pub and if a knowledgeable host or friend can chock it up, put the bung in and prevent it from

dripping, this saves endless bottle-opening. Beer is otherwise available in bottles, cans and 4-litre (7-pint) cans.

Lager-and-lime is refreshing after energetic games.

Besides the standard sparkling and still ciders, there are also vintage and champagne types and champagne perry.

WINE CUPS

This assortment should offer something for every taste; the cost varies of course according to the wine used.

Midsummer Night's Dream cup

ice cubes
1 bottle of Sylvaner
1 bottle of Beaujolais
1 split of lemonade
2 measures of Curaçao
sliced fresh fruit and melon cubes
sugar to taste

Place the ice cubes in a bowl and pour the wines, lemonade and liqueur over them. Add the fruit and sugar to taste. Serve well chilled. Sweet and very pleasant. *About 16 glasses*

Claret and Sauternes frappé

1 bottle of Claret
1 bottle of Sauternes
strawberries and sliced fruit
2 glasses of Curaçao
2 glasses of brandy
juice of 3 lemons
1 large split of soda water
sugar to taste
ice cubes

Place the wines in a bowl, add the fruit and leave for 30 minutes. Add the liqueurs and lemon juice. Just before serving, add the soda water, sugar and ice cubes. Serve well chilled. Slightly sharp, very refreshing. *Makes 22 glasses*

Everyman's bubbly

1 bottle of Graves or Sauternes
1·1 litres (2 pints) soda water

Chill both ingredients and combine just before serving, to make a slightly sparkling and very refreshing drink. *About 16 glasses*

Pride of Oporto

2 lemons
1 bottle of tawny port
60 ml (4 tbsp) Curaçao
1 siphon of soda water

Fish and chip balls (see page 214), Cheese and tomato wedges (see page 212), Rolled sandwiches (see page 215),
Coleslaw clusters (see page 211), Savoury horns (see page 211), Glazed pâté slices (see page 212), Punch Noel (see page 218)

Squeeze the juice of 1 lemon into a bowl and add the port and Curaçao. Slice the second lemon, float it on top and leave for 20 minutes. Fill glasses two-thirds full and top up with chilled soda water. Sharp and refreshing. *About 24 glasses*

Barrier reef

Illustrated in colour on page 213

2 bottles dry white wine
3 measures of brandy
45 ml (3 tbsp) Curaçao
1 split of lemonade
100 g (4 oz) grapes, peeled and seeded
crushed ice
sugar to taste

Mix the wine, brandy, Curaçao, lemonade and grapes. Add the crushed ice and sugar and serve well chilled. Cool and refreshing. *Makes about 20 glasses*

Vermouth cassis

ice cubes
1 bottle of Vermouth
½ bottle of Crème de Cassis
6 splits of soda water
sliced lemon
sugar to taste

Place the ice cubes in a bowl and pour the Vermouth over. Add the other ingredients and serve well chilled. Refreshing and not too sweet. *About 16 glasses*

Punch Noel

Illustrated in colour on page 217

18 cloves
4 lemons
7·5 ml (1 ½ level tsp) mixed spice
900 ml (1 ½ pints) water
3 bottles port
75–100 g (3–4 oz) lump sugar

Stick the cloves into 2 of the lemons. Place in an ovenproof dish and bake in the oven at 180°C (350°F) mark 4 for 30 minutes. Put the mixed spice into a pan with the water, bring to the boil and simmer for 5 minutes. Heat the port to just below boiling point, add the spiced water and the 2 baked lemons. Cover and keep warm on a very low heat for 20 minutes. Meanwhile, rub the lump sugar into the rind of the 2 remaining lemons and add to the punch together with the lemon juice. Re-heat very gently to dissolve the sugar. *Makes 30 glasses*
Note If you wish, a dry red wine can be used instead of the port. When port is the choice, use a cheaper variety.

'SOFT' DRINKS

Allow individual servings of 150–200 ml (¼–⅓ pint) per glass.

Sunshine shake

538-g (19-oz) can orange juice, chilled
1·1 litres (2 pints) milk, chilled
1 orange
fresh mint leaves

Combine the orange juice and milk, preferably in a blender, or failing this, by whisking vigorously with a rotary whisk. Serve in glasses, topped with a slice of orange and a mint leaf. *About 9–12 servings*

Spicy fruit punch

700 ml (1 ¼ pints) canned or fresh
  orange juice
300 ml (½ pint) canned pineapple juice
juice and rind of 1 lemon
2·5 ml (½ level tsp) ground nutmeg
2·5 ml (½ level tsp) ground allspice
6 cloves
175 g (6 oz) sugar
600 ml (1 pint) water
1·1 litres (2 pints) ginger ale

Mix together the fruit juices, lemon rind and spices in a large jug. Put the sugar in the water and heat gently to dissolve; cool slightly and add to the other ingredients. Chill and strain; add the ginger ale before serving. *About 15–20 servings*

Quick quencher

1·1 litres (2 pints) ginger beer, chilled
400 ml (¾ pint) bottled lime juice
ice cubes
fresh mint leaves to garnish

Make this drink just before you wish to serve it. Combine the ginger beer and lime juice, then add the ice cubes and mint. *About 9–12 servings*

Pineapple crush

150 ml (¼ pint) stock syrup (see below)
538-g (19-oz) can pineapple juice
juice of 1 orange and 1 lemon
2 ripe bananas, mashed
1·1 litres (2 pints) ginger ale

To make the stock syrup, which is useful for sweetening all kinds of cold drinks, dissolve 450 g (1 lb) sugar in 300 ml (½ pint) water over a low heat, then bring to the boil; cool and store in a refrigerator to use as required.

Combine the stock syrup with the first 2 ingredients and chill. Just before serving, add the bananas and chilled ginger ale. *About 10–14 servings*

Citrus punch

juice of 2 grapefruit
juice of 2 lemons
juice of 5 oranges
150 ml (¼ pint) canned pineapple juice
150 ml (¼ pint) stock syrup (see
  previous recipe)
4 splits of tonic water
1 lemon, thinly sliced.

Mix the strained fruit juices in a bowl and chill. Just before serving, add the stock syrup and tonic water and decorate with the lemon slices. *About 10 servings*

Pinelime sparkle

538-g (19-oz) can pineapple juice
45 ml (3 tbsp) fresh lemon juice
150 ml (¼ pint) bottled lime juice
50 g (2 oz) icing sugar
2 splits of bitter lemon
slices of pineapple to garnish

Put the pineapple, lemon and lime juices together in a jug, sweeten with the sugar and stir well, then chill. Just before serving add the bitter lemon and the pineapple slices. *About 9–12 servings*

Coffee

Although there are many methods of making coffee, the 'jug' method is still one of the easiest and best. Use a jug of known capacity, warm it and have some boiling water ready. For each 600 ml (1 pint) of water put into the jug 30 ml (2 heaped tbsp) finely ground coffee, then pour on the fast-boiling water, stirring vigorously. Stand the coffee in a warm place for about 5 minutes, stirring once or twice, then leave it undisturbed for a further 5 minutes – it will then be ready. If there appear to be many grounds on the top, stir the surface only very lightly with a small spoon or sprinkle with a few drops of cold water – this should clear it, but if any grounds still remain floating, strain the coffee through a fine strainer or muslin.

If the coffee has to be decanted into another pot, be sure that this also is very hot. When coffee has to be reheated, take care not to let it boil.

For white coffee, combine strained black coffee with an equal amount of hot milk, heated separately. If cream is served, the coffee should be strong and black. Hand the cream separately or pour a dessert-spoonful of it over the back of a spoon into each cup, so that it spreads over the surface of the coffee.

218

Iced coffee

Make a syrup with 100 g (4 oz) sugar and 300 ml (½ pint) water; boil for about 10 minutes, then let it get cold. Chill strong, clear, black coffee and pour into glasses; put a small lump of ice in each glass, sweeten with sugar syrup and top with whipped cream.

COFFEE WITH LIQUEURS

Most liqueurs can be taken with coffee, but some, of course, combine especially well with it.

Coffee to be served in this way should be double-strength – that is, use 75 g (3 oz) coffee per 600 ml (1 pint) of water instead of 40 g (1½ oz).

If a liqueur coffee is served with cream on top, allow it to stand for 5 minutes before drinking, so that the aroma of the liqueur can penetrate and pervade the cream. Do not stir the cream and coffee together, but drink the coffee through the layer of cream.

We give also recipes for two favourite fruit-flavoured brandies which can be made at home to serve with coffee.

Irish or Gaelic coffee

You will need 1 part Irish whiskey to 3 parts double-strength coffee. Warm some small goblets, put 1 measure of whiskey in each glass and add 5 ml (1 level tsp) sugar. Pour in black coffee to within 2·5 cm (1 inch) of the brim and stir to dissolve the sugar completely. Fill the glasses to the brim with chilled double cream, poured over the back of a spoon. Allow to stand for 5 minutes, then drink the coffee through the cream.

Calypso coffee

Allow the following ingredients per glass and proceed as for Irish coffee.

1 measure of Tia Maria
4 measures of double-strength black coffee
thick double cream
5 ml (1 level tsp) sugar

Witch's coffee

Warm some goblet glasses and make sufficient double-strength black coffee. Put 1 measure of Strega in each glass, add 5 ml

(1 level tsp) sugar and pour in 3 measures of coffee; stir to dissolve the sugar. Pour in thick double cream over the back of a spoon and finally sprinkle a little finely grated lemon rind in each glass.

Mexican coffee

Allow the following quantities for each glass and make as for Irish coffee.

1 measure Kahlua
4 measures of double-strength black coffee
thick double cream
5 ml (1 level tsp) sugar

Curaçao coffee

For each glass allow the following ingredients. Make as for Irish coffee and stir with a cinnamon stick.

1 measure of Curaçao
3 measures of double-strength black coffee
sugar to taste
1 cinnamon stick (optional)

Café à la brulot

1 orange
2 × 5-cm (2-inch) sticks of cinnamon
4 whole cloves
3 lumps of sugar
150 ml (¼ pint) Cognac
600 ml (1 pint) double-strength black coffee

Peel off the coloured part of the orange skin in one long, thin ribbon. Place the orange peel, cinnamon sticks, cloves and sugar lumps in a saucepan. Pour in the Cognac, warm it for a moment, then set light to it. While the brandy is still flaming, add the black coffee; as the flame subsides, ladle the coffee into 6 coffee cups.

Liqueur coffee round the world

Make any of the following as for Irish coffee. The quantities are for 1 glass.

Cointreau coffee
1 part of liqueur
2 parts of double-strength black coffee
5 ml (1 level tsp) sugar
thick double cream

Caribbean coffee
1 part of rum
5 parts of double-strength black coffee
5 ml (1 level tsp) sugar
thick double cream

German coffee
1 part of Kirsch
4 parts of double-strength black coffee
5 ml (1 level tsp) sugar
thick double cream

Normandy coffee
1 part of Calvados
3 parts of double-strength black coffee
5 ml (1 level tsp) sugar
thick double cream

Dutch coffee
1 part of Hollands Gin
4 parts of double-strength black coffee
5 ml (1 level tsp) sugar
thick double cream

Russian coffee
1 part of Vodka
5 parts of double-strength black coffee
5 ml (1 level tsp) sugar
thick double cream

Cherry brandy

900 g (2 lb) dark cherries
175 g (6 oz) caster sugar
600 ml (1 pint) brandy

Wash the cherries and cut off the stalks within 0·5 cm (¼ inch) of the fruit. Prick the cherries in several places with a skewer or darning needle, then pack them with alternate layers of sugar into a wide-necked bottle. Pour on the brandy, making sure that the cherries are quite covered. Cork the bottle securely and store in a cool, dark place for at least 2 and preferably 3 months; shake the bottle at intervals. After this time strain off the liqueur and re-bottle it.

Apricot brandy

12 large apricots
225 g (8 oz) caster sugar
600 ml (1 pint) brandy

Halve the apricots and chop into small pieces. Crack the stones, crush the kernels and add to the apricots. Put the fruit and kernels into a bottle and pour on the brandy; shake the bottle well and cork securely. Store in a cool, dark place and shake the bottle at frequent intervals. After 1 month strain the brandy and re-bottle it.

HOME PRESERVING

The principle underlying all preserving is to prevent the decay caused by the growth of minute organisms, yeasts, moulds, and bacteria, which thrive on fruit and vegetables, helped by the chemical action of enzymes. These organisms can all be destroyed by being heated to specified temperatures – different fruits requiring different heats for sterilisation. Once fruits have been sterilised they must be kept securely sealed.

The sugar used in preserving helps in the retention of the natural fruit flavour; in jams, it also helps the keeping qualities, as it prevents the growth of yeasts, which are unable to live in a solution containing 60 per cent or more of sugar.

It is impossible to over-stress the importance of using only fresh, sound fruit, under-ripe rather than over-ripe – in fact, the success of all preserving depends to a large extent on the quality of the fruit.

Jams

Wash the fruit thoroughly.

Cooking The first stage is to cook the fruit, in order to soften it and release the pectin and the acid. This is best done slowly – the fruit and water should only simmer. Extra acid, if needed, is added during this stage. The quantity of water and the cooking time vary for different types of fruit, but the skins must be made really soft, as tough skins in jam are most unpalatable and hard to digest; fruits such as blackcurrants, damsons and plums need at least 30–45 minutes. This preliminary cooking may be done very satisfactorily in a pressure cooker (see page 226).

The addition of sugar Many people imagine there is some advantage in using cane rather than beet sugar, or lump rather than granulated. In fact, there is no difference in the keeping qualities of jam made from any of these sugars. Preserving sugar does have one advantage however – it dissolves more easily.

The sugar must be completely dissolved *before* the mixture comes to the boil again; this is why some recipes state that the sugar should be warmed to help it dissolve more quickly, but this is not essential. Stir the jam while the sugar is dissolving.

Boiling the jam As soon as all the sugar is dissolved, bring the jam rapidly to the boil and boil hard and quickly. (At this stage the traditional large, shallow preserving pan

proves its usefulness, as it enables the jam to boil quickly without boiling over.) Providing the fruit has been properly cooked beforehand, it should now be boiled for about 5–20 minutes, though some jams need as little as 3 minutes.

Testing the setting point There are several reliable ways of deciding whether jam is ready to set or 'jell', but it is at this stage that many people experience difficulty.

Remember when testing jam, particularly in the later stages, that you should always lower the heat, so that it does not go on cooking for too long. If a set is not obtained, continue to boil for a short time.

Of the many different methods of testing, the most common are the 'plate' and the 'flake' test. For the former, 15 ml (1 tbsp) of jam is put on a cold saucer and allowed to cool; if the surface is set and crinkles when it is gently pushed with a finger (see picture on page 221), setting point has been reached. For the 'flake' test, put a wooden spoon in the jam so that it is lightly coated; when cool, the jam should fall from the tilted spoon in flakes rather than in liquid drops.

A very reliable method is to use a sugar thermometer. (This is not expensive and when jam is frequently made, it is a good investment.) When the jam reaches a temperature of 105°C (221°F), and providing the pectin and acid content are correct, setting point has generally been reached. With some jams, a degree higher or lower may give better results, but this is a matter of experience. During testing, keep the thermometer in a jug of boiling water when not in use. Stir the preserve thoroughly before using the thermometer. One note of warning: make sure the thermometer is accurate, checking it from time to time by taking a reading in boiling water – 100°C (212°F).

Potting and storing The yield of jam and number of jars needed is easy to ascertain as the sugar content of the finished jam should not be less than 60 per cent, a recipe that needs 1·4 kg (3 lb) sugar should yield 2·3 kg (5 lb) jam. The jars must be clean and sterilised and should be warmed in an oven just before use. Be sure to buy packets of covers of the correct size for your jars; wax covers in particular must fit exactly, for air spaces increase the risk of mould.

Blackberry and apple jam

3·6 kg (8 lb) blackberries
600 ml (1 pint) water
1·4 kg (3 lb) sour apples
sugar

Place the blackberries in a pan with 150 ml (¼ pint) of the water. Simmer slowly until tender and sieve to remove the seeds. Peel, core and slice the apples, add the remaining 400 ml (¾ pint) water and cook until tender. Mash by beating with a wooden spoon. Add the sieved blackberries, weigh the pulp and add an equal weight of sugar. Stir, bring to the boil and simmer until the jam sets when tested. Pot and cover immediately in the usual way. If the preserving pan is weighed beforehand, the weight of the pulp can easily be calculated.
Yield 4·5 kg (10 lb)

Plum jam

2·7 kg (6 lb) plums
900 ml (1½ pints) water
2·7 kg (6 lb) sugar

Wash the fruit and cut in halves, removing the stones. Put the water, kernels and plums into a pan and bring slowly to boiling point. Simmer gently until the fruit is cooked. Add the sugar, stir until dissolved

Raspberry and strawberry jam (see page 222).

1 Adding ingredients for plum jam to preserving pan. **2** Using 'plate' test to see if jam is ready for setting. **3** Potting. **4** Covering.

and bring to the boil. Boil briskly for about 10–15 minutes and test for jelling. Pot and cover as usual.
Yield 4·5 kg (10 lb).

Blackcurrant jam

1·8 kg (4 lb) blackcurrants
1·7 litres (3 pints) water
2·7 kg (6 lb) sugar

Remove the stalks, wash the fruit and put it into the preserving pan with the water. Simmer gently until it is tender and the

222

---

contents of the pan are considerably reduced. As the mixture becomes thick, stir frequently to prevent burning. Add the sugar, bring to the boil, boil hard for 10 minutes and test on a cold plate for jelling. As soon as it sets, pot and cover immediately.
Yield 4·5 kg (10 lb).

As the skins of blackcurrants are usually very tough, it is important to cook the fruit thoroughly until tender before adding the sugar.

Marrow and ginger jam

1·8 kg (4 lb) prepared marrow
1·8 kg (4 lb) sugar
25 g (1 oz) bruised root ginger
thinly peeled rind and juice of 3 lemons

Peel the marrow, remove the seeds and cut into pieces about 1 cm (½ inch) square. Weigh, place in a basin, sprinkle with about 450 g (1 lb) of the sugar and allow to stand overnight. Tie up the bruised ginger and the thinly peeled lemon rind in a piece of muslin and place, with the marrow and lemon juice, in a preserving pan. Simmer for 30 minutes, add the rest of the sugar and cook gently until the jam sets when tested on a cold plate. Pour into hot, sterilised pots and cover immediately.
Yield 2·7 kg (6 lb).

Gooseberry jam

2·7 kg (6 lb) under-ripe gooseberries
1·1 litres (2 pints) water
2·7 kg (6 lb) sugar

Top and tail and wash the gooseberries, then put them into a pan with the water. Heat slowly at first mashing the fruit as it softens, and continue to cook until the contents of the pan are reduced by about one-third. Add the sugar, stir until it is dissolved and bring back to the boil. Boil briskly for about 15 minutes and test for jelling. Pot and cover the jam in the usual way.
Yield 4·5 kg (10 lb).

Rhubarb ginger

1·1 kg (2½ lb) rhubarb, trimmed
1·1 kg (2½ lb) sugar
25 g (1 oz) root ginger
100 g (4 oz) stem ginger

Wash the rhubarb and cut it into small pieces; put it into a basin with the sugar sprinkled on in layers and leave overnight. Put the contents of the basin into a pan, with the bruised root ginger tied in muslin. Bring to the boil and boil hard for 15 minutes. Add the stem ginger, cut into small pieces, and reboil for 5 minutes or

---

until the rhubarb is clear. Test for jelling pot and cover immediately.
Yield 1·8–2·3 kg (4–5 lb).

Damson jam

2·3 kg (5 lb) damsons
900 ml (1½ pints) water
2·7 kg (6 lb) sugar

Wash the damsons, put them in a pan with the water, bring to the boil and simmer until the fruit is cooked. Add the sugar, stir until dissolved and bring to the boil. Boil quickly removing the stones as they rise. After about 10 minutes' boiling, test for jelling pot and cover.
Yield 4–4·5 kg (9–10 lb) according to the amount of stones removed.

Raspberry jam

Illustrated in colour on page 221

1·8 kg (4 lb) raspberries
1·8 kg (4 lb) sugar

Place the fruit in a pan, heat gently at first necessary adding a very little water), then simmer until the fruit is tender. Add the sugar, stir until dissolved and bring to the boil. Test for a jell and continue to boil until the preserve jells satisfactorily on testing. Pot and cover.
Yield 2·7–3 kg (6–6½ lb).

Strawberry jam (I)

Illustrated in colour on page 221

1·6 kg (3½ lb) strawberries, hulled
juice of 1 lemon
1·6 kg (3 lb) sugar

Put the fruit and lemon juice in a preserving pan and simmer gently until the fruit really soft and the volume of liquid is well reduced. Add the sugar, stir until it has dissolved, then boil rapidly until setting point is reached.
Yield 2·3 kg (5 lb).

Strawberry jam (II)

(Using commercial pectin)

1 kg (2¼ lb) strawberries, hulled
juice of 1 lemon – about 45 ml (3 tbsp)
1·4 kg (3 lb) sugar
½ bottle of commercial pectin

Wash the fruit and put it in the pan with the lemon juice and sugar; leave for 1 hour stirring occasionally. Place over a low heat and when the sugar has dissolved, bring to the boil and boil rapidly for 4 minutes. Remove from the heat, stir in the pectin and leave for 20 minutes before potting, to prevent the fruit from rising.
Yield 2·3 kg (5 lb).

Black cherry jam

1·1 kg (2 ½ lb) black cherries, stoned
150 ml (¼ pint) water
90 ml (6 tbsp) lemon juice
1·4 kg (3 lb) sugar
1 bottle of commercial pectin

Put the prepared fruit in a pan with the water and lemon juice and cook gently with the lid on for 15 minutes, then remove the lid. Add the sugar and stir over a low heat until this is dissolved. Bring to a full rolling boil and boil rapidly for 3 minutes. Remove from the heat, add the bottled pectin and stir well. Cool for 15 minutes, stirring occasionally, to prevent the fruit rising. Pot and cover in the usual way. Yield 2·3 kg (5 lb).

Quince jam

900 g (2 lb) quinces
1·4 litres (2 ½ pints) water
juice of 1 lemon
1·4 kg (3 lb) sugar

Peel, core and slice the quinces. Cook slowly with the water and lemon juice in a preserving pan until the fruit is tender and mashed. Add the sugar, stir until dissolved and bring to the boil. Boil quickly for 10–15 minutes and test for jelling. Pot and cover as usual.
Yield 2·3 kg (5 lb).

Pear jam

1·4 kg (3 lb) pears
thinly pared rind of 1 ½ lemons
45 ml (3 tbsp) lemon juice
600 g (1 lb 5 oz) sugar

Peel and core the pears and cut the flesh into chunks. Boil the cores, peel and lemon rind in 150 ml (¼ pint) water for 10 minutes, then strain. Put the juice in a pan with the pear chunks and lemon juice and simmer gently until the fruit is tender. Add the sugar and stir over a low heat until dissolved. Bring to the boil and boil rapidly until setting point is reached. Pot and cover as usual.
Yield 900g–1·1 kg (2–2 ½ lb).

Jellies

The main requirement for jelly-making is basically the same as for jams – that is, pectin, acid and sugar must all be present in correct proportions. Only fruit which is rich in pectin should be used (eg, crab apples, currants, gooseberries and quinces), though fruit with low pectin and acid

content can be combined with one of the above – giving a variety of delectable flavours.

Apart from washing, the only preparation necessary is to remove any unsound pieces and to slice such fruits as apples and plums. Put into sufficient water to cover – using a little more water for hard-skinned fruits such as red and blackcurrants – and cook slowly and thoroughly, to extract all the pectin and acid. Meanwhile, prepare a jelly bag or a linen cloth by scalding in boiling water and tying it to an upturned stool or chair. When the fruit is ready, strain it through the bag or cloth, allowing the pulp to drain until no more drops fall through – it may be left overnight if more convenient. Avoid pressing or squeezing, which would make the jelly cloudy. Fruits rich in pectin can be boiled twice to increase the extract, in which case the pulp is returned to the pan with about half the original quantity of water and simmered for a further 30 minutes.

Measure the juice and put in a pan with the sugar; the amount added is usually 450 g (1 lb) per 500 ml (1 pint) of juice, but the lower the pectin content, the less the sugar needed. The jelly should set after about 10 minutes' boiling. As soon as setting point has been reached, remove the pan from the heat and quickly remove any scum from the surface, straining the jelly through scalded butter muslin if necessary. Pot and cover as for jams, but use small pots if available.

It is not practicable to quote the yield in jelly recipes because the degree of ripeness of the fruit and the time allowed for the dripping process both affect the quantity of juice obtained.

Elderberry and apple jelly

1·4 kg (3 lb) elderberries
1·4 kg (3 lb) sweet apples
water
sugar

Wash the fruits and slice the apples. Cook separately, using sufficient water to cover in each case. Simmer until tender, then strain through a jelly bag or cloth. Allow 325 g (12 oz) sugar to each 500 ml (1 pint) of the mixed juice and finish in the usual way.

Blackberry and apple jelly

900 g (2 lb) blackberries
900 g (2 lb) crab or cooking apples
600 ml (1 pint) water
sugar

Wash the blackberries and wash and chop the apples, without peeling or coring. Put the fruit in a pan with the water and cook

for about 1 hour, until tender, mashing occasionally with a wooden spoon. Strain through a jelly bag or cloth and allow to drip. Measure the extract and put in a pan with 450 g (1 lb) sugar to each 500 ml (1 pint). Stir until dissolved, bring to the boil and boil rapidly for about 10 minutes, until it jells when tested. Pot and cover.

Crab apple jelly

2·7 kg (6 lb) crab apples
1·7 litres (3 pints) water
cloves or root ginger
sugar

Wash the crab apples and cut into quarters, without peeling or coring. Put into a pan and add the water. Bring to the boil and simmer for about 1 ½ hours, or until the fruit is mashed, adding a little more water if necessary. A few cloves or some root ginger may be added while the apples are cooking, if you think they are lacking in flavour. Strain through a jelly cloth. Measure the extract or juice and put into a pan. Bring to the boil, then add 450 g (1 lb) sugar to each 500 ml (1 pint) of extract. Stir while the sugar is dissolving, allow it to boil briskly for about 10 minutes and test for jelling; pot and cover as usual.

Cranberry and apple jelly

1·4 kg (3 lb) apples
900 g (2 lb) cranberries
water to cover
sugar

Wash the apples and cut into thick slices without peeling or coring. Wash the cranberries and put all the fruit into a pan; add sufficient water to cover and simmer gently until the fruit is thoroughly tender and mashed. Then strain through a jelly cloth, allowing it to drip overnight. Measure the extract, put into a pan and bring to the boil. When boiling, add 450 g (1 lb) sugar to each 500 ml (1 pint) of extract, stir until dissolved, allow it to boil briskly for about 10 minutes, then test for jelling; pour into sterilised jars and cover at once.

This preserve is particularly good with roast turkey, baked ham and other meat, poultry and game dishes.

Black or redcurrant jelly

1·8 kg (4 lb) black or 2·7 kg (6 lb) redcurrants
1·1 litres (2 pints) water
sugar as required

Wash the fruit, but do not remove the stalks. Put into a preserving pan with the water, place over a very low heat and

223

simmer gently until the fruit is thoroughly cooked and all the berries pulped. Strain through a jelly bag and allow to drip for several hours. Measure the extract, put it into a pan and bring to the boil. Add 450 g (1 lb) sugar per 500 ml (1 pint) of extract, stir until dissolved and bring to the boil, then boil briskly for about 7–10 minutes and test for jelling. When the preserve jells, pot and cover.

Mint jelly

2·5 kg (5 ½ lb) tart green apples
1·3 litres (2 ¼ pints) water
1 bunch of mint
1·3 litres (2 ¼ pints) vinegar
sugar
90–120 ml (6–8 tbsp) chopped mint
a few drops of green food colouring

Wash and quarter the apples and place them in a pan with the water and the well-washed bunch of mint. Simmer until the apples are soft and pulped, then add the vinegar and cook for a further 5 minutes. Put into a scalded jelly bag and leave to drip overnight. The next day, measure the extract and return it to the pan with 450 g (1 lb) sugar to each 500 ml (1 pint) of extract. Bring to the boil and boil until setting point is reached. Stir in the chopped mint and a little green colouring and finish in the usual way. Pot and cover.

Windfall apples may be used, providing any bruised parts are cut away.

Redcurrant mint jelly

Follow the recipe above, but adding mint in the same way as directed in the recipe for Mint Jelly. This makes a delicious accompaniment to roast lamb.

Quince jelly

1·8 kg (4 lb) quinces
3·4 litres (6 pints) water
rind and juice of 3 lemons
sugar

Wash the quinces, chop finely (or mince) and simmer in a covered pan with 2·3 litres (4 pints) water until tender – about 1 hour – then strain. Add the lemon juice and rind with the remaining 1·1 litres (2 pints) water to the pulp and simmer for another 30 minutes, the strain again. Mix both extracts and allow 325–450 g (12 oz– 1 lb) sugar to each 500 ml (1 pint). Bring the juice to the boil, stir in the sugar, then bring back to the boil and boil rapidly until setting point is reached. Finish in the usual way, pot and cover.

Marmalades

Although the methods for making marmalade are in the main the same as for other preserves, citrus fruits, with their tougher peels, do need much more preliminary cooking, so a greater proportion of water is needed to allow for evaporation at this stage. Many of the problems in making marmalade could be avoided if it were remembered that during the first cooking the contents of the pan should reduce to rather less than half, if the traditional shallow pan is used. However, if a deep saucepan with a lid is used rather than a preserving pan, less evaporation takes place and less water is needed. Cook marmalade fruits for at least 1 hour in a covered pan after bringing to boiling point, using one-third to half the quantity of water given in the recipe. Then add the sugar and finish in the normal manner, allowing if necessary more time for setting point to be reached. This longer boiling after the addition of sugar gives marmalades a darker colour and mellower flavour, which is particularly advantageous when Seville oranges are not used.

Many recipes advise soaking the chopped fruit and water overnight to soften the peel, and you may find it convenient to divide the operation into two.

There are many ways of preparing the peel, but the choice is largely a matter of personal taste and convenience. The most usual method is to shred the oranges completely before cooking, but some people prefer to cook the whole fruit and then shred it, removing the pips just before the sugar is added. Another method is to quarter the oranges, tie the pips in a muslin bag and cook the quarters with the water and pips – when softened, the peel is easily sliced.

See page 226 for pressure-cooked marmalades.

Seville orange marmalade

1·4 kg (3 lb) Seville oranges
juice of 2 lemons
3·4 litres (6 pints) water
2·7 kg (6 lb) sugar

Scrub the fruit, cut in half and squeeze out the juice and pips. Slice the peel and put in a preserving pan with the lemon juice, water and pips (tied in a muslin bag). Cook gently until the peel is soft and the water is reduced by a half. Remove the bag of pips after squeezing it, add the sugar, stir until this is dissolved, then bring to the boil and boil rapidly until setting point is reached.

Remove any scum and let the marmalade cool slightly before pouring into warmed jars. Cover with waxed discs while still hot and seal when cold.
Yield 4·5 kg (10 lb).

Thick dark marmalade

900 g (2 lb) Seville oranges
1 lemon
2·3 litres (4 pints) water
1·8 kg (4 lb) sugar

Wash the fruit, cut in half and squeeze out the juice. Put the pips in a muslin bag. Cut the peel into thick shreds and put into a pan with the pulp, pips, juice and water. Mark the level of the contents on the outside of the pan, then boil for 2 hours, or until the depth is reduced by rather more than one-third. Remove the bag of pips. Add the sugar and bring to the boil, stirring constantly, until the sugar is dissolved. Boil for 1 ½ hours, or until the colour has darkened and the preserve sets firmly when tested. Pot and cover immediately.
Yield 3·4 kg (6 lb).

Three-fruit marmalade

2 grapefruit
4 lemons
2 sweet oranges
3·4 litres (6 pints) water
2·7 kg (6 lb) sugar

The three sorts of fruit should weigh about 1·4 kg (3 lb) all together. Scrub the fruit, cut in half and squeeze out the juice and pips. Slice the peel, either by hand or in a marmalade cutter, and put in a preserving pan with the juice, the pips (tied in a muslin bag) and the water. Cook gently for about 2 hours, until the peel is quite soft and the liquid is well reduced. Remove the pips, squeeze out the juice and add the sugar. Stir until it has dissolved, then bring to the boil and boil rapidly for 15–20 minutes, to setting point. Pour into warmed jars and cover at once with waxed discs. Seal when cold.
Yield 4·5 kg (10 lb).

Shred marmalade

Illustrated in colour opposite

900 g (2 lb) Seville oranges
juice of 2 lemons
2·6 litres (4 ½ pints) water
1·4 kg (3 lb) sugar

Scrub the oranges and remove the peel, cut off the thick pith and shred 100 g (4 oz) of the peel finely. Cut up the rest of the fruit coarsely and simmer in 1·4 litres (2 ½ pints) water plus the lemon juice in a closed pan

Shred marmalade
(see above).

for 2 hours. Simmer the shreds in a closed pan with 600 ml (1 pint) water until tender. Drain off the liquid from the shreds and add to the pulp. Strain this through a scalded jelly or muslin bag and allow to drip for 15 minutes. Return pulp to pan, add remaining 600 ml (1 pint) water, simmer for a further 20 minutes and strain. When dripping stops, put the liquid in a preserving pan with the sugar. Stir over a medium heat, until the sugar has dissolved, then bring to the boil, add shreds and boil rapidly for 15–20 minutes, until setting point is reached. Skim quickly and allow to cool for about 10 minutes before potting and covering in the usual way.
Yield 2·3 kg (5 lb).

Lime marmalade

Lime marmalade is a refreshingly different breakfast addition.

700 g (1 ½ lb) limes
1·7 litres (3 pints) water
1·4 kg (3 lb) sugar

Scrub the fruit and peel the rinds off thinly, using a potato peeler; shred the peel finely. Squeeze out the lime juice, then shred the rest of the pulp and tie it in muslin. Put the rind, juice, water and bag of pulp into a pan and cook until well reduced. Remove the muslin bag, add the sugar and stir until it has dissolved. Boil rapidly until a set is obtained, pot and cover.
Yield 2·3 kg (5 lb).

Ginger marmalade

5 Seville oranges
3 litres (5 ¼ pints) water
1·4 kg (3 lb) apples
3 kg (6 ½ lb) sugar
225 g (8 oz) preserved ginger
20 ml (4 level tsp) ground ginger

Wash the oranges thoroughly, cut off the rinds and shred these thinly. Squeeze out the juice and put in a pan with the shreds. Tie the pips, pith and stringy parts in muslin and put into a pan. Add 2·8 litres (5 pints) water and boil for 1 ½–2 hours, until the contents of the pan are reduced considerably. Cool, squeeze the juice from the muslin bag and discard contents. Peel and core the apples, stew gently with the remaining 150 ml (¼ pint) water, mash well and combine with the oranges. Add the sugar and gingers, boil for 10–20 minutes and test on a cold plate. When the preserve is boiled sufficiently to set, pot and cover as usual.
Yield about 4·5 kg (10 lb).

Pressure cooking marmalades and jams

If you have a pressure cooker (preferably one with a 3-pressure gauge), it is a good idea to use it for preserving, as it saves quite a bit of time and the fruit retains its flavour and colour.

Rules
1 Always remove the trivet from the pressure pan.
2 Never fill the pan more than half-full.
3 If possible, cook the fruit at 'medium' pressure.
4 Remember that fruit must receive only its preliminary cooking and softening under pressure – never cook a preserve under pressure after adding the sugar (and lemon juice, if used), but boil it up in the open pan.
5 You can adapt any ordinary jam or marmalade recipe for use with a pressure cooker by using half the amount of water stated in the recipe and doing the preliminary cooking of the fruit under pressure.

Processing times at 'medium' pressure

Marrow	1–2 minutes
Gooseberries	3 minutes
Blackcurrants	3–4 minutes
Apples	5 minutes
Damsons, plums and other stone fruit	5 minutes
Quinces	5 minutes
Pears (cooking)	7 minutes
Blackberries and apples combined	7 minutes

Note Soft fruits such as raspberries and strawberries need very little preliminary softening and are therefore not usually cooked in a pressure cooker. When two fruits (eg, blackberries and apples) are combined, the cooking times may vary somewhat.

Seville orange marmalade

900 g (2 lb) Seville oranges
juice of 2 lemons
1·1 litres (2 pints) water
2·3 kg (4 lb) sugar

Wash the fruit and cut off the rind thinly. Peel off the pith, then chop the fruit roughly (on a plate, to collect the juice). Place the pith and pips in a muslin bag and chop the rind into fine strips. Place the fruit, rind, lemon juice, muslin bag of pips and 600 ml (1 pint) of the water in the pressure pan, bring to 'medium' pressure and cook for 10 minutes. Leave the pan to cool and reduce the pressure at room temperature. Remove

the muslin bag, squeezing it well, then ad[d] the remaining water and the sugar. Retur[n] the open pan to a gentle heat and stir unt[il] the sugar dissolves, then bring to th[e] boil and boil rapidly until setting point i[s] reached. Pot and cover as usual.
Yield 3 kg (6 ½ lb).

Three-fruit marmalade

2 oranges
1 grapefruit
2 lemons
900 ml (1 ½ pints) water
1·8 kg (4 lb) sugar

The combined weight of fruit should b[e] about 900 g (2 lb). Wash it and cut int[o] quarters. Tie the pips in a muslin bag. Pu[t] the fruit, muslin bag and 400 ml (¾ pin[t]) water in the pan and pressure-cook a[t] 'medium' pressure for 10 minutes. Allow th[e] pressure to reduce at room temperatur[e] and lift out the muslin bag. Chop the fru[it] finely, then return it to the pan with th[e] remaining water and sugar. When the suga[r] has dissolved, boil rapidly until a set i[s] obtained. Pot and cover as usual.
Yield about 2·7 kg (6 lb).

Grapefruit and lemon marmalade

2 grapefruit – about 900 g (2 lb)
4 lemons – about 450 g (1 lb)
900 ml (1 ½ pints) water
1·4 kg (3 lb) sugar

Wash the fruit and cut off the rind thinl[y]. Peel off the pith, then cut up all the fru[it] roughly. Place the pith and pips in a musl[in] bag and chop the rind into fine strips. Plac[e] the fruit and rind, the muslin bag and 400 m[l] (¾ pint) of the water in the pressure pa[n]. Bring to 'medium' pressure and cook for 1[0] minutes. Allow the pressure to reduce a[t] room temperature, then add the remainin[g] water and sugar. Return the open pan to [a] gentle heat and stir until the sugar ha[s] dissolved, bring to the boil and boil rapidl[y] until a set is obtained – about 15 minute[s]. Pot and cover as usual.
Yield 2–2·3 kg (4 ½–5 lb).

Shred marmalade

450 g (1 lb) Seville oranges
juice and pips of 2 lemons
700 ml (1 ¼ pints) water
700 g (1 ½ lb) sugar

Peel the rind thinly from 2 of the orange[s], cut into fine shreds and tie in a muslin ba[g]. Roughly chop the rest of the fruit, pith an[d] peel. Place the fruit, lemon juice and pip[s], bag of shreds and half the water in th[e] cooker and cook at 'medium' pressure fo[r]

20 minutes. Reduce the pressure at room temperature, then remove the bag of shreds and wash them in cold water. Strain the rest of the contents of the pan through a jelly bag, leaving it overnight. Return the extract and the rest of the water to the pan and bring to the boil, then add the sugar. Boil until setting point is reached and stir in the shreds. Allow to cool for about 15 minutes before potting, so that the shreds do not rise in the jars.
Yield 900 g–1·1 kg (2–2½ lb).

Blackcurrant jam

900 g (2 lb) blackcurrants
300 ml (½ pint) water
900 g (2 lb) sugar

String the fruit, then place it in the pan with the water and cook for 3 minutes at 'medium' pressure. Reduce the pressure at room temperature. Add the sugar, then return the open cooker to a gentle heat and stir until the sugar is dissolved. Boil rapidly until a set is obtained. Pot and cover as usual.
Yield about 1·6 kg (3½ lb).

Apricot conserve

450 g (1 lb) dried apricots
900 ml (1½ pints) water
1·4 kg (3 lb) sugar
juice of 1 lemon
75 g (3 oz) blanched almonds (optional)

Soak the apricots in the water overnight or cover with 600 ml (1 pint) boiling water and leave for 30 minutes. Put the fruit and water into the pan and cook at 'medium' pressure for 10 minutes. Allow the pressure to drop at room temperature, then open the cooker and stir in the sugar, lemon juice and almonds (if used). Bring to the boil and cook without a lid until the jam sets when tested. Pot and cover at once.
Yield 2·3–2·5 kg (5–5½ lb).

This recipe does not give a firmly set jam, but the flavour is very good.

Melon and pineapple jam

900 g (2 lb) prepared melon
225 g (8 oz) prepared pineapple
juice of 3 lemons
1·4 kg (3 lb) sugar

Peel the melon, remove the seeds and cut the flesh into cubes before weighing it. Peel the pineapple and remove the 'eyes' and any brown flesh, cut in cubes and weigh. Cook the fruit with the lemon juice at 'medium' pressure for 10 minutes. Reduce pressure at room temperature, then add sugar and finish in usual way.
Yield 1·8–2 kg (4–4½ lb).

Damson, greengage or plum jam

1·4 kg (3 lb) fruit
150 ml (¼ pint) water
1·4 kg (3 lb) sugar

Wash the fruit and place it in the pan with the water. Cook at 'medium' pressure for 5 minutes, then finish as usual.
Yield about 2·5 kg (5½ lb).

Apple ginger

1·4 kg (3 lb) cooking apples
10 ml (2 level tsp) ground ginger
peel and juice of 1 lemon
300 ml (½ pint) water
1·4 kg (3 lb) sugar
100 g (4 oz) crystallised ginger, chopped

Peel and quarter the apples. Place them in the pan with the ground ginger, lemon juice and water. Tie the apple peel and cores and the lemon peel and pips in a muslin bag and add this. Cook at 'medium' pressure for 5 minutes. Reduce the pressure at room temperature. Remove the muslin bag, add the sugar and crystallised ginger and stir over a gentle heat until the sugar has dissolved. Boil until setting point is reached; pot and cover.
Yield about 1·8 kg (4 lb).

Lemon curd

2 eggs, beaten
50 g (2 oz) butter, cut up
225 g (8 oz) caster sugar
juice and grated rind of 2 lemons

Mix all the ingredients together in a basin, then cover this with a double sheet of greaseproof paper. Place on a trivet in the pressure cooker, pour 300 ml (½ pint) water and 15 ml (1 tbsp) vinegar into the cooker, put on the lid and cook for 12 minutes at 'high' pressure. Reduce the pressure at room temperature. Beat the curd really well before pouring it into warmed jars.
Yield 450 g (1 lb) or just over.

Pressure cooking jellies

The fruit used for jelly making can also be softened in a pressure cooker – this method is particularly useful for those fruits which have hard skins, pips, etc.
1 Prepare the fruit according to any ordinary jelly recipe.
2 Place in the cooker (without the trivet) and add only half the amount of water stated in the recipe.
3 Cook at 'medium' pressure (see the sample times given below), then reduce the pressure at room temperature.
4 Mash the fruit well and pour into the prepared jelly bag. Finish as for ordinary jelly recipes.

Processing times at 'medium' pressure

Gooseberries	3 minutes
Blackcurrants	4 minutes
Damsons	5 minutes
Apples	7 minutes

Fruit preserves

Brandied pineapple

822-g (1 lb 13-oz) can pineapple pieces
3 cloves
5-cm (2-inch) stick of cinnamon
150 ml (¼ pint) brandy or Kirsch

Drain the juice from the pineapple and put it into a saucepan; add the cloves and cinnamon and simmer gently together until of a syrupy consistency. Add the pineapple pieces and then simmer for a further 10 minutes. Remove from the heat and add the brandy or Kirsch. Cool, then pack the fruit into a wide-necked bottle. Pour on syrup and seal. Store in a cool place.

Spiced pears

2·7 kg (6 lb) hard pears
400 g (14 oz) sugar
20 g (¾ oz) salt
1·1 litres (2 pints) water
1·1 litres (2 pints) white vinegar
2 sticks of cinnamon
10 g (¼ oz) whole cloves

Use small or medium-sized pears for this preserve.

Dissolve 50 g (2 oz) of the sugar and the salt in the water and bring to the boil. Peel the pears and if large cut into quarters; add to the boiling water, remove the pan from the heat, cover and leave until cool. Boil together the vinegar, remaining sugar and spices. Remove the pears from the water and drain, then place them in the syrup and bring to the boil. Take from the heat, allow to cool and bring back to the boil. Repeat this process 3 times. Finally, allow to cool and place the pears in small jars. Pour the syrup over them, keeping the surplus, but do not seal. Top up each day for the next 4 days, or until no more syrup is absorbed. Cover as for jam.

Spiced prunes

450 g (1 lb) prunes
cold tea
400 ml (¾ pint) cider vinegar
225 g (8 oz) sugar
7·5 ml (1½ level tsp) mixed spice

Wash the prunes and soak them overnight in the cold tea. Boil together the vinegar, sugar and spice. Cook the prunes in a little of the tea for 10–15 minutes, or until soft; drain. Add 300 ml (½ pint) of the juice to the vinegar. Put the prunes into small jars and cover with syrup. Cover as for jam.

Plum-rum jam

450 g (1 lb) plums, finely chopped
1·1 kg (2½ lb) sugar
2 lemons
30 ml (2 tbsp) dark rum

Put the plums, sugar and lemon juice in a pan. Bring to the boil and boil rapidly for 8–10 minutes, stirring all the time, until a light set is obtained. Remove from the heat and add the rum. Allow to cool, stirring at intervals, for 15 minutes. Pour into jars and seal.

Raspberry liqueur conserve

Put 450 g (1 lb) raspberries and 450 g (1 lb) sugar in separate containers in the oven at 180°C (350°F) mark 4, heat for 15 minutes. Combine them in a large mixing bowl and stir for a few minutes. Leave to stand for 20 minutes. Repeat the stirring and standing 3 times, then add 15 ml (1 tbsp) Kirsch or Cognac, pot in 450-g (1-lb) jars and cover.

Strawberry conserve

1·8 kg (4 lb) small strawberries, hulled
1·8 kg (4 lb) sugar

Wash the strawberries, keeping them whole; place in a large basin in layers with the sugar. Cover and leave for 24 hours. Turn into a pan, bring to the boil, stirring until the sugar dissolves, then boil rapidly for 5 minutes. Return the mixture to the basin, cover and leave for a further 48 hours. Then return it to the pan and boil rapidly until setting point is reached. Cool before potting and covering as usual.

This recipe gives a very lightly set jam, with the whole fruit in a thick syrup.

Lemon curd

4 lemons
4 eggs
450 g (1 lb) sugar
100 g (4 oz) butter

Wash and dry the lemons and grate the rind from each thinly, then halve the fruit and squeeze out all the juice. Strain the juice into a double saucepan and add the grated rind, beaten eggs, sugar and butter. Stir over a gentle heat with a wooden spoon until the sugar and butter are melted and the curd thickens. Don't boil or the mixture will curdle. Pour into sterilised jars and cover at once.

Damson cheese

2·7 kg (6 lb) damsons
300 ml (½ pint) water
sugar

Put the damsons and water in a covered pan and cook slowly until tender. Sieve and weigh the pulp, which should be about 2· kg (5 lb), then cook it in an open pan stirring, until it is reduced to a thick mixture. Add sugar in the proportion of 325–450 (12 oz–1 lb) per 450 g (1 lb) pulp and continue cooking, stirring all the time to prevent burning, until a spoon drawn across the bottom of the pan leaves a clean line. Press the pulp into a warmed mould or straight-sided jar which has been smeared with a little glycerine. Cover with a waxed disc whilst still hot and seal and store as for jams. For serving, the cheese is usually turned out whole on to a small plate or dish

Medlars, blackcurrants, gooseberries and quinces also make excellent cheeses follow the above recipe.

Mincemeat (I)

Illustrated in colour on page 233

225 g (8 oz) currants
225 g (8 oz) sultanas
225 g (8 oz) stoned raisins
225 g (8 oz) cooking apples
100 g (4 oz) mixed candied peel
225 g (8 oz) beef suet
2·5 ml (½ level tsp) mixed spice
grated rind and juice of 1 lemon
225 g (8 oz) moist dark brown sugar
50 g (2 oz) almonds, chopped
75 ml (5 tbsp) brandy

Wash, prepare and chop the fruit together with the suet. Add the rest of the ingredients and mix thoroughly. Leave in a covered container for a week, stirring every day. Pot and seal to make airtight. Keep a few weeks; stir well before using.

Mincemeat (II)

325 g (12 oz) seedless raisins
225 g (8 oz) candied peel
450 g (1 lb) cooking apples
225 g (8 oz) sultanas
225 g (8 oz) currants
225 g (8 oz) suet, finely chopped
325 g (12 oz) brown sugar
grated rind and juice of 1 orange and
**   1 lemon**
2·5 ml (½ level tsp) mixed spice
5 ml (1 level tsp) grated nutmeg
150 ml (¼ pint) brandy or rum
**   (optional)**

Mince twice or finely chop the cleaned and prepared raisins, peel, apples and half the sultanas and currants. Add the remainder of the fruit and the other ingredients, mix well and leave in a covered bowl. Stir every day for a week, then pot, leaving 2·5 cm (1 inch) of space at the top. Cover as jam and keep a few weeks; stir well before using.

Bottled fruits (see page 230

Cranberry cheese

1·7 litres (3 pints) cranberries
900 ml (1 ½ pints) water
700 g (1 ½ lb) sugar

Wash and pick over the cranberries, put in a saucepan with the water and simmer until they are thoroughly tender; if necessary a little more water may be added. When they are cooked, rub through a sieve with a wooden spoon. Wash out the saucepan, return the purée to the pan, add the sugar and bring to the boil, stirring all the time. Boil for 5 minutes, pot and cover.

Cranberry cheese is excellent as an accompaniment to roast game or turkey.

Apple butter

2·7 kg (6 lb) crab apples or windfall
apples
1·1 litres (2 pints) water
1·1 litres (2 pints) dry cider
sugar
5 ml (1 level tsp) powdered cinnamon
2·5–5 ml (½–1 level tsp) ground cloves
(optional)

Wash the fruit, removing any damaged parts, and chop roughly. Simmer in the water and cider until pulpy. Rub it through a sieve and weigh it. Allow 325 g (12 oz) sugar to every 450 g (1 lb) pulp. Return the pulp to the pan and simmer until thick. Add the sugar and the spices and boil until it becomes thick again, stirring frequently. Pot and cover as usual.

PRESERVING PROBLEMS

When jam develops mould This is most often caused by failure to cover the jam with a waxed disc while it is still very hot – this should be done immediately the jam is potted, or it may become infected with mould spores from the air. Alternatively, pots may have been damp or cold when used or insufficiently full or they may have been stored in a damp or warm place. Other possible causes are insufficient evaporation of water while the fruit is being 'broken down' by the preliminary cooking and/or too short boiling after sugar has been added. Mould is not harmful to the jam, but it may affect the flavour slightly. If it is removed, the jam can be boiled up again, re-potted in clean sterilised pots and re-covered; use for cooking purposes.

When tiny bubbles appear Bubbles indicate fermentation, which is usually the result of too small a proportion of sugar in relation to fruit; accurate weighing of fruit and sugar is very important. This trouble can also occur, however, when jam is not

reduced sufficiently, because this too affects the proportion of sugar in the preserve. Fermentation is harmless enough, but it is apt to spoil both flavour and colour. Fermented jam can be boiled up again (see previous paragraph); continue the boiling for a short time if the preserve was not reduced enough in the first instance. Then it can be re-potted and sealed in clean, warm jars and used for cooking purposes.

When peel or fruit rises in jam Strawberry jam and shred marmalade are particularly susceptible to this trouble. It helps if they are allowed to cool for 15–20 minutes and are then given a stir before potting, despite the fact that it is normally advisable to pot all preserves as hot as possible.

When jam crystallises This is usually caused by lack of sufficient acid. You should either use a fruit rich in acid or make sure that acid is added to the fruit during the preliminary softening process. Under-boiling or over-boiling of the jam after the sugar has been added can also cause crystallising, as it will upset the proportion of sugar in the finished jam. Crystallisation may also be due to failure to dissolve the sugar completely before bringing the mixture to the boil.

When jam won't set One cause is the use of over-ripe fruit in which the pectin has deteriorated. Other reasons include under-boiling of the fruit, so that the pectin is not fully extracted; there may also be insufficient evaporation of the water before the sugar is added (this can be remedied by further boiling); or over-cooking after adding the sugar (no remedy).

To ensure a set with fruits deficient in pectin, such as strawberries, it is helpful to add an acid such as lemon juice or citric acid; alternatively, mix with a pectin-rich fruit such as redcurrants, or a pectin extract – commercially made or prepared at home from apples.

Shrinkage of jam on storage This is caused by inadequate covering or failure to store the jam in a cool, dark place.

Bottling fruit

When the season of fresh fruits is at its peak, bottling offers an excellent way of preserving some of these short-lived delights. With a store of bottled fruits, you can enjoy summer tarts and puddings all year round.

THE FRUIT

Illustrated in colour on page 229

Fruit chosen for bottling must be fresh,

sound, free of disease, clean and properly ripe, neither too soft nor too hard. It is wise to select fruits of similar shape, size and ripeness for a given bottle.

Pick over the fruit and remove any that are damaged, as well as any leaves, stems and so on. Then wash and drain it well and pack into jars.

A few fruits require a little extra preparation, as follows:

Apples, pears Peel, core and quarter and drop into a brine solution – 10 ml (2 level tsp) salt to 1·1 litres (2 pints) water – to prevent discoloration. Just before processing, rinse well in fresh water, then drain before packing into the jars.

Peaches Drop the fruit into boiling water for 30 seconds, then transfer to cold water. Skin them, then cut in half and remove the stones. Slice if you wish, and drop into a brine solution, as for apples. Rinse and drain before packing into the jars.

BOTTLING JARS

These are wide-necked glass jars, each covered with a metal sealing disc, with a screw-band to hold it firmly; they can be obtained in 450-g (1-lb) and 900-g (2-lb) sizes. Both the jars and the screw-band can be re-used, but a new sealing disc must be used every time. All jars should be checked before use, to make sure that they can be made quite airtight and that they and the fittings are free from flaws. They must be scrupulously clean, so wash them and rinse in clean hot water; they need not be dried, as the fruit slips more easily into position if the inside of the jar is left slightly wet.

PACKING THE FRUIT

Place the prepared fruit in the jars layer by layer, using a packing spoon or a wooden spoon handle. When a jar is full, the fruit should be firmly and securely wedged in place, without bruising or squashing; the more closely the fruit is packed, the less chance there is of its rising after processing, when it will have shrunk to some extent.

When the jars have been filled all air bubbles should be dispelled by jarring the bottle on the palm of the hand; alternatively, pack in the fruit and add liquid alternately until the bottle is full. Fill the bottles to the brim before putting on the fittings. With wet-pack methods it is essential to loosen screw-bands by a quarter turn before processing, to allow steam and air to escape. If this is not done the bottle may burst.

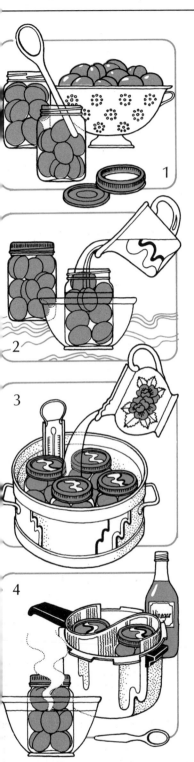

1 Packing fruit into bottling jars. 2 Adding syrup. 3 Adding water to cover bottling jars in a water bath. 4 Jars padded with newspaper ready for bottling in a pressure cooker.

SYRUP FOR PRESERVING

Fruit may be preserved in either syrup or water, but syrup certainly imparts a better flavour and colour to the fruit. The usual proportion of sugar used for syrup is 225 g (8 oz) to 600 ml (1 pint) water, but the amount may be varied according to the sweetness of the particular fruit. Use granulated sugar, dissolve it in half the required amount of water, bring to the boil and boil for 1 minute, then add the remainder of the water. (This method cuts the time required for the syrup to cool.) If the syrup is to be used while still boiling (see below), keep a lid on the pan to prevent evaporation, which would alter its strength. *Note* For pears, add 10 ml (2 tsp) of lemon juice to the prepared syrup for every 450 g (1 lb) of fruit. Bottling syrup can be made with golden syrup instead of sugar, using the same proportions, ie, 225 g (8 oz) syrup to 600 ml (1 pint) water. In this case, put the golden syrup and water into a pan, bring to the boil and simmer for 5 minutes before using.

When the fruit is to be sterilised by the slow water bath method, where the bottles are filled before heating, the syrup is used cold. For the quick water bath method, hot (not boiling) water is poured into the packed jars, which are then processed.

For the wet pack oven method, fill the packed jars with boiling syrup, then process. For the dry pack oven method, boiling liquid is also used, but is not added until after the fruit is processed.

PROCESSING AND TESTING

Sterilise the fruit by one of the methods which are described below, then seal as follows: lift the bottles one at a time on to a wooden surface and screw the band on firmly. When the bottles are cool, test for correct sealing by removing the screwband and trying to lift the bottle by the sealing disc. If the disc holds firm, this shows that a vacuum has been formed as the jar cooled and it is hermetically sealed. If the disc comes off, there is probably a flaw in the rim of the bottle or on the cap. However, if several bottles are unsealed, the processing may have been faulty. The fruit from such jars should be used up at once or transferred to perfect jars and re-processed without delay.

STERILISING

There are two main methods – in the oven or in a water bath.

Oven method This is preferred by many people because quite a number of bottles can be done at one time, and – except for the jars – no special equipment is needed. It is not quite so exact a method as the water bath one, as it is not so easy to maintain a constant temperature and it is easier to over-cook the fruit.

When sterilising fruit by this method, use only one shelf, placed in the middle of the oven, and don't overcrowd the bottles on it, or the heat will not penetrate the fruit evenly.

Water bath method This is considered to be the more exact method, but as it requires some special equipment it is possibly not so commonly used as the above way.

For it you need:

1 A large vessel 5–7·5 cm (2–3 inches) deeper than the height of the bottling jars; a very large saucepan, a zinc bath or a bucket will serve.

2 A thermometer – a sugar-boiling one will do.

3 Bottling tongs (not essential).

See the detailed notes which follow.

OVEN METHOD OF STERILISING

Wet pack Heat the oven to cool 150°C (300°F) mark 2. Fill the packed jars with boiling syrup to within 2·5 cm (1 inch) of the top and put on the discs, but do not put the screw-bands in position. Place the jars 5 cm (2 inches) apart on a solid baking sheet, lined with newspaper to catch any liquid which may boil over. Put in the centre of the oven and cook for the time stated in the table. Remove the jars one by one, screw the bands tightly in place and leave to cool.

Dry pack Pack the bottles with the fruit but do not add any liquid. Cover with the discs and place 5 cm (2 inches) apart on a baking sheet lined as above with newspaper. Cook for the time stated in the table, then remove the jars one at a time (not all together). Use the contents of one jar to top up the others if the fruit has shrunk in the cooking. Fill up at once with boiling syrup and place the discs and screw-bands in place. Leave to cool.

WATER BATH METHOD OF STERILISING

Slow water bath Pack the bottles with fruit and continue as follows:

1 Fill up the bottles with cold syrup.

2 Put the discs and screw-bands in place, then turn the screw-bands back a quarter-turn.

3 Place the bottles in the large vessel and

OVEN METHOD OF STERILISING

The following are the temperatures and processing times recommended by the Long Ashton Research Station:

	Oven – wet pack: Pre-heat oven to 150°C (300°F) mark 2; process as below:	Oven – dry pack: Pre-heat oven to 130°C (250°F) mark ½; process as below:
Soft fruit, in normal packs:		
Blackberries Currants Loganberries Mulberries Raspberries Gooseberries and Rhubarb for pies Apples, sliced	450 g–1·8 kg (1–4 lb) for 30–40 minutes, 2·3–4·5 kg (5–10 lb) for 45–60 minutes.	450 g–1·8 kg (1–4 lb) for 45–55 minutes, 2·3–4·5 kg (5–10 lb) for 60–75 minutes. Not recommended for apples
Soft fruit as above in tight packs; also gooseberries and rhubarb for dessert	450 g–1·8 kg (1–4 lb) for 40–50 minutes, 2·3–4·5 kg (5–10 lb) for 55–70 minutes.	450 g–1·8 kg (1–4 lb) for 55–70 minutes, 2·3–4·5 kg (5–10 lb) for 75–90 minutes.
Stone fruit; dark, whole: Cherries, damsons, whole plums		
Stone fruit; light, whole: Cherries, greengages, plums		Not recommended for light-coloured fruit
Apricots Nectarines Peaches Pineapple Plums, halved	450 g–1·8 kg (1–4 lb) for 50–60 minutes, 2·3–4·5 kg (5–10 lb) for 65–70 minutes.	Not recommended for these fruits
Figs Pears Whole tomatoes	450 g–1·8 kg (1–4 lb) for 60–70 minutes, 2·3–4·5 kg (5–10 lb) for 75–90 minutes.	450 g–1·8 kg (1–4 lb) for 80–100 minutes, 2·3–4·5 kg (5–10 lb) for 105–125 minutes.
Tomatoes, solid pack (halved or quartered)	450 g–1·8 kg (1–4 lb) for 70–80 minutes, 2·3–4·5 kg (5–10 lb) for 85–100 minutes.	Not recommended for solid packs

Note The dry pack oven method is not recommended for fruits which discolour in the air, such as pears, apples and peaches. It will be seen from the above chart that with both oven methods the time required varies not only with the type of fruit, but also with the tightness of the pack and the total load in the oven at one time; the load is calculated according to the total capacity – in 450 g (1 lb) – of the jars.

Mincemeat (see page 228)

cover them with cold water – immersing them completely, if possible, but at least up to the necks.

4 Heat gently on top of the cooker, checking the temperature of the water regularly; raise the temperature to 58°C (130°F) in 1 hour, then to the processing temperature given in the chart in a further 30 minutes.

5 Maintain temperature for time given in chart.

6 Remove the bottles with the tongs (or bale out enough water to remove them with an oven cloth).

7 Place the bottles on a wooden surface one at a time and tighten the screw-bands straight away.

Quick water bath If you have no thermometer, this is a good alternative method to the above. Fill the packed bottles with hot (not boiling) syrup, cover and place in the vessel of warm water. Bring the water to simmering point in 25–30 minutes and keep simmering for the time stated in the table.

PULPED FRUIT

Many people like to bottle soft and stone fruits in this way. Prepare as for stewing, then cover with the minimum of water and stew until just cooked. While still boiling pour into hot bottling jars and place the discs and screw-bands in position. Immerse the bottles in a deep pan lined with newspaper and add hot water to come up to their necks. Raise the temperature to boiling point and maintain for 5 minutes. Remove the bottles and allow to cool. *Note* The fruit may be sieved after stewing and before bottling if you prefer.

Bottling fruit in a pressure cooker

This has the double advantage of shortening the time and ensuring exact control of the temperature. Any pressure cooker will take 450-g (1-lb) bottling jars, but if you want to use larger ones, you will need a pan with a domed lid to give the extra depth.

1 Prepare the fruit as for ordinary bottling, but see also the additional notes in the chart below.

2 Pack into clean, warm bottles, filling completely.

3 Cover with boiling syrup or water to within 0·5 cm (¼ inch) of the top of the bottles.

4 Adjust the metal discs and screw-bands, screwing these tight, then turning them back a quarter-turn. Next, as an extra

234

WATER BATH METHOD OF STERILISING

Fruit	Slow method Raise from cold in 90 minutes and maintain as below:	Quick method Raise from warm – 88°C (100°F) to simmering 88°C (190°F) in 25–30 minutes and maintain for:
Soft fruit, normal packs: Blackberries Currants	74°C (165°F) for 10 minutes	2 minutes
Loganberries Mulberries Raspberries Gooseberries and rhubarb for pies Apple slices	74°C (165°F) for 10 minutes	2 minutes
Soft fruit as above, tight packs; also gooseberries and rhubarb for dessert Stone fruit: Cherries, damsons, whole plums, greengages	82°C (180°F) for 15 minutes	10 minutes
Apricots Nectarines Peaches Pineapple Plums, halved	82°C (180°F) for 15 minutes	20 minutes
Figs Pears Tomatoes (whole)	88°C (190°F) for 30 minutes	40 minutes
Tomatoes, solid pack (halved, quartered)	88°C (190°F) for 40 minutes	50 minutes

precaution, heat the jars by standing them in a bowl of boiling water.

5 Put inverted trivet into pressure cooker and add 900 ml (1 ½ pints) water, plus 15 ml (1 tbsp) vinegar to prevent pan from becoming stained. Bring water to boil.

6 Pack bottles into cooker, making sure they do not touch each other by packing newspaper between.

7 Fix the lid in place, put the pan on the heat and heat until steam comes steadily from the vent.

8 Put on the 'low' pressure control and continue heating gently to take about 3 minutes to reach pressure. Reduce heat and maintain pressure for time given in chart. (Any change in pressure will cause

liquid to be lost from the jars and unde processing may result.)

9 Remove the pan carefully from the hea and reduce the pressure at room tempera ture for about 10 minutes before taking o the lid.

10 Lift out the jars one by one, tighten th screw-bands and leave to cool.

BOTTLING PROBLEMS

When the seal fails Check neck of jar fc chips, cracks or other faults. Inspect sealin disc to make sure that there are no faults o irregularities in the metal or the rubber rir (You must use new sealing disc every time The instructions for each method of sterili

BOTTLING FRUIT IN A PRESSURE COOKER

Fruit	Special preparation	Processing time in minutes at 'low' pressure
Apples	Peel, core and quarter. Keep in brine during preparation to prevent browning. Drain, rinse and pack at once.	1
Apricots	If halved, remove stones	1
Blackberries, Raspberries, Loganberries	Pick over to remove damaged fruit, etc	1
Cherries	Stalk, but leave whole	1
Red-, black- currants	String	1
Damsons	Stalk	1
Gooseberries	Top and tail	1
Peaches	Scald in hot water for a few seconds, then transfer to cold water. Peel, halve and stone; slice if liked. Keep in brine during preparation. Drain, rinse and pack at once	1
Pears	Prepare as for apples. Very hard cooking pears can be pressure-cooked before bottling for about 5 minutes. Add 1·25 ml (¼ level tsp) citric acid or 10 ml (2 tsp) lemon juice to the prepared syrup for every 450 g (1 lb) of pears	5
Plums	Prick skins if left whole; alternatively, cut in half and stone	1
Rhubarb	Wipe and cut in 7·5-cm (3-inch) lengths	1
Strawberries	Not recommended	
Tomatoes	Skin as for peaches; preserve either whole or halved, in brine. Add 1·25 ml (¼ level tsp) citric acid or 10 ml (2 tsp) lemon juice to the prepared brine solution for every 450 g (1 lb) of tomatoes	5
Soft Fruit, solid pack	Place fruit in large bowl, cover with boiling syrup 175 g (6 oz) sugar to 600 ml (1 pint) water, leave overnight. Drain, pack jars as usual and cover with same syrup. Process as usual	3
Pulped Fruit, eg, apples, tomatoes	Prepare as for stewing; pressure-cook with 150 ml (¼ pint) water at 'high' pressure for 2–3 minutes, then sieve. While still hot, fill jars to within 2·5 cm (1 inch) of top, then process. Add 1·25 ml (¼ level tsp) citric acid or 10 ml (2 tsp) lemon juice to the prepared brine solution for every 450 g (1 lb) of tomatoes	1

2 A screw stopper.

3 A cork alone; it must be tied on with wire or string to prevent its being blown off during sterilisation.

Before use the bottles must be sterilised and corks, stoppers, etc, must be submerged under boiling water for at least 15 minutes.

In extracting the juice from the fruit no water is needed except for blackcurrants – 300 ml (½ pint) per 450 g (1 lb) – and blackberries – 300 ml (½ pint) per 2·7 kg (6 lb). There are two methods of carrying out this process.

1 Place the fruit in a bowl over a pan of boiling water, break it up with a wooden spoon and leave until the juice flows freely from the fruit (about 1 hour for 2·7 kg (6 lb)), keeping the pan replenished with boiling water. (This method ensures that the fruit is not over-cooked, which tends to destroy its colour and fresh flavour.)

2 Heat the fruit in a pan with the water (if used), and bring quickly to the boil, stirring constantly. Boil for 1 minute, crushing any whole fruit with a wooden spoon. Tip the fruit into a jelly bag and allow to drain overnight; the next day, press and squeeze the pulp thoroughly to remove all the remaining juice. Usually 325 g (12 oz) sugar is required for each 600 ml (1 pint) of juice. Stir it into the liquid over a gentle heat until dissolved.

Pour syrup into bottles to within 3·5 cm (1½ inch) of top, then seal. Place in a deep pan padded with thick cloth or newspaper. Fill to the base of the corks or stoppers with cold water, then raise to simmering point and maintain this temperature for 20 minutes.

Remove the bottles. If using corks only, seal by brushing over with melted candle wax when the bottles are slightly cooled. Store in a cool, dry place.

ng must be followed exactly – it is particularly important to tighten screw-bands immediately after processing.

When the fruit rises in the jar This does not affect the keeping quality of the fruit, but it does spoil the appearance. It can be due to the use of over-ripe fruit or too heavy a syrup, to over-processing, too high a temperature during the processing or loose packing in the jars.

When mould appears or fermentation takes place These are caused by poor-quality fruit, insufficient sterilising or failure of the bottle to seal.

When fruit is darkened If only the top fruit is attacked, it can be due to fruit not being fully covered by liquid or to under-

processing. If fruit is darkened throughout, this is probably due to using fruit in poor condition, over-processing or failure to store in a cool, dark place.

Fruit syrups and juices

Fruit too ripe for bottling or jam-making is excellent for making syrups; the best are blackberries, blackcurrants, loganberries, raspberries and strawberries.

Any fairly small bottles can be used. Seal them as follows:

1 With a cork, which must be cut off level with the top of the bottle and covered by a screw-cap.

Raspberry or redcurrant syrup

Wash the fruit and drain it thoroughly. Put it into a large basin and stand this over a saucepan of boiling water, then heat slowly until the juice begins to flow, mashing the fruit with a wooden spoon occasionally. Remove from the heat and strain through a jelly-bag. Transfer the pulp to a clean linen cloth, fold over the ends and twist them in opposite directions, to squeeze out as much juice as possible. Measure the extracted juice and add 325 g (12 oz) sugar to every 600 ml (1 pint). Stir thoroughly over a gentle heat until dissolved and pour into sterilised jars. Sterilise as directed above and wrap the bottles in brown paper to keep the

235

syrup a good colour during any length of storage.

Serving suggestions

Use this syrup as a sauce to serve with steamed sponge puddings and similar sweets in the winter, or with ice cream in the summer.

Rose-hip syrup

Rose-hips give a syrup which is particularly rich in vitamin C, and a different method of making is used to ensure that the highest possible amount of the vitamin is retained. The syrup is valuable both for growing children and for those who are suffering from a deficiency of vitamin C in their diet.

Choose hips which are fresh, fully ripe and deep red. Crush, grate or mince them and put at once into boiling water, allowing 1·7 litres (3 pints) per 900 g (2 lb) hips. Bring back to boiling point, then remove from the heat and allow to stand for 10–15 minutes. Strain through a scalded cloth or jelly-bag and when it ceases to drip, return the pulp to the pan with another 900 ml (1½ pints) boiling water. Re-boil and let stand as before for 10 minutes, then strain. Mix the two extracts, pour into a clean pan and reduce by boiling until the juice measures 900 ml (1½ pints). Add 450 g (1 lb) sugar. Stir until dissolved and boil for 5 minutes. Pour while hot into clean, hot bottles and seal at once. Sterilise as for all fruit syrups.

Rose-hip syrup may be taken neat, or diluted to make a drink; alternatively, it may be used in the same ways as Raspberry or Redcurrant Syrup.

Pickles and chutneys

EQUIPMENT

The pans used for pickles, etc, should be made of a thick-gauge metal which is not affected by the acid in the vinegar. The best types are aluminium, stainless steel, or those lined with porcelain or enamel (make sure that the lining is not chipped or damaged in any way). Unlined brass or copper pans must not be used, as the acid reacts with the metal, forming traces of a poisonous salt – copper acetate.

The coverings for pickle and chutney jars should be really airtight, to prevent evaporation of the vinegar.

Suitable types are: **(1)** Special vinegar-proof synthetic 'skin' **(2)** Parchment paper brushed over with melted paraffin wax **(3)** Greaseproof paper covered with a piece of fine cotton dipped in wax **(4)** Properly

236

lacquered metal caps which are lined with discs of a special vinegar-proof paper called ceresin, or with waxed cardboard or with a layer of cork, so that the preserve does not come into contact with the metal and cause corrosion and rusting. Old metal caps should not be re-used unless the lacquer is in perfect condition, and they should always be relined with new ceresin discs.

SPICED VINEGAR FOR PICKLING

The vinegar must be of high quality, with an acetic acid content of not less than 6 per cent; it may be malt, white, wine or cider. To each 1·1 litres (2 pints) add 10 g (¼ oz) each of some or all of the following spices; cloves, peppercorns, allspice, chillies, blade mace, mustard seed and root ginger. (Alternatively, buy them already mixed as 'pickling spice'.)

Bring just to the boil in a covered pan, then remove from the heat, allow to infuse until the vinegar is flavoured – about 2 hours is usually sufficient – and strain.

If you like a very spicy flavour, include the actual spices in the pickle, either in between the layers of vegetables, or placed in the top of each jar – tied if desired in a muslin bag for easy removal.

When filling pickle jars, allow at least 1 cm (½ inch) vinegar above the level of the fruit or vegetable, as a little evaporation is inevitable, but do not let the vinegar come in contact with metal caps.

Allow your pickles and chutneys to mature for 2–3 months (except for cabbage, which is better eaten while still crisp); to preserve their colour, it is best to store them in a dark place.

PICKLES

These can be sweet or sour, and are made from uncooked fruit and vegetables (either left whole or cut up, used singly or mixed), which are preserved in clear spiced vinegar. Piccalilli is an exception, and consists of a combination of vegetables preserved in a special thickened mixture.

The first stage in pickle-making, after the preparation of the fruit or vegetables, is the brining process, which should be 'dry' or 'wet' according to the water content of the particular ingredient. The purpose is to extract liquid and carbohydrates from the tissues, making the pickled food crisp and preventing the growth of bacteria. If the water is not extracted, it dilutes the vinegar, reducing its preserving powers, and also makes it harder for it to penetrate the

tissues. After brining, rinse and drain the fruit or vegetables very thoroughly.

Dry brining is used for watery vegetables such as cucumber, marrow, tomatoes, etc. Place the prepared vegetables in a mixing bowl, sprinkle salt between the layers allowing about 15 ml (1 level tbsp) salt to 450 g (1 lb) vegetables; cover and leave overnight.

Wet brining is used for cauliflower, onions etc. Allow 50 g (2 oz) salt to 600 ml (1 pint) water (sufficient for about 450 g (1 lb) vegetables), place the prepared vegetables in a mixing bowl, cover with the brine and leave overnight. Root vegetables, such as artichokes, and sometimes beetroot, are cooked in half-strength brine until tender.

Spiced vinegar is used for covering most simple pickles. Brewed malt vinegar is most commonly used, but for onions, cauliflower and other light-coloured vegetables, white vinegar may be used.

CHUTNEYS

Chutneys are a blend of fruit and vegetables with vinegar, sugar and spices cooked to a thick consistency; a long simmering time gives a pleasantly smooth mellow flavour. A vast variety of flavours and colours can be obtained by combining different fruits and vegetables, but the final effect should not be too pungent. To ensure the characteristic soft, even texture, the ingredients must be either minced or evenly and finely chopped, and no whole spices should be included.

Pickled onions

Choose small onions or shallots. To make the peeling easier, either do it under cold water, or use a knife and fork. Soak in brine made with 50 g (2 oz) salt to 600 ml (1 pint) water for 24 hours, then drain and wash well. Pack into jars, using a wooden spoon handle, and pour the cold spiced vinegar over. Seal and store.

Pickled red cabbage

1 firm red cabbage
salt
1·1 litres (2 pints) spiced vinegar (see page 238)

Quarter the cabbage, removing the outer leaves and centre stalk. Shred each quarter and place in a large basin, sprinkling each layer with salt. Leave overnight, then rinse and drain thoroughly. Pack loosely into bottles or jars, cover with vinegar and tie down. Do not store for more than 2–3 months, or the cabbage will lose its crispness and colour.

Apple and rhubarb cobbler (see page 138).

Pickled walnuts

green walnuts
brine
spiced vinegar used cold (see page 238)

Wipe the walnuts, prick well and put into a basin, rejecting any that feel hard when pricked. Cover with brine. Allow to soak for 7 days, throw away the brine, cover with fresh brine and re-soak for 14 days. Wash, dry well, spread the walnuts out and expose them to the air until they blacken. Put into pickle jars, pour hot spiced vinegar over and tie down when cold. Store in a cool place for 5–6 weeks before use.

An interesting variation is obtained by pickling walnuts and onions together. Each should be prepared according to the directions given. Place equal quantities of each in jars, arranged in alternate layers, and pour cold spiced vinegar over them.

Apple and onion pickle

325 g (12 oz) tart-flavoured cooking
   apples
325 g (12 oz) onions, skinned
50 g (2 oz) sultanas
9 peppercorns
9 cloves
40 g (1½ oz) chillies
7.5 ml (1½ level tsp) salt
400 ml (¾ pint) vinegar

Chop the apples and onions finely and pack them together with the sultanas in hot, dry jars. Tie the spices in muslin, add the salt to the vinegar and steep the spices in it for 30 minutes. Bring to the boil and simmer for 10 minutes. Pour on the boiling vinegar and tie down. This is ready for use the next day.

Mint pickle

225 g (8 oz) tomatoes
450 g (1 lb) sound cooking apples
300 ml (½ pint) vinegar
225 g (8 oz) sugar
10 ml (2 level tsp) dry mustard
10 ml (2 level tsp) salt
1 stick of cinnamon
5 ml (1 level tsp) peppercorns
1 blade of mace
6 small onions, skinned
25 g (1 oz) sultanas
1 teacupful mint leaves (pressed down)

Cut the tomatoes into four and peel and slice the apples. Boil the vinegar, sugar, condiments and spices together very gently for 30 minutes, then strain. Add the remaining ingredients (except the mint) and simmer for 10 minutes. When the mixture is cold, pack the fruit and onions in jars, sprinkling the chopped mint leaves liberally between the layers. Cover with the

spiced vinegar, cover the jars and leave for a month before use.

Mixed pickles

The following vegetables make a good mixed pickle: Cauliflower, cucumber, green tomatoes, onions and marrow.

Prepare the vegetables, with the exception of the marrow, and soak in brine for 24 hours. Peel the marrow, remove the seeds and cut into small squares, sprinkle with salt and let stand for 12 hours. Drain the vegetables, rinse, pack and cover with cold spiced vinegar, tie down and store for at least 1 month before eating.

Piccalilli

1 large cauliflower
2 cucumbers
900 g (2 lb) shallots
900 g (2 lb) apples
brine
25 g (1 oz) chilli peppers
50 g (2 oz) garlic, skinned
25 g (1 oz) bruised root ginger
25 g (1 oz) black peppercorns
1.1 litres (2 pints) vinegar
50 g (2 oz) cornflour
25 g (1 oz) turmeric
25 g (1 oz) dry mustard

Prepare all the vegetables and the apples as required and cut into neat pieces. Cover with cold brine, leave overnight, drain and pack into hot jars. Boil the chilli peppers, garlic, ginger and peppercorns in the vinegar for 5 minutes, then pour in the cornflour, turmeric and dry mustard, previously blended with a little cold vinegar. Stir and boil for 10 minutes to cook the cornflour. Pour on to the vegetables and fruit and cover in the usual way.

Green tomato chutney

Illustrated in colour on page 240

1.4 kg (3 lb) green tomatoes
225 g (8 oz) cooking apples
225 g (8 oz) onions
25 g (1 oz) salt
100 g (4 oz) prunes
175 g (6 oz) sugar
15 g (½ oz) mustard seed
2.5 ml (½ level tsp) pepper
2.5 ml (½ level tsp) ground allspice
400 ml (¾ pint) vinegar

Wipe the tomatoes and remove the stalks. Peel and core the apples and peel the onions. Put all through a mincer, then add the salt and leave overnight. Soak the prunes overnight. The next day, strain off the liquid from the tomatoes, etc, and turn the pulp into a pan. Stone and chop the

prunes and add to the tomatoes, with the sugar, the spices (tied in muslin), and the vinegar. Simmer gently, stirring occasionally, until reduced to a pulp – about 2 hours. Pot and cover.

Red tomato chutney

Illustrated in colour on page 240

1.8 kg (4 lb) red tomatoes
25 g (1 oz) mustard seed
10 ml (2 level tsp) allspice
2.5 ml (½ level tsp) cayenne pepper
225 g (8 oz) sugar (granulated or
   Demerara)
25 g (1 oz) salt
400 ml (¾ pint) white malt vinegar

Peel the tomatoes by putting them all in boiling water for 1–2 minutes, then plunging them into cold – the skins will then come off easily. Tie the mustard seed and allspice in muslin and add with the cayenne to the tomatoes. Boil until reduced to a pulp (45 minutes) and add the sugar, salt and vinegar. Continue boiling until the right consistency is obtained (45 minutes–1 hour) and bottle in hot sterilised jars. (Take care to reduce the mixture sufficiently, or the chutney will be too liquid.)

Spiced sweet pickle

1.4 kg (3 lb) mixed cucumber, melon
   rinds, and cooking apples
45 ml (3 level tbsp) allspice
45 ml (3 level tbsp) cloves
1 stick of cinnamon
1.1 litres (2 pints) vinegar
700 g (1½ lb) Demerara sugar

Cut the fruit and vegetables into neat pieces. Stew the melon rind in a little water for 15 minutes, then add the cucumber and apple, cook for a further 10 minutes, and drain thoroughly. Tie all the spices in a muslin bag and boil with the vinegar and the sugar for 10 minutes. Add the fruit and vegetables, bring to the boil and simmer for 5 minutes. Drain the mixture well and pack it into hot jars. Boil the vinegar for a further 10 minutes, remove the bag of spices and pour the vinegar into the jars. Cover in the usual way.

Apple chutney

Illustrated in colour on page 240

1.4 kg (3 lb) cooking apples, peeled,
   cored and diced
1.4 kg (3 lb) onions, skinned and
   chopped
450 g (1 lb) sultanas or stoned raisins
rind and juice of 2 lemons
700 g (1½ lb) Demerara sugar
600 ml (1 pint) malt vinegar

Put the apples, onions and sultanas in a large saucepan. Grate the lemon rind, strain the juice, and add both to the pan with the sugar and vinegar. Bring to the boil, reduce the heat, and simmer in the open pan until the mixture is of a thick consistency, with no free liquid. Pot and cover.

Apple and tomato chutney

900 g (2 lb) apples
900 g (2 lb) tomatoes
325 g (12 oz) onions
1 clove of garlic
225 g (8 oz) dried fruit (seeded)
325 g (12 oz) sugar
15 g (½ oz) mustard seed
15 g (½ oz) curry powder
5 ml (1 level tsp) cayenne pepper
salt to taste
900 ml (1½ pints) vinegar

Peel and core the apples and stew in a very little water until they are tender and pulpy. Cut up the tomatoes and chop the onions and the garlic (also the dried fruit if necessary). Add these and the sugar to the prepared fruit. Tie the mustard seed in a piece of muslin and add it, with the remaining ingredients, including the vinegar, and cook gently for about 2 hours. When the chutney reaches the required consistency, pot and cover.

Apricot chutney

900 g (2 lb) dried apricots
225 g (8 oz) onions, skinned
1.4 kg (3 lb) brown sugar
5 ml (1 level tsp) curry powder
5 ml (1 level tsp) cinnamon
5 ml (1 level tsp) allspice
a pinch of cayenne pepper
1.1 litres (2 pints) wine vinegar

Wash the apricots well, cover them with boiling water and leave for 24 hours. Chop the onions, and stew them with a little of the sugar until tender. Strain the apricots and cut into pieces, put into a pan with the sugar, spices, onions and vinegar and simmer until the chutney is thick – about 2 hours. Pot and cover.

Damson chutney

1.6 kg (3½ lb) damsons
2 onions, skinned
1 clove of garlic, skinned
225 g (8 oz) raisins
100 g (4 oz) dates
700 g (1½ lb) brown sugar
1.4 litres (2½ pints) malt vinegar
15 g (½ oz) salt
25 g (1 oz) ground ginger
1.25 ml (¼ level tsp) ground allspice

Wash the fruit. Chop the onions, crush and chop the garlic, chop the raisins and dates. Mix all the ingredients in a pan and simmer for 1½–2 hours very slowly, until the desired consistency is attained. Remove the damson stones. Pour into jars while hot and cover immediately.

Date and apple chutney

450 g (1 lb) apples
450 g (1 lb) dates
225 g (8 oz) onions
50 g (2 oz) sultanas
225 g (8 oz) treacle
2.5 ml (½ level tsp) cayenne pepper
15 g (½ oz) salt
6 cloves
5 ml (1 level tsp) ground allspice
600 ml (1 pint) vinegar

Peel and core the apples, stone the dates if necessary, skin the onions and put all these ingredients through a mincer, together with the sultanas. Put the remaining ingredients in a pan and bring slowly to the boil. Add the minced fruit, etc, and simmer gently until the chutney is of a thick consistency. Pot and cover at once.

Gooseberry chutney

1.4 kg (3 lb) gooseberries
225 g (8 oz) stoned raisins
4 onions, skinned and sliced thinly
15 ml (1 tbsp) crushed mustard seed
2.5 ml (½ level tsp) cayenne pepper
30 ml (2 level tbsp) salt
775 g (1¾ lb) brown sugar
900 ml (1½ pints) vinegar

Put all the ingredients in a pan and cover with the vinegar. Bring to the boil slowly and continue to cook for 2 hours, until the gooseberries are thoroughly pulped. If the vinegar boils away, add a little more. Put the chutney into warm jars and seal immediately.

Pear chutney

1.4 kg (3 lb) pears
450 g (1 lb) onions, skinned
450 g (1 lb) green tomatoes
225 g (8 oz) raisins, seeded
225 g (8 oz) celery
700 g (1½ lb) Demerara sugar
1.25 ml (¼ level tsp) cayenne pepper
1.25 ml (¼ level tsp) ground ginger
15 g (½ oz) salt
5 peppercorns
1.1 litres (2 pints) vinegar

Peel, core and slice the pears, chop the onions, wipe and cut up the tomatoes and cut up the raisins. Put all these ingredients into a pan and cook gently until tender. Add the finely chopped celery, the sugar, the spices and the vinegar and simmer for 4 hours, until the chutney is sufficiently thick. Pot and cover.

Plum and apple chutney

1.4 kg (3 lb) plums
900 g (2 lb) apples
450 g (1 lb) green tomatoes
225 g (8 oz) onions
15 g (½ oz) root ginger
25 g (1 oz) allspice
5 ml (1 level tsp) salt
900 ml (1½ pints) vinegar
700 g (1½ lb) granulated sugar
15 ml (1 tbsp) finely chopped mint

Prepare the fruit and vegetables, stoning the plums, peeling and coring the apples, stalking the tomatoes, and skinning the onions, then chop them up and mix well together. Bruise the ginger and tie in muslin with the allspice. Put everything except the sugar and mint into a saucepan and simmer until the mixture begins to thicken. Add the sugar and mint and cook until quite thick. Remove the bag of spices, pot and cover.

Rhubarb chutney

900 g (2 lb) rhubarb
2 cloves of garlic, skinned
25 g (1 oz) root ginger
peel of 2 lemons
25 g (1 oz) salt
10 ml (2 level tsp) cayenne pepper
450 g (1 lb) sultanas
900 g (2 lb) Demerara sugar
600 ml (1 pint) vinegar

Shred the rhubarb finely and chop the garlic. Crush the root ginger and tie in a piece of muslin with the lemon peel. Put all the ingredients into a pan and simmer gently, stirring frequently, until the mixture thickens. Remove the bag of flavourings and pot the chutney while hot. Keep it for 3 months before using.

Sweet mango chutney

Illustrated in colour on page 240

6 yellow mangoes
150 ml (¼ pint) malt vinegar
175 g (6 oz) Demerara sugar
2 chillies, crushed
40 g (1½ oz) preserved ginger, chopped
2 cloves of garlic, skinned and crushed
40 g (1½ oz) raisins
25 g (1 oz) almonds, blanched
1.25 ml (¼ level tsp) salt

Peel the mangoes, slice the flesh thinly into a pan, add the vinegar and simmer for 10 minutes. Add the sugar and chillies, then cook until the mixture begins to thicken slightly. Add the ginger and garlic and cook

gently for about 30 minutes, stirring occasionally. Add the raisins, almonds and salt, and cook for a further 5 minutes. Pour into hot jars, seal, sterilise and store.

PRESERVING TOMATOES

Tomatoes can be preserved in a variety of ways; the most usual method is to bottle them, but they may also be stored in the form of purée or juice, or made into sauce or chutney.

Bottled tomatoes

Any method used for bottling fruit is suitable for tomatoes; these are the main variations in the preparation:

With no liquid added Dip each tomato in boiling water for about 20 seconds, then remove the skin. Use small tomatoes whole, but halve or quarter larger ones, so that they may be packed really tightly with no air spaces, making it unnecessary to add any water. Mix together 5 ml (1 level tsp) salt, 5 ml (1 level tsp) sugar and 1·25 ml (¼ level tsp) citric acid per 450 g (1 lb) of fruit and sprinkle between the layers of tomatoes.

In their own juice Peel the tomatoes as above and pack tightly into bottles. Stew some extra tomatoes in a covered pan, with 5 ml (1 level tsp) salt to each 900 g (2 lb) fruit, strain the juice, add 1·25 ml (¼ level tsp) citric acid or 10 ml (2 tsp) lemon juice per 450 g (1 lb) of fruit and use to fill up the jars.

Whole unskinned tomatoes (recommended for oven sterilising) Remove the stalks and wash or wipe the tomatoes. Pack into bottles and fill up with a brine made with 10 ml (2 level tsp) salt per 1·1 litres (2 pints) water. Add 1·25 ml (¼ level tsp) citric acid or 10 ml (2 tsp) lemon juice per 450 g (1 lb) of fruit.

For the temperatures and times for bottling tomatoes, see the general bottling tables on pages 232 and 234.

Bottled tomato purée

This method enables poorly shaped tomatoes to be used, though they must be sound and ripe. Wash them and heat in a covered pan with a little water and salt and cook until soft. Rub the pulp through a sieve and return it to the pan, then bring to the boil. Add 1·25 ml (¼ level tsp) citric acid or 10 ml (2 tsp) lemon juice per 450 g (1 lb) of tomatoes, pour at once into hot jars and put the metal sealing discs and screwbands in place. It is very important that this process should be carried out quickly, as the pulp deteriorates if left exposed to the air. Immerse the bottles in a pan of hot water (padded with thick cloth or newspaper), bring to the boil and boil for 10 minutes. Finish and test as usual.

Tomato juice

Simmer ripe tomatoes until soft and rub them through a hair or nylon sieve. To each 1·1 litres (2 pints) of pulp add 300 ml (½ pint) water, 5 ml (1 level tsp) salt, 25 g (1 oz) sugar, a pinch of pepper and 1·25 ml (¼ level tsp) citric acid or 10 ml (2 tsp) lemon juice.

Process the juice as for Tomato Purée.

Red tomato sauce

1·8 kg (4 lb) ripe tomatoes
2 medium onions
25 g (1 oz) salt
a pinch of cayenne pepper
2·5 ml (½ level tsp) paprika pepper
100 g (4 oz) sugar
200 ml (⅓ pint) spiced vinegar (see page 238)
5 ml (1 level tsp) citric acid

Wash and chop the tomatoes, place them in a pan with the peeled and chopped onions and simmer gently until the tomatoes are pulped. Rub through a sieve, return the mixture to the pan and add the remaining ingredients. Simmer, stirring

occasionally, until a creamy consistency is obtained. Add the citric acid. Pour into warm bottles, seal with sterilised corks and brush the top with melted candlewax when cool.

Green tomato sauce

1·4 kg (3 lb) green tomatoes
225 g (8 oz) apples
100 g (4 oz) onions, skinned and sliced
225 g (8 oz) sugar
15 g (½ oz) salt
225 g (8 oz) golden syrup
20 g (¾ oz) peppercorns
2·5 ml (½ level tsp) cayenne pepper
3 cloves
1–2 blades of mace
2·5 ml (½ level tsp) celery seed
400 ml (¾ pint) vinegar
3·75 ml (¾ level tsp) citric acid

Wipe and slice the tomatoes, peel, core and slice the apples, then add the onion, sugar, salt, syrup, spices, etc, and pour the vinegar over them. Boil gently until the sauce is thick, rub it through a fine sieve (adding more vinegar if necessary), then reheat, stirring, and boil until a creamy consistency is obtained. Add the citric acid and pour into warmed sterilised bottles and cover immediately.

Green tomato chutney, Red tomato chutney, Apple chutney (see page 238), Sweet mango chutney (see page 239).

HOME MADE SWEETS

Equipment

If you want to make more than an occasional batch of sweets, it is worthwhile investing in a few pieces of special equipment; they will save time and effort and prevent wasting ingredients. These are the chief requirements:

Sugar-boiling thermometer Necessary for measuring temperature accurately – which often spells the difference between success and failure.

Choose a thermometer which is easy to read and well graduated from 16°C (60°F) to 182°C (360°F) or 232°C (450°F). These thermometers are usually mounted on brass, with a brass or wooden handle; it is useful to have a sliding clip that fits over the side of the pan.

To 'season' a new thermometer, place it in cold water, bring to the boil and leave in the water to cool.

To check a thermometer, try it in boiling water, 100°C (212°F), and note any inaccuracy.

When using the thermometer, shake well so that the mercury thread is unbroken and see that the bulb is completely immersed in the mixture. When the thermometer is not actually in the sweet mixture, stand it in hot water. Clean it very thoroughly, as any sugar crystals left on might spoil the next boiling. Always read a thermometer at eye level.

Saucepan This must be strong and thick-based, to prevent burning and sticking. Cast aluminium is a good choice; enamel or non-stick pans are not suitable, as it is possible that high temperatures may crack the lining.

Spatula A wooden spatula is useful for 'working' fondant mixtures and beating fudges.

Flexible-bladed palette knife One with a stainless steel blade is useful for lifting and shaping sweets.

Marble slab Expensive to buy and not absolutely essential, since an enamelled surface can be used instead. Certain plastic surfaces will also withstand temperatures up to 138°C (280°F), but usually not beyond this.

Rubber fondant mat Consists of a sheet of rubber, 2·5 cm (1 inch) thick, with fancy-shapes impressions into which liquid fondant, jelly or chocolate is run and allowed to set. When the shapes are firm, they can easily be removed by bending back the rubber.

Sugar boiling

This process is the basis of all sweet-making. The sugar is first dissolved in the liquid, then brought to the boil, 100°C (212°F). The temperature continues to rise as the water is evaporated; the syrup thickens and then becomes darker in colour as the temperature rises – at 177°C (350°F) it is a very dark brown.

To measure the temperature really accurately you need a sugar-boiling thermometer (see above), but for simple sweets you can use the homely tests described here.

Smooth 102°C–104°C (215°F–220°F): For crystallising purposes. The mixture begins to look syrupy. To test, dip the fingers in water and then very quickly in the syrup; the thumb will slide smoothly over the fingers, but the sugar clings to the finger.

Soft ball 113°C–118°C (235°F–245°F): For fondants and fudges. When a drop of the syrup is put into very cold water, it forms a soft ball; at 113°C (235°F) the soft ball flattens on being removed from the water, but the higher the temperature, the firmer the ball, until it reaches the next, firm ball, stage.

Firm or hard ball 118°C–130°C (245°F–265°F): For caramels, marsh-mallows and nougat. When dropped into cold water, the syrup forms a ball which is hard enough to hold its shape, but is still plastic.

Soft crack 132°C–143°C (270°F–290°F): For toffees. When dropped into cold water, the syrup separates into threads which are hard but not brittle.

Hard crack 149°C–154°C (300°F–310°F): For hard toffees and rock. When a drop of the syrup is put into cold water, it separates into threads which are hard and brittle.

Caramel 154°C (310°F): For praline and caramels. Shown by the syrup becoming golden brown.

Boiled fondant

150 ml (¼ pint) water (good measure)
450 g (1 lb) granulated sugar
45 ml (3 level tbsp) glucose or a good pinch cream of tartar

Put the water into a pan, add the sugar and let it dissolve slowly. Bring the syrup to the boil, add the glucose or cream of tartar and boil to 116°C (240°F). Sprinkle a little water on a marble slab or other suitable surface, pour on the syrup and leave for a few minutes to cool. When a skin forms round the edges, take the spatula and collect the mixture together, then work it backwards and forwards, using a figure-of-eight movement. Continue to work the syrup, collecting it into as small a compass as possible, until it changes its character and 'grains', becoming opaque and firm. Scrape it off the slab and knead it in the hands until of an even texture throughout. *Note* If no slab is available, the fondant can be 'turned' in a bowl; leave it in the bowl for 15 minutes to cool, 'turn' it in the bowl until thick, then knead it on grease-proof paper.

Fondant creams

Prepare some fondant and knead it well (particularly if it has been stored for some time). To improve the texture and flavour, add a little cream, evaporated milk or melted butter. (If you are using freshly made fondant, add the cream, milk or butter while the fondant is still melted.) Divide the mixture into portions and flavour and colour as required, eg, with lemon, violet, coffee, etc. Roll the fondant out to the required thickness, using a little icing sugar on the board, and cut out with a small cutter or model it by hand.

To obtain fancy shapes, or to make chocolate centres, melt the fondant in a basin over a pan of hot water or in a double saucepan over a very gentle heat; use a little sugar syrup (or a few drops of water) to help to liquefy it. When it is liquid, pour it into moulds in a rubber fondant mat, using a funnel or teaspoon.
Mocha nuts Flavour the liquid fondant with coffee and dip halved walnuts and whole Brazil nuts in it.
Peppermint creams Knead a few drops of oil of peppermint into the fondant, roll out 0·5 cm (¼ inch) thick and cut into rounds with a 2·5-cm (1-inch) cutter.

Toffees

A toffee is basically a simple sugar mixture, requiring to be boiled to a high temperature – 138°C–154°C (280°F–310°F) according to type. These are important points to remember when making toffee:

1 You must use a large, heavy-based pan, as toffee tends to boil over.

2 Don't stir the mixture unless the recipe definitely states this should be done.

3 Move the thermometer from time to time, as the toffee may stick to the bulb and give an inaccurate reading.

4 Keep the heat very low after the mixture reaches 127°C (260°F).

5 Remove the pan from the heat when the mixture has reached a temperature about 2°C (5°F) below the figure require, because the pan holds the heat, so the mixture may be over-boiled. Make sure, however, that the toffee does actually come to the correct temperature.

6 Pour the mixture into the prepared tin as soon as the correct temperature is reached.

Treacle toffee squares

Illustrated in colour on page 244

450 g (1 lb) demerara sugar
150 ml (¼ pint) water
75 g (3 oz) butter
1·25 ml (¼ level tsp) cream of tartar
100 g (4 oz) black treacle
100 g (4 oz) golden syrup

Butter an 18-cm (7-inch) square tin. Dissolve the sugar in the water in a 2·3-litre (4-pint) heavy-based pan over a low heat. Add the remaining ingredients and bring to the boil. Boil to 132°C (270°F) (soft crack stage). Pour into the tin, and when the toffee begins to set mark into squares with a buttered knife. For a variation, make small drops of the toffee mixture on an oiled tin and press a shelled walnut on top of each while still warm. *Makes about 550 g (1¼ lb)*

Peanut brittle

400 g (14 oz) granulated sugar
175 g (6 oz) soft brown sugar
175 g (6 oz) corn syrup or golden syrup
150 ml (¼ pint) water
50 g (2 oz) butter
1·25 ml (¼ level tsp) bicarbonate of soda
350 g (12 oz) unsalted peanuts, chopped

Butter a tin 30·5 × 10 cm (12 × 4 inches) or an 18-cm (7-inch) square tin. Dissolve the sugars, syrup and water over a low heat in a 2·3-litre (4-pint) heavy-based saucepan. Add the butter and bring to the boil; boil very gently to 149°C (300°F) (hard crack stage). Add the bicarbonate of soda and slightly warmed nuts. Pour slowly into the tin and mark into bars when almost set. *Makes about 900 g (2 lb)*

Golden caramels

225 g (8 oz) sugar
50 g (2 oz) glucose
15 ml (1 tbsp) golden syrup
60 ml (4 tbsp) water
60 ml (4 tbsp) milk
vanilla essence

Oil a tin 15 cm × 20·5 cm (6 × 8 inches). Put all the ingredients except the essence in a pan, dissolve the sugar and slowly heat to 124°C (255°F) (hard ball stage), stirring occasionally. Add a little essence, stir and pour the mixture into the tin. Mark with a knife and break into squares when cold. Wrap individually, in waxed paper if possible. *Makes about 350 g (12 oz)*

Butterscotch bars

Illustrated in colour on page 244

225 g (8 oz) granulated sugar
150 ml (¼ pint) water
a pinch of cream of tartar
75 g (3 oz) butter

In a 1·7-litre (3-pint) heavy-based pan, dissolve the sugar in the water. Add a pinch of cream of tartar and boil to 138°C (280°F). Off the heat, add the butter in small pieces. Boil to 149°C (300°F). Remove from the heat and pour into a buttered 15-cm (6-inch) square tin. When the butterscotch starts to set mark into bars with a buttered knife. *Makes about 25*

Chocolate nougatines

Illustrated in colour on page 244

140 g (5½ oz) caster sugar
100 g (4 oz) nibbed almonds

Put the sugar in a heavy-based pan and dissolve over a low heat until liquid, shaking the pan occasionally. Heat until pale caramel colour. Add the almonds and stir with a metal spoon. Turn quickly on to an oiled baking sheet and roll out using a greased lemon or grapefruit (not a rolling pin) to 0·5 cm (¼ inch) thickness. Warm some small metal cutters in star and circle shapes and stamp out quickly. Decorate with piped melted chocolate.

Vanilla fudge

Illustrated in colour on page 244

50 g (2 oz) butter
450 g (1 lb) granulated or caster sugar
150 ml (¼ pint) evaporated milk
150 ml (¼ pint) milk
2·5 ml (½ tsp) vanilla essence

Butter a 15-cm (6-inch) square shallow tin. In a heavy-based large saucepan, heat all ingredients except essence without boiling until the sugar has completely dissolved. Bring to the boil and boil gently to 116°C (240°F), stirring occasionally − this may take up to 30 minutes. Take off the heat, add the vanilla essence and beat until the mixture becomes thick and creamy and 'grains' appear. Pour at once into the tin, using a spatula. Cut into squares when set. *For a cherry variation*, omit the essence and add 60 g (2 oz) glacé cherries, chopped, and a little grated orange rind. *Makes about 450 g (1 lb)*

Chocolate fudge

450 g (1 lb) granulated sugar
150 ml (¼ pint) milk
150 g (5 oz) butter
100 g (4 oz) plain chocolate
50 g (2 oz) honey

Grease a tin 20·5 × 15 cm (8 × 6 inches). Place all the ingredients in a 2·8-litre (5-pint) heavy-based saucepan. Stir over a low heat until the sugar has dissolved. Bring to the boil and boil to 116°C (240°F) (soft ball stage). Remove from the heat, stand the pan on a cool surface for 5 minutes, then beat the mixture until thick, creamy and beginning to 'grain'. Pour into the tin, mark into squares and cut when cold. *Makes about 700 g (1½ lb)*

Marshmallow fudge Add 25 g (8 oz) chopped marshmallows to the mixture before beating; continue as above.

Fruit and nut fudge Add 50 g (2 oz) chopped nuts and 50 g (2 oz) seedless raisins; continue as above.

Date fudge Replace the 150 ml (¼ pint) milk by 150 ml (¼ pint) water and add 75 g (3 oz) finely chopped dates.

Crème de menthe

Illustrated in colour on page 244

30 ml (2 level tbsp) powdered gelatine
400 ml (¾ pint) water
550 g (1 lb 4 oz) icing sugar
30 ml (2 tbsp) lemon juice
5 ml (1 tsp) crème de menthe liqueur
peppermint essence
green food colouring
icing sugar for dredging

Soak the powdered gelatine in 200 ml (⅓ pint) water for 5 minutes. Dissolve the icing sugar in 200 ml (⅓ pint) water in a saucepan, add the gelatine and bring just to the boil. Simmer for 20 minutes, stirring occasionally. Cool slightly, then stir in the lemon juice and liqueur. Add the essence and colour to taste. Pour into a shallow tin to give 1 cm (½ inch) depth. Leave to set

vernight. When firm, unmould, dredge
ith icing sugar, cut into squares and dust
ut edges with more icing sugar.

Marzipan fruits

ustrated in colour opposite

25 g (8 oz) marzipan/almond paste
loves
ed, yellow and green food colouring

Divide the marzipan into four pieces, three
f equal size and one slightly larger.

pples Colour the largest piece of mar-
ipan green by kneading in a few drops of
reen and yellow food colouring. Divide
nto 12 pieces. Roll into small balls, reserv-
ng some of the marzipan for stalks for
ther fruit. Press a clove into the base of
ach apple and invert one in the top for a
talk. Brush with a little undiluted red food
olouring on cotton wool to make rosy
atches.

Oranges Knead a few drops of red and
ellow food colouring into the marzipan
ntil orange in colour. Divide into about 10
ieces and roll each into a ball. Roll over
he surface of a fine grater. Press a clove
nto the base of each.

ananas Colour the marzipan yellow. Roll
mall pieces into banana shapes. Group
ogether in threes, join with a small piece
f green. Mix a few drops of red, yellow and
reen food colouring to make brown col-
uring and paint in brown lines.

ineapples Colour marzipan a yellow
range and divide into 8 pieces. Roll each

into 2-cm (¾-inch) oblongs, rounding off
each end. Make a criss-cross pattern with a
knife and paint in with brown colouring.
With the remaining green marzipan, make
strips of fringes and roll up to form pineapple tops.

Marzipan walnuts

225 g (8 oz) marzipan or almond paste
15 ml (1 level tbsp) chopped walnuts
green food colouring
a few halved walnuts

Knead the marzipan and work in the chopped nuts and a few drops of colouring.
Shape into balls and decorate each with a
walnut half. *Makes about 225 g (8 oz)*

Chocolate truffles

225 g (8 oz) plain chocolate, grated
1 small can evaporated milk
175-g (6-oz) packet trifle sponges,
**   crumbled**
60 g (2 ½ oz) ground almonds
350 g (12 oz) icing sugar, sifted
15–30 ml (1–2 tbsp) rum
chocolate vermicelli or desiccated
**   coconut to decorate**

Put the chocolate and milk in a small
saucepan and heat gently to melt the
chocolate. Off the heat, stir in the remaining ingredients except the vermicelli or
coconut. Allow the mixture to cool. Shape
the mixture into bite-size balls and roll in
vermicelli or coconut, or press into rigid
foil sweet cases. *Makes about 60*

Coconut ice

450 g (1 lb) granulated sugar
150 ml (¼ pint) milk
150 g (5 oz) desiccated coconut
food colouring

Oil or butter a tin 20·5 × 15 cm (8 × 6 inches). Dissolve the sugar in the milk over a
low heat. Bring to the boil and boil gently
for about 10 minutes, or until a temperature of 116°C (240°F) (soft ball stage) is
reached. Remove from the heat and stir in
the coconut. Pour half the mixture quickly
into the tin. Colour the second half and
pour quickly over the first layer. Leave until
half set, mark into bars and cut or break
when cold. *Makes about 550 g (1 ¼ lb)*

Chocolate dates

450 g (1 lb) dessert dates
100 g (4 oz) plain chocolate
15 ml (1 tbsp) boiling water
2·5 ml (½ tsp) vanilla essence
silver balls to decorate

Slit the dates lengthways so that the stones
may be removed without breaking the
fruit. Grate the chocolate into a small pan
and add the boiling water and vanilla essence. Stir over a gentle heat until the
chocolate melts, then stand the pan inside
another saucepan of boiling water so that
the chocolate does not solidify too rapidly.
Open each date and use a teaspoon to fill
with melted chocolate. Gently press the
sides of the dates together and decorate
with silver balls. Allow to set in a cold
place. *Makes about 550 g (1 ¼ lb)*

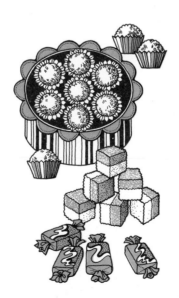

Crème de menthe, Vanilla fudge, Treacle toffee squares,
Butterscotch bars, Chocolate nougatines (see page 243),
Marzipan fruits (see above).

INDEX

Lamb (contd)
Paprika lamb chops 44
Pineapple lamb casserole 63
Roast lamb 43
Rolled stuffed breast of lamb 43
Spiced lamb with aubergines 63
Swiss braised lamb with wine 63
Langues de chat 198
Lardy cake 172
Lasagne al forno 130
Leek 104, 110:
Cheesy stuffed leeks 107
Ham and leeks au gratin 98
Leek and potato soup with meatballs 20
Leek salad 122
Leek and tomato salad 116
Potato and leek soup 20
Lemon:
Lemon buns 192
Lemon butter cream 206
Lemon chiffon cream 158
Lemon coconut sponge 188
Lemon curd 227, 228
Lemon fans 114
Lemon fingers 203
Lemon frosting 206
Lemon gâteau 183
Lemon glacé icing 206
Lemon meringue pie 160
Lemon and oil dressing 126
Lemon satin frosting 206
Lemon sauce 162
Lemon snow 152
Lemon sole 24
Lemon soufflé 143; cold 156
Lemon sponge 134
Lemon yeast buns 175
Lentil:
Lentil and bacon soup 21
Lentil purée (Dhal) 88
Lentil soup 16
Lettuce 114:
Lettuce and bacon salad 122
Lime marmalade 226
Lincolnshire farmhouse dripping cake 182
Liqueur coffees 219
Liqueur glacé icing 206
Liqueur soufflé 143
Liver:
Bacon and liver pie 50
Baked stuffed liver 54
French-style pâté maison 55
Liver hotpot 55
Liver Marsala 55
Liver pilau 133
Liver and vegetable casserole 54
Mexican liver with rice 55
Lobster:
Lobster cocktail 34
Lobster mayonnaise 34
Lobster Newburg 35
Lobster thermidor 34

Loganberry whirls 150
Lyonnaise potatoes 108
Lyonnaise tripe 55

Macaroni cheese 130
Macaroon pastries 196
Macaroons 194
Macheroni alla carbonara 130
Mackerel 24:
Apple-stuffed mackerel fillets 29
Baked stuffed mackerel 29
Madeira cake 178
Madeleines 195
Madras curry 87
Maids of honour 182
Maître d'hôtel butter 71
Malt loaf 179
Mango chutney, sweet 239
Maple satin frosting 206
Marbled cookies 204
Marguerite salad 120
Marmalade 224–6
Marmalade pudding 135
Marmalade (or jam) sauce 135
Marrow 104, 110:
Marrow with cheese sauce 107
Marrow and ginger jam 222
Stuffed marrow 107
Marshmallow creams 203
Marshmallow fudge 243
Marshmallow sauce 142
Marzipan fruits 245
Marzipan walnuts 245
Matabele fried chicken 74
Mayonnaise 126
Meat. See also Beef etc.
To carve meat 68
To choose meat 39
To pickle meat 70
To store meat 39
Italian mixed meat salad 118
Mixed grill 44
Meat balls 20
Meat platter 67
Meat salad mould 116
Party skewers to serve with dips 214
Sauces and accompaniments 71
Mediterranean pasta 130
Melon:
Brandied melon and ginger 147
Filled melon 154
Melon and fruit salad de luxe 147
Melon and pineapple jam 227
Melting moments 204
Meringue balls 162
Meringue nests 186
Meringue pyramid 152
Meringue tops 203
Meringue torte 186
Meringues 196
Merry-go-round cake 191

Mexican coffee 219
Midsummer Night's Dream cup 216
Milk loaf 166
Milk rolls 168
Milk puddings 140–2
Mille-feuilles 160
Mincemeat 228
Mincemeat cookies 204
Mincemeat ring 174
Mincemeat splits 194
Minestrone 13
Mint jelly 224
Mint and onion salad 122
Mint pickle 238
Mint sauce 71
Minute steaks 40
Mixed grill 44
Mixed pickles 238
Mocha butter cream 206
Mocha glacé icing 206
Mont blanc aux marrons 190
Moussaka, Greek aubergine 60
Mousse:
Apple mousse 155
Fish mousse 34
Strawberry mousse 151
Muffins 172
Mulligatawny soup 20
Mushroom 104, 110, 114:
Cold cream of mushroom soup 23
Cream of mushroom soup 14
Curried mushroom salad 119
Mushroom casserole 107
Mushroom omelette 95
Mushroom ring 111
Mushroom salad 122
Mushroom sauce 36, 71
Mushroom-stuffed crisp rolls 91
Paupiettes of sole with mushroom sauce 30
Salad of mushroom and shell-fish 118
Sole with mushrooms 32
'Mushroom' cake 191
Mussel salad 119
Mustard and cress 114
Mutton see Lamb

Noodles milanaise 51
Norfolk cake 180
'Number' birthday cake 191
Nut fruit clusters 199
Nutty-stuffed tomatoes 111
Nutty twists 175

Oatcakes 199
Offal 39, 51–8. See also Brains etc.
Omelettes:
Asparagus omelette 96
Herb omelette 95
Kidney omelette 95
Mushroom omelette 95
Omelette cardinal 95

Omelettes (contd)
Plain omelette 95
Sausage and pepper omelette 96
Soufflé omelettes 96
Spanish omelette 95
Sweet soufflé omelettes 96
Onion 104, 110:
French onion soup 17
Mint and onion salad 122
Onion rings 114
Onion sauce 71
Onion soup 14
Onion soup with cheese 18
Pickled onions 236
Potatoes with onions 107
Stuffed onions 107
Tripe and onions 55
Open sandwiches 215
Orange:
Baked orange soufflé 143
Glazed orange cheesecake 148
Orange ambrosia 147
Orange baskets 151
Orange buns 192
Orange butter cream 206
Orange cookies 204
Orange cream tart 159
Orange frosting 206
Orange glacé icing 206
Orange liqueur gâteau 186
Orange and pineapple cake 186
Orange pudding 139
Orange and raspberry bavarois 151
Orange salad 154
Orange sandwich cake 183
Orange sauce 162
Orange sponge 134
Quick orange buns 196
Seville orange marmalade 224, 226
Shred marmalade 224, 226
Sole with orange 30
Thick dark marmalade 224
Watercress and orange soup 21
Osso bucco 67
Ox tongue, boiled 51
Oxtail:
Oxtail casserole 54
Oxtail hotpot 54
Oxtail soup 16
Oyster 35:
Lamb and oyster hotpot 63

Paella 131
Palmiers 198
Pancakes:
Bacon pancakes 50
Dessert pancakes 142
Ham and cheese pancakes 99
Savoury pancakes 111
Paprika lamb chops 44
Parsley sauce 36